CAMBRII
THE LETTE
D. H. LAWRENCE

THE WORKS OF D. H. LAWRENCE

EDITORIAL BOARD

CONTENTS

ILLUSTRATIONS

(Originals in the Charles Deering McCormick Library, Northwestern University.)

GENERAL EDITOR'S PREFACE

D. H. Lawrence is one of the great writers of the twentieth century – yet the texts of his writings, whether published during his lifetime or since, are, for the most part, textually corrupt. The extent of the corruption is remarkable; it can derive from every stage of composition and publication. We know from study of his MSS that Lawrence was a careful writer, though not rigidly consistent in matters of minor convention. We know also that he revised at every possible stage. Yet he rarely if ever compared one stage with the previous one, and overlooked the errors of typists or copyists. He was forced to accept, as most authors are, the often stringent house-styling of his printers, which overrode his punctuation and even his sentence-structure and paragraphing. He sometimes overlooked plausible printing errors. More important, as a professional author living by his pen, he had to accept, with more or less good will, stringent editing by a publisher's reader in his early days, and at all times the results of his publishers' timidity. So the fear of Grundyish disapproval, or actual legal action, led to bowdlerisation or censorship from the very beginning of his career. Threats of libel suits produced other changes. Sometimes a publisher made more changes than he admitted to Lawrence. On a number of occasions, in dealing with American and British publishers, Lawrence produced texts for both which were not identical. Then there were extraordinary lapses like the occasion when a typist turned over two pages of MS at once, and the result happened to make sense. This whole story can be reconstructed from the introductions to the volumes in this edition; cumulatively they will form a history of Lawrence's writing career.

The Cambridge Edition aims to provide texts which are as close as can now be determined to those he would have wished to see printed. They have been established by a rigorous collation of extant manuscripts and typescripts, proofs and early printed versions; they restore the words, sentences, even whole pages omitted or falsified by editors or compositors; they are freed from printing-house conventions which were imposed on Lawrence's style; and interference on the part of frightened publishers has been eliminated. Far from doing violence to the texts Lawrence would have wished to see published, editorial intervention is essential to recover them. Though we have to accept that some cannot now be recovered in their entirety because

ix

early states have not survived, we must be glad that so much evidence remains. Paradoxical as it may seem, the outcome of this recension will be texts which differ, often radically and certainly frequently, from those seen by the author himself.

Editors have adopted the principle that the most authoritative form of the text is to be followed, even if this leads sometimes to a 'spoken' or a 'manuscript' rather than a 'printed' style. We have not wanted to strip off one house-styling in order to impose another. Editorial discretion may be allowed in order to regularise Lawrence's sometimes wayward spelling and punctuation in accordance with his most frequent practice in a particular text. A detailed record of these and other decisions on textual matters, together with the evidence on which they are based, will be found in the Textual apparatus which records variant readings in manuscripts, typescripts and proofs and printed variants in forms of the text published in Lawrence's lifetime. We do not record posthumous corruptions, except where first publication was posthumous. Significant MS readings may be found in the occasional Explanatory note.

In each volume, the editor's Introduction relates the contents to Lawrence's life and to his other writings; it gives the history of composition of the text in some detail, for its intrinsic interest, and because this history is essential to the statement of editorial principles followed. It provides an account of publication and reception which will be found to contain a good deal of hitherto unknown information. Where appropriate, Appendixes make available extended draft manuscript readings of significance, or important material, sometimes unpublished, associated with a particular work.

Though Lawrence is a twentieth-century writer and in many respects remains our contemporary, the idiom of his day is not invariably intelligible now, especially to the many readers who are not native speakers of British English. His use of dialect is another difficulty, and further barriers to full understanding are created by now obscure literary, historical, political or other references and allusions. On these occasions Explanatory notes are supplied by the editor; it is assumed that the reader has access to a good general dictionary and that the editor need not gloss words or expressions that may be found in it. Where Lawrence's letters are quoted in editorial matter, the reader should assume that his manuscript alone is the source of eccentricities of phrase or spelling.

ACKNOWLEDGEMENTS

To previous editors Roberta Armstrong and Ian MacNiven, I am grateful for the useful base they provided for this volume. For help with rare material in private hands, thanks and special regards are due to Sara Quintanilla of Mexico City; the late Ross Parmenter of Oaxaca and New York; and Philip Peralta-Ramos of New York and Colorado. I am grateful to L. D. Clark, Keith Sagar and others for the example of their work on Lawrence's American period, and also John Worthen for extensive special assistance.

My appreciation is due, as well, to James T. Boulton, Lindeth Vasey, Michael Black, Paul Poplawski and Andrew Brown, all of whom, with Worthen, aided and encouraged me in the course of my editing; and also to Linda Bree and the staff of Cambridge University Press – including Leigh Mueller, who did meticulous sub-editing of the full text for this volume. For help with Lawrence's manuscripts and typescripts in libraries, I am grateful to Cathy Henderson, Richard Workman and the staff of the Harry Ransom Center, University of Texas; Susan Snyder and the staff of Manuscripts and Archives at the Bancroft Library, University of California, Berkeley; William R. Erwin, Jr, and Janie Morris of the Rare Book, Manuscript, and Special Collections Library, Duke University; Adam Marchand and Eva Guggemos of the Beinecke Rare Book and Manuscript Library, Yale University; Scott Krafft, Sigrid P. Perry and the staff of the Charles Deering McCormick Library, Northwestern University, which contains Lawrence's sketches of Pueblo dancers (Illustrations I and II); and the staff of the Rare Book and Manuscript Library, University of Illinois, Champaign-Urbana. I thank these libraries and Gerald Pollinger for permissions to use Lawrence materials. I am grateful to Tina Ferris for permission to consult her site map of the Kiowa Ranch (first produced for the US National Register of Historic Places).

I wish to express high praise for excellent research assistance from Mark Dodd, Diana Archibald, Nathanael Gilbert and Bryce Campbell.

For research time and travel grants in early and intermediate stages of this project, thanks to the Washington State University Department of English and College of Liberal Arts.

xi

CHRONOLOGY

11 September 1885	Born in Eastwood, Nottinghamshire
September 1898–July 1901	Pupil at Nottingham High School
1902–1908	Pupil teacher; student at University College, Nottingham
7 December 1907	First publication: 'A Prelude', in *Nottinghamshire Guardian*
October 1908	Appointed teacher at Davidson Road School, Croydon
November 1909	Publishes five poems in *English Review*
9 December 1910	Death of his mother, Lydia Lawrence
19 January 1911	*The White Peacock* (New York)
19 November 1911	Ill with pneumonia; resigns his teaching post on 28 February 1912
March 1912	Meets Frieda Weekley; they leave for Germany on 3 May
23 May 1912	*The Trespasser*
February 1913	*Love Poems and Others*
29 May 1913	*Sons and Lovers*
1 April 1914	*The Widowing of Mrs. Holroyd* (New York)
13 July 1914	Marries Frieda Weekley in London
26 November 1914	*The Prussian Officer and Other Stories*
30 September 1915	*The Rainbow*; suppressed by court order on 13 November
June 1916	*Twilight in Italy*
July 1916	*Amores*
26 November 1917	*Look! We Have Come Through!*
October 1918	*New Poems*
November 1919–February 1922	In mainland Italy, then Capri and Sicily
20 November 1919	*Bay*
May 1920	*Touch and Go*
9 November 1920	*Women in Love* (New York)
25 November 1920	*The Lost Girl*
15 December 1920	'America, Listen to Your Own' in *New Republic*; Walter Lippmann opposes DHL's celebration of American Indians
February 1921	*Movements in European History*

10 September 1924	Asks E. M. Forster to read 'The Hopi Snake Dance'; death of DHL's father, Arthur John Lawrence
29 September–1 October 1924	Lawrences and Brett in Taos; attend San Geronimo Festival at Taos Pueblo
30 September 1924	DHL sends 'Indians and Entertainment' to Curtis Brown (New York)
October 1924	'The Dance of the Sprouting Corn' (as 'Der Tanz vom Sprießenden Korn') in *Der Neue Merkur*
11–23 October 1924	Lawrences and Brett to Mexico, via Taos and Santa Fe
23–28 October 1924	In Mexico City
between 25 and 28 October 1924	DHL and Brett visit National Museum and Virgin of Guadalupe
26 October 1924	'Indians and Entertainment' in *New York Times Magazine*
31 October 1924	DHL dines with P.E.N. Club, meets Luis Quintanilla
November 1924	'Indians and Entertainment' in the *Adelphi*
2 November 1924	Meets Edward Weston
9 November 1924–14 February 1925	At Oaxaca
before 14 November 1924	DHL calls on Governor Isaac Ibarra in his palace
19 November 1924	Begins second version of 'Quetzalcoatl' (*The Plumed Serpent*)
30? November 1924	Visits Mitla with Donald Miller via Santa Maria del Tule
December 1924	'The Hopi Snake Dance' in *Theatre Arts Monthly*
19?–30? December 1924	Writes four 'Mornings in Mexico' essays
19 December 1924	Suggests that Luis Quintanilla write an article for *Vanity Fair*, to be accompanied by Edward Weston photograph of Lawrence; 'Friday Morning' of 'Mornings in Mexico' ('Corasmin and the Parrots')
20 December 1924	'Saturday Morning' ('Market Day')
21 December 1924	'Sunday Morning' ('Walk to Huayapa'); DHL and Frieda walk to San Andrés Huayapan
29 December 1924	Probably 'Monday Morning' ('The Mozo')
January–February 1925	'The Hopi Snake Dance' in the *Adelphi*
by 10 January 1925	Rewrites Quintanilla's 'Mexico, Why Not?' ('See Mexico After, by Luis Q.') and returns it on 12 January

10 January 1925	DHL sends four 'Mornings in Mexico' essays to Curtis Brown (London)
19 January 1925	Brett leaves Oaxaca for Mexico City
c. 1 February 1925	Finishes _The Plumed Serpent_
1–14 February 1925	DHL seriously ill in Oaxaca with influenza, malaria or typhoid fever
25–26 February 1925	DHL and Frieda to Mexico City via Tehuacan
26 February–25 March 1925	In Mexico City
6–11 March 1925	DHL examined by Mexico City doctors, tuberculosis diagnosed
25–29 March 1925	DHL and Frieda to Santa Fe via El Paso
29 March 1925	In Santa Fe
1–5 April 1925	At Del Monte Ranch
6 April–9 September 1925	At Kiowa Ranch
17 April 1925	DHL tells Nancy Pearn of Curtis Brown (London) that he doesn't want Murry to publish 'Mornings in Mexico' essays
by 12 May 1925	Has asked Curtis Brown (London) to send four 'Mornings in Mexico' essays to the Insel Verlag
14 May 1925	_St. Mawr Together with The Princess_
September 1925–May 1928	In England, France and Italy
10–13 September 1925	DHL and Frieda to New York via Denver; Brett remains at Kiowa
21 September 1925	DHL and Frieda leave for England
by 2 November 1925	'Rosalino' ('The Mozo') in _Insel-Almanach auf der Jahr 1926_
25 November 1925	DHL writes 'A Little Moonshine with Lemon', sends MS to Brett
December 1925	'Corasmin and the Parrots' in _Adelphi_
7 December 1925	_Reflections on the Death of a Porcupine and Other Essays_ (Philadelphia)
January 1926	_The Plumed Serpent_; 'Pan in America' in _Southwest Review_
March 1926	_David_
April 1926	'The Gentle Art of Marketing in Mexico' ('Market Day') in _Travel_; 'A Little Moonshine with Lemon', 'Paris Letter', drawing of 'Pueblo Indian Dancers' (traced version of _The Corn Dance_), etc., in _Laughing Horse_ (special D. H. Lawrence number)
19 April 1926	DHL asks Nancy Pearn to take 'Walk to Huayapa' and 'The Mozo' away from the _Adelphi_

13 May 1926	Advises Nancy Pearn to handle the *Adelphi*'s claim to the remaining 'Mornings in Mexico' essays as she wishes
June 1926	'Mornings in Mexico/Saturday' ('Market Day') in *New Criterion*
November 1926	'Sunday Stroll in Sleepy Mexico' ('Walk to Huayapa') in *Travel*
15 November 1926	Has misgivings about 'half baked' essays for a book suggested by Secker; only feels confident of 'Mornings in Mexico' essays
23 November 1926	Lists planned contents of 'essay book' to Secker; agrees with title *Mornings in Mexico*; wants *The Corn Dance* drawing included; sends Secker *Travel* copy of 'Market Day'
26 November 1926	Sends Secker *Travel* copy of 'Walk to Huayapa'; suggests photographs for *Mornings in Mexico*; offers to write 'a little introduction'
6 December 1926	Asks Curtis Brown (London) to obtain *Theatre Arts Monthly* issues containing 'Dance articles' and illustrations; requests illustrations of 'Indian dances' from Mabel Luhan and offers to dedicate volume to her
8 January 1927	Tells Secker he has not yet received photographs (from Taos and from *Travel*) for *Mornings in Mexico*
12 January 1927	Asks Secker if he received '*Theatre Arts* Magazines' with '"Dance" articles'; suggests March as publication date for *Mornings in Mexico*
17 January 1927	Asks Nancy Pearn if she is 'managing illustrations' for *Mornings in Mexico*
27 January 1927	Believes that *Mornings in Mexico* will appear in 'late spring or early autumn'
February 1927	'The Mozo' in *Adelphi*
8 February 1927	Has still received no illustrations from America for *Mornings in Mexico*; urges Secker to use 'a few pictures'
March 1927	'Walk to Huayapa' in *Adelphi*
15 March 1927	Expecting proofs of *Mornings in Mexico*
27 March 1927	Asks Secker why he decided against illustrations in *Mornings in Mexico*; tells Nancy Pearn he is 'a bit vexed' with Secker

CUE-TITLES

A. Manuscript and typescript locations

DU	Duke University
NWU	Northwestern University
Quintanilla	Sara Quintanilla
UCB	University of California at Berkeley
UIll	University of Illinois at Urbana-Champaign
UT	University of Texas at Austin
YU	Yale University

B. Printed works

(The place of publication, here and throughout, is London unless otherwise stated.)

Brett	Dorothy Brett. *Lawrence and Brett: A Friendship.* Philadelphia: J. B. Lippincott Company, 1933.
KJB	*The Holy Bible Containing the Old and New Testaments (Authorised King James Version)*
Letters, i.	James T. Boulton, ed. *The Letters of D. H. Lawrence.* Volume I. Cambridge: Cambridge University Press, 1979.
Letters, ii.	George J. Zytaruk and James T. Boulton, eds. *The Letters of D. H. Lawrence.* Volume II. Cambridge: Cambridge University Press, 1981.
Letters, iii.	James T. Boulton and Andrew Robertson, eds. *The Letters of D. H. Lawrence.* Volume III. Cambridge: Cambridge University Press, 1984.
Letters, iv.	Warren Roberts, James T. Boulton and Elizabeth Mansfield, eds. *The Letters of D. H. Lawrence.* Volume IV. Cambridge: Cambridge University Press, 1987.
Letters, v.	James T. Boulton and Lindeth Vasey, eds. *The Letters of D. H. Lawrence.* Volume V. Cambridge: Cambridge University Press, 1989.

Letters, vi.	James T. Boulton and Margaret H. Boulton, with Gerald M. Lacy, eds. *The Letters of D. H. Lawrence.* Volume VI. Cambridge: Cambridge University Press, 1991.
Letters, vii.	Keith Sagar and James T. Boulton, eds. *The Letters of D. H. Lawrence.* Volume VII. Cambridge: Cambridge University Press, 1993.
Letters, viii.	James T. Boulton, ed. *The Letters of D. H. Lawrence.* Volume VIII. Cambridge: Cambridge University Press, 2000.
Nehls	Edward Nehls, ed. *D. H. Lawrence: A Composite Biography.* 3 vols. Madison: University of Wisconsin Press, 1957–9.
OED	Sir James A. H. Murray *et al.*, eds. *A New English Dictionary on Historical Principles.* 10 vols. Oxford: Clarendon Press, 1884–1928.
Parmenter	Ross Parmenter. *Lawrence in Oaxaca: A Quest for the Novelist in Mexico.* Salt Lake City: Peregrine Smith Books, 1984.
Phoenix	Edward D. McDonald, ed. *Phoenix: The Posthumous Papers of D. H. Lawrence.* New York: Viking, 1936.
Poems	Vivian de Sola Pinto and Warren Roberts, eds. *The Complete Poems of D. H. Lawrence.* Harmondsworth: Penguin, 1977.
PS	D. H. Lawrence. *The Plumed Serpent (Quetzalcoatl).* Ed. L. D. Clark. Cambridge: Cambridge University Press, 1987.
Reflections	D. H. Lawrence. *Reflections on the Death of a Porcupine and Other Essays.* Ed. Michael Herbert. Cambridge: Cambridge University Press, 1988.
Roberts	Warren Roberts and Paul Poplawski. *A Bibliography of D. H. Lawrence.* 3rd edn. Cambridge: Cambridge University Press, 2001.
Sketches	D. H. Lawrence. *Sketches of Etruscan Places and Other Italian Essays.* Ed. Simonetta de Filippis. Cambridge: Cambridge University Press, 1992.
Studies	D. H. Lawrence. *Studies in Classic American Literature.* Ed. Ezra Greenspan, Lindeth Vasey and John Worthen. Cambridge: Cambridge University Press, 2003.
Tedlock	E. W. Tedlock. *The Frieda Lawrence Collection of D. H. Lawrence Manuscripts: A Descriptive Bibliography.* Albuquerque: University of New Mexico Press, 1948.

INTRODUCTION

When D. H. Lawrence was awaiting publication of the first edition of his book *Mornings in Mexico* (1927), he described it to his sister Emily King as 'a little book of Red Indian and Mexican essays',[1] and it was the focus on indigenous life in the American Southwest and Mexico that unified the volume even then. His sense of the original volume as a unit with 'one basic theme' (vi. 36) had begun to form as early as 1925 when he commented that essays 'on Indian dances' might best be 'kept apart' from the pieces that eventually formed *Reflections on the Death of a Porcupine and Other Essays* (1925).[2] The title 'Mornings in Mexico' belonged in the first place to four essays Lawrence wrote in Oaxaca in 1924–5 while he was working on the last half of his one 'real novel of America' (iv. 457), *The Plumed Serpent*. Like the novel, these essays – which formed half of the original volume *Mornings in Mexico* – take the local Indians as a vital key to national identity and spirit of place. So do the next three of that book's essays, all 'Indian' pieces, followed by 'A Little Moonshine with Lemon', in which Lawrence reminisces in Italy about the Kiowa Ranch in New Mexico. In this present volume, which adds ten essays to the original eight (as well as some early versions), the same American and Native American themes prevail. Although five of the eighteen essays were written in Europe, the preoccupation with America – and 'not the America of the whites' (v. 63) – is evident in nearly all. Only 'Letter from Germany', though sequentially tied to two others, lacks overt reference to the indigenous America. Even 'Paris Letter' attributes a Homeric nobility to Native Americans. Here, in fact, are all the essays Lawrence wrote about Southwestern and Mexican Indians; and they are joined by attempts to capture the essence of Mexico and New Mexico ('See Mexico After, by Luis Q.' and 'New Mexico').

Because he participated in plans for the original *Mornings in Mexico* (along with his English publisher Martin Secker), its contents appear first in this

---

[1] *Letters*, v. 635 [25 January 1927]. Hereafter letters are cited in parenthesis in the text by volume and page number unless accompanied by a footnote.

[2] *Letters*, v. 241, DHL to Harold Mason of Centaur Book Shop and Press, 17 April 1925. Thus the 'Indian' pieces remained available for a later, more thematic volume.

volume. Next come (in chronological order) the essays he wrote in Taos in 1922, those from his following travels in Mexico and Europe in 1922–3, one from the Lawrence ranch (later Kiowa) in 1924, one from Mexico in 1924–5 and a final retrospective study from Europe in 1928. Like the original volume, this one presents a certain bifurcation in its sense of place – divided between Mexico and New Mexico with Europe rather at its margins. Before going to America, Lawrence's mental geography of it was somewhat vague and idealised, linking widely disparate cultures. For example, in the 1920 'Foreword to Studies in Classic American Literature' – first published as 'America, Listen to Your Own' – Americans are urged to turn from Old World standards to 'pick up the life-thread' from 'the Red Indian, the Aztec, the Maya, the Incas'.[3] In America, however, his engagement with specific peoples and issues became much more particularised and even, at times, topical.[4]

The first of these essays to be published, 'Certain Americans and an Englishman', was written late in 1922 when *Aaron's Rod* and *Women in Love* were both prominently on the market (the former having appeared in the spring and the latter having triumphed in September over suppression, based on an obscenity charge). The last essay, 'New Mexico', was written in France in December 1928 when Lawrence had published *Lady Chatterley's Lover* and pirated copies flourished. These essays have interconnections, therefore, with a wide range of his other works.

In fact, he had been thinking about America throughout much of his career,[5] referring to it in 1915, for example, as a goal and an escape from the 'past' for some of the people in *Twilight in Italy*.[6] All during the First World War, Lawrence had imagined a retreat from the conflict, for he felt his heart 'torn out' (ii. 413) by what had happened to civilisation, by the destruction itself and by the suspension of civil liberties which he and his

---

[3] *Studies* (Appendix II), 384:35, 34–5. This essay appeared in the *New Republic*, xxv (15 December 1920), 68–70.

[4] DHL witnessed and wrote about some of the key circumstances that would fuel the later 'Indian New Deal' – Pueblo property rights, Indian boarding schools, and rules against native rituals. The architect of the 'Indian New Deal', John Collier (1884–1968), Commissioner of Indian Affairs (1933–45), wrote about DHL's relations with the Pueblo Indians, stating that they 'accepted him and liked him' and walked uphill to the Kiowa Ranch to honour him 'when they learned of his death' (Nehls, ii. 198).

[5] See *Studies* xxvi–xxxii, for DHL's reading in American literature, and lix–lxvi for his own considerable impact on the criticism of American literature.

[6] See, for example, the character John, whose 'face was set outwards, away from it all—whither, neither he nor anybody knew, but he called it America' (*Twilight in Italy and Other Essays*, ed. Paul Eggert, Cambridge, 1994, 186:40–1).

German-born wife Frieda suffered.[7] The good society which he imagined in 1914, even before the war, was to be an island or a colony both utopian and geographically real; and it was increasingly localised somewhere in America.[8] The prospect of going to America appeared, too, in a cluster of post-war fictions between 1920 and 1923: *The Lost Girl*, the expanded *Dial* version of 'The Fox', *Aaron's Rod* with its vivid dream of a 'lake-city, like Mexico',[9] and *Kangaroo*.[10] In addition, a mystical idea of America entered into the Foreword to *Fantasia of the Unconscious* (1922), which names 'the Amerindians' among those who perpetuated the old myths and rituals of Atlantis and 'the great world previous to ours'.[11] The Maya were mentioned in a similar vision in the first version of 'The Spirit of Place' (1918),[12] which Lawrence rewrote in New Mexico for *Studies in Classic American Literature*, omitting the Atlantean frame of reference. Lawrence had compared himself in 1916 to 'a Columbus who can see a shadowy America before him' (ii. 556), and, like Columbus, he expected a 'new world' that was inevitably different from his projections of it.

Reactions to the publication of 'America, Listen to Your Own' had revealed to Lawrence a profound split in American literary criticism – with advocates of Europeanised models on one hand, typified by the well-known commentator Walter Lippmann, and with proponents of Native American culture on the other, represented by the novelist and essayist Mary Austin, who knew Taos

---

7 DHL chafed at 'having been badgered about . . . kicked out of Cornwall, and pushed about by the police' (*Letters*, iii. 281).

8 DHL adopted its name 'Rananim' in 1914 from the Hebrew music sung by his friend S. S. Koteliansky – ironically, just before the two learned of the declaration of war (*Letters*, ii. 268). Some of the locations associated with this dream included an unnamed island (ii. 266), England itself (ii. 277, 292), Cornwall (ii. 564), perhaps 'California or the South Seas' (iii. 70), the Andes (iii. 173, 174), Palestine (iii. 214, 316), Florida (e.g. ii. 485, 486, 488–92), America's 'far west mountains' (iii. 25), possibly ('a bit') New Mexico (iv. 334, 350) and Mexico (v. 513).

9 Ed. Mara Kalnins (Cambridge, 1988), 288:11.

10 In poetry, too, the same progression is clear. *Birds, Beasts and Flowers* (New York, 1923) illustrates the geographical transition to America because of poems identified with places: not only Europe but also Asia ('Elephant'), Australia ('Kangaroo') and the American Southwest (nine poems located there) – 'Eagle in New Mexico', 'The Blue Jay', 'Bibbles', 'Mountain Lion', 'The Red Wolf', 'Men in New Mexico', 'Autumn at Taos', 'Spirits Summoned West' and 'The American Eagle'. In addition, 'Humming-Bird' was given the location 'Española' (a New Mexico village) although published in one version before DHL's arrival in America; and 'The Evening Land', given the location 'Baden-Baden', confronts white America ('the open tomb of my race', *Poems* 289).

11 In *Psychoanalysis and the Unconscious and Fantasia of the Unconscious*, ed. Bruce Steele (Cambridge, 2004), 63:33, 11–13.

12 *Studies* 169:5.

well.[13] She was a member of the circle around Mabel Dodge Sterne (later Luhan), who would invite the Lawrences to New Mexico. Lawrence had argued in this essay that, while European culture was born of a great creative link between opposites (East and West), it had gone dead, obliging Americans to 'start from Montezuma' and the 'great and lovely life-form, unperfected' that he represented.[14] They must shed the moribund mechanistic civilisation which Lawrence believed was in even further decadence in the United States than in Europe (and therefore closer to rebirth),[15] and find a clue to the future in primordial America. But Lippmann immediately assigned Lawrence to 'the Noble Savage phase'. Americans cannot 'start from Montezuma', he said, because 'there is nothing to start from'. Austin's reply charged Lippmann with 'complacency' over this national ignorance, challenging 'the attitude of a small group of thinkers residing mostly in New York' and calling attention to the surviving 'remnants' of American Indian culture, the successful native struggles in Mexico, and 'a lusty art movement' flourishing on the 'Amerind' foundation.[16] Although Lawrence's position was in fact similar to Austin's, he called her defence 'boring' (iii. 654), and he would later bridle at his association with the appropriation (as he saw it) of Indian subjects by New Mexico artist colonies; because he was seeking popular acceptance in America, he may have been sensitive, too, to the influential Lippmann's broadside national assault.

Whether this criticism contributed or not to Lawrence's later writing about America, he did set about revising his *Studies* radically after his arrival in America – not only removing much of the earlier mystique about the Aztecs but also adopting a new, combative style and a tougher stance towards sentimental primitivism that are evident at times, too, in *Mornings in Mexico*. Lawrence was on an arc of reaction and reassessment, exploring Cooper's

---

[13] Walter Lippmann (1889–1974), influential journalist and author, was a founding editor of the *New Republic*. Mary Hunter Austin (1868–1934), American novelist and poet, author of *The Land of Little Rain* (1903), was a leader of the arts community in Santa Fe and a good friend of Mabel Luhan. See also *The Plays*, ed. Hans-Wilhelm Schwarze and John Worthen (Cambridge, 1999), p. 687, for a note on Austin's place in DHL's drama *Altitude*.

[14] *Studies* 385:11, 1.

[15] Even in 1916, he had explained to Catherine Carswell 'that America, being so much *worse*, falser, further gone than England, is nearer to freedom', having 'dryrotted to a point where the final *seed* of the new is almost left ready to sprout' (*Letters*, iii. 25).

[16] Lippmann, "The Crude Barbarian and the Noble Savage' (with the additional header 'Apropos of Mr. Lawrence'), *New Republic*, xxv (15 December 1920), 70, and Austin, 'Mrs. Austin Protests', *New Republic*, xxv (5 January 1921), 170. See also *Studies* lxii–lxiii on the literatures of 'Nature' and 'Culture' – and on Philip Rahv's 1939 categories 'Paleface' and 'Redskin' in American literature.

theme of a 'communion' between the souls of the races[17] and questioning the possibility of a utopian state, only to return in the end to some of his earlier vision.

But his interest in the United States also had a decidedly practical side, for he was actively attempting to enlarge his American audience in order to earn money. After the suppression of *The Rainbow* in 1915 and the publishers' timidity about *Women in Love*, Lawrence wrote to his agent J. B. Pinker that he must go to America to 'address a new public' and that he could not 'write for America here in England' (iii. 73). That was in 1917, after *Women in Love* had been rejected by Methuen, Duckworth, Secker, and Constable and Co., and Lawrence hoped increasingly for an American audience. Despite repeated attempts, however, he and Frieda were unable to obtain passports until 1919, and they were obliged to accept gifts and loans in order to live. Even in September 1922, from better financial times in America, Lawrence wrote to his principal English publisher, Martin Secker, that his yearly income from England was only about £120: 'Therefore America must have the first consideration. On the English crust I could but starve, now as ever' (iv. 299). Partly due to receptive American periodicals, the New York publisher Thomas Seltzer[18] and the American Robert Mountsier,[19] who had begun to act as Lawrence's agent in 1920 a few months after Pinker's dismissal (iii. 439, 476, 504), Lawrence's fortunes were improving by the time he set sail beyond Europe, first to Ceylon and Australia, then to America across the Pacific. To Mabel Sterne,[20] the American patron of the arts who had offered the Lawrences a house in Taos, New Mexico, he would affirm a certain self-sufficiency as an initial gesture (iv. 269).

[17] *Studies* 209:30–1. 'Fenimore Cooper's Leatherstocking Novels' (First Version) also refers to 'ultimate atonement between races' but the version finds 'an unpassable distance' between them (*Studies* 64:35).

[18] Seltzer (1875–1943), translator, journalist and publisher, born in Russia, grew up in the USA from the age of twelve; he entered the publishing firm Boni and Liveright in 1917, then began Scott and Seltzer in 1918 with Temple Scott. He was DHL's leading publisher for five years (1920–5).

[19] Mountsier (1888–1972), journalist and literary editor at the New York *Sun* (1910), was a friend of DHL when he accepted his position with Lawrence (1920–3) for the US market. Curtis Brown remained DHL's English agent (as he had been since April 1921).

[20] Mabel Dodge Sterne Luhan (1879–1962) was born Mabel Ganson and later married Karl Evans, architect Edwin Dodge, artist Maurice Sterne and Taos Indian leader Antonio (Tony) Lujan (1923) (see footnote 27). She conducted salons in Greenwich Village, Florence and Taos. DHL presented a copy of Seltzer's *Women in Love* to Mabel to commemorate the occasion of their meeting: 'Mabel Sterne / from D. H. Lawrence / on arriving in Taos / 11th September 1922'. He would dedicate *Mornings in Mexico* to 'Mabel Lujan'.

Although he arrived in San Francisco 'penniless', as he wired Mountsier (iv. 287), *The Captain's Doll* had recently sold for $1,000 to *Hearst's International*,[21] and soon he was repaying earlier small loans (e.g. iv. 297, 305) and offering money to his old friend, S. S. Koteliansky (iv. 296–7). The struggle with poverty never really ended for Lawrence, but his 'American period' – actually consisting of three separate periods in New Mexico and three trips to Mexico[22] – was itself remarkably productive, and his publication rate was at its all-time high. The Lawrences' arrival in Taos all but coincided with the propitious outcome on 12 September of a 'suppression' case that had been brought against Seltzer after the publication of *Women in Love* (and two books by other writers). A week after receiving a telegram from Seltzer on his 'triumph' (iv. 296), Lawrence replied, 'I am glad you won that case: now you ought to be able to go freely ahead' (iv. 297). By 17 December, Lawrence could announce to his friend, the writer Catherine Carswell, the sale in America of almost 15,000 copies of W*omen in Love* (iv. 363).

Moreover, in just the next thirteen months, Seltzer published seven of his books: *Fantasia of the Unconscious* and *England, My England* in October 1922, and then, in 1923, *The Captain's Doll* in April, *Studies in Classic American Literature* in August, *Kangaroo* in September, and *Birds, Beasts and Flowers* and *Mastro-don Gesualdo* (Lawrence's translation of Giovanni Verga) in October.[23] In addition, Lawrence was regularly publishing poems, essays and stories in American periodicals. When Lawrence reported his 1922 income to Mountsier for tax purposes, he listed $5,439.67 from American royalties and periodicals (iv. 400), and his balance in the Charleroi Bank was $2,262.86 in the same month.[24] He was by that time, in February 1923, breaking with Mountsier, whose conflicts with Seltzer could not be resolved, and he would begin to detach himself from Seltzer, too, less than a year later, when the

---

[21] *Letters*, iv. 287 n. 2. Seltzer's correspondence with Mountsier indicates that the publisher was responsible for the sale to *Hearst's* and actively conducted other negotiations with periodicals, sometimes attributed by DHL to Mountsier (e.g. *Letters*, iv. 302 to Curtis Brown). *Hearst's* delayed periodical publication and had to relinquish the novella because of Secker's and Seltzer's publication schedules.

[22] His travels within the United States also took him to San Francisco, New Orleans, New York, Chicago and Los Angeles.

[23] Five of these were published first by Seltzer who had already published (besides *Women in Love*) *Sea and Sardinia* and *Psychoanalysis and the Unconscious* in 1921 and *Aaron's Rod* in 1922. Jonathan Cape published *Mastro-don Gesualdo* in 1925.

[24] DHL's diary notes, Tedlock 96. In June 1924 his balance in the Charleroi Bank was holding fairly steady at $2,198.02 (Tedlock 98). On 31 August 1924, he assured his sister Ada Clarke that he had 'plenty': 'I keep a thousand dollars in hand if I can, now' (*Letters*, v. 114).

publisher suffered financial disaster; but both had been important in bringing his work successfully to the American market.

Taos and Del Monte Ranch (September 1922 – March 1923)

'Pueblos and an Englishman'

Lawrence had just turned thirty-seven when he and Frieda arrived in Taos after meeting their hostess Mabel Sterne at Lamy, New Mexico, and lodging overnight at writer Witter Bynner's Santa Fe home, where they also met Willard ('Spud') Johnson, Bynner's secretary and companion.[25] From this little group would come two memoirs of Lawrence, Mabel's *Lorenzo in Taos* and Bynner's *Journey with Genius*, both cited below. Johnson, who became Lawrence's typist on occasion, was co-editor of the little magazine *Laughing Horse*, which later published several of the essays in this volume. Lawrence described his hostess ironically as a cultural 'cooing raven of misfortune' (iv. 351–2). A benefactor in her lifetime to significant artists like Gertrude Stein, Georgia O'Keeffe and Willa Cather,[26] she was a principal instigator of the Taos artists' colony. At the same time, she dedicated herself to causes favourable to Southwestern Indians and married the Taos Indian Tony Lujan in 1923,[27] electing to spell her new married name phonetically.

Lawrence was initially pleased with the 'very pretty adobe house' (v. 313) which she provided about 200 yards from her own home, a mile from the 'plaza' (as the town-centre was termed), and some three miles from the world's largest pueblo on the adjoining Taos Indian Reservation. Next door to the Lawrences was John Collier, the future Commissioner of Indian Affairs

---

[25] Witter Bynner (1881–1968), American poet and playwright, shared some interests with DHL., as in *A Canticle of Pan* (1920) and *Indian Earth* (with its sections 'Chapala Poems' and 'Pueblo Dances'), dedicated to DHL in 1929. Walter Willard ('Spud') Johnson (1897–1968), a founder of *Laughing Horse* (originating at UCB), close friend and once secretary to Witter Bynner in Santa Fe. An early co-editor of *Laughing Horse* was Roy E. Chanslor (1899–1964), who was disciplined by UCB for publishing DHL's review of a controversial book by Ben Hecht in issue no. 4 (December 1922). (See 'Review of *Fantazius Mallare: A Mysterious Oath*', in *Introductions and Reviews*, ed. N. H. Reeve and John Worthen, Cambridge, 2005, pp. 215–17.)

[26] Gertrude Stein (1874–1946), American writer and patron of arts, interacted with famous painters and authors in Paris; Georgia O'Keeffe (1887–1986), American painter, famed for her close-up studies of plants and of New Mexico landscape and architecture; Willa Cather (1873–1947), Pulitzer Prize-winning American writer and managing editor of *McClure's Magazine* (1908), best known for pioneer themes set in the Midwestern and Southwestern USA.

[27] Antonio (Tony) Lujan (d. 1963), activist with John Collier for protection of Pueblo culture; delegate to the First Inter-American Conference on Indian Life held at Patzcuaro, Mexico (1940). He married Mabel Sterne in 1923.

(see footnote 4). Prominent in the nightly conversations that occurred at Mabel's 'big house', Collier was probably one of the activists referred to in 'Certain Americans and an Englishman', yet a comparison of their work suggests certain common interests and a strong possibility of mutual influence (compare Collier's article 'The Red Atlantis' about the Pueblo Indians and Lawrence's evocation of a Mexican Atlantis in *The Plumed Serpent*).[28] But the countryside impressed Lawrence even more than the people: Taos is on a plateau 7,000 feet above sea level, where the desert meets the foothills of the Rocky Mountains and where the sacred lake and mountain of the Taos Indians form a rugged and 'forever unpossessed country' (iv. 314).

Hardly had he arrived in Taos than his hostess sent him with Tony to a gathering of the Jicarilla Apaches at Stone Lake, New Mexico (about 100 miles northwest of Taos), for their mid-September harvest festival, the Go-Jii-Ya. Unlike the Pueblo Indians, who had Spanish land rights to their pueblos, the Jicarilla Apaches had been more migratory and had been moved repeatedly by the US government from southern Colorado, northern New Mexico and elsewhere before an Executive Order brought several bands together in 1887 in this reservation near Dulce, New Mexico. While their ceremonies were distinctively Apache (a Zuni word for 'enemy'), they had interacted with Pueblos historically at least twice – giving protection to isolated refugees during the Pueblo war with the Spanish (after 1680) and taking occasional refuge with Pueblos when the government ousted the Apaches from their lands after the Louisiana Purchase (after 1803). But Apaches were the last American Indians to be subjugated and enclosed by the government. Lawrence had probably learned something about their history at the time of his visit, but he sensed their remoteness from the world he knew. According to Mabel, he wrote about his experience with the Apaches 'when he came back' to Taos,[29] and some of 'Indians and an Englishman' does give the impression of immediacy; his first writing about Indians in America, then, may have occurred on or around 18 September, when he was back in Taos writing letters (iv. 296, iv. 297). On 29–30 September he attended the San Geronimo Festival at Taos Pueblo, and this was the inspiration for the writing that was later called 'Taos'. Meanwhile, the talk of the time was the Bursum Land Bill (see Explanatory notes on 'Certain Americans and an Englishman'), threatening Pueblo Indian land and water rights; and this topic, too, became part of a single essay incorporating the Apache festival, the Taos festival and the Bill.

Lawrence's first reference to this piece (still unnamed) came when he informed Mountsier on 25 October that he was 'doing an article about Indians

---

[28] *Survey* (1 October 1922), 19; *PS* 415:10.
[29] Mabel Dodge Luhan, *Lorenzo in Taos* (New York, 1932), p. 60.

and the Bursum Bill' (iv. 329); two days later he wrote to Mountsier again that he was still busy with the 'article on the Indians' (iv. 330). One problem with the composite approach would have been the fact that the Apaches were not those who lived in the pueblos and whose ancient property rights (previously affirmed by the Spanish, Mexican and American authorities) were under challenge in Congress. Nonetheless, on 30 October he called his work 'Pueblos and an Englishman' to one correspondent, Bessie Freeman,[30] who had accompanied him and Tony into Apache country (iv. 332), though a week later, confusingly, he would call it his 'Indians and an Englishman' article (iv. 336). But this composite piece would eventually be broken up into three essays, 'Indians and an Englishman' (about the Apaches), 'Taos' (about Taos Pueblo) and 'Certain Americans and an Englishman' (about the Bursum Bill).

'Certain Americans and an Englishman', 'Indians and an Englishman', 'Taos'

Lawrence first hoped that the *Dial* could publish the composite article in time to influence an impending Congressional discussion of the Bursum Bill. He sent it to both the *Dial* and Mountsier on 31 October, explaining to the editor Scofield Thayer that the Bursum section would 'be useless' unless published in December (iv. 334). But the *Dial* could not meet this schedule, and *New Republic*, too, was 'a bit stuffed with Bursum Bill', as Lawrence put it on 11 November (iv. 338). Between then and mid-December he reworked the part of the piece which dealt with the Bill, extending it for independent publication in the *New York Times Magazine*, where it appeared as 'Certain Americans and an Englishman'. The national outcries against the Bill – including those of the powerful Federation of Women's Clubs, new Indian rights organisations, and the Taos Indians themselves, who took their case personally to Congress and Wall Street – helped to lead to Congressional hearings in January and February 1923 and to compromise legislation in 1924.[31] But when Lawrence wrote his article about the Bill, December 1922 was still believed to be a decisive date.

---

[30] Elizabeth ('Bessie') Wilkeson Freeman (1876–1951), a friend of Mabel Dodge Luhan since girlhood in New York, met DHL in New Mexico. The two became friends, and he invited her to become part of a utopian ranch community (*Letters*, iv. 333–4).

[31] Pueblo Lands Act (7 June 1924), US Statutes at Large, Washington, D.C., xliii. 636–42. See Kenneth Philp, 'Albert B. Fall and the Protest from the Pueblos, 1921–23', *Arizona and the West*, xii (1970), 237–54; Philp, *John Collier's Crusade for Indian Reform, 1920–1945* (Tucson, 1977); Lawrence C. Kelly, *The Assault on Assimilation: John Collier and the Origins of the Indian Policy Reform* (Albuquerque, 1983); and G. Emlen Hall, 'The Pueblo Grant Labyrinth', in *Land, Water, and Culture: New Perspectives on Hispanic Land Grants*, ed. C. L. Briggs and J. R. Van Ness (Albuquerque, 1987), pp. 67–138.

Mabel had orchestrated literary opposition to the Bursum Bill, urging both Lawrence and Collier – and the writers Mary Austin and Alice Corbin Henderson – to produce articles, then hiring a typist and wiring Walter Lippmann about Lawrence's contribution, asking 'if he could get the article in sections in a daily' (iv. 334). Not only did her plan appropriate the work Lawrence had in hand, but her attempts at micromanagement of his writing meant that he had to ask her to 'send me the MS. of my Bursum article' in order to see if there was a page missing in the typescript (iv. 333). He also wrote to Mountsier that he might send the article straight to the *Dial* 'for quickness' (iv. 329) though he actually sent only a 'duplicate' (i.e. a carbon copy) to the magazine and, presumably, the typescript to Mountsier (iv. 334).[32] But producing topical commentary on demand, for a deadline, was not Lawrence's usual habit. The involvement of his harsh critic Lippmann may have made him particularly resistant. In any case, he informed Mabel of his dislike of fragmenting the article at all: 'I would rather it went in a monthly, whole, than snipped up in a daily' (iv. 333). It seems certain from the extant typescript of 'Indians and an Englishman' (see 'Texts' below) that he revised his article heavily at some time, probably late in October when he reported writing specifically about the Bursum Bill. It is even likely that the composite article (before such revision) had not referred to the Bursum Bill at the outset but that Lawrence had eventually brought the topic to the fore in the writing (it occupies a little more than a page of this typescript). The inclusion of this early political section necessitated the retyping of the opening pages by someone who was using another typewriter. Although the resulting two sections of the typescript – the first seven pages, including p. 6a, typed on one typewriter, and the last five on another – were intended to link up, Lawrence actually had to write an additional line at the top of p. 7 to carry over the sense between the new pages and the old. (A typist's error at the top of p. 7 further compounded the problem, and DHL had to delete a duplicated sentence.) Because of the time factor, it was important not to retype more than necessary. The fact that pp. 1–6a contain rather fewer autograph revisions than the remainder of the typescript is one indication that they represent the later typing.

It is impossible to know if this composite article had ever had an earlier title because none was typed on the new first page, but 'Pueblos and an Englishman' was added by hand in large capital letters, then the first word

---

was deleted and replaced with 'Indians'. Although the section about Taos Pueblo must have been a principal part of the essay at one time, it was now as out of place in the typescript as 'Pueblos' was in the title.

The last page of the surviving typescript was not the last of the essay, for the account clearly continued after 'Indians and an Englishman' as it was published; on p. 11 of the typescript, one paragraph and part of another were deleted by an editor (who drew a bold line in ink and wrote 'Set to here' in the margin). Later pages (now lost) presumably included the material later published as 'Taos'. The unfinished sentence at the end of p. 11 is still about the Apache trip, referring to an 'American woman' – probably Bessie Freeman, to whom Lawrence had written, late in his October writing process, 'You'll see yourself in my "Pueblos and an Englishman" article' (iv. 332). But nowhere is she recognisable, except here. The omission of part of the essay raises questions about the remainder. 'Taos' itself seems to contain editorial intrusions that cannot now be identified (see p. lxxvii below).

Despite his uneasiness at breaking up his work, Lawrence had agreed that Thayer 'could cut the article as he chose' (iv. 334). He meant this to apply to the Bursum Bill material; and on 14 November, he seemed happy enough with news from Gilbert Seldes, the *Dial*'s managing editor, that the work would run 'in their Jan. issue – cutting out the politics' (iv. 340). Yet within less than a month he expressed some resentment, perhaps because he had learned of serialisation or omissions, for he remarked to Mountsier on 12 December, 'Well, Seldes has made a fool of us over that Indian article, and over "Ladybird".'[33] It is unclear what part Lawrence played, if any, in the plan to publish an instalment entitled 'Taos' or to omit at least two paragraphs. Even the earlier of two surviving typescripts entitled 'Taos' only raises questions (see 'Texts' below). This was by far the shortest essay to be extracted from 'Pueblos and an Englishman', yet all extant versions contain internal divisions created by extra spacing. Unless Lawrence actually established segments in it – as he did not do in the longer pieces from 'Pueblos' – the earlier of the two typescripts must itself have been copied

---

33 *Letters*, iv. 358. DHL added: 'Those "mistakes" are always subconscious-intentional, if not deliberate', referring to some 'mistakes' for which Seldes must have apologised. The *Dial* did not publish *The Ladybird* at all, despite 'flirting with' it (iv. 341 n. 1). DHL had probably just received word that Seldes was rejecting it, having made a 'mistake' about accepting it. Moreover, Seldes may have announced that he was rescheduling 'Indians and an Englishman' for February (when it appeared in a shortened form) instead of the promised January and that he was separating it from 'Taos', which appeared in March. Seldes's ambivalence over *The Ladybird* meant that the tale never appeared in a periodical, and delays of this kind cost DHL both profit and publicity.

from the journal, which had published it in this form.[34] It is possible that
the abrupt divisions were occasioned by cuts made by the *Dial* staff. It is
also possible, judging by the amount of Bursum Bill detail finally published
in 'Certain Americans and an Englishman', that the lost pages contained
political material that was excised and recast in 'Certain Americans and an
Englishman'. This is in fact rather likely because the Bursum Bill was a direct
threat to pueblos like Taos Pueblo; the two subject matters were therefore
related. Such an intertextual relationship between them would have explained
why Lawrence did not originally want to divide the parent essay. But –
in the absence of both the manuscript and the latter part of the 'Pueblos'
typescript – it is impossible to be sure about Lawrence's original format.

  'Taos' may be a title supplied by the *Dial* editor, for Lawrence never used
it in correspondence but referred to two 'instalments' of the same 'Indian' or
'Indians' work (e.g. iv. 369, 380, 404). In fact, the *Dial* record itself listed only
'installments' of 'Indians and an Englishman', and the February issue claimed
as much openly in its 'Notes on Contributors': 'Under the title Indians and
an Englishman *The Dial* will publish at varying intervals Mr Lawrence's
impressions of the Southwest.'[35] It has been suggested that the *Dial* staff
changed the title of 'Indians and an Englishman' because they wished to make
it parallel the recent *New York Times Magazine* title 'Certain Americans and
an Englishman'.[36] But Lawrence himself probably printed the title on the
first page. A comparison of the title with Lawrence's printed capital letters
(on dust jacket designs) shows distinct similarity. Just as 'Certain Americans
and an Englishman' somewhat echoes the working title of its parent article
('Pueblos and an Englishman'), so does 'Indians and an Englishman' – and
Lawrence's usual reference in correspondence was to his 'Indian' article.

  Soon after the *Dial* publication of 'Indians and an Englishman', which
included a reproduction of Jan Juta's fiery 1921 portrait of Lawrence, the
writer asked the *Dial* to send a copy to Curtis Brown, reminding Brown
rather pointedly on 10 February that the piece 'might have been acceptable to
several English periodicals' (iv. 380); but it did not appear in England until the
following November's *Adelphi*. The *Dial* publication of 'Taos' was the likely

---

[34] A group of five typescripts at UCB (see Tedlock 186), sharing a distinctive typeface and
format, includes two of the essays in this volume, 'Taos' and 'The Hopi Snake Dance'. The
other three – Roberts E200a ('Life'), Roberts E210a ('Love') and Roberts E338a ('The Reality
of Peace') – have all been judged to be corrected by someone other than DHL (*Reflections* xlii
n. 97), and that is also true of the typescripts of 'Taos' and 'The Hopi Snake Dance', which
played no part in the transmission of those essays to publication in DHL's lifetime.

[35] *Dial*, lxxiv (February 1923), Editor's Note.

[36] Nicholas Joost and Alvin Sullivan, in *D. H. Lawrence and the 'Dial'* (Carbondale, 1970), p. 79.

source for *Cassell's Weekly* (in July), in which the little piece took the strange misnomer 'At Taos, An Englishman Looks at Mexico' without distinguishing New Mexico from the country south of the United States border.[37]

Despite poking barbed fun at the reformers (and the Taos artists) at the beginning of 'Certain Americans and an Englishman', Lawrence, like them, opposed the Bursum Bill and showed a stark awareness of the vulnerability of traditional American Indian centres in the twentieth century. The pueblos were unique stationary locations that the Pueblo Indians had occupied for centuries; here the original Spanish explorers had found the Indians in the sixteenth century, and here (beginning from Taos Pueblo) they had defended their territory in the Pueblo uprising of the next century, driving the Spanish out for over a dozen years and occupying Santa Fe. (Though the Spanish returned, it was the most sustained Indian victory in American history.) The pueblos represented a conundrum, a life-thread that must be carried forward, yet at the same time a manifestation of their past, a past that seemed at odds with the prevailing direction of the dominant culture; and they might be passing away. (This was a common theme of the reformers, as their titles show – e.g. Collier's 'The Pueblos' Last Stand' and Alice Corbin Henderson's 'The Death of the Pueblos'.[38]) Nonetheless, Lawrence acknowledges in 'Taos' the continuing viability of Taos Pueblo, comparing it with European monasteries. Before leaving Europe, he had seen Montecassino, for example, as a 'quick spot' in Italy – so adaptive through the centuries as to be 'not quite dead'.[39] In 'America, Listen to Your Own', he had written of the 'life-thread' that must extend from the Indians' ancient culture to the present;[40] again, in 'Certain Americans and an Englishman', he urges Americans, despite the impending end, to follow the Indians' 'old dark thread' and thus to 'see again as they see'.[41] And in 'Taos', named for the place where the pueblo has stood 'since heaven knows when', he acknowledges 'the slow dark weaving of the Indian life going on still'.[42]

---

37 *Cassell's Weekly* not only retained the internal divisions already discussed but created five more, totalling eight, all set apart from each other by rows of small ornamental icons, as if to suggest that the article consisted of a series of discontinuous impressions.

38 Collier, *Sunset* (February 1923), 21–5; Henderson, *New Republic*, 33 (29 November 1922), 11–13.

39 '*Memoir of Maurice Magnus*', in *Introductions and Reviews*, ed. Reeve and Worthen, 34:25–6. 'Taos' is one of a tiny cluster of DHL texts – along with 'On Human Destiny' and 'Books' – referring in similar terms to the importance of Christian monasteries in the Middle Ages. The essays were preceded in this theme in 1921 by DHL's *Movements in European History*, ed. Philip Crumpton (Cambridge, 1989), 97:3–17.

40 *Studies* 384:35.   41 'Certain Americans and an Englishman' (110:18).

42 'Taos' (126:11–12).

'Indians and an Englishman', however, intensifies the conflict between past and present as the author's attention is riveted by an Apache elder in a sacred kiva. In the evolutionary mode of the time, Lawrence associates him with the primordial ages, declining to relive a tribal experience but acknowledging a deep sense of kinship with the old 'father'.[43] This is his complex but characteristic stand on the necessity of 'progressing' while still cherishing continuity with ancient cultures. Despite the empathetic account of the Taos Indians in 'Taos', an irritated tone creeps into the essays that came from 'Pueblos'; and the relationship with Mabel may account for some of it. Lawrence was wary of being under 'anybody's wing', referring to her at times as a 'padrona' or 'patroness' (iv. 306, 315, 351). He complained to Mountsier of the pressure she put him under: 'I won't have people exerting their wills over me. Whoever does will get a jar. – I'll stick this a month longer, till I have arranged something else' (iv. 330). To Mabel herself he wrote on 7 November that he had already 'more than paid for all the "goodness"' she had offered (iv. 337); and to Bessie Freeman he announced on 24 January, 'I will never see her [Mabel] again' (iv. 372). Instead of simply moving away, however, the Lawrences sought a little distance between themselves and their hostess. Mabel had shown them a ranch she had given her son John Evans on Lobo Mountain, about 20 miles northwest of Taos; the 160-acre spread, with several cabins, was then called the Flying Heart (later Lobo, and then Kiowa), and they thought about renting it.

When they had a trial stay there at the end of October, however, they found the buildings in disrepair and unequal to the approaching needs of winter; they eventually rented cabins on a nearby ranch (Del Monte) from a neighbour and spent the winter there, along with two Danish painters, Knud Merrild and Kai Götzsche.[44] But Lawrence – having suffered an uncomfortable Christmas and New Year avoiding Mabel's 'big house', keeping the peace between Mountsier and Seltzer (who both visited him), and then preparing to dismiss Mountsier[45] – turned to his old panacea of travel, writing to Seltzer, 'And

---

[43] DHL characteristically opposed the regressive lure of the past, as in his comment to Maurice Magnus about the Middle Ages: 'One can't go back' (*Introductions and Reviews*, ed. Reeve and Worthen, 33:26). In *Kangaroo*, ed. Bruce Steele (Cambridge, 1994), the protagonist Richard Lovatt Somers denies being 'the enemy of civilisation' and states, 'I won't give up the flag of our real civilised consciousness' or 'the aware, self-responsible, deep consciousness that we've gained' (348:36, 33–5).

[44] See Merrild, *A Poet and Two Painters: A Memoir of D. H. Lawrence* (1938), pp. 51–69. DHL met Merrild (1894–1954) and Götzsche (b. 1886) at the New Mexico home of the Chicago painter Walter Ufer, of the Taos Society of Artists.

[45] On relations between Seltzer and Mountsier in this period, see David Ellis, *D. H. Lawrence: Dying Game, 1922–1930* (Cambridge, 1998), pp. 84–9.

I want to leave soon . . . It has been ugly enough, M. Sterne and Mountsier' (iv. 378).

Mexico (March–July, September–November 1923)

'Au Revoir, U. S. A.'

Lawrence had thought for some time of writing 'an American novel', mentioning this ambition to Seltzer from Australia in June 1922 (iv. 259); and a false start in Taos – recording Mabel's experiences[46] – helped to turn his imagination southwards. On New Year's Day 1923 he wrote to the painter Jan Juta that he didn't 'want to write here' (in New Mexico) but intended to move on 'into Mexico' (iv. 366). Nonetheless, it was 21 March before the Lawrences crossed the United States border at El Paso, Texas, by train. Two weeks later they visited the ruins of San Juan Teotihuacán, the most extensive pre-Aztec site in Mexico, where sacrifice had once been offered at three gigantic pyramids. Both events are woven into 'Au Revoir, U. S. A.', Lawrence's only essay from this first visit to Mexico. The manuscript has not survived; the piece was published in *Laughing Horse* later the same year.

Although little is known about its composition, it probably occurred soon after 3 April, when the trip to the ruins took place (iv. 417). The Lawrences, who were staying at the Monte Carlo Hotel in Mexico City, were accompanied by Bynner and Johnson, who had joined them a week earlier. To Lawrence's own surprise, perhaps, he had already taken an immediate dislike to 'gruesome Aztec carvings' (iv. 416). In the essay he describes the Pyramid of Quetzalcoatl as an exemplar of a country that honours menacing snake imagery, for the huge fanged heads of the feathered serpent project from the pyramid walls, and a great carved snake runs along its base.[47] But he nevertheless preferred a hot-tempered country with fangs to one of hypocrisy and restrained tensions. 'The blood flows free again in the veins', he wrote to his mother-in-law (iv. 415). And to Nina Witt, a Taos acquaintance, he contrasted Mexico's transient European veneer with the pyramids that 'are impressive still – very: seem to have risen out of the earth: while all the Spanish stuff is just superimposed, extraneous – and collapsing' (iv. 417–18).

[46] 'The Wilful Woman' (so named by Keith Sagar), in *St. Mawr and Other Stories*, ed. Brian Finney (Cambridge, 1983), pp. 197–203.
[47] DHL had almost certainly seen a sculpted serpent from Mexico in the British Museum; well before visiting Mexico, he referred to a 'coiled Aztec rattlesnake carved in stone', in his essay on Hector St John de Crèvecoeur (*Studies* 37:31 and note).

Lawrence was busily seeking a place to write *Quetzalcoatl*, as he would call the first (and indeed the final) version of *The Plumed Serpent*.[48] Although he declared on 21 April, 'I should never be able to write on this continent' (iv. 426), just five days later he discovered the lakeside village that provided the novel's chief setting; and he telegraphed Frieda, 'Chapala paradise. Take evening train' (iv. 435).[49] Before leaving Mexico in July, he had written 479 pages, nearly a complete novel, although only five-eighths of the length of the final version. Still ambivalent about Mexico, Lawrence separated from Frieda in August in New York, where she sailed for England alone. In her absence, he was drawn again to the American West, heading to California and eventually travelling with Kai Götzsche by train and even muleback through rugged western Mexico, then to Guadalajara and Vera Cruz. The main literary product of this period was *The Boy in the Bush*, which Lawrence fashioned from the manuscript of his Australian collaborator, M. L. (Mollie) Skinner (iv. 532), and in which he continued the preoccupation with 'young' if 'awful' gods (iv. 513) that carried over into his Mexican novel and essays.

Europe (November 1923 – March 1924)

'Dear Old Horse, A London Letter'

From Mexico, he gave one explanation for his whereabouts in a letter of 17 October, explaining that New York had caused him 'a revulsion' and the wish 'to go to the uttermost ends of the earth' (iv. 513). But he continued to feel ambivalent about his own 'place' – which, according to Frieda, was England (iv. 513). To Mabel he remembered riding horses near Taos (iv. 515), and to Catherine Carswell he revealed the dream that he might 'start a little centre – a ranch' with adobe houses (iv. 513), a new Mexican version of his old plan for a utopian retreat. With Frieda still urging him to come to England, however, he began to consider Christmas there, though without enthusiasm (iv. 525). From Guadalajara, on the very day before his departure, he told Mabel, 'I feel I belong here . . . This is the Indian *source:* this Aztec and Maya' (iv. 541). But he sailed with Götzsche from Vera Cruz on 22 November, the painter going on to Denmark and Lawrence to Hampstead.

---

[48] While he borrowed the 'plumed serpent' image and the name of the god from some 'awful' sources (as shown in 'Au Revoir, U. S. A.'), the novel is also informed by a tradition of Quetzalcoatl the benign culture-hero (see Appendix V:3 and *PS* 553–4). When *Quetzalcoatl* was at last published in 1995, it was allowed to have the Nahuatl title DHL wished for it whereas the 1926 publication of the final version bore the English translation.

[49] See Witter Bynner, *Journey with Genius: Recollections and Reflections Concerning the D. H. Lawrences* (New York, 1951), p. 79.

During the next weeks, he complained bitterly of Europe. From London, Paris and Baden-Baden, he wrote essays he called 'Letters' – two of them sent to Johnson for *Laughing Horse*. Johnson published the first the following summer as 'Dear Old Horse, A London Letter from D. H. Lawrence'. The third, from Germany, went unnoticed for another ten years, appearing well after Lawrence's death, when the *New Statesman and Nation* brought it out (1934). This last 'Letter', and evidently its two companions as well, belonged to the notebook that later contained 'The Woman Who Rode Away'. Bought in Mexico, the small notebook was in use from November 1923 to June 1924; Lawrence wrote in it from both ends, producing some texts whose alternate leaves bore reversed stamped numbers on the bottom left, as in this case. Nearly every piece was removed from the notebook itself and the contents scattered.[50] The manuscript pages of 'Letter from Germany', which are extant, are stamped 109–11 (reversed), and 'Dear Old Horse, A London Letter' must have been on 134–6 (reversed);[51] similarly, 'Paris Letter' probably occupied 131–3 (reversed). Even texts that are lost can sometimes be 'placed' in the notebook by calculating their length and ascertaining dates of composition.

Most thematically related to the Southwest and Mexico was the first 'Letter', celebrating the so-called turquoise (or blue) horse, revered in Navajo and other Southwestern Indian myth as the steed of the sun.[52] Lawrence's greetings, opening the essay, show that he was responding to the December issue of the *Laughing Horse*, which contained 'Song of the Horse', translated from Navajo by Natalie Curtis Burlin.[53] It had also contained 'Au Revoir, U. S. A.' In a letter of 9 January, Lawrence acknowledged receiving it, telling Johnson, 'Got your *Horse*. Send you an article in shape of letter', adding 'I think I'll try and send you a similar article each month' (iv. 555). Twice in the next three weeks he wrote from Paris to know if the 'little article' – 'that London Letter on Cheval' – had arrived in Santa Fe (iv. 561, 567). He hoped to revise a typescript 'if there is time' (iv. 567), but it is unlikely that he did so. Back in Taos, he wrote to Johnson on 7 April, 'I don't think it's any good

---

[50] The notebook is in the Harry T. Moore estate; see *Reflections* xxxiii n. 53.

[51] Cf. *The Woman Who Rode Away and Other Stories*, ed. Dieter Mehl and Christa Jansohn (Cambridge, 1995), p. xxiii; *Reflections* xxxiii; and Tedlock 134.

[52] See LaVerne Harrell Clark, *They Sang for Horses: The Impact of the Horse on Navajo and Apache Folklore* (Tucson, 1983), pp. 21, 27–31. The 'passion' for blue and turquoise in New Mexico pueblos is mentioned in DHL's *Apocalypse and the Writings on Revelation*, ed. Mara Kalnins (Cambridge, 1980), 128:15–23.

[53] *Laughing Horse*, ix ('Southwest Number'), also contained a review of Burlin's *The Indian Book* (first published in 1907) and news of a Pueblo Indian meeting.

altering the London Letter' (v. 27–8); and the essay appeared the next month in *Laughing Horse*.

This piece contrasts a dark, wintry England with a sunny American Southwest and Mexico. In correspondence, too, Lawrence attributed some of his sense of 'a deadness everywhere' to 'the change from the brightness of Mexico' (iv. 550). Only in the wide-open American spaces is the mythic blue horse still running free. The same day he sent 'Dear Old Horse' to Johnson, Lawrence wrote to Mabel that she should not lose her 'Horse-Sense' – 'It is the Centaur's way of knowledge' – or her sense of humour, a mark of 'the great God Pan' (iv. 555, 556). The piece is part of his 'Pan cluster'.[54] In the 'London Letter', he declares that, while the centaur perished in Europe at the Renaissance, the sacred horse of America is, Pan-like, resurgent, getting the 'last laugh'. The short story 'The Last Laugh', with its laughter of Pan, and 'Jimmy and the Desperate Woman', with its ironic reference to Pan, both written only weeks later, are found in the same notebook with 'Dear Old Horse'.[55]

'Paris Letter'

In the 'Paris Letter', Lawrence continued the theme of the centaur's death, mentioning a Tuileries sculpture of Hercules slaying it; the reference is part of a contrast between finished art and unexhausted reserves of life. Paris is cast as a collection of ponderous old monuments, all weighing down animate life. On 25 January, Lawrence wrote in a similar vein: 'Paris has great beauty – but all like a museum. And when one looks out of the Louvre windows, one wonders whether the museum is more inside or outside – whether all Paris, with its rue de la Paix and its Champs Elysées isn't also all just a sort of museum' (iv. 563). As he shuns palaces in 'Paris Letter', declaring himself a true 'democrat' in opposition to great hereditary 'houses' or dynasties, Lawrence nonetheless argues with some of the stereotypical ideas of democracy. Far better, he thinks, was the natural 'aristocracy' he attributes to American Indians – comparable to the nobility in Homer. Lawrence had arrived in Paris on 23 January (iv. 561, 562) and wrote this essay before 1 February, when he had already 'sent' it to Johnson and stated that he 'definitely' wanted to look at it once more before publication (iv. 567). It is not known whether or not he revised it before its appearance in 1926.

---

[54] See Patricia Merivale, *Pan the Goat-God: His Myth in Modern Times* (Cambridge, Mass., 1969), pp. 194–219, and Mark Kinkead-Weekes, 'Re-Dating "The Overtone"', *D. H. Lawrence Review*, xxv (1993–4), 75–80.

[55] *The Woman Who Rode Away and Other Stories*, ed. Mehl and Jansohn, p. xxiii.

'Letter from Germany'

'Letter from Germany' can be dated because Lawrence says it was written on the last day of his visit there – 19 February 1924: 'We are going to Paris tomorrow, so this is the last moment to write a letter from Germany'.[56] Although mailed to Johnson, it was apparently laid aside and not published until 1934, when it was misdated 1928 by the *New Statesman and Nation* (*Autumn Books Supplement*). Only when Edward D. McDonald included it in *Phoenix* was it properly assigned to 1924,[57] but the 'Letter' was then recognised as an acute, even prophetic statement of the post-war situation in Germany.

His correspondence – e.g. on 9 February to Koteliansky and Secker – shows that, early in his visit, he hoped the change he sensed in Germany was towards some 'manly' self-sufficiency (iv. 574, 576). Nonetheless, ten days later, when he was preparing to leave, he seems to have thought differently. Germany, he states in this essay, is set to repudiate the old European union between southern and northern 'races' and is leaning towards the dangerous East (as he terms it) of Attila the Hun.[58] In terms of his own symbolically charged geography, he warns not only of brewing destruction but of 'evil' that seeks 'to rouse again and work on us – particularly Europe' (iv. 586). In his essay, the post-war mood is set by an account of the hard-fought Marne country, the same deathly location that appears in the short story 'The Border-Line' (the first version of which was written in the same notebook).[59] Even more ominous, in the essay, is the sense that Germany is caught in an almost automatic time lapse, regressing towards medieval and even prehistoric conflicts, not looking towards the future.

After this visit, he was in a hurry to return to America, impelled by discouragement with Europe, a strong desire to get back to his Mexican novel, and worry about Seltzer's financial crisis and long silence. But it was 5 March before the Lawrences actually embarked, along with the painter Dorothy Brett,[60] who had known Lawrence slightly since 1915 and who was the only one to accept his invitation to several friends to make a new life in America.[61]

---

[56] 'Letter from Germany' (149:2–3).   [57] *Phoenix* xv.

[58] See *Studies* 383:19; 'Attila', *Poems* 497; and *Movements in European History*, ed. Crumpton, 69:13–73:35.

[59] *The Woman Who Rode Away*, ed. Mehl and Jansohn, pp. xxiii–xxiv.

[60] Dorothy Brett (1883–1976), daughter of Viscount Esher, was born in London and studied painting at the Slade Institute. She remained in Taos after DHL's departure, becoming a US citizen in 1938. Today she is best known for her paintings of Indian ceremonials.

[61] Ellis, *Dying Game*, pp. 148–52; cf. also Catherine Carswell, *The Savage Pilgrimage: A Narrative of D. H. Lawrence* (1932; 2nd edn, Cambridge, 1981), pp. 205–13, and Brett 20–2.

For a time Brett would become Lawrence's principal typist in America as well
as a faithful friend. His old friend Murry, who had also promised to go, backed
out; but a dialogue of ideas, particularly on religion and self-responsibility,
continued between the two; and Lawrence's essays of the following year
contributed to it.[62]

Taos and Kiowa Ranch (March–October 1924)

'Indians and Entertainment'

The next spring and summer in New Mexico comprised one of Lawrence's
most intense periods of creative energy, eventually producing (among other
things) four of the essays in this volume as well as *St. Mawr*, 'The Woman
Who Rode Away' and 'The Princess'. Back in late March at Mabel Luhan's
Taos compound, Lawrence had again arrived at a time of some crisis for the
Pueblo Indians and was soon caught up in their Easter activities. He produced,
within days, two essays – 'Indians and Entertainment' and 'The Dance of the
Sprouting Corn' – and a poem that sheds light on their genesis. His renewed
focus on Indian ceremonials was sharpened by the Good Friday meeting
(18 April) between Taos Pueblo leaders and the highest officials of the Bureau
of Indian Affairs, who wanted to advance bans against traditional religious
dances and training.[63] To Lawrence it was a 'Consummatum est!' for the
Pueblo people.[64] The poem 'O! Americans' tells the story: 'Today is Easter
Sunday: . . . / On Good Friday the big white men of the Indian Bureau and
big white men from Washington drove out to the pueblo, summoned the old
Indian men, and held a meeting behind closed doors', counselling them against
their 'useless practices' in an effort to integrate them into white mainstream
society.[65] Lawrence, showing little of the pressured spleen of some of his
Bursum Bill writing, sides with the tribe and even, to some unexpected
extent, with the 'artists and long-haired people' who have been accused of
preventing the Indian from becoming a 'hundred-per-cent American'.[66]

On Easter Sunday (20 April), he wrote to Curtis Brown, 'I send a little
article – "Indians and Entertainment"' (v. 36). He had mailed the 'original

---

[62] Catherine Carswell considered *Mornings in Mexico* an 'apologia and manifesto to Middleton
Murry' (*The Savage Pilgrimage*, p. 219 n. 1), and she found this response to Murry clearest
in the 1924 essays on Indian dance (p. 223). See also *The Savage Pilgrimage*, pp. 180–1, 187.

[63] Charles Burke, Commissioner of Indian Affairs (1921–9), came in person to Taos Pueblo
to argue his policy. He believed that the frequent rituals, and training for them, impeded
education and acceptance of federal norms. He was the author of the Burke Act (1906), one
of the founding documents of the assimilationist policy opposed by Collier.

[64] *Poems* 779.   [65] *Poems* 777.   [66] *Poems* 778.

typescript' to A. W. Barmby of Curtis Brown's New York office with advice to concentrate on 'the more serious magazines' (v. 36).[67] While not responding directly to the topical threat, 'Indians and Entertainment' is a defence of the old ceremonies, including accounts of the deer dance, the corn dance and the round dance. It ponders the profound distinction between European theatrical conventions of spectator-and-stage and the Indian enactment of pure 'being' and of taking part in the cycles of nature and the animate universe.

Nancy Pearn, who handled periodical submissions for Curtis Brown (London), wrote on 9 May that she was trying to place 'Indians and Entertainment' with reviews (v. 50),[68] but its first appearance was in the *New York Times Magazine*, which silently cut a large number of its key passages – including the Indian commandment to '*acknowledge the wonder*'[69] – thus considerably altering its focus and ending abruptly on the unexplained note that the Indian dance has no sense of God or of the conscious mind. Since Lawrence did not react in his letters to this mutilation, it is possible he was unaware of it, being preoccupied initially with his third trip to Mexico, then with *The Plumed Serpent*, and finally with life-threatening illness. His faulty recollection in 1926 and 1927 was that *Theatre Arts Monthly* had published this piece (v. 595, 636). Most of it also appeared in the *Adelphi*, but there, too, the last paragraph was omitted; the essay went into *Mornings in Mexico* without it and the paragraph has in consequence never previously been published.[70]

'The Dance of the Sprouting Corn'

On 23 April, Lawrence says he wrote 'The Dance of the Sprouting Corn': 'This is the Wednesday after Easter.'[71] He had been watching the seasonal dance at Santo Domingo,[72] but, although the essay is usually considered a description of that particular corn dance, it must in fact have been a composite. Lawrence knew about the corn dance well enough beforehand (probably at Taos Pueblo) to include it in 'Indians and Entertainment', and on 7 April he sent Johnson a simplified copy of his sketch of two corn dancers, traced by Brett for *Laughing Horse* (v. 27). The more detailed sketch, with a pueblo in the background, went to *Theatre Arts Monthly* before 19 June – when he

---

[67] Barmby represented Curtis Brown in the New York office. After dismissing Mountsier in February 1923, DHL had no American agent until the American office of Curtis Brown took over in spring 1924.

[68] See *Letters*, v. 110 n. 2: the *Adelphi* had accepted it by 22 September.

[69] 'Indians and Entertainment' (67:40).   [70] See Explanatory note on 68:36.

[71] 'The Dance of the Sprouting Corn' (72:8).

[72] On 7 April DHL had asked Johnson about Easter dances at Santo Domingo or San Felipe (v. 27).

mentioned that he expected his 'two little drawings' to accompany a 'little article' that was forthcoming from that journal (v. 59). The second drawing was almost certainly Lawrence's depiction of a *koshare* (a jester-like dance figure), resembling, as in the essay, a deadened corn-cob in need of spring resurrection. (See Illustrations I and II.)[73] But this journal, while publishing the essay and the drawing of the two dancers, used another artist's sketch of a *koshare*.[74]

Still, Lawrence was pleased enough with the appearance of his one drawing and essay to mention them to several correspondents (v. 59, 87, 100, 114, 116). 'The Dance of the Sprouting Corn' was also published with little textual difference in the *Adelphi*, unillustrated, the following month. It is probable that copies were sent to the English and American journals in April at about the same time, and a letter from Nancy Pearn, dated 29 May, shows that Murry had already accepted it before that date.[75] Two months later, Lawrence's sister-in-law Else Jaffe published her translation of the essay in German (also without illustration), and Lawrence commented to Curtis Brown that 'it was very much liked' (v. 173).[76] When *Mornings in Mexico* was in preparation in 1927, Edith Isaacs, editor of *Theatre Arts Monthly*, put together a collection, *Theatre: Essays on the Arts of the Theatre*, which contained 'The Dance of the Sprouting Corn' though not Lawrence's drawing.[77]

'Pan in America'

Soon after the return to New Mexico, Mabel Luhan gave Frieda Lawrence the ranch she had originally shown to the Lawrences at the end of October 1922. Mabel's son John had traded it back to her, making her generosity possible. As a return gift, Lawrence gave Mabel the manuscript of *Sons and Lovers*; and, according to his account to his niece Margaret King: 'Every one

---

[73] See Roberts A37.5, C122 and C139. A37.5 is a 1927 broadside in news-print from Santa Fe, $8\frac{7}{8} \times 6$ in., displaying 'Pueblo Indian Dancers', reproducing the illustration not from C122 (DHL's original, more detailed drawing in *Theatre Arts Monthly*) but from C139 (the traced version from the 1926 *Laughing Horse*) which also appeared on the cover of Secker's *Mornings in Mexico* in 1927.

[74] DHL's sketch of a *koshare* was first printed in *The Letters of D. H. Lawrence*, ed. Aldous Huxley (1932), opposite p. 596.

[75] This letter, and others by Nancy Pearn, are at UT.

[76] 'Der Tanz vom Sprießenden Korn', *Der Neue Merkur*, viii (October 1924), 104–10, probably translated from *Theatre Arts Monthly*. On 17 November DHL suggested that Brown send Else Jaffe a copy of 'The Hopi Snake Dance' to translate (*Letters*, v. 173) but no such translation has been found.

[77] (Boston, 1927), pp. 246–54. This volume was reprinted in 1968. The source was *Theatre Arts Monthly* (Per1).

is very mad with me for giving that MS. The ranch was worth only about $1000, and the MS of *Sons and Lovers* worth three or four thousand – so everybody says. But I don't care' (*Letters*, v. 111). At any rate, the Lawrences did not move to the ranch until May, when they repaired the buildings for occupancy – making adobe bricks, plastering walls and restoring roofs. (See Map 4.)

The property, located 17 miles from Taos, lies 8,600 feet above sea level, surrounded by pine forest and wildlife and prone to 'going wild' (v. 112). 'It's a wonderful place', Lawrence had written the previous autumn, 'with the world at your feet and the mountains at your back, and pine-trees' (iv. 334). It had a rich pioneer history, having been occupied in the 1880s by a gold-miner, who settled under the US Homestead Act, and then tended by farmers, William and Mary McClure, who raised goats – and who had sold the property to Mabel in 1920.[78]

But Lawrence was probably even more captivated by its natural history and its nearness to an ancient Indian route to Taos Pueblo, frequented for hundreds of years by a variety of Indian tribes. In the same Sangre de Cristo Mountains are two Tiwa-speaking pueblos, Taos and Picturis. The Taos Indian workers who assisted Lawrence with repairs must have given him a deepening sense of the ranch's interconnection with native American culture, and, although the Lawrences had already named the ranch Lobo (Spanish, 'Wolf'), in August they renamed it Kiowa Ranch for an Indian tribe that had camped on the hillside long ago (v. 228). Past and present must have seemed to blend when the workers camped 'just above the cabin, under the hanging stars, and we sit with the Indians round the fire, and they sing till late into the night, and sometimes we all dance the Indian tread-dance' (v. 67). In such circumstances, Lawrence began 'Pan in America'.

It exists in two versions, the later one that has been published and an earlier one, already quite advanced on 12 May,[79] a week after the move to the ranch. Although they are separate creations in numerous passages, both emphasise conflict between romantic 'pantheism', especially as developed in American Transcendentalism, and the native spirit of place. Pan is not identified with pastoral fauns but with hunters and is emblematised by a great wild pine tree. The first version makes no direct acknowledgement of the Indians, and Mabel, aware of this version, evidently commented on the lack. In a letter of 14 May, Lawrence protested to her, 'But I had said the things you wrote

[78] See *Letters*, v. 110–11.
[79] DHL wanted Johnson to type the first version of 'Pan in America' (v. 40); even if he did, however, the typescript has not been located.

about the Indians, differently' (v. 43); nonetheless, when he rewrote the essay, he may have borne her hint in mind. The originally generic tree became the huge pine 'on this little ranch under the Rocky Mountains' where once 'the Indians blazed it'[80] – one of five explicit references to native Americans. This particularisation is one of the chief differences between the two versions. It has previously not been known why the essay lay unmentioned and unpublished for nearly a year and a half after its inception. To Mabel, Lawrence stated on 14 May that it was still incomplete: 'I feel a trifle discouraged, don't want to write' (v. 43). In fact, this early version was never finished, but the second writing (though not mentioned in the correspondence) may well have been done fairly soon after the first; they are on identical paper. Certainly, it was his frequent practice to begin a new version of a work soon after abandoning the previous effort, rather than simply revising. Yet similarities between the second 'Pan in America' and the latter part of *St. Mawr* (started probably in June) make it credible that some or all of the second version of the essay dates from later in the summer.

It is now known that Witter Bynner sent the manuscript of the final version to the American scholar Jay B. Hubbell, who was the founding editor of *Southwest Review* from 1924 to 1927. Hubbell noted that he received it from Bynner 'while Lawrence was in the Southwest (or Mexico?)'.[81] Bynner was on the advisory board of the review, sending Hubbell submissions from Taos and Santa Fe writers, and Lawrence must have been aware of this connection. Since the Curtis Brown stamp on the manuscript suggests that it was typed at that agency, it is not known why Lawrence entrusted it – and not a copy – to Bynner. Very possibly he had sent it to be typed, received only the manuscript back, and had no other copy for Bynner. Neither can the time be fixed with certainty, because opportunities to pass the essay to Bynner would have been numerous, especially in the summer of 1924. Still, the 1926 publication in the *Southwest Review* seems late for this dating. Examination of the essay's second version suggests that it may have remained unfinished for some time, then was concluded with a rather cursory last paragraph that seeks to make Pan relevant even to 'the mechanical conquered universe of modern humanity'.[82] Although the ink is of the same kind throughout the manuscript, it appears slightly fainter in the last paragraph (as if the pen had been taken up after an

[80] 'Pan in America' (157:37, 157:39).

[81] Autograph note by Hubbell (at the Perkins Library at DU), attached to the essay's manuscript (second version). In summer 1924, Hubbell had revived the *Texas Review*, expanding it into the *Southwest Review*. Bynner's correspondence with Hubbell (also housed at DU) does not mention the essay.

[82] 'Pan in America' (164:24–5).

interval), and the lines are crammed into a small space at the end of the page. Although Lawrence had projected 'two parts' of the essay (v. 40), the final version never developed a second 'part'. The first version ends when the man rises renewed from a healing sexual encounter with a woman; but the second reveals his veiled fears of being wounded by the woman, as by the moon's dangerous horns, and moves from the love episode into a short commentary about the passing of the old way of life. Mabel Luhan's response to the text, a new feud between her circle and Lawrence's (v. 54, 64, 68, 69, 72, 73, 76) and continuing tension between himself and Frieda[83] – and between Frieda and Brett – may help to explain a certain shrinking away from his frequent theme of the relation between the sexes.

In many ways, the first version illustrates relationships outlined in *Fantasia of the Unconscious*, the man being the purposive 'pioneer' by day while the 'evening and the night', at the 'camp fire', are woman's to restore and replenish him.[84] But stronger female protagonists were rising in Lawrence's imagination, particularly those of *St. Mawr* and *The Plumed Serpent*, and the essay's planned extension may have been diverted into such later works.[85] In *St. Mawr*, for example, Lou Carrington finds no mate as grand as the spirit of place at her Las Chivas Ranch – the spirit of Pan or of a god '*shaggy as the pine-trees*'.[86] Las Chivas is based on Kiowa Ranch, and the descriptions of place in this tale and in 'Pan in America' have strong affinities with each other. In both works, when Lawrence tries to see a future for Indian culture, he feels prevented by the inroads of a false civilisation upon the aboriginal lifestyle – as witness the essay's younger generation and the tale's enigmatic character, Phoenix.[87]

'The Hopi Snake Dance'

The last of the 1924 quartet of essays on Southwestern Indians was 'The Hopi Snake Dance', based on a ceremony the Lawrences attended with Mabel and Tony at Hotevilla, Arizona, on 18 August (v. 100–1). The party later motored through the Navajo lands to the sacred Cañon de Chelly – 'all wild, with great

---

[83] In a letter to Catherine Carswell, DHL stated: 'One doesn't talk any more about being happy – that is child's talk' (*Letters*, v. 47).

[84] In *Psychoanalysis and the Unconscious and Fantasia of the Unconscious*, ed. Steele, 136:29, 31–2.

[85] See also 'The Princess', in the same volume, pp. 159–96, and 'The Woman Who Rode Away', in *The Woman Who Rode Away and Other Stories*, ed. Mehl and Jansohn, pp. 39–71.

[86] *St. Mawr and Other Stories*, ed. Finney, 147:36.

[87] The love and marriage theme would resurface later that year in the final version of *The Plumed Serpent*, which unites the Mexican Indian and European lovers and even projects, mythically, a renewed world harmony (see, e.g., *PS* 414–15).

red cliffs bluffing up', as Lawrence described the area (v. 109). He had been ill – according to Brett, he had haemorrhaged some days before[88] – and was wearied by long periods in the automobile. In a Santa Fe hotel on the way home, he wrote a partly satirical account, 'Just Back from the Snake Dance',[89] on the back of two pages of a letter from Brett. It satirises both tourists and Indians, particularly in the last paragraphs with their American slang terms; and when Lawrence showed it to Mabel she did not conceal her annoyance. 'I had not taken him to the Snake Dance to have him describe it in this fashion', she wrote later,[90] and Lawrence, back in Taos on 23 August, sought to make amends. 'I'll write a sketch for the *Theatre Arts*', he promised, and planned to do a drawing too, something 'not for the *Horse* to laugh at' (v. 103). Although Lawrence does not seem to have done the proposed drawing, his essay 'The Hopi Snake Dance' is the first item in a new notebook dated 26 August and written within days of that date.[91] Since this Hopi essay remained in the bound book, it had to be copied in order to be sent out to Curtis Brown; Brett may have typed it and Lawrence corrected the typescript, though it is just possible that Lawrence mailed a fair longhand copy, considerably revised.

Even though he had mentioned the *Theatre Arts Monthly* to Mabel, he had created in 'The Hopi Snake Dance' a more philosophical essay than he supposed this magazine would favour; both the content and the length gave him pause, and the first editor he contacted, on 30 August, was Murry. Lawrence told him that he was just sending his new essay to Brown and

[88] Brett 139–41.

[89] There is no evidence that DHL wrote the last two words of the title given in the *Laughing Horse* publication of 1924: 'Just Back from the Snake Dance – Tired Out'.

[90] *Lorenzo in Taos*, p. 268.

[91] Inside the notebook front, DHL inscribed '26 August 1924 / D. H. Lawrence / Kiowa Ranch / near Taos New Mexico'. He wrote in it from front to back but sometimes skipped ahead to leave room for a planned work and then found he had too little space; thus the items are not entirely chronological, and there is some overlap of pagination not detailed below. The contents include: 'The Hopi Snake Dance', 1–18 (stamped pp. 1–18); 'Introduction to Bibliography' for Edward D. McDonald's *A Bibliography of the Writings of D. H. Lawrence* (Philadelphia, 1925), published in the volume as 'The Bad Side of Books', 1–4 (pp. 19–22); 'The Princess', 1–53 with numbering error (pp. 23–73), 'Mornings in Mexico' – 'Friday Morning', 1–8 (pp. 74–81); 'Saturday Morning', 1–9 (pp. 82–90); 'Sunday Morning', 1–14 (pp. 91–104); 'Monday Morning', 1–13 (pp. 105–17); 'Resurrection', 1–4 (pp. 118–21); 'See Mexico After, by Luis Q.', 1–8 (pp. 122–9); 'Suggestions for Stories', 1–2 (parts of pp. 129, 130); untitled philosophical fragment, 1–3 (pp. 131–3); notes heading *Noah's Flood* and text of unfinished original version of play, 1–10 (pp. 134–43); 'Mediterranean in January', 1–2 (pp. 144–5); 'Beyond the Rockies', 1–2 (parts of 145, 146); seven blank pages (pp. 147–53); 'Preface to *Black Swans*' [by Mollie Skinner], 1–4 (pp. 154, 155–7); and 'Climbing Down Pisgah', 1–6 (pp. 158–60 and down both sides of the flyleaf and inside the back cover). The last-written of these compositions, 'Beyond the Rockies', was produced in January 1926. The notebook is housed at UT.

wanted Murry to read it despite its length: 'it defines somewhat my position' (v. 109). On the same day he told Nancy Pearn that, if the piece went to Murry, he was 'not to cut it' (v. 110). He even urged E. M. Forster to 'borrow the MS from Jack [Murry]' to read (v. 116): it is all but certain that he meant the copy from Brown's office. On 6 September, Lawrence wrote to Edith Isaacs, as he had to Murry, about his new essay, already having directed that Lida McCord of Curtis Brown send her a copy (no doubt a typescript, as usual). It might be 'far too long and far too speculative' for her magazine, but 'I don't want to cut it down at all: not for anybody' (v. 115). The *Adelphi* could easily have published first if it had not been delayed by financial and managerial problems. Lawrence even had to forfeit some of his expected payment for the essay, writing to Murry: 'If you really cared about it, I'd tell Curtis Brown to let you have it at the price you can afford to pay' (v. 170); and he made the necessary arrangement with Curtis Brown the same day, 17 November (v. 173).

Clearly this essay was special to Lawrence; he told Murry that 'This animistic religion is the only live one ours is a corpse of a religion' (v. 109). He also informed Edith Isaacs that he felt 'rather deeply' about this essay (v. 116). Confident of the quality of his work, he asked Edith Isaacs to show Mabel Luhan (then in New York) the manuscript if she called at the magazine office (v. 116). Although the essay terms the dance itself 'grotesque rather than beautiful', it upholds the dignity of this sacred ritual to put human beings into contact with the cosmic 'dragon', the 'dark sun' to which the serpent is an emissary – the 'source' which is termed 'Sun' simply 'because the other name is too fearful'.[92] Lawrence posits a similar animistic mythology among the peoples of 'all aboriginal America'.[93] Furthermore, he gives credence to the relatively peaceful lifestyle of the Pueblo Indians he has known, asserting that their dragon 'is still somewhat gentle-hearted' in contrast with the Mexican dragon-gods that instilled 'horror'.[94] The two journals adopted different solutions to the problem of the essay's length. *Theatre Arts Monthly* combined paragraphs and created divisions with bold-faced subheadings while the *Adelphi* printed it in two instalments.[95] These publications appear to be the first states of the text after the manuscript to survive.[96]

---

[92] See 'The Hopi Snake Dance' (81:12, 83:4, 86:25, 92:4–6).

[93] 'The Hopi Snake Dance' (83:28); see also 94:12–13. See also Appendix V:1–7.

[94] 'The Hopi Snake Dance' (83:31–2, 83:30).

[95] The third publication, in the *Living Age*, cccxxv (4 April 1925), 47–56, was an abridgement of the *Adelphi* publication.

[96] See footnote 34.

Mexico (October 1924 – March 1925)

'Mornings in Mexico': 'Corasmin and the Parrots', 'Market Day', 'Walk to Huayapa', 'The Mozo'

Lawrence's continuing poor health was one reason for his move to Mexico in autumn 1924; but neither he, Frieda nor Brett could stay in the USA for more than six months at a time without new visas (vii. 94), and he and Frieda probably did not want to spend another winter at such a high altitude (as they had done in 1922–3). The party arrived in Mexico City on 23 October but within the week he and Frieda contracted colds – 'grippe' or 'influenza' (v. 156, 157, 160) – and he looked south for a still warmer climate. Besides, the most significant impetus for the trip to Mexico was his desire to complete his 'American' or 'Mexican' novel – and not in a 'resort' setting, as he now termed Chapala (v. 163), but in a more remote location; Oaxaca appealed to him for its strongly indigenous character as well as for its climate. As he described it to Secker on 9 December: 'The little town of Oaxaca is lonely, away in the south and miles from anywhere except the Indian villages of the hills. I like it: it gives me something' (v. 184). Writing to his good friend Earl Brewster, the American painter who had invited him and Frieda to Ceylon in 1922, he called the Zapotec and Mixtec Indians 'wild' but 'sympatico' (v. 184). The Zapotecs descended from the builders of Monte Albán and Mitla,[97] where the Mixtecs had gained authority in later centuries before the Spanish Conquest (see Appendixes V:2 and VI:1). Both peoples had independently practised advanced calendar arts revealing their skills in astronomy, mathematics and iconic script. They were sculptors and architects, warriors and priests, jewellery-makers and potters; the Zapotec civilisation had been even earlier than the Aztec to the north and basically independent of the Mayan to the south. The Indians of Lawrence's time brought to market the wares – pottery, sculptures, woven blankets and other textiles – for which they are still known today.

Lawrence already knew of Oaxaca as a centre of Zapotec culture,[98] and he referred to this tribe as well as to 'the Maya Indians' when informing his mother-in-law on 2 October that 'there [in Oaxaca] I'd like to finish my

---

[97] The DHL party visited Mitla, as he reported on 7 December (v. 182), and its 'carved courts' appear in *The Plumed Serpent*: 'Hard, four-square, sharp-edged, cutting, zig-zagging Mitla' (79:37–8).

[98] Jaime de Angulo, an anthropologist DHL knew in Taos in 1924, worked in Oaxaca in 1922–3 with Manuel Gamio, a well-known Mexican archaeologist, who wrote to DHL in 1924 (*Letters*, v. 45, 55, 59). But DHL had learned of Oaxaca during his first trip to Mexico and, even while in Europe in 1923–4, he wanted to go there (*Letters*, iv. 545, 592 and 596).

novel' (v. 139).[99] The English Vice-Consul Constantine Rickards, himself an expert on the region's antiquities,[100] put the Lawrences in touch with his brother, Father Edward Rickards, a Roman Catholic priest who rented a wing of his Oaxaca home to the Lawrences while Brett stayed in the Hotel Francia downtown. Although the location had fairly little impact on the scenes in *The Plumed Serpent*, which retained much of their likeness to Chapala, the grounds provided perhaps the best-known setting in *Mornings in Mexico*: as Lawrence described them in a letter of 22 November, three days after moving in, they included 'a very lovely patio, enclosed garden with gigantic trees, coffee-plants, hibiscus flowers, poinsettias – very beautiful' (v. 177). He already had the inspiration for the opening episode of 'Corasmin and the Parrots': 'There are two parrots now sitting in the orange-tree, shrieking Perro! Oh Perro! Perro! (means dog!)' (v. 177–8). Here, while rewriting *The Plumed Serpent* in a ten-week period between late November 1924 and 1 February 1925 (v. 207, 230),[101] Lawrence also wrote the four 'Mornings in Mexico' essays. On 19 December he reported 'doing one or two little articles' which he hoped would 'suit Vanity Fair' (v. 185–6). Lawrence says in 'Corasmin and the Parrots' that Christmas will come the following week, thus indicating that its 'Friday Morning' is probably the same day as the letter. 'Market Day' ('Saturday Morning'), written next, is set on the following day, the Saturday prior to Christmas, 20 December. In 'Walk to Huayapa', it is presumably 'Sunday Morning'; the piece's one reference to Christmas is only a simile, and the solstice is still approaching, for the next day will be the year's shortest.[102] 'The Mozo' spans more than a week's time: from the evening of the walk to Huayapa and the following day of gloom ('Monday Morning') – 22 December – through the Thursday fiesta (Christmas Day was a Thursday) to the following 'Monday Morning' – that is, 29 December.[103] This essay,

---

99 Although DHL was not technically accurate in locating the Maya in Oaxaca (see Gordon Brotherston, *Book of the Fourth World: Reading the Native Americas Through Their Literature* (Cambridge, 1993), pp. 13–20), the ancient calendar art and mythology of this region have some affinities with those of adjacent Mayan culture.

100 Besides collecting artifacts in Oaxaca, where he grew up, Constantine Rickards wrote *The Ruins of Mexico* (1910). A sixteenth-century Mixtec *lienzo* once bore his name as the Rickards Codex (Parmenter 27–8).

101 See *PS* xxxiii.

102 Since 1924 was a leap year, DHL may have been uncertain of the date of the solstice, which can occur variously on 21 or 22 December. But he seems to mean that the date was 21 December, with the solstice 'tomorrow'.

103 See Ross Parmenter's discussion of chronology for 'The Mozo' in his 'Introduction' to *Mornings in Mexico*, ed. Ross Parmenter (Salt Lake City, 1982), p. xxx.

too, uses the imagery of the Nativity – this time for ironic contrast with an Aztec myth about the birth of a flint knife.

On 10 January 1925 Lawrence wrote to Curtis Brown, 'I am sending you four articles – "Mornings in Mexico" – nice and short – via Barmby', adding that he was 'getting ahead with the Mexican novel' and intending to finish it within the month (v. 193). These 'four articles' possess unusual allusiveness. 'Corasmin and the Parrots' proposes a Mesoamerican cosmogony of five 'Suns' or epochs that Lawrence preferred to current scientific theories of evolution; among his direct sources was Lewis Spence, whom he read in Oaxaca,[104] but other influences are also evident.[105] Using the concept of separate creations for humour, irony and even prophecy ('our Sun' is said to be doomed like those before it),[106] Lawrence packed a surprising amount into a short essay, giving it some of the cosmic and apocalyptic contexts of *The Plumed Serpent*. Similarly, 'Market Day' explores not only the Indians' long trek to town, pilgrimage-like, but also the motivations that bring people together in a body – trade and religion. 'Walk to Huayapa' is dense with references to politics and revolutions, underlying topics to which Lawrence brought the experience of one who had been dodging revolts and witnessing their destructiveness.[107] Similarly, political and social issues underlie 'The Mozo', in which Lawrence finally recognises how his Zapotec servant has dared to face reprisals by refusing to be inducted into a victorious rebel army.

---

[104] Brett (203) reported that he read Spence's *Gods of Mexico* (1923) during their stay there.

[105] Books about Mexico that he mentioned in his correspondence include Adolph Bandelier, *The Delight Makers* (New York, 1890) (v. 42); Bernal Díaz del Castillo, *The True History of the Conquest of New Spain* (1632; Maudsley's 5-vol. translation, 1908–16) (*Letters*, iv. 445–6, 452); Manuel Gamio, probably *Forjando patria* (1916) (v. 45); Gutiérrez de Lara and Edgcumb Pinchon, *The Mexican People: Their Struggle for Freedom* (1914) (iv. 394); and T. Philip Terry, *Terry's Guide to Mexico* (rev. edn, New York, 1923) (iv. 374). He is also known to have read Frances Calderón de la Barca's *Life in Mexico* (1843), William Hickling Prescott's *History of the Conquest of Mexico* (New York, 1843), Bandelier's *The Gilded Man* (New York, 1893), Zelia Nuttall's *The Fundamental Principles of Old and New World Civilizations* (Cambridge, Mass., 1901), Alexander von Humboldt's *Vues des cordillères et monuments des peuples indigènes de l'Amérique* (Paris, 1916) and some *Anales* of the National Museum of Mexico (1923), as well as Spence's book. See also *PS* xxv n. 49 and xxxii n. 89, and L. D. Clark, *Dark Night of the Body: D. H. Lawrence's 'The Plumed Serpent'* (Austin, 1964), pp. 103–14. Among many other significant influences was Frederick Carter, whose writing on astrology and the Book of Revelation DHL read in Chapala (*Letters*, iv. 459–61) – later much altered as *The Dragon of the Alchemists* (1926) – and whom he visited in 1924 in Shropshire (iv. 554).

[106] 'Corasmin and the Parrots' (17:26).

[107] DHL's letters consistently revealed the perils even in more quiescent times (e.g. *Letters*, iv. 445; v. 164, 165, 182), and this is a main theme of 'The Mozo'. See Appendix VI:3–4, *PS* 563–7 and Parmenter xxiii–xxxi.

Rosalino emerges as 'one... like myself', as Lawrence puts it, who simply will not be part of a mass movement.[108]

The four essays are in the above order in the black pebbled notebook that also held 'The Hopi Snake Dance' (see footnote 91). It is fitting to their Christmastime date that they are followed immediately by 'Resurrection', which, despite its Easter imagery, belongs to the period of the new year, and by an essay which can be dated to 10 January: 'See Mexico After, by Luis Q.' (see below). On the first page of each of the 'Mornings' essays appears the series title 'Mornings in Mexico'; on another line, after Lawrence's name, is a title designating a specific morning.

On the surviving carbon typescript of the first, Lawrence decisively deleted 'Friday Morning' and wrote 'Corasmin and the Parrots', the title by which it appeared in the *Adelphi* and subsequent publications. Similarly, on the extant carbon typescript of the third essay, he crossed out 'Sunday Morning' and wrote 'Walk to Huayapa' (all in ink). Another title 'Sunday Stroll' (underscored) was inserted in pencil, evidently by an editor at *Travel*, which published it as 'Sunday Stroll in Sleepy Mexico'. (The trip was no 'stroll'; it was a hard 9- or 10-mile trek to and from San Andrés Huayapan, near the mountains northeast of Oaxaca.)[109] The essay appeared in the *Adelphi* as 'Mornings in Mexico / Walk to Huayapa', and 'Walk to Huayapa' is the title Lawrence actually used in correspondence (e.g. v. 580) and in *Mornings in Mexico*. The carbon typescript of 'The Mozo' already bore this typed title, suggesting that the first page had been retyped (by Brett) after the decision to alter the first titles; and this essay first appeared in English in the *Adelphi* as 'Mornings in Mexico / The Mozo'.[110] But its very first appearance was in German as 'Rosalino', translated by Franz Franzius.[111] On 12 May 1925 Lawrence had written to Dr Anton Kippenberg, head of Insel Verlag, saying that he had asked Curtis Brown to send him [Kippenberg] copies of all four 'Mornings in Mexico' sketches: 'If you care for any one of them, will you please use it for this year's Almanach – whichever one you like.' Kippenberg was to post the other three to Lawrence's sister-in-law Else Jaffe: 'Or if you have other use for them, let me know' (v. 252). Lawrence, receiving his copy of the *Almanach* in Baden-Baden later that year, found the article 'amusing... in German', as he wrote to Dr Kippenberg, 2 November 1925

---

108 'The Mozo' (43:38–9).
109 See Parmenter's Introduction to *Mornings in Mexico*, p. xxviii.
110 'The Mozo' was reprinted, abridged, as 'Sons of Montezuma' in the *Living Age*, cccxxxii (1 April 1927), 608–15, from the *Adelphi*.
111 In *Insel-Almanach auf das Jahr 1926* (Leipzig, [1925]), pp. 103–19; not in Roberts.

(v. 331). The copies Kippenberg was sent have not been located, and none of the other three sketches appeared. It is not known why the title 'The Mozo' was not used, as in the *Adelphi*.

The retitling of 'Market Day' (from 'Saturday Morning') is least clear of the four. No typescript survives, and the first published title was 'The Gentle Art of Marketing in Mexico' – which has an editorial ring – in *Travel*, while the second periodical title was 'Mornings in Mexico / Saturday' in the *New Criterion*.[112] Nevertheless, Lawrence called it 'Market Day' in letters (v. 575, 580, 582) and in *Mornings in Mexico*. On 23 November 1926, when he reassembled the four essays for their first printed appearance together in the volume, he placed 'Market Day' last (v. 580), probably as the most panoramic and impressive piece. He emphasised that the four form a unified series (v. 575), and this Cambridge edition presents them as such, following the order he listed for *Mornings in Mexico*.

Delays and misunderstandings impeded the publication of these Mexican essays from the beginning. Lawrence was not altogether pleased that Murry had asked for three of them in April 1925 for the *Adelphi*.[113] In the first place, Lawrence had hoped they would please the 'glossy' press like *Vanity Fair*, but that goal had not materialised. He complained not only that Murry now paid poorly and even came to expect contributions 'gratis' (v. 386; cf. 432, 451–2) as well as delaying publication, but Lawrence also realised the worsening divergence between his and Murry's essential views, often seeing 'Murry's words coming out against me, through people who frequent him', as he informed Nancy Pearn (v. 242). On 29 January 1926 he told her plainly that he 'wouldn't mind a bit' about the lack of money from Murry but could not 'get mixed up in the sickly yellow colour of his *Adelphism*' (v. 386). Although she agreed to stop giving first choice to Murry (v. 242 n. 2), the *Adelphi* had already published 'Corasmin and the Parrots' when Lawrence asked her in April 1926 to 'take the other two from him', only partly because of the threat of non-payment (v. 432). On 13 May, however, he wrote telling her to handle the situation 'just as you think well' (v. 452), and the essays remained at the *Adelphi*, to be printed in February and March 1927, thus appearing while *Mornings in Mexico* itself was nearing production (it came out in June 1927).

---

[112] A separate private printing called *Mornings in Mexico* (Detroit, 1945) contained 'Market Day'. This is almost certainly related to the item called '*Market Day*' (1945) in a catalogue advertisement in 1977 by bookseller William Pieper, described as a Christmas greeting from Mr and Mrs Robert B. Powers (see Roberts A37 and A81.5).

[113] Nancy Pearn had written (1 April 1925): 'Middleton Murry can only pay at the rate of Half a Guinea per page, but I gather you want us to let him have contributions from time to time' (*Letters*, v. 242 n. 1).

'See Mexico After, by Luis Q.'

Only one other essay came from the Oaxaca period: 'See Mexico After, by Luis Q.' Lawrence had hatched a plan to interest *Vanity Fair* in his 'Mornings' essays while boosting the careers of Luis Quintanilla, a young Mexican writer whom he had met at a P.E.N. Club dinner in Mexico City, and the photographer Edward Weston, whom he had met through Quintanilla.[114] Lawrence was a reluctant guest of honour who did not 'like the thought' of going to the P.E.N. dinner on 31 October (v. 157), yet he cultivated a working friendship with the Mexican author, inviting him to write a whimsical piece mentioning Lawrence and Weston (to usher in their respective work). But Lawrence completely recast the resulting essay ('Mexico, Why Not?') about United States tourists in Mexico. Needing to return it, he attempted to erase his handiwork – being so 'conscientious about his erasing' that almost all of his pencil marks were rendered 'illegible' although the pages were clearly 'no longer pristine'.[115] But he had written his own version all out 'again', he told Quintanilla, and would 'get it typed' and send it (v. 195).

This version, presumably close to the one in the 'Hopi Snake Dance' notebook (stamped 122–9), probably differed somewhat from the erased version – which may have been closer to Quintanilla's original. The shortest attempt, a fragment of twenty lines, may be the second manuscript to be written; it is found in a notebook which Frieda kept for studies in Spanish. On 10 January Lawrence wrote to Quintanilla about his typescript, admitting that he 'had to go scribbling' on it because he felt 'the touch' was not 'light enough' (v. 194–5). Two days later Lawrence did send a typescript of the third and last version, stating, 'The little article is yours to do as you like with, entirely' (v. 196). This circumstance explains the byline, 'by Luis Q.', that has been retained in the title. Lawrence now recognised, however, that his own sketch, too, was filled with 'rancour', perhaps from their both having tapped 'a terrible bitterness somewhere deep down between the U.S.A. and Mexico, covered up' (v. 196). It had become a sketch of a sensitive young Mexican writer in a government post, greeting Americans who question constantly whether Mexico is indeed 'American' or not. The essay title derives from a promotional slogan, 'See America First' (meaning the United States),

---

114 *Letters*, v. 185–7, and Parmenter 7–10. Luis Siegfried Quintanilla (1900–80), Paris-born poet and diplomat as well as Professor of English at the University of Mexico (1923–5), was also employed in the government's Foreign Affairs office; Edward Henry Weston (1886–1958), distinguished American photographer.

115 Parmenter 145 and letter from Sara Quintanilla, 28 July 1997, to the editor. MS1 was already illegible when Ross Parmenter saw it while writing *Lawrence in Oaxaca* (letter from Parmenter, 13 March 1997, to the editor).

and is therefore consciously ironic. Quintanilla never tried to publish this piece, partly because he 'did not agree with everything in it'.[116]

Quintanilla was helpful to Brett when Lawrence informed him that she would be returning alone to New Mexico through Mexico City in January.[117] He also visited the Lawrences in Mexico City during the nearly fatal illness that had struck Lawrence down just as he and Frieda were preparing to leave Oaxaca at the beginning of February. Whether or not this attack involved a malarial recurrence, perhaps from Ceylon (see v. 211),[118] or influenza, or typhoid fever, his underlying illness was 'advanced' tuberculosis, and Quintanilla was present when the doctor made this diagnosis.[119] Upon medical advice that Lawrence should return to the ranch rather than risk a voyage to England, Lawrence and Frieda journeyed northwards but were almost turned away at the United States border on health grounds (v. 230). The last summer in New Mexico gave rise to the drama *David* and a number of essays, some of which went into *Reflections on the Death of a Porcupine*.

Italy (November 1925, November 1926 – August 1927)

'A Little Moonshine with Lemon'

Lawrence left New Mexico on the day before his fortieth birthday, 10 September 1925, well aware that he would have difficulty with immigration officials over re-entering the United States.[120] After settling in Italy in mid-November, he was again comparing Europe and America as he had done in Italy in 1920. He wrote 'Europe Versus America' in that month at the Villa Bernarda, Spotorno,[121] emphasising Europe's youthfulness when compared with the age of America. To Blanche Knopf, he wrote on 23 November, 'In America one talks about Europe being old' but one is 'horrorstruck' in Italy at 'America's agedness' (v. 342); and in a letter to Earl and Achsah Brewster two days later, the Mediterranean 'seems . . . so young, after America' (v. 345).

---

[116] Parmenter 148.

[117] Discreetly, DHL mentioned nothing about the domestic difficulties resulting in Frieda's insistence that Brett leave (*Letters*, v. 192).

[118] The city of Oaxaca is said to be too high for the malaria mosquito, unlike the nearby lowlands (Parmenter 318) – but typhoid fever was endemic in the area. See also Ellis, *Dying Game*, p. 235, stating that malaria was common around Mitla, which DHL had visited.

[119] Luis Quintanilla in Nehls, ii. 396.

[120] These officials at El Paso, in late March 1925, had seemed to him to represent 'the Bolshevist method at its crudest' (*Letters*, v. 230). Almost four years later, on 19 January 1929, he told a correspondent, 'I have not forgotten and shall never forget. Sheer degrading insult! No, I don't trust your U.S. "authorities"' (vii. 144).

[121] See *Sketches* lvii–lviii, 199–200.

Almost at this same time came the essay 'A Little Moonshine with Lemon', presumably written on 25 November after the evening festivities. Having drunk St Catherine's wine on that feast day, Lawrence simultaneously watches the moon on the Mediterranean while imagining how it might shine on new snow at the deserted New Mexico ranch.[122] Prominent in his mind is the guardian pine tree near the cabin, the same tree that is a central symbol in 'Pan in America'. Now his 'moonshine' is only a memory, evoking the ghosts of Kiowa.[123]

He evidently wrote to Brett that very night, 'enclosing two little MSS. – one for Spud [Johnson]' (v. 344). The 'one' for Johnson may have been either 'Europe Versus America' or 'A Little Moonshine with Lemon' (v. 344 n. 2), and both essays appeared in the D. H. Lawrence special issue of *Laughing Horse*, in April 1926, along with 'Paris Letter', two of Lawrence's poems[124] and his sketch of the corn dancers in the outline form, probably the same that Brett had traced out in 1924. 'A Little Moonshine with Lemon' was accompanied in print by a photograph of a clay bust of Lawrence's head by Ida Rauh, an actress and sculptress whom he had known in New Mexico.[125]

A slightly incorrect quotation from William Shakespeare's *Julius Caesar* heads all existing typescripts of this essay (no manuscript survives). Brett's ribbon typescript, which Lawrence probably saw, is missing, but in the carbon typescript, the passage appears as an epigraph for an untitled essay: 'Ye Gods, he doth bestride the narrow world / Like a Colossus'.[126] The line probably refers to the author's double identity in the essay – in Italy and yet still in America – as well as applying to the New Mexico pine tree, personified as a giant presence that is rooted in one continent and remembered on another. A later typescript and its carbon copies failed to space the quotation as poetry, thus making it resemble a title, but it is most unlikely that it was intended as a title. Although it cannot be proved that Lawrence, not Johnson, created the title 'A Little Moonshine with Lemon', it echoes the essay's last line and Lawrence made no complaint about it when suggesting in November 1926 that this *Laughing Horse* piece be included in *Mornings in Mexico* (v. 581).

---

[122] Kiowa Ranch was scarcely habitable during the hard winters, when snow was 'often knee deep' and the horses' water could freeze (*Letters*, v. 112). As DHL wrote on 29 July 1925, 'It's the kind of life I like for summer; but the winter would be too stiff' (v. 282).

[123] 'Moonshine', whiskey made and sold illegally during the US Prohibition, is the main ingredient of the hot 'toddy' he describes from memory.

[124] 'Mediterranean in January' and 'Beyond the Rockies' (*Poems* 814–16).

[125] Ida Rauh (1877–1970), actress, sculptress and feminist activist (wife of Max Eastman, then of artist Andrew Dasburg); DHL wrote the role of Michal in *David* for her.

[126] *Julius Caesar*, I. ii. 136–7; I. ii. 130 ('Ye gods'): see Explanatory note on 97:3.

Mornings in Mexico: the volume

None of the specifically Southwestern or Mexican essays had yet been published in book form, and in 1926 George Harrap and Co. began to plan a new essay collection that might have combined some of them with other essays. On 31 August 1926, Lawrence told Nancy Pearn to show Harrap the essays she had on hand, such as 'The Nightingale' (v. 520–1). But Martin Secker soon proposed a volume that would focus specifically on the American pieces, and Lawrence saw the opportunity to bring out the 'Mornings in Mexico' essays as 'a set' (v. 575) along with the best 'dance' articles. His first response to Secker, on 15 November 1926, was rather guarded – he didn't want to publish 'half baked essays' and wondered if the pieces were really 'good enough', apart from the Mexican group (v. 575). Eight days later, however, he wrote to Secker, 'The essay book sounds all right', suggesting the titles 'Days and Dances in Mexico' and 'Mexican Days and Dances' but accepting Secker's choice, *Mornings in Mexico*, as 'a good title' (v. 580–1). The publisher may have favoured it as a parallel to the title of Lawrence's first travel book, *Twilight in Italy* (1916), which Jonathan Cape had just reissued in October 1926, though Lawrence had himself already used 'Mornings in Mexico' for four of the essays.[127]

Lawrence assured Secker from the first contact that he would not have 'Harrap or anybody else' bring out the new essay volume and would keep Curtis Brown from 'going any further' in that direction (v. 575). Since Lawrence disliked 'volumes of oddments' (v. 280), Secker's thematic approach was the right one to fire his interest, and he began at once to seek out texts and illustrations of Indian rituals. He even offered to write an introduction (v. 587), although nothing came of this idea. On 23 November he listed the volume's contents in the order they took in the final volume: the four 'Mornings in Mexico' essays, ending with 'Market Day'; 'Indians and Entertainment'; 'The Dance of the Sprouting Corn'; and 'The Hopi Snake Dance' (v. 580–1). Further, he suggested an additional prose piece, 'the first little article in the *Horse*' – that is, 'A Little Moonshine with Lemon' (v. 581) – and a poem, probably 'Beyond the Rockies'.[128] Although the poem was not included in the volume, the *Laughing Horse* essay became its final item.

---

[127] DHL may have been echoing a section title in a book he had read in 1923, 'Mexico in the Morning', in Frances Calderón de la Barca's *Life in Mexico*, Letter Thirteen; Calderón also refers to *Mornings in the Alameda* by Carlos María de Bustamante (1825–6), Letter Thirty-seven. (See too Clark, *Dark Night of the Body*, p. 104.)

[128] *Poems* 816.

The texts Lawrence sent to Secker for the volume included copies of the journals themselves. On 23 November 1926, for example, he told Secker, 'I enclose a copy of "Market Day"' (v. 581) and 'you have a copy of *The Laughing Horse*' (v. 581) – that is, the one containing 'A Little Moonshine with Lemon'. On 8 January 1927 Lawrence wrote to Secker, 'You got the two copies of *Travel* did you. In one was an anti-Fascist article...' (v. 620). That article was in the November 1926 issue (see v. 620 n. 3), so the other one must have been the April 1926 issue, containing 'Market Day' (probably the copy he had sent in November). Similarly, Lawrence mentioned that he had supplied Secker with the *Theatre Arts Monthly* copy of 'Dance of the Sprouting Corn' (v. 581) and the *Travel* copy of 'Walk to Huayapa' (v. 587); and on 23 November 1926, he commented that he had asked Nancy Pearn to send Secker the 'two copies' of *Theatre Arts Monthly*, presumably including the one with 'The Hopi Snake Dance' (v. 584). Of these sources, Secker would choose to use only 'Market Day' (which followed the *Travel* version since Murry had not published it) and 'A Little Moonshine with Lemon' (which had appeared only in *Laughing Horse*). But Lawrence was also showing his willingness to bring the journal copies themselves to Secker's attention for the future volume. Secker had the *Adelphi* issues close at hand, and four of them – probably the journal copies of 'Corasmin and the Parrots' (December 1925), 'Indians and Entertainment' (November 1924), 'Dance of the Sprouting Corn' (August 1924) and 'The Hopi Snake Dance' (January–February 1925) – were his sources (or possibly typescripts made from them).

The choices were in general fortunate, for it was the *Adelphi* that preserved the best texts of a majority of these essays. In the case of 'Indians and Entertainment', for example, an American version would have been a disaster. Lawrence wrongly believed that this essay had been published by *Theatre Arts Monthly*; in fact, the *New York Times Magazine*'s version was never the elegant publication of his memory but a severely attenuated abridgement (see p. xlv). As *Mornings in Mexico* approached publication in 1927, only 'The Mozo' and 'Walk to Huayapa' were still unpublished. About two months intervened between the *Adelphi*'s 'The Mozo' (February) and the English proofs (April) and only about a month between the *Adelphi*'s 'Walk to Huayapa' (March) and the English proofs; at any rate, the sources might conceivably have been copies of the *Adelphi*. Secker, however, because of the pressure of time, may have borrowed Murry's actual setting-copies or requested that additional typescripts be made, and may have used those.

While planning the volume, Lawrence made repeated attempts to interest Secker in the American publications that had been accompanied by illustrations and to borrow photographs from *Travel* (v. 596) and *Theatre Arts*

Monthly (v. 626, 636, 638). *Travel*, especially, had used photographs of its own with Lawrence's texts. He also asked Mabel Luhan for photographs of Indian dances – 'something a bit suave and beautiful' (v. 594). Above all, he wished one or both of his own drawings of Indian dancers to be included (v. 581, 584). Possibly Lawrence was remembering his own scheme in late 1921 to produce in New Mexico an 'amalgamate book' of essays with illustrations by Jan Juta (iv. 138) – like an American version of *Sea and Sardinia*. Secker may originally have encouraged Lawrence to seek the illustrations, but was probably troubled by the likely cost. Secker had also learned from Knopf (through Curtis Brown) that the American volume would lack pictures, and this fact was probably decisive in his own choice. As late as January and February 1927, Secker had repeatedly failed to reply to Lawrence's anxious inquiries about arrangements and permissions to publish the illustrations (see v. 596, 619, 623). Although he was still contemplating at least a few half-tones as late as March, Secker wrote to Pollinger on 16 May (at Curtis Brown) saying that he and Knopf had reached 'the same no-illustration decision'.[129]

But he did not make this clear to Lawrence, who was still hoping against hope for illustrations when he returned proofs to Secker in mid-April: 'I suppose you won't put pictures in. But I should like you to put just that drawing of the corn dance figures which I made' (vi. 31). Still later he could not help commenting (when planning photographs for *Sketches of Etruscan Places*): 'I'm very much interested to see the *Mornings* with pictures' (vi. 45). On 27 May 1927, when Lawrence discovered what Secker and Knopf had agreed, he wrote to Secker: 'I'm sorry there won't be illustrations in *Mornings* after all. What made you change, at the last moment?' (vi. 68). To Nancy Pearn, on the same day, he was more outspoken: 'I am a bit vexed with Secker about those illustrations to *Mornings in Mexico*. Right up to three weeks ago he said he was putting them in. Not that I insisted at all, but he seemed to want to. Then suddenly he's off. Bella gente [Fine folk]!' (vi. 70). Nonetheless, when Lawrence saw copies of the unillustrated book, he claimed rather unconvincingly, 'I don't mind its not having pictures, really' (vi. 77). And the dust jacket did reprint his sketch of the corn dancers, though only in the simplified *Laughing Horse* version that Brett had traced.

In Lawrence's efforts to include illustrations like those in the American periodicals (e.g. v. 581, 584, 595, 636), he must have forgotten the extent of the liberties some of them had taken with his texts (instances of major reformatting, abridgement and alteration are revealed in the Textual apparatus).

---

[129] Secker Letter-Book, UIll. See *Letters*, vi. 68 n. 1.

He accentuated the volume's New Mexico associations when he dedicated it 'To Mabel Lujan' since, as Lawrence wrote to her, 'to you we really owe Taos and all that ensues from Taos' (vi. 36). When he first suggested this dedication in December 1926, he reassured her indirectly that he was not reprinting essays she especially disliked (like 'Just Back from the Snake Dance'), for he asked diplomatically, 'I only did three Indian articles, didn't I? "Corn Dance", "Snake Dance", and "Indians and Entertainment"' (v. 594). Of this group, only 'The Dance of the Sprouting Corn', in this present volume, has its base-text in an American publication.

The American edition, although printed from different plates and differing occasionally from the English edition, was almost certainly set from the English edition, probably from its proofs. Although his corrected proofs cannot have arrived in England for several days after Lawrence finished correcting them in April, the book was ready, printed and bound six weeks later, for Lawrence acknowledged receipt of two copies on 6 June (vi. 77). This was two months before publication in America, and it would have allowed time for transmission of the text from a copy of the book itself. But it is more likely that Secker sent Knopf a set of corrected proofs as setting-copy; Knopf could have had it more than three months in advance of the appearance of his own edition.

Lawrence had originally expected proofs from Secker at the beginning of 1927, writing on 25 January that he was 'just getting proofs' (v. 635) and inquiring on 15 March, 'Is there a delay?' (v. 655). Though he was still 'expecting the proofs of the Mexican essays' on 24 March (vi. 24), his Etruscan tour with Brewster meant that he did not actually receive them until 12 April and did not correct them until the morning of 13 April (vi. 31). Lawrence had left general arrangements for the American edition to Curtis Brown, commenting offhandedly to Secker, 'He can fix with Knopf' (v. 581); Lawrence believed the two publications 'ought to' be simultaneous but did not know the American publishing schedule (vi. 73). In fact, the first English edition came out in June 1927, followed on 5 August by the first American edition.[130]

---

[130] Secker reprinted the book in the same year and placed it in his New Adelphi Library in April 1930, and Knopf published an inexpensive edition in 1934. The Heinemann Pocket Edition, introduced by Richard Aldington, came out in 1950. Volumes combining *Mornings in Mexico* and *Etruscan Places* (as it was then called) were published by Heinemann in 1956 (reprinted in 1965 and later), and Penguin in 1960 (reprinted in 1967 and later). Twelve of the essays in this present volume were introduced and reprinted in chronological order in *D. H. Lawrence and New Mexico*, ed. Keith Sagar (Salt Lake City, 1982), and also in the Alyscamps / Karl Orend *D. H. Lawrence and New Mexico*, ed. Sagar (Paris and London, 1995).

In correcting the English proofs, Lawrence believed that he had spotted some textual corruption: 'I think they'd missed a line out in one place: not my fault' (vi. 31). If the mistake had been made by the English printer, and Lawrence had attempted to correct it, his effort would have been revealed by the fact that his replacement words would not have corresponded exactly to those of the original setting-copy: he had no access to the texts of his original essays. No such place is, however, apparent. In 'Corasmin and the Parrots', Brett as the original typist had omitted sixteen words about one of the four Aztec 'Suns' of legend;[131] and in 'Walk to Huayapa', exactly one line of Lawrence's manuscript omitted by Brett had described the foothills around Oaxaca as royal blue, lizard-like shapes.[132] In 'The Mozo' she had omitted two sentences about an *'angelito'* in paradise, another about workers at the Oaxaca residence, and another about Rosalino's feelings.[133] In 'Indians and Entertainment', too, the first typing had evidently omitted a dozen words about the nature of progressive creation (in a lost typescript).[134] Similarly, an uncertain number of omissions had occurred in 'The Hopi Snake Dance', including the probably unauthorised loss of fifteen words, present in manuscript, that describe the dancers' body paint.[135] It may have been one of these omissions that Lawrence now noticed; in none of these cases, however, did he make any attempt to correct his text. (In all these cases, this volume restores the missing words.)

We can tell that Knopf was setting either from Secker's revised proofs or from his printed volume since Lawrence made an important change in 'Indians and Entertainment' – an addition of five words – that can only have been introduced in proof; and, significantly, the change appears in both English and American editions.[136] A handful of other variations between the texts of the two volumes result in part from errors introduced by the American printer.[137] The present volume, recognising Lawrence's characteristic method of revising differently on different typescripts, does not follow a fixed

---

[131] See Textual apparatus at 15:28 and note.   [132] See Textual apparatus at 22:5 and note.
[133] See Textual apparatus at 38:20, 41:14 and 42:1 and note on 38:20.
[134] See Textual apparatus at 66:37 and note at 67:6.
[135] See Textual apparatus at 88:12 and note.
[136] See Textual apparatus and Explanatory note on 60:7 (in 'Indians and Entertainment') for this evidence of DHL's work on the proofs. Other examples appear at 31:3 ('Walk to Huayapa') and 38:17 ('The Mozo').
[137] See also Textual apparatus for 'begins' (E1) / 'begin' (A1) (14:7) in 'Corasmin and the Parrots'; 'until' (E1) / 'unto' (A1) (22:1) and 'Rosalino' (E1) / 'Rosalina' (A1) (22:20) in 'Walk to Huayapa'; 'of' (E1) / 'on' (A1) in 'The Mozo' (42:39); 'wounds' (E1) / 'rounds' (A1) (50:8) and 'contact' (E1) / 'contract' (A1) (52:24) in 'Market Day'. Later discrepancies occur in 'The Hopi Snake Dance': 'This' (E1) / 'The' (A1) (81:12) and 'or' (E1) / 'of' (A1) (83:9).

policy favouring either the American or the British periodicals from which the setting-copy typescripts were derived. But the first English edition does have special priority not only because Lawrence paid close attention to it from the first but also because he corrected its proofs (vi. 31).[138]

France (December 1928)

'New Mexico'

Lawrence's 'last word' on the American Southwest was in 'quite a beautiful article on New Mexico', as he described it to Mabel Luhan (vii. 94). 'New Mexico' was written between 19 December 1928, when he first told her he would do it (vii. 71), and Christmas Day, when he enclosed it with a letter to Nancy Pearn, explaining its background: 'The *Survey Graphic* of New York asked me for a 2000 word article, say what I like, on New Mexico, payment $100.00' (vii. 94). (The exact relation between Mabel and the *Survey Graphic* invitation is not clear.) To Mabel he wrote, 'Writing it gave me a real longing to be back', but he acknowledged being mindful of the US immigration restrictions – even though Brett recommended 'creeping in unnoticed' (vii. 94). In March he told Mabel that he feared 'possible unpleasantnesses with authorities or public' if he ever tried to return to America (vii. 203). 'New Mexico' was written at the Hotel Beau Rivage, Bandol, in the south of France, where Lawrence's poor health had apparently stabilised – he even claimed it was better 'poco a poco' (vii. 105). He often worked in bed, just finishing *Pansies*, awaiting the London showing of his paintings by Dorothy Warren, and dispensing copies of the privately printed Florentine edition of *Lady Chatterley's Lover* (vii. 94–5, 113).

His essay praises New Mexico for its silent, imperious beauty – and especially for the indigenous religion that provided 'the greatest experience from the outside world that I have ever had'.[139] He describes a pueblo, San Felipe, that is older and more 'idyllic' than a scene from Theocritus,[140] locating among the Southwestern Indians a surviving tradition predating Christ, ancient Egypt and Moses. The essay even contains a prophecy of a new world deriving from aboriginal America: the authentic America, New Mexico's America, that can render the skyscraper obsolete. Evocation of a golden age mingles

---

[138] Although the Union Square Book Shop catalogue advertised a set of proofs for sale on 30 September 1930 (item no. 68, Roberts E246.2), this set has not been located. It is not known whether they were American or English proofs.
[139] 'New Mexico' (176:11–12).   [140] 'New Mexico' (179:32).

with practical understanding of race relations, which finally depend upon 'individuals . . . on both sides'.[141]

Lawrence valued the essay, fearing at one time that it had gone astray in the mail and lamenting the loss of 'such a good article' (vii. 118). Writing it had filled him with a desire to see New Mexico again, as he told Mabel at Christmas – 'I should like to come in spring even if only to stay the six months allowed by the passport' – but he confessed to being unable to travel (vii. 94). 'New Mexico' did not appear in print during his lifetime; it was published in 1931 along with a reproduction of Georgia O'Keeffe's dramatic *Cross* (1929), in which a huge cross, edged in brilliant light, emerges faintly from darkest shadow. Whether intended or not, the juxtaposition allowed a fitting reflection on the writer whose texts were still structured by Christmas and Easter and saints' days, even at their most iconoclastic.[142]

Reception

Mornings in Mexico elicited completely opposing descriptions – the 'pleasant, sunbaked essays', to the *Saturday Review* writer,[143] presented 'distorted shadows' and 'shining leprosy on a background of darkness' to Carleton Beals of the *Nation*.[144] Beals, despite this unflattering language, nonetheless produced one of the most insightful reviews in this second of two that he published about two weeks apart. Lawrence himself wrote in June 1927, just after Secker's official release of *Mornings in Mexico*: 'I like "Indians and Entertainment" and "Hopi Snake Dance" best: but all women seem to like "Corasmin" best' (vi. 91). 'Corasmin and the Parrots', as the initial essay in the volume, was also a favourite among reviewers, who sometimes ignored the New Mexico essays altogether. The reviews were generally penetrating, and only the occasional commentator, like Thomas Walsh for *Commonweal*, failed to look beyond the exotic surface of the Oaxacan scenes, presided over by the author in his 'easy-chair', nonchalant with 'facile irresponsibility'.[145]

The first review in England, in the *Times Literary Supplement*, sounded several notes that recurred in later responses. One was an awareness of cosmogony, especially in 'Corasmin', creating a *Weltanschauung* for several of

[141] 'New Mexico' (178:19–20).
[142] A lithograph by J. Ward Lockwood – *Taos Signs*, depicting Taos village – appeared at the essay's end.
[143] 'Moods and Phantasies', cxliv (27 August 1927), 281.
[144] 'Acknowledge the Wonder', cxxv (14 September 1927), 257. See also Beals's later notoriously harsh recollection of DHL (Nehls, ii. 227–9).
[145] 'Books', vi (28 September 1927), 505.

the essays, 'a little world-fantasy' concerning the parrots and Corasmin the dog[146] – what the *Saturday Review* called 'a delightful phantasy on the theory of evolution' (p. 281) and Beals in the *Nation* defined as an 'indigenous Bergsonian concept of the time-stream' (p. 258). Conrad Aiken in the *Dial* saw a grotesque nightmare, not a vision, in the spectacle (in 'Corasmin') of 'flamingoes rising' from the 'dark matrix'; to him this was 'tiresomely explicit',[147] apparently unrecognised as part of an Aztec creation myth. But just one reviewer, again Beals of the *Nation*, seemed aware of the full import of that mythology. He referred to the Aztec 'Suns' or epochs in 'Corasmin' and to Lawrence's 'foreboding, with anxiety over the fate of the white monkeys when the present Fifth Sun shatters' (p. 258). In the myth, each 'Sun' is doomed to end in cataclysm, and Lawrence's 'white monkeys' are the cerebral moderns who seem to dominate the present (fifth) epoch but steer it blindly towards its end.

The reviewer of the *Times Literary Supplement* was first, too, to find in the new travel volume 'variations on one theme – the look and nature of the Indians', especially in the person of the mozo Rosalino, who had been 'brutally used in one of the revolutions' (p. 468). The same individualising touch – Rosalino's struggle to escape from mass military conscription – also caught the interest of the reviewer for the *New York Times Book Review*.[148] Genevieve Taggard, in the *New York Herald Tribune Books*, stated that the world had awaited Lawrence's conclusions after his five years of studying the Mexican Indian. What would the 'neurotic, European Lawrence do and decide about him'? The answer came in the striking portrait of 'Rosalindo' even though Lawrence claimed paradoxically that 'you can never understand' the Indians.[149] But controversy surrounded the question of whether Lawrence captured the spirit of such people or simply appropriated it to his own purposes. To Beals, in another notice, this time in the *Saturday Review of Literature*, Lawrence's Indian belongs to 'a primitive race that moves and has its poor being within a greater consciousness' – that of the author's own philosophies.[150] Beals first charged that Lawrence 'simply does not know the Indian' but 'makes of the Indian an image of his own gruesomely brooding soul'. Even to this reviewer, however, this was not true in *Mornings in Mexico* at its best: 'half a dozen sentences alone ring down to the depths and echo back

---

[146] 'Mornings in Mexico' (7 July 1927), 468.
[147] 'Mr Lawrence's Prose', lxxxiii (15 October 1927), 345.
[148] 'Lawrence Presents the Mexicans' (7 August 1927), 2.
[149] 'The Little Ghost in D. H. Lawrence' (7 August 1927), 5.
[150] 'The Divine Tourist', iv (27 August 1927), 68.

to the heights', and in these Lawrence has 'intuitively' captured 'the majestic relation between the Indian and the universe and modern civilization' and has shown 'true understanding of the real Mexico'. In his *Nation* review, entitled 'Acknowledge the Wonder' (a term from 'Indians and Entertainment'), Beals accused Lawrence of 'an inverse sentimentalism'; but Beals could not deny that Lawrence's sense of 'wonder', resembling that of the Indians themselves, made him, though not prone to 'indigenous intimacies', yet 'emotionally coalescent with the whole mainstream of Indian life-consciousness' (p. 258). Moreover, according to the *New York Times Book Review*, Lawrence's study of the Mexican Indians – indeed, of 'the Bloody Aztec Behind the Peon' – might have 'sociological importance', Lawrence having 'penetrated further into the heart of Mexico' than others. In fact, 'Congressmen and others who orate lengthily about Mexico might find Lawrence's volume... of peculiar value' (p. 2). At *Survey*, Halle Schaffner credited his 'sixth sense' with allowing him to enter into 'the qualities and properties of alien lands and peoples' and to 'look two ways' into two cultures, as he recommends in 'Indians and Entertainment'.[151]

Writing style was another hotly contested factor. Peter Quennell in the *New Statesman* conceded the writer's 'genius' but accused him of flippant, vulgar language in *Mornings in Mexico*.[152] Quennell chose 'Walk to Huayapa', with its 'barren' landscape, as the best sketch. Like several other reviewers, he regarded the book as a by-product of *The Plumed Serpent*, of which it 'redistils the essential flavour'. Despite Lawrence's 'masked and grotesque protagonists', the 'embarrassingly strained pitch' of much of *The Plumed Serpent* and the slang quality of *Mornings in Mexico*, Lawrence had captured 'that which is utterly intangible', the 'spark of contact' which, even if expressed only 'vaguely and tentatively', still 'sheds a varying brightness over the whole of his work' (p. 481).

At the same time, several reviewers contrasted the frequently casual style of the new book with well-crafted, lusher descriptions in *Sons and Lovers*. The *Saturday Review of Literature* complained of the 'irritation' and the 'increasingly turbid' quality of Lawrence's language (p. 68). Conrad Aiken, in the *Dial*, also contrasted a prose 'slipshod and journalistic' (in *Mornings in Mexico*) with a description of moonlight and garden scents in *Sons and Lovers* (p. 345). Aiken noted that the slacker style first arose in *Studies in Classic American Literature* along with 'a semi-mystical, semi-psychological jargon' (p. 343). Curiously, Aiken even declared that Lawrence's 'instinct for rhythm

---

[151] 'Lawrence Broods in the Sun', lix (November 1927), 166–7.
[152] 'Mr. Lawrence in Mexico', xix (23 July 1927), 481.

seems to have deserted him' in *Mornings in Mexico* (p. 346), whereas several reviewers claimed exactly the opposite. 'The Dance of the Sprouting Corn' was singled out in the *Nation and Athenaeum* for 'sheer romance' that falls into 'metrical feet',[153] and in the *Saturday Review of Literature* for 'a dithyrambic prose-poetry as consummate as anything in the English language' (p. 68).

If some longed for the author of *Sons and Lovers*, others preferred Lawrence the writer of travel books. Genevieve Taggard, believing that Lawrence was 'sick of the human nightmare', asserted in the *New York Herald Tribune Books*, 'I hope he never tries another novel', adding, 'Lawrence is one of the greatest writers . . . Everything he writes is of first importance, whether right or wrong' (p. 5). The *Independent* praised the book's 'dignified and supple prose', all 'finely written, without affectation of any kind', and applauded the author's emergence 'from the dark valley of Freudian psychology in which his fine talent has wandered far too long'.[154] Halle Schaffner, too, found that Lawrence had 'broken away from the trend of self with its torments' to look at the 'objective and universal' – and 'in each new book it grows, always a-little-more-so' (p. 167). Although the *Saturday Review of Literature* flung the ultimate insult – calling Lawrence 'a super-tourist . . . a kodaker of spiritual knicknacks' (p. 68) – almost all the reviews treated him with seriousness and positive engagement. Clennell Wilkinson, in the *London Mercury*, declared, 'I am determined never again to read anything else of his except his travel-books – and never to miss one of them.'[155]

Texts

'Corasmin and the Parrots'

Base-text is the autograph manuscript (MS) which exists in the notebook now named for 'The Hopi Snake Dance'; it occupies four ruled leaves, each measuring $7\frac{5}{16} \times 9\frac{1}{2}$ in.[156] Dorothy Brett made two typescripts from it: a now missing ribbon copy and a carbon copy (TCC)[157] with the stamp of Curtis Brown (New York) on its first page. Although TCC does not bear the marks of a setting-copy, it contains Lawrence's corrections and revisions (TCCR) and corrections in Brett's hand (TCCC). The missing ribbon copy typescript, similarly but not identically corrected and revised (and just possibly retyped), became the source of the text for the *Adelphi* (Per); the magazine provided

---

153 'Travel and Travellers', xli (13 August 1927), 642.
154 'New Books in Brief Review', cxix (15 October 1927), 389.
155 'Travel and Adventure', xvii (December 1927), 219.
156 Roberts E76a.   157 Roberts E76b.

the setting-copy for Secker's first English edition (E1) and E1 supplied the source (probably a set of proofs) for Knopf's American edition (A1). TCC is a characteristic example of Brett's typing and shows how a variety of corruptions got into the published texts: TCC is filled with unfinished words at the end of lines, duplications, missing words, inaccurate punctuation, omissions and other oddities. One example of the latter was Brett's habit of drawing an accent mark on 'patio' throughout this essay (and its companions) so that Lawrence had to cross out each one individually, creating an ambiguous 'x' over the word each time, which led to some erroneous transcription at the next stage of textual transmission. Lawrence was so concerned with correcting Brett's graphical mistakes that he also failed to spot omissions amounting in one case to more than thirty words. TCC contains more than seventy corrected errors and needed still further correction. It did, however, contain not only Lawrence's responses to error but occasionally his development of his text; and the base-text has been emended sparingly from it.

'Walk to Huayapa'

Base-text is the autograph manuscript (MS),[158] occupying seven ruled leaves in the same notebook as 'Corasmin and the Parrots'. Brett again made two typescripts from MS: a now missing ribbon copy and a carbon copy (TCC)[159] bearing both Lawrence's revisions (TCCR) and corrections in other hands (TCCC), some of them Brett's own and some made when TCC was used as the setting-copy for *Travel* (Per1). The missing ribbon typescript (or just possibly a copy retyped from it) became the source of the other periodical publication, in the *Adelphi* (Per2). We can assume this source because only the greater clarity of the ribbon copy would have allowed for certain key readings that appear in the *Adelphi* but not in *Travel*. A repeated word 'green',[160] for example, was almost completely obliterated in TCC but must still have been visible in the copy from which Per2 was set. Similarly, the word 'those', typed over by Brett, appeared to read 'these' in TCC,[161] but the clearer ribbon typescript must have allowed Murry to distinguish the third and fourth letters correctly. Lawrence may have added other corrections in this lost typescript, thus accounting for other variations in Per2, but it is not possible to trace them to him, as opposed to Murry or someone else. Per2 provided setting-copy for Secker's first English edition (E1), and proofs of E1 were evidently the source

---

[158] Roberts E421.7a.   [159] Roberts E421.7b.   [160] See Textual apparatus at 24:20.
[161] See Textual apparatus at 30:27. Other variants between Per1 and Per2 appear at 24:39, 25:25 and 28:37.

for Knopf's American edition (A1). There is evidence that revision in these proofs affected this essay as it appeared in both E1 and A1. TCC is included in the collation but is not used for emendation unless it agrees with Per2.

'The Mozo'

Base-text is the autograph manuscript (MS),[162] which occupies seven ruled leaves in the same notebook as its three related essays. The carbon type-script (TCC),[163] containing Lawrence's revisions (and one incorrect revision by another hand, TCCC), was the carbon copy of a ribbon typescript that Lawrence would have corrected separately and which probably went to the *Adelphi*, the one periodical publication. Either a copy of the *Adelphi* (Per) or its setting-copy was the source of this essay in Secker's first English edition (E1) and proofs of E1 were probably the source for Knopf's American edi-tion (A1). It is probable that both the ribbon copy and TCC were corrected similarly, and TCC as well as TCCR (Lawrence's revisions) provides lim-ited emendation to base-text. We may underestimate the extent of authorial revision in the ribbon typescript since it cannot be fully determined. But it is clear that it included a new view of the character Rosalino, changing his possible 'Spanish blood' (MS) to 'other Indian blood' (TCC),[164] emphasising his indigenous role, in keeping with features of the essay that were already set in MS. The first publication of the essay, in German (see note 111), has also been consulted, and it is quite possible that the ribbon typescript (pair of TCC) was the source for this translation. The key alterations between MS and TCC appear in all published versions. This essay, like 'Walk to Huayapa', is one of the few to reflect a small revision in proofs for E1 and hence A1.

'Market Day'

The autograph manuscript (MS),[165] consisting of five ruled leaves in the same notebook as its three companions, is the base-text. The copy of the essay in *Travel* (Per1), which Lawrence sent to Secker, provided the text for Secker's first English edition (E1) and proofs of E1 were probably the source for Knopf's American edition (A1). Brett would have typed this essay, as she had the others in its series, in both a ribbon and a carbon copy; but no typescript of 'Market Day' has been found. As with Per1, Per2 (in the *New Criterion*) provides evidence of significant revisions in those missing typescripts. The two publications agree in most but not all substantive variations from MS,

---

[162] Roberts E258a.   [163] Roberts E258b.   [164] See Textual apparatus at 35:7.
[165] Roberts E227.7.

for it is clear that Lawrence followed his usual practice of revising separate copies differently, usually one for England and one for America. MS is the best witness to Lawrence's own punctuation and spelling; but substantives on which Per1 and Per2 agree have generally been adopted unless likely to be based on omission or misreading in the lost typescript (see Note on the texts). The absence of a typescript, however, means that the typing's effects on the text cannot be gauged properly.

'Indians and Entertainment'

The manuscript (MS)[166] occupies seven leaves of ruled loose-leaf notebook paper, $8\frac{3}{8} \times 10\frac{7}{8}$ in. It was possibly typed and corrected by Lawrence, with two typescripts (presumably a ribbon and a carbon copy) becoming likely setting-copies for publication in the *New York Times Magazine* (Per1) and the *Adelphi* (Per2). Both of these typescripts are now missing, but two other identical carbon copies (TCC1–2)[167] are reproductions of MS (not of the first typescript), containing passages that were evidently skipped in the first typing. MS has been adopted as the base-text. It must, however, be emended lightly from a printed source, as Lawrence made corrections in the missing early typescripts (and not in the extant TCC1–2). Per1 is idiosyncratically shortened – the largest of its omissions amounts to nine consecutive paragraphs.[168] Per2 was the source for Secker's first English edition (E1) and proofs of E1 were probably the source for Knopf's American edition (A1). MS is generally emended when Per1 and Per2 agree (see Note on the texts). A key revision in this essay, appearing in E1 and A1, is mentioned above as testimony to Lawrence's work on the Secker proofs for *Mornings in Mexico*. All printed versions of the essay lack a final paragraph that is present in MS and TCC1–2.[169] It is true that Lawrence may have dropped it himself, but there is no evidence of his deletion; given the many excisions in the essay in its American publication, he may not have noticed its absence in both Per1 and Per2 when he prepared for *Mornings in Mexico*. The paragraph is published here for the first time.

---

[166] Roberts E171a.

[167] Roberts E171b and Roberts E171c. Both have title-pages characteristic of Curtis Brown's New York office – and E171b also has the number 8 while E171c bears a longhand note 'Mornings in Mexico / same title' in a hand other than DHL's. Both possess an error in pagination, running 1–4, 4–17; and both are uncorrected.

[168] See Textual apparatus at 67:24. Other main omissions appear at 60:29, 60:35, 61:13, 61:21, 64:22, 66:37 and 68:33.

[169] See Explanatory note at 68:33.

'The Dance of the Sprouting Corn'

The autograph manuscript (MS)[170] was among several sent to Barmby on 30 September 1924 for safekeeping, along with 'Indians and Entertainment'.[171] It was later owned by the late Paul Peralta-Ramos, whose mother Millicent Rogers received it in Taos from Frieda between 1947 and 1953; it passed from him to his son Philip Peralta-Ramos upon his death in 2003 and was reportedly placed at auction at Sotheby's but has not subsequently been located. Tedlock recorded that MS occupies three leaves of ruled loose-leaf notebook paper measuring $8\frac{3}{8} \times 10\frac{7}{8}$ in., but the owner later reported it at $8\frac{3}{8} \times 11\frac{4}{8}$ in.[172] Tedlock stated that Lawrence altered 'Spring Corn' in the original title to 'Sprouting Corn'. No typescript has survived, but it was presumably in the typescript that Lawrence introduced the 'two short paragraphs not in the manuscript' and the very occasional expansion of the text which Tedlock noted.[173] The first periodical publication, in *Theatre Arts Monthly* (Per1), and the second, in the *Adelphi* (Per2), differ at times from each other but were evidently set from copies of the same typing. In his characteristic manner, Lawrence evidently prepared two copies and revised them differently (though not very differently, in this case). For example, the two publications gave slightly different accounts of the post-dance gathering on the kivas – including several extra words in Per1[174] – and Lawrence evidently revised 'ceaseless' to read 'ceaselessly' in one copy of the text (Per2) but not the other.[175] A misreading also occurred in Per2 – 'angle' for 'ankle'; the error was spotted and corrected for the American edition of *Mornings in Mexico* (A1) while, for the English edition (E1), it went unrevised.[176] Per2 provided the source for this essay in Secker's first English edition, and proofs of E1 were the probable source for Knopf's American edition. Per1 has been adopted as base-text because Lawrence was especially pleased with this publication (perhaps not only for its illustrations); he attempted to supply Secker with a copy of it for *Mornings in Mexico* (v. 581). He also permitted Edith Isaacs to reprint it without making changes. Furthermore, Per2 not only included misreading and lacked one phrase of development but also was subjected to modest 'house-styling' that is atypical of Lawrence and lacking in Per1.

---

[170] Roberts E83.5. [171] DHL's diary notes, Tedlock 98.
[172] Tedlock 182; letter from Paul Peralta-Ramos to F. Warren Roberts (30 September 1977).
[173] Tedlock 182. [174] See Textual apparatus at 76:19.
[175] See Textual apparatus at 74:18. [176] See Textual apparatus at 74:7.

'The Hopi Snake Dance'

The manuscript of this essay (MS)[177] is still in its notebook binding (the same one that contains the manuscript of 'Corasmin and the Parrots' and its companion essays), occupying nine sheets of ruled paper, stamped 1–18. Each sheet, therefore, measures $7\frac{15}{16} \times 9\frac{1}{2}$ in. Significant revisions and additions were made to the text after the MS state. But an existing part-carbon copy typescript (TCC)[178] is a late member of a group of typescripts of 'indeterminate date',[179] none corrected by Lawrence: as a copy of Per2, reproducing its segmentation from serialisation, it did not affect the essay's transmission; and collation shows only that it follows Per, not MS (unless Per follows it) or E1 (where it varies from Per). Brett's original typescript and carbon copy have not been located; DHL evidently revised them somewhat differently, in his customary manner, yet most of the same core revisions and additions were in both. More than a dozen likely misreadings or omissions by the original typist can also be detected by comparison with MS. For example, Lawrence refers in MS to the powers of sun and rain as 'invisible', but Per1 and Per2 both followed the inaccurate 'invincible' (evidently from the first typescript); elsewhere, he refers in MS to an experience when 'we who stood near' were close to the released snakes; but all publications read 'we who stood', thus missing the point of nearness to the snakes.[180] These and other lost words (and an entire sentence) are restored,[181] but it is not possible to establish the extent of the impact that revisions in the lost typescript had on the text. This essay in *Theatre Arts Monthly* (Per1), though valued by Lawrence, suffered such extraordinary 'house-styling' that it is unreliable as the principal source of emendations. MS has been adopted as base-text, and accidentals are taken from it; substantive revisions are generally included whenever both Per1 and Per2 agree – except where the first typist's probable misreading or omission of MS seems compelling. When the periodical versions differ from MS and from each other, Per2 (the *Adelphi*) has been preferred because it underwent less editorial interference and it was the source for the essay in Secker's first English edition (E1); proofs of E1 were the likely source for Knopf's American edition (A1). The *Adelphi* was also the source for a reprint in the *Living Age*.[182]

---

[177] Roberts E164a.

[178] Roberts E164b is typed in two segments, corresponding to the serial instalments in the *Adelphi*, betraying its later origin. It bears a number (39), probably from Curtis Brown (New York).

[179] Tedlock 186. See footnote 34.   [180] See Textual apparatus at 81:37 and 91:10.

[181] See p. lxiv and Explanatory note at 81:37.   [182] cccxxv (4 April 1925), 47–56.

Lawrence's independent earlier account of the Hopi Snake Dance, 'Just Back from the Snake Dance', appears in Appendix I. The manuscript (MS) occupies two pages on the back of a letter from Brett to Lawrence; it is almost unreadable because the handwriting is so nearly obliterated by 'bleed-through' ink.[183] A typed copy was required and a typescript (TS), $8\frac{1}{2}$ × 11 in., was made from MS, probably by Willard Johnson; it bears the date 'Aug. 24' on its first page (a month before publication) and contains minor corrections of typographical errors, all probably in Johnson's hand.[184] The periodical publication in *Laughing Horse* (Per) and the first book publication in *The Letters of D. H. Lawrence*, edited by Aldous Huxley, are included in the collation, which suggests that Huxley may have consulted MS. Base-text is MS, emended from TS.

'A Little Moonshine with Lemon'

Although a manuscript was recorded in 1937,[185] it is now unlocated. A surviving carbon typescript (TCC1),[186] beginning not with a title but with an inexact epigraph from Shakespeare's *Julius Caesar*, appears to be one of the copies Lawrence requested of Brett on 25 December 1925 (v. 344); it contains typographical errors, overtyping and some corrections (none substantive) in an indeterminate hand, possibly Lawrence's. But it also reflects significant features of Lawrence's writing process, perhaps especially in the apparently considered choice about the 'ghosts' of Kiowa Ranch that are reproaching 'me', not just 'one'.[187] TCC1 is evidently the carbon copy of the missing ribbon setting-copy for *Laughing Horse* (Per). Per was the source for the essay in Secker's English edition (E1); proofs of E1 were probably the source for Knopf's American edition (A1). TCC1 has been adopted as base-text. A later typescript and two carbon copies (collectively TCC2)[188] are from a separate professional typing; although Lawrence never marked them and although their date is indeterminate, they are very closely related to TCC1, which was their source.[189] The group is included in the collation.

---

[183] Roberts E181.9a.   [184] Roberts E181.9b.

[185] Roberts E203.5a. See also Lawrence Clark Powell, *The Manuscripts of D. H. Lawrence: A Descriptive Catalogue* (Los Angeles, 1937), p. 75.

[186] Roberts E203.5c.   [187] See Textual apparatus at 98:38.   [188] Roberts E203.5b.

[189] Some of the typing accidents of TCC1 directly affected TCC2: for example, the former lacked a period in the construction that should read 'night. Cows', and TCC2 reads 'night cows'. See Textual apparatus at 98:27.

'Certain Americans and an Englishman'

No manuscript has been located. A little more than one page, which was once part of the composite 'Pueblos and an Englishman', is still visible – though deleted by the *Dial* copy editor – in the twelve-page typescript of 'Indians and an Englishman' (TS1).[190] Another typescript (TS2),[191] which appears to derive from the text of the *New York Times Magazine* (Per),[192] was probably prepared in the 1930s at Curtis Brown, perhaps during preparation for the first volume publication, in *Phoenix II* (E1).[193] TS1 has been adopted as base-text for the first four paragraphs of the text in this edition (105:2–106:2). This section is lightly emended from Per (from which it takes its title), and Per is the base-text for the remainder of the essay.

'Indians and an Englishman'

This essay was also originally part of the longer work 'Pueblos and an Englishman'. The manuscript has not been located; a surviving corrected typescript (TS)[194] is composed of both carbon and ribbon sheets and is the work of two typewriters; pages are numbered 1–6, 6a, 7–11 (see p. xxxiv above). Besides bearing the *Dial* stamp and marks by a compositor or editor (TSC), TS contains Lawrence's autograph revisions (TSR), including the title he added and revised in ink. It also contains a political section, crossed out with Lawrence's approval (see p. xxxv above), and a second deleted section (similarly crossed out by an editor) on the last page. It does not appear that Lawrence's approval necessarily extended to this second cut, and the surviving text is reproduced here for the first time. The addition greatly broadens the context for the essay though it ends abruptly in a fragmentary sentence caused by the excision of the last pages, which presumably contained the essay 'Taos'.[195] TS was the setting-copy for the *Dial* (Per1), which was in turn the source for the printing in the *Adelphi* (Per2). An uncorrected fourteen-page carbon typescript (TCC), with title page, may be a copy made at Curtis Brown's direction in 1933.[196] It is closely associated with the first volume publication in *Phoenix* (A1), possibly a carbon of a revised setting-copy. TS is the base-text.

---

[190] Roberts E170.8a contains this section that went on, slightly revised, into 'Certain Americans and an Englishman'.

[191] Roberts E63.3.   [192] Roberts C100.

[193] *Phoenix II: Uncollected, Unpublished and Other Prose Works*, ed. Warren Roberts and Harry T. Moore (1968).

[194] Roberts E170.8a.   [195] See Textual apparatus at 120:28 and Explanatory note at 121:8.

[196] Roberts E170.8b. Brown instructed a typist to make such a copy from a printed source, probably Per1 (28 July 1933, communication in the Curtis Brown archive at UT).

In Appendix II is a variant (LT) consisting of part of 'Indians and an Englishman' and part of 'Certain Americans and an Englishman'; it was included by Mabel Dodge Luhan in *Lorenzo in Taos*. Collation suggests that the fragment is closely related to the parent essay 'Pueblos and an Englishman' before the removal of a section about the Bursum Bill and before the final revisions marked on TS – that is, before DHL changed the title and wrote alterations on that document and before the *Dial* also made changes on the same setting-copy. Like TS, the fragment offers a window onto the organisation and development of the early composite essay.

'Taos'

This essay was originally part of 'Pueblos and an Englishman' and is composed of three short, rather discontinuous sections that the *Dial* (Per1) published after extracting other material for both 'Certain Americans and an Englishman' and 'Indians and an Englishman'; these sections of 'Taos' are separated in Per1 by line spaces, and all publications have perpetuated them. Although this format cannot be traced to Lawrence, this edition adopts it because no other text survives and because Lawrence accepted Per1's plan to remove material about the Bursum Bill and then to publish the remaining text in two instalments. Neither the manuscript nor a setting-copy for Per1 has been located. Per1 was the source for the essay in *Cassell's Weekly* (Per2) – which added rows of tiny icons after each of seven sections and thereby increased the appearance of fragmentation; Per1 was also the source for two later carbon typescripts (TCC1 and TCC2).[197] The tripartite segmentation in these typescripts, not typical of Lawrence but of the *Dial* publication, confirms their late origin. TCC1 bears only a scant trace of a typist's correction, and its exact origin and purpose are unclear (see footnote 34). TCC2, possessing a title-page but no corrections, was probably produced at Curtis Brown (New York) in the 1930s. The incomplete line endings, introducing several variants in A1 (for example, 'Lyon' instead of 'Lyons'),[198] suggest that it could be a carbon copy of the ribbon typescript that led to the first volume publication, in *Phoenix* (A1). The base-text adopted here is Per1.[199]

---

[197] Roberts E388a and Roberts E388b – both bearing the title 'Taos': both contain three divisions. The first is one of a small group of five typescripts at UCB that has been identified and discussed (see footnote 34 above).
[198] See Textual apparatus at 125:17.   [199] Roberts C103.

'Au Revoir, U. S. A.'

This essay is one of a small cluster published in the *Laughing Horse*, from which very few Lawrence manuscripts appear to have survived (an exception is that of 'Just Back from the Snake Dance').[200] No manuscript or typescript for 'Au Revoir, U. S. A.' is extant, but the essay appeared in *Laughing Horse* (Per)[201] about nine months after its creation during Lawrence's first trip to Mexico. Since Johnson was with the Lawrences on this trip, it is possible that he personally took the manuscript with him to the journal's New Mexico headquarters and put it into production after his return. Johnson may sometimes have used Lawrence's manuscripts for setting-copies, saving both time and money – and possibly explaining the absence of surviving typescripts. The first volume publication was in *Phoenix* (A1). The base-text adopted here is Per.

'Dear Old Horse, A London Letter'

As in the case of 'Au Revoir, U. S. A.', no manuscript or typescript survives for 'Dear Old Horse, A London Letter'. Sent to Johnson early in 1924, it appeared in *Laughing Horse* (Per) just four months later.[202] The manuscript had been a part of the notebook that eventually contained 'The Woman Who Rode Away' (see p. xli and footnote 50). A typescript may once have existed; Johnson was doing some other typing for Lawrence in the period before publication of the essay (v. 27). But Lawrence declined to make last-minute revisions, whether in MS or TS (v. 27–8). The first volume publication was in *The Letters of D. H. Lawrence*, ed. Huxley (E1). The base-text adopted here is Per.

'Paris Letter'

The 'Paris Letter', too, was once part of the notebook that came to include 'The Woman Who Rode Away' (see p. xli and footnote 50). Mailed to Johnson within weeks of the dispatch of the 'London Letter', this 'Paris Letter' did not, however, appear until 1926,[203] when *Laughing Horse* included it as part of its special Lawrence issue (Per). The manuscript has not survived, nor has a typescript surfaced. No reason is known for the delay in publication unless it was related to Lawrence's own desire to change the essay (see p. xlii). The

---

[200] See p. lxxv above. Another example of DHL material that survives from *Laughing Horse* is Brett's typescript of 'A Little Moonshine with Lemon'.
[201] Roberts C114.   [202] Roberts C120.   [203] Roberts C139.

first volume publication was in *Phoenix* (A1). The base-text adopted here is Per.

'Letter from Germany'

This piece was also once part of the notebook known for containing 'The Woman Who Rode Away' (see p. xli and footnote 50). The manuscript (MS) consists of three leaves measuring $6\frac{1}{2} \times 8\frac{1}{2}$ in., torn from the notebook to be mailed.[204] It is not known precisely when it was mailed or how it escaped notice for so long. MS was the source of the belated publication in the *Autumn Books Supplement* of the *New Statesman and Nation* (Per) in October 1934. Two carbon typescripts (TCC 1-2)[205] were probably produced in the 1930s for *Phoenix* (A1), which first collected the essay in a volume. Both they and A1 correct several misreadings that were printed in Per; for example, Per had described Strasbourg Cathedral's stones as 'faithful' instead of 'fanciful', and A1 made the correction,[206] no doubt by reference to MS. The base-text adopted here is MS.

'Pan in America'

The essay exists in two independent manuscript versions, the first of which (MS1),[207] written on 12 May 1924, was not quite complete when Lawrence began the second (MS2).[208] Both versions are on identical unruled perforated paper, $7\frac{1}{2} \times 9\frac{1}{2}$ in., MS1 occupying four leaves and MS2 six leaves. No early typescript survives; MS2 itself may have been submitted to the *Southwestern Review* (Per), perhaps through Bynner.[209] Per was evidently the source for an eighteen-page carbon typescript (TCC),[210] which was probably made for the first volume publication in *Phoenix* (A1). The first page of MS2 is marked 'two copies', not in Lawrence's hand; this is no doubt a direction to a typist at Curtis Brown, whose New York stamp it bears. The base-text adopted here is MS2. MS1, which has never been published before, is printed in Appendix III, with Lawrence's deletions and additions indicated.

'See Mexico After, by Luis Q.'

This essay is a complete rewriting of 'Mexico, Why Not?' by the Mexican author Luis Quintanilla. Lawrence began one version of his own and

---

[204] Roberts E197a.   [205] Roberts E197b.   [206] See Textual apparatus at 149:16.
[207] Roberts E300.5a.   [208] Roberts E300.5b.   [209] See footnote 81 above.
[210] Roberts E300.5c, unmarked, has the cover page and format of Curtis Brown's New York office.

completed two others after 30 December 1924, the date on Quintanilla's typescript, and by 10 January 1925. Lawrence first rewrote the essay inter-linearly in pencil on five leaves of Quintanilla's own typescript, measuring $8\frac{1}{2} \times 11$ in.,[211] to create MS1. Because Lawrence erased his own handiwork, MS1 is almost entirely illegible but was presumably the source of both a brief false start (MS2)[212] and the final autograph manuscript (MS3).[213] MS2 occupies a single page of ruled notebook paper, measuring $6\frac{5}{8} \times 8\frac{3}{8}$ in., at the end of Frieda's Spanish notebook. Never incorporated into the final draft, it is transcribed in Appendix IV together with barely decipherable fragments of MS1. MS3 is on four ruled leaves in the notebook containing 'The Hopi Snake Dance' and 'Mornings in Mexico'. Brett made a typescript of it, and a mostly carbon copy (TCC1) survives (with TCC1C);[214] Lawrence revised it and evidently desired a cleaner copy to send to Quintanilla. TCC1 was retyped to incorporate his corrections, and a fair copy produced (TCC2).[215] The typing of TCC2 is, however, not characteristic of Brett and raises the possibility that Lawrence himself was the typist. TS was produced directly from the corrected typescript TCC1, for it embodies not only Lawrence's corrections (TCC1R) but also Brett's inadvertent omissions in TCC1. In the 1930s, when copy was prepared for *Phoenix* (A1), MS3 was chosen as the source, without reference being made to either TCC1 or TS; three identical carbon typescripts (TCC2–4 respectively)[216] – probably duplicates of the lost ribbon-copy probably used as setting-copy – reproduce the material TCC1 omitted but do not include the corrections in TCC1R and TS. A1 repro-duced the text of TCC2–4 accurately but missed Lawrence's further work. The essay's first volume publication, following MS3 only, was in *Phoenix* (A1). MS3 has here been adopted as base-text, emended from TCC1R and TS, forming the first publication to incorporate all revisions.

'New Mexico'

The autograph manuscript has been described in detail[217] but is now lost, and the initial typescript is also missing. On 25 December 1928, Lawrence told Mabel Luhan that he was sending the manuscript to Curtis Brown (London),

---

[211] Roberts E357a.   [212] Roberts E357c.   [213] Roberts E357b.
[214] Roberts E357c.   [215] Roberts E357d.
[216] Roberts E357f (two carbon typescripts) and E357g are in the familiar format of Curtis Brown (New York), and the latter possesses a title-page stamped with Curtis Brown's New York address and a number (13); someone (not DHL) has underlined a Latin term and crossed out a typing error.
[217] Roberts E269a, in Tedlock 194–5; cf. Powell, *The Manuscripts of D. H. Lawrence*, p. 71.

to be typed and sent on to Curtis Brown (New York) for *Survey Graphic* (vii. 94); and ten days later he told Nancy Pearn he hoped it was not lost since it was the 'only copy' (vii. 118). A ribbon typescript (TS) and a carbon typescript (TCC) survive,[218] but neither is stamped by Curtis Brown and neither is that first typescript (or carbon copy) that led to the essay in *Survey Graphic* (Per1) or in *John O'London's Weekly* (Per2), where it was named 'The Spell of New Mexico'. In Lawrence's characteristic fashion, that first typescript and its carbon would have gone, separately, to the American and English journals – perhaps being delayed by Lawrence's death: the former did not publish it until 1931 and the latter until 1932 (with illustrations based on designs by Oliver Holt). There is evidence that the two first typescripts were corrected differently. In Per1, for instance, Lawrence refers to jaded 'Americans who know all about' New Mexico instead of to those who 'know it at all' (Per2).[219] The two early publications appeared with their own distinct 'house-styling', including very different paragraphing, and a few variants. But they are closely related to each other, whereas TS and TCC (both twelve pages) do not derive from Per1 or Per2 but are almost identical with the *Phoenix* essay (A1) and with each other. TS and TCC are from separate professional typings; TCC was probably a carbon copy of the setting-copy for A1 – or a copy of it – but it is uncorrected; and TS was probably copied from TCC. An unknown hand supplied the name and publication date of *Survey Graphic* on the first page of TS and numbered the pages (107–18). In common with these two typescripts, A1 used the Spanish accent incorrectly ('Santa Fé' for 'Santa Fe'), wrote 'Sangre de Cristo, mountains' for 'Sangre de Cristo Mountains', misspelled San Felipe ('San Filipi'), used 'green parrot' as a plural for 'green parrots' and contained other misreadings.[220] Per1 is the base-text.

---

[218] Roberts E269b and Roberts E269c.   [219] See Explanatory note at 176:8.
[220] See Textual apparatus at 176:26, 177:7, 179:29 and 176:30 and Explanatory note at 178:31.

*MORNINGS IN MEXICO AND
OTHER ESSAYS*

NOTE ON THE TEXTS

The base-texts for the essays in this volume are named first, as follows:

'Corasmin and the Parrots': autograph manuscript (MS), 8 pp., UT; emended from DHL's autograph revisions (TCCR) in the carbon copy typescript (TCC), 9 pp., UT; collated also with TCC and TCCC (marks in TCC by another hand); *Adelphi*, iii (December 1925), 480–9, 502–6 (Per); Secker's *Mornings in Mexico* (E1) and Knopf's *Mornings in Mexico* (A1).

'Walk to Huayapa': autograph manuscript (MS), 14 pp., UT; emended from DHL's autograph revisions (TCCR) in the carbon copy typescript (TCC), 16 pp., UIll; collated also with TCC and TCCC (marks in TCC by other hands); *Travel*, xlviii (November 1926), 30–5, 60 (Per1); *Adelphi*, iii (March 1927), 538–54 (Per2); *Mornings in Mexico* (E1) and *Mornings in Mexico* (A1). Additional emendation is made from E1 because of evidence of DHL's revision in proofs for E1.

'The Mozo': autograph manuscript (MS), 13 pp., UT; emended from DHL's autograph revisions (TCCR) in the carbon copy typescript (TCC), 14 pp., UT; collated also with TCC and TCCC (marks in TCC by other hands); *Adelphi*, iv (February 1927), 474–8 (Per); *Mornings in Mexico* (E1) and *Mornings in Mexico* (A1). An additional emendation from E1 follows evidence of DHL's revision in proofs for E1.

'Market Day': autograph manuscript (MS), 9 pp., UT; collated with *Travel*, xlvi (April 1926), 7–9, 44 (Per1); *New Criterion*, v (June 1926), 467–75 (Per2); *Mornings in Mexico* (E1) and *Mornings in Mexico* (A1). Emendations are made when Per1 and Per2 agree in revisions except when misreading or accidental omission of MS is indicated. Single quotation marks, which Per2 used consistently for dialogue, are not recorded unless part of another variant.

'Indians and Entertainment': autograph manuscript (MS), 13 pp., UCB; collated with two identical carbon copy typescripts (TCC1–2), 18 pp. each, UCB and UT; the *New York Times Magazine*, iv (6 October 1924), 3, 11 (Per1); *Adelphi*, ii (November 1924), 494–507 (Per2); *Mornings in Mexico* (E1) and *Mornings in Mexico* (A1). Emendations are made when Per1 and Per2 agree in revisions except when Per1 is excised (leaving Per2 the earliest choice) and except when misreading or accidental omission of MS is detected. Emendation is also made from E1 upon evidence of DHL's revision in proofs for E1. Per1 ends at 67:23 and all other printed versions at 68:32, but this edition includes an additional paragraph.

'The Dance of the Sprouting Corn': *Theatre Arts Monthly*, viii (July 1924), 447–57 (Per1); collated with *Adelphi*, ii (August 1924), 208–15 (Per2); *Mornings in Mexico* (E1) and *Mornings in Mexico* (A1). An autograph manuscript, 6 pp. (once belonging to the Peralta-Ramos family), is noted but presently unlocated.

3

'The Hopi Snake Dance': autograph manuscript (MS), 18 pp., UT; collated with *Theatre Arts Monthly*, viii (December 1924), 836–60 (Per1); *Adelphi*, ii (January–February 1925), 685–92, 764–78 (Per2); *Mornings in Mexico* (E1); *Mornings in Mexico* (A1); and a late carbon copy typescript (TCC), 19 pp., UCB. Emendations are made when Per1 and Per2 agree in revisions except when misreading or accidental omission of MS is indicated. Per1 consistently substitutes 'gray' for DHL's 'grey', and these variants are unrecorded except as part of another entry.

'A Little Moonshine with Lemon': carbon copy typescript (TCC1), 4 pp., UT; collated with a part-ribbon typescript and two carbon copies (TCC2), 5 pp. each, UT; *Laughing Horse*, xiii (April 1926), 1–15 (Per); *Mornings in Mexico* (E1) and *Mornings in Mexico* (A1).

'Certain Americans and an Englishman': part-ribbon and part-carbon typescript (TS1), 2 of 12 pp. (excised), YU, to 106:2, then *New York Times Magazine*, Section iv (24 December 1922), 3, 9 (Per); collated with ribbon copy typescript (TS2), 13 pp., UT, and its following *Phoenix II*, ed. Roberts and Moore (E1).

'Indians and an Englishman': part-ribbon, part-carbon typescript (TS), 12 pp., YU; emended from DHL's autograph revisions in TS (TSR); collated also with TSC (marks in TS by other hands); *Dial*, lxxiv (February 1923), 144–52 (Per1); *Adelphi*, i (November 1923), 484–94 (Per2); carbon copy typescript (TCC), 14 pp., UT; and *Phoenix*, ed. McDonald (A1). All other printed versions end at 120:27, but this edition contains two additional paragraphs.

'Taos': *Dial*, lxxiv (March 1923), 351–4 (Per1); collated with *Cassell's Weekly* (11 July 1923), 535–6 (Per2); two carbon copy typescripts (TCC1 and TCC2), 4 pp. and 6 pp., UCB; and *Phoenix*, ed. McDonald (A1). Per2 added rows of decorative symbols after seven paragraphs, but these are handled in the Textual apparatus only as regular section breaks.

'Au Revoir, U. S. A.': *Laughing Horse*, viii (December 1923), 1–3 (Per); collated with *Phoenix*, ed. McDonald (A1). Throughout, Per presented extra spaces between paragraphs, but this practice is not recorded and not followed.

'Dear Old Horse, A London Letter': *Laughing Horse*, x (May 1924), 3–6 (Per); collated with *Letters*, ed. Huxley (E1).

'Paris Letter': *Laughing Horse*, xiii (April 1926), 11–14 (Per); collated with *Phoenix*, ed. McDonald (A1).

'Letter from Germany': autograph manuscript (MS), 6 pp., UT; collated with *New Statesman and Nation, Autumn Books Supplement*, xiii (October 1934), 481–2 (Per); two carbon copy typescripts (TCC1–2), 7 pp. each, UCB; and *Phoenix*, ed. McDonald (A1).

'Pan in America': autograph manuscript (MS2), 12 pp., DU; collated with *Southwest Review*, xi (January 1926), 102–15 (Per); a carbon copy typescript (TCC), 18 pp., UT; and *Phoenix*, ed. McDonald (A1).

'See Mexico After, by Luis Q': autograph manuscript (MS3), 8 pp., UT; emended from DHL's autograph revisions (TCC1R) in a mostly carbon copy typescript (TCC1), 7 pp., UCB; collated also with TCC1C (marks in TCC1 by an unknown hand); a ribbon copy typescript (TS), 7 pp., Quintanilla; three identical carbon copy typescripts (TCC2–4), 10 pp. each, UCB and UT; and *Phoenix*, ed. McDonald (A1).

'New Mexico': *Survey Graphic*, lxvi (1 May 1931), 153–5 (Per1); collated with 'The Spell of New Mexico', *John O'London's Weekly* (25 June 1932), 423–4 (Per2); a carbon copy typescript (TCC), 12 pp., UCB; a ribbon copy typescript (TS), 12 pp., UT; and *Phoenix*, ed. McDonald (A1).

'Just Back from the Snake Dance': early version of 'The Hopi Snake Dance' (Appendix I): autograph manuscript (MS), 2 pp., YU; collated with the ribbon copy typescript (TS), 4 pp., NWU, containing TSC (marks in TS by another hand); *Laughing Horse*, xi (September 1924), 26–9 (Per); and *Letters*, ed. Huxley (E1).

['Indians and an Englishman' and 'Certain Americans and an Englishman']: early fragment in Luhan (Appendix II): *Lorenzo in Taos*, pp. 52–8 (LT); collated with pp. 1–6a of the part-ribbon, part-carbon typescript named above as base-text for both essays (TS), containing DHL's autograph revisions (TSR) and TSC (marks in TS by other hands), 7 pp., YU; part of *Dial*, lxxiv (February 1923), 144–7 (Per1); and part of *New York Times Magazine*, Section iv (24 December 1922), 3 (Per2). A guide on the right-hand side of the Textual apparatus identifies the fragment with corresponding parts of the two main essays in this text. Quotation marks, at the beginning of all paragraphs, are retained to preserve the fragment's status as a quoted piece, not coming directly from Lawrence. They are recorded in the Textual apparatus only when part of another entry.

'Pan in America': early version (Appendix III): autograph manuscript (MS1), 7 pp., UT, never published before.

['See Mexico After, by Luis Q.']: early fragments (Appendix IV): autograph manuscript (MS1), 8 pp., Quintanilla, and autograph manuscript (MS2), 1 p., UCB.

Silent emendations

Variants between the base-texts, typescripts that affected transmission, early publications and the present text are recorded in the Textual apparatus, except for the instances mentioned above and the following silent exceptions:

1 Errors in transmission of the text have not generally been recorded here, but potentially revealing errors have been included. Omitted full stops or missing quotation marks are silently supplied. Lawrence sometimes omitted or misplaced apostrophes in possessives and contractions (for example 'oclock', 'are nt', 'mother's' for 'mothers''), and these have been regularised.

2 In foreign languages, corrections are not generally supplied in the text (but in Explanatory notes) when a word is part of a dialogue that may contain dialect or intentional phonetic spelling. Diacritical marks in foreign languages have not generally been corrected or supplied unless necessary in proper nouns. In all such cases, alterations have been duly recorded.

3 The printed texts often employed ornamental, large or bold capitals for the first character, word or line of an essay, but these have been recorded in an apparatus entry only in the regular font in use in this edition. In variant titles, bold face has not been recorded. Lawrence's own practice of using upper and lower case has been adopted. This volume has not reproduced superscript letters in the text but renders them in regular type.

4 In typescripts produced by Dorothy Brett, letters and punctuation often had to be supplied at the ends of lines; these alterations have not been recorded unless they introduced variants.

5 Unlike Lawrence's MSS, some typed and printed versions of these essays left extra spaces, especially before or after a question mark or exclamation point. Some published versions also included extra space in contractions (like 'can 't'). Such extra spaces have not been recorded.

6 Lawrence did not usually underline punctuation when indicating that words should be in italics, but the printed texts almost always italicised the punctuation. His own usual practice has been followed, and italic punctuation has not been recorded in an apparatus entry unless part of another variant.

7 Lawrence usually employed double quotation marks, but typescripts or publications sometimes introduced single marks. He usually placed a comma or period inside quotation marks, but this order was occasionally reversed or indeterminate and sometimes the comma or period appears directly under the quotation marks. When doubtful, such punctuation follows his usual practice. While DHL placed spaces between capitals 'D. C.', 'D. F.', 'I. W. W.'s', 'A. F. W.'s' and 'P. J. P.'s', printed versions frequently omitted them; DHL's practice is silently followed. Any missing period in such abbreviations is also supplied silently.

8 'House-styling' by editors and publishers, including Americanisation of Lawrence's British spellings (for example, 'labor' for 'labour', 'color' for 'colour', 'civilization' for 'civilisation', 'realize' for 'realise', 'authorize' for 'authorise', 'center' for 'centre') has been eliminated to reflect DHL's own usual practice. The printed texts often hyphenated 'to-day', 'to-morrow' and 'to-night', whereas Lawrence wrote 'today', 'tomorrow' and 'tonight'; his practice has been followed.

9 Lawrence often used short single-stroke dashes, and Dorothy Brett's typescripts regularly transcribed these in kind while publications generally rendered them as an em, a practice that has been adopted (but not recorded) here.

10 Omitted or illegible letters have not been recorded when numbering fewer than three characters.

MORNINGS IN MEXICO

CORASMIN AND THE PARROTS

Corasmin and the Parrots*

One says Mexico: one means, after all, one little town way south in
the Republic: and in this little town, one rather crumbly adobe house
built round two sides of a garden patio:* and of this house, one spot
on the deep, shady verandah facing inwards to the trees, where there   5
is an onyx table and three rocking chairs and one little wooden chair,
a pot with carnations, and a person with a pen. We talk so grandly, in
capital letters, about Mornings in Mexico. All it amounts to is one little
individual looking at a bit of sky and trees, then looking down at the
page of his exercise book.   10

It is a pity we don't always remember this. When books come out
with grand titles, like *The Future of America* or *The European Situation,**
it's a pity we don't immediately visualise a thin person or a fat person,
in a chair or in bed, dictating to a bob-haired* stenographer or making
little marks on paper with a fountain pen.   15

Still, it is morning, and it is Mexico.* The sun shines. But then,
during the winter, it always shines. It is pleasant to sit out of doors
and write, just fresh enough, and just warm enough. But then it is
Christmas next week, so it ought to be just right.

There is a little smell of carnations, because they are the nearest thing.   20
And there is a resinous smell of ocote wood, and a smell of coffee, and
a faint smell of leaves, and of Morning, and even of Mexico. Because
when all is said and done, Mexico has a faint, physical scent of her own,
as each human being has. And this is a curious, inexplicable scent, in
which there is resin and perspiration and sun-burned earth and urine,*   25
among other things.

And cocks are still crowing. The little mill where the natives have
their corn ground is piffing* rather languidly. And because some women
are talking in the entrance way, the two tame parrots in the trees have
started to whistle.   30

The parrots, even when I don't listen to them, have an extraordinary
effect on me. They make my diaphragm convulse with little laughs,
almost mechanically. They are a quite commonplace pair of green
birds with bits of bluey red, and round, disillusioned eyes and heavy,

overhanging noses. But they listen intently. And they reproduce. This pair whistles now like Rosalino,* in the wild, sliding, Indian fashion of whistling. It is so like Rosalino, who is sweeping the patio with a twig broom; and yet it is* so unlike him, to be whistling full vent, when any of us is around, that one looks at him to see. And the moment one sees him, with his black head bent rather drooping and hidden, as he sweeps, one laughs.

The parrots whistle exactly like Rosalino, only a little more so. And this little-more-so is extremely, sardonically funny. With their sad old long-jowled faces and their flat disillusioned eyes, they reproduce Rosalino and a little-more-so without moving a muscle. And Rosalino, sweeping the patio with his twig broom, scraping the tittering leaves into little heaps, covers himself more and more with the cloud of his own obscurity. He doesn't rebel. He is powerless. Up goes the wild, sliding Indian whistling into the morning, very powerful, with an immense energy seeming to drive behind it. And always, always a little more than lifelike.

Then they break off into a cackling chatter, and one knows they are shifting their clumsy legs, perhaps hanging on with their beaks and clutching with their cold, slow claws, to climb to a higher bough, like rather raggedy green buds climbing to the sun. And suddenly, the penetrating, demonish mocking voices:

"Perro! Oh Perro! Perr-rrro! Oh Perrr-rro! Perro!"

They are imitating somebody calling the dog. *Perro* means dog. But that any creature should be able to pour such a suave, prussic acid sarcasm over the voice of a human being calling a dog, is incredible. One's diaphragm chuckles involuntarily. And one thinks: *Is it possible?* Is it possible that we are so absolutely, so innocently, so *ab ovo** ridiculous?

And not only is it possible, it is patent. We cover our heads in confusion.

Now they are yapping like a dog: exactly like Corasmin. Corasmin is a little, fat, curly white dog who was lying in the sun a minute ago, and has now come in to the verandah shade, walking with slow resignation, to lie against the wall near my chair. "Yap-yap-yap! Wouf! Wouf!! Yapyapyapyap!!" go the parrots, exactly like Corasmin when some stranger comes into the zaguan. Corasmin and a little-more-so.

With a grin on my face I look down at Corasmin. And with a silent, abashed resignation in his yellow eyes, Corasmin looks up at me, with a touch of reproach. His little white nose is sharp, and under his eyes there are dark marks, as under the eyes of one who has known much trouble. All day, he does nothing but walk resignedly out of the sun, when the sun gets too hot, and out of the shade, when the shade gets too cool. And bite ineffectually in the region of his fleas.

Poor old Corasmin: he is only about six, but resigned, unspeakably resigned. Only not humble. He does not kiss the rod.* He rises in spirit above it, letting his body lie.

"Perro! Oh Perr-rro! Perr-rro! Perr-rr-rro!!" shriek the parrots, with that strange, penetrating, antediluvian malevolence that seems to make even the trees prick their ears. It is a sound that penetrates one straight at the diaphragm, belonging to the ages before brains were invented.* And Corasmin pushes his sharp little nose into his bushy tail, closes his eyes because I am grinning, feigns to sleep; and then, in an orgasm of self-consciousness, starts up to bite in the region of his fleas.

"Perr-rro! Perr-rro!" And then a restrained, withheld sort of yapping. The fiendish rolling of the Spanish 'r',* malevolence rippling out of all the vanished, spiteful aeons. And following it, the small, little-curly-dog sort of yapping. They can make their voices so devilishly small and futile, like a little curly dog. And follow it up with that ringing malevolence that swoops up the ladders of the sunbeams right to the stars, rolling the Spanish 'r'.

Corasmin slowly walks away from the verandah, his head drooped, and flings himself down in the sun. No! He gets up again, in an agony of self-control, and scratches the earth loose a little, to soften his lie. Then flings himself down again.

Invictus!* The still unconquered Corasmin! The sad little white curly pendulum oscillating ever slower and slower between the shadow and the sun.

"In the fell clutch of circumstance
I have not winced nor cried aloud!
Under the bludgeonings of chance
My head is bloody, but unbowed."*

But that is human bombast, and a little too ridiculous even for Corasmin. Poor old Corasmin's clear yellow eyes! He is going to be master of his own soul, under all the vitriol those parrots pour over him. But he's not going to throw out his chest in a real lust of self-pity. That belongs to the next cycle of evolution.

I wait for the day when the parrots will start throwing English at us, in the pit of our stomach. They cock their heads and listen to our gabble. But so far, they haven't got it. It puzzles them. Castilian,* and Corasmin, and Rosalino come more natural.

Myself, I don't believe in evolution,* like a long string hooked on to a First Cause,* and being slowly twisted in unbroken continuity through the ages. I prefer to believe in what the Aztecs called Suns:* that is, Worlds successively created and destroyed. The sun itself convulses, and the worlds go out like so many candles when somebody coughs* in the middle of them. Then subtly, mysteriously, the sun convulses again, and a new set of worlds begin to flicker alight.

This pleases my fancy better than the long and weary twisting of the rope of Time and Evolution, hitched on to the revolving hook of a First Cause. I like to think of the whole show going bust, *bang!*—and nothing but bits of chaos flying about. Then out of the dark, new little twinklings reviving from no-where, no-how.

I like to think of the world going pop! when the lizards had grown too unwieldy,* and it was time they were taken down a peg or two. Then the little humming birds beginning to spark in the darkness, and a whole succession of birds shaking themselves clean of the dark matrix, flamingoes rising upon one leg like dawn commencing, parrots shrieking about at mid-day, *almost* able to talk, then peacocks* unfolding at evening like the night with stars. And apart from these little, pure birds, a lot of unwieldy skinny-necked monsters bigger than crocodiles barging through the mosses till it was time to put a stop to them. When someone mysteriously touched the button, and the sun went bang, with smithereens of birds bursting in all directions. Only a few parrot eggs and peacock eggs and eggs of flamingo snuggling in some safe nook, to hatch on the next Day, when the animals arose.

Up reared the elephant,* and shook the mud off his back. The birds watched him in sheer stupefaction. *What? What in heaven's name is this wingless, beakless old perambulator?*

No good, oh birds! Curly little white Corasmins ran yapping out of the new undergrowth, till parrots, going white at the gills, flew off into the ancientest recesses. Then the terrific neighing of the wild horse was heard in the twilight for the first time, and the bellowing of lions through the night.

And the birds were sad. What is this? they said. A whole vast gamut of new noises. A universe of new voices.

Then the birds under the leaves hung their heads and were dumb. No good our making a sound, they said. We are superseded.

The great, big, booming, half-baked birds were blown to smithereens. Only the real little feathery individuals hatched out again and remained. This was a consolation. The larks and warblers cheered

up, and began to say their little say, out of the old "Sun," to the new
Sun. But the peacock, and the turkey, and the raven, and the parrot
above all,* they could not get over it. Because, in the old days of the
Sun of Birds, they had been the big guns. The parrot had been the old
boss of the flock. He was so clever.   5

Now he was, so to speak, up a tree. Nor dare he come down, because of
the toddling little curly white Corasmins, and such-like, down below.
He felt absolutely bitter. That wingless, beakless, featherless, curly,
mis-shapen bird's-nest of a Corasmin had usurped the face of the
earth, waddling about, whereas his Grace,* the heavy-nosed old Duke   10
of a parrot, was forced to sit out of reach up a tree, dispossessed.

So, like the riff-raff up in the gallery at the theatre, aloft in the
Paradiso of the vanished Sun, he began to whistle and jeer. Yap-yap!
said his new little lordship of a Corasmin. "Ye Gods!" cried the parrot. "Hear him forsooth! *Yap-yap!* he says! Could anything be more   15
imbecile? *Yap-yap!* Oh Sun of Birds, hark at that! *Yap-yap-yap! Perro!
Perr-rro! Oh Perr-rr-rro!*"

The parrot had found his cue. Stiff-nosed, heavy-nosed old duke of
the birds, he wasn't going to give in, and sing a new song, like those fool
brown thrushes and nightingales. Let them twitter and warble. The   20
parrot was a gentleman of the old school. He was going to jeer now!
Like an ineffectual old aristocrat.

"*Oh, Perr-rro! Perr-rro-o-o-o!*"

The Aztecs say there have been four Suns, and ours is the fifth. The
first Sun, a Tiger, or a Jaguar,* a night-spotted monster of rage, rose out 25
of no-where and swallowed it, with all its huge, mercifully-forgotten
insects along with it. The second Sun blew up in a great wind: that was
when the big lizards must have collapsed. The third Sun went in a rain,
of fire, presumably. This singed out the unwanted birds. The fourth
Sun* bust in water, and drowned all the animals that were considered   30
unnecessary, together with the first attempts at animal man.

Out of the floods rose our own Sun, and little naked man. "Hello!"
said the old elephant. "What's that noise?" And he pricked his ears,
listening to a new voice on the face of the earth. The sound of man,
and *words* for the first time. Terrible unheard-of sound! The elephant 35
dropped his tail and ran into the deep jungle, and there stood looking
down his nose.

But little white curly Corasmin was fascinated. *Come on! Perro! Perro!*
called the naked two-legged one. And Corasmin, fascinated, said to
himself: "Can't hold out against that name. Shall have to go!" so off he 40

trotted, at the heels of the naked one. Then came the horse, then the elephant, spellbound at being given a name.* The other animals ran for their lives, and stood quaking.

In the dust, however, the snake, the oldest dethroned king of all,* bit his tail once more* and said to himself: *Here's another! No end to these new lords of creation! But I'll bruise his heel!* *Just as I swallow the eggs of the parrot, and lick up the little Corasmin-pups.*

And in the branches, the parrot said to himself: *Hello! What's this new sort of half-bird? Why he's got Corasmin trotting at his heels! Must be a new sort of boss! Let's listen to him, and see if I can't take him off.*

Perr-rro! Perr-rr-rro-o-o! Oh Perro!

The parrot had hit it.

And the monkey,* cleverest of creatures, cried with rage when he heard men speaking. *Oh, why couldn't I do it!* he chattered. But no good, he belonged to the old Sun. So he sat and gibbered across the invisible gulf in time, which is the "other dimension" that clever people gas about: calling it "fourth dimension,"* as if you could measure it with a foot-rule,* the same as the obedient other three dimensions.

If you come to think of it, when you look at the monkey you are looking straight into the other dimension. He's got length and breadth and height all right, and he's in the same universe of Space and time* as you are. But there's another dimension. He's different. There's no rope of evolution linking him to you, like a navel-string. No! Between you and him there's a cataclysm and another dimension. It's no good. You can't link him up. Never will. It's the other dimension.

He mocks at you and gibes at you and imitates you. Sometimes he is even more *like* you than you are yourself. It's funny, and you laugh just a bit on the wrong side of your face. It's the other dimension.

He stands in one Sun, you in another. He whisks his tail in one Day,* you scratch your head in another. He jeers at you, and is afraid of you. You laugh at him, and are frightened of him.

What's the length and the breadth, what's the height and the depth* between you and me? says the monkey.

You get out a tape measure, and he flies into an obscene mockery of you.

It's the other dimension, put the tape-measure away, it won't serve.

"Perro! Oh Perr-rro!" shrieks the parrot.

Corasmin looks up at me, as much as to say:

"It's the other dimension. There's no help for it. Let us agree about it."

And I look down into his yellow eyes, and say:

"You're quite right, Corasmin, it's the other dimension. You and I, we admit it. But the parrot won't, and the monkey won't, and the crocodile won't, neither will the earwig. They all wind themselves up and wriggle inside the cage of the other dimension, hating it. And those that have voices jeer, and those that have mouths bite, and the insects that haven't even mouths, they turn up their tails and nip with them, or sting. Just behaving according to their own dimensions: which, for me, is the other dimension."

And Corasmin wags his tail mildly, and looks at me with real wisdom in his eyes. He and I, we understand each other in the wisdom of the other dimension.

But the flat, saucer-eyed parrot won't have it. Just won't have it.

"Oh Perro! Perr-rro! Perr-rro-o-o-o! Yap-yap-yap!"

And Rosalino, the Indian mozo, looks up at me with his eyes veiled by their own blackness. He won't have it either: he is hiding and repudiating. Between us also is the gulf of the other dimension, and he wants to bridge it with the foot-rule of three-dimensional space. He knows it can't be done. So do I. Each of us knows the other knows.

But he can imitate me, even more than life-like. As the parrot can him. And I have to laugh at his *me*, a bit on the wrong side of my face, as he has to grin on the wrong side of his face when I catch his eye as the parrot is whistling *him*. With a grin, with a laugh we pay tribute to the other dimension. But Corasmin is wiser. In his clear yellow eyes is the self-possession of full admission.

The Aztecs said this world, our Sun, would blow up from inside, in earthquakes.* Then what will come, in the other dimension, when we are superseded?

WALK TO HUAYAPA

Walk to Huayapa*

Curious is the psychology of Sunday. Humanity enjoying itself is on the whole a dreary spectacle, and holidays are more disheartening than drudgery. One makes up one's mind: on Sundays and on fiestas I will stay at home, in the hermitage of the patio, with the parrots and Corasmin and the reddening coffee-berries. I will avoid the sight of people "enjoying themselves"—or trying* to, without much success.

Then comes Sunday morning, with the peculiar looseness of its sunshine. And even if *you* keep mum,* the better-half* says: Let's go somewhere.

But thank God, in Mexico at least one can't set off in the "machine."* It is a question of a meagre horse and a wooden saddle: or a donkey: or what we called as children "Shank's pony;"* the shanks referring discourteously to one's own legs.

We will go out of the town. "Rosalino, we are going for a walk to San Felipe de las Aguas.* Do you want to go, and carry the basket?"

"*Como no, Señor!*"*

It is Rosalino's inevitable answer, as inevitable as the parrots' *Perro!* "Como no, Señor!"—"How not, Señor!"

The Norte, the north-wind, was blowing last night, rattling the worm-chewed window-frames.

"Rosalino, I am afraid you will be cold in the night."

"*Como no, Señor!*"

"Would you like a blanket?"

"*Como no, Señor!*"

"With this you will be warm?"

"*Como no, Señor!*"

But the morning is perfect, in a moment we are clean out of the town. Most towns in Mexico, saving the Capital,* end in themselves, at once. As if they had been lowered from heaven on a napkin,* and deposited, rather foreign, upon the wild plain. So, we walk round the wall of the church and the huge old monastery enclosure, that is now barracks for the scrap-heap soldiery,* and at once, there are the hills.

21

"I will lift up mine eyes unto the hills, whence cometh my strength."*
At least one can always do *that*, in Mexico. In a stride, the town
passes away. Before us lies the gleaming, pinkish-ochre of the valley flat, wild and exalted with sunshine. On the left, quite near, bank
the stiffly-pleated mountains, all their pleats and folds full of a royal-
blue shade. Above the first lizard-claws of* the foot-hills, that press
savannah-coloured into the savannah of the valley, the mountains are
clothed smokily with pine, *ocote*, and like a woman in a gauze rebozo,
they rear in a rich blue fume, that is almost corn-flower blue in the
clefts. It is their characteristic, that they are darkest, bluest at the top.
Like some splendid lizard with a wavering, royal-blue crest down the
ridge of his back, and pale belly, and soft, pinky-fawn claws on the
plain.

Between the pallor of the claws, a dark spot of trees, and white dots
of a church with twin towers. Further away, along the foot-hills,* a
few scattered trees, white dot and stroke of a hacienda, and a green
green square of sugar-cane. Further off still, at the mouth of a cleft of
a canyon, a dense little green patch of trees, and two spots of proud
church.

"Rosalino, which is San Felipe?"

"Quién sabe, Señor!" says Rosalino, looking at the villages beyond
the sun of the savannah with black, visionless eyes. In his voice is the
inevitable flat resonance of aloofness, touched with resignation, as if to
say: It is not becoming to a man to know these things.—Among the
Indians, it is not becoming to know anything, not even one's own name.

Rosalino is a mountain boy, an Indian from a village two days' walk
away. But he has been two years in the little city, and has learnt his
modicum of Spanish.

"Have you never been to any of these villages?"

"No Señor. I never went."

"Didn't you want to?"

"Como no, Señor!"

The Americans would call him a dumb bell.*

We decide for the farthest speck of a village in a dark spot of trees.
It lies so magical, alone, tilted on the fawn-pink slope, again as if a
dark-green napkin with a few white, tiny buildings had been lowered
from heaven and left, there at the foot of the mountains, with the deep
groove of a canyon slanting in behind. So alone, and as it were detached
from the world in which it lies, a spot.

Nowhere more than in Mexico does human life become isolated, external to its surroundings, and cut off tinily from the environment. Even as you come across the plain to a big city like Guadalajara, and see the twin towers of the cathedral* peering around in loneliness like two lost birds side by side on a moor, lifting their white heads to look 5 around in the wilderness, your heart gives a clutch, feeling the pathos, the isolated tinyness of human effort. As for building a church with one tower only, it is unthinkable. There must be two towers, to keep each other company in this wilderness world.

The morning is still early, the brilliant sun does not burn too much. 10 Tomorrow is the shortest day. The savannah valley is shadeless, spotted only with the thorny ravel of mesquite bushes. Down the trail that has worn grooves in the turf—the rock is near the surface—occasional donkeys with a blue-hooded woman perched on top come tripping in silence, twinkling a shadow. Just occasional women taking a few 15 vegetables to market. Practically no men. It is Sunday.

Rosalino, prancing behind with the basket, plucks up his courage to speak to one of the women passing on a donkey. Is that San Felipe where we are going?—No, that is not San Felipe.—What then is it called?— It is called Huayapa.*—Which then is San Felipe?—That one!—she 20 points to her right.

They have spoken to each other in half-audible, crushed tones, as they always do, the woman on the donkey, and the woman with her on foot, swerving away from the basket-carrying Rosalino. They all swerve away from us, as if we were potential bold bad brigands. It 25 really gets one's pecker up.* The presence of the Señora* only half reassures them. For the Señora, in a plain hat of bluey-green woven grass, and a dress of white cotton with black squares on it, is almost a monster of unusualness. *Prophet art thou, bird, or devil?** the women seem to say, as they look at her with keen black eyes. I think they choose 30 to decide that she is more of the last.

The women look at the woman, the men look at the man. And always with that same suspicious, enquiring, wondering look, the same with which Edgar Allan Poe must have looked at his momentous raven.

Prophet art thou, bird, or devil? 35

Devil, then, to please you! one longs to answer, in a tone of Nevermore.

Ten o'clock, and the sun getting hot. Not a spot of shade, apparently, from here to Huayapa. The blue going thinner on the mountains, and an indiscernible vagueness, of too-much light, descending on the plain. 40

The road suddenly dips into a little crack, where runs a creek. This again is characteristic of these parts of America. Water keeps out of sight. Even the biggest rivers, even the tiny brooks. You look across a plain on which the light sinks down, and you think: Dry! Dry! Absolutely dry!
5   You travel along, and suddenly come to a crack in the earth, and a little stream is running in a little walled-in valley bed, where is a half-yard of green turf, and bushes, the palo-blanco with leaves, and with big white flowers like pure white, crumpled cambric.*—Or you may come to a river a thousand feet sheer below you. But not in this valley. Only the
10 stream.

"Shade!" says the Señora, subsiding under a steep bank.

"Mucho calor!"* says Rosalino, taking off his extra-jaunty, big straw hat, and subsiding with the basket.

Down the slope are coming two women on donkeys. Seeing the
15 terrible array of three people sitting under a bank, they pull up.

"Adios!" I say, with firm resonance.

"Adios!" says the Señora, with diffidence.

"Adios!" says the reticent Rosalino, his voice like the shadow of ours.

"Adios! Adios! Adios!" say the women, in suppressed voices,
20 swerving neutral past us on their self-contained, sway-eared asses.

When they have passed, Rosalino looks at me to see if I shall laugh. I give a little grin, and he gives me back a great explosive grin, throwing back his head in silence, opening wide his mouth and showing his soft pink tongue, looking along his cheeks with his saurian black eyes in an
25 access of *farouche** derision.

A great hawk, like an eagle, with white bars at the end of its wings, sweeps low over us, looking for snakes. One can hear the hiss of its pinions.

"Gabilan!"* says Rosalino.
30 "What is it called in the *idioma?*"*

"Psia!"—He makes the consonants explode and hiss.

"Ah!" says the Señora. "One hears it in the wings! *Psia!*"

"Yes," says Rosalino, with black eyes of incomprehension.

Down the creek, two native boys, little herdsmen, are bathing, stoop-
35 ing with knees together and throwing water over themselves, rising gleaming dark coffee-red in the sun, wetly. They are very dark, and their wet heads are so black, they seem to give off a bluish light, like dark electricity.

The great cattle which they are tending slowly plunge through the
40 bushes, coming upstream. At the place where the path fords the stream,

a great ox stoops to drink. Comes a cow after him, and a calf, and a
young bull. They all drink a little at the stream, their noses delicately
touching the water. And then the young bull, horns abranch, stares
fixedly, with some of the same Indian wonder-and-suspicion stare, at
us sitting under the bank.   5

Up jumps the Señora, proceeds uphill, trying to save her dignity.
The bull, slowly leaning into motion, moves across-stream like a ship
unmoored. The bathing lad on the bank is hastily fastening his calico
pantaloons round his ruddy-dark waist. The Indians have a certain rich
physique, even this lad. He comes running short-step down the bank,   10
uttering a bird-like whoop, his dark hair gleaming bluish. Stooping for
a moment to select a stone, he runs athwart the bull, and aims the stone
sideways at him. There is a thud, the ponderous, adventurous young
animal swerves docilely round towards the stream. *Becerro*! cries the
boy, in his bird-like piping tone, selecting a stone to throw at the calf. 15

We proceed in the blazing sun, up the slope. There is a white line at
the foot of the trees. It looks like water running white over a weir. The
supply of the town water comes this way. Perhaps there is a reservoir.
A sheet of water! How lovely it would be, in this country, if there were
a sheet of water with a stream running out of it! And those dense trees 20
of Huayapa behind.

"What is that white, Rosalino? Is it water?"

"El blanco? Si, agua, Señora!" says that dumb bell.

Probably, if the Señora had said: Is it milk?—he would have replied
in exactly the same way: Si, es leche, Señora!—Yes, it is milk!   25

Hot, silent, walking only amidst a weight of light, out of which one
hardly sees, we climb the spurs towards the dark trees. And as we draw
nearer, the white slowly resolves into a broken, whitewashed wall.

"Oh!" exclaims the Señora in real disappointment. "It isn't water.
It's a wall!"   30

"Si, Señora! Es panteón!"—(They call a cemetery a panteón, down
here.)

"It is a cemetery!" announces Rosalino, with a certain ponderous, pleased assurance, and without afterthought. But when I suddenly laugh at the absurdity, he also gives a sudden broken yelp of   35
laughter.—They laugh as if it were against their will, as if it hurt them,
giving themselves away.

It was nearing midday. At last we got into a shady lane, in which
were puddles of escaped irrigation water. The ragged semi-squalor of
a half tropical lane, with naked trees spouting out spiky scarlet flowers, 40

and bushes with biggish yellow flowers, sitting rather wearily on their stems, led to the village.

We were entering Huayapa. *Ia Calle de las Minas*, said an old notice. *Ia Calle de las Minas*,* said a new, brand-new notice, as if in confirmation. *First Street of the Mines.*—And every street had the same old and brand-new notice: 1st Street of the Magnolia: 4th Street of Enrique Gonzalez: very fine!

But the First Street of the Mines was just a track between the stiff living fence of organ cactus, with poinsettia trees holding up scarlet mops of flowers, and mango trees, tall and black, stonily drooping the strings of unripe fruit. The Street of the Magnolia was a rocky stream-gutter disappearing to nowhere from nowhere, between cactus and bushes. The Street of the Vasquez was a stony stream-bed, emerging out of tall, wildly-tall reeds.

Not a soul anywhere. Through the fences, half-deserted gardens of trees and banana plants, each enclosure with a half-hidden hut of black adobe bricks crowned with a few old tiles for a roof, and perhaps a new wing made of twigs. Everything hidden, secret, silent. A sense of darkness among the silent mango trees, a sense of lurking, of unwillingness. Then actually some half-bald curs barking at us across the stile of one garden, a forked bough over which one must step to enter the chicken-bitten enclosure. And actually a man crossing the proudly-labelled: Fifth Street of the Independence.

If there were no church to mark a point in these villages, there would be nowhere at all to make for. The sense of nowhere is intense, between the dumb and repellent living fence of cactus. But the Spaniards, in the midst of these black, mud-brick huts, have inevitably reared the white, twin-towered magnificence of a big and lonely, hopeless church; and where there is a church there will be a plaza. And a plaza is a Zócalo, a hub. Even though the wheel does not go round, a hub is still a hub. Like the old Forum.*

So we stray diffidently on, in the maze of streets which are only straight tracks between cactuses, till we see *Reforma*,* and at the end of *Reforma*, the great church.

In front of the church is a rocky plaza leaking with grass, with water rushing into two big, oblong stone basins. The great church stands rather ragged, in a dense forlornness, for all the world like some big white human being, in rags, held captive in a world of ants.*

On the uphill side of the plaza, a long low white building with a shed in front, and under the shed, crowding, all the short-statured men of the

pueblo,* in their white cotton clothes and big hats. They are listening
to something: but the silence is heavy, furtive, secretive. They stir like
white-clad insects.

Rosalino looks sideways at them, and sheers away. Even we lower
our voices to ask what is going on. Rosalino replies, *sotto voce*, that they
are making asuntos. But *what* business? we insist. The dark faces of the
little men under the big hats look round at us suspiciously, like dark gaps
in the atmosphere. Our alien presence, in this vacuous village, is like
the sound of a drum in a churchyard. Rosalino mumbles unintelligibly.
We stray across the forlorn yard into the church.

Thursday was the day of the Virgin of the Soledad,* so the church
is littered with flowers, sprays of the wild yellow flower trailing on the
floor. There is a great Gulliver's Travels' fresco picture of an angel
having a joy-ride on the back of a Goliath.* On the left, near the altar
steps, is seated a life-size Christ—rather undersized:* seated upon a
little table, wearing a pair of woman's frilled knickers, a little mantle
of purple silk dangling from his back, and his face bent forward gazing
fatuously at his naked knee, which emerges from the needlework frill
of the drawers. Across from him, a living woman is half hidden behind
a buttress, mending something, sewing.

We sit silent, motionless, in the whitewashed church ornamented
with royal blue and bits of gilt. A barefoot Indian with a high-domed
head comes in and kneels with his legs close together, his back stiff,
at once very humble and resistant. His cotton jacket and trousers are
long-unwashed rag, the colour of dry earth, and torn, so that one sees
smooth pieces of brown thigh, and brown back. He kneels in a sort
of intense fervour for a minute, then gets up and childishly, almost
idiotically begins to take the pieces of candle from the candlesticks. He
is the verger.

Outside the gang of men is still pressing under the shed. We insist on
knowing what is going on. Rosalino, looking sideways at them, plucks
up courage to say plainly that the two men at the table are canvassing for
votes: for the government, for the state, for a new governor,* whatever
it may be. Votes! Votes! The farce of it! Already on the wall of the
long low building, on which one sees, in blue letters, the word *Justizia,*
there are pasted the late political posters, with the loud announcement:
Vote For This Mark* ◎! Or another: Vote For This Mark ◉! My
dear fellow, this is when democracy becomes real fun. You vote for one
red ring inside another red ring, and you get a Julio Echegaray. You
vote for a blue dot inside a blue ring, and you get a Socrate Ezequiel

Tos.* Heaven knows what you get for the two little red circles on top of one another **8**. Suppose we vote, and try. There's all sorts in the lucky bag.* There might come out a name like Peregrino Zenón Cocotilla.*

Independence! Government by the People, of the People, for the People!* We all live in the Calle de la Reforma, in Mexico.

On the bottom side of the plaza is a shop. We want some fruit.—*Hay frutas?* Oranges, or bananas?—*No, Señor.*—No fruits?—*No hay!*—Can I buy a cup?—*No hay.*—Can I buy a jícara, a gourd-shell that we might drink from?—*No hay!*

No hay! means *there isn't any!* and it's the most regular sound made by the prevailing dumb bells of the land.

"What is there, then?"—A sickly grin. There are, as a matter of fact, candles, soap, dead and withered chiles, a few dried grass-hoppers, dust, and stark bare wooden pigeon-holes. Nothing, nothing, nothing. Next door is another little hole of a shop. *Hay frutas?*—*No hay!*—*Qué hay?*—*Hay tepache!*

"Para borracharse!" says Rosalino, with a great grin.

Tepache is a fermented drink of pineapple rinds and brown sugar: to get drunk on, as Rosalino says. But mildly drunk. There is probably mescal too, to get brutally drunk on—*

The village is exhausted in resource. But we insist on fruit. Where, *where* can I buy oranges or bananas? I see oranges on the trees, I see banana plants.

"Up there!"—The woman waves with her hand as if she were cutting the air upwards.

"That way?"

"Yes."

We go up the Street of Independence. They have got rid of us from the plaza.

Another black hut with a yard, and orange trees beyond.

"Hay frutas?"

"No hay!"

"Not an orange, nor a banana?"

"No hay!"

We go on. *She* has got rid of us. We descend the black rocky slope to the stream, and up the other side, past the high reeds. There is a yard with heaps of maize in a shed, and two tethered bullocks: and a bare-bosomed, black-browed girl.

"Hay frutas?"

"No hay!"

"But yes! There are oranges—there!"

She turns and looks at the oranges on the trees at the back, and imbecilely answers:

"No hay!"

It is a choice between killing her and hurrying away.

We hear a drum and a whistle. It is down a rocky black track that calls itself the Street of Benito Juárez:* the same old gent who stands for all this obvious Reform, and Vote For ◉.

A yard with sheds round. Women kneading the maize dough, *masa*, for tortillas. A man lounging. And a little boy beating a kettle-drum sideways, and a big man playing a little reedy wooden whistle, rapidly, endlessly, disguising the tune of *La Cucaracha*.* They won't play a tune unless they can render it *almost* unrecognisable.

"Hay frutas?"

"No hay!"

"Then what is there?"*

A sheepish look, and no answer.

"Why are you playing music?"

"It is a fiesta."

My god, a feast! That weary *masa*, a millstone in the belly. And for the rest, the blank, heavy, dark-grey barrenness, like an adobe brick. The drum-boy rolls his big Indian eyes at us, and beats on, though filled with consternation. The flute man glances, is half appalled, and half resentful, so he blows harder. The lounging man comes and mutters to Rosalino, and Rosalino mutters back: four words.

Four words in the idioma, the Zapotec language. We retire, pushed silently away.

"What language do they speak here, Rosalino?"

"The *idioma*."

"You understand them? It is Zapoteca, same as your language?"

"Yes Señor."

"Then why do you always speak in Spanish to them?"

"Because they don't speak the *idioma* of my village."

He means, presumably, that there are dialect* differences. Anyhow he asserts his bit of Spanish, and says *Hay frutas?*

It was like a *posada*.* It was like the Holy Virgin on Christmas Eve, wandering from door to door looking for a lodging in which to bear her child: Is there a room here? *No hay!* The same with us. *Hay frutas? No hay!* We went down every straight ant-run of that blessed village. But at last we pinned a good-natured woman. "Now tell us, *where* can we buy oranges? We see them on the trees. We want some to eat."

"Go," she said, "to Valentino Ruiz.* He has oranges. Yes, he has oranges, and he sells them." And she cut the air upwards with her hand.

From black hut to black hut went we, till at last we got to the house of Valentino Ruiz. And lo! it was the yard with the "fiesta." The lounging man was peeping out of the gateless gateway as we came, at us.

"It is the same place!" cried Rosalino, with a laugh of bashful agony.

But we don't belong to the ruling race for nothing. Into the yard we march.

"Is this the house of Valentino Ruiz? Hay naranjas? Are there oranges?"

We had wandered so long, and asked so often, that the masa was made into tortillas, the tortillas were baked, and a group of people were sitting in a ring on the ground, eating them. It was the fiesta.

At my question up jumped a youngish man, and a woman, as if they had been sitting on a scorpion each.

"Oh señor," said the woman, "there are few oranges, and they are not ripe, as the señor would want them. But pass this way."

We pass up to the garden, past the pink roses, to a little orange tree with a few yellowish green oranges.

"You see, they are not ripe as you will want them," says the youngish man.

"They will do."—Tropical oranges are always green. These, we found later, were almost insipidly sweet.

Even then, I can only get three of the big, thick-skinned, greenish oranges. But I spy sweet limes, and insist on having five or six of those.

He charges me three cents apiece for the oranges: the market price is two for five cents: and one cent each for the *limas*.

"In my village," mutters Rosalino when we get away, "oranges are five for one cent."

Never mind! It is one o'clock. Let us get out of the village, where the water will be safe, and eat lunch.

In the plaza, the men are just dispersing, one gang coming down hill. They watch us as if we were a coyote, a zopilote, and a white she-bear* walking together in the street.

"Adios!"

"Adios!" comes the low roll of reply, like a roll of cannon-shot.

The water rushes down-hill in a stone gutter beside the road. We climb up the hill, up the Street of the Camomile, alongside the rushing water. At one point it crosses the road unchanneled, and we wade through it. It is the village drinking supply.

At the juncture of the roads,* where the water crosses, another silent white gang of men. Again: *Adios!* and again the low, musical, deep volley of *Adios!*

Up, up wearily. We *must* get above the village, to be able to drink the water without developing typhoid.

At last, the last house, the naked hills. We follow the water across a dry maize-field, then up along a bank. Below is a quite deep gully. Across is an orchard, and some women with baskets of fruit.

"Hay frutas?" calls Rosalino, in a half-voice. He is getting bold.

"Hay!" says an old woman, in the curious half voice. "But not ripe."

Shall we go down into the gully into the shade? No, someone is bathing among the reeds below, and the aqueduct water rushes along in the gutter here above.—On, on, till we spy a wild guava tree over the channel of water. At last we can sit down and eat and drink, on a bank of dry grass, under the wild guava tree.

We put the bottle of lemonade in the aqueduct to cool. I scoop out a big half-orange, the thick rind of which makes a cup.

"Look, Rosalino! The cup!"

"La taza!" he cries, soft tongued, with a bark of laughter and delight.

And one drinks the soft, rather lifeless warmish Mexican water. But it is pure.

Over the brink of the water-channel is the gully, and a noise, chock! chock! I go to look. It is a woman, naked to the hips, standing washing her other garments upon a stone. She has a beautiful full back, of a deep orange colour, and her wet hair is divided and piled. In the water, a few yards upstream, two men are sitting naked, their brown-orange bodies giving off a glow below in the shadow, also washing their clothes. Their wet hair seems to steam blue-blackness. Just above them is a sort of bridge, where the water divides, the channel-water taken from the little river, and led along the top of the bank.

We sit under the wild guava tree in silence, and eat. The old woman of the fruit, with naked breast and coffee-brown naked arm, her undergarment fastened on one shoulder, round her waist an old striped sarape for a skirt, and on her head a blue rebozo piled against the sun, comes marching down the aqueduct with black bare feet, holding three or four chirimoyas to her bosom. Chirimoyas are green custard-apples.

She lectures us, in slow, heavy Spanish.

"This water, here, is for drinking. The other, below, is for washing. This, you drink, and you don't wash in it. The other, you wash in, and you don't drink it."—And she looked inquisitively at the bottle of lemonade, cooling.

5   "Very good, we understand."

Then she gave us the chirimoyas. I asked her to change the peso: I had no change.

"No, Señor!" she said. "No Señor. You don't pay me. I bring you these, and may you eat well. But the chirimoyas are not ripe: in two or
10   three days they will be ripe. Now, they are not. In two or three days they will be. Now they are not. You can't eat them yet. But I make a gift of them to you, and may you eat well. Farewell. Remain with God."

She marched impatiently off along the aqueduct.

Rosalino waited to catch my eye. Then he opened his mouth and
15   showed his pink tongue and swelled out his throat like a cobra, in a silent laugh after the old woman.

"But," he said, in a low tone, "the chirimoyas are not good ones."

And again he swelled in the silent, delighted, derisive laugh.

He was right. When we came to eat them, three days later, the
20   custard-apples all had worms in them, and hardly any white meat.

"The old woman of Huayapa!" said Rosalino, reminiscent.

However, she had got the bottle. When we had drunk the lemonade, we sent Rosalino to give her the empty wine-bottle, and she made him another sententious little speech. But to her, the bottle was a treasure.

25   And I, going round the little hummock behind the wild guava tree, to throw away the papers of the picnic, came upon a golden brown young man with his shirt just coming down over his head, but over no more of him. Hastily retreating, I thought again what beautiful suave rich skins these people have, a sort of richness of the flesh. It goes, perhaps, with
30   the complete absence of what we call "spirit."*

We lay still for a time, looking at the tiny guavas and the perfect, soft, high blue sky overhead, where the hawks and the ragged-winged zopilotes sway and diminish. A long, hot way home. But *mañana es otro día*. Tomorrow is another day.* And even the next five minutes are far
35   enough away, in Mexico, on a Sunday afternoon.

THE MOZO

The Mozo

Rosalino really goes with the house, though he has been in service here only two months. When we went to look at the place, we saw him lurking in the patio, and glancing furtively under his brows. He is not one of the erect, bantam little Indians that stare with a black, incomprehensible, but somewhat defiant stare. It may be Rosalino has a distant strain of other Indian blood, not Zapotec.* Or it may be he is only a bit different. The difference lies in a certain sensitiveness and aloneness, as if he were a mother's boy. The way he drops his head and looks sideways under his black lashes, apprehensive, apprehending, feeling his way, as it were. Not the bold male glare of most of the Indians, who seem as if they had never had mothers at all.

The Aztec gods and goddesses are, as far as we have known anything about them, an unlovely and unloveable lot.* In their myths, there is no grace or charm, no poetry. Only this perpetual grudge, grudge, grudging, one god grudging another, the gods grudging men their existence, and men grudging the animals. The goddess of love* is goddess of dirt and prostitution, a dirt-eater, a horror, without a touch of tenderness. If the god wants to make love to her, she has to sprawl down in front of him, blatant and accessible.

And then after all, when she conceives and brings forth, what is it she produces? What is the infant god she tenderly bears? Guess, all ye people, joyfully triumphant!*

You never could.

It is a stone knife.*

It is a razor-edged knife of blackish-green flint, the knife of all knives, the veritable Paraclete of knives.* It is the sacrificial knife with which the priest makes a gash in his victim's breast, before he tears out the heart, to hold it smoking to the sun. And the Sun, the Sun behind the sun,* is supposed to suck the smoking heart greedily, with insatiable appetite.

This then is a pretty Christmas Eve. Lo, the goddess is gone to bed, to bring forth her child. Lo! ye people, await the birth of the saviour, the wife of a god is about to become a mother.*

35

Tarumm-tarahh! *Tarumm-tarahh!* blow the trumpets. The child is born. Unto us a son is given.* Bring him forth, lay him on a tender cushion. Show him then to all the people.

See! See! See him upon the cushion, tenderly new-born and reposing? Ah, qué bonito! Oh what a nice, blackish, smooth, keen stone knife!

And to this day, most of the Mexican Indian women seem to bring forth stone knives. Look at them, these sons of incomprehensible mothers, with their black eyes like flints, and their stiff little bodies as taut and as keen as knives of obsidian.* Take care they don't rip you up.

Our Rosalino is an exception. He drops his shoulders just a little. He is a bit bigger, also, than the average Indian down here. He must be about five feet four inches. And he hasn't got the big, obsidian, glaring eyes. His eyes are smaller, blacker, like the quick black eyes of a lizard. They don't look at one with the obsidian stare. They are just a bit aware that there is another being, unknown, at the other end of the glance. Hence he drops his head with a little apprehension, screening himself as if he were vulnerable.

Usually, these people have no correspondence with one at all. To them, a white man or a white woman is a sort of phenomenon, just as a monkey is a sort of phenomenon. Something to watch, and wonder at, and laugh at, but not to be taken on one's own plane.

Now the white man is a sort of extraordinary white monkey* that, by cunning, has learnt lots of semi-magical secrets of the universe, and made himself boss of the show. Imagine a race of big white monkeys got up in fantastic clothes, and able to kill a man by hissing at him; able to leap through the air in great hops, covering a mile in each leap; able to transmit his thoughts by a moment's effort of concentration to some great white monkey or monkeyess, a thousand miles away: and you have, from our point of view, something of the picture that the Indian has of us.

The white monkey has curious tricks. He knows, for example, the time. Now to a Mexican and an Indian, time is a vague, foggy reality. There are only three times: en la mañana, en la tarde, en la noche: in the morning, in the afternoon, in the night. There is even no mid-day, and no evening.

But to the white monkey, horrible to relate there are exact spots of time, such as five o'clock, half-past nine. The day is a horrible puzzle of exact spots of time.

The same with distance: horrible invisible distances called two miles, ten miles. To the Indian, there is near, and far, and very near and very far. There is two days or one day. But two miles are as good as twenty to him, for he goes entirely by his feeling. If a certain two miles feels far to him, then it is far, it is *muy lejos*! But if a certain twenty miles *feels* near and familiar, then it is not far. Oh no, it is just a little distance. And he will let you set off in the evening, for night to overtake you in the wilderness, without a qualm. It is not far.

But the white man has a horrible, truly horrible, monkey-like passion for invisible exactitudes. *Mañana*, to the native, may mean tomorrow, three days hence, six months hence, and never. There are no fixed points in life, save birth, and death, and the fiestas. The fixed points of birth and death evaporate spontaneously into vagueness. And the priests fix the fiestas. From time immemorial priests have fixed the fiestas,* the festivals of the gods, and men have had no more to do with time. What should men have to do with time?

The same with money. These centavos and these pesos, what do they mean after all? Little discs that have no charm. The natives insist on reckoning in invisible coins, coins that don't exist here, like *reales* or *pesetas*. If you buy two eggs for a *real*, you have to pay twelve-and-a-half centavos. Since half a centavo also doesn't exist, you or the vendor forfeit the non-existent.*

The same with honesty, the *meum* and the *tuum*.* The white man has a horrible trick of remembering, even to a centavo, even to a thimbleful of mescal. Horrible! The Indian, it seems to me, is not naturally dishonest. He is not naturally avaricious, has not even any innate cupidity. In this he is unlike the old peoples of the Mediterranean, to whom possessions have a mystic meaning, and a silver coin a mystic white halo, a *lueur** of magic.

To the real Mexican, no! He doesn't care. He doesn't even *like* keeping money. His deep instinct is to spend it at once, so that he needn't have it. He doesn't really want to keep anything, not even his wife and children. Nothing that he has to be responsible for. Strip, strip, strip away the past and the future, leave the naked moment of the present disentangled. Strip away memory, strip away forethought and care: leave the moment, stark and sharp and without consciousness, like the obsidian knife. The before and the after are the stuff of consciousness. The instant moment is forever keen with a razor-edge of oblivion, like the knife of sacrifice.

But the great white monkey has got hold of the keys of the world, and the black-eyed Mexican has to serve the great white monkey, in order to live. He has to learn the tricks of the white monkey-show, time of the day, coin of money, machines that start at a certain second, work that is meaningless and yet is paid for with exactitude, in exact coin. A whole existence of monkey-tricks and monkey-virtues. The strange monkey-virtue of charity, the white monkeys nosing round to *help*, to *save*! Could any trick be more unnatural? Yet it is one of the tricks of the great white monkey.

If an Indian is poor, he says to another: I have no food. Give me to eat.—Then the other hands the hungry one a couple of tortillas. That is natural. But when the white monkeys come round, they peer at the house, at the women, at the children. They say: Your child is sick. *Si Señor*! What have you done for it?—*Nothing. What is to be done?*—You must make a poultice. I will show you—.

Well, it is very amusing, this making hot dough to dab on the baby. Like plastering a house with mud.* But why do it twice? Twice is not amusing. The child will die. Well then, it will be in paradise. How nice for it! That's just what God wants of it, that it shall be a cheerful little angel among the roses of paradise.* Poor baby, it will die. But then, how nice to die and be an *angelito* in paradise. What could be better!

How tedious of the white monkey coming with the trick of salvation, to rub oil on the baby, and put poultices on it, and make you give it medicine in a spoon at morning, noon, and night. Why morning, noon, and night? Why not just any-time, any-when? It will die tomorrow if you don't do these things today! But tomorrow is another day, and it is not dead now, so if it dies at another time, it must be because the other times are out of hand.*

Oh the tedious, exacting white monkeys, with their yesterdays and todays and tomorrow.* Tomorrow is always another day, and yesterday is part of the encircling never. Why think outside the moment? And inside the moment one does not think. So why pretend to think. It is one of the white monkey-tricks. He is a clever monkey. But he is ugly, and he has nasty white flesh.* We are not ugly, with screwed-up faces, and we have good warm-brown flesh. If we have to work for the white monkey, we don't care. His tricks are half amusing. And one may as well amuse oneself that way as any other. So long as one is amused.

So long as the devil does not rouse in us, seeing the white monkeys forever mechanically bossing, with their incessant tick-tack of work.*

Seeing them get the work out of us, the sweat, the money, and then taking the very land from us, the very oil and metal out of our soil.*

They do it! They do it all the time. Because they can't help it. Because grasshoppers can but hop, and ants can carry little sticks, and white monkeys can go tick-tack, tick-tack, do this, do that, time to work, time to eat, time to drink, time to sleep, time to walk, time to ride, time to wash, time to look dirty, tick-tack, tick-tack, time, time, time, time, time. Oh, cut off his nose and make him swallow it.

For the *moment* is changeless as an obsidian knife, and the heart of the Indian is keen as the moment that divides past from future, and sacrifices them both.

To Rosalino, too, the white monkey-tricks are amusing. He is ready to work for the white monkeys, to learn some of their tricks, their monkey-speech of Spanish, their tick-tack ways. He works for four pesos a month, and his food: a few tortillas. Four pesos are two American dollars: about nine shillings. He owns two cotton shirts, two pairs of calico pantaloons, two blouses, one of pink cotton, one of darkish flannelette, and a pair of sandals. Also, his straw hat that he has curled up to look very jaunty, and a rather old, factory-made, rather cheap shawl, or plaid rug with fringe. Et praeterea nihil.*

His duty is to rise in the morning and sweep the street in front of the house, and water it. Then he sweeps and waters the broad, brick-tiled verandahs, and flicks the chairs with a sort of duster made of fluffy reeds. After which he walks behind the cook—she is very superior, had a Spanish grandfather,* and Rosalino must address her as *Señora*— carrying the basket to market. Returned from the market, he sweeps the whole of the patio, gathers up the leaves and refuse, fills the panier basket,* hitches it up on to his shoulders and holds it by a band across his forehead, and thus a beast of burden, goes out to deposit the garbage at the side of one of the little roads leading out of the city. Every *little* road leaves the town between heaps of garbage, an avenue of garbage blistering in the sun.

Returning, Rosalino waters the whole of the garden and sprinkles the whole of the patio. This takes most of the morning. In the afternoon, he sits without much to do. If the wind has blown or the day was hot, he starts again at about three o'clock, sweeping up leaves, and sprinkling everywhere with an old watering can.

Then he retreats to the entrance-way, the zaguan, which, with its big doors and its cobbled track, is big enough to admit an ox-wagon. The zaguan is his home: just the door-way. In one corner is a low wooden

bench about four feet long and eighteen inches wide. On this he screws
up and sleeps, in his clothes as he is, wrapped in the old sarape.

But this is anticipating.—In the obscurity of the zaguan he sits and
pores, pores, pores over a school-book, learning to read and write. He
can read a bit, and write a bit. He filled a large sheet of foolscap with
writing: quite nice. But I found out that what he had written was a
Spanish poem, a love-poem with *no puedo olvidar* and *voy a cortar*—
the rose, of course.* He had written the thing straight ahead, without
verse-lines or capitals or punctuation at all, just a vast string of words,
a whole foolscap sheet full. When I read a few lines aloud,* he writhed
and laughed in an agony of confused feelings. And of what he had
written he understood a small, small amount, parrot-wise, from the top
of his head. Actually, it meant just words, sound, noise, to him: noise
called Castellano, Castilian. Exactly like a parrot.

From seven to eight he goes to the night-school, to cover a bit more
of the foolscap. He has been going for two years. If he goes two years
more, he will perhaps really be able to read and write six intelligible
sentences: but only Spanish, which is as foreign to him as Hindustani*
would be to an English farm-boy. Then if he can speak his quantum of
Spanish, and read it and write it to an uncertain extent, he will return
to his village two days' journey on foot into the hills, and then, in time,
he may even rise to be alcalde, or head-man of the village, responsible
to the government. If he were alcalde he would get a little salary. But
far more important to him, is the glory: being able to boss.

He has a paisano, a fellow-countryman, to sleep with him in the
zaguan, to guard the doors. Whoever gets into the house or patio,
must get through these big doors. There is no other entrance, not even
a needle's eye.* The windows to the street are heavily barred. Each
house is its own small fortress. Ours is a double square, the trees and
flowers in the first square, with the two wings of the house. And in
the second patio, the chickens, pigeons, guinea-pigs, and the big heavy
earthenware dish or tub, called an apaxtle, in which all the servants can
bathe themselves, like chickens in a saucer.

By half-past nine at night Rosalino is lying on his little bench, screwed
up, wrapped in his shawl, his sandals, called huaraches, on the floor.
Usually he takes off his huaraches when he goes to bed. That is all his
preparation. In another corner, wrapped up, head and all, like a mummy
in his thin old blanket, the paisano, another lad of about twenty, lies
asleep on the cold stones. And at an altitude of five thousand feet, the
nights can be cold.

Usually everybody is in by half past nine, in our very quiet house. If not, you may thunder at the big doors. It is hard to wake Rosalino. You have to go close to him, and call. That will wake him. But don't touch him. That would startle him terribly. No one is touched unawares, except to be robbed or murdered.

"Rosalino! estan tocando!"*—"Rosalino! they are knocking!"

At last there starts up a strange, glaring, utterly lost Rosalino. Perhaps he just has enough wit to pull the door-catch.—One wonders where he was, and what he was, in his sleep, he starts up so strange and wild and lost.

The first time he had anything to do for me was when the van was come to carry the bit of furniture to the house. There was Aurelio, the dwarf mozo of our friends,* and Rosalino, and the man who drove the wagon. But there *should* have been also two proper cargadores, porters for carrying things. Aurelio was willing, but not the carter. "Help them!" said I to Rosalino. "You give a hand to help." But he winced away, muttering: "No quiero!—I don't want to."

The fellow, I thought to myself, is a fool. He thinks it's not his job, and perhaps he is afraid of smashing the furniture. Nothing to be done but to leave him alone.

We settled in, and Rosalino seemed to like doing things for us. He liked learning new monkey tricks from the white monkeys. And since we started feeding him from our meals, and for the first time in his life he had real soups, meat stews, or a fried egg, he loved to do things in the kitchen. He would come with sparkling black eyes: "Hé comido el caldo. Grazias!"*—"I have eaten the soup. Thank you!"—And he would give a strange, excited little yelp of a laugh.

Came the day when we walked to Huayapa, on the Sunday, and he was very thrilled. But at night, in the evening when we got home, he lay mute on his bench—not that he was really tired. The Indian gloom, which settles on them like a black marsh-fog, had settled on him. He did not bring in the water—let me carry it in by myself.

Monday morning, the same black, reptilian gloom, and a sense of hatred. He hated us. This was a bit flabbergasting, because he had been so thrilled and happy the day before. But the revulsion had come. He didn't forgive himself for having felt free and happy with us. He had eaten what we had eaten, hard-boiled eggs and sardine sandwiches and cheese, he had drunk out of the orange-peel *taza*, which delighted him so much. He had had a bottle of gazeosa, fizz, with us, on the way home, in San Felipe.*

And now, the reaction. The flint knife. He had been happy, *therefore* he was being exploited. He had been equal with us, on the same footing, *therefore*, we were scheming to take another advantage of him. We had some devilish white monkey trick up our sleeve, we wanted to get at his *soul*, no doubt, and do it the white monkey's damage. We wanted to get at his heart, did we! But his heart was an obsidian knife.

He hated us, and gave off a black steam of hate, that filled the patio and made one feel sick. He did not come to the kitchen, he did not carry the water. Leave him alone.

At lunch-time on Monday, he said he wanted to leave. Why?—He said he wanted to go back to his village.

Very well. He was to wait just a few days, till another mozo was found.

At this, a glance of pure, reptilian hate from his black eyes.

He sat motionless on his bench all the afternoon, in the Indian stupor of gloom, and profound hate. In the evening, he cheered up a little, and said he would stay on, at least till Easter.

Tuesday morning. More stupor of gloom and hate. He wanted to go back to his village at once.—All right! No one wanted to keep him against his will. Another mozo would be found at once.

He went off in the numb stupor of gloom and hate, a very potent hate, that could affect one in the pit of one's stomach, with nausea.

Tuesday afternoon, and he thought he would stay.

Wednesday morning, and he wanted to go.

Very good. Enquiries made, another mozo was coming on Friday morning. It was settled.

Thursday was fiesta.* Wednesday, therefore, we would go to market, the Niña*—that is the mistress—myself, and Rosalino with the basket. He loved to go to market with the *patrones*. We would give him money and send him off to bargain for oranges, pitahayas, potatoes, eggs, a chicken, and so forth. This he simply loved to do. It put him into a temper to see us buying without bargaining, and paying ghastly prices.

He bargained away, silent almost, muttering darkly. It took him a long time, but he had far greater success than even Natividad, the cook. And he came back in triumph, with much stuff and little money spent.

So again that afternoon, he was staying on. The spell was wearing off.

The Indians of the hills have a heavy, intense sort of attachment to their villages. Rosalino had not been out of the little city for two years.

Suddenly finding himself in Huayapa, a real Indian hill-village, the
black Indian gloom of nostalgia must have made a crack in his spirits.
But he had been perfectly cheerful—perhaps too cheerful—till we got
home.

Again, the Señorita had taken a photograph of him.* They are all   5
crazy to have their photographs taken. I had given him an envelope and
a stamp, to send a photograph to his mother. Because in his village,
he had a widowed mother, a brother, and a married sister. The family
owned a bit of land, with orange trees. The best oranges come from the
hills, where it is cooler.   10

Seeing the photograph, the mother, who had completely forgotten
her son, as far as any keen remembering goes, suddenly, like a cracker
going off* inside her, wanted him: at that very moment. So she sent an
urgent message.

But already it was Wednesday afternoon. Arrived a little fellow in   15
white clothes, smiling hard. It was the brother from the hills. Now,
we thought, Rosalino will have someone to walk back with. On Friday,
after the fiesta, he could go.

Thursday, he escorted us with the basket to the fiesta. He bargained
for flowers, and for a serape which he didn't get, for a carved jícara   20
which he did get, and for a number of toys. He and the Niña and the
Señorita ate a great wafer of a pancake with sweet stuff on it. The
basket grew heavy. The brother appeared, to carry the hen and the
extra things. Bliss.

He was perfectly happy again. He didn't want to go on Friday. He   25
didn't want to go at all. He wanted to stay with us, and come with us to
England when we went home.

So, another trip to the friend, the Mexican who had found us the
other mozo. Back* to put off the other boy again: but then they are like
that.   30

And the Mexican, who had known Rosalino when he first came down
from the hills and could speak no Spanish, told us another thing about
him.

In the last revolution*—a year ago—the revolutionaries of the winning side wanted more soldiers, from the hills. The alcalde of the   35
hill-village was told to pick out young men and send them down to the
barracks in the city. Rosalino was among the chosen.

But Rosalino refused, said again *No quiero*! He is one of those, like
myself,* who have a horror of serving in a mass of men, or even of being
mixed up with a mass of men. He obstinately refused. Whereupon   40

the recruiting soldiers beat him with the butt of their rifles till he lay unconscious, apparently dead.

Then, because they wanted him at once, and he would now be no good for some time, with his injured back, they left him, to get the revolution over without him.

This explains his fear of furniture-carrying, and his fear of being "caught."

Yet that little Aurelio, the friend's mozo, who is not above four feet six in height, a tiny fellow, fared even worse. He too is from the hills. In his village, a cousin of his gave some information to the *losing* side in the revolution. The cousin wisely disappeared.

But in the city, the winning side seized Aurelio, since he was the *cousin* of the delinquent. In spite of the fact that he was the faithful mozo of a foreign resident, he was flung into prison. Prisoners in prison are not fed. Either friends or relatives bring them food, or they go very, very thin. Aurelio had a married sister in town, but *she* was afraid to go to the prison, lest she or her husband should be seized. The master, then, sent his new mozo twice a day to the prison with a basket: the huge, huge prison, for this little town of a few thousands.*

Meanwhile the master struggled and struggled with the "authorities"—friends of the people—for Aurelio's release. Nothing to be done.

One day the new mozo arrived at the prison with the basket, to find no Aurelio. A friendly soldier gave the message Aurelio had left. "Adios a mi patron.* Me llevan."—Oh fatal words: *me llevan!* they are taking me off. The master rushed to the train: it had gone, with the dwarf, plucky little mozo, into the void.

Months later, Aurelio reappeared. He was in rags, haggard, and his dark throat was swollen up to the ears. He had been taken off, two hundred miles into Vera Cruz State.* He had been hung up by the neck, with a fixed knot, and left hanging for hours. Why? To make the cousin come to save his relative: put his own neck into a running noose. To make the absolutely innocent fellow confess: what? Everybody knew he was innocent. At any rate, to teach everybody better next time. Oh brotherly teaching!

Aurelio escaped, and took to the mountains. Sturdy little dwarf of a fellow, he made his way back, begging tortillas at the villages, and arrived, haggard, with a great swollen neck, to find his master waiting, and another "party" in power. More friends of the people.

Tomorrow is another day. The master nursed Aurelio well, and Aurelio is a strong, if tiny fellow, with big, brilliant black eyes that for the moment will trust a foreigner, but none of his own people. A dwarf in stature, but perfectly made, and very strong. And very intelligent, far more quick and intelligent than Rosalino.

Is it any wonder that Aurelio and Rosalino, when they see the soldiers with guns on their shoulders marching towards the prison with some blenched prisoner between them—and one sees it every few days— stand and gaze in a blank kind of horror, and look at the *patron*, to see if there is any refuge?

Not to be *caught*! not to be *caught*! It must have been the prevailing motive of Indian-Mexican life since long before Montezuma marched his prisoners to sacrifice.*

MARKET DAY

Market Day*

This is the last Saturday before Christmas. The next year will be momentous, one feels. This year is nearly gone.

Dawn was windy, shaking the leaves, and the rising sun shone under a gap of yellow cloud. But at once it touched the yellow flowers that rise above the patio wall, and the swaying, glowing magenta of the bougainvillea, and the fierce red outbursts of the poinsettia. The poinsettia is splendid,* the flowers very big, and of a sure, stainless red. They call them Noche Buenas, flowers of Christmas Eve.* These tufts throw out their scarlet sharply, like red birds ruffling in the wind of dawn as if going to bathe, all their feathers alert. This for Christmas, instead of holly-berries. Christmas seems to need a red herald.

The yucca* is tall, higher than the house. It too is in flower, hanging an arm's-length of soft creamy bells, like a yard-long* grape-cluster of foam. And the waxy bells break on their stems in the wind, fall noiselessly from the long creamy bunch, that hardly sways.

The coffee berries are turning red. The hibiscus flowers, rose-coloured, sway at the tips of the thin branches, in rosettes of soft red.

In the second patio, there is a tall tree of the flimsy acacia sort.* Above itself it puts up whitish fingers of flowers, naked on the blue sky. And in the wind these fingers of flowers in the bare blue sky sway, sway with the reeling, roundward motion of tree tips in a wind.

A restless morning, with clouds lower down, moving also with a larger roundward motion. Everything moving. Best to go out in motion too, the slow roundward motion like the hawks.

Everything seems slowly to circle and hover towards a central point, the clouds, the mountains round the valley, the dust that rises, the big, beautiful, white-barred hawks, gabilanes, and even the snow-white flakes of flowers upon the dim palo blanco tree. Even the organ cactus, rising in stock-straight clumps, and the candelabrum cactus,* seem to be slowly wheeling and pivoting upon a centre, close upon it.

Strange that we should think in straight lines, when there are none, and talk of straight courses, when every course, sooner or later, is seen

to be making the sweep round, swooping upon the centre. When space
is curved,* and the cosmos is sphere within sphere, and the way from
any one point to any other point is round the bend of the inevitable,
that turns as the tips of the broad wings of the hawk turn upwards,
5   leaning upon the air like the visible* half of the ellipse.

If I have a way to go, it will be round the swoop of a bend, impinging
centripetal towards the centre. The straight course is hacked out in
wounds, against the will of the world.

Yet the dust advances like a ghost along the road, down the valley
10   plain. The dry turf of the valley-bed gleams like soft skin, sunlit and
pinkish ochre, spreading wide between the mountains that seem to
emit their own darkness, a dark-blue vapour translucent, sombering
them from the humped crests downwards. The many-pleated, noiseless
mountains of Mexico.

15   And away on the foot-slope lie the white specks of Huayapa,* among
its lake of trees. It is Saturday, and the white dots of men are threading
down the trail over the bare humps to the plain, following the dark
twinkle movement of asses, the dark nodding of the woman's head as
she rides between the baskets. Saturday, and market-day, and morning,
20   so the white specks of men, like sea-gulls on ploughland, come ebbing
like sparks from the palo blanco, over the fawn undulating of the valley
slope.

They are dressed in snow-white cotton, and they lift their knees in
the Indian trot, following the ass where the woman sits perched between
25   the huge baskets, her child held tight in the blue rebozo, at the brown
breast. And girls in long, full, soiled cotton skirts running, trotting,
ebbing along, after the twinkle-movement of the ass. Down they come,
in families, in clusters, in solitary ones, threading with ebbing, running,
barefoot movement noiseless towards the town, that blows the bubbles
30   of its church-domes* above the stagnant green of trees, away under the
opposite fawn-skin hills.

But down the valley middle comes the big road, almost straight. You
will know it by the tall walking of the dust, that hastens also towards the
town, overtaking, overpassing everybody. Overpassing all the dark little
35   figures and the white specks that thread tinily, in a sort of underworld,
to the town.

From the valley villages and from the mountains the peasants and
the Indians are coming in with supplies, the road is like a pilgrimage,*
with the dust in greatest haste, dashing for town. Dark-eared asses and
40   running men, running women, running girls, running lads, twinkling

donkeys ambling on fine little feet, under twin great baskets with tomatoes and gourds, twin great nets of bubble-shaped jars, twin bundles of
neat-cut faggots of wood, neat as bunches of cigarettes, and twin net-
sacks of charcoal. Donkeys, mules, on they come, great panier baskets
making a rhythm under the perched woman, great bundles bouncing   5
against the sides of the slim-footed animals. A baby donkey, trotting
naked after its piled-up dam,* a white, sandal-footed man following
with the silent Indian haste, and a girl running again on light feet.

Onwards, on a strange, ebbing current of haste. And slowly rowing
among the foot-travel, the ox-wagons rolling solid wheels below the   10
high nets of the body. Slow oxen, with heads pressed down nosing to
the earth, swaying, swaying their great horns as a snake sways itself, the
shovel-shaped collar of solid wood pressing down on their necks like
a scoop. On, on between the burnt-up turf and the solid, monumental
green of the organ cactus. Past the rocks and the floating palo blanco   15
flowers, past the towsled dust of the mesquite bushes.* While the dust
once more, in a greater haste than anyone, comes tall and rapid down
the road, overpowering and obscuring all the little people: as in a
cataclysm.

They are mostly small people, of the Zapotec race:* small men with   20
lifted chests and quick, lifted knees, advancing with heavy energy in the
mist of dust. And quiet, small, round-headed women running barefoot,
tightening their blue cotton rebozos round their shoulders, so often
with a baby in the fold. The white cotton clothes of the men so white,
that their faces are invisible, places of darkness under their big hats.   25
Clothed darkness, faces of night, quickly, silently, with inexhaustible
energy advancing to the town.

And many of the Serranos,* the Indians from the hills, wearing their
little conical black felt hats, seem capped with night, above the straight
white shoulders. Some have come far, walking all yesterday in their   30
little black hats and black-sheathed sandals. Tomorrow they will walk
back. And their eyes will be just the same, black and bright and wild,
in the dark faces. They have no goal, any more than the hawks in the
air, and no course to run, any more than the clouds.

The market is a huge roofed-in place.* Most extraordinary is the   35
noise that comes out, as you pass along the adjacent street. It is a huge
noise, yet you may never notice it. It sounds as if all the ghosts in the
world were talking to one another, in ghost-voices, within the darkness
of the market structure. It is a noise something like rain, or banana
leaves in a wind. The market full of Indians, dark-faced, silent-footed,   40

hush-spoken, but pressing in in countless numbers. The queer hissing murmur of the Zapotec *idioma*,* among the sounds of Spanish, the quiet, aside-voices of the Mixtecas.*

5

To buy and to sell, but above all, to commingle. In the old world, men make themselves two great excuses for coming together to a centre, and commingling freely in a mixed, unsuspicious host. Market and religion. These alone bring men, unarmed, together since time began. A little load of firewood, a woven blanket, a few eggs and tomatoes are excuse enough for men, women and children to cross the foot-weary miles

10

of valley and mountain. To buy, to sell, to barter, to exchange. To exchange, above all things, human contact.

That is why they like you to bargain, even if it's only the difference of a centavo. Round the centre of the covered market, where there is a basin of water, are the flowers: red, white, pink roses in heaps, many-

15

coloured little carnations, poppies, bits of larkspur, lemon and orange marigolds, buds of madonna lilies, pansies, a few forget me nots. They don't bring the tropical flowers. Only the lilies come wild from the hills, and the mauve red orchids.

"How much this bunch of cherry-pie heliotrope?"

20

"Fifteen centavos."

"Ten."

"Fifteen."

You put back the cherry-pie, and depart. But the woman is quite content. The contest, so short even, brisked her up.

25

"Pinks?"

"The red ones, señorita? Thirty centavos!"

"No. I don't want red ones. The mixed."

"Ah!" The woman seizes a handful of little carnations of all colours. Carefully puts them together. "Look, Señorita. No more?"

30

"No, no more. How much?"

"The same. Thirty centavos."

"It is much."

"No, Señorita, it is not much. Look at this little bunch. It is eight centavos."—Displays a scrappy little bunch. "Come then, twenty-five."

35

"No! Twenty-two."

"Look!" She gathers up three or four more flowers, and claps them to the bunch. "Two *reales*, Señorita."

It is a bargain. Off you go with multicoloured pinks, and the woman has had one more moment of contact, with a stranger, a perfect stranger.

An intermingling of voices, a threading together of different wills. It is life. The centavos are an excuse.

The stalls go off in straight lines, to the right, brilliant vegetables, to the left, bread and sweetened buns. Away at the one end, cheeses, butter, eggs, chickens, turkeys, meat. At the other, the native woven blankets and rebozos, skirts, shirts, handkerchieves. Down the far side, sandals and leather things.

The serape men spy you, and whistle to you like ferocious birds, and call "Señor! Señor! Look!" Then with violence one flings open a dazzling blanket, while another whistles more ear-piercingly still, to make you look at his blanket. It is a veritable den of lions and tigers, that spot where the serape men have their blankets piled on the ground. You shake your head, and flee.

To find yourself in the leather avenue.

"Señor! Señor! Look! Huaraches! Very fine, very finely made! Look Señor!"

The fat leather man jumps up and holds a pair of sandals at one's breast. They are of narrow woven strips of leather, in the newest Paris style, but a style ancient to these natives.* You take them in your hand, and look at them quizzically, while the fat wife of the huarache man reiterates: "Very fine work. Very fine. Much work!"

Leather men usually seem to have their wives with them.

"How much?"

"Twenty *reales.*"

"Twenty!"—in a voice of surprise and pained indignation.

"How much do you give?"

You refuse to answer. Instead, you put the huaraches to your nose. The huarache man looks at his wife, and they laugh aloud.

"They smell," you say.

"No, señor, they don't smell!"—and the two go off into fits of laughter.

"Yes, they smell. It is not American leather."*

"Yes, señor, it is American leather. They don't smell, Señor. No, they don't smell."—He coaxes you till you wouldn't believe your own nose.

"Yes, they smell."

"How much do you give?"

"Nothing, because they smell."

And you give another sniff, though it is painfully unnecessary. And in spite of your refusal to bid, the man and wife go into fits of laughter, to see you painfully sniffing.

You lay down the sandals, and shake your head.

5 "How much do you offer?" reiterates the man, gaily.

You shake your head mournfully, and move away. The leather man and his wife look at one another and go off into another fit of laughter, because you smelt the huaraches, and said they stank.

They did. The natives use human excrement for tanning leather.*
10 When Bernal Díaz came with Cortés* to the great market-place of Mexico City, in Montezuma's day,* he saw the little pots of human excrement in rows for sale, and the leather-makers going round sniffing to see which was the best, before they paid for it. It staggered even a fifteenth-century Spaniard. Yet my leather man and his wife think
15 it screamingly funny that I smell the huaraches before buying them. Everything has its own smell, and the natural smell of huaraches is what it is. You might as well quarrel with an onion for smelling like an onion.

The great press of the quiet natives, some of them bright and clean, many in old rags, the brown flesh showing through the rents in the
20 dirty cotton. Many wild hillmen, in their little hats of conical black felt, with their wild, staring eyes. And as they cluster round the hat-stall, in a long, long suspense of indecision before they can commit themselves, trying on a new hat, their black hair gleams blue-black, and falls thick and rich over their foreheads, like gleaming, bluey-black feathers. And
25 one is reminded again of the blue-haired Buddha, with the lotus at his navel.*

But already the fleas are travelling under one's clothing.

Market lasts all day. The native inns are great dreary yards with little sheds, and little rooms around. Some men and families who have
30 come from far, will sleep in one or other of the little stall-like rooms. Many will sleep on the stones, on the earth, round the market, anywhere. But the asses are there by the hundred, crowded in the inn-yards, drooping their ears with the eternal patience of the beast that knows better than any other beast that every road curves round to the same
35 centre of rest, and hither and thither means nothing.*

And towards nightfall the dusty road will be thronged with shadowy people and unladen asses and new-laden mules, urging silently into the country again, their backs to the town, glad to get away from the town, to see the cactus and the pleated hills, and the trees that mean a village.

In some village they will lie under a tree, or under a wall, and sleep. Then the next day, home.

It is fulfilled, what they came to market for. They have sold and bought. But more than that, they have had their moment of contact and centripetal flow. They have been part of a great stream of men flowing to a centre, to the vortex of the market-place. And here they have felt life concentrate upon them, they have been jammed between the soft hot bodies of strange men come from afar, they have had the sound of strangers' voices in their ears, they have asked and been answered in unaccustomed ways.

There is no goal, and no abiding-place, and nothing is fixed, not even the cathedral towers. The Cathedral towers are slowly leaning, seeking the curve of return. As the natives curved in a strong swirl, towards the vortex of the market. Then on a strong swerve of repulsion, curved out and away again, into space.

Nothing but the touch, the spark of contact. That, no more. That, which is most elusive, still the only treasure. Come, and gone, and yet the clue itself.

True, folded up in the handkerchief inside the shirt, are the copper centavos, and maybe a few silver pesos. But these too will disappear as the stars disappear at daybreak, as they are meant to disappear. Everything is meant to disappear. Every curve plunges into the vortex and is lost, re-emerges with a certain relief and takes to the open, and there is lost again.

Only that which is utterly intangible, matters. The contact, the spark of exchange. That which can never be fastened upon, forever gone, forever coming, never to be detained: the spark of contact.

Like the evening star,* when it is neither night nor day. Like the evening star, between the sun and the moon, and swayed by neither of them. The flashing intermediary, the evening star that is seen only at the dividing of the day and night, but then is more wonderful than either.

INDIANS AND ENTERTAINMENT

Indians and Entertainment*

We go to the theatre* to be entertained. It may be *The Potters*, it may be
Max Reinhardt, *King Lear* or *Electra*.* All entertainment.
We want to be taken out of ourselves. Or not entirely that. We want
to become spectators at our own show. We lean down from the plush   5
seats like little gods in a democratic heaven, and see ourselves away
below there, on the world of the stage, in a brilliant artificial sunlight,
behaving comically absurdly, like Pa Potter, yet getting away with it,
or behaving tragically absurdly, like King Lear, and not getting away
with it: rather proud of not getting away with it.   10
    We see ourselves: we survey ourselves: we laugh at ourselves: we weep
over ourselves: we are the gods above of our own destinies. Which is
very entertaining.
    The secret of it all, is that we detach ourselves from the painful
and always solid trammels of actual existence, and become creatures of 15
memory and of spirit-like consciousness. We are the gods and there's the
machine,* down below us. Down below, on the stage, our mechanical or
earth-bound self stutters or raves, Pa Potter or King Lear. But however
Potterish or Learian we may be, while we sit aloft in plush seats we are
creatures of pure consciousness, pure spirit, surveying those selves of 20
clay who are so absurd or so tragic, below.
    Even a little girl trailing a long skirt and playing at being Mrs Paradiso
next door, is enjoying the same sensation. From her childish little
consciousness she is making Mrs Paradiso, creating her according to
her own fancy. It is the little individual consciousness lording it, for the 25
moment, over the actually tiresome and inflexible world of actuality.
Mrs Paradiso in the flesh is a thing to fear. But if I can play at being
Mrs Paradiso, why, then I am a little Lord Almighty, and Mrs Paradiso
is but a creation from my consciousness.
    The audience in the theatre is a little democracy of the ideal con-   30
sciousness.* They all sit there, gods of the ideal mind, and survey with
laughter or tears the realm of actuality.
    Which is very soothing and satisfying so long as you believe that
the ideal mind is the actual arbiter. So long as you instinctively feel

that there is some supreme, universal ideal consciousness swaying all destiny.

When you begin to have misgivings, you sit rather uneasily on your plush seat.

5   Nobody really believes that destiny is an accident. The very fact that day keeps on following night, and summer, winter, establishes the belief in universal law, and from this to a belief in* some great hidden mind in the universe is an inevitable step for us.

A few people, the so-called advanced, have grown uneasy in their
10   bones about the Universal Mind.* But the mass are absolutely convinced. And every member of the mass is absolutely convinced that he is part and parcel of this Universal Mind. Hence his joy at the theatre. His even greater joy at the cinematograph.*

In the moving pictures he has detached himself even further from
15   the solid stuff of earth. There, the people are truly shadows: the shadow-pictures are thinkings of his mind. They live in the rapid and kaleidoscopic realm of the abstract. And the individual watching the shadow-spectacle sits a very god, in an orgy of abstraction, actually dissolved into delighted, watchful spirit. And if his best girl sits beside him,
20   she vibrates in the same ether, and triumphs in the same orgy of abstraction. No wonder this passion of dramatic abstraction becomes a lust.

That is our idea of entertainment.

You come to the Indian and ask him about his. He hasn't got one.

The Indians dance around the drum singing. They have their great
25   spectacular dances, Eagle dance, Corn dance. They have the dancing, singing procession between the fires at Christmas. They have their sacred races, down the long track.*

White people always, or nearly always, write sentimentally about the Indians. Even a man like Adolf Bandelier.* He was not a sentimental
30   man. On the contrary. Yet the sentimentality creeps in, when he writes about the thing he knows best, the Indian.

So it is with all of them, anthropologists and myth-transcribers and all. There is that creeping note of sentimentality through it all, which makes one shrug one's shoulders and wish the Indians to hell, along
35   with a lot of other bunk.

You've got to de-bunk the Indian, as you've got to de-bunk the Cowboy.* When you've de-bunked the Cowboy, there's not much left. But the Indian bunk is not the Indian's invention. It is ours.

It is almost impossible for white people to approach the Indian with-
40   out either sentimentality or dislike. The common healthy vulgar white

usually feels a certain native dislike of these drumming aboriginals. The highbrow invariably lapses into sentimentalism like the smell of bad eggs.

Why?—Both the reactions are due to the same feeling in the white man. The Indian is not in line with us. He's not coming our way. His whole being is going a different way from ours. And the minute you set eyes on him you know it.

And then, there's only two things you can do. You can detest the insidious devil for having an utterly different way from our own great way. Or you can perform the mental trick, and fool yourself and others into believing that the befeathered and bedaubed darling is nearer to the true ideal gods, than we are.

This last is just bunk, and a lie. But it saves our appearances. The former feeling, of instinctive but tolerant repulsion, the feeling of most ordinary farmers and ranchers and mere individuals in the west, is quite natural, it is only honesty to admit it.

The Indian way of consciousness is different from and fatal to our way of consciousness. Our way of consciousness is different from and fatal to the Indian's.* The two ways, the two streams are never to be united. They are not even to be reconciled. There is no bridge, no canal of connection.

The sooner we realise and accept this, the better, and leave off trying, with fulsome sentimentalism, to render the Indian in our own terms.

The acceptance of the great paradox of human consciousness is the first step to a new accomplishment.

The consciousness of one branch of humanity is the annihilation of the consciousness of another branch. That is, the life of the Indian, his stream of conscious being, is just death to the white man. And we can understand the consciousness of the Indian only in terms of the death of our own consciousness.

And let not this be turned into another sentimentalism. Because the same paradox exists between the consciousness of white men and Hindoos or Polynesians or Bantu.* It is the eternal paradox of human consciousness. To pretend that all is one stream is to cause chaos and nullity. To pretend to express one stream in terms of another, so as to identify the two, is false and sentimental. The only thing you can do is to have a little Ghost inside you which sees both ways, or even many ways.* But a man cannot *belong* to both ways, or to many ways. One man can belong to one great way of consciousness only. He may even change from one way to another. But he cannot go both ways at once. Can't be done.

So that, to understand the Indian conception of entertainment, we have to destroy our own conception.

Perhaps the commonest entertainment among the Indians is singing round the drum, at evening, when the day is over. European peasants* will sit round the fire and sing. But they sing ballads or lyrics, tales about individuals or individual, personal experience. And each individual identifies the emotion of the song with his own emotion.

Or the wild fishermen of the Outer Hebrides* will sing in their intense,* concentrated way, by the fire. And again, usually, the songs have words. Yet sometimes not. Sometimes the song has merely sounds, and a marvellous melody. It is the seal drifting in to shore on the wave, or the seal woman,* singing low and secret, departing back from the shores of men, through the surf, back to the realm of the outer beasts, that rock on the waters and stare through glistening, vivid, mindless eyes.

This is approaching the Indian song. But even this is pictorial, conceptual far beyond the Indian point. The Hebridean still sees himself human, and *outside* the great naturalistic influences, which are the dramatic circumstances of his life.

The Indian, singing, sings without words or vision. Face lifted and sightless, eyes half closed and visionless, mouth open and speechless, the sounds arise in his chest, from the consciousness in the abdomen.* He will tell you it is a song of a man coming home from the bear hunt: or a song to make rain: or a song to make the corn grow: or even, quite modern, the song of the church bell on Sunday morning.*

But the man coming home from the bear hunt is any man, all men, the bear is any bear, every bear, all bear. There is no individual, isolated experience. It is the hunting, tired, triumphant demon of manhood which has won against the squint-eyed demon of all bears. The experience is generic, non-individual. It is an experience of the human blood-stream, not of the mind or spirit. Hence the subtle, incessant, insistent rhythm of the drum, which is pulsated like the heart, and soulless, and un-escapable. Hence the strange blind unanimity of the Indian men's voices. The experience is one experience, tribal, of the blood-stream. Hence, to our ears, the absence of melody. Melody is individualised emotion, just as orchestral music is the harmonising again of many separate, individual emotions or experiences. But the real Indian song is non-individual, and without melody.* Strange, clapping, crowing, gurgling sounds, in an unseizable subtle rhythm, the rhythm of the heart in her throes: from a parted, entranced mouth, from a chest powerful and free, from an abdomen where the great blood-stream surges in the dark, and surges in its own generic experiences.

This may mean nothing to you. To the ordinary white ear, the Indian's singing is a rather disagreeable howling of dogs to a tom-tom. But if it rouses no other sensation, it rouses a touch of fear amid the hostility. Whatever the spirit of man may be, the blood is basic.

Or take the song to make the corn grow. The dark faces stoop forward, in a strange race darkness. The eyelashes droop a little in the dark, ageless, vulnerable faces. The drum is a heart beating with insistent thuds. And the spirits of the men go out on the ether, vibrating in waves from the hot, dark, intentional blood, seeking the creative presence that hovers forever in the ether, seeking the identification, following on down the mysterious rhythms of the creative pulse, on and on into the germinating quick of the maize that lies under the ground, there, with the throbbing, pulsing, clapping rhythm that comes from the dark, creative blood in man, to stimulate the tremulous, pulsating protoplasm* in the seed-germ, till it throws forth its rhythms of creative energy, into rising blades of leaf or stem.

Or take the round dances,* round the drum. These may or may not have a name. The dance, anyhow, is primarily a song. All the men sing in unison, as they move with the soft, yet heavy bird-tread* which is the whole of the dance. There is no drama. With bodies bent a little forward, shoulders and breasts loose and heavy, feet powerful but soft, the men tread the rhythm into the centre of the earth. The drums keep up the pulsating heart-beat. The men sing in unison, though some will be silent for moments, or even minutes. And for hours, hours it goes on: the round dance.

It has no name. It has no words. It means nothing at all. There is no spectacle, no spectator.

Yet perhaps it is the most stirring sight in the world, in the dark, near the fire, with the drums going, the pine-trees standing still, the everlasting darkness, and the strange lifting and dropping, surging, crowing, gurgling, aah-h-h-ing! of the male voices.

What are they doing? Who knows! But perhaps they are giving themselves again to the pulsing, incalculable fall of the blood, which forever seeks to fall to the centre of the earth, while the heart, like a planet pulsating in an orbit, keeps up the strange, lonely circulation* of the separate human existence.

But what we seek, passively, in sleep, they perhaps seek, actively, in the round dance. It is the homeward pulling of the blood, as the feet fall in the soft, heavy rhythm, endlessly. It is the dark blood falling back from the mind, from sight and speech and knowing, back to the great central source where is rest and unspeakable renewal. We whites, creatures of spirit, look upon sleep and see only the dreams that lie as debris of the day, mere bits of wreckage from the day-Consciousness. We never realise the strange falling back of the dark blood into the downward rhythm, the rhythm of pure forgetting and pure renewal.

Or take the little dances round the fire, the mime dances, when two men put on the eagle feathers and take the shield on their arm, and dance the pantomime of a fight, a spear dance.* The rhythm is the same, really, the drums keep up the heart-pulsation, the feet the peculiar bird-tread, the soft, heavy, bird-like step that treads as it were towards the centre of the earth. But there is also the subtle leaping towards each other of the two shield-sheltered naked ones, feathered with the power of the eagle. The leaping together, the coming close, the circling, wary, stealthy avoidance and retreat, always on the same rhythm of drum-beats, the same regular, heavy-soft tread of moccasined feet.

It is the dance of the naked blood-being, defending his own isolation in the rhythm of the universe. Not skill nor prowess, not heroism. Not man to man. The creature of the isolated, circulating blood-stream dancing in the peril of his own isolation, in the overweening of his own singleness. The glory in power of the man of the single blood-stream. The peril of the man whose heart is suspended, like a single red star, in a great and complex universe, following its lone course round the invisible sun of our being, amid the strange wandering array of other hearts.

The other men look on. They may or may not sing. And they see themselves in the power and peril of the lonely heart, the creature of the isolated blood-circuit. They see also, subsidiary, the skill, the agility, the swiftness, the daunting onrush that make the warrior. It is practice as well as mystery.

Or take the big, spectacular dances, like the deer dance, the corn dance. The deer dance in the New Year.* The people crowded on the roofs of the pueblo, women, children, old men, watching. The two long lines of men, hunters, facing one another. And away at the stream which comes running swiftly from among the cotton-wood trees, the watchers, watching eagerly. At last, over the log bridge,* two maidens leading the animals: two maidens in their black shawls and wide white deer-skin top-boots, dancing with a slow, delicate-footed rhythm, facing out, then facing in, and shaking their gourd rattles delicately, marking the rhythm as the drums mark it. Following the maidens, all the animals: men in two columns, and each man an animal, leaning forward each on two slim sticks which are his forelegs, with the deer-skin over him, the antlers branching from his head: or the buffalo hide, from whose shaggy mane his bent head peers out: or a black bear, or a wolf. There they come, the two long lines of wild animals, deer, buffalo, bear, wolf, coyote, and at the back, even tiny boys, as foxes, all stepping on those soft, pointed toes, and moving in slow silence under the winter sun, following the slow, swinging progress of the dancing maidens.

Everything is very soft, subtle, delicate. There is none of the hardness of representation. They are not representing something, not even playing. It is a soft, subtle *being* something.

Yet at the same time it is a game, and a very dramatic naïve spectacle. The old men trot softly alongside, laughing, showing all their wrinkles. But they are experiencing a delicate, wild inward delight, participating in the natural mysteries. They tease the little boys under the fox-skins, and the boys, peeping with their round black eyes, are shy and confused. Yet they keep on in the procession, solemnly, as it moves between the ranks of the wild hunters. And all eyes are round with wonder, and the mystery of participation. Amused too, on the merely human side of themselves. The gay touch of amusement in buffoonery does not in the least detract from the delicate, pulsing wonder of solemnity, which comes from participating in the ceremony itself.

There you have it all, the pantomime, the buffoonery, the human comicalness. But at the same time, quivering bright and wide-eyed in unchangeable delight of solemnity, you have the participating in a natural wonder. The mystery of the wild creatures led from their fastnesses, their wintry retreats and holes in the ground, docilely fascinated by the delicacy and the commanding wistfulness of the maidens who went out to seek them, to seek food in the winter, and who draw after them, in a following, the wild, the timid, the rapacious animals, following in gentle wonder of bewitchment, right into the haunts of men, right into the camp and up to the hunters. The two long lines of wild animals delicately and slowly stepping behind the slow gyration of the two dark-fringed maidens, who shake their gourd rattles in a delicate, quick, three-pulse rhythm, and never change their wide dark eyes, under the dark fringe. It is the celebration of another triumph, the triumph of the magical wistfulness of woman, the wonderful power of her seeking, her yearning, which can draw forth even the bear from his den.

Now drama, we are told, has developed out of these ceremonial dances. Greek drama arose this way.* But from the Indian's ceremonial dance to the Greek's early religious ceremony is still a long step. The Greeks usually had some specified deity, some specific God to whom the ceremony was offered. And this God is the witness, the essential audience of the play. The ceremony is *performed* for the gratification of the god. And here you have the beginning of the theatre, with players and audience.

With the Indians it is different. There is strictly no god. The Indian does not consider himself as created, and therefore external to God, or the creature of God. To the Indian there is no conception of a defined God. Creation is a great flood, forever flowing, in lovely and terrible waves. In everything, the shimmer of creation,* and never the finality of the created. Never the distinction between God and God's Creation,* or between Spirit and Matter. Everything, everything is the wonderful shimmer of creation, it may be a deadly shimmer like lightning or the anger in the little eyes of the bear, it may be the beautiful shimmer of the moving deer, or the pine-boughs softly swaying under snow. Creation contains the unspeakably terrifying enemy, the unspeakably lovely friend, as the maiden who brings us our food in dead of winter,* by her passion of tender wistfulness. Yet even this tender wistfulness is the fearful danger of the wild creatures, deer and bear and buffalo, which find their death in it.

There is, in our sense of the word, no God. But all is Godly. There is no Great Mind directing the universe. Yet the mystery of creation, the wonder and fascination of creation shimmers in every leaf and stone, in every thorn and bud, in the fangs of the rattle-snake and in the soft eyes of a fawn. Things utterly opposite are still pure wonder of creation. There is no Creator: only the endless quivering unfolding of creation, in* the yell of the mountain-lion, and the breeze in the aspen leaves. The Apache warrior in his war-paint,* shrieking the war-cry and cutting the throats of the old women, still he is part of the mystery of creation. He is godly as the growing corn. And the mystery of creation makes us sharpen the knives and point the arrows in utmost determination against him. It must be so. It is part of the wonder. And to every part of the wonder we must answer in kind.

The Indian accepts Jesus on the Cross amid all the rest of the wonders. The presence of Jesus on the Cross, or the pitiful Mary Mother*

does not in the least prevent the strange intensity of the war-dance.
The brave comes home with a scalp.* In the morning he goes to mass.
Two mysteries! The soul of man is the theatre in which every mystery
is enacted. Jesus, Mary, the snake-dance, red blood on the knife: it is
all the rippling of this untellable flood of creation, which, in a narrow   5
sense, we call Nature.*

There is no division between actor and audience. It is all one.

There is no God looking on. The only god there is, is involved all
the time in the dramatic wonder and inconsistency of creation. God is
immersed, as it were, in creation, not to be separated or distinguished.   10
There can be no Ideal God.

And here finally you see the difference between Indian entertainment
and even the earliest form of Greek drama. Right at the beginning of
Old World dramatic presentation there was the onlooker, if only in
the shape of the God Himself, or the Goddess Herself, to whom the   15
dramatic offering was made. And this God or Goddess resolves, at last,
into a Mind occupied by some particular thought or idea. And in the
long course of evolution, we ourselves become the gods of our own
drama. The spectacle is offered to us. And we sit aloft, enthroned in the
Mind, dominated by some one exclusive idea, and we judge the show.   20

There is absolutely none of this in the Indian dance. There is no
God. There is no Onlooker. There is no Mind. There is no dominant
idea. And finally, there is no judgment: absolutely no judgment.*

The Indian is completely embedded in the wonder of his own drama.
It is a drama that has no beginning and no end, it is all-inclusive. It   25
can't be judged, because there is nothing outside it, to judge it.

The mind is there merely as a servant, to keep man pure and true to
the mystery, which is always present. The mind bows down before the
creative mystery, even of the atrocious Apache warrior. It judges, not
the good and the bad, but the lie and the true. The Apache warrior,   30
in all his atrocity, is true to his own creative mystery. And as such, he
must be fought. But he cannot be called a *lie* on the face of the earth.
Hence he cannot be classed among the abominations,* the cowards and
the liars: those who betray the wonder.

The Indian, so long as he is pure, has only two great negative   35
commandments.*

Thou shalt not lie.

Thou shalt not be a coward.

Positively, his one commandment is:

Thou shalt acknowledge the wonder.   40

Evil lies in lying and in cowardice. Wickedness lies in witchcraft; that is, in seeking to prostitute the creative wonder to the individual mind and will, the individual conceit.

And virtue? Virtue lies in the heroic response to the creative wonder, the utmost response. In the man, it is a valiant putting forth of all his strength to meet and to run forward with the wonder. In woman it is the putting forth of all herself in a delicate, marvellous sensitiveness, which draws forth the wonder to herself, and draws the man to the wonder in her, as it drew even the wild animals from the lair of winter.

You see this so plainly in the Indian races. Naked, and daubed with clay to hide the nakedness, and to take the anointment of the earth; stuck over with bits of fluff of eagle's down, to be anointed with the power of the air, the youths and men whirl down the racing track, in relays. They are not racing to win a race. They are not racing for a prize. They are not racing to show their prowess.

They are putting forth all their might, all their strength, in a tension that is half anguish, half ecstasy, in the effort to gather into their souls more and more of the creative fire, the creative energy which shall carry their tribe through the year, through the vicissitudes of the months, on, on in the unending race of humanity along the track of trackless creation. It is the heroic effort, the sacred heroic effort which men must make and must keep on making. As if hurled from a catapult the Indian youth throws himself along the course, working his body strangely, incomprehensibly. And when his turn comes again, he hurls himself forward with greater intensity, to greater speed, driving himself, as it were, into the heart of the fire. And the old men along the track encourage him, urge him with their green twigs, laughingly, mockingly, teasingly, but at the same time with an exquisite pure anxiety and concern.

And he walks away at last, his chest lifting and falling heavily, a strange look in his eyes, having run with the changeless god who will give us nothing unless we overtake him.

But what is the good of talking about it all. The Indians are losing too, in the long race. They too prefer to sit passive at the moving pictures, now. Their form of entertainment is nearly finished. The dollar is blotting the mystery out for ever, from their race as from ours.*

THE DANCE OF THE SPROUTING CORN

Illustration I *The Corn Dance*, sketch by D. H. Lawrence (by 1924)

The Dance of the Sprouting Corn*

Pale, dry, baked earth, that blows into dust of fine sand. Low hills of
baked pale earth, sinking heavily, and speckled sparsely with dark dots
of cedar bushes. A river on the plain of drought,* just a cleft of dark,
reddish-brown water, almost a flood. And over all, the blue, uneasy,   5
alkaline sky.

A pale, uneven, parched world where a motor-car rocks and lurches
and churns in sand. A world pallid with dryness, inhuman with a faint
taste of alkali. Like driving in the bed of a great sea that dried up
unthinkable ages ago,* and now is drier than any other dryness, yet still   10
reminiscent of the bottom of the sea, sandhills sinking, and straight,
cracked mesas, like cracks in the dry-mud bottom of the sea.

So, the mud church standing discreetly outside, just outside the
pueblo, not to see too much. And on its facade of mud, under the tim-
bered mud-eaves, two speckled horses rampant, painted by the   15
Indians, a red piebald and a black one.*

Swish! Over the logs of the ditch-bridge, where brown water is
flowing full. There below is the pueblo,* dried mud like mud-pie houses,
all squatting in a jumble, prepared to crumble into dust and be invisible,
dust to dust returning, earth to earth.*   20

That they don't crumble is the mystery. That these little squarish
mud-heaps endure for centuries after centuries, while Greek marble
tumbles asunder, and cathedrals totter, is the wonder. But then, the
naked human hand with a bit of new soft mud is quicker than time,*
and defies the centuries.   25

Roughly the low, square, mud-pie houses make a wide street where
all is naked earth save a door-way or a window with a pale-blue sash.
At the end of the street, turn again into a parallel wide, dry street. And
there, in the dry, oblong aridity, there tosses a small forest that is alive;
and thud-thud-thud goes the drum, and the deep sound of men singing   30
is like the deep soughing of the wind, in the depths of a wood.

You realise that you had heard the drum from the distance, also the
deep, distant roar and boom of the singing, but that you had not heeded,
as you don't heed the wind.

Illustration II Sketch of a *koshare* by D. H. Lawrence (probably 1924)

It all tosses like young, agile trees in a wind. This is the dance of the sprouting corn, and everybody holds a little, beating branch of green pine.* Thud-thud-thud-thud-thud! goes the drum, heavily the men hop and hop and hop, sway, sway, sway, sway go the little branches of
5 green pine. It tosses like a little forest, and the deep sound of men's singing is like the booming and tearing of a wind deep inside a forest. They are dancing the Spring Corn Dance.

This is the Wednesday after Easter, after Christ Risen and the corn germinated. They dance on Monday and on Tuesday. Wednesday is
10 the third and last dance of this green resurrection.

You realise the long lines of dancers, and a solid cluster of men singing near the drum. You realise the intermittent black-and-white fantasy of the hopping Koshare, the jesters, the Delight-Makers.* You become aware of the ripple of bells on the knee-garters of the dancers, a continual
15 pulsing ripple of little bells; and of the sudden wild, whooping yells from near the drum. Then you become aware of the seed-like shudder of the gourd-rattles, as the dance changes, and the swaying of the tufts of green pine-twigs stuck behind the arms of all the dancing men, in the broad green arm-bands.

20 Gradually comes through to you the black, stable solidity of the dancing women, who poise like solid shadow, one woman behind each

rippling, leaping male. The long, silky, black hair of the women, streaming down their backs, and the equally long, streaming, gleaming hair of
the males, loose over broad, naked, orange-brown shoulders.

Then the faces, the impassive, rather fat, golden-brown faces of the
women, with eyes cast down, crowned above with the green tableta,   5
like a flat tiara.* Something strange and noble about the impassive,
barefoot women in the short black cassocks, as they subtly tread the
dance, scarcely moving, and yet edging rhythmically along, swaying
from each hand the green spray of pine-twig out-out-out-out, to the
thud of the drum, immediately behind the leaping fox-skin of the men   10
dancers. And all the emerald-green, painted tabletas, the flat wooden
tiaras shaped like a castle gateway, rise steady and noble from the soft,
slightly bowed heads of the women, held by a band under the chin.
All the tabletas down the line, emerald green, almost steady, while the
bright black heads of the men leap softly up and down, between.   15

Bit by bit you take it in. You cannot get a whole impression, save of
some sort of wood tossing, a little forest of trees in motion, with gleaming
black hair and gold-ruddy breasts that somehow do not destroy the
illusion of forest.

When you look at the women, you forget the men. The bare-armed,   20
bare-legged, barefoot women with streaming hair and lofty green tiaras,
impassive, downward-looking faces, twigs swaying outwards from
subtle, rhythmic wrists; women clad in the black, prehistoric short
gown* fastened over one shoulder, leaving the other shoulder bare, and
showing at the arm-place a bit of pink or white under-shirt; belted also   25
round the waist with a woven woollen sash, scarlet and green on the
handwoven black cassock. The noble, slightly submissive bending of
the tiara-ed head. The subtle measure of the bare, breathing, bird-like
feet, that are flat, and seem to cleave to earth softly, and softly lift away.
The continuous outward swaying of the pine-sprays!   30

But when you look at the men, you forget the women. The men are
naked to the waist, and ruddy-golden, and in the rhythmic, hopping
leap of the dance their breasts shake downwards, as the strong, heavy
body comes down, down, down, down, in the downward-plunge of
the dance. The black hair streams loose and living down their backs,   35
the black brows are level, the black eyes look out unchanging from
under the silky lashes. They are handsome, and absorbed with a deep
rhythmic absorption, which still leaves them awake and aware. Down,
down, down they drop, on the heavy, ceaseless leap of the dance, and
the great necklaces of shell-cores* spring on the naked breasts, the   40

neck-shell flaps up and down, the short white kilt of woven stuff, with the heavy woollen embroidery, green and red and black,* opens and shuts slightly to the strong lifting of the knees: the heavy whitish cords that hang from the kilt-band at the side sway and coil forever down the side of the right leg, down to the ankle, the bells on the red-woven garters under the knees ripple without end and the feet in buckskin boots, furred round the ankle with a beautiful band of skunk fur, black with a white tip, come down with a lovely, heavy, soft precision, first one, then the other, dropping always plumb to earth. Slightly bending forward, a black gourd rattle in the right hand, a small green bough in the left, the dancer dances the eternal dropping leap, that brings his life down, down, down, down from the mind, down from the broad, beautiful, shaking breast, down to the powerful pivot of the knees, then to the ankles, and plunges deep from the ball of the foot into the earth, towards the earth's red centre, where these men belong, as is signified by the red earth with which they are smeared.*

And meanwhile, the shell-cores from the Pacific sway up and down, ceaseless, on their breasts. Mindless, without effort, under the hot sun, unceasing, yet never perspiring nor even breathing heavily, they dance on and on. Mindless, yet still listening, observing. They hear the deep, surging singing of the bunch of old men, like a great wind soughing. They hear the cries and yells of the man waving his bough by the drum. They catch the word of the song, and at a moment, shudder the black rattles, wheel, and the line breaks, women from men, they thread across to a new formation. And as the men wheel round, their black hair gleams and shakes, and the long fox-skin sways, like a tail.

And always, when they form into line again it is a beautiful long straight line, flexible as life, but straight as rain.

The men round the drum are old, or elderly. They are all in a bunch, and they wear day dress, loose cotton drawers,* pink or white cotton shirts, hair tied up behind with the red cords, and banded round the head with a strip of pink rag, or white rag, or blue. There they are, solid like a cluster of bees, their black heads with the pink rag circles all close together, swaying their pine-twigs with rhythmic, wind-swept hands, dancing slightly, mostly on the right foot, ceaselessly, and singing, their black bright eyes absorbed, their dark lips pushed out, while the deep strong sound rushes like wind, and the unknown words form themselves in the dark.

Suddenly the solitary man pounding the drum swings his drum round, and begins to pound on the other end, on a higher note, pang-pang-pang! Instead of the previous brumm! brumm! brumm! of the bass note. The watchful man next the drummer yells and waves lightly, dancing on bird-feet. The Koshare make strange, eloquent gestures to the sky.

And again the gleaming bronze-and-dark men dancing in the rows shudder their rattles, break the rhythm, change into a queer, beautiful two-step, the long lines suddenly curl into rings, four rings of dancers, the leaping, gleaming-seeming men between the solid, subtle, submissive blackness of the women who are crowned with emerald green tiaras, all going subtly round in rings. Then slowly they change again, and form a star. Then again, unmingling, they come back into rows.

And all the while, all the while the naked Koshare are threading about. Of bronze-and-dark men dancers there are some forty-two, each with a dark, crowned woman attending him like a shadow. The old men, the bunch of singers in shirts and tied-up black hair, are about sixty in number, or sixty-four. The Koshare are about twenty-four.

They are slim and naked, daubed with black-and-white earth, their hair daubed white and gathered upwards to a great knot on top of the head, whence springs a tuft of corn-husks, dry corn-leaves.* Though they wear nothing but a little black square cloth, front and back, at their middle, they do not seem naked, for some are white with black spots, like a leopard, and some have broad black lines or zigzags on their smeared bodies, and all their faces are blackened with triangles or lines till they look like weird masks. Meanwhile their hair, gathered straight up and daubed white and sticking up from the top of the head with corn husks, completes the fantasy. They are anything but natural. Like blackened ghosts of a dead corn cob, tufted at the top.

And all the time, running like queer spotted dogs they weave nakedly through the unheeding dance, comical, weird, dancing the dance-step naked and fine, prancing through the lines, up and down the lines, and making fine gestures with their flexible hands, calling something down from the sky, calling something up from the earth, and dancing forward all the time. Suddenly as they catch a word from the singers, name of a star, of a wind, a name for the sun, for a cloud, their hands soar up and gather in the air, soar down with a slow motion. And again, as they catch a word that means earth, earth deeps, water within the earth, or red-earth-quickening, the hands flutter softly down, and draw up the water, draw up the earth-quickening, earth to sky, sky to earth, influences above to influences below, to meet in the germ-quick of corn, where life is.

And as they dance, the Koshare watch the dancing men. And if a fox-skin is coming loose at the belt, they fasten it as the man dances, or they stoop and tie another man's shoe. For the dancer must not hesitate to the end.

5   And then after some forty minutes, the drum stops. Slowly the dancers file into one line, woman behind man, and move away, threading towards their kiva,* with no sound but the tinkle of knee-bells in the silence.

But at the same moment, the thud of an unseen drum, from beyond,
10   the soughing of deep song approaching from the unseen. It is the other half, the other half of the tribe coming to continue the dance. They appear round the Kiva—one Koshare and one dancer leading the rows, the old men all abreast, singing already in a great strong burst.

So, from ten o'clock in the morning till about four in the afternoon,
15   first one half, then the other. Till at last, as the day wanes, the two halves meet, and the two singings like two great winds surge one past the other, and the thicket of the dance becomes a real forest. It is the close of the third day.*

Afterwards, the men and women crowd on the low, round towers of
20   the kivas, and take off their ceremonial dress, while the Koshare run round jesting and miming, and taking big offerings from the women, loaves of bread and cakes of blue-maize meal. Women come carrying big baskets of bread and guayava, on two hands, an offering.

And the mystery of germination—not procreation, but *putting forth*,
25   resurrection, life springing within the seed, is accomplished. The sky has its fire, its waters, its stars, its wandering electricity, its winds, its fingers of cold. The earth has its reddened body, its invisible hot heart, its inner waters and many juices and unaccountable stuffs. Between them all, the little seed: and also man, like a seed that is busy and
30   aware. And from the heights and from the depths man, the caller, calls: man, the knower, brings down the influences, and brings up the influences, with his knowledge: man, so vulnerable, so subject, and yet even in his vulnerability and subjection, a master, commands the invisible influences, and is obeyed. Commands in that song, in
35   that rhythmic energy of dance, in that still-submissive mockery of the Koshare. And he accomplishes his end, as master. He partakes in the springing of the corn, in the rising and budding and earing of the corn. And when he eats his bread, at last, he recovers all he once sent forth, and partakes again of the energies he called to the corn, from out of the
40   wide universe.

THE HOPI SNAKE DANCE

The Hopi Snake Dance*

The Hopi country is in Arizona, next the Navajo country, and some
seventy miles north of the Santa Fe railroad.* The Hopis are pueblo
Indians,* village Indians, so their reservation is not large. It consists of a
square tract of greyish, unappetising desert, out of which rise three tall,   5
arid mesas, broken off in ragged, pallid rock. On the top of the mesas
perch the ragged, broken, greyish pueblos, identical with the mesas on
which they stand.

The nearest village, Walpi,* stands in half ruin high, high on a narrow
rock top where no leaf of life ever was tender. It is all grey, utterly dry,   10
utterly pallid, stone and dust, and very narrow. Below is all the stark
light of the dry Arizona sun.

Walpi is called the "first mesa." And it is at the far edge of Walpi you
see the withered beaks and claws and bones of sacrificed eagles,* in a
rock cleft under the sky. They sacrifice an eagle each year, on the brink,   15
by rolling him out and crushing him so as to shed no blood. Then they
drop his remains down the dry cleft in the promontory's farthest grey
tip.

The trail winds on, utterly bumpy and horrible, for thirty miles,
past the second mesa, where Chimopova is, on to the third mesa. And   20
on the Sunday afternoon of the 17th August, black automobile after
automobile lurched and crawled across the grey desert, where low grey
sage scrub was coming to pallid yellow. Black hood followed crawling
after black hood, like a funeral cortège. The motorcars, with all the
tourists, wending their way to the third and farthest mesa, thirty miles   25
across this dismal desert where an odd water windmill spun, and odd
patches of corn blew in the strong desert wind, like dark-green women
with fringed shawls blowing and fluttering, not far from the foot of the
great, grey, up-piled mesa.

The snake-dance* (I am told) is held once a year, on each of the   30
three mesas in succession. This year of grace 1924, it was to be held in
Hotevilla, the last village on the furthest western tip of the third mesa.

On and on bumped the cars. The lonely second mesa lay in the
distance. On and on, to the ragged ghost of the third mesa.

79

The third mesa has two main villages, Oraibi, which is on the near edge, and Hotevilla, on the far. Up scrambles the car, on all its four legs, like a black-beetle straddling past the school house and store down below, up the bare rock and over the changeless boulders, with a surge and a sickening lurch to the sky-brim, where stands the rather foolish church. Just beyond, dry, grey, ruined, and apparently abandoned, Oraibi, its few ragged stone huts. All these cars come all this way, and apparently nobody at home.

You climb still, up the shoulders of rock, a few more miles, across the lofty, wind-swept mesa, and so you come to Hotevilla, where the dance is, and where already hundreds of motor cars are herded in an official camping-ground, among the piñon bushes.

Hotevilla is a tiny little village of grey little houses, raggedly built with undressed stone and mud around a little oblong plaza, and partly in ruin. One of the chief two-storey houses on the small square is a ruin, with big square window-holes.

It is a parched grey country of snakes and eagles, pitched up against the sky. And a few dark-faced, short, thickly-built Indians have their few peach-trees among the sand, their beans and squashes on the naked sand under the sky, their springs of brackish water.

Three thousand people* came to see the little snake-dance this year, over miles of desert and bumps. Three thousand, of all sorts, cultured people from New York, Californians, onward pressing tourists, cowboys, Navajo Indians, even negroes: fathers, mothers, children, all ages, colours, sizes of stoutness, dimensions of curiosity.

What had they come for?* Mostly, to see men hold *live rattlesnakes** in their mouths. *I never did see a rattlesnake, and I'm crazy to see one!* cried a girl with bobbed hair.

There you have it. People trail hundreds of miles, avidly, to see this circus-performance* of men handling live rattlesnakes that may bite them any minute: even do bite them. Some show, that!

There is the other aspect, of the ritual dance. One may look on from the angle of culture, as one looks on while Anna Pavlova dances with the Russian ballet.*

Or there is still another point of view, the religious. Before the snake-dance begins, on the Monday, and the spectators are packed thick on the ground round the square, and in the window holes, and on all the roofs, all sorts of people greedy with curiosity, a little speech is made to them all, asking the audience to be silent and respectful, as this is a sacred religious ceremonial of the Hopi Indians, and not a public entertainment. Therefore, please, no clapping or cheering or applause, but remember you are, as it were, in a Church.

The audience accepts the implied rebuke in good faith, and looks round with a grin at the "Church." But it is a good-humoured, very decent crowd, ready to respect any sort of feelings. And the Indian with his "religion" is a sort of public pet.

From the cultured point of view,* the Hopi snake dance is almost nothing, not much more than a circus turn, or the games that children play in the street. It has none of the impressive beauty of the Corn Dance at Santo Domingo,* for example. The big pueblos of Zuni, Santo Domingo, Taos* have a cultured instinct which is not revealed in the Hopi snake-dance. This last is grotesque rather than beautiful, and rather uncouth in its touch of horror. Hence the thrill, and the crowd.

As a cultured spectacle, it is a circus turn: men actually dancing round with snakes, poisonous snakes, dangling from their mouths.

And as a religious ceremonial: well, you can either be politely tolerant, like the crowd to the Hopis; or, you must have some spark of understanding of the sort of religion implied.

"Oh, the Indians," I heard a woman say, "they believe we are all brothers, the snakes are the Indian's brothers, and the Indians are the snakes' brothers. The Indians would never hurt the snakes: they won't hurt any animal. So the snakes won't bite the Indians. They are all brothers, and none of them hurt anybody."

This sounds very nice, only more Hindoo* than Hopi. The dance itself does not convey much sense of fraternal communion. It is not in the least like St. Francis preaching to the birds.*

The animistic religion,* as we call it, is not the religion of the Spirit. A religion of spirits, yes. But not of Spirit. There is no One Spirit. There is no One God. There is no Creator. There is strictly no God at all: because all is alive.* In our conception of religion, there exists God and His Creation: two things. We are creatures of God, therefore we pray to God as the Father, the Saviour, the Maker.

But strictly, in the religion of aboriginal America, there is no Father, and no Maker. There is the great living source of life: say the Sun of existence: to which you can no more pray than you can pray to Electricity. And emerging from this Sun are the great potencies, the invisible* influences which make shine and warmth and rain. From these great inter-related potencies of rain and heat and thunder emerges the seed of life itself, corn, and creatures like snakes. And beyond these, men, persons. But all emerge separately. There is no oneness,

no sympathetic identifying oneself with the rest. The law of isolation is
heavy on every creature.

Now the Sun, the rain, the shine, the thunder, they are alive. But they
are not persons or people. They are alive. They are vast manifestations
5 of living activity. But they are not personal gods.

Everything lives. Thunder lives, and rain lives, and sunshine lives.
But not in the personal sense. How is man to get himself into relation
with the vast living convulsions of rain and thunder and sun, which are
conscious and alive and potent, but like the vastest of beasts, inscrutable
10 and incomprehensible. How is man to get himself into relation with
these, the vastest of cosmic beasts?

It is the problem of the ages of man. Our religion says, the cosmos
is Matter, to be conquered by the Spirit of Man. The yogi, the fakir,
the saint* try conquest by abnegation and by psychic powers. The real
15 conquest of the cosmos is made by science.

The American Indian sees no division into Spirit and Matter, God
and Not-God.* Everything is alive, though not personally so. Thunder
is neither Thor nor Zeus.* Thunder is the vast living thunder asserting
itself like some incomprehensible monster, or some huge reptile-bird
20 of the pristine cosmos.

How to conquer the dragon-mouthed thunder! How to capture the
feathered rain!

We make reservoirs and irrigation ditches and artesian wells. We
make lightning conductors, and build vast electric plants. We say it is
25 a matter of science, energy, force.

But the Indian says No! It all lives. We must approach it livingly, with
profound respect, but also with desperate courage. Because man must
conquer the cosmic monsters of living thunder and live rain. The rain
that slides down from its source, and ebbs back subtly, with a strange
30 energy generated between its coming and going, an energy which, even
to our science, is of life: this, man has to conquer. The serpent-striped,
feathery Rain.

We make the conquest by dams and reservoirs and windmills. The
Indian, like the old Egyptian, seeks to make the conquest from the
35 mystic will within him, pitted against the Cosmic Dragon.*

We must remember, to the animistic vision there is no perfect God
behind us, who created us from His knowledge, and foreordained all
things. No such God. Behind us lies only the terrific, terrible, crude
Source, the mystic Sun, the well-head of all things. From this mystic
40 Sun emanate the Dragons, Rain, Wind, Thunder, Shine, Light. The

Potencies or Powers. These bring forth earth, then reptiles, birds and
fishes.*
   The Potencies are not gods. They are Dragons. The Sun of Creation
itself is a dragon most terrible, vast and most powerful, yet even so,
less in being than we. The only gods on earth are men.* For gods, like   5
man, do not exist beforehand. They are created and evolved gradually,
with aeons of effort, out of the fire and smelting of life. They are the
highest thing created, smelted between the furnace of the Life-Sun, and
beaten on the anvil of the rain, with hammers of thunder and bellows
of rushing wind. The cosmos is a great furnace, a dragon's den,* where   10
the heroes and demi-gods, men, forge themselves into being. It is a
vast and violent matrix, where souls form like diamonds in earth, under
extreme pressure.
   So that gods are the outcome, not the origin. And the best gods that
have resulted, so far, are men. But gods are frail as flowers, which have   15
also the godliness of things that have won perfection out of the terrific
dragon-clutch of the cosmos. Men are frail as flowers.* Man is as a
flower, rain can kill him or succour him, heat can flick him with a bright
tail, and destroy him: or, on the other hand, it can softly call him into
existence, out of the egg of chaos.* Man is delicate as a flower, godly   20
beyond flowers, and his lordship is a ticklish business.
   He has to conquer, and hold his own, and again conquer all the time.
Conquer the powers of the cosmos. To us, science is our religion of
conquest. Hence, through science, we are the conquerors and resultant
gods of our earth. But to the Indian, the so-called mechanical processes   25
do not exist. All lives. And the conquest is made by means of the living
will.*
   This is the religion of all aboriginal America, Peruvian, Aztec,
Athabascan: perhaps the aboriginal religion of all the world.* In Mexico, men fell into horror of the crude, pristine gods, the dragons. But   30
to the pueblo Indian, the most terrible dragon is still somewhat gentle-
hearted.*
   This brings us back to the Hopi. He has the hardest task, the stub-
bornest destiny. Some inward fate drove him to the top of those parched
mesas, all rock and eagles, sand and snakes and wind and sun and alkali.   35
There he had to conquer. Not merely, as we should put it, the natural
conditions of the place. But the mysterious life-spirit that reigned there.
The eagle and the snake.*
   It is a destiny as well as another. The destiny of the animistic soul of
man, instead of our destiny of Mind and Spirit. We have undertaken   40

the scientific conquest of forces, of natural conditions. It has been comparatively easy, and we are victors. Look at our black motor cars like beetles working up the rock-face at Oraibi. Look at our three thousand tourists, gathered to gaze at the twenty lonely men who dance in the tribe's snake-dance!

The Hopi sought the conquest by means of the mystic, living will that is in man, pitted against the living will of the dragon-cosmos. The Egyptians long ago made a partial conquest by the same means. We have made a partial conquest by other means. Our corn doesn't fail us: we have no seven years of famine,* and apparently need never have. But the other thing fails us, the strange inward Sun of life; the pellucid monster of the rain never shows us his stripes. To us, heaven switches on daylight, or turns on the shower-bath. We little gods are gods of the machine only. It is our highest. Our cosmos is a great engine. And we die of ennui. A subtle dragon stings us in the midst of plenty. *Quos vult perdere Deus, dementat prius.**

On the Sunday evening* is a first little dance in the plaza at Hotevilla, called the Antelope dance.* There is the hot, sandy, oblong little place, with a tuft of green cottonwood boughs stuck like a plume at the south end, and on the floor at the foot of the green, a little wooden lid of a trap-door. They say the snakes are under there.

They say that the twelve officiating men of the snake clan of the tribe have for nine days been hunting snakes in the rocks. They have been performing the mysteries for nine days, in the kiva,* and for two days they have fasted completely. All these days they have tended the snakes, washed them with repeated lustrations, soothed them, and exchanged spirits with them. The spirit of man soothing and seeking and making interchange with* the spirits of the snakes. For the snakes are more rudimentary, nearer to the great convulsive powers. Nearer to the nameless Sun, more knowing in the slanting tracks of the rain, the pattering of the invisible feet of the rain-monster from the sky. The snakes are man's next emissaries to the rain-god. The snakes lie nearer to the source of potency, the dark, lurking, intense sun at the centre of the earth.* For to the cultured animist, and the pueblo Indian is such, the earth's dark centre holds its dark sun, our source of isolated being, round which our world coils its folds like a great snake. The snake is nearer the dark sun, and cunning of it.

They say—people say—that rattle-snakes are not travellers. They haunt the same spots on earth, and die there. It is said also that the

snake-priests (so-called) of the Hopi, probably capture the same snakes
year after year.

Be that as it may. At sundown* before the real dance, there is the
little dance called the Antelope Dance. We stand and wait on a house
roof. Behind is tethered an eagle; rather dishevelled he sits on the   5
coping, and looks at us in unutterable resentment. See him, and see how
much "brotherhood" the Indian feels with animals!—at best, the silent
tolerance that acknowledges dangerous difference.—We wait without
event. There are no drums, no announcements. Suddenly into the
plaza, with rude, intense movements, hurries a little file of men. They   10
are smeared all with grey and black, and are naked save for little kilts
embroidered like the sacred dance-kilts in other pueblos, red and green
and black on a white fibre-cloth.* The fox-skins hang behind. The feet
of the dancers are pure ash-grey. Their hair is long. The first is a heavy
old man with heavy, long, wild grey hair and heavy fringe. He plods   15
intensely forward, in the silence, followed in a sort of circle by the other
grey-smeared, long-haired, naked, concentrated men. The oldest men
are first: the last is a short haired boy of fourteen or fifteen. There are
only eight men—the so-called antelope priests. They pace round in a
circle, rudely, absorbedly, till the first heavy, intense old man with his   20
massive grey hair flowing, comes to the lid on the ground, near the tuft
of kiva-boughs. He rapidly shakes from the hollow of his right hand a
little white meal on the lid, stamps heavily, with naked right foot, on the
meal, so the wood resounds, and paces heavily forward. Each man, to
the boy, shakes meal, stamps, paces absorbedly on in the circle, comes   25
to the lid again, shakes meal, stamps, paces absorbedly on, comes a third
time to the lid, or trap-door, and this time spits on the lid, stamps and
goes on. And this time the eight men file away behind the lid, between
it and the tuft of green boughs. And there they stand in a line, their
backs to the kiva-tuft of green, silent, absorbed, bowing a little to the   30
ground.

Suddenly paces with rude haste another file of men. They are naked,
and smeared with red "medicine,"* with big black lozenges of smeared
paint on their backs. Their wild heavy hair hangs loose, the old, heavy,
grey-haired men go first, then the middle aged, then the young men,   35
then last, two short-haired, slim boys, school-boys. The hair of the
young men, growing after school,* is bobbed round.

The grown men are all heavily built, rather short, with heavy but
shapely flesh, and rather straight sides. They have not the archaic slim
waists of the Taos Indians. They have an archaic squareness, and a   40

sensuous heaviness. Their very hair is black, massive, heavy. These are the so-called snake priests, men of the snake clan. And tonight, they are eleven in number.

They pace rapidly round, with that heavy wild silence of concentra-
5   tion characteristic of them, and cast meal and stamp upon the lid, cast meal and stamp in the second round, come round and spit and stamp in the third.—For to the savage, the animist, to spit may be a kind of blessing, a communion, a sort of embrace.

The eleven snake-priests form silently in a row, facing the eight
10   grey-smeared antelope-priests across the little lid, and bowing forward a little, to earth. Then the antelope priests, bending forward, begin a low, sombre chant, or call, that sounds wordless, only a deep, low-toned, secret Ay-a! Ay-a! Ay-a! And they bend from right to left, giving two shakes to the little, flat white rattle in their left hand, at each shake,
15   and stamping the right foot in heavy rhythm. In their right hand, that held the meal, is grasped a little skin bag, perhaps also containing meal.

They lean from right to left, two seed-like shakes of the rattle each time, and the heavy, rhythmic stamp of the foot, and the low, sombre, secretive chant-call each time. It is a strange low sound, such as we never
20   hear, and it reveals how deep, how deep the men are in the mystery they are practising, how sunk deep below our world, to the world of snakes, and dark ways in the earth, where are the roots of corn, and where the little rivers of unchanneled, uncreated life-passion run like dark, trickling lightning, to the roots of the corn and to the feet and
25   loins of men, from the earth's innermost dark sun.* They are calling in the deep, almost silent snake-language, to the snakes and the rays of dark emission from the earth's inward "Sun."

At this moment, a silence falls on the whole crowd of listeners. It is that famous darkness and silence of Egypt,* the touch of the other
30   mystery. The deep concentration of the "priests" conquers, for a few seconds, our white-faced flippancy, and we hear only the deep Háh-ha! Háh-ha! speaking to snakes and the earth's inner core.

This lasts for a minute or two. Then the antelope priests stand bowed and still, and the snake priests take up the swaying and the deep chant,
35   that sometimes is so low, it is like a mutter underground, inaudible. The rhythm is crude, the swaying unison is all uneven. Culturally, there is nothing. If it were not for that mystic, dark-sacred concentration.

Several times, in turn, the two rows of daubed, long-haired, in-sunk men facing one another take up the swaying and the chant. Then that too
40   is finished. There is a break in the formation. A young snake-priest takes

up something that may be a corn-cob—perhaps an antelope-priest
hands it to him,—and comes forward, with an old, heavy, but still
shapely snake priest behind him dusting his shoulders with the feathers,
eagle-feathers presumably, which are the Indian's hollow prayer-sticks.
With the heavy, stamping hop they move round in the previous circle,　5
the young priest holding the cob curiously, and the old priest prancing
strangely at the young priest's back, in a sort of incantation, and brushing the heavy young shoulders delicately with the prayer-feathers. It is
the God-vibration that enters us from behind, and is transmitted to the
hands, from the hands to the corn-cob. Several young priests emerge,　10
with the bowed head and the cob in their hands and the heavy older
priest hanging over them behind. They tread round the rough curve
and come back to the kiva, take perhaps another cob, and tread round
again.

That is all. In ten or fifteen minutes it is over. The two files file　15
rapidly and silently away. A brief, primitive performance.

The crowd disperses. They were not many people. There were no
venomous snakes on exhibition, so the mass had nothing to come for.
And therefore, the curious immersed intensity of the priests was able
to conquer the white crowd.　20

By afternoon on the next day the three thousand people had massed
in the little plaza, secured themselves places on the roofs and in the
window-spaces, everywhere, till the small pueblo seemed built of people
instead of stones. All sorts of people, hundreds and hundreds of white
women, all in breeches like half-men, hundreds and hundreds of men　25
who had been driving motor-cars, then many Navajos, the women in
their full long skirts and tight velvet bodices, the men rather lanky,
long-waisted, real nomads.* In the hot sun and the wind which blows
the sand every day, every day in volumes round the corners, the three
thousand tourists sat for hours and hours, waiting for the show. The　30
Indian policemen cleared the central oblong, in front of the kiva. The
front rows of onlookers sat thick on the ground. And at last, rather
early, because of the masses awaiting them, suddenly, silently, in the
same rude haste, the antelope priests filed absorbedly in, and made
the rounds over the lid, as before. Today, the eight antelope priests　35
were very grey. Their feet were ashed pure grey, like suede soft boots:
and their lower jaw was pure suède grey, while the rest of the face was
blackish. With that pale-grey jaw, they looked like corpse-faces with the
swathing-bands.* And all their bodies ash-grey smeared, with smears
of black, and a black cloth today at the loins.　40

They made their rounds, and took their silent position behind the lid, with backs to the green kiva tuft: an unearthly grey row of men with little skin bags in their hands. They were the lords of shadow, the intermediate twilight, the place of after-life and before-life,* where house the winds of change. Lords of the mysterious, fleeting power of change.

Suddenly, with abrupt silence, in paced the snake-priests, headed by the same heavy man with solid grey hair like iron. Today they were twelve men, from the old one, down to the slight, short-haired, erect boy of fourteen. Twelve men, two for each of the six worlds, or quarters:* east, north, south, west, above and below. And today they were in a queer ecstasy. Their bodies were smeared dark red, with black lozenges on the back, like snake marks.* Their faces were black, showing the whites of the eyes. And they wore small black loin-aprons. They were the hot, living men of the darkness, lords of the earth's inner vital rays, the black sun of the earth's vital core, from which dart the speckled snakes, like beams.

Round they went, in rapid, uneven, silent absorption, the three rounds. Then in a row they faced the eight ash-grey men, across the lid. All kept their heads bowed towards earth, except the young boys.

Then, in the intense, secret, muttering chant, the grey men began their leaning from right to left, shaking the hand, one-two, one-two, one-two, and bowing the body each time from right to left, left to right, above the lid in the ground, under which were the snakes. And their low, deep, mysterious voices spoke to the spirits under the earth, not to men above the earth.

But the great crowd was on tenterhooks for the snakes, and could hardly wait for the mummery* to cease. There was an atmosphere of inattention and impatience. But the chant and the swaying passed from the grey men to the black-faced men, and back again, several times.

This was finished. The formation of the two lines broke up. There was a slight crowding to the centre, round the lid. The old antelope priest (so-called) was stooping. And before the crowd could realize anything else, a young snake-priest* emerged, bowing reverently, with the neck of a pale, delicate rattle-snake held between his teeth, the little, naïve, bird-like head of the rattle-snake quite still, near the black cheek, and the long, pale, yellowish, spangled body of the snake dangling like some thick, beautiful cord. On paced the black-faced young priest, with the wondering snake dangling from his mouth, pacing in the original circle, while behind him, leaping almost on his shoulders, was the oldest, heavy priest, dusting the young man's shoulders with the feather-prayer-sticks, in an intense, earnest anxiety of concentration such as I have only seen in the old Indian men, during a religious dance.

Came another young black-faced man out of the confusion, with another snake dangling and writhing a little from his mouth, and an elder priest dusting him from behind with the feathers: and then another: and another: till it was a confusion, probably, of six, and then four young priests with snakes dangling from their mouths, going round, apparently, three times in the circle. At the end of the third round, the young priest stooped, and delicately laid his snake on the earth, waving him away, away, as it were, into the world. He must not wriggle back to the kiva bush.

And after wondering a moment, the pale, delicate snake steered away with a rattle-snake's beautiful movement, rippling and looping, with the small, sensitive head lifted like antennae, across the sand to the massed audience squatting solid on the ground around. Like soft, watery lightning went the wondering snake at the crowd. As he came nearer, the people began to shrink aside, half mesmerised. But they betrayed no exaggerated fear. And as the little snake drew very near, up rushed one of the two black-faced young priests who held the snake-stick, poised a moment over the snake in the prayer concentration of reverence which is at the same time conquest, and snatched the pale long creature delicately from the ground, waving him in a swoop over the heads of the seated crowd, then delicately smoothing down the length of the snake with his left hand, stroking and smoothing and soothing the long, pale, bird like thing; and returning with it to the kiva, handed it to one of the grey-jawed antelope priests.

Meanwhile, all the time, the other young priests were emerging with a snake dangling from their mouths. The boy had finished his rounds. He launched his rattle-snake on the ground, like a ship, and like a ship, away it steered. In a moment, after it went one of those two young black-faced priests who carried the snake-sticks and were the snake-catchers. As it neared the crowd, very close, he caught it up and waved it in the air* dramatically, his eyes glaring strangely out of his black face. And in the interim, that youngest boy had been given a long, very handsome bull-snake, by the priest at the hole under the kiva boughs. The bull-snake is not poisonous. It is a constrictor. This one was six feet long, with a sumptuous pattern. It waved its pale belly, and pulled its neck out of the boy's mouth. With two hands he put it back. It pulled itself once more free. Again he got it back, and managed to hold it. And then, as he went round in his looping circle, it coiled its handsome folds twice round his knee. He stooped, quietly, and as quietly as if he were untying his garter, he unloosed the folds. And all the time, behind him, an old priest was intently brushing the boy's thin straight shoulders with the feathers. And all the time, the snakes seemed strangely gentle, naïve, wondering, and almost willing, almost in harmony with the men. Which of course was the sacred aim. While the boy's expression remained quite still and simple, as it were candid, in a candour where he and the snake should be in unison. The only dancers who showed signs of being wrought-up were the two young snake-catchers, and one of these, particularly, seemed in a state of actor-like uplift, rather ostentatious. But the old priests had that immersed, religious intentness which is like a spell, something from another world.

The young boy launched his bull-snake. It wanted to go back to the kiva. The snake-catcher drove it gently forward. Away it went, towards the crowd, and at the last minute, was caught up into the air. Then this snake was handed to an old man sitting on the ground in the audience, in the front row. He was an old Hopi of the snake clan.

Snake after snake had been carried round in the circles, dangling by the neck from the mouth of one young priest or another, and writhing and swaying slowly, with the small, delicate snake-head held as if wondering and listening. There had been some very large rattle-snakes, unusually large, two or three handsome bull-snakes, and some racers, whip-snakes. All had been launched, after their circuits in the mouth, all had been caught up by the young priests with the snake-sticks, one or two had been handed to old snake-clan men in the audience, who sat holding them in their arms as men hold a kitten. The most of the snakes, however, had been handed to the grey antelope men who stood in the row, with their backs to the kiva bush. Till some of these ash-smeared men held armfuls of snakes, hanging over their arms like wet washing. Some of the snakes twisted and knotted round one another, showing pale bellies.

Yet most of them hung very still and docile. Docile, almost sympathetic, so that one was struck only by their clean, slim length of snake nudity, their beauty like soft, quiescent lightning. They were so clean, because they had been washed and anointed and lustrated by the priests, in the days they had been in the kiva.

At last all the snakes had been mouth-carried in the circuits, and had made their little out-running excursion to the crowd, and had been handed back to the priests in the rear. And now the Indian policemen, Hopi and Navajo,* began to clear away the crowd that sat on the ground, five or six rows deep, around the small plaza. The snakes were all going   5
to be set free on the ground. We must clear away.

We recoiled to the further end of the plaza. There, two Hopi women were scattering white corn-meal on the sandy ground. And thither came the two snake-catchers, almost at once, with their arms full of snakes. And before we who stood near had realized it, the snakes were   10
all writhing and squirming on the ground, in the white dust of meal, a couple of yards from our feet. Then immediately, before they could writhe clear of each other and steer away, they were gently, swiftly snatched up again, and with their arms full of snakes, the two young priests went running out of the plaza.   15

We followed slowly, wondering, towards the western, or north-western edge of the mesa. There the mesa dropped steeply, and a broad trail wound down to the vast hollow of desert brimmed up with strong evening light, up out of which jutted a perspective of sharp rock and further mesas and distant sharp mountains: the great, hollow,   20
rock-wilderness space of that part of Arizona, submerged in light.

Away down on the trail, small, dark, naked, rapid figures with arms held close, were the two young men, running swiftly down to the hollow level, and diminishing, diminishing, running across the hollow towards more stark rocks of the other side. Two small, rapid, intent, dwindling   25
little human figures. The tiny dark sparks of men. Such specks of gods.

They disappeared, no bigger than stones, behind rocks in shadow. They had gone, it was said, to lay down the snakes before a rock called the snake-shrine, and let them all go free. Free, to carry the messages and thanks to the dragon-gods who can give and withhold.   30
To carry the human spirit, the human breath, the human prayer, the human gratitude, the human command which had been breathed upon them in the mouths of the priests, transferred into them from those feather-prayer-sticks which the old wise men swept upon the shoulders of the young, snake-bearing men, to carry this back, into the vaster,   35
dimmer, inchoate regions where the monsters of rain and wind alter-nated in beneficence and wrath. Carry the human prayer and will-power into the holes of the winds, down into the octopus heart of the rain-source.* Carry the corn-meal which the women had scattered, back to that terrific, dread and causeful dark sun which is at the earth's core,   40

that which sends us corn out of the earth's nearness, sends us food or death, according to our strength of vital purpose, our power of sensitive will, our infallible courage.

It is a battle, a wrestling all the time. The Sun, the nameless Sun, source of all things, which we call Sun because the other name is too fearful, this, this vast dark protoplasmic sun from which issues all that feeds our life, this original One is all the time willing and unwilling. Systole, diastole,* it pulses its willingness and its unwillingness, that we should live and move on, from being to being, manhood to further manhood. Man, small, vulnerable man, the farthest adventurer from the dark heart of the first of suns, into the cosmos of creation. Man, the last god won into existence. And all the time, he is sustained and threatened, menaced and sustained from the Source, the innermost sun-dragon. And all the time, he must submit and he must conquer. Submit to the strange beneficence from the Source, whose ways are past finding out. And conquer the strange malevolence of the Source, which is past comprehension also.

For the great dragons from which we draw our vitality are all the time willing and unwilling that we should have being. Hence only the heroes snatch manhood, little by little, from the strange den of the Cosmos.

Man, little Man, with his consciousness and his will must both submit to the great origin-powers of his life, and conquer them. Conquered by man who has overcome his fears, the snakes must go back into the earth with his messages of tenderness, of request, and of power. They go back as rays of love to the dark heart of the first of suns. But they go back also as arrows shot clean by man's sapience and courage, into the resistant, malevolent heart of the earth's oldest, stubborn core. In the core of the first of suns, whence man draws his vitality, lies poison as bitter as the rattle-snake's. This poison man must overcome, he must be master of its issue. Because, from the first of suns come travelling the rays that make men strong and glad and gods who can range between the known and the unknown. Rays that quiver out of the earth as serpents do, naked with vitality. But each ray charged with poison for the unwary, the irreverent, and the cowardly. Awareness, wariness, is the first virtue in primitive man's morality. And his awareness must travel back and forth, back and forth, from the darkest origins out to the brightest edifices of creation.

And amid all its crudity, and the sensationalism which comes chiefly out of the crowd's desire for thrills, one cannot help pausing in reverence before the delicate, anointed bravery of the snake-priests (so-called) with the snakes.

They say the Hopis have a marvellous secret cure for snake-bites.* They say the bitten men are given an emetic drink, after the dance, by the old women, and that they must lie on the edge of the cliff and vomit, vomit, vomit. I saw none of this. The two snake-men who ran down into the shadow came soon running up again, running all the while, and steering off at a tangent, ran up the mesa once more, but beyond a deep, impassable cleft. And there, when they had come up to our level, we saw them across the cleft distance washing brown and naked, in a pool: washing off the paint, the medicine, the ecstasy, to come back into daily life and eat food. Because for two days they had eaten nothing, it was said. And for nine days they had been immersed in the mystery of the snakes, and fasting in some measure.

Men who have lived many years among the Indians say they do not believe the Hopi have any secret cure. Sometimes priests do die of bites, it is said. But a rattle snake secretes his poison slowly. Each time he strikes he loses his venom, until, if he strike several times, he has very little wherewithal to poison a man. Not enough, not half enough to kill. His glands must be very full charged with poison, as they are when he emerges from winter-sleep, before he can kill a man outright. And even then, he must strike near some artery.

Therefore, during the nine days in the kiva, when the snakes are bathed and lustrated, perhaps they strike their poison away into some inanimate object. And surely they are soothed and calmed with such things as the priests, after centuries of experience, know how to administer to them.

We dam the Nile and take the railway across America.* The Hopi smooths the rattle-snake and carries him in his mouth, to send him back into the dark places of the earth, an emissary to the inner powers.

To each sort of man his own achievement, his own victory, his own conquest. To the Hopi, the origins are dark and dual, cruelty is coiled in the very beginnings of all things, and circle after circle creation emerges towards a flickering, revealed godhead. With man as the godhead so far achieved, waveringly and forever incomplete, in this world.

To us and to the orientals, the God-head was perfect to start with,* and man makes but a mechanical excursion into a created and ordained universe, an excursion of mechanical achievement, and of yearning for the return to the perfect Godhead of the beginning.

To us, God was in the beginning, Paradise and the Golden Age have been long lost,* and all we can do is to win back.

To the Hopi, God is not yet, and the Golden Age lies far ahead. Out of the dragon's den of the cosmos, we have wrested only the beginnings of our being, the rudiments of our godhead.

Between the two visions lies the gulf of mutual negation. But ours was the quickest way, so we are conquerors for the moment.

The American aborigines are radically, innately religious. The fabric of their life is religious. But their religion is animistic, their sources are dark and impersonal, their conflict with their "gods" is slow, and unceasing.

This is true of the settled pueblo Indians and the wandering Navajo, the ancient Maya and the surviving Aztec.* They are all involved at every moment, in their old, struggling religion.

Until they break in a kind of hopelessness under our cheerful, triumphant success. Which is what is rapidly happening. The young Indians who have been to school for many years are losing their religion, becoming discontented, bored, and rootless. An Indian with his own religion inside him *cannot* be bored. The flow of the mystery is too intense all the time, too intense, even, for him to adjust himself to circumstances which really are mechanical. Hence his failure. So he, in his great religious struggle for the Godhead of man, falls back beaten. The Personal God who ordained a mechanical cosmos gave the victory to his sons, a mechanical triumph.

Soon after the dance is over, the Navajo begin to ride down the western trail, into the light. Their women, with velvet bodices and full, full skirts, silver and turquoise tinkling thick on their breasts, sit back on their horses and ride down the steep slope, looking wonderingly around from their pleasant, broad, nomadic, Mongolian faces.* And the men, long, loose, thin, long-waisted, with tall hats on their brows and low-sunk silver belts on their hips, come down to water their horses at the spring. We say they look wild. But they have the intent remoteness of their religion, their animistic vision, in their eyes, they can't see as we see. And they cannot accept us. They stare at us as the coyotes stare at us: the gulf of mutual negation between us.

So, in groups, in pairs, singly, they ride silently down into the lower strata of light, the aboriginal Americans riding into their shut-in reservations. While the white Americans hurry back to their motor cars, and soon the air buzzes with starting engines, like the biggest of rattle-snakes buzzing.

A LITTLE MOONSHINE WITH LEMON

A Little Moonshine with Lemon*

"Ye Gods, he doth bestride the narrow world
Like a Colossus—!"*

There is bright moon, so that even the vines make a shadow and the
Mediterranean has a broad white shimmer between its dimness. By the   5
shore, the lights of the old houses twinkle quietly, and out of the wall of
the headland emerges the glare of a locomotive's lamps. It is a feast-day,
St. Catherine's day,* and the men are all sitting round the little tables,
down below, drinking wine or Vermouth.

And what about the ranch, the little ranch in New Mexico? The time   10
is different there: but I too have drunk my glass to St. Catherine, so I
can't be bothered to reckon. I shall consider that there too, the moon is
in the south-east standing, as it were, over Santa Fe, beyond the bend
of those mountains of Picoris.*

Sono io! say the Italians. I am I! Which sounds simpler than it is.   15

Because which I am I, after all, now that I have drunk a glass also to
St. Catherine, and the moon shines over the sea, and my thoughts, just
because they are fleetingly occupied by the moon on the Mediterranean,
and ringing with the last farewell: *Dunque, Signore! di nuovo*—!*—must
needs follow the moon-track south-west, to the great South-west, where   20
the ranch is.

They say: *in vino veritas.** Bah! they say so much! But in the wine
of St. Catherine, my little ranch, and the three horses down among
the timber. Or if it has snowed, the horses are gone away, and it is
snow, and the moon shines on the alfalfa slope, between the pines, and   25
the cabins are blind. There is nobody there. Everything shut up. Only
the big pine-tree in front of the house, standing still and unconcerned,
alive.

Perhaps when I have a *Weh* at all, my Heimweh* is for the tree in
front of the house, the overshadowing tree whose green top one never   30
looks at. But on the trunk one hangs the various odds and ends of iron
things.* It is so near. One goes out of the door, and the tree-trunk is
there, like a guardian angel.

The tree-trunk, and the long work table, and the fence. Then beyond, since it is night, and the moon shines, for me at least, away beyond is a light, at Taos, or at Ranchos de Taos.* Here, the castle of Noli* is on the western sky line. But there, no doubt it has snowed, since even
5   here the wind is cold. There it has snowed, and the nearly-full moon blazes wolf-like, as here he never blazes, risen like a were-wolf over the mountains. So there is a faint hoar shagginess of pine-trees, away at the foot of the alfalfa field, and a grey gleam of snow in the night, on the level desert, and a ruddy point of human light, in Ranchos de Taos.
10 And beyond, you see them even if you don't see them, the circling mountains since there is a moon.

So, one hurries indoors, and throws more logs on the fire.

One doesn't either. One hears Giovanni* calling from below, to say Goodnight! He is going down to the village for a spell.—*Vado giù,*
15 *Signor Lorenzo! Buona notte!**

And the Mediterranean whispers in the distance, a sound like in a shell. And save that somebody is whistling the night is very bright and still. The Mediterranean, so eternally young, the very symbol of youth. And Italy, so reputedly old, yet forever so childlike and naive. Never,
20 never for a moment able to comprehend the wonderful, hoary age of America, the continent of the afterwards.*

I wonder if I am here, or if I am just going to bed at the ranch. Perhaps looking in Montgomery Ward's catalogue* for something for Christmas, and drinking moonshine and hot water, since it is cold. Go
25 out and look if the chickens are shut up warm: if the horses are in sight: if Susan, the black cow,* has gone to her nest among the trees, for the night. Cows don't eat much at night. But Susan will wander in the moon. It makes her uneasy. And the horses stamp round the cabins.

In a cold like this, the stars snap like distant coyotes, beyond the
30 moon. And you'll see the shadow of actual coyotes, going across the alfalfa field.* And the pine-trees make little noises, sudden and stealthy, as if they were walking about. And the place heaves with ghosts. That place, the ranch, heaves with ghosts. But when one has got used to one's own home-ghosts, be they never so many, and so potent, they are like
35 one's own family, but nearer than the blood. It is the ghosts one misses most, the ghosts there, of the Rocky Mountains* that never go beyond the timber and that linger, like the animals, round the water-spring. I know them, they know me: we go well together. But they reproach me for going away. They are resentful too.

Perhaps the snow is in tufts on the greasewood bushes. Perhaps the blue jays fall in a blue, metallic cloud out of the pine tree* in front of the house, at dawn, in the terrific cold, when the dangerous light comes watchful over the mountains, and touches the desert far-off, far-off, beyond the Rio Grande.*   5

And I, I give it up.—There is a choice of vermouth, Marsala, red wine or white.* At the ranch, tonight, because it is cold, I should have moonshine, not very good moonshine, but still, warming: with hot water and lemon, and sugar, and a bit of cinnamon from one of those little red Schilling's tins.* And I should light my little stove in the bed-   10
room, and let it roar a bit, sucking the wind. Then dart to bed, with all the ghosts of the ranch cosily round me, and sleep till the very coldness of my emerged nose wakes me. Waking, I shall look at once through the glass panels of the bedroom door, and see the trunk of the great pine tree, like a person on guard, and a low star just coming over the   15
mountain, very brilliant, like someone swinging an electric lantern.

Si verra la primavera
Fiorann' le mandorline—*

Ah well, let it be vermouth, since there's no moonshine with lemon and cinnamon. Supposing I called Giovanni, and told him I wanted un   20
poco di chiar' di luna, con cannella e limone – – –*

OTHER ESSAYS 1922–1928

CERTAIN AMERICANS AND
AN ENGLISHMAN

Certain Americans and an Englishman*

I* arrive in New Mexico at a moment of crisis. I suppose every man always does, here. The crisis is a thing called the Bursum Bill, and it affects the Pueblo Indians.* I wouldn't know a thing about it, if I needn't. But it's Bursum Bursum Bursum!! the Bill! the Bill! the Bill! Twitchell, Twitchell, Twitchell!! O Mr. Secretary Fall, Fall, Fall! O Mr. Secretary Fall!* you bad man, you good man, you Fall, you Rise, you Fall!!! The Joy Survey,* Oh Joy, No Joy, Once Joy, now Woe! Woe! Whoa!* Whoa Bursum! Whoa Bill! Whoa-a-a!—like a Lindsay Boom-Boom bellowing* it goes on in my unwonted ears, till I have to take heed. And then I solemnly sit down in a chair and read the Bill, the Bill, the Printed Bursum Bill, Section one-two-three-four-five-six-seven, whereas and wherefore and heretobefore, right to the damned and distant end. Then I start the Insomuch-as of Mr. Francis Wilson's Brief* concerning the Bill. Then I read Mr. C's passionate article against, and Mrs. H's hatchet-stroke summary against, and Mr. M's sharp-knife jugglery *for* the Bill.* After which I feel I'm getting mixed up, and Bear Ye One Another's Bursum.* Then Lamb-like, ram-like, I feel I'll do a bit of butting too, on a stage where every known animal butts.

But first I toddle to a corner and, like a dog when music is going on in the room, put my paws exasperatedly over my ears, and my nose to the ground, and groan softly. So doing I try to hypnotise myself back into my old natural world, outside the circus-tent, where horses don't buck and prance so much, and where not every lady is leaping through the hoop and crashing through the paper confines of the universe at every hand's turn.*

Try to extricate my lamb-like soul into its fleecy isolation, and then adjust myself. Adjust myself to that much-talked-of actor in the Wild West show,* the Red Indian.

Don't imagine, indulgent reader, that I'm talking *at* you or down to you; or trying to put something over on you. No, no, imagine me lamb-like and bewildered muttering softly to myself, between soft groans,

trying to make head-or-tail of myself in my present situation. And then
you'll get the spirit of these effusions.

The Indian is not an American citizen.* He is apparently in the
position of a defenceless nation protected by a benevolent Congress.

5 He is an American subject, but a member of a dominated, defenceless
nation which Congress undertakes to protect and cherish. The Indian
Bureau* is supposed to do the cherishing.

Around about the pueblos live Mexican and American settlers who
are American citizens, who do pay taxes and who do vote. They have

10 cattle ranches, sheep ranches, little farms, and so on, and are most of
them in debt.

These are the first two items: the dark spots of the protected pueblos; the hungry, unscrupulous frontier population squatting, rather
scattered and rather impoverished, around.

15 There is plenty of land: sage brush desert. All depends on water. The
pueblos, of course, are pitched upon the waters.* The beautiful Taos
Valley culminates in Taos Pueblo.* The ranches and farms straggle
round and try to encroach on this watered place. Six miles away is a
deserted Mexican village, waterless.

20 Already you have a situation.

Now, when the United States took over New Mexico in 1848,*
Congress decided to abide by all the conditions established by Spain
and old Mexico in this State. Congress also, apparently, decreed that
to each pueblo belonged the four square leagues of land surrounding

25 the pueblo; whether in accordance with ancient Spanish grant or not,
isn't for me to say. Anyhow, there it is. Taos Pueblo owning four
square leagues, which is thirty-six square miles of land immediately
surrounding the pueblo; measuring a league in each direction from the
centre of the pueblo. There are 800 Indians in the pueblo. But much of

30 the land is dry desert or stony hill. True, some of the desert might be
irrigated—if the water were there to irrigate it with, or if the Indians
would make the effort.

At the same time Congress will abide by all the old Spanish or
Mexican grants, titles, and so forth, which were in existence at the time

35 of the taking over of this territory.

Immediately a problem. Because the Indian four square leagues has
been much of it for centuries occupied by Spanish or Mexican or white
settlers. There they sit. Taos Plaza, that is the white village of Taos,
stands itself entirely within the four square leagues decreed to Taos

40 Pueblo. There are Spanish grants from governors; there are Mexican

grants; and there are forged grants, forged deeds. Well, then, a terrible problem. For Taos Plaza has probably been standing for at least 200 years.* Almost as old as New York.

Terrible problem! Why hasn't the place run with blood? Because the Indian never measured any leagues, but tilled his land around the pueblo itself. Much of the space intervening between the pueblo and the plaza is just sage desert. And this definite uncontested Indian land—uncontested for the moment, that is, so long as there is no Bursum bill—lies between plaza and pueblo as a sort of frontier. Nobody cut anybody's throat, because the occasion didn't arrive. Many squatters squat within the bounds of these four square leagues, but they are beyond a no-man's land still of sage desert, away from the heart where the pueblo rises, among the cotton-wood trees, and tills its land around the waters.

Thus the situation.

Then the highbrows come and say: "Poor Indian, dear Indian!* why, all America ought to belong to him! Why look you now at the injustice that has been done to him! Not only has all America been snatched from him, but even his four square leagues are invaded by vile white men, greedy white men, hateful white men!"

So sing the highbrow palefaces.* Till the Indian gradually begins to get his tail up.

Luckily for us he is few; unluckily for himself. Because if the tiny prairie dog yaps too hard at the western American airedale,* alas for prairie dogs!

Now things begin to stir. It is time this business of grants and titles was settled. Old Spanish grants to Spaniards versus these four square leagues. Taos Plaza versus Taos Pueblo. Spanish grants, Mexican titles, forged deeds suddenly fluttering into life in a breath of hot wind of contest. Four square leagues flying away on the wings of old Spanish grants, which Congress is bound to validify, and the Indian perching on his big toe end, trying to poise on four square inches. Or, vice versa, an appeal to Congress, and Congress is sovereign majesty, and the Indians can come and take their brooms and sweep old José or old Fernandez or old Maria,* with all Taos village, pell-mell over the border of the four square leagues, into limbo.

Not that the Indian is likely to take Congress by the ear and do it. The Indian is afflicted with the lovable malady of laissez-faire.* But then you never know what some of those white highbrows* will be up to, these palefaces who love the dear Indian, the poor Indian, and who

would like to see all America restored to him, let alone four square
leagues, which is thirty-six square miles.

Now I believe the lands of some of the pueblos, sadly, very sadly
enough, have been eaten right up by encroachments. But let me not be
5   very sad. Taos isn't sad. Let me stay by Taos.

It will be obvious to everybody that a move had to be made about these
leagues and these grants. And New Mexico made the move. Senator
Bursum is the black knight* who has hopped on to the four leagues.
His famous Bursum bill has passed the Senate and comes before the
10 House, presumably this month (December).*

And here is the Bursum bill: an absolute checkmate to Pueblo, highbrow and all. It is the frontiersman biting off as much as he can chew.

"A bill to ascertain and settle land claims of persons not Indian,
within Pueblo Indian land, land grants, and reservations in the State of
15 New Mexico."

A court called the District Court of the United States for the District
of New Mexico shall assume jurisdiction over all crimes, offenses, &c.,
committed within the areas of pueblo grants, by any person, Indian or
non-Indian, so long as the Indians are occupying that land or claim that
20 land.

(So this nice New Mexico court, which knows just what it wants for
itself, takes a first modest step.)

2. This court shall have exclusive original jurisdiction in all suits of a
civil nature, in all suits involving any right or title to any land within the
25 said pueblo reservations, also in all suits involving property of Indians,
also in all suits involving any question of internal government of any of
the said pueblos. (Which means that the old, autonomous tribal body
of the pueblo* is placed at the mercy of this distant district court.)

4. All persons or corporations who have had possession of lands
30 within the pueblo grants since prior to the Guadalupe Hidalgo Treaty
of 1848* shall be entitled to a decree in their favour for all lands
so possessed. In proof, secondary evidence shall be admissible and
competent.

5. All persons who have held possession of lands within the pueblo
35 grants for more than ten years previous to July, 1910, without colour
of title * * * shall be entitled to a decree in their favour for all lands so
possessed. But in return to the Indians, the Secretary of the Interior*
shall have some other bit of adjacent land allotted to the Pueblo if
any such land be available. (None of the available land is any good.)

Otherwise the Pueblo shall be compensated in cash, as the Secretary thinks fit.

6. Pueblos shall have the right to the use of just as much water as they use at this minute (even though this amount be sadly insufficient to irrigate the present fields). But if any dam or reservoir be made, damming up the pueblo supplies, then all the surplus water and the control thereof shall be adjudicated according to the laws of the State of New Mexico.

7. All proceedings under this act shall be without cost to parties.

8. All suits under this act must be brought within five years.

9. The "Joy Surveys" (which were made to give evidence as to how Indian lands had been wrongly invaded) shall be accepted as prima facie evidence.

12. That any person or persons making any claim whatsoever to any lands within pueblo grants, whether they squatted on it only yesterday, may, with approval of the court, purchase the land at the court's valuation, and the money paid shall be held by the Secretary of the Interior on behalf of the Indians. (Which means that if I want a chunk of pueblo land I put a fence around it and pay the Secretary of the Interior a sum which the court will, if it likes me, kindly make as small as possible, and the Indian sits staring at the Charybdis of me and the Scylla* of Mr. Secretary Fall and holding out his hand for a bit of charity bread.)

It is obvious this means the scattering of the Pueblos. The squatters and Mexicans interested—and where land grabbing is the game, every neighbour is interested—openly declare that the pueblos will be finished in ten years. That is, five years for the claims to be all made and five for their final enforcement. And then the Indians will have merged. They will be scattered day labourers through the States and the nucleus will be broken.

The great desire to turn them into white men will be fulfilled as far as it can be fulfilled. They will all be wage earners, and that's enough. For the rest, lost, mutilated intelligences.

As it is, the Pueblos are slowly disbanding; there are the Indian schools, a doom in themselves.* The young men all speak American. They go as hired labourers. And man is like a dog—he believes in the hand that feeds him. He belongs where he is fed.

The end of the Pueblos.* But at least let them die a natural death. To me the Bursum bill is amusing in its bare-facedness—a cool joke. It startles any English mind a little to realize that it may become law.

Let the Pueblos die a natural death. The Bursum bill plays the Wild West scalping trick* a little too brazenly. Surely the great Federal Government is capable of instituting an efficient Indian Commission* to inquire fairly and settle fairly. Or a small Indian office that knows
5 what it's about. For Heaven's sake keep these Indians out of the clutches of politics.

Because, finally, in some curious way, the pueblos still lie here at the core of American life. In some curious way, it is the Indians still who are American. This great welter of whites is not yet a nation, not yet a
10 people. The Indians keep burning an eternal fire, the sacred fire* of the old dark religion. To the vast white America, either in our generation or in the time of our children or grandchildren, will come some fearful convulsion. Some terrible convulsion will take place among the millions of this country, sooner or later. When the pueblos are gone. But oh, let
15 us have the grace and dignity to shelter these ancient centres of life, so that, if die they must, they die a natural death. And at the same time, let us try to adjust ourselves again to the Indian outlook, to take up an old dark thread from their vision,* and see again as they see, without forgetting we are ourselves.

20 For it is a new era we have now got to cross into. And our own electric light won't show us over the gulf. We have to feel our way by the dark thread of the old vision. Before it lapses, let us take it up.

Before the pueblos disappear, let there be just one moment of reconciliation between the white spirit and the dark.*

25 And whether there be this moment of reconciliation or not, let us prevent Jack Grab and Juan Arrapar* from putting their foot on the pueblos.

Besides, if the Bursum bill passes, what a lively shooting match will go on between all the jacks and the juans who claim the bits of land in
30 question, ten claimants to every inch!

And then, again, what business is it of mine, foreigner and newcomer?

INDIANS AND AN ENGLISHMAN

Indians and an Englishman*

Supposing one fell on to the moon,* and found them talking English, it would be something the same as falling out of the open world plump down here in the middle of America. "Here" means New Mexico, the South West, wild and woolly and artistic and sage-brush desert.*

It is all rather like comic opera played with solemn intensity. All the wildness and woollyness and westernity and motor-cars and art and sage and savage are so mixed up, so incongruous, that it is a farce, and everybody knows it. But they refuse to play it as farce. The wild and woolly section insists on being heavily dramatic, bold and bad on purpose; the art insists on being real American and artistic; motor-cars insist on being thrilled, moved to the marrow; high-brows insist on being ecstatic, Mexicans insist on being Mexicans, squeezing the last black drop of macabre joy out of life, and Indians wind themselves in white cotton sheets like Hamlet's father's ghost,* with a lurking smile.

And here am I, a lone lorn* Englishman, tumbled out of the known world of the British Empire on to this stage: for it persists in seeming like a stage to me, and not like the proper world.

Whatever makes a proper world, I don't know. But surely two elements are necessary: a common purpose and a common sympathy. I can't see any common purpose. The Indians and Mexicans don't even seem very keen on dollars. That full moon of a silver dollar* doesn't strike me as overwhelmingly hypnotic out here. As for a common sympathy or understanding, that's beyond imagining. West is wild and woolly and bad on purpose, commerce is a little self-conscious about its own pioneering importance— Pioneers, Oh Pioneers!*—high-brow is bent on getting to the bottom of everything and saving the lost soul down there in the depths, Mexican is bent on being Mexican and not yet Gringo, and the Indian is all the things that all the others aren't. And so everybody smirks at everybody else, and says tacitly: "Go on, you do your little stunt, and I'll do mine," and they're like the various troupes in a circus, all performing at once, with nobody for Master of Ceremonies.*

It seems to me, in this country, everything is taken so damn seriously that nothing remains serious. Nothing is so farcical as insistent drama. Everybody is lurkingly conscious of this. Each section or troupe is quite willing to admit that all the other sections are buffoon stunts. But it itself is the real thing, solemnly bad in its badness, good in its goodness, wild in its wildness, woolly in its woollyness, arty in its artiness, deep in its depths, in a word, earnest.

In such a masquerade of earnestness, a bewildered straggler out of the far-flung British Empire, myself! Don't let me for a moment pretend to *know* anything. I know less than nothing. I simply gasp like a bumpkin in a circus ring, with the horse-lady leaping over my head, the Apache war-whooping in my ear, the Mexican staggering under crosses* and bumping me as he goes by, the artist whirling colours across my dazzled vision, the high-brows solemnly declaiming at me from all the cross-roads. If, dear reader, you, being the audience who has paid to come in, feel that you must take up an attitude to me, let it be one of amused pity.

One has to take sides. First, one must be either pro-Mexican or pro-Indian; then, either art or intellect: then, republican or democrat: and so on. But as for me, poor lost lamb, if I bleat at all in the circus-ring, it will be my own shorn lonely bleat of a lamb who's lost his mother.*

The first Indians I really saw were the Apaches in the Apache Reservation of this state.* We drove in a motor-car, across desert and mesa, down canyons and up divides and along arroyos and so forth, two days, till at afternoon our two Indian men ran the car aside from the trail and sat under the pine-tree to comb their long black hair and roll it into the two roll-plaits that hang in front of their shoulders, and put on all their silver-and-turquoise jewellery and their best blankets: because we were nearly there. On the trail were horsemen passing, and wagons with Ute Indians and Navajos.*

"Da donde viene, Usted?"......*

We came at dusk from the high shallows and saw on a low crest the points of Indian tents, the tepees,* and smoke, and silhouettes of tethered horses and blanketted figures moving. In the shadow a rider was following a flock of white goats that flowed like water. The car ran to the top of the crest, and there was a hollow basin with a lake in the distance, pale in the dying light. And this shallow upland basin, dotted with Indian tents, and the fires flickering in front, and crouching blanketted figures, and horsemen crossing the dusk from tent to tent, horsemen in big steeple hats* sitting glued on their ponies, and bells tinkling, and dogs yapping, and tilted wagons trailing in on the trail below, and a smell of woodsmoke and of cooking, and wagons coming in from far off, and tents pricking on the ridge of the round *vallum*,* and horsemen dipping down and emerging again, and more red sparks of fires glittering, and crouching bundles of women's figures squatting at 5 a fire before a little tent made of boughs, and little girls in full petticoats hovering, and wild barefoot boys throwing bones at thin-tailed dogs, and tents away in the distance, in the growing dark, on the slopes, and the trail crossing the floor of the hollows in the low dusk.

There you had it all, as in the hollow of your hand. And to my heart, 10 born in England and kindled with Fenimore Cooper,* it wasn't the wild and woolly west, it was the nomad nations gathering still in the continent of hemlock trees and prairies. The Apaches came and talked to us, in their steeple black hats, and plaits wrapped with beaver fur, and their silver and beads and turquoise. Some talked strong American, 15 and some talked only Spanish. And they had strange lines in their faces.

The two kivas, the rings of cut aspen trees stuck in the ground like the walls of a big hut of living trees, were on the plain, at either end of the race-track.* And as the sun went down, the drums began to beat, the drums with their strong-weak, strong-weak pulse that beat 20 on the plasm of one's tissue. The car slid down to the south kiva. Two elderly men held the drum, and danced the pàt-pat, pàt-pat,* quick beat on flat feet, like birds that move from the feet only, and sang with wide mouths, Hie! Hie! Hie! Hỳ-a! Hỳ-a! Hỳ-a! Hie! Hie! Hie! Ay-away-away!!* Strange dark faces with wide, shouting mouths 25 and rows of small, close-set teeth, and strange lines on the faces, part ecstasy, part mockery, part humorous, part devilish, and the strange, calling, summoning sound in a wild song-shout, to the thud-thud of the drum. Answer of the same from the other kiva, as of a challenge accepted. And from the gathering darkness around, men drifting slowly 30 in, each carrying an aspen-twig,* each joining to cluster close in two rows upon the drum, holding each his aspen twig inwards, their faces all together, mouths all open in the song-shout, and all of them all the time going on the two feet, pàt-pat, pàt-pat, pàt-pat, to the thud-thud of the drum and the strange, plangent yell of the chant, edging inch 35 by inch, pàt-pat, pàt-pat, pàt-pat, sideways in a cluster along the track, towards the distant cluster of the challengers from the other kiva, who were sing-shouting and edging onwards, sideways in the dusk, their faces all together, their leaves all inwards, towards the drum, and their feet going pàt-pat, pàt-pat, on the dust, with their buttocks stuck out 40 a little, faces all inwards shouting open-mouthed to the drum, and half laughing, half mocking, half devilment, half fun. *Hie! Hie! Hie! Hie-away-awaya!* The strange yell, song, shout rising so lonely in the dusk, as if pine-trees could suddenly, shaggily sing. Almost a pre-animal sound, full of triumph in life, and devilment against other life, and mockery, and humorousness, and the pàt-pat, pàt-pat of the rhythm. Sometimes more youths coming up, and as they draw near laughing they give the war-whoop, like a turkey giving a startled shriek* and then gobble-gobbling with laughter—Ugh!—the shriek half laughter, then the gobble-gobble-gobble like a great demoniac chuckle. The chuckle in the war whoop.—They produce the gobble from the deeps of the stomach, and say it makes them feel good.*

Listening, an acute sadness, and a nostalgia, unbearable yearning for something, and a sickness of the soul came over me. The gobble-gobble chuckle in the whoop surprised me in my very tissues. Then I got used to it, and could hear in it the humanness, the playfulness, and then, beyond that, the mockery and the diabolical, pre-human, pine-tree fun of cutting dusky throats and letting the blood spurt out unconfined. Gobble-agobble-agobble, the unconfined loose blood, gobble-agobble, the dead, mutilated lump, gobble-agobble-agobble, the fun, the greatest man-fun. The war-whoop!

So I felt. I may have been all wrong, and other folk may feel much more natural and reasonable things. But so I felt. And the sadness and the nostalgia of the song-calling, and the resinous continent of pine-trees and turkeys, the feet of birds treading a dance, far-off, when man was dusky* and not individualised.

I am no ethnologist. The point is, what is the feeling that passes from an Indian to me, when we meet. We are both men, but how do we feel together? I shall never forget that first evening when I first came into contact with Red Men, away in the Apache country. It was not what I had thought it would be. It was something of a shock. Again something in my soul broke down, letting in a bitterer dark, a pungent awakening to the lost past, old darkness, new terror, new root-griefs, old root-richnesses.

The Apaches have a cult of water-hatred; they never wash flesh or rag. So never in my life have I smelt such an unbearable sulphur-human smell as comes from them when they cluster: a smell that takes the breath from the nostrils.

We drove the car away half a mile or more, back from the Apache hollow, to a lonely ridge, where we pitched camp under pine trees. Our two Indians made the fire, dragged in wood, then wrapped themselves in their best blankets and went off to the tepees of their friends. The night was cold and starry.

After supper I wrapped myself in a red serape up to the nose, and went down alone to the Apache encampment. It is good, on a chilly night in a strange country, to be wrapped almost to the eyes in a good Navajo blanket. Then you feel warm inside yourself, and as good as invisible, and the dark air thick with enemies. So I stumbled on, startling the hobbled horses that jerked aside from me. Reaching the rim-crest one saw many fires burning in red spots round the slopes of the hollow, and against the fires, many crouching figures.* Dogs barked, a baby cried from a bough shelter, there was a queer low crackle of voices. So I stumbled alone over the ditches and past the tents, down to the kiva. Just near was a shelter with a big fire in front, and a man, an Indian, selling drinks, no doubt Budweiser beer and grape juice, nonintoxicants.* Cowboys in chaps and big hats* were drinking too, and one screechy, ungentle cow-girl in khaki. So I went on in the dark up the opposite slope. The dark Indians passing in the night peered at me. The air was full of a sort of sportiveness, playfulness, that had a jeering, malevolent vibration in it, to my fancy. As if this play were another kind of harmless-harmful warfare, overbearing. Just the antithesis of what I understand by jolliness: ridicule. Comic sort of bullying. No jolly, free laughter. Yet a great deal of laughter. But with a sort of gibe in it.

This, of course, may just be the limitation of my European fancy. But that was my feeling. One felt a stress of will, of human wills, in the dark air, gibing even in the comic laughter. And a sort of unconscious animosity.

Again a sound of a drum down below, so again I stumbled down to the kiva. A bunch of young men were clustered—seven or eight round a drum, and standing with their faces together loudly and mockingly singing the song yells, some of them treading the pat-pat, some not bothering. Just behind was the blazing fire and the open shelter of the drink tent, with Indians in tall black hats and long plaits in front of their shoulders, and bead-braided waistcoats, and hands in their pockets; some swathed in sheets, some in brilliant blankets, and all grinning, laughing. The cowboys with big spurs still there, horses' bridles trailing, and cow-girl screeching her laugh. One felt an inevitable silent gibing, animosity in each group, one for the other. At the same time, an absolute avoidance of any evidence of this.

The young men round the drum died out and started again. As they died out, the strange uplifted voice in the kiva was heard. It seemed to me the outside drumming and singing served to cover the voice within the kiva.

5 The kiva of young green trees was just near, two paces only. On the ground outside, boughs and twigs were strewn round to prevent anyone's coming close to the enclosure. Within was the firelight. And one could see through the green of the leaf-screen, men round a fire inside there, and one old man, the same old man always facing the open
10 entrance, the fire between him and it. Other Indians sat in a circle, of which he was the key. The old man had his dark face lifted, his head bare, his two plaits falling on his shoulders. His close-shutting Indian lips were drawn open, his eyes were as if half veiled, as he went on and on, on and on, in a distinct, plangent, recitative voice,* male and yet strangely
15 far off and plaintive, reciting, reciting, reciting like a somnambulist, telling, no doubt, the history of the tribe interwoven with the gods.* Other Apaches sat round the fire. Those nearest the old teller were stationary, though one chewed gum all the time and one ate bread cake and others lit cigarettes. Those nearer the entrance rose after a time,
20 restless. At first some strolled in, stood a minute, then strolled out, desultory. But as the night went on, the ring round the fire inside the wall of green young trees was complete, all squatting on the ground, the old man with the lifted face and parted lips and half-unseeing eyes going on and on, across the fire. Some men stood lounging with the
25 half-self-conscious ease of the Indian behind the seated men. They lit cigarettes. Some drifted out. Another filtered in. I stood wrapped in my blanket in the cold night, at some little distance from the entrance, looking on.

A big young Indian came and pushed his face under my hat to see
30 who or what I was.

"Buenos!"*

"Buenos!"

"Que quiere?"

"No hablo espagnol."
35 "Oh only English, eh?—You can't come in here."

"I don't want to."

"This Indian Church."

"Is it?"

"I don't let people come, only Apache, only Indian."
40 "You keep watch?"

"I keep watch, yes; Indian church, eh?"

"And the old man preaches?"

"Yes, he preaches."

After which I stood quite still and uncommunicative. He waited for
a further development. There was none. So, after giving me another
look, he went to talk to other Indians, sotto voce, by the door.

The circle was complete, groups stood behind the squatting ring,
some men were huddled in blankets, some sitting just in trousers and
shirt, in the warmth near the fire, some wrapped close in white cotton
sheets. The firelight shone on the dark, unconcerned faces of the listeners, as they chewed gum, or ate bread, or smoked a cigarette. Some
had big silver ear-rings swinging, and necklaces of turquoise. Some had
waistcoats all bead braids. Some wore store shirts and store trousers,*
like Americans. From time to time one man pushed another piece of
wood on the fire.

They seemed to be paying no attention, it all had a very perfunctory
appearance. But they kept silent, and the voice of the old reciter went
on blindly, from his lifted, bronze mask of a face with its wide-opened
lips. They furl back their teeth as they speak, and they use a sort of
resonant tenor voice, that has a plangent half-sad, twanging sound,
vibrating deep from the chest. The old man went on and on, for hours,
in that urgent, far-off voice. His hair was grey, and parted, and his two
round plaits hung in front of his shoulders on his shirt. From his ears
dangled pieces of blue turquoise, tied with string. An old green blanket
was wrapped round above his waist, and his feet in old moccasins
were crossed before the fire. There was a deep pathos, for me, in the
old, mask-like, virile figure, with its metallic courage of persistence,
old memory, and its twanging male voice. So far, so great a memory.
So dauntless a persistence in the piece of living red earth seated on the
naked earth, before the fire; this old, bronze-resonant man with his eyes
as if glazed in old memory, and his voice issuing in endless plangent
monotony from the wide, unfurled mouth.

And the young men, who chewed chewing gum and listened without
listening. The voice no doubt registered on their under-consciousness,
as they looked around, and lit a cigarette, and spat sometimes aside.
With their day-consciousness they hardly attended.

As for me, standing outside, beyond the open entrance, I was no
enemy of theirs; far from it. The voice out of the far-off time was not
for my ears. Its language was unknown to me. And I did not wish
to know. It was enough to hear the sound issuing plangent from the

bristling pine-tree darkness of the far past, to see the bronze mask of the face lifted, the white, small, close-packed teeth showing all the time. It was not for me, and I knew it. Nor had I any curiosity to understand. The soul is as old as the oldest day, and has its own hushed echoes, its own far-off tribal understandings sunk and incorporated. We do not need to live the past over again. Our darkest tissues are twisted in this old tribal experience, our warmest blood came out of the old tribal fire. And they vibrate still in answer, our blood, our tissue. But me, the conscious me, I have gone a long road since then.* And as I look back, like memory terrible as blood-shed, the dark faces round the fire in the night, and one blood beating in me and them. But I don't want to go back to them, ah never. I never want to deny them, or break with them. But there is no going back. Always onward, still further.* The great devious onward-flowing stream of conscious human blood. From them to me, and from me on.

I don't want to live again the tribal mysteries my blood has lived long since. I don't want to know as I have known, in the tribal exclusiveness. But every drop of me trembles still alive to the old sound, every thread in my body quivers to the frenzy of the old mystery. I know my derivation. I was born of no virgin, of no Holy Ghost. Ah no, these old men telling the tribal tale were my fathers. I have a dark-faced, bronze-voiced father far back in the resinous ages. My mother was no virgin. She lay in her hour with this dusky-lipped tribe-father. And I have not forgotten him. But he, like many an old father with a changeling son, he would like to deny me. But I stand on the far edge of their fire light and am neither denied nor accepted. My way is my own, old red father; I can't cluster at the drum any more.*

Just near, the young men were still standing clustered on the drum and singing and treading unevenly, holding the tom-tom drum in their midst and clustering on it as on some nucleus. And all the time the thud-thud of the drum, the half-hearted rhythm, the halfhearted bird-tread of the dance, the half-hearted wild song. And all the time the horse-play and the jokes and the laughter.

The night was getting late, and the cowboys had ridden off, white men had lapsed out. A new sound came into the voices, a new savagery in the air. The dark eyes of the Apache loungers by the drink-booth seemed to grow bigger, with a sort of dark glare, like the glare of a night animal. The individual, that lonely phenomenon evolved through struggle of ages, was lapsing right out again, the one bloodstream was swimming before their eyes. They looked at me strangely, as if they could not see me, but sensed my presence like an irritant in the night, as a mountain lion might feel the rankling of a thorn in his flesh without knowing where or what it was. And I, I stood in my isolate individuality,* and let them look. They didn't want me there, so at last I went slowly away, out of the hollow and over the rim, and across the darkness to find my own lonely camp, where I imagined the American woman* who was camp-companion had gone to bed tired. The camp was over the brow of a*

5

TAOS

Taos

The Indians say Taos is the heart of the world.* Their world, maybe. Some places seem temporary on the face of the earth: San Francisco for example.* Some places seem final. They have a true nodality. I never felt that so powerfully as, years ago, in London.* The intense powerful nodality of that great heart of the world. And during the war that heart, for me, broke. So it is. Places can lose their living nodality. Rome, to me, has lost hers. In Venice one feels the magic of the glamorous old node that once united East and West, but it is the beauty of an afterlife.*

Taos pueblo* still retains its old nodality. Not like a great city. But, in its way, like one of the monasteries of Europe. You cannot come upon the ruins of the old great monasteries of England, beside their waters, in some lovely valley, now remote, without feeling that here is one of the choice spots of the earth, where the spirit dwelt.* To me it is so important to remember that when Rome collapsed, when the great Roman Empire fell into smoking ruins, and bears roamed in the streets of Lyons,* and wolves howled in the deserted streets of Rome, and Europe really was a dark ruin, then, it was not in castles or manors or cottages that life remained vivid. Then those whose souls were still alive withdrew together and gradually built monasteries, and these monasteries and convents, little communities of quiet labour and courage, isolated, helpless, and yet never overcome in a world flooded with devastation, these alone kept the human spirit from disintegration, from going quite dark, in the Dark Ages. These men made the Church, which again made Europe, inspiring the martial faith of the Middle Ages.*

Taos pueblo affects me rather like one of the old monasteries. When you get there you feel something final. There is an arrival. The nodality still holds good.

But this is the pueblo. And from the north side to the south side,* from the south side to the north side, the perpetual silent wandering intentness of a full-skirted, black-shawled, long-fringed woman in her wide white deerskin boots, the running of children, the silent sauntering of dark-faced men, bare-headed, the two plaits in front of their thin

shoulders, and a white sheet like a sash swathed round their loins.*
They must have something to swathe themselves in.

And if it were sunset, the men swathing themselves in their sheets like
shrouds, leaving only the black place of the eyes visible. And women,
darker than ever, with shawls over their heads, busy at the ovens.* And
cattle being driven to sheds. And men and boys trotting in from the
fields, on ponies. And as the night is dark, on one of the roofs, or more
often on the bridge, the inevitable drum-drum-drum of the tom-tom,*
and young men in the dark lifting their voices to the song, like wolves
or coyotes crying in music.

There it is then, the pueblo, as it has been since heaven knows when.
And the slow dark weaving of the Indian life going on still, though
perhaps more waveringly. And oneself, sitting there on a pony, a far-
off stranger with gulfs of time between me and this. And yet, the
old nodality of the pueblo still holding, like a dark ganglion* spinning
invisible threads of consciousness. A sense of dryness, almost of weariness, about the pueblo. And a sense of the inalterable. It brings a sick
sort of feeling over me, always, to get into the Indian vibration. Like
breathing chlorine.

The next day in the morning we went to help erect the great stripped
may-pole.* It was the straight, smoothed yellow trunk of a big tree.
Of course one of the white boys took the bossing of the show. But the
Indians were none too ready to obey, and their own fat dark-faced boss
gave counter-orders. It was the old, amusing contradiction between
the white and the dark races. As for me, I just gave a hand steadying
the pole as it went up, outsider at both ends of the game.

An American girl came with a camera, and got a snap of us all
struggling in the morning light with the great yellow trunk. One of the
Indians went to her abruptly, in his quiet, insidious way.

"You give me that kodak.* You ain't allowed take no snaps here. You
pay fine—one dollar." She was frightened, but she clung to her camera.

"You're not going to take my kodak from me," she said.

"I'm going to take that film out. And you pay one dollar, fine, see."
The girl relinquished the camera, the Indian took out the film.

"Now you pay me one dollar, or I don't give you back this kodak."
Rather sullenly, she took out her purse and gave the two silver half-
dollars. The Indian returned the camera, pocketed the money, and
turned aside with a sort of triumph. Done it over one specimen of the
white race.

There were not very many Indians helping to put up the pole.

"I never see so few boys helping put up the pole," said Tony Romero*
to me.

"Where are they all?" I asked. He shrugged his shoulders.*

Dr. West, a woman doctor from New York who has settled in one of
the villages, was with us. Mass was being said inside the church, and   5
she would have liked to go in. She is well enough known too. But two
Indians were at the church-door, and one put his elbow in front of her.

"You Catholic?"

"No, I'm not."

"Then you can't come in."   10

The same almost jeering triumph in giving the white man—or the
white woman—a kick. It is the same the whole world over, between
dark-skin and white. Dr. West, of course, thinks everything Indian
wonderful. But she wasn't used to being rebuffed, and she didn't like
it. But she found excuses.   15

"Of course," she said, "they're quite right to exclude the white
people, if the white people can't behave themselves. It seems there were
some Americans, boys and girls, in the church yesterday, insulting the
images of the saints, shrieking, laughing, and saying they looked like
monkeys. So now no white people are allowed inside the church."   20

I listened and said nothing. I had heard the same story at Buddhist
temples in Ceylon.* For my own part, I have long since passed the stage
when I want to crowd up and stare at anybody's spectacle, white man's
or dark man's.

I stood on one of the first roofs of the north pueblo. The iron bell of   25
the church began to bang-bang-bang. The sun was down beyond the
far-off, thin clear line of the western mesa, the light had ceased glowing
on the piñon-dotted foot-hills* beyond the south pueblo. The square
beneath was thick with people. And the Indians began to come out of
church.   30

Two Indian women brought a little dressed-up Madonna to her
platform in the green starting-bower.* Then the men slowly gathered
round the drum. The bell clanged. The tom-tom beat. The men slowly
uplifted their voices.* The wild music resounded strangely against
the banging of that iron bell, the silence of the many faces, as the   35
group of Indians in their sheets and their best blankets, and in their
ear-rings and brilliant scarlet trousers, or emerald trousers, or purple
trousers, trimmed with beads, trod the slow bird-dance sideways, in

feet of beaded moccasins, or yellow doeskin moccasins, singing all the
time like drumming coyotes, slowly down and across the bridge to the
south side, and up the incline to the south kiva. One or two Apaches
in their beaded waist-coats and big black hats were among the singers,
distinguishable by their thick build also. An old Navajo chief was among
the encouragers.

As dusk fell, the singers came back under a certain house by the south
kiva, and as they passed under the platform they broke and dispersed,
it was over. They seemed as if they were grinning subtly as they went:
grinning at being there in all that white crowd of inquisitives. It must
have been a sort of ordeal, to sing and tread the slow dance between
that solid wall of silent, impassive white faces. But the Indians seemed
to take no notice. And the crowd only silently, impassively watched.
Watched with that strange, static American quality of *laisser faire** and
of indomitable curiosity.

AU REVOIR, U. S. A.

Au Revoir, U. S. A.

"Say au revoir
But not goodbye
This parting brings
*A bitter sigh . . . ."** 5

It really does, when you find yourself in an unkempt Pullman* trailing through endless deserts, south of El Paso,* fed on doubtful scraps at enormous charge and at the will of a rather shoddy smallpox-marked Mexican Pullman-boy who knows there's been a revolution and that his end is up.* Then you remember the neat and nice nigger who looked 10 after you as far as El Paso, before you crossed the Rio Grande into desert and chaos, and you sigh, if you have time before a curse chokes you.

Yet, U. S. A., you do put a strain on the nerves. Mexico puts a strain on the temper. Choose which you prefer. Mine's the latter. I'd rather 15 be in a temper than be pulled taut. Which is what the U. S. A. did to me. Tight as a fiddle string, tense over the bridge of the solar plexus.* Any how the solar plexus goes a bit loose and has a bit of play down here.

I still don't know why the U. S. A. pulls one so tight and makes one 20 feel like a chicken that is being drawn. The people on the whole are quite as amenable as people anywhere else. They don't pick your pocket, or even your personality. They're not unfriendly. It's not the people. Something in the air tightens one's nerves like fiddle strings, screws them up, squeak-squeak! . . . till one's nerves will give out nothing but 25 a shrill fine shriek of overwroughtness. Why, in the name of heaven? Nobody knows. It's just the spirit of place.*

You cross the Rio Grande, and change from tension into exasperation. You feel like hitting the impudent Pullman waiter with a beer-bottle. In the U. S. A. you don't even think of such a thing. 30

Of course, one might get used to a state of tension. And then one would pine for the United States. Meanwhile one merely snarls back at the dragons of San Juan Teotihuacán.*

131

It's a queer continent—as much as I've seen of it. It's a fanged continent. It's got a rattle-snake coiled in its heart, has this democracy of the New World. It's a dangerous animal, once it lifts its head again. Meanwhile, the dove still nests in the coils of the rattlesnake, the stone coiled rattlesnake of Aztec eternity.* The dove lays her eggs on his flat head.

The old people had a marvellous feeling for snakes and fangs, down here in Mexico. And after all, Mexico is only the sort of solar plexus of North America. The great paleface overlay hasn't gone into the soil half an inch. The Spanish churches and palaces stagger, the most ricketty things imaginable, always just on the point of falling down.* And the peon still grins his Indian grin behind the Cross. And there's quite a lively light in his eyes, much more so than in the eyes of the Northern Indian. He knows his gods.

These old civilisations down here, they never got any higher than Quetzalcoatl.* And he's just a sort of feathered snake. Who needed the smoke of a little heart's-blood now and then, even he.

"Only the ugly is aesthetic now," said the young Mexican artist.* Personally, he seems as gentle and self-effacing as the nicest of lambs. Yet his caricatures are hideous, hideous without mirth or whimsicality. Blood-hideous. Grim, earnest hideousness.

Like the Aztec things, the Aztec carvings. They all twist and bite. That's all they do. Twist and writhe and bite, or crouch in lumps. And coiled rattle-snakes, many, like dark heaps of excrement.* And out at San Juan Teotihuacán where are the great pyramids of a vanished, pre-Aztec people, as we are told—and the so-called Temple of Quetzalcoatl*—there, behold you, huge gnashing heads jut out jagged from the wall-face of the low pyramid, and a huge snake stretches along the base, and one grasps at a carved fish, that swims in old stone and for once seems harmless. Actually a harmless fish!

But look out! The great stone heads snarl at you from the wall, trying to bite you:—and one great dark green blob of an obsidian eye, you never saw anything so blindly malevolent: and then white fangs. Great white fangs, smooth today, the white fangs, with tiny cracks in them. Enamelled. These bygone pyramid-building Americans, who were a dead-and-gone mystery even to the Aztecs, when the Spaniards arrived,* they applied their highest art to the enamelling of the great fangs of these venomous stone heads, and there is the enamel today, white and smooth. You can stroke the great fang with your finger and see. And the blob of an obsidian eye looks down at you.

It's a queer continent. The anthropologists may make what prettiness they like out of myths. But come here, and you'll see that the gods bit. There is none of the phallic pre-occupation of the old Mediterranean.* Here they hadn't got even as far as hotblooded sex. Fangs, and cold serpent folds, and bird-snakes with fierce cold blood and claws. I admit that I feel bewildered. There is always something a bit amiably comic about Chinese dragons* and contortions. There's nothing amiably comic in these ancient monsters. They're dead in earnest about biting and writhing, snake-blooded birds.

And the Spanish white superimposition, with rococo church-towers among pepper-trees and column cactuses, seems so ricketty and temporary, the pyramids seem so indigenous, rising like hills out of the earth itself. The one goes down with a clatter, the other remains.

And this is what seems to me the difference between Mexico and the United States. And this is why, it seems to me, Mexico exasperates, whereas the U. S. A. puts an unbearable tension on one. Because here in Mexico the fangs are still obvious. Everybody knows the gods are going to bite within the next five minutes. While in the United States, the gods have had their teeth pulled, and their claws cut, and their tails docked, till they seem real mild lambs. Yet all the time, inside, it's the same old dragon's blood. The same old aboriginal American dragon's blood.

And that discrepancy of course is a strain on the human psyche.

DEAR OLD HORSE, A LONDON LETTER

Dear Old Horse, A London Letter*

Yesterday came the Horse,* capering a trifle woodenly, and today a fall of snow. Enough bright white snow on the ground to make a bit of daylight. I've been here exactly a month, in London, and day has never broken all the time. A dull, heavy, mortified half-light that seems to take the place of day in London in winter. I can't stand it.

However, with a bit of snow-brightness in the air, and a bit of a rather wooden neigh from the Horse in my ears, I prick up and write you a London Letter.

Dear old Azure Horse, Turquoise Horse, Hobby Horse, Trojan Horse* with a few scared heroes in your belly; Horse, laughing your Horse Laugh, you do actually ramp in with a bit of horse sense. I'm all for horse sense, O Horsie! Come down to it, and it's the Centaur.* Good old Horse, be patted, and be persuaded to grin and to be a Centaur getting your own back.

Even if you're only a hobby Horse, with a wooden head and a Spoodle* on your broom-stick flanks, you're welcome just now. Very welcome. Here's an apple. Be tempted, like Adam,* and take it. And for the sake of all horses, be braver than Adam, who only bit a bite out and dropped the main. Eat up the whole gaudy apple, O Horse. Let's have the centaur back.

Dear old Horse, you'd never be azure or turquoise here in London. Oh, London is awful: so dark, so damp, so yellow-grey, so mouldering piecemeal. With crowds of people going about in a mouldering, damp, half-visible sort of way, as if they were all mouldering bits of rag that had fallen from an old garment. Horse, Horse, be as hobby as you like, but let me get on your back and ride away again to New Mexico. I don't care how frozen it is, how grey the desert, how cold the air, in Taos, in Lobo,* in Santa Fe. It isn't choky, it is bright day at daytime, and bright dark night at night. And one isn't wrapped like a mummy in winding-sheet after winding-sheet of yellow, damp, unclean, cloyed, ancient, breathed-to-death so-called air. Oh Horse, Horse, Horse, when you kick your heels you shatter an enclosure every time. And over here the Horse is dead: he'll kick his heels no more. I don't know whether it's the Pale Galilean who has triumphed,* or a paleness paler than the pallor even of Jesus. But a yellow and jaundiced paleness has triumphed over here, the Turquoise Horse has been long dead, and churned into sausages. I find it unbearable.

5   Let the horse laugh. I'm all for a horse that laughs. Though I don't care for him when he merely sniggers.*

I'm all for a horse, it's not even the Houyhnhnms.* They aren't blue enough for me. It's a turquoise centaur who laughs, who laughs longest and who laughs last. I believe in him. I believe he's there, over the desert

10   in the south-west. I believe if you'll cajole him with a bit of proper corn, he'll come down to Santa Fe and bite your noses off and then laugh at you again.

Two-legged man is no good. If he's going to stand steady, he must stand on four feet. Like the Centaur. When Jesus was born, the spirits

15   wailed round the Mediterranean: Pan is dead. Great Pan is dead.* And at the Renaissance the centaur gave a final groan, and expired. At least, I seem to remember him lamenting and about to expire, in the Uffizi.*

It would be a terrible thing if the Horse in us died forever:* as he seems to have died in Europe. How awful it would be, if at this present moment

20   I sat in the yellow mummy-swathings of London atmosphere—the snow is melting—inside the dreadful mummy-sarcophagus of Europe,* and didn't know that the blue horse was still kicking his heels and making a few sparks fly, across the tops of the Rockies.* It would be a truly sad case for me.

25   As it is, I say to myself: Bah! In Lobo, in Taos, in Santa Fe the Turquoise Horse is waving snow out of his tail, and trotting gaily to the blue mountains of the far distance. And in Mexico his mane is bright yellow on his blue body, so streaming with sun, and he's lashing out again like the devil, till his hoofs are red.* Good old Horse!

30   But talking seriously,* Man must be centaur. This two-legged forked radish* is going flabby.

The Centaur's Lament! Not at all. The laugh of the Turquoise Man Horse. Let the forked radish do the lamenting.

In modern symbolism, the Horse is supposed to stand for the pas-

35   sions. Passions be blowed. What does the Centaur stand for, Chiron or any other of that quondam four-footed gentry.* Sense! Horse Sense. Sound, powerful, four-footed Sense, that's what the Horse stands for. Horse sense, I tell you. That's the Centaur. That's the blue horse of the ancient Mediterranean, before the pale Galilean or the extra pale Ger-

40   man or Nordic gentleman conquered. First of all, Sense, Good Sense,

Sound Sense, Horse Sense. And then, a laugh, a loud, sensible Horse Laugh.* After that these same passions, glossy and dangerous in the flanks. And after these again, hoofs, irresistible, splintering hoofs, that can kick the walls of the world down.*

Horse-sense, Horse-laughter, Horse-passion, Horse-hoofs: ask the 5 Indians if it is not so.

Tell me the Horse is dead? Tell me the Centaur has died out? It may easily be so, in Europe here, since the Renaissance. But in the wide blue skies of the southwest, and far-away south over Mexico: over the grey deserts and the red deserts beneath the Rockies and the Sierra Madre;* 10 down the canyons and across the mesas and along the depths of the barrancas goes the Turquoise Horse, uneasy, bethinking himself, and just on the point of bursting into a loud laugh, after all, laughing longest and laughing last.

Ask the Indians, if there isn't a little blue foal born every year, in the 15 pueblos, out of the old dark earth-coloured mottled mare.* Tell me the centaur can't beget centaurs?—Ask the Indian, ask the Navajo, ask the Mexican under his big hat.*

It's no good. I've got to ride on a laughing horse. The forked radish has ceased to perambulate. I've got to ride a laughing horse. And I 20 whistle for him, call him, spread corn for him, and hold out an apple to him here in England. No go! No answer! The poor devil's dead and churned into Cambridge sausages.* Flabby flaccid forked radishes, sausages, pairs of sausages in dead skins: these seem to drift about in the soup of the London air. 25

There's no answer. There's no blue cave to stable the Turquoise Horse, here. There's no dark earth-coloured mare to bear his foals. There's no far-away blue distance for him to roam across. He's dead.

And yet I've got to ride, centaur, on a blue stallion.

So, thanks be to the oldest of Gods, comes a wooden little Laughing 30 Horse sliding down from the blue air of the Rockies, riding on his hobby stick like a rocket, summoning me to mount and away.

Hurray! Hup-a-la! Up we go! Like a witch on a broom-stick,* riding West.

PARIS LETTER

Paris Letter*

I promised to write a letter to you from Paris. Probably I should have forgotten, but I saw a little picture–or sculpture–in the Tuileries, of Hercules slaying the Centaur,* and that reminded me. I had so much rather the Centaur had slain Hercules, and men had never developed souls. Seems to me they're the greatest ailment humanity ever had. However, they've got it.

Paris is still monumental and handsome. Along the river where its splendours are, there's no denying its man-made beauty. The poor, pale little Seine* runs rapidly north to the sea, the sky is pale, pale jade overhead, greenish and Parisian, the trees of black wire stand in rows, and flourish their black wire brushes against a low sky of jade-pale cobwebs, and the huge dark-grey palaces rear up their masses of stone and slope off towards the sky still with a massive, satisfying suggestion of pyramids.* There is something noble and man-made about it all.

My wife says she wishes that grandeur still squared its shoulders on the earth. She wishes she could sit sumptuously in the river windows of the Tuileries, and see a royal spouse—who wouldn't be me—cross the bridge at the head of a tossing, silk and silver cavalcade.* She wishes she had a bevy of ladies-in-waiting around her, as a peacock has its tail, as she crossed the weary expanses of pavement in the Champs Elysées.*

Well, she can have it. At least, she can't. The world has lost its faculty for splendour, and Paris is like an old, weary peacock that sports a bunch of dirty twigs at its rump, where it used to have a tail. Democracy has collapsed into more and more democracy, and men, particularly Frenchmen, have collapsed into little, rather insignificant, rather wistful, rather nice and helplessly commonplace little fellows who rouse one's mother-instinct and make one feel they should be tucked away in bed and left to sleep, like Rip Van Winkle,* till the rest of the storms rolled by.

It's a queer thing to sit in the Tuileries on a Sunday afternoon and watch the crowd drag through the galleries. Instead of a gay and wicked court, the weary, weary crowd, that looks as if it had nothing at heart to keep it going. As if the human creature had been dwindling and

143

dwindling through the processes of democracy, amid the ponderous ridicule of the aristocratic setting, till soon he will dwindle right away.

Oh, those galleries. Oh, those pictures and those statues of nude, nude women: nude, nude, insistently and hopelessly nude. At last the eyes fall in absolute weariness, the moment they catch sight of a bit of pink-and-white painting, or a pair of white marble fesses.* It becomes an inquisition;* like being *forced* to go on eating pink marzipan icing. And yet there is a fat and very undistinguished bourgeois with a little beard and a fat and hopelessly petit bourgeoise* wife and awful little girl, standing in front of a huge heap of twisting marble, while he, with a goose-grease unctuous simper, strokes the marble hip of the huge marble female, and points out its niceness *to his wife*. She is not in the least jealous. She knows, no doubt, that her own hip and the marble hip are the only ones he will stroke without paying various prices, one of which, and the last he could pay, would be the price of the spunk.

It seems to me the French are just worn out. And not nearly so much with the late great war as with the pink nudities of women. The men are just worn out, making offerings on the shrine of Aphrodite in elastic garters.* And the women are worn out, keeping the men up to it. The rest is all nervous exasperation.

And the table. One shouldn't forget that other, four-legged mistress of man, more unwitherable than Cleopatra.* The table. The good kindly tables of Paris, with Coquilles Saint Martin, and escargots and oysters and Chateaubriands* and the good red wine. If they can afford it, the men sit and eat themselves pink. And no wonder. But the Aphrodite in a hard black hat opposite, when she has eaten herself also pink, is going to insist on further delights, to which somebody has got to play up. Weariness isn't the word for it.

May the Lord deliver us from our own enjoyments, we gasp at last.—And he won't. We actually have to deliver ourselves.

One goes out again from the restaurant comfortably fed and soothed with food and drink, to find the pale-jade sky of Paris crumbling in a wet dust of rain; motor-cars skidding till they turn clean around, and are facing south when they were going north: a boy on a bicycle coming smack, and picking himself up with his bicycle pump between his legs: and the men still fishing, as if it were a Sisyphus penalty,* with long sticks fishing for invisible fishes in the Seine: and the huge buildings of the Louvre and the Tuileries* standing ponderously, with their Parisian suggestion of pyramids.

And no, in the old style of grandeur I never want to be grand. That sort of regality, that builds itself up in piles of stone and masonry, and prides itself on living inside the monstrous heaps, once they're built is not for me. My wife asks why she can't live in the Petit Palais,* while she's in Paris. Well, even if she might, she'd live alone.

I don't believe any more in democracy. But I can't believe in the old sort of aristocracy,* either, nor can I wish it back, splendid as it was. What I believe in is the old Homeric aristocracy, when the grandeur was inside the man, and he lived in a simple wooden house. Then, the men that were grand inside themselves, like Ulysses,* were the chieftains and the aristocrats by instinct and by choice. At least we'll hope so. And the Red Indians only knew the aristocrat by instinct.* The leader was leader in his own being, not because he was somebody's son or had so much money.

It's got to be so again. They say it won't work. I say, why not? If men could once recognise the natural aristocrat when they set eyes on him, they can still. They can still choose him if they would.

But this business of dynasties is a weariness. House of Valois, House of Tudor!* Who would want to be a House, or a bit of a House! Let a man be a man, and damn the House business. I'm absolutely a democrat as far as that goes.

But that men are all brothers and all equal is a greater lie than the other. Some men are always aristocrats.* But it doesn't go by birth. A always contains B, but B is not contained in C.

Democracy, however, says that there is no such thing as an aristocrat. All men have two legs and one nose, ergo, they are all alike. Nosily and leggily, maybe. But otherwise, very different.

Democracy says that B is not contained in C, and neither is it contained in A. B, that is, the aristocrat, does not exist.

Now this is palpably a greater lie than the old dynastic lie. Aristocracy truly does not go by birth. But it still goes. And the tradition of aristocracy will help it a lot.

The aristocrats tried to fortify themselves inside these palaces and these splendours. Regal Paris built up the external evidences of her regality. But the two-limbed man inside these vast shells died, poor worm, of over-encumbrance.

The natural aristocrat has got to fortify himself inside his own will, according to his own strength. The moment he builds himself external evidences, like palaces, he builds himself in, and commits his own doom. The moment he depends on his jewels, he has lost his virtue.

It always seems to me that the next civilisation won't want to raise these ponderous, massive, deadly buildings that refuse to crumble away with their epoch and weigh men helplessly down. Neither palaces nor cathedrals nor any other hugenesses. Material simplicity is after all the highest sign of civilisation. Here in Paris one knows it finally. The ponderous and depressing museum that is regal Paris. And living humanity like poor worms struggling inside the shell of history, all of them inside the museum. The dead life and the living life, all one museum.

Monuments, museums, permanencies and ponderosities are all anathema. But brave men are forever born, and nothing else is worth having.

LETTER FROM GERMANY

Letter from Germany*

We are going back to Paris tomorrow, so this is the last moment to write a letter from Germany. Only from the fringe of Germany too.

It's a miserable journey from Paris to Nancy, through that Marne country,* where the country still seems to have had the soul blasted out of it, though the dreary fields are ploughed and level, and the pale wire trees stand up. But it is all void and null. And in the villages, the smashed houses in the street rows, like rotten teeth between good teeth.

You come to Strasburg,* and the people still talk Alsatian German, as ever, in spite of French shop signs. The place feels dead. And full of cotton goods, white goods, from Mülhausen,* from the factories that once were German. Such cheap white cotton goods, in a glut.

The cathedral-front rearing up high and flat and fanciful, a sort of darkness in the dark, with round rose windows and long, long prisms of stone.* Queer, that men should have ever wanted to put stone upon fanciful stone to such a height, without having it fall down. The gothic!* I was always glad when my card castles fell. But these goths and alemans* seemed to have a craze for peaky height.

The Rhine is still the Rhine, the great divider.* You feel it as you cross. The flat, frozen, watery places. Then the cold and curving river. Then the other side, seeming so cold, so empty, so frozen, so forsaken. The train stands and steams fiercely. Then it draws through the flat Rhine plain, past frozen pools of flood-water, and frozen fields, in the emptiness of this bit of occupied territory.*

Immediately you are over the Rhine, the spirit of place has changed. There is no more attempt at the bluff of geniality. The marshy places are frozen. The fields are vacant. There seems nobody in the world.

It is as if the life had retreated eastwards. As if the Germanic life were slowly ebbing away from contact with western Europe, ebbing to the deserts* of the east. And there stand the heavy, ponderous round hills of the Black Forest,* black with an inky blackness of Germanic trees, and patched with a whiteness of snow. They are like a series of huge, involved black mounds, obstructing the vision eastwards. You

149

look at them from the Rhine plain, and know that you stand on an actual border, up against something.

The moment you are in Germany, you know. It feels empty, and somehow, menacing. So must the Roman soldiers have watched those black, massive round hills: with a certain fear, and with the knowledge that they were at their own limit. A fear of the invisible natives. A fear of the invisible life lurking among the woods.* A fear of their own opposite.

So it is with the French: this almost mystic fear. But one should not insult even one's fears.

Germany, this bit of Germany, is very different from what it was two and a half years ago, when I was here. Then it was still open to Europe. Then it still looked to western Europe for a re-union, for a sort of reconciliation. Now that is over. The inevitable, mysterious barrier has fallen again, and the great leaning of the Germanic spirit is once more eastwards; towards Russia, towards Tartary.* The strange vortex of Tartary has become the positive centre again, the positivity of western Europe is broken. The positivity of our civilisation has broken. The influences that come, come invisibly out of Tartary. So that all Germany reads *Men Beasts and Gods*,* with a kind of fascination. Returning again to the fascination of the destructive East, that produced Attila.*

So it is at night. Baden Baden* is a little quiet place, all its guests gone. No more Turgenevs or Dostoevskys or Grand Dukes or King Edwards* coming to drink the waters. All the outward effect of a world-famous watering place. But empty now, a mere Black Forest village with the wagon-loads of timber going through, to the French.

The Rentenmark, the new Gold Mark of Germany,* is abominably dear. Prices are high in England, but English money buys less in Baden than it buys in London, by a long chalk.* And there is no work— consequently no money. Nobody buys anything, except absolute necessities. The shop keepers are in despair. And there is less and less work.

Everybody gives up the telephone—can't afford it. The tram-cars don't run, except about three times a day to the station. Up to the Annaberg, the suburb, the lines are rusty, no trams ever go. The people can't afford the ten Pfennigs for the fare. Ten pfennigs is an important sum now: one penny. It is really a hundred Milliards of Marks.*

Money becomes insane, and people with it.

At night the place is almost dark, economising light. Economy, economy, economy—that too becomes an insanity. Luckily the government keeps bread fairly cheap.

But at night you feel strange things stirring in the darkness, strange feelings stirring out of this still-unconquered Black Forest. You stiffen your backbone and you listen to the night. There is a sense of danger. It is not the people. They don't seem dangerous. Out of the very air comes a sense of danger, a queer, *bristling* feeling of uncanny danger.*

Something has happened. Something has happened which has not yet eventuated. The old spell of the old world has broken, and the old, bristling, savage spirit has set in. The war did not break the old peace-and-production hope of the world, though it gave it a severe wrench. Yet the old peace-and-production hope still governs, at least the consciousness. Even in Germany it has not quite gone.

But it feels as if, virtually, it were gone. The last two years have done it. The hope in peace-and-production is broken. The old flow, the old adherence is ruptured. And a still older flow has set in. Back, back to the savage polarity of Tartary, and away from the polarity of civilised Christian Europe.* This, it seems to me, has already happened. And it is a happening of far more profound import than any actual event. It is the father of the next phase of events.

And the feeling never relaxes. As you travel up the Rhine valley, still the same latent sense of danger, of silence, of suspension. Not that the people are actually planning or plotting or preparing. I don't believe it for a minute. But something has happened to the human soul, beyond all help. The human soul recoiling now from unison, and making itself strong elsewhere. The ancient spirit of pre-historic Germany coming back, at the end of history.

The same in Heidelberg.* Heidelberg full, full, full of people.* Students the same, youths with rucksacks the same, boys and maidens in gangs, come down from the hills. The same, and not the same. These queer gangs of Young Socialists,* youths and girls, with their non-materialistic professions, their half mystical assertions, they strike one as strange. Something primitive, like loose roving gangs of broken, scattered tribes, so they affect one. And the swarms of people somehow produce an impression of silence, of secrecy, of stealth. It is as if everything and everybody recoiled away from the old unison, as barbarians lurking in a wood recoil out of sight. The old habits remain. But the bulk of the people have no money. And the whole stream of feeling is reversed.

So, you stand in the woods above the town and see the Neckar flowing green and swift and slippery out of the gulf of Germany, to the Rhine. And the sun sets slow and scarlet into the haze of the Rhine valley. And the old, pinkish stone of the ruined castle* across looks sultry, the marshalry is in shadow below, the peaked roofs of old, tight Heidelberg compressed in its river gateway* glimmer and glimmer out. There is a blue haze.

And it all looks as if the years were wheeling swiftly backwards, no more onwards. Like a spring that is broken, and whirls swiftly back, so time seems to be whirling with mysterious swiftness to a sort of death. Whirling to the ghost of the old Middle Ages of Germany, then to the Roman days, then to the days of the silent forest and the dangerous, lurking barbarian.

Something about the Germanic races is unalterable. White skinned, elemental, and dangerous. Our civilisation has come from the fusion of the dark-eyes with the blue. The meeting and mixing and mingling of the two races has been the joy of our ages. And the Celt has been there, alien, but necessary as some chemical reagent to the fusion.* So the civilisation of Europe rose up. So these Cathedrals and these thoughts.

But now the Celt is the disintegrating agent. And the Latin and southern races are falling out of association with the northern races, the northern Germanic impulse is recoiling towards Tartary, the destructive vortex of Tartary.

It is a fate, nobody now can alter it. It is a fate. The very blood changes. Within the last three years, the very constituency of the blood has changed, in European veins. But particularly in Germanic veins.

At the same time, we have brought it about ourselves—by a Ruhr occupation, by an English nullity, and by a German false will.* We have done it ourselves. But apparently it was not to be helped.

Quos vult perdere Deus, dementat prius.*

PAN IN AMERICA

Pan in America

At the beginning of the Christian era, voices were heard off the coasts of Greece, out to sea, on the Mediterranean, wailing: "Pan is dead! Great Pan is dead!"*

The father of fauns and nymphs, satyrs and dryads and naiads* was dead, with only the voices in the air to lament him. Humanity hardly noticed.

But who was he, really? Down the long lanes and overgrown ridings* of history we catch odd glimpses of a lurking rustic god with a goat's white lightning in his eyes. A sort of fugitive, hidden among leaves, and laughing with the uncanny derision of one who feels himself defeated by something lesser than himself.

An outlaw, even in the early days of the gods. A sort of Ishmael* among the bushes.

Yet always his lingering title: The Great God Pan. As if he was, or had been, the greatest.

Lurking among the leafy recesses, he was almost more demon than god. To be feared, not loved or approached. A man who should see Pan by daylight fell dead,* as if blasted by lightning.

Yet you might dimly see him in the night, a dark body within the darkness. And then, it was a vision filling the limbs and the trunk of a man with power, as with new, strong-mounting sap. The Pan power! You went on your way in the darkness secretly and subtly elated with blind energy,* and you could cast a spell, by your mere presence, on women and on men. But particularly on women.

In the woods and the remote places ran the children of Pan, all the nymphs and fauns of the forest and the spring and the river and the rocks. These, too, it was dangerous to see by day. The man who looked up to see the white arms of a nymph flash as she darted behind the thick wild laurels, away from him, followed helplessly. He was a nympholept.* Fascinated by the swift limbs and the wild, fresh sides of the nymph, he followed forever, forever, in the endless monotony of his desire. Unless came some wise being who could absolve him from the spell.

But the nymphs, running among the trees and curling to sleep under the bushes, made the myrtles blossom more gaily, and the spring bubble up with greater urge, and the birds splash with a strength of life. And the lithe flanks of the faun gave life to the oak groves, the vast trees hummed with energy. And the wheat sprouted like green rain returning out of the ground, in the little fields, and the vine hung its black drops in abundance, urging a secret.

Gradually, men moved into cities. And they loved the display of people better than the display of a tree. They liked the glory they got of overpowering one another in war. And above all, they loved the vainglory of their own words, the pomp of argument and the vanity of ideas.

So Pan became old and grey-bearded and goat-legged, and his passion was degraded with the lust of senility. His power to blast and to brighten dwindled. His nymphs became coarse and vulgar.

Till at last, the old Pan died, and was turned into the devil of the Christians. The old god Pan became the Christian devil, with the cloven hoofs and the horns, the tail, and the laugh of derision. Old Nick, the Old Gentleman* who is responsible for all our wickednesses, but especially our sensual excesses, this is all that is left of the great god Pan.

It is strange. It is a most strange ending for a god with such a name. Pan! All! That which is everything has goats' feet and a tail! With a black face!

This really is curious.

Yet this was all that remained of Pan, except that he acquired brimstone and hell-fire,* for many, many centuries. The nymphs turned into the nasty-smelling witches of a Walpurgis night,* and the fauns that danced became sorcerers riding the air, or fairies no bigger than your thumb.

But Pan keeps on being re-born, in all kinds of strange shapes. There he was, at the Renaissance. And in the eighteenth century he had quite a vogue. He gave rise to an "ism"; and there were many Pantheists, Wordsworth one of the first.* They worshipped Nature in her sweet-and-pure aspect, her Lucy Gray aspect.

"Oft have I heard of Lucy Gray," the school child began to recite, on examination day.

"So have I," interrupted the bored inspector. Lucy Gray, alas, was the form that William Wordsworth thought fit to give to the Great God Pan.

And then he crossed over to the young United States: I mean Pan did. Suddenly he gets a new name. He becomes the Oversoul,* the Allness of everything. To this new Lucifer Gray* of a Pan, Whitman sings the famous *Song of Myself.* "I am All, and All is Me." That is: "I am Pan and Pan is me."

The old goat-legged gentleman from Greece thoughtfully strokes his beard, and answers:

"All A is B, but all B is not A."

Aristotle* did not live for nothing. All Walt is Pan, but all Pan is not Walt.

This, even to Whitman, is incontrovertible. So the new American pantheism collapses.

Then the poets dress up a few fauns and nymphs, to let them run riskily—oh, would there were any risk!—in their private "grounds." But alas, these tame guinea pigs soon became boring. Change the game.

We still *pretend* to believe that there is One mysterious Something-or-other back of Everything, ordaining all things for the ultimate good of humanity. It wasn't back of the Germans in 1914,* of course, and whether it's back of the bolshevist* is still a grave question. But still, it's back of _us_,* so that's all right.

Alas, poor Pan! Is this what you've come to. Legless, hornless, face-less, even smileless, you are less than everything or anything, except a lie.

And yet here, in America, the oldest of all old Pan is still alive. When Pan was greatest, he was not even Pan. He was nameless and unconceived, mentally. Just as a small baby new from the womb may say Mama! Dada!* Whereas in the womb it said nothing, so humanity, in the womb of Pan, said nought. But when humanity was born into a separate idea of itself, it said *Pan*!

In the days before man got too-much separated off from the universe, he *was* Pan, along with all the rest.

As a tree still is. A strong-willed, powerful thing-in-itself, reaching up and reaching down. With a powerful will of its own it thrusts green hands and huge limbs at the light above, and sends huge legs and gripping toes down, down between the earth and rocks, to the earth's middle.*

Here, on this little ranch under the Rocky Mountains,* a big pine tree rises like a guardian spirit in front of the cabin where we live. Long, long ago the Indians blazed it. And the lightning, or the storm has

cut off its crest. Yet its column is always there, alive and changeless, alive and changing. The tree has its own aura of life. And in winter the snow slips off it, and in June it sprinkles down its little catkin-like pollen-tips, and it hisses in the wind, and it makes a silence within a
5   silence. It is a great tree, under which the house is built. And the tree is still within the allness of Pan. At night, when the lamplight shines out of the window, the great trunk dimly shows, in the near darkness, like an Egyptian column,* supporting some powerful mystery in the over-branching darkness. By day, it is just a tree.

10   It is just a tree. The chipmunks skeeter a little way up it, the little black-and-white birds, tree-creepers, walk quick as mice on its rough perpendicular, tapping: the blue jays* throng in its branches, high up, at dawn, and in the afternoon you hear the faintest rustle of many little wild doves alighting in its upper remoteness. It is a tree, which is still
15   Pan.

And we live beneath it, without noticing. Yet sometimes, when one suddenly looks far up and sees those wild doves there, or when one glances quickly at the inhuman-human hammering of a woodpecker, one realises that the tree is asserting itself as much as I am. It gives
20   out life, as I give out life. Our two lives meet and cross one another, unknowingly: the tree's life penetrates my life, and my life, the tree's. We cannot live near one another, as we do, without affecting one another.

The tree gathers up earth-power from the dark bowels of the earth,
25   and a roaming sky-glitter from above. And all unto itself, which is a tree, woody, enormous, slow but unyielding with life, bristling with acquisitive energy, obscurely radiating some of its great strength.

It vibrates its presence into my soul, and I am with Pan. I think no man could live near a pine-tree and remain quite suave and supple
30   and compliant.* Something fierce and bristling is communicated. The piney sweetness is rousing and defiant, like turpentine, the noise of the needles is keen with aeons of sharpness. In the volleys of wind from the western desert, the tree hisses and resists. It does not lean eastward at all. It resists with a vast force of resistance, from within itself, and its
35   column is a ribbed, magnificent assertion.

I have become conscious of the tree, and of its interpenetration into my life. Long ago, the Indians must have been even more acutely conscious of it, when they blazed it to leave their mark on it.

I am conscious that it helps to change me, vitally. I am even conscious
40   that shivers of energy cross my living plasm, from the tree, and I become

a degree more like unto the tree, more bristling and turpentiney, in Pan. And the tree gets a certain shade and alertness of my life, within itself.

Of course, if I like to cut myself off, and say it is all bunk, a tree is merely so much lumber not yet sawn, then in a great measure I shall *be* cut off. So much depends on one's attitude. One can shut many, many doors of receptivity in one's self: or one can open many doors that are shut.

I prefer to open my doors to the coming of the tree. Its raw earth-power and its raw sky-power, its resinous erectness and resistance, its sharpness of hissing needles and relentlessness of roots, all that goes to the primitive savageness of a pine-tree, goes also to the strength of a man.

Give me of your power, then, oh tree! And I will give you of mine.

And this is what men must have said, more naively, less sophisticatedly, in the days when all was Pan. It is what, in a way, the aboriginal Indians still say, and still *mean*, intensely: especially when they dance the sacred dance, with the tree: or with the spruce twigs tied above their elbows.*

Give me your power, oh tree, to help me in my life. And I will give you my power: even symbolized in a rag torn from my clothing.

This is the oldest Pan.

Or again, I say: "Oh you, you big tree, standing so strong and swallowing juice from the earth's inner body, warmth from the sky, beware of me. Beware of me, because I am strongest. I am going to cut you down and take your life and make you into beams for my house, and into a fire. Prepare to deliver up your life to me."

Is this any less true than when the lumberman glances at a pine-tree, sees if it will cut good lumber, dabs a mark or a number upon it, and goes his way absolutely without further thought or feeling? Is he truer to life? Is it truer to life, to insulate oneself entirely from the influence of the tree's life, and to walk about in an inanimate forest of standing lumber, marketable in St. Louis, Mo?* Or is it truer to life to know, with a pantheistic sensuality, that the tree has its own life, its own assertive existence, its own living relatedness to me: that my life is added to or militated against, by the tree's life.

Which is really truer?

Which is truer, to live among the living, or to run on wheels?

And who can sit with the Indians around a big camp-fire* of logs, in the mountains at night, when a man rises and turns his breast and his

curiously-smiling bronze face away from the blaze, and stands volup-
tuously warming his thighs and buttocks and loins, his back to the fire,
faintly smiling the inscrutable Pan-smile* into the dark trees surrounding, without hearing him say, in the Pan-voice: "Aha! Tree! Aha! Tree!
5   Who has triumphed now? I drank the heat of your blood into my face
and breast, and now I am drinking it into my loins and buttocks and
legs, Oh tree! I am drinking your heat right through me, Oh tree! Fire is
life, and I take your life for mine. I am drinking it up, Oh tree, even into
my buttocks. Aha! Tree! I am warm! I am strong! I am happy, Tree,
10   in this cold night in the mountains!"

And the old man, glancing up and seeing the flames flapping in flamy
rags at the dark smoke, in the upper fire-hurry towards the stars and
the dark spaces between the stars, sits stonily and inscrutable; yet one
knows that he is saying: "Go back, Oh fire! Go back like honey! Go
15   back, honey of life, to where you came from, before you were hidden
in the tree. The trees climb into the sky and steal the honey of the sun,
like bears stealing from a hollow tree-trunk. But when the tree falls and
is put on to the fire, the honey flames and goes straight back to where
it came from. And the smell of burning pine is as the smell of honey."
20   So the old man says, with his lightless Indian eyes. But he is careful
never to utter one word of the mystery. Speech is the death of Pan, who
can but laugh and sound the reed-flute.

Is it better, I ask you, to cross the room and turn on the heat at
the radiator, glancing at the thermometer and saying: "We're just a bit
25   below the level, in here"? Then to go back to the newspaper!

What can a man do with his life but live it? And what does life
consist in, save a vivid relatedness between the man and the living
universe that surrounds him. Yet man insulates himself more and more
into mechanism, and repudiates everything but the machine and the
30   contrivance of which he himself is master, God in the machine.*

Morning comes, and white ash lies in the fire-hollow, and the old
man looks at it broodingly.

"The fire is gone," he says in the Pan silence, that is so full of
unutterable things. "Look! there is no more tree! We drank his warmth,
35   and he is gone. He is way, way off in the sky, his smoke is in the blueness,
with the sweet smell of a pine-wood fire, and his yellow flame is in the
sun. It is morning, with the ashes of night. There is no more tree. Tree
is gone. But perhaps there is fire among the ashes. I shall blow it, and
it will be alive. There is always fire, between the tree that goes and the
40   tree that stays.—One day I shall go—"

So they cook their meat, and rise, and go in silence.

There is a big rock towering up above the trees, a cliff. And silently a man glances at it. You hear him say, without speech:

"Oh you big rock! If a man fall down from you, he dies. Don't let me fall down from you. Oh you big pale rock, you are so still, you know lots of things. You know a lot. Help me then, with your stillness. I go to find deer. Help me find deer."

And the man slips aside, and secretly lays a twig, or a pebble, some little object in a niche of the rock, as a pact between him and the rock. The rock will give him some of its radiant-cold stillness and enduring presence, and he makes a symbolic return, of gratitude.

Is it foolish? Would it have been better to invent a gun, to shoot his game from a great distance, so that he need not approach it with any of that living stealth and preparedness with which one live thing approaches another. Is it better to have a machine in one's hands, and so avoid the life-contact: the trouble! the pains! Is it better to see the rock as a mere nothing, not worth noticing because it has no value, and you can't eat it as you can a deer?

But the old hunter steals on, in the stillness of the eternal Pan, which is so full of soundless sounds. And in his soul he is saying: "Deer! Oh you thin-legged deer! I am coming! Where are you, with your feet like little stones bounding down a hill? I know you. Yes, I know you. But you don't know me. You don't know where I am, and you don't know me, anyhow. But I know you. I am thinking of you. I shall get you. I've got to get you. I got to, so it will be.*—I shall get you, and shoot an arrow right in you."

In this state of abstraction, and subtle, hunter's communion with the quarry—a weird psychic connection between hunter and hunted—the man creeps into the mountains.

And even a white man who is a born hunter, must fall into this state. Gun or no gun! He projects his deepest, most primitive hunter's consciousness abroad, and finds his game, not by accident, nor even chiefly by looking for signs, but primarily, by a psychic attraction, a sort of telepathy: the hunter's telepathy. Then when he finds his quarry, he aims with a pure, spell-bound volition. If there is no flaw in his abstracted huntsman's *will*, he cannot miss. Arrow or bullet, it flies like a movement of pure will, straight to the spot. And the deer, once she has let her quivering alertness be overmastered or stilled by the hunter's subtle, hypnotic, *following* spell, she cannot escape.

This is Pan, the Pan-mystery, the Pan-power. What can men who sit at home in their studies, and drink hot milk and have lambs-wool slippers on their feet, and write anthropology, what *can* they possibly know about men, the men of Pan?

5   Among the creatures of Pan, there is an eternal struggle for life, between lives. Man, defenceless, rapacious man, has needed the qualities of every living thing, at one time or other. The hard, silent abidingness of a rock, the surging resistance of a tree, the still evasion of a puma, the dogged earth-knowledge of the bear, the light alertness of
10   the deer, the sky-prowling vision of the eagle: turn by turn man has needed the power of every living thing. Tree, stone, or hill, river, or little stream, or water-fall, or salmon in the fall—man can be master, and complete in himself, only by assuming the living powers of each of them, as the occasion requires.

15   He used to make himself master by a great effort of will, and sensitive, intuitive cunning, and immense labour of body.

Then he discovered the "idea." He found that all things were related by certain *laws*. The moment man learned to abstract, he began to make engines that would do the work of his body. So, instead of concentrating
20   upon his quarry, or upon the living things which made his universe, he concentrated upon the engines or instruments which should intervene between him and the living universe, and give him mastery.

This was the death of the great Pan. The idea and the engine came between man and all things, like a death. The old connection, the old
25   Allness, was severed, and can never be ideally restored. Great Pan is dead.

Yet what do we live for, except to live? Man has lived to conquer the phenomenal universe. To a great extent, he has succeeded. With all the mechanisms of the human world, man is to a great extent master of all
30   life, and of most phenomena.

And what then? Once you have conquered a thing, you have lost it. Its real relation to you collapses.

A conquered world is no good to man. He sits stupefied with boredom upon his conquest.

35   We need the universe to live again, so that we can live with it. A conquered universe, a dead Pan, leaves us nothing to live with.

You have to abandon the conquest, before Pan will live again. You have to live to live, not to conquer. What's the good of conquering even the North Pole,* if after the conquest you've nothing left but an inert
40   fact? Better leave it a mystery.

It was better to be a hunter in the woods of Pan, than it is to be a clerk in a city store. The hunter hungered, laboured, suffered tortures of fatigue. But at least he lived in a ceaseless living relation to his surrounding universe.

At evening, when the deer was killed, he went home to the tents, and threw down the deer-meat on the swept place before the tent of his women.* And the women came out to greet him softly, with a sort of reverence, as he stood before the meat, the life-stuff. He came back spent, yet full of power, bringing the life-stuff. And the children looked with black eyes at the meat, and at that wonder-being, the man, the bringer of meat.

Perhaps the children of the store-clerk look at their father with a *tiny* bit of the same mystery. And perhaps the clerk feels a fragment of the old glorification, when he hands his wife the paper dollars.

But about the tents the women move silently. Then when the cooking-fire dies low, the man crouches in silence and toasts meat on a stick, while the dogs lurk round like shadows, and the children watch avidly. The man eats as the sun goes down. And as the glitter departs, he says: "Lo, the sun is going, and I stay. All goes, but still I stay. Power of deer-meat is in my belly, power of sun is in my body. I am tired, but it is with power.—There the small moon gives her first sharp sign. So! So! I watch her. I will give her something, she is very sharp and bright, and I do not know her power. Lo! I will give the woman something for this moon, which troubles me above the sunset, and has power. Lo! how very curved and sharp she is! Lo! how she troubles me!"

Thus, always aware, always watchful, subtly poising himself in the world of Pan, among the powers of the living universe, he sustains his life and is sustained. There is no boredom, because *everything is* alive and active, and danger is inherent in all movement. The contact between all things is keen and wary: for wariness is also a sort of reverence, or respect. And nothing, in the world of Pan, may be taken for granted.

So when the fire is extinguished, and the moon sinks, the man says to the woman: Oh woman, be very soft, be very soft and deep towards me, with the deep silence. Oh woman, do not speak and stir and wound me with the sharp horns of yourself. Let me come into the deep, soft places, the dark soft places deep as between the stars. Oh, let me lose there the weariness of the day: let me come in the power of the night.—Oh, do not speak to me, nor break the deep night of my silence and my power. Be softer than dust, and darker than any flower. Oh woman, wonderful is the craft of your softness, the distance of your dark depths. Oh open silently the deep that has no end, and do not turn the horns of the moon* against me—

This is the might of Pan, and the power of Pan.

And still, in America, among the Indians, the oldest Pan is alive. But here also, dying fast.

It is useless to glorify the savage. For he will kill Pan with his own hands, for the sake of a motor-car. And a bored savage, for whom Pan is dead, is the stupefied image of all boredom.

And we cannot return to the primitive life, to live in teepees* and hunt with bows and arrows.

Yet live we must. And once life has been conquered, it is pretty difficult to live. What are we going to do, with a conquered universe?*

The Pan relationship, which the world of man once had with all the world, was better than anything man has now. The savage, today, if you give him the chance, will become more mechanical and unliving than any civilised man. But civilised man, having conquered the universe, may as well leave off bossing it. Because when all is said and done, life itself consists in a live relatedness between man and his universe;—sun, moon, stars, earth, trees, flowers, birds, animals, men, everything—and not in a "conquest" of anything by anything. Even the conquest of the air* makes the world smaller, tighter, and more airless.

And whether we are a store-clerk or a bus-conductor, we can still choose between the living universe of Pan, and the mechanical con-quered universe of modern humanity. The machine has no windows. But even the most mechanised human being has only got his windows nailed up, or bricked in.

SEE MEXICO AFTER, BY LUIS Q.

See Mexico After, by Luis Q.*

My home's in Mexico.
That's where you want to go.
Life's one long *cine* show . . . .*

As a matter of fact I am a hard-worked, lean individual poked in the   5
corner of a would-be important building in Mexico D. F.*
That's that.
I am—married, so this is not a matrimonial ad. But I, as I said,
am lean, pale, hard-worked, with indiscriminate fair hair and, I hope,
nice blue eyes. Anyhow they aren't black. And I am young. And I am   10
Mexican: oh don't doubt it for a second. Mejicano soy. La-la-la-la! I'll
jabber your head off in Spanish. But where is my gun and red sash!*
Ay-de-mi! That's how one sighs in Spanish. I am sighing because
I am Mexican, for who would be a Mexican? Where would he be if
he was one?—I am an official—without doubt important, since every   15
four-farthing sparrow* etc.—And being an important official, I am
always having to receive people. Receive. Deceive. Believe. Rather,
they're not usually people. They're almost always commissions.
   "Please to meet you, Mister," they say. "Not American, are you?"
   I seize my chin in trepidation. "Good God! Am I?" There is a   20
Monroe doctrine,* and there is a continent, or two continents. Am I
American?—by any chance?
   "Pardon me one moment!" I say, with true Mexican courtesy.
   And I dash upstairs to the top floor—the fourth—no elevators—
to my little corner office that looks out over the flat roofs and bubbly   25
church-domes and streaks of wire of Mexico D. F., I rush to the window,
I look out, and ah!—Yes! *Qué tal? Amigo!* How lucky you're there! Say,
boy, will you tell me whether you're American or not? Because if you
are, I am.
   This interesting announcement is addressed to my old friend Popo,   30
who is lounging his heavy shoulders under the sky, smoking a cigarette
end, à la Mexicaine.* Further, since I'm paid to give information, Popo
is the imperturbable volcano, known at length as Popocatepetl,* with

the accent on the tay, so I beg you not to put it on the cat, who is usually loitering in the vicinity of Mexico D. F.

No, I shan't tell you what the D. F. is: or *who* it is. Take it for yourself if you like. I never come pulling the tail of your D. C.—Washington.*

5   Popo gives another puff to his eternal cigarette, and replies, as every Mexican should:

"Quien sabe?"*

"Who knows?—Ask me another, boy!"*

Ca!—as a matter of fact, we don't say *Caramba!* very much. But
10   I'll say it to please. I say it. I tear my hair. I dash downstairs to the Committee, or rather Commission, which is waiting with bated breath (mint) to know whether I'm American or not. I smile ingratiatingly.

"Do pardon me for the interruption, gentlemen. (One of them is usually a lady, but she's best interpreted by *gentlemen*.) You ask me, am
15   I American?—Quien sabe?"

"Then you're *not*."

"Am I not, gentlemen? Ay-de-mi!"

"Ever been in America?"

Good God! Again? Ah, my chin, let me seize thee!
20   Once more I flee upstairs and poke myself out of that window; and say *Oiga! Viejo!*—Oiga! is a very important word.* And I am in the Bureau of Information.

"*Oiga! Viejo!* Are you in America?"

"Quien sabe!" He bumps the other white shoulder at me. Snow!
25   "Oh gentlemen!" I pant. "Quien sabe!"

"Then you haven't."

"But I've been to New York."

"Why didn't you say so!"

"Have I then been to America?"
30   "Hey! Who's running this Information Bureau?"

"I am. Let me run it."

So I dart upstairs again, and address myself to Popo.

"Popo! I have been to America, via New York, and you haven't."

Down I dart, to my Commission. On the way I remember how
35   everything—I mean the loud walls—in New York, said SEE AMER-ICA FIRST.* —Thank God! I say to myself, wiping my wet face before entering to the Commission: On American evidence, I've seen him, her, or it. But whether en todo or en parte, Quién sabe!

I open the door, and I give a supercilious sniff. Such are my American
40   manners.

I am just smelling my Commission.—As usual! I say to myself, snobbishly: *Oil*!

There are all sorts and sizes of commissions, every sort and size and condition of commission.* But oil predominates. Usually, I can smell oil down the telephone.

There are others.—Railway Commissions, Mines Commissions, American Women's Christian Missions, American Bankers' Missions, American Bootleggers Missions,* American Episcopalian, Presbyterian, Mormon, and Jewish Missions, American Tramps Missions——

I, however, in my little office, am Mohammet. If you would like to see Mexico summed up into one unique figure, see me, à la Mohammet, in my little office, saying: Let these mountains come to *me*.*

And they come. They come in whole ranges, in sierras, in Cordilleras. I smell oil, and I see the backbone of America walking up the stair-case (no elevators). I hear the sound of footsteps, and behold the entire Sierra Madre* marching me-wards. Ask me if* leave Mohammet with cold feet! Oh, I am *muy Mejicano*, I am!

I feel I am still SEEING AMERICA FIRST, and they are seeing Mexico after. I feel myself getting starrier and stripeyer* every day, I see such a lot of America first.

But what happens to them, when they see Mexico after?

Quien sabe!

I am always murmuring: You see, Mexico and America are not in the same boat.

I want to add: They're not even floating on the same ocean. I doubt if they're gyrating in the same cosmos.

But superlatives are not well-mannered.

Still, it is hard on a young man like me to be merely Mexican, when my father, merely by moving up the map a little while he was still strong and lusty, might have left me hundred-per-cent-plus American. I'm sure I should have been plus.

It is hard on me, I say. As it is hard on Popo. He might have been Mount Brown or Mount Abraham.* How can any mountain, when you come to think of it, be Popocatepetl?—and *tay*-petl at that!

There there! let me soothe myself.

In fact, I am always a little sorry for the Americans who come seeing Mexico after.—"I am left such a long way behind!" as the burro said when he fell down an abandoned mine.

Still, the Commissioners and missioners often stay quite brisk. They really do wonders. They put up chimneys and they make all sorts of wheels go round. The Mexicans are simply enraptured. But after a while, being nothing but naughty boys and greasers,* they are pining to put their spokes in those wheels. Mischief, I tell you. *Brummm*! go the spokes! And the wheels pause to wonder, while the bits fly. That's fun!

Other gentlemen who are very sharp-eyed, seeing Mexico after, are the political see-ers. America is too hot for them,* as a rule, so they move into cool, cool Mexico. They are some boys, they are! At least, so they tell me. And they belong to weird things that only exist as initials, such I. W. W.'s and A. F. L.'s* and P. J. P.'s.—Give me a job, say these gentlemen, and I'll take the rest.

Why certainly, what could be more accommodating! Whereupon instantly, these gentlemen acquire the gift of Spanish, with an almost Pentecostal suddenness;* they pat you on the shoulder and tell you sulphureous Mexican stories which certainly you would never have heard but for them. Oh hot stuff! Hot dog! They even cry aloud *Perro caliente*!*—and the walls of the city quake.

Moreover they proceed to organise our Labour, after having so firmly insisted that we haven't any. But we produce some, for their sakes. And they proceed to organize it: without music. And in throes of self-esteem they cry: Ah, Mexico's the place. America can't touch it! God bless Mexico!

Whereupon all the Mexicans present burst into tears.

You want no darn Gringoes and gringo capital down here! they say. We cross ourselves rapidly! Absit omen.*

But alas, these thrilling gentlemen always leave us. They return with luggage, having come without, to AMERICA.

Well, adios! eh, boy? Come up there one day. Show you something. Tears, the train moves out.

No, I am Mexican. I might as well be Jonah in the whale's belly,* so perfectly, so mysteriously am I nowhere.

But they come. They come as tourists, for example, looking round the whale's interior.

"My wife's a college graduate," says the he-man.

She looks it. And she may thank her lucky stars—Rudolph Valentino* is the first-magnitude—she will go on looking it all her days.

Ah, the first time she felt Rudolfino's Italianino-Argentino-swoon-between-o kisses! On the screen, of course.—Ah, that first time!

On the back porch, afterwards: Bill, I'm so tired of clean, hygienic kisses.

Poor Bill spits away his still-good, five-cents, mint-covered Wrigley's* chewing-gum gag, and with it, the last straw he had to cling to.

Now, aged thirty-five, and never quite a Valentino, he's brought her to see Mexico after—she'd seen Ramon Novarro's face, with the skin-you-love-to-touch.* On the screen, of course.

Bill has brought her south. She has crossed the border with Bill. Ah, her eyes at the Pullman window!* Where is the skin I would love to touch? they cry. And a dirty Indian pushes his black face and glaring eyes towards her, offering to sell her enchiladas.*

It is no use *my* being sorry for her. Bill is better-looking than I am. So she re-falls in love with Bill, the dark-eyed flour-faced creatures* make such eyes at him, down here. Call them women! Down-trodden things!

The escaped husband is another one. He drinks, swears, looks at all the women meaningly over a red nose, and lives with a prostitute. Hot *dog*!

Then the young lady collecting information! Golly!* Quite nice-looking too. And the things she does! One would think the invisible unicorn that protects virgins* was ramping round her every moment. But it's not that. Not even the toughest bandit, not even Pancho Villa,* could carry off all that information, though she as good as typed out her temptation to him.

Then the home-town aristocrats, of Little Bull, Arizona, or of Old Hat, Illinois.* They are just looking round for something: seeing Mexico after: and very rarely finding it. It really is extraordinary the things there are in Little Bull and in Old Hat, that there aren't in Mexico. Cold slaw,* for example! Why, in Little Bull—!

San Juan Teotihuacán! Hey, boy, why don't you get the parson to sprinkle him with a new tag.* Never stand a name like that for half a day, in Little Bull, Illinois. Or was it Arizona?

Such a pity, to have to see Mexico after you've seen America first: or at least, Little Bull, which is probably more so.

The ends won't meet. America isn't just *a* civilisation, it is CIVILISATION. So what is Mexico? Beside Little Bull, what is Mexico?

Of course Mexico went in for civilisation long, long, long ago. But it got left.

The snake crawled on, leaving his tail behind him.* The snake crawled, lap by lap, all round the globe, till it got back to America. And by that time he was some snake, was civilisation. But where was his tail? He'd forgotten it?

Hey, boy! What's that?

Mexico!

Mexico!—the snake didn't know his own tail. *Mexico!* Garn!* That's nothing. It's mere nothing, but the darn silly emptiness where I'm not. Not yet.

So he opens his mouth, and Mexico, his old tail, shivers.

But before civilisation swallows its own tail, that tail will buzz. For civilisation's a rattler:* anyhow Mexico is.

NEW MEXICO

New Mexico*

Superficially, the world has become small and known. Poor little globe of earth, the tourist trots around you as easily as they trot round the Bois or round Central Park.* There is no mystery left, we've been there, we've seen it, we know all about it. We've done the globe, and the globe   5
is done.

This is quite true, superficially. On the superficies, horizontally, we've been everywhere, and done everything, we know all about it. Yet the more we know, superficially, the less we penetrate, vertically. It's all very well skimming across the surface of the ocean, and saying you   10
know all about the sea. There still remain the terrifying under-deeps, of which we have utterly no experience.

The same is true of land travel. We skim along, we get there, we see it all, we've done it all. And, as a rule, we never once go through the curious film which railroads, ships, motor-cars and hotels stretch over   15
the surface of the whole earth. Pekin is just the same as New York,* with a few different things to look at; rather more Chinese about, etc. Poor creatures that we are, we crave for experience, yet we are like flies that crawl on the pure and transparent mucous-paper in which the world, like a bon-bon, is wrapped so carefully that we can never get at   20
it, though we see it there all the time as we move about it, apparently in contact, yet actually as far removed as if it were the moon.

As a matter of fact, our great-grandfathers, who never went any-where, in actuality had more experience of the world than we have, who have seen everything. When they listened to a lecture with lantern-   25
slides,* they really held their breath before the unknown, as they sat in the village school-room. We, bowling along in a rickshaw in Ceylon, say to ourselves: It's very much what you'd expect: we really know it all.

We are mistaken. The know-it-all state of mind is just the result of   30
being outside the mucous-paper wrapping of civilisation. Underneath is everything we don't know and are afraid of knowing.

I realised this with shattering force when I went to New Mexico. New Mexico, one of the United States, part of the U.S.A. New Mexico, the

175

picturesque reservation and playground of the Eastern States, very
romantic, old Spanish, Red Indian, desert-mesas, pueblos, cow-boys,
penitentes, all that film-stuff.* Very nice, the great Southwest; put on
a sombrero and knot a red kerchief round your neck, to go out in the
great free spaces.

That is New Mexico wrapped in the absolutely hygienic and shiny
mucous-paper of our trite civilisation. That is the New Mexico known
to most of the Americans who know all about it.* But break through
the shiny sterilised wrapping, and actually touch the country, and you
will never be the same again.

I think New Mexico was the greatest experience from the outside
world that I have ever had. It certainly changed me for ever. Curious as
it may sound, it was New Mexico that liberated me from the present era
of civilisation, the great era of material and mechanical development.
Months spent in holy Kandy, in Ceylon, the holy of holies of southern Buddhism,* had not touched the great psyche of materialism and
idealism which dominated me. And years, even, in the exquisite beauty
of Sicily, right among the old Greek paganism* that still lives there,
had not shattered the essential Christianity on which my character was
established. Australia was a sort of dream or trance, like being under a
spell, the self remaining unchanged, so long as the trance did not last
too long. Tahiti, in a mere glimpse, repelled me; and so did California,*
after a stay of a few weeks. There seemed a strange brutality in the spirit
of the western coast, and I felt: Oh, let me get away!

But the moment I saw the brilliant, proud morning shine high up
over the deserts of Santa Fe, something stood still in my soul, and I
started to attend. There was a certain magnificence in the high-up day,
a certain eagle-like royalty, so different from the equally pure, equally
pristine and lovely morning of Australia,* which is so soft, so utterly
pure in its softness, and betrayed by green parrots flying. But in the
lovely morning of Australia one went into a dream. In the magnificent
fierce morning of New Mexico one sprang awake, a new part of the soul
woke up suddenly, and the old world gave way to a new.

There are all kinds of beauty in the world, thank God, though ugliness
is homogeneous. How lovely is Sicily, with Calabria across the sea
like an opal, and Etna with her snow* in a world above and beyond!
How lovely is Tuscany, with little red tulips wild among the corn;*
or bluebells at dusk in England, or mimosa in clouds of pure yellow
among the grey-green dun foliage of Australia,* under a soft, blue,
unbreathed sky! But for a *greatness* of beauty I have never experienced

anything like New Mexico. All those mornings when I went with a hoe
along the ditch to the canyon, at the ranch,* and stood, in the fierce,
proud silence of the Rockies, on their foot-hills, to look far over the
desert to the blue mountains away in Arizona,* blue as chalcedony,
with the sage-brush desert sweeping grey-blue in between, dotted with 5
tiny cube-crystals of houses: the vast amphitheatre of lofty, indomitable
desert, sweeping round to the ponderous Sangre de Cristo Mountains
on the east, and coming up flush at the pine-dotted foot-hills of the
Rockies!* What splendour! Only the tawny eagle could really sail out
into the splendour of it all. Leo Stein* once wrote to me: "It is the 10
most aesthetically-satisfying landscape I know."—To me it was much
more than that. It had a splendid, silent terror, and a vast, far-and-wide
magnificence which made it way beyond mere aesthetic appreciation.
Never is the light more pure and overweening than there, arching with
a royalty almost cruel over the hollow, uptilted world. For it is curious 15
that the land which has produced modern political democracy at its
highest pitch should give one the greatest sense of overweening, terrible
proudness and mercilessness: but so beautiful, God! so beautiful! Those
that have spent morning after morning alone there pitched among
the pines above the great proud world of desert will know, almost 20
unbearably, how beautiful it is, how clear and unquestioned is the
might of the day. Just day itself is tremendous there. It is so easy to
understand that the Aztecs gave hearts of men to the sun.* For the
sun is not merely hot or scorching, not at all. It is of a brilliant and
unchallengeable purity and haughty serenity which would make one 25
sacrifice the heart to it. Ah, yes, in New Mexico the heart is sacrificed
to the sun, and the human being is left stark, heartless, but undauntedly
religious.

And that was the second revelation out there. I had looked over all the
world for something that would strike me as religious. The simple piety 30
of some English people, the semi-pagan mystery of some Catholics in
southern Italy, the intensity of some Bavarian peasants, the semi-ecstasy
of Buddhists or Brahmins:* all this had seemed religious all right, as
far as the parties concerned were involved, but it didn't involve me. I
looked on at their religiousness from the outside. For it is still harder 35
to feel religion at will, than to love at will.*

I had seen what I felt was a hint of wild religion in the so-called
devil dances of a group of naked villagers from the far-remote jungle
in Ceylon, dancing at midnight under the torches, glittering wet with
sweat on their dark bodies as if they had been gilded, at the celebration 40

of the Pera-hera in Kandy, given to the Prince of Wales.* And the utter dark absorption of these naked men, as they danced with their knees wide apart, suddenly affected me with a *sense* of religion, I *felt* religion for a moment. For religion is an experience, an uncontrollable, sensual experience even more so than love: I use sensual to mean an experience deep down in the senses, inexplicable and inscrutable.

But this experience was fleeting, gone in the curious turmoil of the Pera-hera, and I had no permanent feeling of religion till I came to New Mexico and penetrated into the old human race-experience there. It is curious that it should be in America, of all places, that a European should really experience religion, after touching the old Mediterranean and the East. It is curious that one should get a sense of living religion from the Red Indians, having failed to get it from Hindus or Sicilian Catholics or Cinghalese.*

Let me make a reservation. I don't stand up to praise the Red Indian as he reveals himself in contact with white civilisation. From that angle, I am forced to admit he may be thoroughly objectionable. Even my small experience knows it. But also I know he *may* be thoroughly nice, even in his dealings with white men. It's a question of individuals, a good deal, on both sides.

But in this article I don't want to deal with the everyday or superficial aspect of New Mexico, outside the mucous-paper wrapping. I *want* to go beneath the surface. And therefore the American Indian in his behaviour as an American citizen doesn't really concern me. What concerns me is what he is, or what he seems to me to be, in his ancient, ancient race-self and religious self.

For the Red Indian seems to me much older than Greeks or Hindus or any Europeans or even Egyptians. The Red Indian, as a civilised and truly religious man, civilised beyond tabu and totem,* as he is in the south, is religious in perhaps the oldest sense, and deepest, of the word.* That is to say, he is a remnant of the most deeply religious race still living. So it seems to me.

But again let me protect myself. The Indian who sells you baskets on Albuquerque station or who slinks around Taos plaza* may be an utter waster and an indescribably low dog. Personally, he may be even less religious than a New York sneak-thief. He may have broken with his tribe, or his tribe itself may have collapsed finally from its old religious integrity, and ceased, really, to exist. Then he is only fit for rapid absorption into white civilisation, which must make the best of him.

But while a tribe retains its religion and keeps up its religious practices, and while any member of the tribe shares in those practices, then
there is a tribal integrity and a living tradition going back far beyond the
birth of Christ, beyond the pyramids, beyond Moses.* A vast, old religion which once swayed the earth lingers in unbroken practice there in   5
New Mexico, older, perhaps, than anything in the world save Australian
aboriginal* tabu and totem, and that is not yet religion.

You can feel it, the atmosphere of it, around the pueblo. Not, of
course, when the place is crowded with sight-seers and motor-cars.
But go to Taos pueblo* on some brilliant snowy morning, and see the   10
white figures on the roof: or come riding through at dusk on some
windy evening, when the black skirts of the silent women blow around
the white wide boots, and you will feel the old, old root of human
consciousness still reaching down to depths we know nothing of: and of
which, only too often, we are jealous. It seems it will not be long before   15
the pueblos are uprooted.

But never shall I forget watching the dancers, the men with the fox-
skin swaying down from their buttocks, file out at San Geronimo,* and
the women with seed-rattles following. The long, streaming, glistening
black hair of the men. Even in ancient Crete long hair was sacred in a   20
man, as it is still in the Indians. Never shall I forget the utter absorption
of the dance, so quiet, so steadily, timelessly rhythmic, and silent, with
the ceaseless down-tread, always to the earth's centre, the very reverse
of the upflow of Dionysiac or Christian ecstasy.* Never shall I forget the
deep singing of the men at the drum, swelling and sinking, the deepest   25
sound I have heard in all my life, deeper than thunder, deeper than the
sound of the Pacific Ocean, deeper than the roar of a deep waterfall: the
wonderful deep sound of men calling to the unspeakable depths.

Never shall I forget coming into the little pueblo of San Felipe*
one sunny morning in spring, unexpectedly, when bloom was on the   30
trees in the perfect little pueblo more old, more utterly peaceful and
idyllic than anything in Theocritus,* and seeing a little casual dance.
Not impressive as a spectacle, only, to me, profoundly moving, because
of the truly terrifying religious absorption of it.

Never shall I forget the Christmas dances at Taos,* twilight, snow,   35
the darkness coming over the great wintry mountains and the lonely
pueblo, then suddenly, again, like dark calling to dark,* the deep Indian
cluster-singing around the drum, wild and awful, suddenly rousing
on the last dusk as the procession starts. And then the bonfires leaping

suddenly in pure spurts of high flame, columns of sudden flame forming an alley for the procession.

Never shall I forget the khiva of birch-trees, away in the Apache country, in Arizona this time,* the teepees and flickering fires, the neighing of horses unseen under the huge dark night, and the Apaches all abroad, in their silent moccasined feet: and in the khiva, beyond a little fire, the old man reciting, reciting in the unknown Apache speech, in the strange wild Indian voice that re-echoes away back to before the Flood,* reciting apparently the traditions and legends of the tribe, going on and on, while the young men, the *braves* of today, wandered in, listened, and wandered away again, overcome with the power and majesty of that utterly old tribal voice, yet uneasy with their half-adherence to the modern civilisation, the two things in contact. And one of these *braves* shoved his face under my hat, in the night, and stared with his glittering eyes close to mine. He'd have killed me then and there, had he dared. He didn't dare: and I knew it: and he knew it.

Never shall I forget the Indian races,* when the young men, even the boys, run naked, smeared with white earth and stuck with bits of eagle fluff for the swiftness of the heavens, and the old men brush them with eagle feathers, to give them power. And they run in the strange hurling fashion of the primitive world, hurled forward, not making speed deliberately. And the race is not for victory. It is not a contest. There is no competition. It is a great cumulative effort. The tribe this day is adding up its male energy and exerting to the utmost: for what? To get power, to get strength: to come, by sheer cumulative, hurling effort of the bodies of men, into contact with the great cosmic source of vitality which gives strength, power, energy to the men who can grasp it, energy for the year of attainment.

It was a vast old religion, greater than anything we know: more darkly and nakedly religious. There is no God, no conception of a god. All is god. But it is not the pantheism* we are accustomed to, which expresses itself as "God is everywhere, god is in everything." In the oldest religion, everything was alive, not supernaturally but naturally alive. There were only deeper and deeper streams of life, vibrations of life more and more vast. So rocks were alive, but a mountain had a deeper, vaster life than a rock, and it was much harder for a man to bring his spirit, or his energy, into contact with the life of the mountain, and so draw strength from the mountain, as from a great standing well of life, than it was to come into contact with the rock. And he had to put forth a greater religious effort. For the whole life-effort of man was to get his life into direct contact with the elemental life of the cosmos, mountain-life, cloud-life, thunder-life, air-life, earth-life, sun-life. To come into immediate *felt* contact, and so derive energy, power, and a dark sort of joy. This effort into sheer, naked contact, *without an intermediary or mediator*, is the real meaning of religion. And at the sacred races the runners hurled themselves in a terrible cumulative effort, through the air, to come at last into naked contact with the very life of the air, which is the life of the clouds, and so of the rain.

It was a vast and pure religion, without idols or images, even mental ones. It is the oldest religion, a cosmic religion the same for all peoples, not broken up into specific gods or saviours or systems. It is the religion which precedes the god-concept, and is therefore greater and deeper than any god-religion.

And it lingers still, for a little while, in New Mexico: but long enough to have been a revelation to me. And the Indian, however objectionable he may be on occasion, has still some of the strange beauty and pathos of the religion that brought him forth and is now shedding him away into oblivion. When Trinidad,* the Indian boy, and I planted corn at the ranch, my soul paused to see his brown hands softly moving the earth over the maize in pure ritual. He was back in his old religious self, and the ages stood still. Ten minutes later he was making a fool of himself with the horses. Horses were never part of the Indian's religious life, never would be. He hasn't a tithe of the feeling for them that he has for a bear, for example. So horses don't like Indians.

But there it is: the newest democracy ousting the oldest religion! And once the oldest religion is ousted, one feels the democracy and all its paraphernalia will collapse, and the oldest religion, which comes down to us from man's pre-war days, will start again. The sky-scraper will scatter on the winds like thistledown, and the genuine America, the America of New Mexico, will start on its course again. This is an interregnum.

APPENDIX I

JUST BACK FROM THE SNAKE DANCE

SUPPLEMENTARY NOTE ON THE TEXT

Although an early version of 'The Hopi Snake Dance', the text is an independent creation: see Introduction, p. l, Note on the texts and Textual apparatus.

Just Back from the Snake Dance*

One wonders what one went for—what all those people went for. The Hopi country is hideous—a clayey pale-grey desert with death-grey mesas, sticking up like broken pieces of ancient, dry, grey bread. And the hell of a bumpy trail, for forty miles. Yet car after car lurched and bobbled and ducked across the dismalness, on Sunday afternoon.

The Hopi country is some forty miles across, and three stale mesas jut up in its desert. The dance was on the last mesa, and on the furthest brim of the last mesa, in Hotevilla. The various Hopi villages are like broken edges of bread crust, utterly grey and arid, on the top of these mesas: and so you pass them: first Walpi: then unseen Chimopova: then Oraibi, on the last mesa: and beyond Oraibi, on the same mesa, but on a still higher level of grey rag-rock, and away at the western brim, is Hotevilla.

The pueblos of little grey houses are largely in ruin, dry,* raggy bits of disheartening ruin. One wonders what dire necessity or what Cain-like stubbornness drove the Hopis to these dismal grey heights and extremities!* Anyhow once they got there there was evidently no going back. But the pueblos are mostly ruin. And even then, very small.

Hotevilla is a scrap of a place with a plaza no bigger than a fair-sized back yard: and the chief house on the square, a ruin. But into this plaza finally three thousand onlookers piled. A mile from the village was improvised the official camping ground, like a corral with hundreds of black motor cars. Across the death-grey desert, bump and lurch, came strings of more black cars, like a funeral cortège. Till everybody had come—about three thousand bodies.*

And all these bodies piled in the little oblong plaza, on the roofs, in the ruined windows, and thick around on the sandy floor, under the old walls: a great crowd. There were Americans of all sorts, wild west and tame west, American women in pants, an extraordinary assortment of female breeches: and at least two women in skirts, relics of the last era. There were Navajo women in full skirts and velvet bodices:* there were Hopi women in bright shawls: a negress in a low-cut black blouse and a black sailor hat: various half breeds: and all the men to match. The ruined house had two wide square window holes; in the one was posed an apparently naked young lady with a little black hat on. She laid her naked handsome arm like a white anaconda along the sill, and posed as Queen Semiramis seated and waiting.* Behind her, the heads of various Americans to match: perhaps movie people. In the next window hole, a poppy-show of Indian women in coloured shawls and glistening long black fringe above their conventionally demure eyes.—Two windows to the west!

And what had they all come to see?*—come so far, over so weary a way, to camp uncomfortably? To see a little bit of a snake dance in a plaza no bigger than a back-yard? Eight grey-daubed antelope priests— (so-called)—and a dozen black-daubed snake-priests (so-called). No drums, no pageantry. A hollow muttering. And then one* of the snake priests hopping slowly round with the neck of a pale, bird-like snake nipped between his teeth, while six elder priests dusted the six younger, snake-adorned priests with prayer feathers, on the shoulders, hopping behind like a children's game. Like a children's game—Old Roger is dead and is low in his grave!* After a few little rounds, the man set his snake on the sand, and away it steered, towards the massed spectators sitting around. And after it came a snake priest with a snake stick, picked it up with a flourish from the shrinking crowd, and handed it to an antelope priest in the background. The six young men renewed their snake as the eagle his youth*—sometimes the youngest, a boy of fourteen or so, had a rattle snake ornamentally drooping from his teeth, sometimes a racer, a thin whip snake, sometimes a heavier bull-snake, which wrapped its long end round his knee like a garter—till he calmly undid it. More snakes, till the priests at the back had little armfuls, like armfuls of silk stockings that they were going to hang on the line to dry.

When all the snakes had had their little ride in a man's mouth, and had made their little excursion towards the crowd, they were all gathered, like a real lot of wet silk stockings—say forty—or thirty— and let to wriggle all together for a minute in meal, corn-meal, that the women of the pueblo had laid down on the sand of the plaza. Then hey—presto!*—they were snatched up like fallen washing, and the two priests ran away with them westward, down the mesa, to set them free among the rocks, at the snake-shrine (so-called).

And it was over. Navajos began to ride to the sunset, black motor cars began to scuttle with their backs to the light. It was over.

And what had we come to see, all of us? Men with snakes in their mouths, like a circus?* Nice clean snakes, all washed and cold-creamed

by the priests (so-called). Like wet, pale silk stockings. Snakes with
little, naïve, bird-like heads, that bit nobody, but looked more harmless
than doves?* And funny men with blackened faces and whitened jaws,
like a corpse band?

A show? But it was a tiny little show, for all that distance.   5

Just a show! The South west is the great playground of the white
American. The desert isn't good for anything else. But it does make
a fine national playground. And the Indian, with his long hair and his
bits of pottery and blankets and clumsy home-made trinkets, he's a
wonderful live toy to play with. More fun than keeping rabbits, and   10
just as harmless. Wonderful, really, hopping round with a snake in
his mouth. Lots of fun! Oh, the wild west is lots of fun: the Land of
Enchantment.* Like being right inside the circus-ring: lots of sand, and
painted savages jabbering, and snakes and all that. Come on, boys! Lots
of fun!   15

The great South-west, the natural circus-ground. Come on, boys;
we've every bit as much right to it as anybody else. Lots of fun!

As for the hopping Indian with his queer muttering gibberish and
his dangling snake—Why, he sure is cute! He says he's dancing to make
his corn grow. What price irrigation, Jimmy?* He says the snakes are   20
emissaries to his rain god, to tell him to send rain to the corn on the
Hopi Reservation, so the Hopis will have lots of corn meal. What price
a spell of work on the railway, Jimmy? Get all the corn-meal you want
with two dollars a day, anyhow.—

But oh, dry up!* Let every man have his own religion. And if there   25
wasn't any snake dance we couldn't come to see it. Miss lots of fun.
Good old Hopi, he sure is cute with a rattler between his teeth. You
sure should see him, boy.* If you don't, you miss a lot.

APPENDIX II

['*INDIANS AND AN ENGLISHMAN*' *AND* '*CERTAIN AMERICANS AND AN ENGLISHMAN*']: *EARLY FRAGMENT*

SUPPLEMENTARY NOTE ON THE TEXT

Although Luhan's fragment (LT) lacks a title, it corresponds in most substantives to the first six pages (plus a few lines) of the TS Roberts E170.8a, once called 'Pueblos and an Englishman' (see Introduction, pp. xxxiii–xxxvii). The sections 191:2–192:21 and 193:16-195:16 give variants of material that became parts of 'Indians and an Englishman' in the *Dial* (Per1); similarly, 192:22–193:15 is a variant of material that formed part of 'Certain Americans and an Englishman' in the *New York Times Magazine* (Per2). See Note on the texts and Textual apparatus.

[In *Lorenzo in Taos*]

"Supposing one fell on to the moon, and found them talking English; it would be something the same as falling out of the open world plump down here in the middle of America. 'Here' means New Mexico, the South West, wild and woolly and artistic and Indian* and sage-brush desert.

"It is all rather like comic opera played with solemn intensity. All the wildness and woollyness and westernity and motor-cars and art and sage and savage are so mixed up, so incongruous, that it is a farce, and everybody knows it. But they refuse to play it as farce. The wild and woolly section insists on being heavily dramatic, bold and bad on purpose; the art insists on being real American and artistic; motor-cars insist on being thrilled, moved to the marrow; high-brows insist on being ecstatic, Mexicans insist on being Mexicans, squeezing the last black drop of macabre joy out of life, and Indians wind themselves in white cotton sheets like Hamlet's father's ghost, with a lurking smile.

"And here am I, a lone lorn Englishman, tumbled out of the known world of the British Empire on to this stage: for it persists in seeming like a stage to me, and not like the proper world.

"Whatever makes a proper world, I don't know. But surely two elements are necessary: a common purpose and a common sympathy. I can't see any common purpose. The Indians and Mexicans don't even seem very keen on dollars. That full moon of a silver dollar doesn't strike me as overwhelmingly hypnotic out here. As for a common sympathy or understanding, that's beyond imagining. West is wild and woolly and bad on purpose, commerce is a little self-conscious about its own pioneering importance—Pioneers, Oh Pioneers!—high-brow is bent on getting to the bottom of everything and saving the lost soul down there in the depths, Mexican is bent on being Mexican and not yet Gringo, and the Indian is all the things that all the others aren't. And so everybody smirks at everybody else, and says, tacitly: 'Go on. You do your little stunt, and I'll do mine'—and they're like the various troupes in a circus, all performing at once, with nobody for Master of Ceremonies.

"It seems to me, in this country, everything is taken so damn seriously that nothing remains serious. Nothing is so farcical as insistent drama. Everybody is lurkingly conscious of this. Each section or troupe is quite willing to admit that all the other sections are buggoon stunts. But it itself is the real thing, solemnly bad in its badness, good in its goodness, wild in its wildness, woolly in its woollyness, arty in its artiness, deep in its depths, in a word, earnest.

"In such a masquerade of earnestness, a bewildered straggler out of the far-flung British Empire is myself! Don't let me for a moment pretend to *know* anything. I know less than nothing. I simply gasp like a bumpkin in a circus-ring, with the horse-lady leaping over my head, the Apache war-whooping in my ear, the Mexican staggering under crosses and thorns and bumping me as he goes by, the artist whirling colours across my dazzled vision, the high-brows solemnly declaiming at me from all the cross-roads. If, dear, you, being the audience who has paid to come in, feel that you must take up an attitude to me, let it be one of amused pity.

"One has to take sides. First, one must be either pro-Mexican or pro-Indian: then, either art or intellect: then, republican or democrat: and so on. But as for me, poor lost lamb, if I bleat at all in the circus-ring, it will be my own shorn lonely bleat of a lamb who's lost his mother.

"But I arrive at a moment of crisis. I suppose every man always does, here. The crisis is a thing called the Bursum Bill, and it affects the Pueblo Indians. I wouldn't know a thing about it, if I needn't. But Bursum Bursum Bursum!! the Bill! the Bill! the Bill! Twitchell, Twitchell, Twitchell!! O Mr. Secretary Fall, Fall, Fall! Oh Mr. Secretary Fall! you bad man, you good man, you Fall, you Rise, you Fall!!! The joy Survey, Oh Joy. No Joy, Once Joy, now Woe! Woe! Whoa! Whoa Bursum! Whoa Bill! Whoa-a-a!

"Like a Lindsay Boom-Boom bellowing it goes on in my unwonted ears, till I *have* to take heed. And then I solemnly sit down in a chair and read the Bill, the Bill, the Printed Bursum Bill, Section one-two-three-four-five-six-seven, whereas and heretobefore, right to the damned and distant end. Then I start the Insomuch-as of Mr. Francis Wilson's Brief concerning the Bill. Then I read Mr. C's passionate article against, and Mrs. H's hatchet-stroke summary against, and Mr. M's sharp-knife jugglery *for* the bill. After which I feel I'm getting mixed up, and Bear ye one another's Bursum. Then lamb-like, ram-like, I feel I'll do a bit of butting too, on a stage where every known animal butts.

"But first I toddle to a corner and, like a dog when music is going on in the room, put my paws exasperatedly over my ears and my nose to the ground, and groan softly. So doing, I try to hypnotise myself back into my old natural world, outside the circus-tent, where horses don't buck and prance so much, and where not every lady is leaping through the hoop and crashing through the paper confines of the universe at every hand's turn.

"Try to extricate my lamb-like soul into its fleecy isolation, and then adjust myself. Adjust myself to that much-talked-of actor in the Wild West Show, the Red Indian.

"Don't imagine, indulgent reader, that I'm talking *at* you or down to you, or trying to put something over you. No no, imagine me lamb-like and bewildered, muttering softly to myself, between soft groans, trying to make head-or-tail of myself in my present situation. And then you'll get the spirit of these effusions.

"The first Indians I really saw were the Apaches in the Apache Reservation of this state. We drove in a motor-car, across desert and mesa, down canyons and up divides and along arroyos and so forth, two days, till at afternoon our two Indian men ran the car aside from the trail and sat under a pine-tree to comb their long black hair and roll it into the two roll-plaits that hang in front of their shoulders, and put on all their silver and turquoise jewellery and their best blankets: because we were nearly there. On the trail were horsemen passing, and wagons with Ute Indians and Navajos.

"'Da donde viene, Usted?' . . .

"We came at dusk from the high shallows and saw on a low crest the points of Indian tents, the tepees, and smoke, and silhouettes of tethered horses and blanketed figures moving. In the shadow a rider was following a flock of white goats flowed like water. The car ran to the top of the crest, and there was a hollow basin with a lake in the distance, pale in the dying light. And this shallow upland basin dotted with Indian tents, and the fires flickering in front, and crouching blanketed figures, and horsemen crossing the dusk from tent to tent, horsemen in big steeple hats sitting glued on their ponies, and bells tinkling, and dogs yapping, and tilted wagons trailing in on the trail below, and a smell of wood-smoke and of cooking, and wagons coming in from far off, and tents pricking on the ridge of the round *vallum*, and horsemen dipping down and emerging again, and more red sparks of fires glittering, and crouching bundles of women's figures squatting at a fire before a little tent made of boughs, and little girls in full petticoats hovering, and wild, barefoot boys throwing bones at thin-tailed dogs, and tents away in the distance, in the growing dark, on the slopes, and the trail crossing the floor of the hollow, in the low dusk.

"There you had it all, as in the hollow of your hand. And to my heart, born in England and kindled with Fenimore Cooper, it wasn't the wild and woolly west, it was the nomad nations still in the continent of hemlock trees and prairies. The Apaches came and talked to us, in their steeple black hats, and plaits wrapped with beaver fur, and their silver and beads and turquoise. Some talked strong American, and some talked only Spanish; and they had strange lines in their faces.

"The two kivas, the rings of cut aspen trees stuck in the ground like the walls of a big hut of living trees, were on the plain, at either end of the race-track. And as the sun went down, the drums began to beat, the drums with their strong-weak, strong-weak pulse that beat on the plasm of one's tissue. The car slid down to the south kiva. Two elderly men held the drum and danced the pat-pat, pat-pat quick beat on flat feet, like birds that move from the feet only, and sang with wide mouths, Hie! Hie! Hie! Hy-a! Hy-a! Hy-a! Hie! Hie! Hie! Ay-away-away—!! Strange dark faces with wide, shouting mouths and rows of small, close-set teeth, and strange lines on the faces, part ecstasy, part mockery, part humorous, part devilish, and the strange, calling, summoning sound in a wild song-shout, to the thud-thud of the drum. Answer of the same from the other kiva, as of a challenge accepted. And from the gathering darkness around, men drifting slowly in, each carrying an aspen-twig, each joining to cluster close in two rows upon the drum, holding each his aspen twig inwards, their faces all together, mouths all open in the song-shout, and all of them all the time going on the two feet, pát-pat, pát-pat, pát-pat, to the thud-thud of the drum and the strange, plangent yell of the chant, edging inch by inch, pát-pat, pát-pat, pát-pat, sideways in a cluster along the track, towards the distant cluster of the challengers from the other kiva, who were sing-shouting and edging onwards, sideways in the dusk, their faces all together, their leaves all inwards, towards the drum, and their feet going pát-pat, pát-pat, on the dust, with their buttocks stuck out a little, faces all inwards shouting open-mouthed to the drum, and half laughing, half mocking, half devilment, half fun. *Hie! Hie! Hie!—Hie—away—awaya!* The strange yell, song, shout rising so lonely in the dusk, as if pine-trees could suddenly, shaggily sing. Almost a pre-animal sound, full of triumph in life, and devilment against other life, and mockery, and humorousness, and the pát-pat, pát-pat of the rhythm. Sometimes more youths coming up, and as they draw near, laughing, they give the war-whoop, like a turkey giving a startled squeal and then gobble-gobbling with laughter—*Ugh!*— the shriek half laughter, then the gobble-gobble-gobble like a great demoniac chuckle. The chuckle in the war whoop.

"Listening, an acute sadness, and a nostalgia, unbearable, yearning for something, and a sickness of the soul came over me. The gobble-gobble chuckle in the whoop surprised me in my very tissues. Then I got used to it, and could hear in it the humour, the playfulness, and then, beyond that, the mockery and the diabolical, pre-human, pine-tree fun of cutting dusky throats and letting the blood spurt out unconfined. Gobble-agobble-agobble, the unconfined, loose blood, gobble-agobble-agobble, the dead, mutilated lump, gobble-agobble, agobble, the fun, the greatest man-fun.

"So I felt. I may have been all wrong, and other folks may feel much . . . ."

APPENDIX III

PAN IN AMERICA: EARLY VERSION

SUPPLEMENTARY NOTE ON THE TEXT

The text is 'Pan in America' (MS1): see Introduction, pp. xlvii–xlviii. The following symbols are used:

< > = Deletion by DHL in manuscript
{}   = Revision by DHL in manuscript

Pan in America

At the beginning of the Christian era, voices were heard off the coast of Greece, a little way out to sea, on the Mediterranean, wailing: *Pan is dead! Great Pan is dead!*

And dead he was, for Europe. He must have been failing, for a long 5 time. As father of fauns and satyrs, nymphs and dryads he was already an old man, with grey in his goatee beard. Pan, the great Pan, grown elderly.

As a matter of fact, down the long lanes and the overgrown ridings of history, it is hard to catch a glimpse of him whom we should call the 10 Great God Pan. The father of fauns and nymphs, Pan of the goat hoofs, is <lordling> {boss} of a side-show only, even in the days of Homer. Hermes and Aphrodite* are the smooth-skinned, bright-faced gods. Pan is a half-animal, half-demon gentleman, who easily becomes <the Satan> {Old Nick} of the Christians, the lewd old father of the 15 lower half in man.

The Great God Pan! Where is he? Not this lewd old father of the lower half of man.

Look further into the thickets. As unrevealed lord of the mysteries of nature he is still in some disgrace, an outlaw, even at the very beginning 20 of our history. The Great God Pan! As far as we can see, he was never actually great, even in his exile. Dethroned, potent as an outlaw, to be feared, and then to be derided. Therein lies his greatness, apparently. And then, with the old world <being> Christianised, he is dead. *Great Pan is dead.* 25

We revived him later, and in our own day he has had some vogue. The goat-legged, elderly, lewd gentleman with a gleam of hate in his eyes, reappearing in our rapidly-thinning thickets, by night, and exerting a considerable sway over a half-demoralised populace. *The great god Pan!* Where is the Allness and the Greatness, however? This goat-eyed 30 luster is not All, is he? And he scarcely seems great.

In modern poetry, we have to take him on trust. < In actuality,> {Actually,} we know he stands, in modern life, for a rather elderly lewdness.

The Great God Pan!

<But> A hundred years ago, or thereabouts, the name of Pan was {significantly} heard on men's lips, as it will always be heard, from time to time, as long as men last, and always meaning a different thing.

5   William Wordsworth, we say, was a pantheist. Pantheism! Pantheism was, <almost> {and is,} a religion in itself. And if ever America had any *original* religion of her own—we speak of the Anglo-Saxon America*—it was this same pantheism. Emerson, Thoreau,* Whitman, they are the great American pantheists. Call it Transcendentalism if you

10 like, <but> it is an attempt at an ideal pantheism. The Allness, the Everything, from which Whitman makes the Song of Myself. The Oversoul,* which pervades everything.

I think, in the Emersonian *Oversoul*, in Whitman's *All Things*, in Wordsworth's *Nature*,* we approach, from the far side, a glimpse of the

15 real Great God Pan, who ruled before Zeus or Ra.* But it is a ghost we see, a resurrection in the spirit, and the flesh "redeemed."

Even Whitman was a redeemer. He redeemed the flesh and its functions into pure consciousness, into spirituality.

The modern pantheism—and it is the religion of all our really great

20 moderns—is essentially redemptive. Everything is God and God is everything. Very good! But it is a stupendous and dangerous cliche. From it, we begin to rationalise, and then God help us.

This one phrase, *Everything is God*, is the inspiration of practically all modern thought and feeling. *All is God*—and hence *All is Good*.

25 Pantheism!

But analyse it, and you will see that this rationalised monotheism,* or pantheism, is still dualistic. Monotheism is bound to be pantheistic, the moment you think about it. And pantheism is really a dilemma, with its *Everything is God,* and the rational corollary, *Everything is Good*.

30 Because Everything is *not* good, no matter how we may rationalise. It is *not* good to kiss the leper, or embrace the syphilitic prostitute,* or commit crimes: no matter how we rationalise.

Hence the inevitable dualism of our sort of pantheism. Emerson was the wisest, when he lifted up the Oversoul out of everything, and

35 above everything. Everything is now God, because it is permeated by the Oversoul, the Universal Spirit. In fact, it is the Universal Spirit *in* everything that makes everything God, and Good.

But you have the fatal dualism of the thing itself, and the spirit that is in it. The old Matter and Spirit dilemma.* Spirit is all good, or God,

40 and Matter is just negative, not-God.

Whitman's attempt to break down this quite sound dualism was only an attempt, in the end, further to spiritualise Matter, by making it a term of consciousness. Sex, or a prostitute, once they are reduced to complete mental consciousness, are no longer impure.

But the point is, that Sex and prostitutes, as ideas, or entities of the ideal consciousness, are still not the same as our actual sex that does things to us, or the actual prostitute with her fee. You have rationalised, but it hasn't helped you really.

And here we have to give up our modern religion, the modern or ideal pantheism which is at the back of every {positive} idea and every {profound} emotion today. Monotheism lands us into pantheism, and pantheism leaves us in hopeless dilemma. Which is where we are.

But our own modern Pan, our modern Great God Pan, the great Spirit which lurks in Everything and permeates everywhere, might help us, if we are capable of a great revulsion, to look far, far down the vistas of the ancient forest of history, and catch some glimpse of the <ancient Great God> {primeval Pan}. Before the gentleman with the brown face and horns and goat legs was visualised, before the hosts of nymphs and dryads, fauns and satyrs were discriminated among the flowers and fruit, <an older,> {a greater,} darker, more mysterious presence. The Pan who was Everything, and a very great god, among the most ancient of trees. When trees were trees, and spoke aloud, without needing any dryad to voice them. When waters in themselves went running and intending, and no nymph could rise out of them, to leave them spiritless.

Because after all, this faun and nymph business was the first step in the Spirit and Matter split. The nymphless spring of water was matter spiritless.

The great Pan was not even a god. He was not even *he*. Only Pan, All.

And that, even that was an abstraction.

In the oldest of days, the day of Pan, of All, there was no God or gods.* Go back beyond the Greeks with their passion for intellectualisation, and back beyond the image-makers and idol-worshippers, who felt their ideas clumsily in stone,* and you come, as one travelling deeper and deeper into an unbroken, living forest, to the old world of Pan, of All.

And here, in the shadow of huge trees, there is no god and not-god, there are no gods and anti-gods. There is no Spirit, there is no Matter. There is only Pan.

Not even the Great God Pan. How can you have a Great God All? Just Pan, which is <first> the exclamation of the infant human spirit, when it is born as spirit, or abstract consciousness. Just as a child out of the womb says Ma-ma-ma! or Da-da! In the womb it said nothing. So the human mind, in the womb of Pan, said nought, and Pan was not conceived. Just as, to the unborn child, the mother is not conceived, and no sound of Ma-ma! is uttered.

When the mind of man first emerged from the womb of Pan, like an infant it spoke a primary syllable, *Pan!*—or *Ra!* The first syllable of the born mind.

But before the mind was born into separateness, with a power of creating its own abstract reality, its own spiritual world, or imaginary world, or ideal world, before the First Word, or Logos* was uttered, then mankind lived in the world of the unconceived, unspoken Pan. Man himself *was* Pan, along with all the rest.

Then the tree grew up as a thing in itself, a strong-willed powerful thing reaching up and reaching down. With a powerful will of its own it thrust green hands and huge limbs at the light above, at the sun, and sent huge legs and gripping toes down, down between the earth and rocks, to the earth's middle. And man, his little, naked, vulnerable lordship, sheltered under the leaves, ate the fruit, and said: Tree, oh Tree, you strong one doing your own deed, be my friend, and I will be yours. Bring me up strength, power, from the dark vitals of the ground, that I cannot get to. Bring it me up, and give it to me, when I sit down beneath you. Bring it me up, and let it enter me through my hams and haunches, as I sit under your body. And I will bring you triumphs. I will give you the thrill of my power, the trophies of my strength.—And oh, Tree, reach me down the glitter of the sky, the sparkling power of the sun, pass them on to me, down your trunk. Be my friend and do this for me, so I can have sun-power in my breast and hands, earth-power in my feet and belly, and my back may be strong as the trunk of a tree! Oh Tree! And I will give you my wandering power, and tell you the things I see, for I can walk and see and hunt in distant places. And I will bring you things back, Oh Tree!

Then, in those days, when the world was still Pan, one man would find, perhaps, one particular tree that was his friend and his giver. Or perhaps a whole tribe would find one tree—or one grove of trees.

And to other trees they would say: Oh you, you trees, standing so strong and swallowing warmth from the sun, juice from the earth's inner body, beware of me! Beware of me, for I am the strongest. I am coming to cut you down and make fire of you.

And as the fire burned, the men of Pan would say, sitting before the blaze with their breasts, or turning their backs and buttocks to the warmth: "Aha! Tree! I have conquered you! I have you, Tree! I am drinking the heat of your blood into my breast, into my loins and buttocks, Oh Tree! I am drinking it up. I am warm, I am strong, I am happy with strength, laughing with the cup of your strength, Tree, on this cold night of the hills."

And looking up, seeing the flames flapping in flamy rags, upwards to the stars, and the faint dark smoke hurrying in haste towards the dark spaces between the stars, he would say, spreading his hands in expansive gratification: "Aha! Look at the sun-stuff going back to the stars, which are like solitary bees from the sun's hive, and the flames go up to them like their own honey! And see the smoke making haste to the dark blue sky, to fill it in, lest it should get empty, and the scent of pine going up in the night, to lie in the sky till the trees fetch it down again, as a bear fetches honey from a comb in a hollow trunk!"*

And in the morning, seeing the white ash in the fire-hollow, he would say broodily to himself: "Look, there is no more tree! The tree has gone away. I have drunk the warmth of his blood, and his yellow blood has all gone back into the sky, to the stars, and the stars will fly back, like bees, to the sun with it. His dark smoke and leaves have gone into the spaces of the sky, that is blue and dark with the sweet breath of <dead> {burnt} trees and burnt things. And his white bone-ash lies here, to go down into the ground again. The ground will suck it in, so that the ground never get no smaller, no weaker. This is strong food for the ground, like meat to a man is ash to the ground that eats it up.—No, there is no more tree. Tree is gone. But I am a strong man this morning, to talk to that stone that is keeping so still. It keeps so still, it knows something. I am going to ask it to tell me, how I find the deer."

To the great pale rock he goes, and silently contemplates it, in silence communing with it. "You big rock, you be my friend. I give you lots of things. I bring things down to you, like I bring a big tree down. You big pale rock, you tell me now where I find deer. You tell me which way I go!"

And in a state of communion, a certain throb will enter him, and he will take a direction. And then a new communion will begin. "Deer, oh you thin-legged deer, where are you, with your feet like little stones bounding down a hill! I know where you are, so don't you forget it. I

know where you are, and I'm coming after you. I've got to get one of
you. You see! No matter what you do, you've got to come against my
arrows this day, you know it. You got to fall down with my arrows in
you. No good running. I am coming, you got to die from me. I got to
kill you, you got to die. I am thinking of you, you deer. I know you,
and I am thinking of you. And when I am thinking of you hard, very
hard, no good you trying to get away, you got to be caught, you got to
be shot. I am telling you—"

In this state of concentration, intense *sensual* abstraction, the hunter
goes on, mile after mile, seeing only hunt-signs, on and on, his whole
sensual self summed up in one intense, concentrated spell, casting the
spell over the deer he is tracking down. And according as his power
of concentration and of projecting his will, his desire, his hunt-passion
over his quarry is greater or less, so is he a better or a feebler hunter.
A great hunter can so concentrate that he <trails> {tracks} the deer
almost infallibly, has the creature under his spell from the first sign of
its existence, or even before that. And when he aims, he aims with pure,
spell-bound volition. And unless something has failed in his will, in his
spirit, he can hardly miss. The arrow flies like a live thing, intent to one
spot. And the deer, using all her cunning, cannot evade it, unless her
quivering wariness can escape from the sort of <mesmerism> {power}
the hunter casts over her.

It is a contest in being. And man, powerful, defenceless, unprovided
man, needs the qualities of every living thing, at one time or another.
The peculiar silent clairvoyance of the puma,* the bead-eyed resentful
earth-knowledge of the bear, the terrible, hot-throated blood-lust of the
wolf, the sensitiveness of the deer, the all-seeingness, all-knowingness
of the eagle: turn by turn he needs the power of every living thing. Nay,
of every existing thing, tree, or stone, or hill, or little river, or water-fall,
or salmon in the water. He can be master only by assuming the *being*
of each thing, one after another. Only by acquiring the *power* of the
deer, the eagle, the mountain-lion, the stream of water, the pine-tree,
the sun, and the middle earth, can he live, and keep himself alive, and
be himself, and be a man.

Then at last, at evening one day, he goes back to the camp place,
where the few families are. And he throws the deer-meat down on a
clean place before the tents, and the women come out and greet him
softly, with a sort of reverence, as he <comes home bringing> {stands
before} the meat, the life-stuff, coming back full of power. And the

little children look with big black eyes at the meat, and at the hero, the bringer of meat, and feel humble and proud because of his power.

And they light fires and toast meat, and eat, and the dogs lurk round like shadows. Then the man sits by the low cooking fire as the sun sets, and watching the sinking sun as he eats his meat, he says: "Lo, the sun is going, and I am staying. All goes, and I stay. I have the power of deer-meat in my belly, and the power of the sun in my arms, as he goes and I stay. Now the small moon is coming forward. I must watch her carefully, she may be my enemy, and hurt me in the night. I must be aware of her, I must go forward to her to where she shines, to speak to her, because she is white and powerful, and she may be my friend too, during the night, lest anything befall me while I sleep."

Always aware, always watchful, subtly poising himself amid the many presences, in the world of Pan.

And to the woman he says: Oh woman, be very soft, be very soft and deep with soft silence. Oh woman, you are dark like the dark places between the stars, your eyes and hair are dark and your flesh is soft and there is no end to its soft depth. Oh woman, with your dark soft spirit, draw me into the deeps of the dark places between the stars, draw me deep, deep into the dark soft places, that I may travel very far in the sightless direction, go very far in your darkness and softness, and gather much unseen power in the places that are softer than dust, and darker than any flower. Oh woman, the craft of your softness, the distance of your dark depths, open silently, flower of night, let there be no hardness and no knot in you, oh flower that is so deep it has no end, oh space between the stars.*

Then in the morning he says: That woman gave me a great deal of power. The depth of that woman is so deep, it goes behind the sun. And the way is open to me, in her. I must bring her back meat, and the power of the world.*

APPENDIX IV

[*'SEE MEXICO AFTER, BY LUIS Q.'*]:
EARLY FRAGMENTS

SUPPLEMENTARY NOTE ON THE TEXT

Texts are 'By Luis Q.' (MS1) and 'See Mexico After / by Luis Q.' (MS2): see Introduction, pp. lvii–lviii, lxxix–lxxx. The letters A–G are editorial conveniences, not by DHL. The following symbols are used:

... = Discontinuous text due to erasures by DHL
[ ] = Uncertain word

I
By Luis Q.*

(A) SEE AMERICA FIRST . . . of Popo* smoking . . . the [stump] of a cigarette. Hé, Viejo . . . American.

(B) . . . see it first—and then I see it again . . . gentle reader, so that I am always seeing it first in all its gentleness. And ah, how happy I [should] be if I knew . . . reader, I was SEEING AMERICA FIRST.

(C) So I am a Mexican, all for my father's fault, and whether or not I see . . . myself as an American first or a fowl from the coasts of the ichthyopophagi* who is to tell?

Who is an American? . . . Or am I one? . . . You are so American.

(D) I have to put all my powers . . . for fear of lapsus-linguaes, or lapsi linguarum.* Because you see, I am never quite sure of myself. I ask myself, in self-[conscious] spirit: Am I American First?—Because you see, I am Mexican, and there are slips between cups and lips.* Nasty ones. I daren't quaff too hastily from the cup in which the stars are floating like bits of . . .

(E) Oh dear reader . . . pardon me, gentle reader . . . States. We are the United State[s] . . . we call the United States of the North, you call *yourselves* the United States of *America*.

(F) Gentlemen, you smell of oil . . . [Are] you a continent, or are you [merely] a commission?

(G) Then there's the husband and wife . . . *My wife's a college graduate.* She looks it. She can thank her lucky stars—Rudolph Valentino is the chief of them—that she'll go on looking it to her dying day. Ah, the first time she felt the kisses of Rudolfino—Italianino-Argentino!—on the screen of course. Ah, that first time! And on the porch afterwards: Bill, I'm so tired of hygienic kisses. Poor Bill spit out his still-good five-cents mint-coated chewing gum. And with it his last . . . still secretly pining for unhygienic kisses—and after she [saw] Ramon Navarro's face, with the . . .

II
See America After
by Luis Q.

What is America?
Where is America?
Why is America?
SEE AMERICA FIRST.
There was I, a tender and impressionable youth, innocently sent to America—Oh! not very long ago!—by an old but still tender and impressionable father, to learn what's what, and the first commandment that roared at me from every Sinai of a bill-board, was SEE AMERICA FIRST.*
Why should I see it?
How can I help seeing it?
Where is it, what is it, why is it?
On revient toujours a son premier amour.*
Let me confess, I am a Mexican. The worst of Mexicans is, they ought to be swarthy, with a red sash. Whereas I am an ordinary fairish young man in an American suit. I apologise, I really do.
The worst of America is, one never knows where it is. I used to think old Popo—I mean "our" Mexican volcano; at length, Popocatapetl—was perched like an old cock with a white tail on top of the American continent. Apparently he's not. When I asked an American if Popo was in America, he said quite nicely "Why no. He's not."

APPENDIX V

MESOAMERICAN AND SOUTHWESTERN AMERICAN MYTH

MESOAMERICAN AND SOUTHWESTERN
AMERICAN MYTH

1 Overview

No worldview is more prevalent in Mesoamerican and Southwestern Indian mythology than that of successive worlds – the five 'Suns' or epochs of the Aztecs and Maya, the four of the Hopis and New Mexico Pueblos, and the four (or more) of other American Indians in the Pueblo circle of influence. These cosmogonies posited the development of life through several attempts by a god or gods to create humans and animals in a changing habitat that alternately nurtured and destroyed. Lawrence suggests a global similarity in some of the views of these widely diverse peoples – he associates it with animism – and it is possible to see this myth in such terms, as an elaboration of interrelationships among all natural things. This is particularly true since the prior worlds were often said to be underground and the emergence of human life was considered analogous to that of a plant (in a Mayan myth, the true human was fashioned of maize) or to a series of metamorphoses through various animal forms – almost like links in a rudimentary scheme of what we call 'evolution'. Yet their worlds were said to be discontinuous, closed off from each other by cyclic cataclysms.

To Mesoamericans, the universe was intricately layered in space and time. Both Aztecs and Maya believed it to have thirteen heavens and nine underworlds as well as four pre-worlds. The universe was visualised as a quaternity, based on the four cardinal directions, four winds and four colours – plus the nadir and zenith with their own winds and emblems. Most Southwestern Indians subscribe to similar four-fold geocosmic patterns.

In this volume, Lawrence mentions the Teotihuacános, Maya, Zapotecs and Aztecs of Mexico; the ancient Peruvians (eventually Incas) of South America; and the eastern Pueblos (especially the Taos), Hopis, Navajos, Apaches and Utes. (In addition, he refers to the Kiowas, though not by name, in 'Pan in America'.) The rituals of all these peoples possessed dual focus on this world and the next. Their religions have been called cults of the rain gods because, dwelling in challenging landscapes, they petitioned the ultimate powers for rain and good crops. Another great theme was the interplay of life and death and the paradox of death and rebirth, often represented by twin gods or demi-gods (one in this world and one in the afterworld). In Mexico, great ball-courts symbolised deadly cosmic games between mortals and gods. In the Southwest, racetracks allowed human athletes to challenge, and participate with, the gods in their efforts to keep the universe on course, forestalling chaos.

Lawrence knew Teotihuacán to be influential upon the Aztecs ('Au Revoir, U. S. A.'), and his use of Aztec material is known, primarily in *The Plumed Serpent* (see Clark's Introduction and his Appendixes I–III). Lawrence knew less about the Maya but learned aspects of their creation tales through cognate Aztec myths. The ancient

213

Zapotec culture he knew chiefly through its monumental architecture, which he saw for himself while living in Oaxaca. But the supernatural Seven Macaw or Great Parrot of the Maya (as in the *Popul vuh* in Quiché Mayan) and the elaborate bird gods of the Zapotecs – richly illustrated in graphic arts of Oaxaca – seem to find an echo in the first essay of his *Mornings in Mexico* ('Corasmin and the Parrots').

2 Ancient Mexico and Peru

(A) Teotihuacán

Human gathering in Mexico goes back more than ten millennia – and far longer if new finds and DNA dating are the criteria. Lawrence does not mention the Olmec culture (from 1200 BC), whose antiquity was not recognised in his day; but it left its imprint on later civilisations both in Mexico and in Central America. Among great archaeological excavations of Lawrence's time were those in the Valley of Mexico, at Teotihuacán, near Mexico City, in 1917–22, and those in southernmost Mexico – Mayan Chiapas and the Yucatan Peninsula – in 1923. By the 1920s, too, Peruvian Cuzco and Macchu Picchu had been excavated for a decade (1911–16) and were already on the tongues of readers and some tourists. Lawrence could have learned that the classic Maya pyramids overlapped in time with the Zapotec florescence, the decline of Teotihuacán ('place of the gods' to the later settlers) and the rise of the Toltecs. New leaders had emerged after AD 900, the Toltec culture adopting and building upon the Teotihuacán, and the Mixtec grafting itself onto the Zapotec. Around the same time, the Mayan civilisation experienced a new phase of growth, influenced by the Toltecs, who exported the culture hero Quetzalcoatl (the 'feathered serpent') to Yucatan (as Kukulcan) and Guatemala (as Gukumatz).

(B) Mayan

In Mayan myth, successive attempts at human life had failed; and the four separate 'worlds', consecutively destroyed, could be defined by their end products of fish, birds, monkeys and other mammals. The maize essence of the authentic humans in the fifth (present) world underlined the significance of the agricultural lifestyle that nurtured the great indigenous American civilisations. Mayan animism channelled itself through a vast sacred hierarchy with flamboyant gods of sun and moon, reptile and bird, plant and animal, human and superhuman.

(C) Zapotec and Mixtec

The Zapotecs told two myths about their own creation – that they had come up into this world through a series of lower underground worlds and, alternatively, that they had been transfigured into humans from trees and animals. Aside from the creator (who could not be described), their most prominent deity was a rain god Cocijo ('lightning'), emblematised by a sky-serpent and an earth-jaguar (perhaps a survival of the Olmecs' favourite jaguar emblem); other Zapotec immortals included a sun god, a serpent god and bird gods.

Although the Zapotecs called themselves *Be'ena'a* ('the people'), they also became known as the 'Cloud People' (Mixtec *Nusabi*) because of a legend that they were spirits, ancient progenitors. Both the Zapotec and the Mixtec languages are part of the Otomanguean language family, each with a wide range of dialects that can be inaccessible to one another (see 'Walk to Huayapa' and 'The Mozo').

The Mixtecs – who appropriated the Zapotec monuments at Monte Albán and Mitla by 1200 (see Appendix VI:1) – also had multiple nature gods, deifying the sun (Taandoco), for example, and the corn plant. Their myths assigned their own creation to a god couple who had turned two tall trees into the first man and woman.

After the Aztecs overwhelmed their neighbouring tribes in the fifteenth century, Zapotecs and Mixtecs initially faced them together as a common enemy but they eventually differed in their approaches. Lawrence was historically correct to assert (in 'The Mozo') that the Aztec emperor, Montezuma (Montezuma II), had taken Oaxacan prisoners for sacrifice – both Zapotecs and Mixtecs, whose common villagers provided human 'tribute'.

After the Spanish Conquest, Zapotecs were decimated by diseases and conflict but were resurgent in the twentieth century, joining as Serranos in some of the historic events of state. Although they took some part in the War for Mexican Independence from Spain in 1810, Zapotecs were particularly prominent in later revolutionary activities, from Mexico's great first constitutional President Benito Juárez in the nineteenth century (hero of the Wars of Reform in the 1850s) to the Serrano generals (in the Mexican Revolution of 1910) who unseated Oaxaca's governor (Vigil) in Lawrence's time and became his successors (see notes on 'Walk to Huayapa'). It was one of these governors whom Lawrence met. Porfirio Díaz himself, the long-time Mexican president who was ejected by the revolution, was Oaxacan – and partly Mixtec – and he had fought along with Juárez in 1862 against the French Maximilian.

(D) Peruvian

Lawrence's reference to early Peruvians ('The Hopi Snake Dance'), though it is brief, greatly expands his overview of Indian civilisation into South America. It evokes the Inca Empire, which rose later than the Aztec but had only a century of dominance before the Spanish conquistador Francisco Pizzaro (*c.* 1471–1541) subdued it. Peru had already seen thousands of years of social growth, including its alliance with the pan-Andean Tiahuanacan Empire, on Lake Titicaca, in today's Bolivia (fl. AD 600–800) before the Incas became dominant at their sacred centre, Cuzco. Remarkably, despite significant geographic barriers (like the Andes), Inca legend had some affinities with Mexican in that it assumed successive creations and recognised bird, serpent and jaguar gods. And everywhere, *apus* ('spirit') and *huaca* or *waka* ('sacred things') were represented by a wide range of natural and supernatural phenomena.

3 Aztec

The Aztecs migrated from the Far North, through Canada and the Southwest, into the Valley of Mexico around AD 1200. They spoke Nahuatl – in the same Uto-Aztecan family as Hopi and the Aztec-Tanoan linguistic stock of many other Pueblo Indians. In their legends, the Aztecs told of their emergence through several underground caves into their original settlement in Aztlán ('place of the heron' or 'place of whiteness'), an idyllic homeland which has been located variously in northern Mexico, on an island off the Mexican coast, and even on the Colorado Plateau north of the present Hopi and Navajo Reservations of Arizona. In legend, the Aztec trek into central Mexico was led by the fierce war god Huitzilopochtli, and it was he who prophesied that the group would found their great civilisation (Tenochtitlan, now Mexico City) on the spot where an eagle stood on a prickly-pear cactus with a serpent in its beak. This image of bird and snake became the emblem of Mexico (as in 'Au Revoir, U. S. A.'), appearing even on the national flag. Illustrated codexes revealed a further significance in the fruit of this cactus, which represented a heart as the desired food of the gods; and one myth told how the cactus grew from the particular heart of one of Huitzilopochtli's victims. Even before arriving at their goal, the Aztecs had grown acquainted with Toltec culture in Tula. Reaching their foretold destination, they discovered Teotihuacán itself, though long abandoned, and sought to assimilate its imagery and power to their own expansion.

In the Aztec version of successive 'Suns' (see 'Corasmin and the Parrots'), the creator Ometeotl – 'Lord and Lady of Sustenance' – reigned with four sons, all called Tezcatlipoca (white, black, blue and red, respectively), associated in most versions with the cardinal directions – and one of them often identified with Huitzilopochtli. When the four resolved themselves into a duality between Tezcatlipoca ('smoking mirror') – a god of sheer chaotic power – and Quetzalcoatl ('plumed serpent') – a more humanistic god and yet a great sky-dragon – the two alternated as the immediate makers of the subsequent epochs. First Tezcatlipoca produced the dark, earthy 'Sun' of the jaguar – possibly recalling the Olmec deity – and the giants of that age were destroyed by fierce beasts. Then Quetzalcoatl made a new 'Sun' of wind, whose pre-human forms were destroyed by hurricanes, leaving monkeys behind (see word-play on monkeys in 'The Mozo'). Tezcatlipoca rose again to turn the rain god Tlaloc ('sprouting earth') into the third 'Sun'; but Quetzalcoatl rained fire upon it, and the inhabitants metamorphosed into birds. The fourth 'Sun', instituted again by Quetzalcoatl, was physically composed of the water goddess Chalchiuhtlicue ('lady of the jade skirt') and ended in massive floods that transformed survivors into fish. At last, the fifth world had to be made, so the gods gathered at Teotihuacán and sacrificed themselves in a great blaze, thus transforming themselves into the present 'Sun' and all the heavenly bodies.

Only Quetzalcoatl (the Morning Star) could visit the underworld through his twin Xolotl (the Evening Star) and yet return, so he went into the nether regions to secure ancient bones from which to form the human race. He revitalised the bones with his own blood, and the Mother Goddess mixed them in a bowl of creation, forming people for the fifth 'Sun' (the present world). But this fifth age, too, would end in earthquake at some future time (as suggested at the end of 'Corasmin and the Parrots').

To extend the epoch and postpone this doom, the inhabitants must compensate the gods for their trouble – and must keep them at their posts in the sky – by sacrifices of their own. This covenant of exchange was central to the Aztec religion, which greatly increased the demand for human sacrifice that had already been a part of earlier cultures. The Aztecs' own tribal deity, Huitzilopochtli, was especially demanding of such tribute, but so was his mother Coatlicue the earth goddess, and so, even, was the god Quetzalcoatl (see 'Au Revoir, U. S. A.').

As a culture hero, Quetzalcoatl (it was said) had supplied the people with maize, taught them arts and ceremonies to go with a sedentary life, and made a calendar to facilitate recurring rituals. The god was further humanised when combined in communal memory with a king who was his namesake: that Quetzalcoatl's enlightened reign among the Toltecs of Tula fostered peace and artistic invention, forbidding human sacrifice. When he grew old and departed in self-immolation, the god was expected to return cyclically, perhaps as a fair-haired immortal.

The Aztec earth goddess (see 'The Mozo') went by many names and often displayed serpent features – e.g. Coatlicue ('lady of the serpent skirts') and Cihuacoatl ('serpent woman'). She was also Tonantzin and Toci ('our mother' and 'our grandmother'). These goddesses were frequently interchangeable with one another and with Tlazolteotl ('devourer of filth' and, as a confessor, 'devourer of sin'), goddess of love and sex and mother of the maize god, Cinteotl. Among other earth goddesses were Xochiquetzal ('quetzal flower'), associated with birds and flowers and yet a queen of the dead, and Itzpapalotl ('obsidian butterfly'), who was identified with flowers and maize and yet had a name that recalled the obsidian knife of sacrifice. Moon goddesses, like Huitzilopochtli's sister Coyolxauhqui ('golden bells'), were typically surrounded by skulls in pictographs.

The goddess who gave birth to a stone knife ('The Mozo') was the mother goddess, sometimes called Tonacaciuatl ('lady of sustenance', an aspect of Ometeotl). Her knife/son was sky-born among the gods but was cast to earth – where it/he shattered into a thousand gods. Tezcatlipoca himself was closely identified with his sacred stone, obsidian, the traditional substance for sacrificial instruments. One of his identities was that of Itzli, the threatening 'stone knife god'. The Aztec Calendar Stone, or Sunstone, which Lawrence saw in Mexico City, depicts the sun god Tonatiuh ('Sun' of the fifth world) with a stone knife for a tongue, emblematic of the god's thirst for sacrifice. Montezuma II followed ancient tradition when he subjected prisoners to ritual execution in the great temples of the gods, as Hernán Cortés discovered upon his conquest in 1520.

4 Rio Grande Pueblo

New Mexico contains some of the oldest human traces in the Americas, dating back to late Pleistocene times, when hunters roamed its northern expanse seeking mammoths and other now-extinct game. In Lawrence's time, prehistoric bison bones were found near Folsom, New Mexico (about 130 miles n.e. of Questa and Kiowa Ranch), and the site was excavated in the 1920s, yielding the distinctive arrow projectiles – called 'Folsom points' – that first showed American settlement preceding the Ice Age. But the Pueblo Indians are believed to have more immediate ancestors in the Anasazi (Navajo for 'Ancient Ones') who, around AD 750, developed from a basketmaker culture to a 'Puebloan' phase in which they built huge communal dwellings (their Pueblo Bonita, or 'beautiful pueblo', at Chaco Canyon, New Mexico, contained over 700 rooms). Their centre was the Four Corners area where four states meet today, and they influenced outlying villages over as much as 40,000 square miles. For uncertain reasons, their civilisation declined around the end of the thirteenth century, and inhabitants presumably scattered to such locations as the Rio Grande Valley, western New Mexico, and the Hopi region of northeastern Arizona. The ruins of the Anasazi pueblos and highway systems inspired early Spanish observers to associate them with Aztec buildings and to name one site 'Aztec'. But researchers have not conclusively proved the exact link between the cultures, aside from evidence of trade.

Among the oldest continuously occupied Pueblo villages or complexes are Oraibi in Hopi land and Taos, the former nearly 900 years old and the latter at least 600–700 (and located near an older site). Each pueblo was independent, and several languages flourished (in at least two linguistic stocks) from the eastern pueblos (on the Rio Grande) to the western pueblos like Zuni (near the Arizona line), and the Hopi villages (in northeastern Arizona). At Taos, the language is Tiwa (in the Aztec-Tanoan group); at Santo Domingo ('The Dance of the Sprouting Corn') and San Felipe ('New Mexico'), it is eastern Keres (in the Hokan-Siouan). Twelve Hopi villages (by twentieth-century count) speak Hopi (in the Uto-Aztecan group), but one speaks Tewa (in the Aztec-Tanoan), and the Zuni language is related to no other. A particular Shoshonean dialect relates Hopi linguistically to the Ute and Comanche tongues as well as to the Aztec.

Pueblo Indians believed that their people had come up through three underground levels, or worlds, into this fourth world, emerging at the *sipapu* ('world-navel'), which varied in location with the people: to the Taos Indians it was at their sacred Blue Lake – in the forested mountains high above the pueblo – while some Hopis located it in the Grand Canyon and Navajos placed it in the Four Corners area. Nearly all Pueblo accounts assign life to ultimate deific figures. In a Taos Indian creation legend, for example, the Sun Father and Moon Mother originally mated over Blue Lake, and life forms spilled from the Big Dipper (Ursa Major) into the lake, from which they emerged.

A system of correspondences connecting the earth, heavens and under-worlds was basic to Pueblo mythology. Similarly, man-made representations, such as emblems on garments and symbolic structures, could affect their cosmic counterparts. The Pueblos posited that their underground kiva formed a microcosm of the universe, symbolising the successive underworlds and 'before' and 'after' (see 'The Dance of the Sprouting Corn', 'The Hopi Snake Dance', 'Taos' and 'Indians and an Englishman', for its Apache structure). A hole in the floor represented the nadir with its *sipapu* while the hole in the roof allowed access by way of a ladder to the present, or 'fourth world', and a view of the overhead zenith, with heavenly bodies by which the ritual calendar was set. An altar was placed at the level of the 'second world' and a ladder was elevated to rest on the third. The kivas developed from domestic pithouses, underground dwellings that offered protection from the elements before the Pueblo Indians moved into apartment-style complexes. When pithouses became obsolete as homes, they continued as sacred centres. The earliest Spanish account of the Rio Grande pueblos commented on the great number and superiority of kivas at Taos Pueblo.

In the kiva and in the surrounding countryside, the young men were prepared for their initiation into full community life. The eastern Pueblos were each organised not only into clans and sodalities but also into *moieties* or 'halves' – 'Summer People' and 'Winter People' (or northern and southern) – who had responsibilities for carrying out the ceremonials during half of the year. The western (Hopis) were organised by matrilineal clans and were matrilocal as well, women owning the property and husbands moving into their wives' and mothers-in-law's homes. But ownership at Taos was not generally in the maternal line.

It was with a sense of cosmic geography that the builders of Taos Pueblo placed one huge high-rise on the north side of their river and another on the south. The Pueblo race track (as in 'Indians and Entertainment', 'The Hopi Snake Dance', 'New Mexico') and the Apache track (in 'Indians and an Englishman') were cosmographically laid out, being located at Taos where legend says the Sun Father once fell from his lofty post to the earth, on the pueblo's north side, and darkened the world. The people had to coax him back into the sky, and the biennial footraces (May and September) were designed to help him on his course by the collective will of the people.

Pueblo deity could manifest itself through animals as well as anthropo-morphic gods. One myth maintained that, upon emerging from Blue Lake into this world, the Taos people were led by an eagle that dropped feathers to mark their proper home. Moreover, when they were facing starvation, a deer sought them out, offered itself as food and taught the people to use bows and arrows. Such lifesaving incidents are thought to be commemorated today in the Eagle Dance and the Deer Dance, just as the acquisition and growth of maize are celebrated in the Corn Dance (see 'Indians and Entertainment' and 'Dance of the Sprouting Corn').

While Spain occupied the pueblos in the sixteenth century, America's first revolt against Spain was by the Pueblo Indians, 140 years before Mexico threw off Spanish rule (see Appendix VI:3, 5). The assault was planned at Taos Pueblo under the leadership of the San Juan Indian Popé, urged on by abuses in the mission system; and all the pueblos – including those of Hopi – coordinated their actions to oust the enemy completely. The Pueblos occupied Santa Fe for twelve years before the Spanish return in 1692. At Mexican independence (1821), the pueblos became Mexican territory and, after the Spanish-American War, US territory. The church at Taos was razed by the US Army, and all its occupants destroyed, when they were believed to be rebels who, with Mexican forces, killed the first US governor in 1847.

The Rio Grande Pueblos, while strongly maintaining their own traditional obser-vances, are also Roman Catholics (see 'Taos'); and some of their ceremonies have Spanish and Mexican origins – like the Matachines dance, believed to be based on a medieval Morisca (Moorish) dance, combined with Spanish and Mexican influences – the latter introducing the characters Montezuma and his virgin bride. A maypole is part of this tradition (as in English Morris dance and drama), but the maypole Lawrence describes at Taos Pueblo ('Taos') probably derives from an indigenous custom.

5 Hopi

The Hopis take their name from their own term for themselves, *Hopitu*, meaning 'peaceable people'. Lawrence wonders (in 'Just Back from the Snake Dance') what extremity could have called them to their remote, forbidding landscape. In fact, they are thought to have scattered to such fastnesses in flight from the unpleasant conditions of the Anasazi decline. Furthermore, some Hopi villages relocated during the seventeenth-century Pueblo Rebellion, moving from the more accessible land at the foot of the mesa to high fortresses in their resolution to avoid and repel the Spanish. In this aim, they were ultimately more successful than the Rio Grande Pueblos in that they never reinstated the missionary priests and even went to war against a Hopi village that wanted to welcome them back.

The Pueblo mythology that has been studied most thoroughly is the Hopi (called *Moquis* in early ethnographic studies). Leading gods included the creator, Taiowa the Sun Spirit – not the physical sun but its shining essence – and Masauwu (*maasi* means 'grey'), the guardian of this present earth and, at the same time, the death god. In varying tales, he had two aspects, one attractive and one frightful. 'Spider Woman' or 'Spider Grandmother' (Gogyeng Sowuhti), who had both human and arachnid forms, aided Taiowa in creating life, and later guided and protected humans, even having a part in the Snake Dance narratives told in the kiva (as below). Another figure with deific status was Palolokong (or Avanyu in Tewa), the Great Water Serpent with feathers – not precisely the Aztec 'plumed serpent' yet a figure that may descend similarly from Mexico.

In their emergence stories, the Hopis lived in a dark cave (*Tokpela* or 'endless space') and were tended by 'Ant People' when Taiowa destroyed the first world for its imperfections. The pre-human remnant was then led by Spider Woman to the second underground world; but it had to be destroyed in an ice age. Spider Woman took the surviving band to the third world, where they became full humans; but this society lacked piety and did not keep the peace, so Taiowa sent great floods to submerge it. All along the way, the chosen ones had been assisted by insects, reptiles and animals. Now they sent a message to the fourth world, above them, asking permission from Masauwu to enter his domain (Túwaqachi, 'world complete'). In most versions, they climbed a great reed or bamboo upwards and then took reed boats across the flood waters.

To the Hopis, the diverse peoples of the world all emerged with them from the third world – including the 'white brother', sometimes called Pahana, who was to go his own way in the fourth world but return to them at its end, before the rise of a fifth. Resembling the Aztec myth that reportedly caused Montezuma to welcome Cortés, this tale of the lost brother may have motivated the Hopis to accept the Spanish initially, but they rectified their error forcefully in the Pueblo Rebellion. The myth has cognate forms among Navajos as well as Pueblos.

The best-known Hopi rituals are those of the Snake Dance ('The Hopi Snake Dance'), discussed in ethnologists' reports since the late nineteenth century. The pre-dance ceremonials in the kiva recount the journey of the culture-hero Tiyo ('Boy') back into a pre-world, the underworld of snakes. Tiyo sailed down the Colorado River through the Grand Canyon in a hollow log and there re-entered *sipapu*, being directed by Spider Woman and meeting the god-like 'Snake People', then returning home with treasure, secrets of the Snake Dance, and a Snake Woman as a bride. (Some versions include maize, or knowledge of growing it, among his acquisitions.) The children of Tiyo and the Snake Woman were initially feared, being distinguished by snake characteristics; but this lineage flourished, and, in some tales, Tiyo's brother married the Snake Woman's sister, whereupon the two brothers founded the Snake and Antelope Clans that still present the Hopi Snake Dance jointly. In the Hopi myth of successive worlds, both snake and antelope also had their places, the former usually identified with the first world and the latter with the fourth.

The purpose of the dance is to send serpents back to the gods as intermediaries to petition for rain, fertility and good crops. The Snake Dancers were said to relate to the world 'below' while the Antelope Dancers partly represented the 'above', because an antelope's antlers are located at the kopavi or crown of the head through which, to the Hopis, life entered and departed, and through which the gods might communicate. During the nine days preceding the dance, there was a symbolic wedding of Antelope and Snake representatives, and dramatic songs told these histories of the clans.

Lawrence's 'lords of shadow', who know 'after-life and before-life' ('The Hopi Snake Dance', 88:34), suggest the Kachinas who were said to visit the villages annually. They were spirits or 'cloud people' from the otherworld (including both nature entities and dead ancestors). The Hopis believed that these trans-dimensional figures once lived among them but withdrew to their sacred centre in the San Francisco Peaks near Flagstaff, Arizona. Nonetheless, they left this retreat annually, returning to be with the people from the winter solstice to the end of July – being embodied by masked dancers. The Hopis anticipated an afterlife among the Kachinas even though they told of another Hell-like place of the dead (probably influenced by Spanish contact).

The Hopi Indian Reservation is on ancient Hopi grounds, lying above the spectacular Painted Desert in northeastern Arizona on the southern edge of the Colorado Plateau. It was established in 1882 by the US government (see also notes on 'The Hopi Snake Dance').

6 Athabascan (Navajo and Apache)

Members of the Athabascan or Athapascan language group (*Na-Dene*), Navajos and Apaches ('The Hopi Snake Dance' and 'Indians and an Englishman') were once nomadic hunters and gatherers, believed to have been among the last bands to cross the Bering Straits from Asia. They arrived in the Southwest only a century or so before the Spanish discovery of them, by Coronado's men, in the 1540s. The name 'Navajo' (from *Navahu*, which in Tewa means 'cultivated fields') was adopted by the Spanish to distinguish the more pastoral nomads, who farmed, from their wandering Apache relatives. The Navajos, now the largest tribe in the USA, became herders as well as farmers. The name 'Apache' (from a Yuma word for 'fighting men' and Zuni for 'enemy') accurately points to the Apaches' expertise as warriors and raiders who were the last American Indians to defend their nomadic lifestyle and independence from the US government (as previously from the Spanish, Mexicans and numerous other tribes) before being placed on reservations late in the nineteenth century. The Navajos called themselves the *Dineh*, and the Apaches were the *Tinde* or *Ndee* among themselves (all three meaning 'the people').

Both Navajos and Apaches were, like Hopis, matricentric and organised in clans. Both held some core beliefs that were similar to those of the Pueblos, but the Navajos added their own 'beauty way', emphasising their particular sense of *Hozhoni* ('balance' or 'harmony', often translated as 'beauty'); and Apaches subscribed to a similar vision of a full-circle pathway of life in concord with natural surroundings and spiritual forces. Navajo ceremonies attempted to foster openness to the *diyin din* or *Yei* ('divine heroes' or 'holy people') who could move among them, somewhat like the Kachinas among the Hopis. Even the Navajo hogan (a dwelling or ceremonial structure) was viewed as a model of the universe, facing east to facilitate the entry of the *Yei*. Somewhat similarly, the Apaches could be visited by the *Gaa'he* or *Gans* ('mountain spirits') – sometimes said to live in the San Francisco Peaks, like the Hopi Kachinas. They were honoured in the Apache wickiups or tepees, which had ceremonial significance (see 'Indians and an Englishman') just as did the Navajo hogans. Dancers impersonated the 'mountain spirits', wearing black masks and body paint, in rituals that were sometimes associated with miraculous healing.

One of the most powerful Navajo deities, like a similar Apache goddess, was Changing Woman, an earth deity who was honoured in four aspects as a personification of the seasons. Somewhat like the Hopi Spider Woman, she could change her aspect, renewing her youth by whirling around to each of the four directions. Beyond Changing Woman and the Navajo *Yei,* there was an ultimate deity too holy to be named. The Apaches told of the goddess's mating with the Sun, bearing hero-twins who battled evil forces. But beyond these intermediaries and beyond the Apache *Gans* was Life-Giver.

Both Navajos and Apaches believed that they once passed through underground worlds into the present world (usually the fourth, occasionally the fifth or more). Like the Hopis, they told of having climbed some natural 'ladder', like a sunflower stalk or a reed, into the upper world. Both had a strong sense of place, bounded on each side by particular mountain landmarks that were identified with certain colours and animals – as in Navajo descriptions of the multi-hued horses that represented the cardinal compass points (see 'Dear Old Horse'). Like other Southwestern Indians, both Navajos and Apaches remain receptive to their natural surroundings. They are known for coming-of-age ceremonies, and the Apache elder's attempt to tutor the youths (in 'Indians and an Englishman') is a representative example of their preparation for such rites.

The Jicarilla Apaches (Spanish 'Little Basket' for their fine baskets), whom Lawrence describes, had been influenced by life on the Great Plains, having followed the buffalo herds. They had ranged from Colorado into Oklahoma and south into Texas before being confined late in the nineteenth century to the New Mexico reservation. The harvest festival that Lawrence attended (the *Go-Jii-Yah*) was an annual thanksgiving for crops and game, prosperity and ongoing seasons. The *Llaneros* ('plains people') and *Olleros* ('mountain-valley people'), the 'halves' of the tribe, competed annually in the races; they represented two geographically diverse Apache bands that had united. The activities of the festival are said to look back hundreds of years to nomadic days when two clans met periodically in the course of their travels. After both were placed on the same reservation, they codified the meetings, setting the date in September. The present Jicarilla Reservation dates back to 1887 and was extended in 1908.

In 1862–3, the Navajos (and Mescalero Apaches) had been removed by the US Army from their ancestral landmarks and herded into the Bosque Redondo Reservation, near Fort Sumner, New Mexico – a 400-mile 'Long Walk' for Navajos from their sacred canyon in Arizona. After massive loss of Indian life in this internment, the US government signed a treaty (1868) establishing the Navajos' Reservation on their old land, where today it completely surrounds the Hopi Reservation (see above under 'Hopi') and is the largest reservation in the USA (larger than nine small states put together). The respective Hopi and Navajo boundaries have been redrawn many times, never to the mutual satisfaction of both parties.

7 Other

(A) Ute

The Ute Indians ('Indians and an Englishman') were nomadic hunters of the Great Basin and Southwest – concentrated in western Colorado, eastern Utah, and far northern Arizona and New Mexico. Little is certain about their origin, but they had entered the region by the sixteenth century. They called themselves *Guche* ('the people') but the Spanish referred to them as *Yuta*, apparently mistaking them for the *Yuttahih* (Apache for 'highland people', meaning the Navajos). Their language, like that of the Hopis and many other Southwesterners, is in the Uto-Aztecan group, and their myths tell about their emergence from underground worlds and their gratitude to natural forces that assisted them. With the coming of the Spanish horse into the Southwest, they journeyed widely on horseback in search of buffalo. In 1880, the Utes were placed in reservations (southern Utes in Utah and northern Utes in Colorado).

(B) Kiowa

When Lawrence referred to the past Indians at his Kiowa Ranch, he meant the Kiowas ('Pan in America'). They had migrated early in the eighteenth century from the Montana mountains to the southern Great Plains, ranging from western Colorado and Kansas to Oklahoma, following the buffalo herds. The Kiowa, in their Kiowa-Tanoan language, called themselves the *Kwuda* ('coming-out people') for their myth of emergence from the underground through a hollow log; but their more common name was *Kiowa* (from *Kai-i-gwu*, 'principal people'). Nomadic hunters and warriors, the Kiowas raided in New Mexico but took the Kiowa Trail to the Taos Trade Fairs – annual harvest events at Taos Pueblo. They practised the Sun Dance (outlawed by the US government in 1882, partly because it included self-mutilation as a 'sacrifice' to the cosmic powers). Although Lawrence learned that one of the Kiowa campsites lay on the Kiowa Ranch property, the people themselves were long gone. The Kiowas, with the Comanches and others, were moved in 1868 to a reservation in Oklahoma; when it was opened to white settlement after 1900, the Indians were given individual allotments.

Further reference

See Introduction, footnotes 98–100, 104–5, and references to Gordon Brotherston and Harold Courlander in Explanatory notes, as well as the following.

Mesoamerica

Adams, Richard E. W., and Murdo J. MacLeod, eds., *The Cambridge History of the Native Peoples of the Americas*, 3 vols. Vol. ii: *Mesoamerica* (Cambridge, 2000).

Blanton, Richard E., Gary M. Feinman, Stephen A. Kowalewski and Linda M. Nichols, *Ancient Oaxaca* (Cambridge, 1999).

Flannery, Kent V., and Joyce Marcus, eds., *The Cloud People: Divergent Evolution of the Zapotec and Mixtec Civilizations* (New York, 1983).

Marcus, Joyce, and Kent V. Flannery, *Zapotec Civilization: How Urban Society Evolved in Mexico's Oaxaca Valley* (New York, 1996).

Miller, Mary, and Karl Taube, *Gods and Symbols of Ancient Mexico and the Maya* (New York, 1993).

Sahagún, Fray Bernardino de, *A History of Ancient Mexico: Anthropological, Mythological, and Social, 1547–1577*, trans. Fanny R. Bandelier, from the Spanish of Carlos María de Bustamante (1829) (Nashville, Tenn., 1932).

Spores, Ronald, *The Mixtecs in Ancient and Colonial Times* (Norman, Okla., 1984).

Taube, Karl, *Aztec and Maya Myths* (Austin, Tex., 1993).

Southwestern USA

Locke, Raymond F., *The Book of the Navajo* (Los Angeles, 1976).

Taube, Karl, 'The Teotihuacán Cave of Origin: The Iconography and Architecture of Emergence Mythology in Mesoamerica and the Southwest', *Anthropology and Aesthetics*, xii (Autumn 1986), 51–82.

'The Teotihuacán Spider Woman', *Journal of Latin American Lore*, ix.2 (1983), 107–89.

Tiller, Veronica Velarde, *The Jicarilla Apache Tribe: A History* (Lincoln, Nebr., 1992).

Waters, Frank, with Oswald White Bear Fredericks, *The Book of the Hopi* (New York, 1963).

Wood, Nancy, *Taos Pueblo* (New York, 1989).

APPENDIX VI

HISTORY TIMELINES

History Timelines

1 Pre-Columbian Mexico

Before 10000 BC	Human life (radiocarbon dating)
1500–200 BC	Various formative cultures
100 BC – AD 750	Teotihuacán flourishes
AD 200–750	Monte Albán (Zapotec) built and flourishes
500	Mitla (Zapotec) flourishes
650–800	Palenque (Mayan) built and flourishes
650–900	Chichén Itzá (Mayan) built and flourishes
900–1200	Tula (Toltec) rises to dominance
900–1200	Chichén Itzá (Toltec-Mayan) has second productive period
1200–1300	Northern tribes (Mexica, also called 'Nahuatl' or 'Aztec') invade central Mexico
1200–1521	Mixtecs control Monte Albán and Mitla
1325	Tenochtitlan (Aztec) founded (site of Mexico City)
1400–1521	Aztec Empire rises
1480	Montezuma (Moctezuma) II born
1517–21	Hernán Cortés conquers Mexico; Emperor Montezuma II dies (1520)

2 Peru

Before 9000 BC	Human societies in place
1500–300 BC	Rise of formative cultures
AD 1100	Cuzco (Inca) established
1534	Francisco Pizarro conquers Peru

3 Republic of Mexico

1821	Mexico gains independence from Spain
1824	First Republican Constitution
1857	Another Constitution
1855–9	Reform Laws adopted; Benito Juárez of Oaxaca is provisional president
1861	By French invasion, a Mexican Empire is imposed under Ferdinand Maximilian Joseph (Habsburg)
1867	French withdrawal, at US and Mexican insistence; Maximilian executed
1867–72	Juárez reelected but dies in office
1876	Porfirio Díaz of Oaxaca becomes president (in power thirty-five years)
1910	Francisco I. Madero of Coahuila elected president but Mexican Revolution begins
1913–14	Victoriano Huerta seizes presidency, opposed by coalition of generals: Alvaro Obregón from Sonora, Emiliano Zapata from Morelos, Venustiano Carranza from Coahuila, and Doroteo Arango ('Pancho Villa') from Chihuahua

1917	Modern Constitution adopted
1917–20	Venustiano Carranza becomes president but is shot fleeing Mexico
1920–4	Alvaro Obregón elected president
1923	Adolfo de la Huerta revolts against President Obregón and successor Plutarco Elías Calles

4 Oaxaca

1821–1923	See 'Republic of Mexico' above
1923–4	Governor Manuel García Vigil withdraws Oaxaca from federal union, joins de la Huerta Revolt; Serranos oppose him successfully; Vigil executed (1924)
1924	Isaac Ibarra, Zapotec leader, becomes provisional governor (meets DHL); Onofre Jiménez, Zapotec leader, succeeds him by election

5 Southwestern United States

Before 10000 BC	Ice Age man lives in America (evidence excavated at Folsom, New Mexico, in 1920s; later at Clovis, New Mexico)
8000 BC	Indigenous settlements already in place
AD 1–1300	Anasazi (ancestors of Pueblo Indians) form civilisation on Colorado Plateau of New Mexico, Arizona, Utah and Colorado
1300–1450	Anasazi disperse, probably into Arizona (Hopi), western New Mexico (Zuni) and Rio Grande watershed (Taos and elsewhere)
1450–1520	Utes and Athabascans (Apaches and Navajos) interact with Pueblos
1500s–1800s	Taos Pueblo Trade Fairs flourish
1500s–1880s	El Camino Real, trade route between Mexico City and Taos, flourishes
1514	Spanish *Requerimiento* first administered in the New World (forced conversion)
1540	Francisco Vazquez de Coronado seeks fabled 'seven cities of Cibola', sending emissaries to Taos and Oraibi (Hopi)
1590	Gaspar Castaño de Sosa leads expedition to Santo Domingo region
1598	Juan de Oñata claims Hopi and Rio Grande pueblos – including Taos, Santo Domingo and San Felipe – for Spanish crown and Roman Catholic Church and makes Santo Domingo an administrative centre
1608	La Villa Real de la Santa Fe de San Francisco de Asis (Santa Fe) founded (capital of Spanish, Mexican and US territories)
1613–15	Spanish village formed near Taos Pueblo (later relocated)
1680	Pueblo Rebellion begins at Taos under Popé of San Juan Pueblo (Taos church burned), driving Spanish out of New Mexico; Pueblo Indians occupy Santa Fe
1692–3	Don Diego de Vargas leads Spanish back to Santa Fe
1696	Pueblo resistance continues briefly at Taos and elsewhere; Hopis refuse new missions

1716–25	Ranchos de Taos forms near present town of Taos on Spanish land grant (separate from eventual village of Taos)
1795–6	Taos (town) relocated at present site on Spanish land grant and takes name Don Fernando de Taos
1820s–80s	Santa Fe Trail, trade and pioneer route from Missouri to Santa Fe and Pacific Ocean, flourishes
1821	Mexican Independence from Spain places New Mexico and contiguous lands under Mexican government
1846–8	Mexican War waged between USA and Mexico
1847	Mexican and Pueblo rising against USA includes killing of new territorial governor, Charles Bent, in Taos; Taos Indians, in refuge at San Geronimo Church, Taos Pueblo, destroyed in retaliation by US Army (church burned)
1848	Treaty of Guadalupe Hidalgo (USA gains part or all of present New Mexico, Arizona, Utah, Nevada, California, Texas, Colorado, Wyoming, Kansas and Oklahoma)
1850	New Mexico Territory declared (present Arizona, New Mexico, southern Colorado, Utah and Nevada)
1853	Gadsden Purchase (USA gains additional land in present New Mexico and Arizona)
1880	Transcontinental Railroad reaches Santa Fe
1912	New Mexico becomes US state
1914	Arizona becomes US state
1922	Bursum Bill passes US Senate but is recalled after heavy opposition
1923	Hearings on Bursum Bill substitutes in US Senate and House of Representatives
1924	Pueblo Lands Act passes

APPENDIX VII

MAPS

MAPS

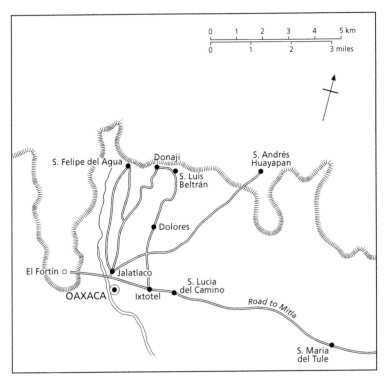

MAP 1 Oaxaca villages (*c.* 1924–5), map adapted from Ross Parmenter

233

MAP 2 Rio Grande Pueblos, Del Monte Ranch and Kiowa Ranch (*c.* 1922–5)

MAP 3 Southwestern USA and Mexico (*c.* 1923–5)

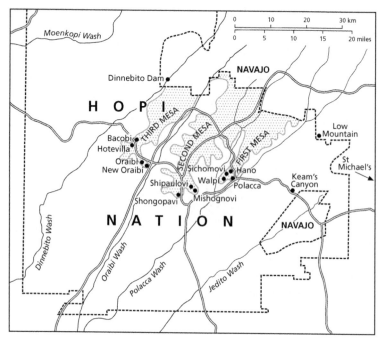

MAP 4 Hopi villages (*c.* 1924)

MAP 5 Europe (*c.* 1922–8)

EXPLANATORY NOTES

EXPLANATORY NOTES

Corasmin and the Parrots

11:1 **Corasmin and the Parrots**   Both the dog ('more pug than poodle') and the parrots belonged to the Lawrences' landlord, the Revd Edward Arden Rickards (1879–1941), a Roman Catholic priest who was a native of Oaxaca though born of British parents (Parmenter 30, 42). See a photograph of DHL and Frieda with Rickards and a parrot (Ellis, *Dying Game*, Illustration 20; Parmenter, Plate 11). This essay and the next three were written in Oaxaca, Mexico (see Introduction, pp. lii–lv).

11:4 **one little town [11:2]...in the Republic...adobe house... garden patio:**   Oaxaca City is some 200 miles s. of Mexico City in the state of Oaxaca. Mexico became a federal republic with its first Constitution (1824), after gaining its independence from Spain three years earlier; and later Constitutions of 1857 and 1917 continued the same form of government. The house where DHL and Frieda lived, from 20 November 1924 to 14 February 1925, is at Pino Suarez 600 (43 in DHL's time) but was altered considerably in later years. It is traditional in Mexico for a house to be built of adobe and to possess a central garden or patio. See Glossary for 'adobe', 'patio' and other Spanish and Indian terms.

11:12 *The Future of America... The European Situation,*   Possibly *The Future in America* by H. G. Wells (1906) – which predicted increased prosperity for the USA – and *What Is Coming: A European Forecast* by Wells (1916) – containing 'The new map of Europe'. Or he may be using representative titles to suggest similarly named publications – e.g. Leopold Godowski's *The Future of America* (St Louis, 1915) and Walter Lichtenstein's *The European Situation* (New York, 1924).

11:14 **bob-haired**   Short-haired, in the fashion of the period.

11:16 **it is morning, and it is Mexico.**   A reference to the title of the four-piece series in which this essay stands first. Madame Calderón de la Barca's *Life in Mexico*, which DHL read (see Introduction, footnote 105), includes a section called 'Mexico in the Morning' ('Letter the Thirteenth'); she also cites *Mornings in the Alameda* (1825–6) by Don Carlos Bustamante (in her 'Letter the Thirty-seventh').

11:25 **urine,**   The word had been omitted in the typescript, as shown in the surviving TCC, where DHL added 'urine' clearly in longhand (but the *Adelphi* printed 'wine').

11:28 **piffing**   Rendered 'puffing' in previous publications, Lawrence's word 'piffing' (MS, p. 1), possibly from 'piffle', is an onomatopoeic construction that may suggest the sound of an Indian corn-grinding mill. 'Piff' (also 'piff-paff') is an imitative interjection representing the sound of a projectile as it travels through the air; and 'pifaro' (Spanish) is a wind instrument with a high reedy sound, related to Italian 'piffero', French 'fifre', German 'Pfeife' and English 'fife'. *OED* also gives 'piffling' as a verbal substantive, but DHL seems to have coined 'piffing' as a progressive verb.

12:2 **Rosalino,** The Lawrences' servant, a young Zapotec Indian (b. *c.* 1904) from Santa Maria Zoogochi in the Sierra de Juárez Mountains. Cf. Parmenter 84–5 and Brett 175, 178–80, 195.

12:4 **it is** The revision in TCCR shows that DHL was the source, in typescript (p. 2), for this variation from MS, which appears in all printed versions. The same is true of several other alterations that developed his text (not simply correcting typographical error), including 'cold' at 12:20 (TCCR, p. 2) and 'our Sun' at 17:26 (TCCR, p. 9).

12:28 *ab ovo* Literally, 'from the egg' – in its inception, from the beginning (Latin).

13:5 **kiss the rod.** 'To accept chastisement or correction submissively' (*OED*). See *Richard II* by Shakespeare (1564–1616), in which the deposed king is blamed for not acting like 'a lion and a king of beasts' but, instead, choosing to face his 'correction mildly, kiss the rod' (II. i). Among other literary references is another by Shakespeare, in *Two Gentlemen of Verona* (I. ii).

13:10 **diaphragm . . . before brains were invented.** Cf. *Fantasia of the Unconscious,* ed. Steele: 'The first seat of our primal consciousness is the solar plexus, the great nerve-centre situated in the middle-front of the abdomen', where 'we know as we can never mentally know' (79:7–8, 17). DHL's source is probably James M. Pryse, whose *Apocalypse Unsealed* (New York, 1910) he had read by 1917 (*Letters,* iii. 150).

13:15 **the Spanish 'r',** In Spanish, the 'r' is pronounced as a dental or uvular trill. The repetition of 'r' in DHL's renditions of 'Perro' suggest this rolling sound.

13:25 **Invictus!** 'Unconquered!' (Latin). The poem 'Invictus', by William Ernest Henley (1849–1903), was written in 1875 and published in his *Echoes* (1888). DHL refers to it elsewhere – e.g. 'A Modern Lover', *Love Among the Haystacks and Other Stories,* ed. John Worthen (Cambridge, 1987), 35:21–2; '. . . . . Love Was Once a Little Boy', *Reflections* 345:6–9; the final versions of 'Edgar Allan Poe', 'Nathaniel Hawthorne and *The Scarlet Letter*' and 'Whitman' (*Studies* 67:33–4, 87:28–9, 158:22–3). The present quotation (13:28–31) is from Henley's second stanza ['. . . aloud,']. The subsequent allusion (13:33–4) is to the poem's closing lines: 'I am the master of my fate: / I am the captain of my soul.'

13:39 **Castilian,** The refined Spanish spoken in mainland Spain, as distinguished from the Galician and Catalan dialects and from all American Spanish. In Mexico, it was a mark of European education and high social class and was accordingly disdained by some revolutionaries.

14:1 **I don't believe in evolution,** Cf. *Fantasia of the Unconscious,* ed. Steele: 'I do not believe in evolution, but in the strangeness and rainbow-change of ever-renewed creative civilisations' (64:18–19). Cf. also 'Him With His Tail in His Mouth': 'Evolution sings away at the same old song' (*Reflections* 309:37–8).

14:2 **First Cause,** That which originally created the universe. Cf. Madame Helena Petrovna Blavatsky, *The Secret Doctrine* (1888): 'the Absolute . . . is the First Cause (Plato's *Logos*) the original and eternal IDEA' (i. 214). DHL knew this theosophical work by August 1917 (*Letters*, iii. 150).

14:3 **what the Aztecs called Suns:** The five Aztec 'Suns', like much other Mesoamerican mythology, dealt with the development of life through separate epochs and cataclysms: out of these ends of the world, survivors had their interludes of dominance, from reptiles and birds to monkeys and other mammals like dogs (sometimes in reverse order). In the fifth 'Sun' the human race emerged, but this 'Sun' was doomed to perish one day, too. See also Appendix V:1, 3; Brotherston, *Book of the Fourth World*, pp. 221–8; and *PS* 553–9.

14:5 **somebody coughs** DHL had first written 'a bomb bursts' in MS (p. 4) but substituted a more organic agent. Some of the other revisions in MS follow, with '< >' indicating excision and '{}' revision: 13:12 <'a spasm'> {'an orgasm'} (p. 3); 14:29 <'old'> {'oh'} (p. 5); 15:10 <'and the sly'> {'waddling'} (p. 5); and 16:27 <'we'> {'you'} and <'our'> {'your'} (p. 7). At 14:39, 'hatched out again' was squeezed between lines in MS (p. 5) to explain how some birds survived, creating a link between 'Suns'; and at 15:1–2 'to the new Sun', also added to MS (p. 5), sharpened this continuity.

14:14 **lizards . . . too unwieldy,** 'Humming-Bird' notes that 'little lizards, they say, were once big' (*Poems* 372).

14:18 **peacocks** In the poem 'Turkey-Cock', DHL casts the peacock as a representative of the old order: 'Has the peacock had his day . . . ?' (*Poems* 371). The peacock is among DHL's repeated symbols, as in *The White Peacock* (1911) and the short story 'Wintry Peacock' (1921).

14:26 **elephant,** The poem 'Elephant' describes this animal as 'the hugest, oldest of beasts' (*Poems* 388).

15:3 **the parrot above all,** In one widespread Mesoamerican myth, a great parrot (Seven Parrot, or Seven Macaw) presided over the third epoch or 'Sun' (see note on 14:3). Illustrations of huge parrot-like birds, surmounting the world's cardinal points, appear in Spence, *Gods of Mexico*, 58–60. Like the parrot, the turkey (15:2) was one of the thirteen Aztec 'fliers' or bird signs. Native to America, turkeys were associated in DHL's poem 'Turkey-Cock' with 'those sombre, dead, feather-lustrous Aztecs, Amerindians' (*Poems* 371). See also Appendix V:2–3.

15:10 **his Grace,** Proper mode of referring to a duke.

15:25 **Tiger . . . Jaguar,** A ferocious beast of the cat family, usually said to be a jaguar (*Felis onca*), ended the first Aztec 'Sun'. Although a tiger differs from a jaguar and does not occur wild in the Americas, the word 'tiger' is sometimes applied to a jaguar or a cougar.

15:30 **third Sun . . . . The fourth Sun** The omission of one of the 'Suns' by Brett in TS may have gone unnoticed by DHL because Tlaloc and Chalchuihtlicue, the god and goddess associated with the third and fourth creations respectively, were both identified with water. See Appendix V:3.

Although someone attempted to normalise 'bust' to 'burst' (TCCC, p. 7), DHL was clearly using a diction that echoes back to 14:10.

16:2 **given a name.** Cf. Genesis ii. 19–20.

16:4 **the snake, the oldest dethroned king of all,** In DHL's poem 'Snake', the snake is 'one of the lords / Of life' (*Poems* 351), and in one draft of *The Plumed Serpent*, 'the great First Cause' is 'like a dragon coiled at the very centre of all the cosmos' (542, column 2). Cf. Ramón's teaching: 'At the heart of this earth sleeps a great serpent, in the midst of fire . . . The snake of the world is huge, and the rocks are his scales, trees grow between them' (*PS* 196:26–7). This description accords with an Aztec idea of a primal Quetzal-Snake – cf. Spence, *Gods of Mexico*, 13, identifying the original 'earth-monster' as a 'dragon'. Cf. Genesis iii. 1–14.

16:5 **bit his tail once more** The Uroboros, a circular serpentine sign that represents eternity and infinity, is part of the emblem of the Quetzalcoatl movement in *The Plumed Serpent*: an eagle 'within the ring of a serpent that had its tail in its mouth' (118:33–4). In fact, DHL designed such an emblem, which was stamped on the front cover of the first American edition of the novel. In 'Him With His Tail in His Mouth', he was tired of the image: 'It seems to me time somebody gave that serpent of eternity another dummy to suck' (*Reflections* 309:8–9). See also 'The Crown' on 'the infinite with its tail in its mouth' (*Reflections* 267:27), and a similar reference in Blavatsky, *The Secret Doctrine*, i. 253.

16:6 **But I'll bruise his heel!** In Genesis iii. 15, God addresses the serpent: 'And I will put enmity between thee and the woman, and between thy seed and her seed; it shall bruise thy head, and thou shalt bruise his heel' (*KJB*).

16:10 *take him off.* Imitate him (colloquial).

16:13 **monkey,** In most versions of the Aztec creation myth, the earth's populace turns into monkeys at the end of one of the 'Suns' – usually the second or fourth. See also 'The Mozo' (pp. 36–9 and notes at 36:29 and 38:34), and *The Plumed Serpent* (250:13–255:34) for word-play on the human 'monkey'.

16:17 **"fourth dimension,"** DHL had read and annotated Peter D. Ouspensky's *Tertium Organum: A Key to the Enigmas of the World*, trans. N. Bessaraboff and C. Brangdon (1920), dealing with this concept, probably in 1923 in New Mexico. He refers directly to the 'other dimension' or the 'Fourth Dimension' elsewhere – e.g. 'The Crown', as revised in 1925 (*Reflections* 304:7); 'Him with His Tail in His Mouth' (*Reflections* 313–17); and 'Reflections on the Death of a Porcupine' (*Reflections* 358–63). In the last, it is equated with that which 'the old people called heaven' (*Reflections* 363:13); in *The Plumed Serpent*, it is an 'infinite room' where 'the soul is at home in its own dream' and 'where alone can the human family assemble in immediate contact' (126:14, 18, 32–3). In 'Corasmin and the Parrots', the 'other dimension' is adapted to the myth of separate creations (see note on 14:3 and Appendix V:1–3). 'Fourth dimension' theories arose partly from Albert Einstein's ideas, first announced in 1905 and 1916, proposing a four-dimensional space–time continuum in defiance of the Euclidean idea of space as separate from time. In addition, the concept of a 'fourth dimension' had appeared in H. G. Wells

(1866–1946), *The Time Machine* (1895). See also Richard O. Young, '"Where Even the Trees Come and Go": D. H. Lawrence and the Fourth Dimension', *D. H. Lawrence Review*, xiii (1980), 30–44.

16:18 **a foot-rule,** A measuring rod one foot (twelve inches) long.

16:21 **universe of Space and time** 'The Crown' and 'Reflections on the Death of a Porcupine' (*Reflections* 304:7–8, 358:38–40) contain statements that the 'fourth dimension' is outside space and time. In *The Plumed Serpent* it lies 'inside the axis of our wheeling space' and at 'the very centre of time' (126:15, 21).

16:29 **Day,** DHL wrote about 'the Greater Day', as a new epoch or dimension, in 'The Flying-Fish', which he began to dictate to Frieda during his nearly fatal illness only two and a half months after writing 'Corasmin and the Parrots' (see *St. Mawr and Other Stories*, ed. Finney, pp. 209ff.).

16:32 **the length and the breadth . . . the height and the depth** Cf. Ephesians iii. 18 (*KJB*): 'to comprehend . . . what is the breadth, and length, and depth, and height' [of the love of Christ].

17:27 **The Aztecs . . . our Sun, . . . in earthquakes.** Aztec prophecy for a future time. See Appendix V:1, 3 and note on 14:3.

Walk to Huayapa

21:1 **Walk to Huayapa** The essay's first publication, in *Travel*, was accompanied by ten photographs showing a fiesta in a Mexican marketplace, a quiet street ('NO ONE HURRIES IN THE LAND OF MAÑANA'), 'MUSIC AND DANCING IN THE CHURCH YARD', sales of handicrafts and other street scenes ('A Sunday Stroll in Sleepy Mexico', pp. 30–5). See also note on 23:20.

21:7 **trying** The suggestion is that people may try 'enjoying themselves' rather unsuccessfully (MS, p. 1). But notice (in Textual apparatus) an alternate reading in E1, suggesting it is the narrator who will 'try' to avoid the sight but not very successfully. Although a revision in Secker's proofs by DHL is possible, a misreading in E1 is equally likely and MS has been retained.

21:9 **keep mum,** To be silent – from 'an inarticulate sound made with closed lips' (*OED*).

21:9 **better-half** Spouse; perhaps from the 'better part', sometimes 'soul' (*OED*).

21:11 **the "machine."** The automobile.

21:13 **"Shank's pony;"** Sometimes also 'Shank's mare', referring to travel on foot (*OED*).

21:16 **San Felipe de las Aguas.** See notes on 23:20 and 41:40.

21:17 **"*Como no, Señor!*"** 'How . . . !' (Spanish). In these essays, DHL seldom used the acute accent mark on Spanish interrogatories; neither did he use it on the Spanish 'Si' for 'Yes' (as at 25:23 and following). It is significant that some of his main characters are speakers of dialect (see note on 41:6). See also the Glossary for this and subsequent Spanish passages.

21:29 **the Capital,** Mexico City, capital of Mexico, comprised numerous *colonias* (or neighbourhoods), even in 1924, when it was already spreading towards the limits of the Distrito Federal in which it is located. Guadalajara (23:3), capital of the state of Jalisco, was second to Mexico City in size, as it is today.

21:30 **from heaven on a napkin,** Medieval iconography sometimes depicts a white napkin as the conveyance between earth and heaven, lifting up the souls of saints. Examples include paintings of St James and St Josias in Stoke Orchard, Gloucestershire (twelfth century), and of St Erasmus in Chippenham, Cambridgeshire (probably fifteenth century).

21:33 **the church... monastery enclosure... soldiery,** The Church of El Patrocinio in Oaxaca city, a former Bethlehemite monastery, which was converted first into a seminary (the Seminario Pontifico y Conciliar de la Santa Cruz) and then into a military hospital.

22:1 **"I will lift up mine eyes unto the hills, whence cometh my strength."** Psalms cxxi. 1 (*KJB*) ['... from whence... my help'].

22:6 **their pleats... lizard-claws of** Eye-skip by Brett was responsible for the omission of sixteen words of MS (p. 2) from TCC (p. 2).

22:15 **away, along the foot-hills,** Originally 'down' in MS (p. 2), the expansion was one of several by which DHL added to the sense of landscape. Similar interlinear additions in MS were: at 23:5, 'on a moor' (p. 3), and at 24:8–10, three sentences 'Or you... the stream' (p. 4).

22:33 **The Americans... dumb bell.** 'A stupid person' (slang), not confined to American English (*OED*).

23:4 **the twin towers of the cathedral** The Cathedral of Guadalajara, started in 1561 and consecrated in 1618, suffered an earthquake that damaged both towers in 1848. They were rebuilt taller than before.

23:20 **Huayapa.** San Andrés Huayapan, n.e. of Oaxaca in the foothills, one of four villages in the region – including San Felipe del Agua, Donaji, and San Luis Beltrán (see Map 1). Villagers generally omit the 'n' from 'Huayapan' when pronouncing it (Parmenter 115), but census records inscribe it.

23:26 **gets one's pecker up.** In TCC, an unknown hand – perhaps that of a compositor for Peri (*Travel*) – crossed out 'pecker' and wrote 'dander' (p. 4). The alteration probably occurred because, in American slang, the term 'pecker' had come to refer to the penis. However, in the expression 'to keep one's pecker up', 'pecker' commonly means 'resolution, courage' (*OED*), and DHL's term suggests the particular irritation (the 'strain on the temper') he feels in Mexico ('Au Revoir, U. S. A.', 131:14–15). In November 1924 DHL had written to Edward McDonald, 'Myself, I don't know American slang, and I'm sure pecker isn't improper in English. If it is, tant mieux' (*Letters*, v. 176).

23:26 **the Señora** Frieda Lawrence, also 'the better-half' (see note at 21:9).

23:29 *Prophet art thou, bird, or devil?* 'The Raven' (1845), by American writer Edgar Allan Poe (1809–49), contains the twice-repeated line, '"Prophet!" said I, "thing of evil! – prophet still, if bird or devil!"' (lines 85, 91). 'Nevermore' (23:37) is the raven's constant response to the speaker.

24:8 **the palo-blanco . . . big white flowers like pure white, crumpled cambric.** The palo blanco tree's sweet-smelling white flowers sometimes give it another name, *palo dulce* or 'sweet wood'. But the flowers may be those of the *cazaguate*, which give nearby Monte Albán the name 'White Mountain' (Parmenter 116). Cambric is a fine white linen cloth, named for its home in Cambrai, France; it has a soft, glossy surface and is often preferred for fashion accessories and backing for fancy needlecraft.

24:12 **"Mucho calor!"** December in Oaxaca state is sunny, past the rainy season, and the daytime heat can rise to 70° or 80° Fahrenheit in some areas.

24:25 *farouche* Both 'shy and awkward, or sullen' and 'savage, wild or fierce' (French). Both meanings seem to apply.

24:29 **"Gabilan!"** Commonly 'Gavilán' (Spanish), but DHL may intend a dialect pronunciation.

24:30 *idioma?* In the state of Oaxaca, 200 non-Spanish dialects have been recorded, a number of them related to Zapotec. DHL commented to his niece Margaret King on 22 November 1924, 'Our boy, Rosalino, is a Zapotec – it's taken him two years to learn the bit of Spanish he knows' (*Letters*, v. 178). See also Appendix V:2.

26:4 *Ia Calle . . . Ia Calle de las Minas,* DHL did not use the Spanish 'La' but the Roman numeral I with the superior letter 'a' (I^a) for *Prima,* the number (First) that is part of the street name. The 'First Street of the Mines' was named for the mountain mines of the region; Parmenter, who followed in DHL's footsteps through Huayapa in 1962, found both a street of the 'Mines' and one of the 'Mine' – the latter being the one DHL seems to have taken (120). Some of the other street names concern national politics – e.g. 'Street of the Independence' (26:23), which recognises Mexico's independence from Spain.

26:31 **And a plaza [26:29] . . . Zócalo . . . old Forum.** A 'Zócalo' (Spanish), or 'plaza', is a marketplace and civic centre, an urban or village 'hub' like the Roman forum. See 'Taos', p. 125 and notes on 125:9 and 125:14.

26:33 *Reforma,* Many Mexican cities and towns have streets named Reforma in honour of the Laws of Reform (1856–9) by which Benito Pablo Juárez (1806–72) sought to redistribute the land of large property owners and the Roman Catholic Church; see also note on 29:7. Agrarian reform was still at issue in the Mexican Revolution (1910–20), as through much of the twentieth century. DHL wrote to Murry that the Indians fell prey to 'awful agitators' who 'pump bits of socialism over them', adding, 'And socialism here is a farce of farces: except very dangerous' (*Letters*, v. 168).

26:38 **like some big white human being, in rags, held captive in a world of ants.** See H. G. Wells, 'The Empire of the Ants' (1905), in which an army of ants threatens 'civilisation' in a Latin American setting (*The Complete Short Stories of H. G. Wells* [1927], pp. 92–108). See also Wells, *The First Men in the Moon* (1901), describing the ragged Cavor's captivity among the ant-like Selenites (chs. XII, XXVI). Cf. also DHL's 'insects' (27:3) and Wells's Selenites as 'insects' (ch. XI) or 'insect men' (ch. XVI).

27:1 **pueblo,** DHL was evidently thinking of the New Mexico pueblos, where Indian tribes were concentrated in large communal buildings – unlike the smaller dwellings of the Mexican hill communities.

27:11 **Virgin of the Soledad,** The Virgin of Solitude, closely linked to the Virgin of Sorrows, is one of the most venerated aspects of the Virgin Mary in Mexican churches and especially in Oaxaca, where she is patron saint. The Lawrences had attended a fiesta honouring her at Oaxaca's Church of Soledad de Santa Cruz in December 1924. In *The Plumed Serpent*, Cipriano thinks of Kate in terms of the Soledad: 'The wonder, the mystery, the magic that used to flood over him as a boy and a youth, when he kneeled before the babyish figure of the Santa Maria de la Soledad, flooded him again. He was in the presence of the goddess, white-handed, mysterious, gleaming with a moon-like power and the intense potency of grief' (71:23–7).

27:14 **Gulliver's Travels' fresco... Goliath.** In *Gulliver's Travels* (1726), by Jonathan Swift (1667–1745), the protagonist appears as a giant among the tiny Lilliputians. Goliath is the Philistine champion, described as a giant, slain by the young David (1 Samuel 17.4–7, 40–57). The fresco DHL describes features a huge St Christopher carrying the Christ child.

27:15 **a life-size Christ—rather undersized:** This image, called *El Señor de la Humildad Páciente* ('the Lord of Patient Humility'), belonged in a side niche but was placed at the altar for the festival of Soledad because the Soledad is linked with Christ's Passion through Mary's suffering at the foot of the cross.

27:33 **for the government, for the state, for a new governor,** Although Rosalino says the men are canvassing for votes, the 1924 election was over, and Onofre Jiménez (b. 1888) had been installed as governor of Oaxaca on 1 December 1924, succeeding Isaac M. Ibarra (1888–1972), the federal senator and provisional governor whom DHL met in the Municipal Palace in November (*Letters*, v. 167, 170). Ibarra himself had replaced Manuel García Vigil (1882–1924) when the latter was shot earlier the same year (see Appendix VI:4 and note on 43:34).

27:35 **Justizia,** The sign designates the town council hall, the Sala Municipal.

27:37 **This Mark** The voting symbol is drawn by hand in MS (p. 9) and TCC (p. 10) by DHL or Brett. Similarly hand-drawn symbols appear at 28:2 and 29:8 (MS, pp. 9, 10; TCC, pp. 10, 11).

28:1 **Julio Echegaray... Socrate Ezequiel Tos.** These names were additions to MS (p. 9), where DHL crossed out the original words and left only 'rabid agrarista' (a fanatical supporter of agrarian reform) still legible (though cancelled) under Tos ('Cough'). The name Socrate Ezequiel probably echoes the name of Plutarco Elías Calles (1877–1945), president of Mexico (1924–8), as did the name Socrates Tomás Montes in *The Plumed Serpent*. Calles was known in part for furthering agrarian policy on models set initially by Juárez. See Appendix VI:3–4.

28:3 **lucky bag.** 'A bag, at fairs and bazaars, in which, on payment of a small sum, one dips one's hand and draws an article of greater or less value' (*OED*), a term that was being superseded in the 1920s by 'lucky dip'.

28:3 **Peregrino Zenón Cocotilla.** The surname was 'Quintanilla' in MS (p. 9) but was changed in typescript (p. 10) to the 'Cocotilla' of all published versions, no doubt as a courtesy to the writer and diplomat Luis Quintanilla whom DHL had met in Mexico City (*Letters*, v. 162ff.; Nehls, ii. 368–70, 520–1). See also Introduction, pp. lvii–lviii, footnote 114 and note on 167:1.

28:5 **Government by the People, of the People, for the People!** Abraham Lincoln (1809–65), in the 'Gettysburg Address' ['of the people, by the people, for the people'], delivered on 19 November 1863 to commemorate the Union dead of the Civil War battle at Gettysburg, Pennsylvania. In *Apocalypse and the Writings on Revelation*, ed. Mara Kalnins (Cambridge, 1983), DHL terms Lincoln 'a half-evil saint who *almost* believes in the utter destruction of power' (69:5–6).

28:20 **Tepache [28:18]. . . drunk on—** When this essay appeared in *Travel*, an editor wrote, in the caption under a photograph: 'the peon falls back on *tepache*. . . or. . . the deadly *mescal*' ('A Sunday Stroll in Sleepy Mexico', p. 31) because of dangerous drinking water. DHL added the words about the effect of *mescal* between lines in MS (p. 9), apparently to qualify his statement about *tepache*. Rosalino's comment is in Spanish slang.

29:7 **the Street of Benito Juárez:** A Zapotec Indian, born in the mountains near Oaxaca, Juárez is Mexico's national hero. He led the Liberal movement that created the Constitution of 1857 and the Reform Laws (see note on 26:33). He became provisional president of Mexico but was ousted by French invaders who forced the Habsburg Maximilian upon Mexico as its emperor. Juárez defeated him (1867) and was again elected president twice but died in office (1872).

29:12 **La Cucaracha.** 'The Cockroach' is the title of one of the Mexican Revolution's best-known folkloric 'corridos' – anonymous story-telling songs with political associations; in this case, many versions favour 'Pancho Villa' (see also note on 40:8).

29:16 **"Then what is there?"** The TCCR reading (p. 14) – "Then what is happening here?" – was written only because DHL's original line (MS, p. 10) had been omitted by Brett.

29:34 **dialect** In revising typescript (TCCR, p. 12) DHL replaced 'dialectic' (MS, p. 11), choosing the word more associated with language inflection, not a term more prevalent in philosophical discourse.

29:36 **a *posada*.** Often 'Las posadas' ('the inns'), a Mexican Christmas custom observed for nine days leading up to the holiday. Participants form a procession, all carrying candles, and stop at each other's homes to reenact the Virgin Mary's search for a room in Bethlehem. They are turned away from the doors repeatedly but at last congregate at one of the stops for refreshments and entertainment. The *posadas* can range from large community events to intimate family gatherings. Cf. 29:38: **Is there a room here?** ['there was no room for them in the inn'] (Luke ii. 7, *KJB*). Cf. also 30:6: **And lo!** ['And, lo'] (Luke ii. 9).

30:3 **Valentino Ruiz.** An actual villager whose house was at 12 Calle de Magnolia (Parmenter 122).

30:35 **a coyote, a zopilote, and a white she-bear** DHL termed himself a 'dog' and a 'red wolf' in 'The Red Wolf', written in Taos (*Poems* 404, 405). A *zopilote* is a wild scavenger bird. The 'white she-bear' refers to Frieda's fairness and solidity and perhaps also to her white checked garment.

31:3 **juncture of the roads,** DHL probably made this correction, from 'junction of roads' (MS, p. 12), in the proofs he corrected for the first English edition; the word may convey an intensified sense of confrontation (as in 'at this juncture') to such a meeting at the crossroads. Corrections in these proofs were evidently few: see also notes on 38:17 and 60:7.

32:30 **complete absence of what we call "spirit."** But this does not preclude the 'soul' to DHL, who adopted the pre-Socratic distinction between 'spirit' and 'soul', holding that the 'soul' can be 'conceived of as being the blood itself' – e.g. *Apocalypse and the Writings on Revelation*, ed. Kalnins (189:5). See also *Apocalypse* 136:5–6 ('soul, spirit, and the eternal I'). The 'spirit', on the other hand, he often associated with excessive consciousness.

32:34 *mañana es otro día.* **Tomorrow is another day.** A common saying in Spanish America. Cf. 'The Mozo' (38:30) and also *The Escaped Cock*, in *The Virgin and the Gipsy and Other Stories*, ed. Michael Herbert, Bethan Jones and Lindeth Vasey (Cambridge, 2005): 'Tomorrow is another day' (163:22–3).

The Mozo

35:7 **other Indian blood, not Zapotec.** 'Spanish blood' in MS (p. 1). The alteration to 'other Indian blood' is also in the first publication (*Insel-Almanach*, p. 103); see Introduction, p. lv and footnote 111. This change first appears in Brett's typescript (TCC, p. 1), along with the new title and a few new words, 'here' (at 35:2) and 'have known' (at 35:13); this page is a ribbon copy (unlike the following carbon pages). DHL must have made so many alterations on the page that Brett retyped it, probably in both ribbon and carbon copies; as was his custom, he would have made no distinction between the two. The other copy (or else the corrected first page) must have been incorporated into the missing ribbon copy (which presumably went to the *Insel-Almanach*). DHL considered the Zapotecs fierce (*Letters*, v. 167), possibly because of their ancient warrior class and certainly because of their prominence in the Mexican Revolution. After finishing the essay, which highlights the mozo's nostalgia for his Indian village, DHL would understandably have seen the logic of this change. It is entirely in keeping with the revisions in TCC, in DHL's own hand, that increase Rosalino's difficulty with Spanish (40:3–23) and emphasise his Indian identity.

35:14 **The Aztec gods and goddesses ... unloveable lot.** The Aztec world scheme is based upon radical dualism and conflict, as epitomised in the battle for dominance between Quetzalcoatl (the 'plumed serpent') and Tezcatlipoca (or Huitzilopochtli), associated with darkness and violence. Similarly, the earth goddess Coatlicue (in a variety of names) was often identified with death as well as life; she had a hideous, inhuman appearance in art, with serpentine characteristics and a necklace of human hearts. See also Appendix V:3; Spence, *Gods of Mexico*, 91–116, 223–8; and *PS* 553–9.

35:17 **The goddess of love** Tlazolteotl, an aspect of the earth goddess, was variously known as goddess of love, of the moon, and of excrement. In *The Plumed Serpent*, Ramón tells Kate, 'There have been some pretty goddesses, I assure you, in the Aztec pantheon' (255:22–3). See also Appendix V:3 and Clark's notes on *PS* 236:8 and 322:35.

35:23 **all ye people, joyfully triumphant!** Echoes the Christmas hymn 'O Come, All Ye Faithful' ['joyful and triumphant'], initially 'Adeste fideles' by John Francis Wade (1711–86), trans. Frederick Oakley (1802–80) and others, traditionally sung to Wade's music for his original Latin. The *Adelphi* altered DHL's wording, increasing the line's resemblance to the hymn.

35:25 **a stone knife.** In one legend, the earth mother (in the name Tonacaciuatl) gave birth to a flint knife, the precursor of the demi-gods. See Appendix V:3 and Michel Graulich, *Myths of Ancient Mexico*, trans. Bernard R. Ortiz and Thelma Ortiz de Montellano (Norman, Oklah., 1997), pp. 172–5.

35:27 **Paraclete of knives.** The 'Paraclete' (Greek) is the third person of the Christian trinity, the Holy Spirit, intercessor between human and divine.

35:30 **And the Sun . . . behind the sun,** Cf. 'The Hopi Snake Dance' (86:25–7, 92:4–7), 'The Flying Fish' (*St. Mawr and Other Stories*, ed. Finney, 210:11–12) and *The Plumed Serpent*: 'through the sun . . . the dark sun, the same that made the sun and the world' (123:3–4).

35:34 **Lo, the goddess [35:32] . . . a mother.** The angel Gabriel says to the Virgin Mary, 'And, behold, thou shalt . . . bring forth a son' (Luke i. 31–2, *KJB*); 'he shall save his people from their sins' (Matthew i. 21, *KJB*); and 'that holy thing which shall be born of thee shall be called the Son of God' (Luke i. 35, *KJB*).

36:2 **Unto us a son is given.** Cf. Isaiah ix. 6.

36:9 **obsidian.** A black, vitreous stone from which knives and arrowheads were made, obsidian had great religious significance, being especially sacred to Tezcatlipoca. See Appendix V:3; Spence, *Gods of Mexico*, pp. 37–9; and Graulich, *Myths of Ancient Mexico*, p. 108.

36:23 **white monkey** John Galsworthy's novel *The White Monkey* (1924) also uses the image of a 'white monkey' in a critique of modern civilisation.

37:15 **From time immemorial . . . fiestas,** Elaborate pre-Columbian calendar systems, devised by priests, set feast days, weeks and even hours for tributes to a wide variety of gods and goddesses. After the Spanish Conquest, the Roman Catholic feast days replaced many of the indigenous ones. See Appendix V:1–3 and Spence, *Gods of Mexico*, 268, 359–70.

37:22 **the non-existent.** A 'real' (Spanish for 'royal'), amounting to one-eighth of a peso, is like the US 'bit' or one-eighth of a dollar that has no corresponding coin. For the historic Spanish colonial 'real' and the eight-real piece, and for other terms of Mexican currency, see the Glossary.

37:23 **the *meum* and the *tuum*** Literally, 'what is mine and what is yours' (Latin).

37:28 **a *lueur*** A 'gleam' or 'glow' (French). When referring to people of the ancient Near East who lost the 'golden age', DHL says that 'gold fell from glory and became money' (*Apocalypse and the Writings on Revelation*, ed. Kalnins, 128:28–9).

38:17 **mud.** The change in E1 from 'masa' (MS, p. 5), or bread dough, indicates DHL's correction of Secker's proofs for *Mornings in Mexico*.

38:20 **roses of paradise.** Cf. the Christian heaven in *The Plumed Serpent*: 'the dead have peace among the scentless rose-trees, in the Paradise of God' (124:35–6). The typist skipped from this 'paradise' to the essay's next instance of the word, omitting seventeen words – which are restored in this edition from MS (p. 5). TCC also omitted twelve words at 41:14–15 ('two proper . . . but not', MS, p. 9) and fifteen at 42:1–2 ('*therefore* he . . . same footing', MS, p. 9), in the latter case skipping from one instance of '*therefore*' to the next.

38:28 **the other times are out of hand.** Previously 'God wants it so' (MS, p. 5) but changed by DHL in TCC (p. 5), apparently to further the variations on time.

38:30 **their yesterdays and todays and tomorrow.** In *The Plumed Serpent*, Ramón also emphasises the 'Now': 'a man in a deep sleep has no tomorrow, no yesterday nor today, but only is . . . Now, and forever Now' (176:3–5). See also DHL's own view, in 'Poetry of the Present' (*Poems* 181–3).

38:34 **a clever monkey . . . ugly . . . nasty white flesh.** In *The Plumed Serpent*, similarly, white foreigners are 'the clever ones' whose 'faces are ugly' (256:37, 257:2).

38:40 **tick-tack of work.** Cf. *Study of Thomas Hardy and Other Essays*, ed. Bruce Steele (Cambridge, 1985), 10:34 ('the tick-tack of birth and death') and 11:28 ('birth and death are a tick-tack'); 'The Crown', *Reflections* 281:22–3 ('time, which shall tick forth from us as from a clock'); and *Women in Love*, ed. David Farmer, John Worthen and Lindeth Vasey (Cambridge, 1987), 464:16–17 ('the wheels within wheels of people—it makes one's head tick like a clock').

39:2 **the very oil and metal out of our soil.** Cf. *The Plumed Serpent*, condemning the exploiters: 'They want gold, they want silver from the mountains, / And oil, much oil from the coast' (256:23–4). The 'greedy ones' are associated with their machines, and 'their wills are like their machines of iron' (257:3). But Mexicans may 'Take back our lands and silver and oil, take the trains and the factories and the automobiles' (257:17–18).

39:20 **Et praeterea nihil.** 'And nothing more' (Latin).

39:25 **she is very superior, had a Spanish grandfather,** European birth was the basis of the Mexican class system before independence from Spain and continued to affect social standing in the twentieth century. The Lawrences' cook, Natividad, was employed by Father Rickards along with some of her family. 'Señora' not only means 'Mrs' but is a respectful term for a woman with some authority.

39:28 **panier basket,** 'Bread basket' (French, from Latin 'panarium'). The typical large wicker baskets used to carry produce in rural Mexico, usually slung double across the back of a donkey or horse (see 51:4) or carried singly on the shoulders and back.

40:8 **a Spanish poem . . . the rose, of course.** Not simply a love poem, as DHL supposed, 'La Adelita' exists in several versions as a popular 'corrido' of the Mexican Revolution. DHL quotes from the first stanza of one:

> Adelita se llama la joven
> a quien yo quiero y no puedo olvidar,
> en el mundo yo tengo una rosa
> y con el tiempo la voy a cortar.

> (Adelita's the name of the maiden
> Whom I love and cannot forget;
> In the world I possess a rose
> And in time I am going to cut [pluck] it.)

Adelita is sometimes a sweetheart left behind or a camp-follower or a 'soldadero', one of the woman freedom-fighters who marched with the armies. One version has been attributed to Sergeant Antonio del Rio Armenta, who referred to an army nurse. See Maria Herrera-Sobek, *The Mexican Corrido: A Feminist Analysis* (Bloomington, Ind., 1990), p. 108, and note on 29:12.

40:10 **When I read a few lines aloud,** DHL helped Rosalino generously with his studies (Brett 172). See Ellis, *Dying Game*, on the relatively low Spanish literacy rate in Oaxaca (p. 210), due to its many dialects (as in 'Walk to Huayapa').

40:18 **Hindustani** Historically, a language group in n.w. India, including Hindi and Urdu; the Hindi dialect of Delhi, a widely used trade language for centuries, today usually called simply 'Hindi'.

40:28 **a needle's eye.** 'It is easier for a camel to go through the eye of a needle, than for a rich man to enter into the kingdom of God' (Matthew xix. 24, *KJB*); cf. also Mark x. 25, Luke xviii. 25.

41:6 **estan tocando!"** DHL uses diacritical marks lightly in the Spanish of these essays: he may be representing dialect since this is not the first language of the Zapotec Indian speaker. See also notes on 21:17, 24:29, 41:26, 114:31 and 118:31.

41:13 **Aurelio, the dwarf mozo of our friends,** Inocente Cruz, from the Sierra de Juárez Mountains, was a servant of Hermann Kull (1889–1967), a Swiss dentist educated in the USA, and his Lithuanian wife Carola Kull (1886–1966), an amateur artist; from these friends in Oaxaca the Lawrences learned Inocente's and Rosalino's backgrounds. When Rosalino wanted to go home, the Kulls arranged a replacement for him. It is likely that DHL changed Inocente's name in the essay to afford him political safety in a still volatile political environment. See Brett 187–9; Parmenter 60, 65–82; *Letters*, v. 174 n. 2.

41:26 **Grazias!"** Although the Spanish spelling would commonly be 'Gracias', Rosalino presumably has an accent from his *'idioma'*.

41:40 **San Felipe.** This passage suggests that the Lawrence party's return from Huayapa to Oaxaca was through San Felipe, which they had missed on the first half of the Sunday walk (see 21:15–16, 23:18–20).

42:27 **fiesta.** The Thursday fiesta in 1924 was Christmas Day. In the original order of these essays, before DHL placed 'Market Day' last in the 'Mornings in Mexico' series (see Introduction), the set culminated with 'The Mozo', giving an increased prominence to this fiesta.

42:28 **the Niña** Frieda Lawrence. In *The Plumed Serpent*, Kate muses on the meaning of this Spanish word for 'Child', 'the honorable title for a mistress'; she recognises a 'slight note' of 'mockery' in this address (110:1–3, 19–20).

43:5 **the Señorita . . . a photograph of him.** Photographs by Dorothy Brett captured many activities of the Lawrence party in and around Oaxaca – see a selection of prints in Parmenter, including one of Rosalino (Plate 25).

43:13 **like a cracker going off** A firecracker, presumably, or a 'Christmas cracker' – a gift-wrapped tube that pops to expel a treat or gift.

43:29 **Back** A typing error in TCC (p. 12) caused DHL to supply a new word 'Now', but the intended word is retrieved from MS (p. 11).

43:34 **the last revolution** The revolt in 1923 by Adolfo de la Huerta (d. 1955) against Mexican President Alvaro Obregón (1880–1928) and his chosen successor Calles concerned Oaxaca directly when Governor Vigil joined it (see note on 27:33). On 12 January 1924, when the city was attacked by Serranos backing Obregón, Vigil's forces won – hence were 'the winning side' (45:5) and the Serranos 'the *losing* side' (45:3). But the tables were turned in April. It is likely that the soldiers who tried to induct Rosalino, like those who punished Aurelio in reprisal for the Serrano revolt (Parmenter 76–7), were Vigil's *Huertistas* while the troops the mozos continued to avoid were those of Obregón, Calles and their Serrano generals Ibarra and Jiménez. All five regarded themselves as liberal democratic leaders. See also Appendix VI:3–4.

43:39 **those, like myself,** Cf. the chapter 'Nightmare' in *Kangaroo* for DHL's wartime experiences as a non-combatant. He describes in a letter (1916) the 'degradation' he felt when he was 'marched like a criminal through the streets' to his own military inspection in Bodmin (*Letters*, ii. 618).

44:19 **this little town of a few thousands.** In the 1921 census, the population of Oaxaca was just over 27,000 – and DHL estimated it at 30,000 in November 1924 (*Letters*, v. 164). Since the 1909 census recorded over 36,000, these figures show a sharp decline in population during the revolutionary years. The disproportionately 'huge prison' (68:4), overcrowded with political prisoners since Governor Vigil's time (Parmenter 75), was near DHL's own lodgings.

44:25 **Adios a mi patron.** 'Farewell my master' or 'Farewell my benefactor' (Spanish). See note on 41:6.

44:30 **Vera Cruz State.** Located on the e. coast of the Gulf of Mexico, adjoining six other states of Mexico, including Oaxaca. It has Mexico's most important seaport (Vera Cruz), making it a strategic location in the revolt and an early stronghold of de la Huerta's forces (see note on 43:34).

45:13 **before Montezuma . . . to sacrifice.** DHL rightly implies that the practice of human sacrifice was much older than the time of Montezuma II (1480–1520), who ordered ritual sacrifice of captured enemies. In passages that DHL excised from *The Plumed Serpent* before publication, he states that 'the life-hope was dead, there was an instinct of death-worship in the Aztecs' (509–10). In the published novel, however, he still voices his faith in more benign origins: 'the older Indians, who knew [Quetzalcoatl] before the Aztecs raised their deities to heights of horror and vindictiveness' (58:35–6).

Market Day

49:1 **Market Day** The essay's first publication, in *Travel*, was accompanied by six photographs: a 'typical Mexican street scene', burros carrying goats' milk to town, a Mexican feast day, street musicians and Mexican market scenes ('The Gentle Art of Marketing in Mexico', pp. 7–9).

49:8 **splendid,** Although both periodical publications include the additional word 'very' (see Textual apparatus), DHL had cancelled it in MS. It is likely that the typist did not notice the deletion.

49:9 **Noche Buenas, flowers of Christmas Eve.** Cf. *PS* 430:39. DHL's term for the *flor de Nochebuena* ('flower of Christmas Eve'), called 'poinsettia' in English to commemorate Joel R. Poinsett, an ambassador to Mexico who introduced its seeds into the USA. Native to southern Mexico and Central America, it is known for its tapering scarlet bracts like petals. See Kate's thoughts in *The Plumed Serpent*: 'How awful, Christmas with hibiscus and poinsettia!' (430:40).

49:13 **yucca** A giant arborescent plant, related to the 'century plant'; see also Glossary.

49:14 **yard-long** This was DHL's alteration in MS, which originally read 'great' (p. 1). Other changes to MS include: 51:6 <'little'> {'baby'} (p. 3); 51:21 <'trotting'> {'advancing'} (p. 4); and 55:18 <'life'> {'clue'} (p. 9).

49:20 **a tall tree of the flimsy acacia sort** Probably a *guaje* (Nahuatl), a white-trunked flowering 'locust' tree of the mimosa family.

49:31 **candelabrum cactus** These cactuses display towering fleshy stems in symmetrical arrangement around a central matrix.

50:2 **When space is curved,** According to Albert Einstein's general theory of relativity (1916), gravity is a curvature of space–time. Cf. also note on 16:17.

50:5 **visible** Although both Per1 and Per2 read 'invisible', 'visible' is clear in MS (p. 2). It is likely that the error occurred in Brett's typing and was therefore in both ribbon and carbon copies that went to the two periodicals. Other misreadings or omissions in the first typing are likely, as at 53:4, where 'sweetened' and 'cheeses' (MS, p. 6) were replaced until now by 'sweet' and 'cheese'. See also the note on 49:8 and Textual apparatus.

50:15 **Huayapa,** See note on 23:20.

50:30 **the bubbles of its church-domes** Cf. *The Plumed Serpent*, describing 'a huge old church ... its domes, like bubbles inflated' (50:22–3) and 'lingering, tall, handsome churches whose domes are like inflations that are going to burst' (78:40–79:1).

50:38 **the road is like a pilgrimage,** In *Quetzalcoatl: The First Version of 'The Plumed Serpent'*, ed. Louis L. Martz (Redding Ridge, Conn., 1995), Kate Burns sees Mexico in terms of 'her old visions of Israelites in deserts, and Abraham seeking water' (134).

51:7 **dam** A female parent, usually of a four-legged animal but related linguistically to the word 'dame' (*OED*).

51:16 **organ cactus [51:15]... palo blanco flowers... mesquite bushes.** See also the 'stiff living fence' formed by organ cactus and the flowering palo blanco trees in 'Walk to Huayapa' (26:8–9, 24:7–8). The mesquite's fan-like compound leaves, tough thorns, and crooked branches can form impenetrable windbreaks on the Oaxaca uplands, clothing the trees and bushes in a canopy of dust. See also Glossary and notes on 49:20 and 49:31.

51:20 **Zapotec race:** See Introduction (p. lii) and Appendix V:1 and 2. DHL described the Zapotecs in November 1924: 'Zapotec Indians, small, but very straight and alert and alive: really very nice' (*Letters*, v. 164).

51:28 **Serranos,** 'Mountain-dwellers' (Spanish), the Indian inhabitants (mostly Zapotec) of the high elevations around Oaxaca, named Sierra de Juárez for the national hero who was born there. The term had complex political significance since Serranos had supported, variously, both de la Huerta and Obregón in the course of the 1920s (see note on 43:34).

51:35 **The market is a huge roofed-in place.** Constructed in 1893, this market in downtown Oaxaca – the Mercado Benito Juárez – was eventually altered to roof in the patio as well as the stalls; a new market at the edge of town threatened its existence in 1974, but it was saved by the efforts of its vendors (Parmenter, *Mornings in Mexico*, Salt Lake City, 1982, pp. xxvii–xxviii). DHL wrote in November 1924, 'There is a big market humming like a bee-hive, where one can buy anything, from roses to horse-shoes' (*Letters*, v. 164); but by the next day he was more conscious of its 'babel' and 'hubbub' (*Letters*, v. 167). According to widespread custom at Mexican markets, the vendors 'like you to bargain' (52:12).

52:2 **Zapotec *idioma*,** See note on 24:30.

52:3 **Mixtecas.** The Mixtec Indians flourished in mountainous northern Oaxaca from AD 1200 to 1521, having gained control of key Zapotec sites through both force and diplomatic alliances. See Appendix V:2.

53:19 **the newest Paris style... ancient to these natives.** Sandals with leather lattice-work and straps, like the native *huaraches*.

53:32 **American leather."** US leather: presumably, leather tanned according to strict standards.

54:9 **The natives... human excrement for tanning leather.** Bernal Díaz del Castillo (*c.* 1492–1581), Spanish soldier and historian who was with Cortés, reported his discovery (though not in Mexico City) that dung was sold for the tanning of leather. But Parmenter says the practice was not continued in DHL's time, the tanning agent in Oaxaca being from oak tree barks and a fruit-like tamarind called *cascalote* (56–7). DHL sought out Díaz's *The True History of the Conquest of New Spain* (5 vols., 1632) for his work on *The Plumed Serpent* (*Letters*, iv. 445).

54:10 **Cortés**   Hernán Cortés (1485–1547), Spanish conqueror of Mexico (1521). He received honours in Spain, being named the Marquis of the Valley of Oaxaca, and the Conquest ushered in centuries of subjection of the Mexican people to European viceroys.

54:11 **the great market-place . . . in Montezuma's day,**   The great plaza or *zócalo* of Tenochtitlan (Mexico City) was a bustling centre of trade even in pre-Columbian times. Along one axis was an open area crowded with craftsmen, vendors and merchants hawking wares. The Aztec temple, with its twin altars to Huitzilopochtli the war god and Tlaloc the rain god, was on the present location of the Metropolitan Cathedral, and Montezuma's palace stood where the National Palace is today. Montezuma II was the Aztec emperor during the Spanish Conquest. Although DHL had once (1918) regarded him as 'a decadent and sensitive character', drawn to the Europeans by 'mystic sympathy, mystic desire' (*Studies* 173:5–6, 172:37–8), he had learned from Díaz and others (Introduction, footnote 105).

54:26 **the blue-haired Buddha, with the lotus at his navel.**   Historically, Buddha was Sakyamuni, Siddhartha, or Gautama Buddha of northern India (*c.* 563–483 BC), but recurrent Buddhas (reflecting a universal model) are also part of this tradition. In both conventional and theosophical Buddhism, blue is a primary colour of the 'Buddha rays' that often emanate from the head of an image of Buddha as 'The Enlightened One'. He is sometimes represented in painting with glowing dark-blue hair and in sculpture with *lapis lazuli* inlaid in the head. DHL has combined Buddha with Tantrism such as he found in Pryse, *Apocalypse Unsealed* (see note on 13:10). In this system, the manipura or navel 'lotus', or centre of fulfillment, is at the solar plexus, located behind the navel and in front of the lumbar ganglion. See *Psychoanalysis and the Unconscious*, ed. Steele, on 'the lotus of the navel' (21:12–13). For a Buddhist lotus mantra in a book DHL knew by 1906 (*Letters*, i. 46), see Edwin Arnold, *The Light of Asia* (1879), viii. 289.

54:35 **the beast that knows [54:33] . . . hither and thither means nothing.**   In the poem 'The Ass', DHL says 'the ass is a primal creature, and never forgets', remembering alike 'The Steppes of Tartary, / And Jesus on a meek ass-colt: mares: Mary escaping into Egypt: Joseph's cudgel' (*Poems* 379, 380). A possible reference to the circular quest of the protagonist / ass in *The Golden Ass* (second century AD) by Apuleius.

55:28 **Like the evening star,**   Venus as morning and evening star had sacred significance in Mesoamerican mythology and is a ubiquitous symbol in *The Plumed Serpent*, signifying the revivified Quetzalcoatl and a new life for Mexico. Ramón's followers call themselves 'Men of the Morning and the Evening Star' (178:37); and he tells them 'the day should not turn into glory, / And the night should not turn deep, / Save for the morning and evening star, upon which they turn' (339:35–7). When he performs Kate's marriage to Cipriano, the two meet 'at twilight, between the night and the day' under 'the unfading star' (329:8, 9). While Quetzalcoatl was more associated in legend with the morning star, the evening star was the particular emblem of his 'twin' Xolotl. For the evening star in DHL's early writing, cf., for instance, 'A Modern Lover', 'The Fly in the Ointment' and 'The Witch à la Mode', all in *Love*

Among the Haystacks and Other Stories, ed. Worthen, 29:1–3, 49:13, 54:28–31. It is clear that DHL felt a personal relationship with it, as with Orion.

Indians and Entertainment

59:1 **Indians and Entertainment**   The essay's first publication, in the *New York Times Magazine*, was illustrated by a drawing of Plains Indian dancers by the Blackfoot Indian artist Lone Wolf. The scene seems unrelated to the Pueblo dancers of the essay (p. 3).

59:2 **We go to the theatre**   DHL had cancelled the first sentence in MS, 'The theatre is a place of entertainment' (p. 1), but its echo remains in the title.

59:3 *The Potters…* **Max Reinhardt,** *King Lear* **or** *Electra.*   *The Potters,* a comedy dramatised by J. P. McEvoy (1897–1958) from his *Chicago Tribune* stories, opened in December 1923 in Plymouth, Massachusetts. It concerned the amiable but bumbling Pa Potter and the efforts of his family to make ends meet. Max Reinhardt, originally Goldmann (1873–1943), Austrian theatrical director, produced a wide range of dramas by Sophocles (*c.* 498–406 BC), Shakespeare, August Strindberg (1849–1912), George Bernard Shaw (1856–1950) and others. Reinhardt was touring in the USA in 1923. *King Lear* is a tragedy by Shakespeare. Both Sophocles and Euripides (*c.* 484–407 BC) wrote tragedies named *Electra* for the doomed heroine of the house of Atreus, battling the will of the gods – a subject inherited from the *Oresteia* of Aeschylus (*c.* 525–456 BC).

59:17 **We are the gods and there's the machine,**   DHL often plays with the idea of the *deus ex machina,* a 'god' that was lowered mechanically onto the Greek and Roman stage to resolve some otherwise insoluble problem. He means that the self manufactures itself as god. See also note on 160:30.

59:31 **ideal consciousness.**   DHL opposed Platonism and idealism as well as Transcendental concepts of consciousness. He attributed to the Greeks 'the great passion for the ideal, the passion for translating all consciousness into terms of spirit and ideal or idea' (early 'Whitman', *Studies* 403:20–1). In 'A Propos of *Lady Chatterley's Lover*', he states: 'We have to go back, a long way, before the idealist conceptions began, before Plato, before the tragic idea of life arose, to get on to our feet again' (*Lady Chatterley's Lover and 'A Propos of Lady Chatterley's Lover'*, ed. Michael Squires, Cambridge, 1993, 330:13–15).

60:7 **and from this to a belief in**   The passage appears first in E1, replacing the words 'And from universal law' (MS, p. 2); it is likely that DHL made the alteration in the lost Secker proofs.

60:10 **Universal Mind.**   A particular preoccupation of the theosophist Madame Blavatsky, who sought to unite the idealism of Immanuel Kant (1724–1804) with Vedantic and hermetic concepts of a great mind to which smaller minds all belong (*The Secret Doctrine*, i. 601–3).

60:13 **cinematograph.**   A pioneering device to project moving images (eventually motion pictures), patented in 1895 by Louis and Auguste Lumière in Paris. See Mr May's criticism of the cinematograph films in *The Lost Girl*: 'Pictures don't have any life except in the people who watch them. And that's why they like them. Because they make them feel that they are everything' (*The Lost Girl*, ed. John Worthen, Cambridge, 1981, 116:12–14).

60:27 **Eagle dance, Corn dance [60:25]... the fires at Christmas... sacred races, down the long track.** For the most part, DHL is describing ceremonies at Taos Pueblo, 3 miles n. of the town of Taos, New Mexico. In the Pueblo Eagle Dance, male dancers impersonate eagles, seen as emissaries from humans to the powers that provide rain and fertility. The Corn Dance occurs regularly each spring and summer in most pueblos, including Taos, featuring both men and women petitioning for good crops. Huge bonfires are lighted at Taos Pueblo every Christmas Eve, when the Indians form a procession outside the Church of San Geronimo and sing hymns (*alabados*). Foot races are held at this pueblo each 3 May, at the beginning of planting season, and again on 30 September (the feast of the patron saint San Geronimo), traditionally the end of the growing season. (See Appendix V:4.)

60:29 **Adolf Bandelier.** The American archaeologist Adolph Francis Alphonse Bandelier (1840–1914), author of *The Delight Makers* (1890, 1916) – which Mabel Luhan sent to DHL in May 1924, probably in the illustrated second edition. It tells of prehistoric Pueblo Indians and the popular clowns, *Koshare* or 'Delight Makers', who still play tricks and provide amusement at fiestas.

60:37 **de-bunk the Indian... de-bunk the Cowboy.** Wild West shows and pulp-fiction 'Westerns' promoted both glamourised and debased stereotypes of American Indians and 'cowboys' – cow herders – of the US frontier days. See also notes on 66:33 and 105:30.

61:19 **Our way of consciousness... the Indian's.** An apparent error in the missing first typescript, rendering 'Indians' for 'Indian's' (MS, p. 4), led to confusion in all previous publications. (TCC1–2, p. 4, repeat the same error.) One of DHL's characteristic themes is the alternating opposition and interplay of two states of consciousness, like English and Italian in *The Lost Girl*, with a mediating factor between them. See the 'meeting ground' or 'star' between Indian and 'white' at the marriage of Cipriano and Kate in *The Plumed Serpent* (331:7, 20).

61:33 **Hindoos or Polynesians or Bantu.** In the 'Epilogue' to *Movements in European History*, ed. Crumpton, 'different directions' are taken by diverse races and nationalities, all unique 'branches on the one tree of mankind' – including 'the Hindu' and 'the negroes and the Polynesians' (256:12–14); nonetheless, the European 'growing tip' may need to be 'grafted' outside itself: 'Our idea and our ideal begin to peter out' (256:33, 257:13, 15–16). In *Kangaroo*, ed. Steele, DHL refers to a mystery 'which white men have struggled so long against, and which is the clue to the life of the Hindu': 'The other mystic relationship between men, which democracy and equality try to deny and obliterate. Not any arbitrary caste or birth aristocracy. But the mystic recognition of difference and innate priority' (107:25–6, 27–30). DHL would have known of Bantu power in ancient Africa because in 1918 he read *The Voice of Africa*, 2 vols. (1913), by the German ethnologist Leo Frobenius, trans. Rudolf Blind (*Letters*, iii. 233).

61:38 **a little Ghost inside you . . . both ways, or even many ways.** See 'Foreword' to *Sons and Lovers*, in which the 'glad cry' of self, poised between Father and Son, 'is the Holy Ghost the Comforter' (ed. Helen Baron and Carl Baron, Cambridge, 1992, 427:12–13); 'The Crown', in which an 'utter relation' between 'two eternities' is 'the Unrevealed God: what Jesus called the Holy Ghost' (*Reflections* 300:29, 33–4); *Study of Thomas Hardy*, ed. Steele, 80:2, 87–8, 126–7; and 'The Theatre' (1915 version) in *Twilight in Italy*, ed. Eggert, 148:14. In *The Plumed Serpent* this scheme is applied to the union of two individuals: 'The good ghost of me goes down the distance / To the Holy Ghost. / Oh you, in the tent of the cloven flame / Meet me, you I like most', for each has 'his own way forever, but towards / The hoverer between' (441:9–12, 13–14).

62:6 **European peasants** See, for example, the Bavarian peasants who 'sing strangely in the mountain fields' in 'The Crucifix Across the Mountains' (*Twilight in Italy*, ed. Eggert, 93:23), and the Italian folk musicians in 'The Dance' (pp. 170–1).

62:10 **the wild fishermen of the Outer Hebrides** In Cornwall in 1917, DHL sang Hebridean folk songs which, according to Catherine Carswell, he 'howled' in sounds he 'ingenuously supposed to be the Gaelic' and imitated 'the noise made by a seal' (*The Savage Pilgrimage*, pp. 90–1). See DHL's thinly fictionalised account of the wartime authorities who suspected the Lawrences of being spies because of the songs: 'Somers had had in his pocket the words of one of the Hebridean Folk Songs . . . On a bit of paper in his jacket-pocket, the words which have no meaning in any language apparently, but are just vocal, almost animal sounds: the Seal Woman's Song—This they had taken.

> "Ver mi hiu—ravo na la vo— —
> Ver mi hiu—ravo ho-ro i— —
> Ver mi hiu—ravo na la vo—an catal—
> Traum—san jechar—'"
>
> (*Kangaroo*, ed. Steele, 245:3–12)

The composer and music critic Cecil Gray introduced the Lawrences to *Songs of the Hebrides* (1909–21) by Marjory Kennedy-Fraser (1857–1930), and DHL called the transcribed Gaelic originals both 'marvellous' (*Letters*, iii. 164) and 'songs of the damned' (*Letters*, iii. 180).

62:11 **intense,** Substituted for 'low' in MS (p. 5), one of several small changes by DHL, including: 63:38 <'though'> {'while'} (p. 7); 64:26 <'inimical'> {'complex'} (p. 8); and 65:35 <'women'> {'hunters'} (p. 10).

62:14 **seal woman,** A well-known figure in Hebridean folk song is a female 'selkie' or seal-woman whose life is divided between human and seal identities. One song, 'The Seal-Woman's Croon' published by Kennedy-Fraser (*Songs of the Hebrides*, i. 15–17), tells of a woman transformed into a seal by a spell that allows only occasional returns. In *Kangaroo*, Somers identifies with the woman while he stands on the Pacific shore: 'Now he understood the yearning in the seal-woman's croon, as she went back to the sea, leaving her husband and her children of warm flesh' (ed. Steele, 125:22–4). Possibly DHL also knew of the opera *The Seal-Woman* (1924) by Granville Bantock (1868–1946), for which Kennedy-Fraser supplied the libretto. See also the idea of a speaking seal in *Women in Love*, ed. Farmer, Vasey and Worthen (427:2).

62:24 **the consciousness in the abdomen.** A reference to the solar plexus, a chakra and one of the Yogic centres of consciousness (see note on 13:10).

62:27 **quite modern, the song of the church bell on Sunday morning.** A reference to a song – 'tune the church bell of the Indians' – exists in the early form of the drama *David* (but was later deleted); it names the tune as a musical setting for part of Psalm viii (*The Plays*, ed. Schwarze and Worthen, note on 487:33, and its Appendix V). DHL heard the Taos Indians sing to the ringing of their church bell (see 'Taos', 127:25–6, 127:33–5). The Taos bells represent the relatively 'modern' religion brought by the Franciscan missionaries with Spanish contact. The present San Geronimo Church, built in 1850, has twin bells. But the 'old' bell with its belltower also survives from the church that the US Army destroyed just after the Spanish-American War. The original church, built in 1619, was burned sixty-one years later during the Pueblo Rebellion that ousted the Spanish (see Appendix V:4 and Appendix VI:5).

62:40 **without melody.** See also the singing in *The Plumed Serpent* by a Mexican Indian 'in the fashion of the old Red Indians': 'For a long time, no melody at all was recognisable' and 'There was no recognisable rhythm, no recognisable emotion' though the sound reached 'the most ancient and everlasting soul of all men' (126:9, 25–6, 29, 31–2). DHL's music for *David* (1926, performed 1927) was influenced by the style of Southwestern Indian chants.

63:19 **the tremulous, pulsating protoplasm** See 'Foreword' to *Sons and Lovers*, ed. Baron and Baron: 'that quivering, shimmering flesh of flesh, which is the same, unchanged forever, a constant stream, called if you like Protoplasm, the eternal, the unquestioned, the infinite of the "Rose", the Flesh, the Father—which were more properly, the Mother' (470:28–32). Cf. also *Study of Thomas Hardy*, ed. Steele, identifying a man's 'body' with 'his vital tissue, the very protoplasm in him' (119:20).

63:21 **the round dances,** Round dances are common among American Indian tribes, but the Taos Indians perform a characteristic side step in the Taos Round Dance. Dancers form two concentric wheels – an outer one, where participants move clockwise, and an inner one, where others move counterclockwise. Witter Bynner (1881–1968) describes a social 'Circle Dance', model for the Plaza dance in *The Plumed Serpent*, that was popular in New Mexico: 'concentric dancing with a drummer seated at the core of it' (*Journey with Genius*, p. 265).

63:23 **bird-tread** One of the most characteristic steps in American Indian dances is the stomp step, a flat-footed trot. The toe–heel action is performed while the dancer stands in a slightly forward-tilting posture with the knee raised. A Pueblo variation includes a stylised lift of the foot and solid stamp. See also Bynner, *Journey with Genius* (p. 209).

63:39 **circulation** Both periodicals printed 'circulating', probably because of the typist's original misreading. See also 65:38 ('three-pulse' not 'three-pulsed', MS, p. 10) and note on 61:19 ('Indian's'). In addition, several words were evidently skipped in the missing first typing by Brett (see Textual apparatus).

64:12 **the mime dances [64:10] ... a spear dance.** In the spear dance, two men bearing spears and shields dance a pantomime of single combat. See also *The Plumed Serpent*, in which Cipriano has imported 'the shield and spear dance' into Mexico, having learned it from northern American Indians (364:31). Two of his men are 'naked save for a breech-cloth and the scarlet feathers on their head, dancing the old spear-dance, whooping challenge in the firelight' (351:14–16); Cipriano also performs it, 'the dance of the two warriors, champions in the midst of the dense ring of soldiers' (364:38–9).

64:35 **The deer dance in the New Year.** At Christmas and again on 6 January at Taos Pueblo, dancers traditionally perform the Deer Dance (or, alternately, the Buffalo Dance). Two women lead columns of male dancers, masquerading as animals – deer, buffalo, black bear, wolf, coyote, fox and the like – from a site outside the pueblo into its plaza. In part, the dance recognises a sacred deer that saved the Taos people from starving (see Appendix V:4). Some dancers wear deer hides and antlers while clown figures (see *Koshare* in Glossary) appear in black and white paint, shooting the 'deer' with miniature bows and arrows and occasionally slinging a dancer over their shoulders and running out of the circle. At the end, they place bits of fresh venison in the mouths of some participants.

64:39 **on the roofs of the pueblo [64:35] ... the stream ... the log bridge,** At Taos Pueblo, the roofs form flat terraces that are reached by ladders, platforms where people can gather to watch ceremonies. The Pueblo de Taos River is the 'stream' that runs from the sacred Blue Lake high in the Sangre de Cristo Mountains through the pueblo site, where it passes cottonwood trees, flows under a wooden bridge, and separates the north and south pueblo structures before entering the Rio Grande Gorge 6 miles to the north.

66:4 **Greek drama arose this way.** Tradition says that Thespis (sixth century BC) first introduced dialogue into the Greek dithyrambic rituals for the god Dionysus by adding a separate actor in addition to the chorus. Aristotle (384–322 BC) tells in his *Poetics* (Pt iv) how the tragedians Aeschylus and Sophocles (see note on 59:3) each added an additional actor. Accompanying the stately tragedies (fl. fifth century BC) were bawdier satyr plays, probably descended from fertility worship, that influenced Greek comedy. Medieval Christianity, while originally hostile to theatre, developed dramatic tropes like the Easter dialogue between the women at Christ's tomb and an angel who asks them, 'Quem quaeritis?' – 'Whom seek ye?' (as based on Christ's words to Mary Magdalene, 'Whom seekest thou?' in John xx.15, *KJB*).

66:15 **shimmer of creation,** The word 'shimmer' is a DHL staple: cf. *Letters*, i. 255; *Sons and Lovers*, ed. Baron and Baron, 183:2–5; and *The Rainbow*, ed. Mark Kinkead-Weekes (Cambridge, 1989), 126:6. See also the following repetitions of the word: 66:18, 66:19, 66:28.

66:16 **distinction between God and God's Creation,** Cf. *Apocalypse and the Writings on Revelation*, ed. Kalnins: 'The very oldest ideas of man are purely religious, and there is no notion of any sort of God or gods. God and gods enter when man has "fallen" into a sense of separateness and loneliness' (131:5–8). Before that, 'the individual was hardly separated out' and 'the tribe lived breast to breast, as it were, with the cosmos' (130:31, 32). See also note below on 82:17.

66:22 **the maiden who brings us our food in dead of winter,** A Taos Indian version of the 'goddess of beasts' derives from the tribe's hunting heritage. In Europe, Paleolithic cave paintings depict a fertility goddess, guardian of surrounding wild animals. Similar is the iconography of the Greek Artemis (Roman Diana), the virgin goddess, paradoxically the patron of wild things and their huntress. The stag was sacred to Artemis, and deer were among the characteristic sacrifices to her. See Anne Baring and Jules Cashford, *The Myth of the Goddess: Evolution of an Image* (1999), pp. 70–1, 122–3, 320–32. In one Taos tale, the women find signs of deer on the mountain and save the tribe from hunger (Blanche Grant, *The Taos Indians*, Taos, 1925, p. 92).

66:32 **There is no . . . creation, in** Both Per1 and Per2 omit these words, present in MS (p. 11) and TCC1–2 (pp. 13–14), probably skipped by the first typist when her eye skipped from 'wonder of creation' to 'creation, in', thus missing the twelve intervening words.

66:33 **Apache warrior in his war-paint,** The Apache Indians were among the most fictionalised Indian tribes in European 'Westerns', in which they figured as both bloodthirsty maurauders and noble models of courage. Feared by foes for their fierce war skills, Apache armies resisted the US government for decades until the late nineteenth century. Their 'renegades' were still hunted by the Army as late as 1906 and rumours of their continuing threat lingered into the 1920s. But the last great Apache general, Geronimo (Goyathlay) (1829–1909), had surrendered in 1886.

66:40 **The presence of Jesus on the Cross, or the pitiful Mary Mother** Jesus was somewhat assimilated to models of indigenous culture-heroes like Poseyemu (Tewa), and the Virgin Mary was identified with the Pueblo Earth Mother whose plaster image the Taos Indians carried from the church to bless the fields. (See 'Taos', 127:31–2, for the Madonna in the 'starting-bower'.) In 1680, when the Indians burned the first Taos church, a painting of the Virgin Mary was spared; moreover, a Taos woman rescued the Virgin's statue from the doomed second church in 1847.

67:2 **The brave comes home with a scalp.** A reference to the custom of collecting scalps of enemies during the Indian wars (see note on 110:2). No American tribe practised it in DHL's time.

67:6 **which . . . we call Nature.** This passage is adopted from Per2; its source must have been an authorial addition at the (now missing) typescript stage. Per1 is abridged at this point and so does not contain it. Cf. *Apocalypse and the Writings on Revelation*, ed. Kalnins: 'What is our petty little love of nature— Nature!!—compared to the ancient magnificent living with the cosmos, and being honoured by the cosmos!' (76:24–6).

67:23 **absolutely no judgment.** This was the end of the essay in Per1.

67:33 **abominations,** The plural reading is accepted from Per2 despite a singular in MS (p. 12) because the use of 'among' and the plurals 'cowards' and 'liars' shows that DHL intended more than one.

67:36 **great negative commandments.** 'Thou shalt not', as in the Ten Commandments (e.g., 'Thou shalt not kill', Exodus xx. 13), as distinguished in the Bible from the positive commandments reiterated by Christ: 'Thou shalt love the Lord thy God with all thy heart, and with all thy soul, and with all thy mind, and with all thy strength' and 'Thou shalt love thy neighbour as thyself' (Matthew xxii. 37, xxii. 39; cf. Deuteronomy vi. 5 and Leviticus xix. 18, *KJB*). See also 'a Thou Shalt Not commandment' ('On Being Religious', *Reflections* 170:27–8) and 'the Christian Community today, in its perpetual mean thou-shalt-not' (*Apocalypse and the Writings on Revelation*, ed. Kalnins, 72:15–16).

68:36 **But what [68:33]...as from ours.** Although this unpublished paragraph from MS (p. 13) could possibly have been omitted by DHL himself (see Introduction, pp. xlv, lxxii), it expresses a fear that he repeats elsewhere in these essays, as also through the character Phoenix, caught up in the 'thrill and excitement' of 'motor cars and moving-pictures' (*St. Mawr and Other Stories*, ed. Finney, 136:14–15).

The Dance of the Sprouting Corn

71:1 **The Dance of the Sprouting Corn** DHL had first written 'Spring Corn' but revised it to read 'Sprouting Corn' (see Introduction, p. lxxiii). This ritual is sometimes called 'the Dance of Green Corn' to distinguish it from a celebration of Yellow Corn (a harvest dance). The essay's first publication, in *Theatre Arts Monthly*, appeared with four illustrations: DHL's sketch of corn dancers (see also Introduction, pp. xlv–xlvi, and Illustration I), a sketch by Robert Edmond Jones of the blessing of horses at Acoma Pueblo, a *koshare* sketch supplied by Miss A. E. White, and a sketch of a Pueblo Basket Dance (pp. 449–52).

71:4 **A river on the plain of drought,** Landscape and architectural details in the text locate this dance at Santo Domingo Pueblo (see Introduction, pp. xlv–xlvi), 25 miles s. of Santa Fe on the Rio Grande. Annual precipitation on the New Mexico Plateau ranges from less than 10 inches to a rare 20. Nevertheless, Santo Domingo has suffered flood damage. All but one of New Mexico's nineteen pueblos are located on the Rio Grande – which flows 1,900 miles from southwest Colorado to the Gulf of Mexico and, in Mexico, is called the Rio Bravo del Norte.

71:10 **the bed of a great sea that dried up unthinkable ages ago,** In the Paleozoic era, much of New Mexico lay under a shallow sea, and fossils of marine life are often found in sandstone and limestone formations.

71:16 **the mud church [71:13]...two speckled horses rampant...a red piebald and a black one.** The Church of the Pueblo of Santo Domingo (St Dominic) is a multi-level painted adobe structure, with a tall stepped belfry and a railed balcony over the entrance. It dates from 1886, when it replaced a mission church that had been destroyed by flooding on the Rio Grande. Beneath the eaves on the upper balcony is the mural of running horses, perhaps representing day and night or east and west. Ladders lead to each level in pueblo style.

71:18 **the pueblo,** Santo Domingo (where the Keres or Keresan language is spoken) is sometimes called 'Heart of the Pueblos'. Much of the village dates to the seventeenth century, but substantial portions of the pueblo were lost to nineteenth-century floods and rebuilt, so that both ancient and modern building styles are present. Santo Domingo got its name and patron saint (St Dominic) when it was claimed for Spain in 1598, becoming the ecclesiastical centre and missionary headquarters for the early Franciscans in New Mexico.

71:20 **dust to dust returning, earth to earth.** The Order for the Burial of the Dead, committing the dead body to the earth: 'ashes to ashes, dust to dust' (Book of Common Prayer). See also Genesis iii. 19, in which God states, after the fall of man, 'dust thou art, and unto dust shalt thou return' (*KJB*).

71:24 **the naked human hand . . . quicker than time,** Cf. DHL's 'Things Men Have Made', about products of 'wakened hands' that 'are awake through years with transferred touch, and go on glowing / for long years . . . warm still with the life of forgotten men who made them' (*Poems* 448). DHL's 'quick' has a special meaning as 'quick and alive': 'The quick is God-flame, in everything' ('The Novel', in *Study of Thomas Hardy and Other Essays*, ed. Steele, 183:28, 182:40–183:1). As the 'living plasm' itself, 'it inhales the future, it exhales the past, it is the quick of both, and yet it is neither' ('Poetry of the Present', *Poems* 182).

72:3 **a little, beating branch of green pine.** Various tree branches are commonly carried or worn during Pueblo dances to symbolise the earth's fertility, which can summon further fertility by a kind of sympathetic attraction.

72:13 **the hopping Koshare, the jesters, the Delight-Makers.** These figures have great antiquity and spiritual significance as representatives of deific, ancestral and other spirits. They are held to be benign, correcting behaviour through a form of mockery. See Illustration II and notes on 60:29 (Bandelier's *The Delight Makers*) and 64:35.

73:6 **the green tableta, like a flat tiara.** The dance is sometimes called the 'tableta dance' because of this headdress, which depicts rain clouds on its high castle-like crown.

73:24 **the black, prehistoric short gown** The traditional black or dark brown woollen garment wrapped around the woman's body, fastening on the right shoulder and leaving the left shoulder bare; it is cinched at the waist by tying the sash. See *The Plumed Serpent*, in which Kate fastens her wedding gown that has 'no sleeves nor arm-holes' (328:31–2): 'Then she remembered the old Indian way, and tied the string over her left shoulder: rather, slipped the tied string over her left shoulder, leaving her arms and part of her right breast bare, the slip gathered full over her breasts' (328:31–2, 33–6).

73:40 **the great necklaces of shell-cores** Santo Domingo is known for its shell jewellery. The Pueblo trade region extended westward into California, source of shells from the Pacific Ocean, even at a prehistoric date.

74:2 **short white kilt... embroidery, green and red and black,** See note on 85:13.

74:16 **the red earth with which they are smeared.** Cf. *Sketches:* 'In the early days, men smeared themselves with scarlet when they took on their sacred natures. The Red Indians still do it. When they wish to figure in their sacred and portentous selves, they smear their bodies all over with red' (50:22–5). In *The Plumed Serpent*, Cipriano wears body paint of 'oil and red earth-powder' (365:37). See also the poem 'For the Heroes Are Dipped in Scarlet', in which 'the loveliest is red all over, rippling vermilion' (*Poems* 689).

74:30 **loose cotton drawers,** The everyday Pueblo trousers were short and unfitted with slits on the lower outer legs.

75:19 **daubed with black-and-white earth [75:17]... dry corn-leaves.** The *koshare* wear body paint of dark clay or charcoal and kaolin, a chalky white clay, forming patterns of stripes, zigzags, triangles, and dots from head to toe. The corn tufts on their heads form 'horns' and hint of the dryness of death awaiting the crop's rebirth.

76:7 **their kiva,** The kiva is a ceremonial structure that symbolises the successive 'underworlds' through which, in legend, the people emerged into the present (their fourth world): see Glossary and Appendix V:4.

76:18 **the third day.** The three days of the festival, at Easter, have both indigenous and Christian significance. DHL captures the latter in the biblical phrase associated with Creation and Resurrection (cf. Genesis i. 13, Hosea vi. 2, Luke xxiv. 7 and I Corinthians xv. 4).

The Hopi Snake Dance

79:1 **The Hopi Snake Dance** The essay's first publication, in *Theatre Arts Monthly*, was accompanied by seven illustrations: Hopis 'dancing in procession' before the Snake Dance, Walpi Pueblo on its mesa, Oraibi Pueblo, Hopi Kachina dancers and Kachina dolls, and drawings provided by Miss A. E. White of a Snake Priest and an Antelope Priest, respectively (pp. 839–42, 853–4).

79:3 **The Hopi country... north of the Santa Fe railroad.** The Hopi and Navajo Reservations were established in the nineteenth century in northeastern Arizona on ancestral grounds (see Appendix V:5). The Hopi villages occupy three jagged mesas – themselves projections of Black Mesa – 200 miles due w. of Taos, encircled by the Navajo. The Atchison, Topeka and Santa Fe railroad came to New Mexico in 1878, running from Lamy (near Santa Fe) to Los Angeles. The Lawrences, with Mabel Dodge Luhan and Tony Lujan, made part of their trip on what would become the historic Route 66, 'the highway beside the railroad that goes through the Navajo Reservation', as Mabel puts it in *Lorenzo in Taos* (p. 257). Instead of passing through Holbrook

(Arizona), however, the Lawrence party veered northward from Gallup (New Mexico) to St Michael's, a Franciscan mission town on the Navajo Reservation, and crossed all three Hopi mesas on their way to Hotevilla in Arizona (see Map 4). In MS (p. 1) the word 'railroad' appears partly blotted but not deleted; on the same page, the apparent capital 'c' in 'Navajo country' is very possibly an example of DHL's tendency, at times, to loop his lower-case 'c', so that capital and plural are difficult to distinguish. All parallel instances of 'country' in the opening paragraphs of MS and of 'Just Back from the Snake Dance' (MS, p. 1) are uncapitalised; and this form is adopted here as DHL's intention and usual practice.

79:4 **The Hopis are pueblo Indians,** Like the Pueblo Indians of New Mexico, the Hopis live in villages. But they consider themselves separate and are distinguished from the eastern (New Mexico) Pueblos by language, religion (seldom Catholic) and geographic isolation. See also Appendix V:5.

79:9 **Walpi,** The name is Hopi for 'Place of the Gap' since the community occupies the tip of a 600-foot-high mesa, First Mesa. It was moved from the base of the mesa to the top after the Pueblo Rebellion (1680) for greater safety from the Spanish. **Chimopova** (79:20) is DHL's phonetic spelling of Shongopovi (Shongopavi) or Shungopavi, the ceremonial centre of Second Mesa, also settled at its present location in the seventeenth century. Tony Lujan spelled it 'Chimopavi', as cited in Mabel Dodge Luhan's *Winter in Taos* (New York, 1935), p. 215. **Hotevilla** (79:32), settled in 1906 by a group from Oraibi, is a strongly traditional village on Third Mesa, where the two sites of **Oraibi** (80:1) are also located – [Old] Oraibi and New Oraibi, the former being one of the earliest settlements in the New World (from AD 1100).

79:14 **sacrificed eagles,** Every spring the Hopis gather fledgeling golden eagles from nests on the cliffs, sacrificing them as emissaries to the gods. The Hopis, uniquely, were exempted from federal rules protecting these birds, but their right to gather them in national parks was challenged late in the twentieth century.

79:30 **snake-dance** The Snake Dance alternates every other year with the Flute Dance in different Hopi villages: in Hotevilla, where DHL saw it, it falls in even-numbered years; in Walpi and Oraibi, in odd-numbered years. The term 'Hopi Snake Dance' actually refers to more than a week of separate activities. The central dance is a petition for rain and fertility, offering snakes as emissaries to the rain god. It is the culmination of nine days of preparation in two kivas – those of the Snake Clan (where snakes are gathered in an underground chamber) and the Antelope Clan (which summons clouds), balancing the powers of earth and sky. Preparatory rites teach the tribe's prehistory with 'Snake People' in the earth's centre (see Appendix V:5 and Harold Courlander, *The Fourth World of the Hopi*, Albuquerque, 1971, pp. 82–95). Public events of the week include two dances (beginning with the Antelope Dance), two footraces and a 'corn scramble' in which participants vie to catch choice foods and plants that are tossed into a crowd. See also note on 84:18.

80:21 **Three thousand people** In 'Just Back from the Snake Dance', DHL wrote the same figure, but someone – perhaps Willard Johnson – changed it to read 'eight hundred' as it appeared in *Laughing Horse* (see Appendix I). But there was no effort to make this change in 'The Hopi Snake Dance'. The more likely number of tourists at that time was 800, even at a large dance in Hotevilla.

80:26 **What had they come for?** See the more elaborated reference in 'Just Back from the Snake Dance' (at 186:9, 186:39), echoing Christ's repeated words to those who sought out John the Baptist in the wilderness (Appendix I). Cf. Luke vii. 24, 25, 26.

80:26 *rattlesnakes* Members of the *Viperidae* family, most common in the US Southwest and Mexico. They get their name from their 'rattles', hard segments of skin at the ends of their tails that make a characteristic hissing or rattling sound when they are roused to strike. Their venomous bite can be lethal.

80:30 **circus-performance** Even before Wild West Shows, circuses staged improvised Indian rituals, following the lead of entertainment entrepreneur Phineas Taylor Barnum (1810–91), who housed American Indian dancers at his American Museum in New York as early as 1843.

80:34 **Anna Pavlova...Russian ballet.** Russian ballet dancer (1885–1931) who performed with Sergei Diaghilev's Compagnie des Ballets Russes (founded 1909). Forming her own dance company, she toured in Europe and the USA after 1911 and settled in Paris. See also *Mr Noon*, ed. Lindeth Vasey (Cambridge, 1984), 255:22–256:5; *Women in Love*, ed. Farmer, Vasey and Worthen, 91:22; and *The First 'Women in Love'*, ed. John Worthen and Vasey (Cambridge, 1998), 80:13 and notes.

81:7 **cultured point of view,** DHL originally used the word 'cultural' three times within a few lines (MS, pp. 3–4), but the considerable change of meaning to 'cultured' in all three instances (81:27, 81:11, 81:14) is in both Per1 and Per2 and has been accepted as DHL's. Elsewhere in the essay, 'cultured' is an attribute of sophisticated, perhaps superficial, society at 80:22–3 ('cultured people from New York'). He had written to Mabel Luhan in April 1922, 'I wish I could come to America without meeting the awful "cultured" Americans' (*Letters*, iv. 226). But DHL also calls the Pueblo Indian 'a cultured animist' at 84:34 (MS, p. 7).

81:10 **the Corn Dance at Santo Domingo,** See notes on 'The Dance of the Sprouting Corn', beginning at 72:3.

81:11 **The big pueblos of Zuni, Santo Domingo, Taos** Zuni Pueblo – the largest in New Mexico in population and acreage – is near the Arizona border, 170 miles n.w. of Albuquerque. The Zuni population (1,640 in 1910) was twice that of Santo Domingo and three times that of Taos Pueblo.

81:24 **Hindoo** While the Hopis and other Pueblo Indians often profess aspects of totemism, associating animals with gods, ancestors and founders of clans, the Hindu religion (India's ancient Vedic faith) goes further. Because the human and animal souls are linked in the process of transmigration, Hindus extend their non-violence principle to the animal world. DHL may be thinking, too, of the Jainists (dating to India's sixth century BC), who go to such extremes of *Ahimsa* ('no violence') that they avoid stepping on, or breathing in, an insect.

81:26 **St. Francis preaching to the birds.** Giovanni Francesco Bernardone (1182–1226), Italian founder of the Franciscan order. His *Canticle of the Sun* praises all creatures as brothers, and he is said to have preached to the birds, addressing them as 'My sisters the birds' (*Little Flowers of St. Francis*, trans. W. Heywood, 1906, p. 26). Frieda painted a picture of DHL as St Francis with birds and fishes (at UT). See DHL's comment on St Francis and the birds in *Letters*, iii. 712. After this line and at subsequent points in the essay (see Textual apparatus), Peri inserted subheadings, but there is no evidence that DHL authorised them.

81:30 **animistic religion [81:27]...all is alive.** DHL points elsewhere to 'one underlying religious idea' – that of an animistic universe – in ancient Asia, Egypt, Babylonia, the Pacific islands and 'aboriginal America': 'The whole thing was alive, and had a great soul, or anima: and in spite of one great soul, there were myriad roving, lesser souls; every man, every creature and tree and lake and mountain and stream was animate, had its own peculiar consciousness' (*Sketches* 57:34, 10–14). Cf. also *The Plays*, ed. Schwarze and Worthen, pp. lxx–lxxi, cxxi–cxxii with note on 439:30.

81:30 **alive.** This word was substituted in MS for 'godly', apparently as part of the expanding focus on animism. Other changes in MS include: 79:3 <'reservation'> {'railroad'} (p. 1); 79:13 <'in'> {'at the far edge'} (p. 1); 79:15 <'against'> {'under'} (p. 1); 81:27 <'by no means'> {'not'} (p. 4); 82:27 <'profound'> {'desperate'} (p. 5); 84:28 <'embracing'> {'making interchange with'} (p. 7); 84:30 <'nearer to'> {'more knowing in'} (p. 7); 86:24 <'corn plant'> {'the corn'} (p. 9); 87:15 <'Then it is finished'> {'That is all'} (p. 10); 88:24 <'where the'> {'under which'} (p. 11); 90:10 <'harmony'> {'unison'} (p. 13); and 91:38 <'caverns'> {'holes'} (p. 15). DHL added a total of eight lines interlinearly to MS in addition to a number of words; and he deleted words (e.g. 81:11: 'for a moment' was removed from 'not for a moment revealed', p. 4).

81:37 **invisible** Although rendered 'invincible' in previous publications, 'invisible' in MS (p. 4) was surely misread by Brett as the original typist. For other apparent misreadings or omissions in the missing first typescript, see notes on 88:13, 88:34 and 89:35, and see Textual apparatus.

82:14 **The yogi, the fakir, the saint** A yogi is a member of an ascetic Hindu order, devoted to the god Siva, that teaches freedom of the self from body, mind and will. A fakir, an initiate in the Muslim Sufi order, may seem to defy physical laws through the practice of devotional religious exercises (e.g., lying on a bed of nails without pain). In popular European usage, the two are often conflated and associated with magic or miraculous experiences of mind over matter. In Roman Catholic practice, a saint is a person of extraordinary holiness who may be canonised only when associated with miracles beyond natural explanation.

82:17 **no division into Spirit and Matter, God and Not-God.** DHL traces a split between 'Me' and 'Not-Me' not only to 'the empirical and ideal systems of philosophy', dividing spirit and body, but also to rationales for modern science and industrialism based on the spiritual 'Not-Me': 'It was this religious belief which expressed itself in science' *(Twilight in Italy*, ed. Eggert, 120:2–3, 36–7, 121:15). See also notes on 59:31 and 66:16.

82:18 **neither Thor nor Zeus.** Thor was the Norse god of thunder and strength; Zeus was the most powerful of the Greek Olympians (Roman Jove or Jupiter), a god of thunderbolts, ruler of heaven and earth. But to the Pueblo Indians, a feathered serpent (appearing on some ceremonial garments) signifies thunder by its wings (like the stylised Hopi 'thunderbird'). Although no manuscript evidence now survives, DHL must have added a cluster of imagery to the (now missing) typescripts (sources for Per1 and Per2) suggesting a 'plumed serpent' instead of an anthropomorphic god: 'huge reptile-bird' (82:19), 'dragon-mouthed' (82:21), 'feathered' (82:22) and 'The serpent-striped, feathery Rain' (82:31–2).

82:35 **like the old Egyptian . . . Cosmic Dragon.** The struggle was reflected in the Egyptian myth of the cosmic serpent or dragon, Apophis, which daily strove to swallow the solar barque of the sun on its journey through the night (or otherworld); the encounter was mirrored in initiation ceremonies like those of Isis and Osiris. Most of the Egyptian gods – including Sebek the crocodile-god, Set the antagonist of the sun god, and even Amon the early sun god (later Amon-Ra) – had snake aspects to signify conquest of the elementary chthonic powers as well as identification with them. The Pharaoh wore the 'double crown' of Horus (a hawk or vulture) and of Set (the *uraeus*, a cobra or asp). DHL describes the 'sensual being' and 'magnificent central positivity' by which the 'lords of Egypt' related to their surroundings ('The Two Principles', first version, *Studies* 268:31, 33, 36) and later credits the Egyptians with maintaining 'the spark between man and the living universe' ('Him with His Tail in His Mouth', *Reflections* 316:13). See also *Women in Love*, ed. Farmer, Vasey and Worthen, 318:10–24.

83:2 **From this mystic Sun [82:39] . . . reptiles, birds and fishes.** See the Mesoamerican creation myth in Appendix V:1–2 and in a section DHL excised from *PS* 541–3.

83:5 **The only gods on earth are men.** Cf. a passage DHL excised from *The Plumed Serpent* in final revision: 'Tell them the only gods are men', says Ramón despite referring also to 'the One at the centre' of creation (541).

83:10 **The cosmos is a great furnace, a dragon's den,** See Ramón's 'Fourth Hymn' of Quetzalcoatl in *The Plumed Serpent*: 'There are dragons of sun and ice, dragons of the moon and the earth, dragons of salty water, dragons of thunder; there is the spangled dragon of the stars at large. And far at the centre, with one unblinking eye, the dragon of the Morning Star' (259:13–17). See also passages that DHL excised from the final novel: there is a firebreathing 'Wonder-dragon at the centre of the cosmos', where 'Fires cannot die, and waters cannot perish, because all the time they come invisibly from the deeps of all the cosmos, and differently, having moved substantial in the created worlds, they return' (*PS* 542).

83:17 **Men are frail as flowers.** DHL compares human and plant life in 'Study of Thomas Hardy': 'the rising flower thrusts and pushes at the heart of us, strives and wrestles', and 'the flower is the culmination and climax, the degree to be striven for' (*Study of Thomas Hardy and Other Essays*, ed. Steele, 12:13, 39). In 'The Crown', too, DHL describes a human 'state of blossoming' – 'from the delicate blue speedwells of childhood, to the equally delicate, frail farewell flowers of old age' ('The Crown', *Reflections* 286:10–12). See also 'Flowers and Men', *Poems* 683.

83:20 **the egg of chaos.** In Egyptian mythology, the cosmic serpent Apophis coiled itself around the egg of chaos to hatch the sun. See also Blavatsky's chapter 'The Mundane Egg' in *The Secret Doctrine*, in which an invisible bird 'dropped an Egg into Chaos, which Egg became the Universe' (i. 359).

83:27 **the living will.** As opposed to earlier DHL 'will' (wilfulness, as in the unfinished story 'The Wilful Woman'). See also 'the mystic, living will' at 84:6. There may be an echo of *In Memoriam* (1850) by Alfred, Lord Tennyson (1809–92): 'O living will that shalt endure / When all that seems shall suffer shock' (section cxxxi).

83:29 **This is the religion... Peruvian, Aztec, Athabascan:... all the world.** Ancient Peruvians revered the sun's deified energy and other natural forces, developing into the Inca Empire (fl. 1440). The Aztec Empire (fl. 1400) amounted to a theocracy with its powerful priestly class preoccupied with gods that controlled the sun, moon, rain and other phenomena. Members of the Athabascan language group – Navajos and Apaches who entered the US Southwest after 1400 – diverged in some concepts, but both subscribed to the idea that many natural objects had spirits that could be propitiated. (See Appendix V:1–6, VI:1–5.)

83:32 **In Mexico [83:29]... pueblo Indian... still somewhat gentle-hearted.** Bynner reports that DHL was so aghast at human sacrifice and 'the death presence in Mexico' in April 1923 that he had to be reminded of the Pueblos with their *koshare*, representing more amiable forces (*Journey with Genius*, p. 42). See also note on 60:29.

83:38 **The eagle and the snake.** Both are natural denizens of the US Southwest and Mexico but had sacred significance to Indians of these regions. See also Appendix V:3 and note on 82:18.

84:10 **seven years of famine,** Cf. Genesis xli. 27, xli. 30. Joseph the Hebrew prophet presided in Egypt over the stored supplies that sustained his people through a seven-year famine.

84:16 **_Quos vult perdere Deus, dementat prius._** More commonly 'Quos Deus vult perdere...' ('Whom God wishes to destroy, he first makes mad' (Latin)), anonymous though sometimes wrongly attributed to Sophocles or Euripides (see note on 59:3). The passage was appended to a scholium in the *Antigone* of Sophocles and expresses a common theme of Greek tragic drama (see Ruth Padel, *Whom Gods Destroy: Elements of Greek and Tragic Madness*, Princeton, 1995). Another popular form reads 'gods' for 'God', and a well-known variant ['... Jupiter...'] is quoted in the *Homeri Gnomologia* (1660) of James Duport (1606–79). See also *Letters*, iii. 48; the essay 'Love' (*Reflections* 11:31); the final version of 'Hawthorne's Blithedale Romance' and the first version of 'Fenimore Cooper's Anglo-American Novels' (*Studies* 98:29, 206:30).

84:17 **On the Sunday evening** In Per1, *Theatre Arts Monthly*, this line is the first after a subheading. But in Per2, the *Adelphi*, it is the first in the essay's second instalment although DHL left no direction for serialisation.

84:18 **Antelope dance.** In addition to representing rain clouds, the Antelope Priests celebrate the myth of human emergence from earth and the analogous growth of plants into upper air. While the 'trap-door' represents the *sipapu* to the underworld, the kisi, or cottonwood bower, illustrates fertility in this present or 'fourth' world (see Appendix V:5). The winner of the day's race goes to the Antelope kiva, receiving a sacred gourd of water, cornmeal and prayer-sticks to bless the future crops. As the thunder of antelope hoofs is said in legend to summon the clouds, the Antelope dancers shake their rattles and stamp the earth; traditionally wearing cloud symbols on their ceremonial kilts, they are regarded as rain-makers.

84:24 **for nine days, in the kiva,** During these days, dramatic songs and gestures tell and reenact the background of the Snake Dance (see Appendix V:5).

84:28 **making interchange with** Revising the original MS, DHL increased the active reciprocity connecting man and snake by crossing out 'embracing' and substituting these words (p. 7). On the same page, he increased the activity of consciousness, writing 'more knowing in' instead of the discarded 'nearer to' (84:30).

84:34 **the dark, lurking, intense sun at the centre of the earth.** See also *The Plumed Serpent*: 'the dark sun at the back of the day-sun' and 'the Master-Sun, the dark one' (123:31, 124:15).

85:3 **At sundown** The words 'on the Sunday', part of an insertion by DHL in MS (p. 8), were possibly missed by Brett, as the first typist, because 'sundown' and 'Sunday' looked similar; but they could have been deleted by DHL on the ground that he had already referred to the Sunday once. For the full passage, see Textual apparatus.

85:13 **little kilts embroidered like the sacred dance-kilts ... a white fibre-cloth.** The short skirt-like cotton kilts are embroidered in wool with bright sacerdotal glyphs such as zigzag lines for lightning and semicircles for rain clouds. Like many other Pueblo men, the Hopi men have traditionally woven their own ceremonial garments with such stylisation that they may vary little from village to village.

85:33 **smeared with red "medicine,"** Pigments from certain plants and minerals were believed to confer ceremonial power or 'medicine' to the wearer. See *Sketches*: 'The American Indian will tell you. The red paint, it is medicine, make you see!—But he means medicine in a different sense from ours. It is deeper even than magic' (50:32–4). 'Hopi Red Dye' is derived from amaranth (*Amaranthus*), and distinctive reds also come from pulverized hematite and from the 'Indian Paintbrush' plant (*Castilleja*).

85:37 **The hair of the young men, growing after school,** The US Bureau of Indian Affairs established both day schools and larger government boarding schools (1870s), requiring students to conform to 'white' standards, including cutting their hair. By August during summer vacation, however, their hair would be growing again into the accustomed longer tribal style although still retaining the rounded contour of the bob. Hotevilla was the scene of particularly notorious intrusion by federal troops in 1911 when the elders refused to send the young people away to boarding school; the armed forces entered their homes and removed the children, imprisoning some of the Hopi fathers.

86:25 **to the roots of the corn and to the feet and loins of men, from the earth's innermost dark sun.** Cf. *Sketches*: 'the serpent represented the vivid powers of the inner earth... the quick powers that run up the roots of plants and establish the great body of the tree, the tree of life, and run up the feet and legs of man' (164:29–165:4).

86:29 **that famous darkness and silence of Egypt,** Ancient Egyptian initiation rites, perhaps as described by Blavatsky. Mirroring the soul's death journey in *The Book of the Dead*, the initiate was kept in dark silence and 'deep sleep' for three days while laid inside a sarcophagus in a temple crypt or cave; just before the third day, he was carried to the initiation place to be awakened by the dawning light as the culmination of the mystery of Osiris (*The Secret Doctrine*, ii. 558). DHL also knew the Isis mysteries in *The Golden Ass* of Apuleius, XI, and elsewhere.

87:28 **many Navajos...real nomads.** Along with the Apaches, Navajos were once wandering sub-Arctic hunters and gatherers (see also Appendix V:6). During contacts with the sedentary Pueblo Indians, the Navajos learned fine weaving; and their colourful dyes and durable weaves became renowned. The women's traditional dress features voluminous gathered skirts, often with multiple tiers, and long-sleeved, tucked bodices, both modelled on Spanish and US frontier women's styles that modified their indigenous dress. Although their prior clothing was of fur and buckskin, they gained wool, cotton, suede-like velvet and baize from the Spanish trade. They frequently unravelled commercial fabrics and wove them anew with their own threads.

87:39 **like corpse-faces with the swathing-bands.** Mummies, like the Egyptian dead who were wrapped in bands of linen, the head showing slight indentations at the mouth and eyes and the jaw appearing sunken. According to Sir James George Frazer (1854–1941), in *The Golden Bough: A Study in Magic and Religion*, 3rd edn (1906–15), 12 vols., this funerary custom followed the rites of Osiris (v, ch. XXXVIII). DHL had read Frazer in 1914 (*Letters*, ii. 470).

88:4 **the lords of shadow...after-life and before-life,** Chthonic powers and intermediaries: similar to the Hopi Kachinas (*katsinas*, 'honoured spirits') – supernatural entities that were said to visit the Hopis for six months of the year. Dancers impersonated them, and children and adults alike kept carved wooden images or 'dolls' depicting the various Kachinas. The powerful lord of earthly death, Masauwu, was sometimes placed among the Kachinas; he controlled the passage to and from this world, and, in his deathly aspect, he appeared with a fiery red or skull-like face and wore dark clothing. Grey signified the nadir direction or the underworld. See also Appendix V:5.

88:10 **the six worlds, or quarters:**   To Pueblo Indians, as to Aztecs, there were
six directions, including not only the cardinal four but also the nadir and the
zenith. See *The Plumed Serpent* on the six winds, including one 'that blows
down to the middle of earth' and one 'that blows upward' (225:33–5).

88:13 **Their bodies were smeared . . . like snake marks.**   The first typescript
(missing), by Brett, omitted this fifteen-word sentence, exactly one line, that
appears in MS (p. 11) but in no other state of the text. Her eye would have
skipped from 'Their' to the next sentence, which also begins 'Their'.

88:28 **mummery**   Performance by silent mummers, actors in traditional pantomime dramas. See note above on 64:12 and also 'A Prelude', *Love Among
the Haystacks*, ed. Worthen, pp. 8–11 and note on 8:22; and *The Rainbow*, ed.
Kinkead-Weekes, p. 130 and note on 130:25.

88:34 **snake-priest**   Although both periodical publications read 'priest', MS (p. 12)
shows that DHL distinguishes this 'snake-priest' from the 'antelope-priest' in
the same paragraph. It is probable that a typing error by the first typist had
omitted part of the compound.

89:35 **in the air**   The first typescript must have lacked these words, present in MS
(p. 13) but not in any publication; the words 'in the', reappearing in the next
line, must have persuaded Brett that the phrase was repeated. On the same
page, she missed the words 'behind him' (90:5), probably because of eye-skip
from the preceding 'all the time' to the same phrase in the next line (90:6).

91:4 **Indian policemen, Hopi and Navajo,**   The Bureau of Indian Affairs would
have hired both. In 1878, the US Congress approved funds for the Indian
Police, and the Snyder Act of 1921 further provided for law enforcement on
the reservations.

91:39 **the octopus heart of the rain-source.**   In passages that DHL excised from
The Plumed Serpent, Ramón describes 'the centre of the cosmos' as 'A centre
of life like some watchful octopus' that can affect 'the waters over the earth' as
well as 'the fires inside the earth' (p. 541).

92:8 **Systole, diastole,**   In Emerson's essay 'Compensation' (1841), these terms
are used to explain polarities in nature. DHL also uses this metaphor in 'Foreword' to *Sons and Lovers*, ed. Baron and Baron, 471:31–2; *Study of Thomas
Hardy*, ed. Steele, 7:18–20; and 'The Reality of Peace', *Reflections* 27:14, 21
and 36:32–3. The Emerson essay was included in the *International Library of
Famous Literature*, xv, 7105–22, which the Lawrence family owned, acquiring
the 20-vol. set in 1901 at the death of William Ernest Lawrence (see Cue-titles
to *Sons and Lovers*, p. xvi).

93:3 **a marvellous secret cure for snake-bites.**   As early as 1897, Jesse Walter
Fewkes speculated that the Hopis take an emetic after the dance ('Tusayan
Snake Ceremonies', *Annual Reports of the Bureau of American Ethnology*, 16).
Theodore Roosevelt (1858–1919), who attended the Hopi Snake Dance at Walpi
in 1913 and recorded his experience in *A Book-Lover's Holiday in the Open*
(1916), mentioned the possibility that the Indians take medicine to prevent
snakebite poisoning but inclined, instead, to the theory that some people have

a natural capacity to control snakes just as some have a gift of bee-keeping (ch. III).

93:28 **We dam the Nile and take the railway across America.** The Aswan Dam was built over the Nile in Egypt between 1899 and 1901, and the Makwar Dam (today's Sennar Dam) was built over the Blue Nile in Sudan after the First World War (completed 1925). The first transcontinental railway in America was completed in 1869, when the Central Pacific and Union Pacific Railroads met at Promontory Point, Utah. The Northern Pacific spanned the country in 1883 at Gold Creek, Montana Territory, and the Atchison, Topeka, and the Santa Fe reached Santa Fe in 1880 and Los Angeles in 1887.

93:36 **To us and to the orientals, the God-head was perfect to start with,** In the Judaeo-Christian tradition, Jehovah is absolute good. DHL may also have in mind a concept of the Absolute as Brahman (Hindu) or as embodied in the third (universal) body of the Buddha in Mahayana Buddhism.

94:2 **Paradise and the Golden Age have been long lost,** Jewish, Islamic and Christian religions teach the 'fall' from perfection in Eden, and DHL's phrasing may echo the title of *Paradise Lost* (1667) by John Milton (1608–74). Classical mythology, from Hesiod (fl. 700 BC?) to Ovid (43 BC – *c.* AD 17), outlines a cycle of 'ages', beginning with the 'golden age' of the Greek Kronos (Roman Saturn) and degenerating to the 'iron age'. Similarly, in ancient India, the Laws of Manu (*c.* 200 BC – AD 200) describe the 'Krita' or 'golden age' as the highest, with succeeding ages of decline (*Laws of Manu*, i: 81–6). An apocalyptic vision was codified among the Aztecs, too, who looked back nostalgically to their mythic homeland 'Aztlan' and forecast the cataclysmic end of their era (see note on 14:3 and Appendix V:5). Hopi legends posit an original closeness to nature along with conditions of continual struggle.

94:13 **settled pueblo Indians...wandering Navajo...ancient Maya... surviving Aztec.** See Appendix V:1–6.

94:29 **Mongolian faces.** One theory of the origin of American Indians is that they journeyed through Mongolia, crossing from Asia into Alaska by way of the Bering Straits.

A Little Moonshine with Lemon

97:1 **A Little Moonshine with Lemon** On the choice of title, see the Introduction, p. lix. DHL's word-play combines the Italian moonlight at the Villa Bernarda, Spotorno, and the illegal American 'moonshine', bootleg whiskey that was plentiful in the USA during the American Prohibition on alcoholic beverages (1920–33). DHL reviewed John Allen Krout's *The Origins of Prohibition* (New York, 1925) for the *New York Herald Tribune* (31 January 1926), sending the review to Curtis Brown on 21 November 1925, two days before moving into the villa. Although the Eighteenth Amendment to the US Constitution banned the manufacture, distribution and sale of alcoholic beverages – and the Volstead Act (1919) made it law – individual home brewers and the black market circumvented the law, often working stills and making deliveries by night in 'moonlight'. Only after DHL's death did the Twenty-first Amendment (1933) repeal the Eighteenth.

97:3 **"Ye Gods, he doth bestride the narrow world / Like a Colossus – !"**
In Shakespeare's *Julius Caesar*, Cassius speaks to Brutus, comparing Caesar
to the Colossus of Rhodes ['Why, man . . . a Colossus'] and continuing: 'and
we petty men / Walk under his huge legs' (I. ii. 136–9). 'Ye Gods' derives
from earlier lines by Cassius to Brutus: 'Ye gods, it doth amaze me / A man
of such a feeble temper should / So get the start of the majestic world, /
And bear the palm alone!' (I. ii. 130–3). The Colossus of Rhodes, one of the
'Seven Wonders of the Ancient World', was the gigantic statue of Apollo (Greek
Helios) on the Greek island of Rhodes at the entrance of Mandraki Harbour,
where the Aegean Sea meets the Mediterranean. Built to the design of sculptor
Chares of Lindos *c.* 292–280 BC, it was destroyed by earthquake *c.* 226 BC,
becoming associated in common parlance with the rise and fall of power. The
statue was, in legend, more than 110 feet tall, straddling the harbour with one
foot on either side. While this pose is today doubted, it may explain Lawrence's
choice of this epigraph for an essay that situates him in two places at once, with
one base in Italy and one in New Mexico.

97:8 **St. Catherine's day,** 25 November was established in the tenth century as
the Catholic holy day for the fourth-century Catherine of Alexandria, patron
saint of philosophers and unmarried women. St Catherine was said to have
been tortured on a spiked wheel, and later martyred, for refusing a bigamous
marriage to Roman Emperor Maxentius. The historical accuracy of her story
was questioned in 1969, and the church removed the day from the calendar.

97:14 **Santa Fe . . . mountains of Picoris.** The name, usually spelt 'Picuris', is
the same as that of the Picuris Pueblo of the same region. Santa Fe, the capital
of New Mexico, is 75 miles s. of Taos, marking the convergence of a high
desert plateau (7,100 feet above sea level) with the Rocky Mountains. The
Picuris or Picoris Mountains, also s. of Taos, form an arm of the Sangre de
Cristo Mountains, themselves part of the southern Rocky Mountains. See
DHL's poem 'Mountain Lion', referring to 'the snow of the Sangre de Cristo
mountains, the ice of the mountains of Picoris' (*Poems* 402).

97:15 *Sono io!* 'It's I' or 'I am I' (Italian).

97:19 *Dunque, Signore! di nuovo—!* 'Well, Sir! Again!' (Italian).

97:22 *in vino veritas.* 'In wine is truth' (Latin).

97:29 *Weh . . .* **Heimweh** 'Homesickness' (German). 'Weh' alone is 'pain' or
'sadness'.

97:32 **But on the trunk . . . iron things.** The Lawrences used the massive tree
trunk at their Kiowa Ranch as an adjunct of their kitchen, hanging household
items on it. Moreover, '**the long work table**' (98:1) was DHL's utility table,
near the cabin, and '**the fence**' (98:1) was a white picket fence that separated
the cabin and tree from the Lawrences' vegetable garden. Georgia O'Keeffe's
painting of the pine tree (*The Lawrence Tree*) captured its appearance in 1929,
and it is still there in the twenty-first century. See also the description of the
tree in 'Pan in America', 157:37–159:2 and notes.

98:3 **Ranchos de Taos.** Village s. of Taos, New Mexico, originally settled by the
Spanish in the eighteenth century (see Map 2 and Appendix VI:5).

98:3 **the castle of Noli** The Castle of Monte Ursino (*c.* 1100) lies inside the city walls of Noli, now a small village near Spotorno but once a maritime republic in its own right. The town is nearly 10 miles from Savona, nearly 40 from Genoa.

98:13 **Giovanni** In a letter to Blanche Knopf, dated 23 November 1925 from the Villa Bernarda, DHL referred to the 'contadino Giovanni downstairs' (v. 343) – Giovanni Rossi, who did errands and general services for the Lawrences. He lived in the basement while they occupied the three storeys above. The Lawrences had rented the dwelling, on the Ligurian Riviera, from Angelo Ravagli the same day, just over two and a half months after leaving New Mexico.

98:15 *Vado giù.... Buona notte*! 'I'm going down... Good night!' (Italian).

98:21 **the wonderful, hoary age of America, the continent of the afterwards.** In 'Europe Versus America', DHL furthers this thinking: 'Even these countries of the Mediterranean, which have known quite a bit of history, seem to me much, much younger even than Taos, not to mention Long Island, or Coney Island' (*Sketches* 200:2–4). In the 1920 'Foreword to Studies in Classic American Literature' ('America, Listen to Your Own'), DHL refers to Americans as 'a young race' (*Studies* 384:7) but reminds them of American Indian, Aztec, Maya and Inca antiquity, urging them to look back 'towards Montezuma' (384:36–7). But in *Kangaroo*, ed. Steele, he is aware of age in another sense: Somers refers to the archaeologist Flinders Petrie (1853–1942) – whom DHL mentions to correspondents (iv. 240, 264) – to claim that a colony is not younger but may be 'even older' than its parent, 'one step further gone' (49:26).

98:23 **Montgomery Ward's catalogue** Catalogues were issued periodically by the first American mail-order giant, Montgomery Ward's, founded in 1872 by Aaron Montgomery Ward (1844–1913) of Chicago. The Christmas issue was always especially popular, coming at a time when customers were eager for gift ideas. Ward's great success launched a mail-order age, and in 1946 the Grolier Society in New York chose the Montgomery Ward catalogue as one of 100 American books most influential on life and culture in the USA.

98:26 **Susan, the black cow,** See also DHL's description of Susan in '......Love Was Once a Little Boy' (*Reflections* 332:29–334:31), and the painting of Susan in *The Kiowa Ranch* (oil) by Dorothy Brett with additions by DHL and Frieda (1925). On 18 December 1925, DHL asked William Hawk, 'Have you sold Susan, the black-eyed?' (*Letters*, v. 358).

98:31 **stars... like distant coyotes... actual coyotes, going across the alfalfa field.** Cf. Lou Carrington's ranch, based on Kiowa Ranch, in *St. Mawr and Other Stories*, ed. Finney, 30–3: 'great stars sitting on the mountain's edge seemed to be watching like the eyes of a mountain lion... Then the coyotes in the near canyon howled and sobbed, and ran like shadows over the snow.'

98:36 **the Rocky Mountains** Taos is located on the southernmost range of the Rocky Mountains. The 'Rockies', comprising at least 100 separate mountain ranges, extend 3,000 miles in length, from their rise in western Canada to their mighty terminus in New Mexico and Arizona.

99:2 **the blue jays fall . . . out of the pine tree**   The incorrect plurals 'pine trees' (Per) and 'pine-trees' (E1, A1), diverging from TCC1 (p. 2), have previously blunted the identification of the 'Lawrence Tree' in this passage. See also DHL's poem 'The Blue Jay': 'From the pine-tree that towers and hisses like a pillar of shaggy cloud / Immense above the cabin / Comes a strident laugh . . .' (*Poems* 375). Signed 'Lobo' (the ranch's name before Kiowa), the poem may refer to the same tree: by late 1922, when it was written, the Lawrences were living at Del Monte Ranch but had also stayed at their future Kiowa Ranch (*Letters*, iv. 335–6).

99:5 **Rio Grande.**   The river flows 6 miles e. of Taos and part of its steep canyon (to 800 feet deep) is visible from the ranch. In *St. Mawr*, too, Lou Carrington watches the 'vast strand of the desert' below, where only 'a blackish crack' shows the 'otherwise invisible canyon of the Rio Grande' with the mountains 'beyond everything' (*St. Mawr and Other Stories*, ed. Finney, 145:29, 39, 40). See note on 71:4.

99:7 **vermouth, Marsala, red wine or white.**   Cf. DHL's letter to Blanche Knopf in November 1925: 'I've got my little stock of red and white wine – from the garden of this house' (v. 342).

99:10 **Schilling's tins.**   Schilling Spice Company, founded by August Schilling in the late nineteenth century, was one of the leading American providers of spices. Its trademark tins were usually red, white and blue with the company's or the spice's name in white on a red field. They are still marketed today in the Schilling name although by another owner (McCormick Consumer Products since 1947).

99:18 **Si verra la primavera / Fiorann' le mandorline—**   'Spring will come / The almonds will flower' (Italian), quoted also in 'The Dance', in *Twilight in Italy*, ed. Eggert, 171:17–18, with 'mandoline' for 'mandorline' – not quite 'correct Italian', DHL indicates there (171:25). TCC1 (p. 2) is much less exact (see Textual apparatus) and is emended to the language in Per since DHL recommended the essay to Secker in that form (see Introduction, p. lx). This song, which musicians performed at San Gaudenzio, continued in a rather improper mode: 'Vienn' di basso le Trentine / Coi 'taliani far' l'amor' ('From below, the Trentine women will come / To make love with Italian men', *Twilight in Italy*, 171:19–20).

99:21 **un poco di chiar' di luna, con cannella e limone – – –**   'A bit of moonlight, with cinnamon and lemon' (Italian).

Certain Americans and an Englishman

105:1 **Certain Americans and an Englishman**   The essay's first publication, in the *New York Times Magazine*, bears the following editorial headnote: 'Mr. Lawrence, the British novelist whose books are generally best sellers in his own country and sometimes over here, arrived in San Francisco, a few weeks ago, on his way to spend a long vacation on a ranch. Upon

reaching New Mexico he heard much talk about the Pueblo land controversy, and became so interested in it that he wrote the accompanying article. Since then the Bursum bill, which would have taken away the Pueblos' lands, has been buried in a Congressional committee, and probably it
will never see the light again.' On the same page is an artist's sketch of a
pueblo, with Pueblo Indians in the foreground, and a caption quoting DHL
on assimilationist policy: 'The great desire to turn them into white men'
(p. 3).

105:2 **I** Because this essay was extracted from a larger whole (see Introduction,
pp. xxxiii–xxxvi), the earliest extant source begins 'But I'. The excision of
the first word was part of the revision that DHL undertook to make the essay
independent; thus the opening wording is adopted from the first publication
(Per).

105:4 **Bursum Bill... Pueblo Indians.** US Senator Holm O. Bursum (1867–
1953), of New Mexico, had introduced a Bill into Congress to allow settlers on Pueblo land to legitimise their claims despite the Pueblo land and
water rights – rights held by national treaties and aboriginal settlement.
The Bill (S. 3855) had passed in the US Senate in September 1922 and
was expected to come before the House of Representatives by the end of
the year, but rising protests intervened. See Introduction, p. xxxiii, and footnote 31.

105:7 **Twitchell... Mr. Secretary Fall!** Ralph Emerson Twitchell (1859–1925),
Santa Fe lawyer and historian and a political appointee in the US attor-
ney general's office, drafted part of the Bursum Bill at the behest of Albert
B. Fall. Fall (1861–1944), Bursum's predecessor as US senator from New
Mexico, was Secretary of the Interior (1921–3) under President Warren
G. Harding until, implicated in the Teapot Dome scandal, he resigned his
office.

105:8 **The Joy Survey,** After New Mexico's statehood (1912), the Office of Indian
Affairs had directed Francis Joy and associates, of the General Land Office, to
conduct field surveys to determine and mark the boundaries of Indian Pueblos
and the claims of all non-Indians. There had also been a survey in 1907.

105:9 **Whoa!** Traditional English and American interjection, usually a command
to a horse ('Halt!').

105:10 **Lindsay... bellowing** The American poet Nicholas Vachel Lindsay
(1879–1931) was well known for reciting his poems with bombastic sound
effects and syncopated rhythms – performances that the poet called
'the Higher Vaudeville'. His poem 'General William Booth Enters into
Heaven' (1913) begins with the stage direction 'Bass drum beaten loudly';
and another, 'The Congo' (1914), contains repetitions of 'Boom, boom,
BOOM' and 'boomlay, BOOM'. See also the final version of 'Herman
Melville's "Moby Dick"': 'Boom! as Vachel Lindsay would say' (*Studies*
147:7).

105:15 **Mr. Francis Wilson's Brief** Francis Cushman Wilson (1876–1952), who
had served in the Territory of New Mexico as US attorney for the Pueblo

Indians (1909–14), was retained to oppose the Bursum Bill and wrote one of the substitute Bills that came before Congress.

105:17 **Mr. C's passionate article...Mrs. H's hatchet-stroke...Mr. M's sharp-knife jugglery *for* the Bill.** John Collier wrote 'The Red Atlantis'; Alice Corbin Henderson (1881–1949), American poet, co-founder with Harriet Monroe of *Poetry* magazine, authored 'The Death of the Pueblos' (see Introduction, footnotes 4, 28, 38). Mr M is possibly Arthur Rochfort Manby (1859–1929), an unscrupulous land speculator who was known for 'juggling' funds, attacking a local editor with a knife, and reporting to the Bureau of Indian Affairs on Mabel's activities with Tony Lujan and the Taos Indians – reports that threatened her political programme with scandal. Manby's biographer reports that, embittered by the loss of his own land through his mismanagement, Manby was 'delighted' by the 'turmoil among Indian, Spanish, and Anglo residents alike that raised the question of just who owned...the whole valley' (Frank Waters, *To Possess the Land*, Chicago, 1973, p. 173). On Manby, see *Letters*, v. 550 and vii. 486, 547.

105:18 **Bear Ye One Another's Bursum.** Cf. St Paul's advice to the Galatians ['...burdens'] (vi. 2, *KJB*).

105:27 **leaping through the hoop and crashing through the paper...at every hand's turn.** A favourite trick of circus acrobats was to jump through a papered hoop, on foot or on horseback. The term 'at every hand's turn' means 'in every case or chance' (slang).

105:30 **the Wild West show,** Wild West Shows peaked in popularity after 1883, when William Frederick Cody (1846–1917) originated the Buffalo Bill Cody Wild West Show, taking it to Queen Victoria's Golden Jubilee in 1887. Besides parading defeated Indian leaders, Cody and other such showmen staged Indian dances and battles. The shows spread from America to Europe, as in DHL's Natcha-Kee-Tawara, 'strictly a Red Indian troupe' of European performers, in *The Lost Girl*, ed. Worthen, 120:10. Such shows usually included 'cowboys' performing sharpshooting and trick riding. By 'Red Indian' DHL simply means 'American Indian', probably without recognising it as racial slang.

106:3 **The Indian is not an American citizen.** The Indian Citizenship Act was passed by Congress in 1924, providing a uniform franchise for American Indians. Because of the Indian tribes' uneven history, the vote had been sporadically granted and tribes had been handled severally both as sovereign nations and as wards of Congress. With the Dawes Act (1887) and Burke Act (1906), Congress envisioned 'assimilation' that would end the tribal system (and federal benefits) in exchange for standardised national status. In opposition, Collier favoured strong tribal structures but nonetheless advocated full US citizenship.

106:7 **Indian Bureau** The Bureau of Indian Affairs is in the Department of the Interior (having moved from the War Department in 1849). It administers Indian lands and services, including education and health care.

106:16 **pitched upon the waters.** Possible echo of Joshua xi. 5, where the kings 'pitched together at the waters' at Merom for their fight with Joshua; or of Numbers xxxiii. 9, where the children of Israel 'pitched' near 'fountains of water' (*KJB*).

106:17 **Taos Valley... Taos Pueblo.** The valley is actually a high plateau with the pueblo situated hundreds of feet above the town on both banks of the Rio Pueblo de Taos, and the Taos Indians have 'prior right' to the region's surface water and deep groundwaters – a claim based on geography, aboriginal possession and agreements with three nations (Spain, Mexico and the USA). Already in 1540, Pedro de Castañeda, chronicler for Francisco de Coronado (1510–54), took note of the swift river that ran through Taos Pueblo and the steep river banks in the vicinity (1596; *The Journey of Coronado, 1540–1542*, trans. and ed. George Parker Winship, New York, 1904 [1896], Pt i, ch. XXII). The 'waterless' village (106:19) is possibly suggested by Agua del Lobo ('water of the wolf'), a 'ghost town' that rose and failed between 1880 and 1905, or Arroyo Seco ('dry stream'); although the latter was not 'deserted' and not without water, it contains historic ruins and lost a historic water rights suit when the pueblo asserted its primary right to water from the Rio Lucero in 1823.

106:21 **when the United States took over New Mexico in 1848,** By the Treaty of Guadalupe Hidalgo, which ended the Mexican War, most of the present state of New Mexico (along with land that became six other states) was transferred from Mexico to the USA in 1848. The Gadsden Purchase (1853) further readjusted national boundaries, adding to southern Arizona and New Mexico. Although the USA accepted the land grants and titles that had been awarded during Spanish colonialism and the following Mexican period, grants often overlapped because of informal sale and barter of property, careless grant practices by the two prior governments, the illegal 'squatting' DHL mentions, and serious differences in measurement. The Spanish *vara* was originally one pace by a grown man, and a league was the distance a horseman could cover in an hour on even ground and at a normal gait; the Mexicans standardised the *vara*, and the US territorial authorities set still another standard. Moreover, the confusion over ownership attracted unscrupulous speculators.

107:3 **For Taos Plaza... at least 200 years.** The town of Taos first sprang up around the pueblo's Spanish mission (established in 1610–12) but moved to the present site, on a Spanish land grant, in 1795–6 and was incorporated in 1934. Its plaza is the main square where downtown shops are located. The pueblo has its own plaza, dating to the fourteenth and fifteenth centuries. New York City was founded in 1612 and charterted in 1897.

107:16 **"Poor Indian, dear Indian!** Probably based on the line 'Lo, the poor Indian' by Alexander Pope (1688–1744) in his *Essay on Man* (1733–4), iv. 99, celebrating the natural piety in the 'untutored mind' of an American Indian. The expression 'poor Lo' became a synonym for the Indian, when regarded as a sentimentalised 'child of nature'.

107:21 **highbrow palefaces.** A 'highbrow' (Anglo-American slang) was an intellectual or urbane person of erudite tastes, an identity much discussed in the culture debates of the early twentieth century. A 'paleface' was a white person (a term attributed to several indigenous American tribes).

107:24 **the tiny prairie dog... the western American airedale,** Prairie dogs are small, burrowing rodents of the squirrel family that occupy the western USA from Canada to Mexico; their distinctive high-pitched bark resembles that of some canines. The Airedale is a large terrier, first bred in Yorkshire, known as an effective police dog and bold battlefront dog.

107:35 **old José or old Fernandez or old Maria,** Generic names, Spanish for Joseph, Ferdinand and Mary. But the Spanish names – used also by the Pueblo Indians (and by Mexican Indians) as well as by the Mexican settlers – suggest the complexity of the issues raised.

107:38 **laissez-faire.** DHL does not mean the economic doctrine of free trade associated with Adam Smith (French, 'laissez-faire'*)* but the verb compound 'let it be' or 'let [people] do [as they choose]' (French, 'laisser-faire'). See also 128:14.

107:39 **those white highbrows** Taos was known as a haven for socially liberal artists and intellectuals after the formation in 1912 of the Taos Society of Artists. Mabel had mobilised many of them in the effort to defeat the Bursum Bill by publicising Indian culture and grievances, an undertaking spearheaded nationally by the American Federation of Women's Clubs, led by Stella Atwood; the club's American Indian Defense Association, represented by Collier; the Eastern (New York) Association on Indian Affairs, led by Amelia Elizabeth White; and the Indian Rights Association (Philadelphia), represented by S. M. Brosius. Writers and artists who signed a petition against the Bursum Bill included Lawrence, Vachel Lindsay, Carl Sandburg, Edgar Lee Masters, Zane Grey and Taos painters Victor Higgins and Walter Ufer.

108:8 **black knight** A 'villain' (slang), possibly related here to *A Game of Chess* (1624) by Thomas Middleton, about a Spaniard's attempt to corrupt England as part of the power politics between the two nations.

108:10 **comes before the House, presumably this month (December).** See note on 105:4.

108:28 **the old, autonomous tribal body of the pueblo** When the Spanish first contacted the Rio Grande Pueblos in 1540, they found representative councils of elders already in place (Castañeda, *The Journey of Coronado*, Pt ii, chs. III–IV); these bodies governed along with priests (*caciques* or spiritual leaders). Collier called the pueblos 'the oldest self-governing democratic institutions in the Western Hemisphere' ('The Pueblos' Last Stand', as in Introduction, footnote 38) and presented the Pueblo method as a model of tribal self-government for other tribes. See also DHL's praise of the American Indian 'aristocrat', chosen by merit and not heredity, in 'Paris Letter' (145:12).

108:31 **the Guadalupe Hidalgo Treaty of 1848** Cf. note on 106:21. The Mexico City neighbourhood where the US–Mexico treaty was negotiated: it was named for Our Lady of Guadalupe and Miguel Hidalgo y Costilla (1753–1811), the Revolutionary priest whose 'Grito de Dolores' in 1810 (a cry for reform) launched the War for Mexican Independence against Maximilian and entrenched national interests, leading the rebel army under a banner of Our Lady of Guadalupe. (The apparition of Guadalupe came in 1531 to the indigenous convert called Juan Diego [Cuauhtlatoazin], canonised in 2002.) The spelling 'Guadaloupe' in Per may represent DHL's conflation of the spelling of the Mexico City site with that of the French West Indies colony of Guadeloupe.

108:37 **Secretary of the Interior** Secretary Fall (see note on 105:7).

109:21 **Charybdis... Scylla** One of DHL's most characteristic metaphors, referring to Odysseus' impossible choice between two dangers when steering his ship between the monster Scylla and the whirlpool Charybdis (Homer, *Odyssey*, xii).

109:34 **the Indian schools, a doom in themselves.** The young Indians were sent to boarding schools to assimilate them into 'white' culture (see Introduction, footnote 63, and note on 85:37). DHL's poem 'O! Americans' describes 'the old American aborigines' after a Good Friday meeting at Taos Pueblo (1924) with 'the big white men of the Indian Bureau': 'What does it mean, they say? / That our boys must stay at school until they are eighteen, and not be allowed to absent themselves for ceremonies and ceremonial preparations? / Then our life is finished, our day is over completely. / *Consummatum est!*' (*Poems* 777, 779).

109:37 **The end of the Pueblos.** A common theme of the time was that the pueblo-dwelling way of life was being driven out of existence by modern encroachment; see Collier and Henderson in note 105:17 and Introduction, footnote 38.

110:2 **Wild West scalping trick** 'Scalping', American slang for 'cheating' or 'fleecing' by a confidence artist, derives from the practice by some American Indian warriors and others of collecting the scalps and hair of their enemies as trophies of war. Wild West Shows sometimes presented pantomimes of such frontier activity. See *The Lost Girl*, ed. Worthen, in which Ciccio, impersonating a brave in the Natcha-Kee-Tawara troupe, 'wore scalp-fringed trousers' (135:10). Although popularly attributed exclusively to the Indians, 'scalping' was known to occur on both sides of the Indian wars.

110:3 **Indian Commission** Perhaps the same as Bureau of Indian Affairs (see also note on 106:7).

110:10 **an eternal fire, the sacred fire** In *St. Mawr*, the American setting suggests 'the holy fire in the old temples' of the Vestal Virgins and the 'Apollo mystery of the inner fire' (*St. Mawr and Other Stories*, ed. Finney, 138:38, 139:31). Marcus Tullius Cicero (106–43 BC) referred to the 'eternal flame' in the Roman temples of Vesta (*De legibus*, ii); and many other faith traditions throughout the world, including those of various US and Mexican Indian tribes, assert the sacredness of fire.

110:18 **to take up an old dark thread from their vision,** Cf. the 1920 'Foreword to Studies in Classic American Literature' (first published as 'America, Listen to Your Own') – Americans must grasp 'the life-thread' not from Europe but from the American Indians (*Studies* 384:35) – and *The Plumed Serpent*, in which Kate thinks, 'We must go back to pick up old threads. We must take up the old, broken impulse that will connect us with the mystery of the cosmos again, now we are at the end of our own tether' (138:5–7). Probably also a reference to Ariadne's 'dark thread' as the guide out of a labyrinth (Greek).

110:24 **Before the pueblos disappear . . . reconciliation between the white spirit and the dark.** See the first version of 'Fenimore Cooper's Anglo-American Novels': although 'the Red Indian lives unappeased and inwardly destructive in the American', Cooper 'very beautifully gives the myth of the atonement, the communion between the soul of the white man and the soul of the Indian' (*Studies* 209:20–1).

110:26 **Jack Grab and Juan Arrapar** Coined surnames based on the verbs 'to grab' (English) and 'to seize' (Spanish from Catalan). Both first names are versions of the common name 'John'.

Indians and an Englishman

113:2 **Supposing one fell on to the moon,** Possibly an echo of the literal fall onto the moon in H. G. Wells, *The First Men in the Moon*, chs. VI–VIII (see also note on 26:38).

113:5 **wild and woolly and artistic and sage-brush desert.** 'Wild and woolly' (American frontier term), a rugged style of dress and behaviour sometimes affected by tourists and artists in the western USA; possibly refers to unkempt hair and beard of frontiersmen or to sheepskin and fur clothing that was common on the range. Sagebrush is a deciduous perennial shrub of the aster family that gives the distinctive silvery hue of its leaves to many arid landscapes of the American Southwest.

113:15 **in white cotton sheets like Hamlet's father's ghost,** Among the Taos Indians, a traditional men's outer garment was a white, sheet-like cotton wrap. In Shakespeare's *Hamlet* (*c.* 1602), the ghost of Hamlet's father wears armour (I. i. 60–1, I. ii. 254, I. iv. 52), but productions have sometimes substituted the loose grave cerements associated popularly with ghosts. In theatres, DHL had seen 'the spectral form of Hamlet's father both sheeted and cased in tin', and in January 1913 he attended an Italian version in which the ghost 'was wrapped down to the knees in a great white cloth' ('The Theatre', 1913 and 1915 versions, *Twilight in Italy*, ed. Eggert, 77:31–2, 149:18–19).

113:16 **lone lorn** Mrs Gummidge in *David Copperfield* (1850) by Charles Dickens (1812–70) calls herself a 'lone lorn creetur'.

113:22 **full moon of a silver dollar**   Reference to US materialism, symbolised by the silver dollar (authorised in 1792 by the US Coinage Act). The 'full moon' suggests the dollar's round, shiny appearance and magnetism, continuing the moon imagery of the opening paragraph.

113:26 **Pioneers, Oh Pioneers!**   An allusion to 'Pioneers! O Pioneers!' (1865, 1881) by Walt Whitman (1819–92), American poet and father of free verse. See also *The Pioneers* (1823), first of the 'Leatherstocking' novels by James Fenimore Cooper (1789–1851), and the novel *O Pioneers* (1913) by Willa Sibert Cather (1873–1947). DHL discussed Whitman and Cooper in *Studies in Classic American Literature*, which he was revising in 1922, and would visit Cather in 1924. All three of these American writers referred to the settlers on the Western US frontier.

113:33 **Master of Ceremonies.**   Announcer who introduces speakers or theatrical acts to the public: a prominent figure in the circus and Wild West Show, the Master of Ceremonies often wore formal attire and kept order.

114:12 **the Apache war-whooping . . . the Mexican staggering under crosses** Obsolete stereotype of an Apache warrior, probably based on pulp fiction or Wild West Shows (see note on Apaches at 66:33). New Mexico's Hispanic Catholics included members of 'Los Hermanos Penitentes' (a lay brotherhood) who carried full-size crosses, practised self-flagellation and staged human Crucifixion scenes during Holy Week until they were officially banned and reconstituted in the nineteenth century. When the Lawrences lived in Mabel's 'two-story' house in Taos (as they did during Lent in 1924), they were adjacent to a Penitente morada (chapter house) on Calvary Road, with 'a great, stark cross at the end of it'; and DHL, who objected to this 'medieval survival', kept his windows closed in order to avoid hearing the zealous sufferers (Luhan, *Lorenzo in Taos*, pp. 187, 188). Cf. DHL's 'Men in New Mexico': 'The Penitentes lash themselves till they run with blood' (*Poems* 408).

114:21 **a lamb who's lost his mother.**   Following this passage in TS (the setting-copy for *Dial*), 34 typed lines were excised by the editor at the *Dial* to form the basis for the opening passages of 'Certain Americans and an Englishman'.

114:23 **the Apaches in the Apache Reservation of this state.**   The Jicarilla Apache Reservation, which DHL visited, is at Stone Lake, near Dulce, in northern New Mexico. The Jicarillas hold this harvest festival annually in September. DHL never saw the other Apache Reservation (Mescalero), in the southern part of the state. See also Appendix V:6.

114:30 **Ute Indians and Navajos.**   The nearest Ute reservation is centred in southern Colorado adjoining Utah and New Mexico, where the Utes were well established by AD 1500. The Navajo Reservation, the largest in the USA, is primarily in northeastern Arizona but extends into Utah and northwestern New Mexico, close to the Jicarilla Apache Reservation. See also notes on 79:3 and 87:28.

114:31 **"Da donde viene, Usted?"** 'Where are you from?' (Spanish). Possibly dialect since DHL is reporting what he heard among these Apache Indians. See also entries at 41:6 and 118:31.

114:33 **tepees,** See Glossary. Unlike western Apaches, the eastern Apaches (including the Jicarilla) adopted Plains Indian tepees while they were buffalo-hunting nomads (see Appendix V:6). But wickiups (circular structures of brush and mud) were more characteristic Apache dwellings and ceremonial centres.

114:40 **big steeple hats** Many American Indians considered headwear a symbol of power, and tall-crowned felt or beaver hats, sometimes with braid or plume, were used in both Mexican and US trade with them. Black hats of the 'Hardee' style, worn by Civil War officers (1860–4) and the later US Cavalry (to 1872), were prized; and the 'stovepipe' hat, popularised by Abraham Lincoln, was marketed long past its fashionable period. A 'steeple' may also suggest the high, conical crown of a Mexican sombrero (which Southwestern Indians also wore).

115:3 **the round *vallum*,** Usually a man-made rampart but, in this case, a natural formation.

115:11 **kindled with Fenimore Cooper,** James Fenimore Cooper (1789–1851), American novelist, author of *The Pioneers* (1823), *The Last of the Mohicans* (1826), *The Prairie* (1827), *The Pathfinder* (1840), *The Deerslayer* (1841) – all in the 'Leatherstocking' series about a white settler's adventures among the American Indians on the US frontier. Cooper is also known for his 'Anglo-American' novels like *The Spy* (1821) and *The Pilot* (1823) about white settlement in America. In 1919, DHL published two essays about Cooper in the *English Review* – 'Fenimore Cooper's Anglo-American Novels' and 'Fenimore Cooper's Leatherstocking Novels' – and rewrote them in New Mexico in 1922 (about the same time he was writing this present essay) for the final version of *Studies in Classic American Literature*.

115:19 **two kivas ... race-track.** Ceremonial chambers (see note on 76:7) and a track where races are held for ritual purposes. These 'kivas' are not in the Pueblos' underground pithouse-style but in the style of the Apache dwelling, with a structure of tree-boughs, which was itself invested with sacred symbolism. The two chambers provide headquarters for the two clans that compete annually in the races (see Appendix V:6 and note on 121:8). On Pueblo races, see Appendix V:4–5; 'Indians and Entertainment' and 'The Hopi Snake Dance'; and notes on 60:27 and 84:18.

115:22 **pàt-pat, pàt-pat,** Although it is not certain whether DHL or someone else drew the accent marks in TS (p. 6) to emphasise the rhythm in this onomatopoeic phrase – as well as marks at 115:24, 115:34, 115:36, 115:40 and 116:6 – it is most likely that he authorised them (it is unlikely that an editor would have introduced them); DHL's unquestioned manuscript revisions appear on the same page, and the accent marks, too, are adopted here. Accent marks also appear in several parallel instances in the early fragment of this essay reported by Mabel Luhan (see Appendix II).

115:25 **Hie! Hie! Hie! . . . Ay-away-away!!**   Apparently DHL's phonetic rendition of supposed Athabascan language.

115:31 **each carrying an aspen-twig,**   See note on 72:3.

116:8 **shriek**   Substituted by DHL in TS for 'squeal' (p. 6). For additional revisions, see Textual apparatus and note on 117:11.

116:12 **deeps of the stomach . . . feel good.**   See note on 13:10 about the solar plexus.

116:26 **when man was dusky**   See 'Grapes' from *Birds, Beasts and Flowers*: 'When the vine was rose, the Gods were dark-skinned' and 'Once God was all negroid, as now he is fair' (*Poems* 286).

117:11 **of the hollow . . . crouching figures.**   DHL added this passage in longhand to TS (p. 7), crossing out some duplication and completing the sentence that began on the previous page. The revision linked the two sections of the typescript, produced on different typewriters (see Introduction, p. xxxiv).

117:16 **Budweiser beer . . . non-intoxicants.**   As soon as national Prohibition of alcoholic drinks went into effect in the USA in 1920 (see note on 97:1), the Anheuser-Busch brewing company (makers of Budweiser beer) marketed 'near beer', an alcohol-free pilsner, as well as fruit-flavoured beverages. The Budweiser trademark was registered in the USA in 1876.

117:16 **Cowboys in chaps and big hats**   See Glossary for 'chaps'. The big felt hats, 'cowboy hats' or 'ten-gallon hats' (from Spanish 'sombrero galoneado' or 'festooned hat') had brims four to six inches broad. The most popular frontier style was the 'Boss of the Prairie' (also 'Hat of the West'), created in 1865 by the Philadelphia hat-maker John B. Stetson (1820–1906), who was impressed by the even wider-brimmed Mexican sombrero.

118:14 **recitative voice,**   In opera's *stile recitativo* (Italian) or 'recitative style', usually employed for dialogue between arias, a text is spoken in a rapid, syllabic manner to instrumental accompaniment.

118:16 **the history of the tribe interwoven with the gods.**   Apaches believed their migration was led by a supreme force (see Appendix V:6).

118:31 **"Buenos!"**   A contraction for 'Buenos días', 'Buenas tardes' or 'Buenas noches': 'Good day', 'Good evening' or 'Good night' (Spanish). At 118:33, **"Que quiere?"** 'What do you want?' (Spanish); at 118:34, **"No hablo espagnol."** 'I don't speak Spanish' (Spanish). This spelling is unusual in America (not Spanish 'Español') and, whether intentionally or not, adds to the 'foreign' character of the speaker (DHL, 'an Englishman'). See also note on 114:31 and Glossary.

119:13 **store shirts and store trousers,**   Clothing bought in shops, as distinguished from the garments made by the Apache people in their own traditional styles.

120:9 **The soul is [120:4] . . . road since then.**   DHL is repeating a common model of evolution, tracing human development from a tribal (primitive) stage to a cultured (modern) achievement. A somewhat different view was in fact inherent in DHL's disagreement with Walter Lippmann in 1920 about native American art (see Introduction, pp. xxvii–xxviii). But see, for example, H. G. Wells, *The Outline of History* (1920): humans have progressed from a 'tribal' stage – through a Neolithic period – to arrive at 'the *Age of Cultivation*, the age of the white man in Europe' (pp. 54, 81, 92); Wells claimed that America lagged '6,000 years behind the Old World' (pp. 153–4). DHL referenced this book with irony in *St. Mawr* in 1924 (*St. Mawr and Other Stories*, ed. Finney, 65:12).

120:13 **But there is no going back. Always onward, still further.** In the essay 'On Human Destiny', DHL describes progress: 'Man, poor, conscious, forever-animal man, has a very stern destiny, from which he is never allowed to escape. It is his destiny that he must move on and on, in the thought-adventure' (*Reflections* 208:24–7). But see also *Fantasia of the Unconscious*, ed. Steele: 'The business of living is to travel away from the source. But you must start every single day fresh from the source' (191:35–7). See also Introduction, footnote 43, and note on 110:18.

120:27 **I can't cluster at the drum any more.** But see 'New Mexico', crediting the New Mexico Indians with giving DHL his greatest experience of religion (178:9–14, 178:27–32). Following this line is the additional section of the essay, never published before, which ends in TS (p. 11) with a sentence fragment because of the *Dial*'s deletion of material belonging to both 'Indians and an Englishman' and 'Taos' (see Introduction, p. xxxv).

121:3 **isolate individuality,** Contrast with 116:26 ('dusky and not individualised').

121:6 **the American woman** Bessie Freeman (see Introduction, p. xxxiii and footnote 30).

121:8 **Just near [120:28] . . . over the brow of a** This final section from TS (p. 11), once part of the composite 'Pueblos and an Englishman', has never been published before. It was deleted by the *Dial* for Per1 and ends with a fragmentary sentence.

Mabel Dodge Luhan supplied two additional paragraphs by DHL (besides the fragment in Appendix II), associating them with this essay. They are, she stated, 'descriptive of the happenings of the following day' (after the events in 'Indians and an Englishman'):

"We waited three hours for the race to begin, and it was over in half an hour. Then the two groups of racers clustered on their drums again at opposite ends of the track, the drumming began, the ritual song, and slowly the two groups advanced to meet in the centre of the course. They should dance the bird tread all the way, but only the elder ones do so. The others just shuffle. Like the white boy, who stares with a kind of half-ashamed, half-defiant outcast look from side to side.

"The groups meet in the centre, and circle round each other, continuing the singing, while there is a great whooping of the elders. The crowd presses close, and gorgeous Apache women on big horses fling little round loaves of bread, and apples, and small peaches, at random into the cluster of dancers, who catch and pick up from the ground such things as they want. The daubed racers are dully singing, the two drums thud; only the white boy glowers silent.

Then the two sides have passed one another, and proceed to their respective goals. There is one tall, lanky young Indian with a square of red cloth hanging at his rear. One of the elders lifts this hind flap and switches the small, loinclothed posterior of the lanky one as he passes . . . ." (*Lorenzo in Taos*, p. 58).

Taos

125:2 **The Indians say Taos is the heart of the world.** Like most other Southwestern tribes, Taos Indians design their kivas to represent the universe, centred on the world's navel. And each tribe has myths of origin that involve nearby geographical centres, like the Blue Lake of the Taos Indians (see Appendix V:4).

125:4 **San Francisco for example.** San Francisco was colonised after 1776 by the Spanish on the site of an ancient Ohlone Indian settlement. The Gold Rush in 1849 brought overnight crowding and notoriety, and the 1906 earthquake and fire, devastating the city, could have added to DHL's sense of its impermanence. He was there for five days on 4–8 September 1922, calling it 'a sort of never-stop Hades' to Mountsier and 'very noisy and iron-clanking and expensive' to Catherine Carswell (*Letters*, iv. 290, 291).

125:5 **years ago, in London.** See DHL's essay 'Why I Don't Like Living in London' ('Dull London', originally published in the *Evening News*, 3 September 1928): 'Twenty years ago, London was to me thrilling, thrilling, thrilling, the vast and roaring heart of all adventure. It was not only the heart of the world, it was the heart of the world's living adventure.' But it was later 'as if the whole air were impregnated with chloroform or some other pervasive anaesthetic, that . . . takes the edge off everything, whether nice or nasty' (*Late Essays and Articles*, ed. James T. Boulton, Cambridge, 2004, 121:18–21, 121:8–10). In the final version of 'The Spirit of Place', DHL states: 'The Island of Great Britain had a wonderful terrestrial magnetism or polarity of its own, which made the British people. For the moment, this polarity seems to be breaking' (*Studies* 17:27–9). See also *The White Peacock*, ed. Andrew Robertson (Cambridge, 1987), pp. 264, 281–2.

125:9 **Rome [125:7] . . . Venice . . . once united East and West . . . an afterlife.** See 'The Spirit of Place': 'There was a tremendous polarity in Italy, in the city of Rome. And this seems to have died. For even places die' (*Studies* 17:26–7). In *Movements in European History*, 'The Roman Empire is the most wonderful the world has ever known: not because of its size, but because of its strange unity and singleness'; however, 'the Eternal City, Rome herself, Mistress of the World, became an object of contempt' as 'real power' shifted (12:16–18, 16:36–7, 39). Venice was 'mistress of the eastern seas' after the Fourth Crusade (1201–4) and 'every year more brilliant' during the Renaissance (*Movements in European History*, ed. Crumpton, 132:9–10, 165:24–5), a beneficiary and successor of the Byzantine confluence of East and West. But a character in *Aaron's Rod*, ed. Kalnins, states that post-war 'Venice is a strange back-water' with its 'lingering Venetian families' – 'Rather like the Byzantines – lingering on into far ages' (270:15, 36, 33–4). In 1920, DHL found Venice 'melancholic with its dreary bygone lagoons' and 'lovely to look at, but very stagnant as regards life' (*Letters*, iii. 590, 608).

125:10 **Taos pueblo**   Taos Pueblo dates back at least to the fourteenth and fifteenth centuries. It was visited in 1540 by Hernando de Alvarado, a captain for Francisco de Coronado (1510–54), and was claimed for Spain in 1598 by Juan de Oñate (*c.* 1550 – *c.* 1626). See also Appendix VI:5; Appendix V:4; and note on 106:17. In the second periodical publication, in *Cassell's Weekly* (Per2), p. 535, an asterisk appeared after 'pueblo', referring to a note at the bottom of the page: 'Pueblo is a name given to a village in North Mexico inhabited by Roman Catholic Indians.' DHL was referring to Taos Pueblo in New Mexico, not to 'a town in North Mexico'; it is true that the Taos Pueblo's church is Roman Catholic.

125:14 **one of the choice spots of the earth, where the spirit dwelt.**   See also DHL's 1922 'Introduction' to the *Memoir of Maurice Magnus*, tracing Monte-cassino in these terms, relating the spot to the 'sacred grove', temples 'before Christ was born', and the age of 'the great Cyclopean wall . . . built even before the pagan temples' (p. 57).

125:17 **Lyons,**   The spelling 'Lyon', in *Phoenix* (A1), probably resulted from an incomplete line end in the typescript (as in TCC2, p. 1), not from a preference for the French spelling. But DHL did use both spellings in *Letters* – e.g., 'Lyon' (vii. 208) and 'Lyons' (vii. 241), – often the former.

125:26 **To me [125:14] . . . when Rome collapsed . . . the Middle Ages.**   See also 'On Human Destiny', celebrating 'tiny monasteries of monks' who 'kept the eternal light of man's undying effort at consciousness alive'; and 'Books', describing 'the little fortified monasteries, the little arks floating and keeping the adventure afloat' (*Reflections* 199:35–6, 207:11–13). These essays are preceded in this theme by *Movements in European History*, ed. Crumpton, 97:3–17. DHL had read G. W. Kitchin's *A History of France* (Oxford, 1873), stating that Gaul was 'abandoned to beasts of prey' after the fall of Rome but that 'Christianity alone seemed to retain vigour and power over men' (62, 64–5).

125:30 **from the north side to the south side,**   See note on 64:39.

126:1 **a full-skirted [125:32] . . . long-fringed woman . . . a white sheet . . . swathed round their loins.**   The women's styles combined indigenous and Spanish features. For the men's 'sheets', see note on 113:15.

126:5 **the ovens.**   The ovens are large round outdoor adobe structures called 'hornos' (Spanish), still used today.

126:8 **on the bridge . . . the tom-tom,**   The dance procession often begins at the bridge (see the Deer Dance in 'Indians and Entertainment' and note on 64:35). The 'tom-tom' is a hand drum.

126:15 **ganglion**   Galen (second century AD) first used the word to describe a nerve complex. Today, an aggregate centre of nerve cell bodies interconnected in the nervous system; a mass of grey matter within the brain or spinal cord.

126:21 **may-pole.** It is possible to date the ceremony by the raising of the pole in late September for the San Geronimo festival (30 Sept.), which DHL attended in 1922. Athletic youths competed at climbing the pole, around 30 feet in height, in order to obtain the gifts attached to the top – food items – that would be used at the community feast.

126:30 **"You give me that kodak.** Almost all pueblos forbade tourist photographs at sacred ceremonies. The brand name 'Kodak' refers to a popular hand-held camera, sold by the Eastman Kodak Company (founded in Rochester, New York, in 1892 by inventor George Eastman).

127:1 **Tony Romero** Antonio Romero was governor of Taos Pueblo in 1924 (Kelly, *The Assault on Assimilation*, p. 309). He was also a leader in the Pueblo councils that resisted measures like the Bursum Bill.

127:3 **his shoulders.** Following this passage in all surviving states of the text (none earlier than Per1), an extra vertical space appears, as also after 127:24 ('dark man's'). In TCC1, the passage comes at the bottom of a page (p. 3), but there are two copy-reading symbols for paragraphing, indicating that extra space is intended. In *Cassell's Weekly* (Per2), there are seven divisions of the same kind, each with a row of decorative icons in addition to vertical spacing. See Introduction, p. lxxvii.

127:22 **Buddhist temples in Ceylon.** In 1922, DHL visited Ceylon, where his friend Earl Brewster was a daily student at a Buddhist temple (*Letters*, iv. 216) and where DHL visited temples he considered 'vulgar' (iv. 225, 226).

127:28 **piñon-dotted foot-hills** The piñon is a variety of small coniferous pine tree (see Glossary).

127:32 **a little dressed-up Madonna . . . in the green starting-bower.** See note on 66:40.

127:34 **The bell clanged. The tom-tom beat. The men slowly uplifted their voices.** See 'the song of the church bell', 62:27 and note.

128:14 *laisser faire* See note on 107:38.

Au Revoir, U. S. A.

131:5 *"Say au revoir /* [131:2] *. . . A bitter sigh . . . ."* A popular song 'Say "Au Revoir" But Not "Goodbye"' (1893) with words and music by Harry Kennedy. One of the earliest songs recorded by Edison, it should not be confused with the First World War song with a similar name, 'Au Revoir But Not Goodbye Soldier Boy' (1917) with words by Lew Brown. In 1918 E. T. Paull adapted Kennedy's song to wartime with additions to the lyrics.

131:6 **Pullman** In 1865 the American inventor George Pullman (1831–97) patented the Pullman 'sleeping car', allowing train seats to be converted into beds at night.

131:7 **El Paso,** Leading city on the Mexican–US border, located nearly 600 miles w. of Dallas, Texas, on the Rio Grande River – the international boundary – at a primary centre of east–west and north–south traffic. The

Lawrences' 1923 trip through El Paso (which this essay records) was the first of three, for they journeyed to Mexico by the same route in 1924 and made the return trip to New Mexico the same way. (See Map 3.)

131:10 **Mexican Pullman-boy...a revolution...end is up.** The train employee who took care of the sleeping cars. Workers were supposed to be the beneficiaries of the Mexican Revolution, which ousted the autocratic President Porfirio Díaz (1830–1915) in 1911 and won a new Constitution in 1917. But revolt continued even in 1923, when Adolfo de la Huerta opposed President Obregón and his successor Calles and when 'Pancho Villa' was assassinated (see Appendix VI:3–4 and notes on 26:33, 43:34 and 171:23). It was sometimes difficult to tell which side was 'up', but all sides professed their sympathy with the common people, as opposed to earlier aristocratic and authoritarian regimes.

131:17 **the solar plexus.** DHL identifies the human solar plexus, 'in the middle of you' near the navel, with pre-mental consciousness, the sympathetic nervous system and 'dynamic life-activity' (*Fantasia of the Unconscious*, ed. Steele, 74:11, 75:2); see also notes on 13:10 and 62:24. He further suggests that Mexico functions like a geographical solar plexus, near the 'navel' of America, between North and South.

131:27 **the spirit of place.** Cf. the title of the first chapter of *Studies*.

131:33 **San Juan Teotihuacán.** The town 30 miles n.e. of Mexico City, named for St John by conquistadors, is the site of the ancient pyramids that the Aztecs found deserted. The Pyramid of the Sun (third largest in the world), the Pyramid of the Moon, and the Temple of Quetzalcoatl date back to 100–200 BC but were abandoned 500 years later (see Appendix V:2).

132:5 **the dove still nests...rattlesnake of Aztec eternity.** See 'American Eagle': 'The dove of Liberty sat on an egg / And hatched another eagle', but DHL questions whether this American eagle is 'a sucking-dove', a pelican, or a 'prosperity-gander' that 'lays the golden egg' (*Poems* 413, 414). See also note on 16:5 about the Uroboros.

132:11 **The Spanish churches and palaces...on the point of falling down.** In *The Plumed Serpent*, the churches are 'barren' and in an odd disrepair despite their imposing dominance: 'You get a sense of plaster, of mortar, of whitewash, of smeared blue-wash or grey-wash, and of gilt laid on and ready to peel off' (277:1–5). During Mexico's revolutions, DHL adds, churches were often employed 'for stables and for barracks' or transformed 'into schools, and concert-halls, and cinematograph theatres' (278:11–13). The neo-Aztec transformation of the fictional Sayula church (ch. XVIII) plays upon this tenuous quality of Christian and European influence in Mexico (278–87). See also 'Walk to Huayapa', 50:29–30 and note.

132:16 **Quetzalcoatl.** The ancient Mexican god Quetzalcoatl had dual characteristics, as a feathered bird-snake or 'plumed serpent'. Like other Mexican gods, he was frequently worshipped by human sacrifice. Although DHL had learned that this practice was prevalent throughout ancient Mesoamerica, he conceived it as a late symptom of decadence; and his Kate Leslie, in *The Plumed Serpent*, prefers 'the older Indians, who knew [Quetzalcoatl] before the Aztecs raised their deities to heights of horror and vindictiveness' (58:35–6). In final excisions from this novel, 'the life-hope was dead, there was an instinct of death-worship in the Aztecs' when they sacrificed at the temple of Huitzilopochtli (509–10). See also Appendix V:3.

132:18 **the young Mexican artist.** DHL met Miguel Covarrubias (1902–57), once a student of Diego Rivera (1886–1957), in April 1923. See also 'young Garcia', who discusses modern Mexican frescoes with Kate in *The Plumed Serpent*, stating: 'But they are meant to be ugly' (51:10, 53:27). According to Bynner's *Journey with Genius*, Covarrubias spoke similarly (pp. 29–30).

132:24 **coiled rattle-snakes ... heaps of excrement.** Cf. DHL's description of sculptures in the Mexican National Museum in Mexico City: 'Snakes coiled like excrement, snakes fanged and feathered beyond all dreams of dread' (*PS* 79:21–2). See also Introduction, footnote 47, on his earlier reference to a rattlesnake sculpture.

132:27 **Temple of Quetzalcoatl** The Pyramid of the Plumed Serpent (AD 100–300) – called Quetzalcoatl – is at the southern end of the Avenue of the Dead on an elevated Ciudadela (citadel arena) at Teotihuacán. Its stepped platforms mount to an open temple area, lavishly decorated with undulating stone serpents. Superimposed on them are protruding heads of more massive feathered serpents, alternating with other high-relief heads (possibly of Tlaloc the rain god). See also *The Plumed Serpent*: 'The House of Quetzalcoatl wreathed with the Snake of all snakes, his huge fangs white and pure today as in the lost centuries when his makers were alive' (79:24–7).

132:37 **These bygone pyramid-building Americans ... when the Spaniards arrived,** Unknown even to the Aztecs, the builders may have been the ancestors of the Toltecs, whose culture the Aztecs emulated when they arrived in the Valley of Mexico in the thirteenth century. See also Appendixes V:1–2, VI:1.

133:3 **none of the phallic pre-occupation of the old Mediterranean.** The principal Greek father-god Zeus (Roman Jove) was known for his dalliances with women, including Io, Alcmene, Leda, Leto, Semele and Europa; and the jealousy of his wife Hera (Roman Juno) is central to many myths. Aphrodite (Roman Venus) was goddess of love, and Dionysus (Roman Bacchus), Eros (Roman Cupid) and Pan were also linked with eroticism. See notes to 35:14 and 35:17 on principal Aztec gods and goddesses.

133:7 **Chinese dragons** The *taotie* image of a frightful reptilian beast, appearing on sacrificial vessels by the second century BC, is thought to be an early form of the Chinese dragon; but the creatures became increasingly graceful, elongated and colourful, with long serpentine bodies, and were often represented in playful poses in the arts and crafts, dances and parades. Chinese myths tell of cosmic dragons that could mount to the heavens or rule under the seas.

Dear Old Horse, A London Letter

137:1 **Dear Old Horse, A London Letter** DHL wrote this piece from London
as a letter to Willard ('Spud') Johnson, to be published in his 'little magazine'
Laughing Horse. The words 'A London Letter' were probably added by Johnson to explain the essay's origin, but the present edition accepts it because
this term is in the essay and parallels the titles of DHL's next two essays
'Paris Letter' and 'A Letter from Germany'; DHL may well have authorised the full title. DHL's nickname for Johnson, co-founder of the magazine (see Introduction, footnote 25), was 'Spoodle' (see Textual apparatus for
137:2).

137:2 **Yesterday came the Horse,** The 'Horse' was the December 1923 issue
of the journal *Laughing Horse*, then housed in Santa Fe. See Introduction,
p. xli.

137:11 **Azure Horse, Turquoise Horse, Hobby Horse, Trojan Horse** In one
Navajo myth with Pueblo variants, the cardinal compass points are represented
by horses belonging to the Sun; their models on earth were once semi-precious
stone images that came to life, and the 'blue' or steel-grey horse was of turquoise
surrounded by a cloud of dazzling mineral dust. The cardinal 'blue' horse is
often called the Sun's favourite – the son of the Sun, reborn not only daily but
yearly, emerging from the dark earth-cave where the sun sets. The north (night,
winter) was represented by either a black or a dappled mount, while blue was
for the south (the zenith, summer), the colour of the sky as well as the turquoise.
(See also Introduction, footnote 52.) **Hobby Horse** (from Old English *hobin*,
a 'nag'), a standard figure accompanying English Morris dances in which
someone impersonated a horse by wearing a wicker frame or straddling a stick
with a horse's head. A child's toy 'Hobby Horse' was related to such models
but was mounted on rockers or wheels. A French children's expression for
'Hobby Horse' gave its name to the early twentieth-century art movement
Dada (1916–22). **Trojan Horse** (Homer, *Odyssey*, iv, viii, xi; Vergil, 70–19 BC,
Aeneid, ii; Dante Alighieri, 1265–1321, *Inferno*, Canto xxvi), a large, hollow
wooden horse which the Greeks gave the Trojans as a gift during the Trojan
War – only to emerge armed from its belly after the structure was brought
within the city walls and the city slept. Odysseus and his heroes had hidden
inside.

137:13 **the Centaur.** The Centaur, with the body of a horse but the torso and head
of a human, was usually associated with licence and wildness, but sometimes
with wisdom, healing powers and practical knowledge. In *The Boy in the
Bush*, ed Paul Eggert (Cambridge, 1996), the hero is called 'more animal than
human, like a centaur, as if he were one blood with the horse, and had the
centaur's superlative horse-sense, its non-human power, and wisdom of hot
blood-knowledge' (121:15–18).

137:17 **a Spoodle** See note on 137:1.

137:18 **like Adam,** Although the Bible does not mention an apple but an anonymous fruit and says nothing about sex at the time of the Fall (Genesis iii.

6–12), DHL often relies on John Milton's interpretation in *Paradise Lost*, which includes both (Bks viii–ix).

137:29 **Lobo,** 'Wolf' (Spanish), the name of the mountain where the ranch – later the Lawrence ranch – was located near San Cristobal.

138:1 **the Pale Galilean who has triumphed,** One of DHL's most characteristic literary allusions, from 'Hymn to Proserpine' (1866) by Algernon Charles Swinburne (1837–1909): 'Thou hast conquered, O pale Galilean; the world has grown grey from thy breath' (line 35). Based on a Latin passage attributed to Julian the Apostate, the line is supposedly spoken by a pagan worshipper at the time of Constantine's proclamation of the Christian faith in Rome (AD 313).

138:6 **sniggers.** In *Laughing Horse*, an extended space follows this word, indicating the end of a paragraph; since the next line lacks indentation, it is supplied here from E1.

138:7 **Houyhnhnms.** In *Gulliver's Travels* (1726) by Jonathan Swift (1667–1745), the Houyhnhnms are intelligent horses who rule over the Yahoos, a race of brutes resembling human beings (Pt iv, chs. I-X).

138:15 **When Jesus was born ... Great Pan is dead.** Cf. 'Pan in America', 155:2–4 and note.

138:17 **lamenting and about to expire, in the Uffizi.** Probably a reference to *Pallas Subduing a Centaur* (often called *Pallas and the Centaur*), an allegorical painting on the civilising power of mind over brute instincts, by Sandro Filipepi (Botticelli) (1445–1510). As the goddess of wisdom Pallas Athena grasps him by the hair, she holds a guard's pike-like halberd and the centaur looks around with dismay. The painting is one of the treasures of the Uffizi Gallery in Florence (founded in 1581).

138:18 **if the Horse in us died forever:** In a 1929 letter to Frederick Carter, DHL stated that 'the great effort of pre-spiritual man was to get himself the *powers* – the *honours and powers and might* – the Mana – of the vivid beasts' *(Letters,* vii. 545). See also *Apocalypse and the Writings on Revelation*, ed. Kalnins: 'Far back, far back in our dark soul the horse prances', being 'the symbol of surging potency and power of movement, of action, in man' (101:26, 102:3–4).

138:21 **the yellow mummy-swathings ... the dreadful mummy-sarcophagus of Europe,** DHL wrote to Alfred Stieglitz from Hampstead on 17 December 1923: 'I feel ... buried alive, under the yellow air and the vast inertia' *(Letters,* iv. 543). See also Birkin's sense of being 'in some Egyptian tomb' at Breadalby in *Women in Love*, ed. Farmer, Vasey and Worthen (98:36–7); and the view of England, from shipboard, as a grey 'coffin' in *The Lost Girl*, ed. Worthen (294:24) and *Kangaroo*, ed. Steele (258:32).

138:23 **the Rockies.** The Rocky Mountains, forming the 'backbone' of western North America, include a number of rugged, glaciated mountain ranges and contain the headwaters of major rivers of the Great Plains and US West Coast regions – including the Arkansas, Yellowstone, Missouri, Colorado, Columbia, Snake and Rio Grande. See also note on 98:36.

138:29 **And in Mexico [138:27]... his hoofs are red.** Probably a reference to the dry, sunny climate of Mexico's high desert plateau as well as to the Mexican Revolution which was still in progress (see Appendix VI:3–4). DHL wrote to Witter Bynner on 17 December 1923, 'I only hope Mexico will stop "revoluting"' (*Letters*, iv. 547). Of the major leaders of the revolution, most had already met violent deaths.

138:30 **seriously,** The name 'Spoodle' follows in Huxley's version (see Textual apparatus and note on 137:1).

138:31 **This two-legged forked radish** See Shakespeare's *Henry IV, Part Two*: 'Like a man made after supper of a cheeseparing: when a' was naked, a' was, for all the world, like a forked radish, with a head fantastically carved upon it with a knife' (III. ii); and *Sartor Resartus: The Life and Opinions of Herr Teufelsdröckh* (1833–4), by Thomas Carlyle (1795–1881), quoting 'a forked Radish with a head fantastically carved' (iv, 'Adamitism'). See also DHL, 'Introduction to Pictures': 'Man is anything from a forked radish to an immortal spirit' (*Late Essays and Articles*, ed. Boulton, 168:2).

138:36 **Chiron... that quondam four-footed gentry.** As early as the ninth century BC, Homer refers to Chiron as the 'most righteous' of the Centaurs (*Iliad*, xi) and Dante calls him 'the great Centaur' (*Inferno*, Canto xii). He was the learned tutor of the Greek physician Asclepius and the heroes Jason, Achilles and Hercules. While Chiron was the son of Chronos, the other Centaurs were children of Ixion, known for their wildness and animality, often mentioned as drunken followers of Dionysus. Their home was Thessaly. See also 143:4.

139:2 **a loud, sensible Horse Laugh.** 'Horse Sense' is common sense, and DHL adds merriment to his definition. He wrote to Mabel Dodge Luhan on 9 January 1924 to keep her 'power to laugh a bit': 'Don't go back on your common horse-sense. It is the centaur's way of knowledge' (*Letters*, iv. 555).

139:4 **hoofs, that can kick the walls of the world down.** See also Ursula Brangwen's encounter with horses, their 'great hoofs flashing bright' (*The Rainbow*, ed. Kinkead-Weekes, 453:6–7), and Lou Carrington's response to St. Mawr: 'It was... as if the walls of her own world had suddenly melted away' (*St. Mawr and Other Stories*, ed. Finney, 30:37–8).

139:10 **the Sierra Madre;** Several mountain ranges go by this name. Near Santa Fe, the Rocky Mountains extend into the Sierra Madre Mountains, which join the north–south Sierra Madre of Mexico – itself divided into the Sierra Madre Oriental, from El Paso along the Gulf of Mexico, and the Sierra Madre Occidental, from Arizona along the Gulf of California. These ranges meet and link with the Sierra Madre del Sur that continues into Central America.

139:16 **a little blue foal... out of the old dark earth-coloured mottled mare.** See note on 137:11 and Introduction, footnote 52. To the Navajo, the changing colours of the Sun's mount followed both diurnal and annual patterns, and some Pueblo tales take similar lines.

139:18 **the Mexican under his big hat.** The Mexican sombrero (from 'sombra', Spanish for 'shade') was related to a wide-brimmed Spanish hat but had an even wider brim and a high, conical crown, often with a band of braid or silver conchos and a chin-strap. Brett's cover design for the first edition of *The Plumed Serpent* (Knopf) shows such hats.

139:23 **Cambridge sausages.** An insulting suggestion that the meat is horse-meat because of the nearness of Newmarket, the racing and horse-trading centre. See also Aaron Sisson's dream of a human skin stuffed 'as the skin of a Bologna sausage' (*Aaron's Rod*, ed. Kalnins, 286:19).

139:33 **a witch on a broom-stick,** In European folklore, witches fly through the air while riding a broomstick. The image may arise from pagan fertility rites in which a rod or broom was imagined to have the magic properties of a shaman's wand.

Paris Letter

143:1 **Paris Letter** The essay is one of three written from the Lawrences' European travel locations in 1924. See Introduction, p. xlii, and note on 137:1. (See Map 5.)

143:4 **Hercules slaying the Centaur,** A famous art scene is the battle between Hercules and the centaur Nessus, who had attempted to assault his wife Dejanira. Hercules is also shown in his accidental killing of Chiron and is occasionally depicted (instead of Theseus) fighting the centaurs at a Lapith wedding when they tried to abduct the bride. Although the picture DHL saw is unidentified, the Louvre and the Bibliothèque Nationale both contained scenes like these on Greek and Etruscan pottery of the fifth and sixth centuries BC. DHL could also have been thinking of sculptures of *Theseus Killing the Minotaur* (1847) and *Lapith and Centaur* (1848), both in the Tuileries gardens, by Antoine Louis Barye (1796–1875). And he probably would have known *Fight Between the Centaurs and the Lapiths* by Piero di Cosimo (1461–1521), in the National Gallery, London.

143:10 **Seine** The chief river of Paris, arising in Burgundy in n.e. France and flowing 482 miles to the English Channel. Paris is divided by the Seine into the Right Bank and the Left Bank. The trees (143:11–12) are probably the plane trees lining the river banks; though slow to lose their leaves, they have bare, dark boughs in late January, when the essay was written.

143:15 **the huge dark-grey palaces [143:13] . . . suggestion of pyramids.** DHL was not wrong to sense an Egyptian influence. The Louvre instituted its Egyptian Museum in 1827, aided by Napoleonic collections, new excavations and the French Institute of Oriental Archaeology. The Obelisk of Luxor (weighing 230 tons), a gift from the viceroy of Egypt (Mohammed Ali), was installed in 1836 at one end of the Tuileries gardens at the Place de la Concorde. In 1867, Egypt sent a celebrated exhibition to Paris, which was shown in a small Egyptian temple approached by an avenue of sphinxes; and the Petit Palais displayed important Egyptian art at the 1900 World Exposition and thereafter.

143:19 **the river windows of the Tuileries [143:17]...a royal spouse...the bridge...silk and silver cavalcade.** Only the gardens remain of the Tuileries Palace, started by Catherine de Médicis (1519–89), wife of Henri II (1519–59), but its windows once commanded the Seine on one side. A residence of several early kings of France before Louis XIV (1638–1715) moved the court to Versailles, the Tuileries later housed Louis XVI (1754–93) and Marie Antoinette (1755–93) in their last years; and it was the principal residence of Napoleon Bonaparte (1769–1821) after 1800, the Restoration kings and Napoleon III (1808–73). The bridge is probably the Pont Neuf ('New Bridge', actually the oldest on the Seine), completed by Henri IV (1553–1610), connecting the Tuileries to the Left Bank and a small island where royal entertainments could be held. The view of the bridge was unimpeded (without buildings) by royal command, but venders, performers and social strollers frequented it.

143:21 **Champs Elysées.** A celebrated east–west boulevard, 230 feet wide and lined by chestnut and plane trees, the Champs Elysées runs through the heart of Paris, being one of twelve avenues that converge at the Arc de Triomphe. Named for the Greek Elysian Fields, the avenue – once a path planned in 1616 by Marie de Médicis and a fashionable eighteenth-century walkway used by Marie Antoinette – was given much of its modern form under Napoleon III in the nineteenth century.

143:29 **Rip Van Winkle,** In the story by the American author Washington Irving (1783–1859), Van Winkle slept for twenty years in the Catskill Mountains of New York and woke to find the world changed by the US Revolution. Irving wrote the tale under two of his pseudonyms, attributing it to Diedrich Knickerbocker but publishing it in *The Sketch Book of Geoffrey Crayon* (1819).

144:6 **white marble fesses.** Sculptured buttocks (French *fesses*).

144:7 **inquisition;** From 'inquiro' (Latin), 'to inquire into'. Popularly refers to ecclesiastical measures to combat heresy, supposedly by questioning, torture and compulsion – especially the Spanish Inquisition of the fifteenth century.

144:9 **bourgeois...petit bourgeoise** Middle-class; lower-middle-class, small business owners and their workers.

144:19 **Aphrodite in elastic garters.** The Greek goddess of love (Roman Venus). The image suggests a painting in the style of Henri de Toulouse Lautrec (1864–1901), French post-impressionist painter of subjects like *Woman Adjusting her Garter*, or Amedeo Modigliani (1884–1920), Italian Expressionist painter known for the mannered distortion and odd accessories of his nudes like *Nude with a Hat* – a black hat (see 144:25–6 on 'Aphrodite in a hard black hat').

144:22 **more unwitherable than Cleopatra.** Cleopatra VII (69–30 BC), of the Macedonian Ptolemaic Dynasty in Egypt, last of the pharaohs, married to Ptolemy XIII, Ptolemy XIV and Mark Antony, lover of Julius Caesar. See Shakespeare's *Antony and Cleopatra*: 'Age cannot wither her, nor custom stale / Her infinite variety' (II. ii).

144:24 **Coquilles Saint Martin, and escargots . . . and Chateaubriands**   Scallops in a creamy wine sauce, sometimes served in shells (French 'coquilles'); snails; . . . a beef delicacy, sliced and mixed with Bearnaise or another sauce, probably created around 1822 for François Vicomte de Chateaubriand (1768–1848).

144:36 **a Sisyphus penalty,**   In the mythic underworld, Sisyphus was forced to roll a stone up a steep hill endlessly since the stone always rolled back down when it reached the top (Homer, *Odyssey*, XI). Although Homer gives no reason for the punishment, other accounts mention his avarice, deceit and betrayal of the gods' secrets to mortals. One solar myth links him with the sun that perpetually rises and falls below the horizon.

144:38 **the huge buildings of the Louvre and the Tuileries**   Originally a fortress started around 1220 by Philippe Auguste (1165–1223), the Louvre became one of the largest palace complexes in the world, displaying medieval, Renaissance and neoclassic features as commissioned by eleven kings and renovated by Napoleon I and Napoleon III. An intermittent residence of the kings of France until the late seventeenth century, it was a repository of important royal art collections as early as François I (1498–1547), and much of the Louvre became a public museum nearly 250 years later (1793) after the French Revolution. See also note on the Tuileries at 143:19.

145:4 **the Petit Palais,**   Built in 1900 for the Paris World Exposition, the regal structure stands between the Champs Elysées and the Arena Alexandre III, housing a wide range of art.

145:7 **democracy . . . the old sort of aristocracy,**   DHL, sceptical of 'democracy' as he saw it, was nonetheless a spokesman for 'the right, the sacred duty' to practice 'natural aristocracy' (*Letters*, iv. 226). In contrast to the old hereditary aristocracy, this society would depend on the citizens' 'new reverence for their heroes' and 'new regard for their comrades' ('Education of the People', *Reflections* 166:12).

145:10 **like Ulysses,**   Although Ulysses was the son and heir of King Laertes of Ithaca, his power as hero of the *Odyssey* depended on his wit and perseverance. While to Dante, he was a false counsellor (*Inferno*, Canto xxvi), to Homer he was a stalwart leader. See also 145:8 on 'the old Homeric aristocracy'.

145:12 **the Red Indians only knew the aristocrat by instinct.**   DHL would have known the Pueblo Indian way of electing chief officers and voting in councils of elders (see note on 108:28), of being born into clan membership but advancing through rites of passage. Collier, too, referred in 1923 to the 'Homeric laughter heard in the Pueblos' ('The Pueblos' Last Stand', 22).

145:19 **House of Valois, House of Tudor!**   The French House of Valois, a branch of the Capetian Dynasty, ruled from the accession of Philippe VI (1328) to the death of Henri III (1589). England's House of Tudor began with the accession of Henry VII (1485) and ended at the death of Elizabeth I (1603).

145:23 **Some men are always aristocrats.**   See also 'Aristocracy': 'Men of the sun, whether Chinese or Hottentot or Nordic, or Hindu or Esquimo, if they touch the sun in the heavens, are lords of the earth. And together they will form the aristocracy of the world' (*Reflections* 376:34–7). The same essay opposes the 'new (a new-old) aristocracy, completely unmysterious and scientific: the aristocracy of money' (*Reflections* 368:31–2).

Letter from Germany

149:1 **Letter from Germany** The essay's first publication, in 1934 in the *New Statesman and Nation*, bore the following headnote: '[*This letter, written by D. H. Lawrence in 1928, shows a remarkable sensitiveness to the trend of events in Germany at a time when Hitlerism, as we know it, hardly existed.*]' (p. 481). The actual date of composition was later recognised as 1924, when the Lawrences were in Europe between stays in America (see Introduction, p. xliii).

149:5 **from Paris to Nancy, through that Marne country,** Nancy is a city on the main line from Paris to Strasbourg, a route taken periodically by the Lawrences when en route to Frieda's family home in Baden-Baden (see Map 5). The Marne area of France was the site of fierce warfare during the First World War (the Battle of the Marne in 1914 and the Second Battle of the Marne in 1918); the vicinity had been a battleground for centuries, as when the Frankish King Clovis defeated the Romans near Soissons in 486 (*Movements in European History*, ed. Crumpton, pp. 88–9), about 50 miles n. of the Marne. See also 'The Border Line' in which Katharine Farquhar recognises the location: 'the ghastly Marne country, century after century digging the corpses of frustrated men into its soil. The border country where the Latin races and the Germanic neutralise one another into horrid ash' (*The Woman Who Rode Away and Other Stories*, ed. Mehl and Jansohn, 83:2–4).

149:9 **Strasburg,** Strasbourg, in Alsace on a Roman site of the first century BC, became part of France in the seventeenth century but was annexed to Germany in 1871 after the Franco-Prussian War. Although the Treaty of Versailles (1919) returned Alsace and Lorraine to France, large numbers of the people (particularly in Alsace) continued to speak German. Strasbourg was once a free imperial city of the Holy Roman Empire.

149:11 **Mülhausen,** [Mühlhausen], in Alsace, about 80 miles s. of Strasbourg, known for its textile industry. An imperial free city in the Middle Ages, it became part of France in the eighteenth century and part of Germany from the Franco-Prussian War to the First World War. The river is the Ill River.

149:15 **The cathedral-front [149:13]... prisms of stone.** The red sandstone front of the Cathedral of Notre Dame in Strasbourg is in the Gothic style, mostly from the thirteenth century but dating back to the twelfth. The tower is topped by a fifteenth-century spire 466 feet tall, once making this the tallest building in Europe. See DHL's description in 'The Border Line': 'And like a great ghost, a reddish flush in its darkness, the uncanny cathedral... looking down like darkness out of darkness, on the pigmy humanness of the city. It was built of reddish stone, that had a flush in the darkness, like dark flesh. And vast, an incomprehensibly tall, strange thing, it looked down out of the night. The great rose window poised high seemed like a breast of the vast

Thing, and prisms and needles of stone shot up, as if it were plumage, dimly, half-visible in heaven' (*The Woman Who Rode Away and Other Stories*, ed. Mehl and Jansohn, 84:32–40).

149:16 **The gothic!** The Gothic architectural style, ascribed in the Renaissance to the 'Goths' or barbarians, was one of the most distinctive of Europe, arising in twelfth-century France and spreading quickly to Early English cathedral construction – e.g. Canterbury's choir and Lincoln's nave. Reaction to the Gothic style is a recurrent motif in DHL – e.g. Paul Morel's preference for the 'horizontals' of the older Norman form over the ascetic 'perpendicular lines' of Gothic in *Sons and Lovers*, ed. Baron and Baron, 215:9, 14. Other examples include the scenes at Lincoln Cathedral in *The Rainbow*; Aaron Sisson's ambivalence at Milan Cathedral in *Aaron's Rod*; and Somers's recoil at the dream of 'a huge, pale-grey bulk of a cathedral, an old gothic cathedral', as recalled in *Kangaroo*: 'He had now a horror of vast superincumbent buildings . . . Even the cathedrals . . . Horrible, inert, man-moulded weight. Heavy as death' (ed. Steele, 346:22–4, 34–5, 38–9).

149:17 **goths and alemans** Both Germanic 'barbarian' tribes that fought against Rome – the Alemanni coalition in the third century, the Visigoths and Ostrogoths in the fifth. Their national arts probably contributed centuries later to Gothic architectural form. In *Movements in European History*, ed. Crumpton, DHL describes the Goths as warriors driven towards Rome by a 'great impulse' (53:13); and in 'Germans and English' (1927) he notices the Wandervögel, German youths in Italy as if in a 'mystery' of migration (*Sketches* 247:28–9) – in them, the Italians 'see again the Goths and the Vandals passing with loud and guttural speech, i barbari' (248:18–19). The Alemanni, whose name gave France the term 'Allemagne' for Germany, settled largely in Swabia, the present western and southwestern Baden-Württemberg, Alsace and northeastern Switzerland.

149:19 **The Rhine is still the Rhine, the great divider.** In Roman days, DHL wrote, the Rhine was one of the main 'barriers between savage and civilised Europe', a barrier that failed in 407 when the previously Roman-fortified Rhine frontier yielded to massive numbers of Germanic people moving southwards, not to be turned back (*Movements in European History*, ed. Crumpton, 59:38–9).

149:24 **occupied territory.** After the First World War, the Treaty of Versailles (1919) gave Alsace-Lorraine up to French occupation. See also note on 152:28 about the Ruhr occupation.

149:30 **deserts** Originally 'wildness' in MS (p. 2). Among other changes in MS were: 149:30 <'low'> {'ponderous'} (p. 2); 151:22 <'changes'> {'relaxes'} (p. 4); and 151:37 <'savages'> {'barbarians'} (p. 5 unpaginated).

149:31 **Black Forest,** Forest of wooded hills and valleys in southwest Germany, where the Danube and Neckar Rivers arise; bordered by the Rhine and Switzerland, near Baden-Baden in the north and Freiburg in the south. See also DHL's description of German forest in Roman days in *Movements in European History*, ed. Crumpton: 'To the south . . . the whole country was covered by a vast forest of dark fir and pine-trees, tracts of which still remain' (45:12–14).

150:7 **A fear of the invisible life lurking among the woods.** DHL expands upon this idea in *Movements in European History*, ed. Crumpton: 'In their camps along the Rhine the Roman soldiers . . . told terrible stories of the land confronting them, stories of wolves, and growling bears . . . stories of lurking, deadly Germans; stories of horrible sacrifices in groves dark as night; stories of demons that howled through the trees in the blackness, of wolves that turned into ghastly, blood-drinking women—and so on' (46:14–20). From the Black Forest in 1921, DHL recalls the presence there of the Roman legions: 'No wonder they thrilled with horror when, deep in the woods, they found the skulls and trophies of their dead comrades upon the trees' (*Fantasia of the Unconscious*, ed. Steele, 87:29–31).

150:16 **eastwards; towards Russia, towards Tartary.** Cf. also the invasions from 'Middle Asia' that broke 'first on Russia': 'And every time the black swarm broke out of the east, the white clouds of German and Slavonic barbarians came rolling over Europe to the south'; DHL locates the Huns in 'that immeasurable basin of dreary land called Tartary or Scythia' (*Movements in European History*, ed. Crumpton, 65: 7–11, 16).

150:20 *Men Beasts and Gods*, [*Beasts, Men and Gods*], published in 1922 by Ferdinand Ossendowski (1876–1945), a Polish-born explorer and writer who told about his life in Siberia in the wake of the Russian Revolution, when 'the Heart of Asia' was swept with political and religious ferment and hardship. He reported prophecies from Central Asia that there would be a huge migration, 'the last march of the Mongols', and that the entire earth would be 'emptied' by war and moral collapse (ch. XLIX). Most unusual of all was the story Ossendowski learned about a subterranean civilisation of Agharti, ruled by 'the King of the World' as a refuge for vanished peoples – like those who fled Jenghis Khan – from which the world may expect eventual assistance. The prophecy was attributed to this king himself.

150:21 **Attila.** Attila the Hun (AD 406–53) was called 'the Scourge of God' (Edmund Gibbon, *The History of the Decline and Fall of the Roman Empire*, 6 vols., 1776–89, i. ch. XXXIV) for conquering much of the Roman Empire between Gaul and the Caspian Sea and from Greece to Russia and northern Europe. In 'Blessed Are the Powerful', DHL refers to 'Attila's charred ruins and emptied spaces' but adds, 'If it must be a scourge, let it be a scourge of God' (*Reflections* 328:1, 12). In *Movements in European History*, ed. Crumpton, DHL tells how 'the Huns destroyed the Roman world' (65:11–12). Yet Attila is termed 'perhaps the greatest barbarian conqueror that ever lived', whose 'people loved him' (69:25, 26). See also DHL's poem 'Attila' (*Poems* 497).

150:22 **Baden Baden** German city in today's Baden-Württemberg, 108 miles s. of Frankfurt and 69 n.e. of Freiburg. Baden is famous for its thermal hotsprings, popular with the Romans in the first century and with European royalty, especially in the nineteenth century.

150:23 **Turgenevs or Dostoevskys or Grand Dukes or King Edwards**   Ivan
Turgenev (1818–83), Russian author of *Fathers and Sons* (1862), lived in
Baden-Baden and Paris much of his adult life and made the former the setting
of his novel *Smoke* (1867). Fyodor Dostoevsky (1821–81), Russian author of
Crime and Punishment (1866) and *The Brothers Karamazov* (1880), stayed in
Baden-Baden several times during the 1860s and had a famous confronta-
tion there with Turgenev. Friedrich I (1826–1907), Grand Duke of Baden,
promoted the building of the Friedrichsbad ('old bath') that opened in 1877.
Edward VII of England (1841–1910), while still Prince of Wales, was a frequent
visitor.

150:27 **The Rentenmark, the new Gold Mark of Germany,**   In 1923, due to
hyperinflation of the currency, a new mark was adopted, the Rentenmark
which was equivalent to a trillion old marks and 100 new Rentenpfennig; and,
in 1924, these were to become the gold-backed Reichsmark and Reichspfennig.
Financial hardship was severe because of the inflation itself and the cure –
savings and pensions disappeared along with businesses and employment –
and general discontent helped to make it possible for Adolf Hitler (1889–1945)
to gain an audience and to become Nazi leader and Chancellor of Germany.

150:29 **by a long chalk.**   'By a long way, by many degrees': perhaps based on the
tallying of game scores (as in dominoes) with chalk; the longer the notations,
the higher the scores.

150:37 **Ten pfennigs . . . a hundred Milliards of Marks.**   A Rentenpfennig was
a hundredth part of a Rentenmark. A Milliard is a thousand millions.

151:8 **a queer, *bristling* feeling of uncanny danger.**   'Bristling' is one of DHL's
key words, originating in the description of the threatening ash tree outside
the Morel family home (*Sons and Lovers*, ed. Baron and Baron, 85:4) and
ranging into extended meditations about power, as in DHL's recollection of
the uncanny fear of the Roman legions when they encountered the Hercynian
forests 'bristling with indomitable energy' (*Fantasia of the Unconscious*, ed.
Steele, 87:26). In the first version of 'The Border-Line', in the same German
forest setting after the First World War, a ghost returns from death as a 'Tree
of Life' with 'pine-bristles' (*The Woman Who Rode Away and Other Stories*,
ed. Mehl and Jansohn, 293:24). In 'The Princess', the deathly New Mexico
setting is described 'bristling with grey dead trees among grey rock' and amid
'the bristling black feathers of spruce' (*St. Mawr and Other Stories*, ed. Finney,
179:19, 181:25). The 'bristling' imagery – also appearing in *The Rainbow*, *Mr.
Noon*, *Movements in European History*, *The Captain's Doll*, 'The Princess' and
elsewhere – characteristically associates dread and danger with a tree shape
that usually manifests itself at night. See also 'Pan in America' (158:26, 158:30
and 159:1) and notes on 149:31, 150:7 and 157:36.

151:19 **the polarity of civilised Christian Europe.**   Cf. 'In the early
Middle Ages Europe was one great realm as it has never been since. It was not
strictly Europe, but Christendom . . . . A man counted himself first a Christian, then a Norman or a Saxon, and after that a Frenchman or an Englishman
as might be' (*Movements in European History*, ed. Crumpton, 116:2–3, 5–7).
DHL often refers to the European balance between Southern and Northern

peoples: 'The fusion of the two opposites brought us the greatness of modern days: just as the hostility of the two brings disaster, now as in the old past' (*Movements in European History*, ed. Crumpton, 52:7–9). Similarly, East and West had come into a volatile but productive contact: 'Hence Venice' (*Studies* 383:19).

151:29 **Heidelberg.** Heidelberg, famous for its castle and university of medieval origins, is in Baden-Württemberg, 50 miles s. of Frankfurt on the Neckar River, which flows into the Rhine Valley at nearby Mannheim.

151:29 **people.** An indentation in MS, following this word, is actually caused by a page number on the notebook sheet and does not signal a new paragraph.

151:32 **These queer gangs of Young Socialists,** The Social Democrats, moderate centrist Socialists, were the leaders in the coalition that formed the Weimar Republic in 1919. But some of the 'Young Socialists' were actually extremists like those who had already staged a Socialist rebellion during the war (the 'Wilhelmshaven Revolt') or the Spartacists, Communist-leaners who rebelled in October 1923 in Hamburg, a month before Hitler led his 'right wing' *putsch* in Bavaria (unsuccessful at that time).

152:4 **the old, pinkish stone of the ruined castle** Heidelberg Castle was built of red sandstone in a variety of styles during 400 years, beginning in the fourteenth century. But it was destroyed in the Thirty Years War, razed by the French twice during the seventeenth century and burned after lightning struck it in 1764. Still it dominates the city, lying just above it on a high eminence. The castle was once the home of the Palatine Counts and Electors.

152:6 **river gateway** The 'old bridge' includes a gateway with twin towers topped by spiked caps, dating to the eighteenth century.

152:18 **And the Celt ... to the fusion.** DHL often criticises the Welsh Lloyd George, Prime Minister of the United Kingdom (1916–22), as in 'The Proper Study', 'On Coming Home' and 'Blessed Are the Powerful', *Reflections* 171:40, 181:16, 324:13, 28 and 15. In *Movements in European History*, ed. Crumpton, DHL praises the old Arthurian Celts and credits the power of their Druids, but attributes their decline to 'quarrelsome clans', 'luxury and folly' (79:1, 4–5). In *The Plumed Serpent*, Kate Leslie is Irish, as was her revolutionary husband Joachim.

152:28 **a Ruhr occupation ... an English nullity ... a German false will.** In 1923, France and Belgium protested against late German payment of the First World War reparations by occupying the Ruhr region along the Ruhr River and north on the Lippe – the nation's pre-eminent manufacturing and mining centre. In passive resistance, the Weimar government paid the workers to go on strike, thus depleting the national treasury and contributing to its own financial crisis. The Dawes Plan (named for an American banker who led an international committee on reparations) was adopted: it called for the withdrawal of the occupying forces, provided gradual instalments for payment, and promised international loans. While England condemned the French action, it joined in the Dawes provisions that many Germans considered punishing.

152:30 **Quos vult perdere Deus, dementat prius.**   One of DHL's favourite quo-
tations (see note on 84:16).

Pan in America

155:4 **"Pan is... is dead!"**   Cf. 'Dear Old Horse, A London Letter' (138:14–
15). Traditionally Pan was a pastoral deity, half-man and half-goat, who
was patron of shepherds and flocks, hunters and woods. The post-Homeric
'Hymn to Pan' first tried to explain his association with 'All' (iii. 2). But
the tradition of his death originated in the *Moralia* ('De defectu oracu-
lorum') of Plutarch (*c.* AD 46–120) and the interpretation of it by Eusebius
(*c.* AD 265–340), to whom Pan, like other pagan deities, was a demon destined
to be cast out by Christ. Later glosses pinpointed Pan's death at the time of
the Advent or the Crucifixion. In another tradition, Pan was identified with
Christ by Paulus Marsus (*c.* 1482). But DHL's 1923–4 'Pan cluster' employs
opposition instead of harmony between Pan and Christ.
  Perhaps the most popular English poem on Pan's death is Elizabeth Barrett
Browning's 'The Dead Pan' (1844); but Ezra Pound's 'Pan Is Dead', in his
Ripostes (1912), begins with the exact words ending DHL's opening sentence.
A work of more immediacy to DHL may have been *A Canticle of Pan* (New
York, 1920) by Witter Bynner (1881–1968), which combines the traditions
of Plutarch and Marsus. See also Introduction, footnote 54, and *The Woman
Who Rode Away and Other Stories*, ed. Mehl and Jansohn, note on 122:27.

155:5 **fauns and... and naiads**   Minor classical nature deities: fauns and satyrs,
located in and around woodlands, had horns and the legs of goats; nymphs
were beautiful young females who lived in, and animated, particular natural
settings – dryads in trees and naiads in bodies of water, fountains or springs.
Fauns and satyrs were generally followers of Dionysus (Roman Bacchus), but
some were of Pan's train, as were some nymphs. Pan was not literally their
father but their leader.

155:8 **ridings**   Roads or paths 'specially intended for persons riding' (*OED*);
ancient administrative units in Britain and Scandinavia (from Norse, 'thrid-
ings'). In the twelfth-century laws of Edward the Confessor, a riding was a
'third part' of a county.

155:13 **Ishmael**   Genesis xvi. 8–15, xxi. 9–20. As the son of a bondwoman, Ishmael
was sent away into the wilderness by his father Abraham, thus becoming
an archetypal example of the outcast; in Islam, nonetheless, he is regarded
as a great progenitor of the faithful. DHL may also refer to the 'pariah-like
Ishmael' Bush (*Studies* 61:8), a renegade pioneer in Fenimore Cooper's *The
Prairie* (1827), or to Ishmael, the wandering narrator of Herman Melville's
Moby-Dick (1851).

155:19 **A man... fell dead,**   Although the idylls of Theocritus show Pan to be
frightening if troubled in his mid-day nap after hunting (i. 15–18), another
story – attributed by Eusebius to Porphyry (*c.* 232–304) – told how nine
persons, upon beholding Pan, fell dead. The 'revival' of Pan in 1890s and
Edwardian literature often featured a 'Gothic' Pan or Pan figure, a source of

calamities, as in 'The Great God Pan' (1894) by Arthur Machen (1863–1947). DHL was familiar with some of Machen's work by 1909 (*Letters*, i. 107) and received more in July 1924 (*Letters*, v. 79).

155:24 **blind energy,** A revision in MS, previously 'power' (p. 1). Among other revisions in MS are: 156:9 <'men'> {'people'} (p. 2); 158:2 <'It is a presence having'> {'The tree has'} (p. 5); 158:6 <'womb'> {'allness'} (p. 5); 158:19 <'always there'> {'asserting itself'} (p. 5); 158:20 <'fertilise'> {'cross'} (p. 5); 158:21 <'enters'> {'penetrates'} (p. 5); 158:27 <'energy'> {'strength'} (p. 5); 158:32 <'resistance'> {'sharpness'} (p. 5); 159:39 <'the men of Pan'> {'a man rises and'} (p. 7); 161:37 <'conscious gesture'> {'movement of pure will'} (p. 9); 162:5 <'trees'> {'creatures'} (p. 10); 162:16 <'sympathetic'> {'intuitive'} (p. 10); 162:24 <'knife'> {'death'} (p. 10); 162:28 <'conquered'> {'succeeded'} (p. 10); 162:37 <'give up'> {'abandon'} (p. 10); 163:9 <'with'> {'bringing'} (p. 11); 163:30 <'among'> {'inherent in'} (p. 11); 163:30 <'relation to'> {'contact between'} (p. 11); and 163:36 <'the moon'> {'yourself'} (p. 12). See also notes on 158:30, 161:25, 163:7 and 164:13.

155:31 **nympholept.** One 'caught' or bewitched by a nymph and filled with mad ecstasy. Cf. 'A Nympholept' (1891) by Algernon Charles Swinburne (1837–1909).

156:19 **Old Nick, the Old Gentleman** Terms for the Devil. Samuel Butler (1612–80) suggests in *Hudibras*, iii.1, that 'our Old Nick' derives his name from the Italian Niccolò Machiavelli, or 'Nick Machiavel' (1469–1527), but the name has also been derived from a much earlier Danish sea god. The Devil is also referred to as 'the old one', referring to 'his primeval character', and 'the old gentleman (in black)' (*OED*). DHL easily detected in *The Scarlet Letter* (1850) by Nathaniel Hawthorne (1804–64) a figure of the Satan of Massachusetts witchcraft: 'the Black Man that haunts the forest round us' (*Studies* 94:40–95:1).

156:26 **brimstone and hell-fire,** Cf. Revelation xix. 20, in which Satan is to be cast into a 'lake of fire burning with brimstone' (*KJB*).

156:27 **witches of a Walpurgis night,** Cf. *Letters*, i. 419. A German legend says that witches gather on the eve of May Day, 30 April, on Brocken Peak in the Harz Mountains. The following day is dedicated to St Walpurgis, an eighth-century English missionary to Germany.

156:33 **Pantheists, Wordsworth one of the first.** Believers in the doctrine that God is in all nature. Cf. DHL's definition in MS1 (Appendix III), 200:5–37. In *Apocalypse and the Writings on Revelation*, ed. Kalnins, DHL seems almost to agree: to 'the ancient consciousness', a rock or a pool of water 'is God' (95:16–17). But he calls depictions of nature by William Wordsworth (1770–1850) 'Sweet-Williamish' in '. . . . . . Love Was Once a Little Boy' (*Reflections* 336:13) and satirises him in a letter of 1922 (*Letters*, v. 308). The '**Lucy Gray aspect**' (156:34) refers to Wordsworth's 'Lucy Gray; or, Solitude' (1800), in which Lucy is called 'The sweetest thing that ever grew / Beside a human door' (lines 8–9). 'Oft have I heard of Lucy Gray' (156:35) is Lawrence's version of the poem's first line ['Oft I had heard of Lucy Gray']. This poem was a favourite elocution piece. Cf. 'On Human Destiny' with its 'Wordsworthian Lucy' of low vitality and nearly a 'simpleton's' nature (*Reflections* 204:2–4).

157:2 **Oversoul,** The supreme animating spirit of the universe, unifying all things, according to the Transcendentalism of Ralph Waldo Emerson (1803–82), as in 'The Over-Soul', in *Essays: First Series* (1841), which DHL requested in 1917 (*Letters*, iii. 66). But DHL's 'Democracy' opposes the view that 'a Great Mind floats in space: God, the Anima Mundi, the Oversoul'; rather, 'the actual living quick' is 'the creative reality' (*Reflections* 76:38–9, 77:3–4). Cf. also his comment about a primrose: 'all the oversouling in the world won't melt it [a primrose] out into a Williamish oneness' ('. . . . . Love Was Once a Little Boy', *Reflections* 335:6–7).

157:3 **Lucifer Gray** Lucifer was the fallen angel (Isaiah xiv. 12) associated with Satan. A 'Lucifer Gray' would resemble the Americans whose 'goody-goody' façades conceal 'demons', as DHL says in 'Nathaniel Hawthorne and *The Scarlet Letter*' (*Studies* 81:14, 20).

157:4 *Song of Myself.* A poem by Whitman, included in his *Leaves of Grass* (1855). DHL quotes from it elsewhere, objecting to the poet's 'Allness' (*Studies* 151:33–9).

157:9 **Aristotle** Greek philosopher (see note on 66:4), a student of Plato, he diverged from his master in stressing observation of 'real' nature; hence he is often seen as a father of science. DHL is emphasising his work on logic – the *Organon*, including four books on analytics and one on sophism. Among Aristotle's other books were thirteen in *Metaphysics* and ten in the *Nichomachean Ethics*.

157:18 **Germans in 1914,** The First World War (1914–18).

157:19 **bolshevist** Originally a member of the wing of the Social Democratic Party of Russia that formed its Communist Party. The Bolsheviks had wrested control of their country in 1917 soon after the overthrow of the Czar. In 1924 the country's future course – and that of the party – was unclear.

157:20 *us,* DHL underlined the word twice (MS, p. 4), but the double emphasis was lost in TCC (p. 5) and all publications of the essay.

157:27 **a small baby . . . Mama! Dada!** Cf. 'First Glimmerings of Mind' in *Fantasia of the Unconscious*, ed. Steele (pp. 105–11).

157:36 **As a tree . . . earth's middle.** Cf. *Fantasia of the Unconscious*, ed. Steele, describing a great Black Forest tree that is 'vast and powerful and exultant in his two directions', 'a huge, savage, thoughtless soul': 'He thrusts himself tremendously down to the middle earth . . . and he turns himself about in high air' (86:34–6, 28–30). The association between Pan and roots is longstanding in DHL – e.g. a letter to E. M. Forster: 'Don't you see Pan is the undifferentiated root and stem drawing out of unfathomable darkness' (*Letters*, ii. 275).

157:37 **little ranch . . . Rocky Mountains,** The setting is Kiowa Ranch (though still called 'Lobo' until August 1924), with 'the pine-trees coming down the mountain' (*Letters*, v. 46). Near the cabin was the huge pine that the Indians marked long ago for purposes of identification – likely the Kiowa Indians, who 'used to camp on the hill' (*Letters*, v. 228). See Introduction, pp. xlvi–xlvii.

158:8 **Egyptian column,** Probably more than a dark column: Egyptian worshippers raised a huge 'Djied' column or pillar during the Osiris ritual just before the new year. They addressed the resurrected god in the column, recalling the fact that Osiris' body floated down the Nile in a chest and eventually became embedded in the supporting column of a house. Here Isis in Search found him and conceived Horus, an act involving regeneration and rebirth. The pillar was often depicted as a tree, suggesting the Tree of Life at the world's axis, and it was sometimes given the form of the ankh cross. Cf. Blavatsky, *The Secret Doctrine*, esp. ii. 546–7, 558–9, and Baring and Cashford, *The Myth of the Goddess*, pp. 228–30, 233–4.

158:12 **blue jays** See note 99:2 on DHL's poem 'The Blue Jay' about these birds with crested heads and bright blue backs.

158:30 **remain quite suave and supple and compliant.** In MS (p. 5), DHL had made this substitution for 'a true self-abnegating Christian', a line that would have furthered the Pan–Christ conflict mentioned in the note on 155:4.

159:18 **aboriginal Indians [159:15]...their elbows.** Cf. 'The Dance of the Sprouting Corn' and Illustrations I and II.

159:32 **St. Louis, Mo?** A commercial centre on the Mississippi River between the US Eastern states and the Far West as well as between North and South. 'Mo' (rhymes with 'Oh') is an American slang term based on a contraction for 'Missouri' (from the US postal code).

159:38 **Indians around a big camp-fire** The passage apparently reflects the Lawrences' experiences (see Introduction, p. xlvii).

160:3 **Pan-smile** Cf. 'The Last Laugh', in *The Woman Who Ran Away and Other Stories*, ed. Mehl and Jansohn, pp. 122–37.

160:30 **God in the machine.** One of DHL's favourite terms for egoistic, manipulative will, derived in part from Greek drama's *Deus ex Machina* and in part from the mechanistic view of the universe. Cf. the invocation to the *Deus ex Machina* in *Mr. Noon*, ed. Vasey, 92:34–40; the explanation of the body as machine and the will as 'god' in *Fantasia of the Unconscious*, ed. Steele (95:3–9); the imagery of aeroplane flight for the self as god in 'Education of the People' (*Reflections* 131:28–132:8); and related meanings in 'On Being a Man' and 'Accumulated Mail' (*Reflections* 214:36 and 242:18).

161:25 **it will be.** These words in MS (p. 9) replaced 'you know it. But you don't know me.—I am finding you. I am finding you, hard, hard! Ever so hard, I am knowing you. So'. DHL was attempting to reproduce the syntax and intensity of the hunter.

162:39 **conquering even the North Pole,** In 1924 Admiral Richard Evelyn Byrd (1888–1957), an American naval officer and explorer, was preparing to fly over the 'Pole', as he did the following year; and dangerous, arduous attempts to reach it by air, by land and ice, and even under the sea continued throughout most of the twentieth century. It was first visited in 1909 by Robert Edwin Peary (1856–1920), also an American naval officer and explorer, and his claim was upheld by successive investigations that arose for decades because of a well-publicised but discredited denial of Peary's achievement by Frederick A. Cook (1865–1940).

163:7 **women.**   Substituted in MS (p. 11) for 'wife, or his wives'. Cf. the bigamy issue in the last two chapters of *The Boy in the Bush*, ed. Eggert, and DHL's statement that men may, in an early Mormon style, 'have more than one wife, in the coming America' (*Studies* 91:16–17).

164:3 **horns of the moon**   Cf. *Apocalypse and the Writings on Revolution*, ed. Kalnins: 'Oh beware of the angry Artemis of the night heavens, beware of the spite of Cybele, beware of the vindictiveness of horned Astarte' (77:16–18). The three goddesses, who had lunar aspects, were also associated with horns because of widespread bull sacrifice in the ancient Mediterranean and Near East. The Phoenician mother goddess Astarte, dating back before the fifteenth century BC, was often depicted crowned with the horns of a cow or bull, signifying fertility out of death, or with the 'horned' crescent moon. The horned altar at Delos was dedicated to Artemis, Greek goddess of the hunt and of childbirth, being associated with the new moon as Hecate is with the dark moon. Cybele, the Anatolian and Roman mother goddess, was also associated with the moon and with sacrifice. Cf. Baring and Cashford, *The Myth of the Goddess*, pp. 44–5, 320–9, 405–10.

164:10 **live in teepees**   The Kiowa Indians, who travelled with teepees (see Glossary), probably erected them on the ranch hillside during their past camping trips (see note on 114:33).

164:13 **Yet...universe?**   These three sentences were substituted in MS (p. 12) by DHL for the line 'Yet we must live to live not to conquer life, or be superior to it.'

164:22 **conquest of the air**   In 1903, Orville and Wilbur Wright (1871–1948, 1867–1912) achieved the first powered flight in a heavier-than-air machine. The first transatlantic flight was in 1919, the first transglobal in 1924.

See Mexico After, by Luis Q.

167:1 **See Mexico After, by Luis Q.**   DHL wrote 'by Luis Q.' in order to suggest that the Mexican writer Luis Quintanilla should put his own name on the article despite the rewriting by DHL. Nonetheless, the phrase has been retained in the title; the comma is adopted from the A1 title, where the same choice was made to include the name in this abbreviated form and on the same line with the title.

167:4 **My home's in Mexico. /...Life's one long *cine* show....**   Apparently DHL composed the song. 'Cine', a slang contraction for 'cinema'.

167:6 **Mexico D. F.**   Mexico City is in the Distrito Federal (Spanish, 'Federal District').

167:12 **But where is my gun and red sash!** Stereotype popularised by screen stars and flamboyant Mexican bandits and generals of the Revolutionary period (1910–20s). One popular fictional Mexican with a silk cummerbund was the foppish Don Diego de la Vega (El Zorro), based on the pulp novels of Johnston McCully (1853–1958) and played on the silent screen by Douglas Fairbanks, Sr, in *The Mark of Zorro* (1920, 1924).

167:16 **four-farthing sparrow** DHL is thinking of the tradition of the 'fifth sparrow' based on the discrepancy between Christ's words in Matthew x. 29 (*KJB*) – 'Are not two sparrows sold for a farthing?' – and those in Luke xii. 6 (*KJB*) – 'Are not five sparrows sold for two farthings?' (The merchant, it was said, had given the buyer an extra sparrow for a double order.) The trope was a favourite of DHL's collaborator Mollie Skinner, as shown by the title of her later autobiography *The Fifth Sparrow* (Sydney, 1972). In fact, two different Greek words in the Bible, both translated as 'farthing', account for the apparent anomaly. A farthing was an English coin worth less than a cent.

167:21 **Monroe doctrine,** A historic formulation of US foreign policy, the doctrine was delivered in 1823 by President James Monroe (1758–1831), warning other countries to stay out of the Americas. Critics sometimes called it a means of protecting US power in the region.

167:32 **à la Mexicaine.** 'In the Mexican manner' (French).

167:33 **Popocatepetl,** Named by the Aztecs ('Smoking Mountain' in Nahuatl), Popocatepetl is a large active volcano 45 miles s.e. of Mexico City and over 17,800 feet high. Its eruptions span centuries – being recorded in the fourteenth–sixteenth centuries as well as in the 1920s and the 1990s. An Aztec legend says that the warrior Popocatepetl was in love with the maiden Ixtaccihautl (now the name of a nearby volcano, 'Sleeping Woman', over 17,300 feet high); when she believed he was untrue to her, she committed suicide and he built the two volcanic mounds to memorialise their love. She lies supine, covered with a blanket of snow, and he stands upright and snow-capped like a guard. Both mountains belong to the Sierra Nevada range, in the Volcánica Transversal, which intersects with both the Sierra Madre Occidental and the Sierra Madre Oriental (see note on 139:10).

168:4 **D. C.—Washington.** The 100-square-mile plot of land for the US seat of government, located between Virginia and Maryland, was designated 'District of Columbia' for Christopher Columbus (1451–1506), and the new capital city ('Federal City') became 'Washington' for George Washington (1732–99).

168:7 **Quien sabe?** 'Who knows?' (Spanish). DHL used the accent mark on this construction very infrequently in these essays. But he was reproducing language as he heard it for a particular character sketch.

168:8 **boy!"** The term has the same force in the essay as it still does in the USA: there are demeaning racial or ethnic implications in calling a grown man a 'boy'.

168:21 **Oiga! is a very important word.** 'Attention!', combined with 'Viejo!' ('Old One!') for a term of respect.

168:36 **SEE AMERICA FIRST.** A popular slogan adopted by the Great Northern Railway of the USA in 1906 to promote a resort in Montana; it was also used to advocate the establishment of Glacier National Park (1910) and subsequently repeated in a variety of marketing strategies, guidebooks and campaigns for tourist attractions. The phrase is attributed to Fred Kiser (1878–1955), official photographer for the Great Northern Railway; and Charles Fletcher Lummis (1859–1928), Southwestern writer and editor, also claimed the term. See Marguerite S. Shaffer's *See America First: Tourism and National Identity, 1880–1940* (Washington, D.C., 2001).

169:4 **every sort and size and condition of commission.** Echo of the Church of England prayer for 'all sorts and conditions of men' (*Book of Common Prayer*).

169:8 **Bootleggers Missions,** Relates to makers of illegal whiskey. Some of the 'Missions' – Mormon and Jewish – are in Quintanilla's own typescript.

169:13 **I...am Mohammet [169:11]...Let these mountains come to** *me.* Based on a legendary incident in the ministry of Mohammed (571–632), founder of Islam, in which he was challenged to produce a miracle. Francis Bacon (1561–1626), 'Of Boldness', in *Essays* (1625), tells of the Prophet's response when he could not summon a peak to come to him: 'If the hill will not come to Mahomet, Mahomet will go to the hill.' Later versions generally used 'mountain' for 'hill'.

169:17 **entire Sierra Madre** See notes on 139:10 and 167:33. These mountains are rich in minerals.

169:17 **if** There appears to be a missing word after 'if'; therefore, *Phoenix II* added '[sic]' after this word; the word is missing in all states of the text.

169:20 **starrier and stripeyer** The US flag is composed of stars and stripes.

169:34 **Mount Brown or Mount Abraham.** Mount Brown (over 8,000 feet) in Glacier National Park, Montana, was a touted attraction for visitors; Mount Abraham (over 4,000 feet) was located in the Green Mountains of Vermont on the earliest long-distance hiking trail in the USA (1910–30), attracting tourists from nearby Lake George and Lake Champlain. Plans were underway in the 1920s for Green Mountain National Forest (1932), containing Mount Abraham. See also note on 168:36.

170:4 **greasers,** A crude slang term for 'Mexicans'.

170:9 **too hot for them,** American gangster slang: 'too threatening' – placing them in danger of being detected.

170:12 **I. W. W.'s and A. F. L.'s** Industrial Workers of the World (IWW), a workers' organisation, formed in 1905 in Chicago, in response to the AFL's acceptance of capitalism and refusal to accept unskilled labourers. The IWW was involved in a number of strikes and protests in the 1920s but declined in public favour during the First World War (to which the IWW was opposed). The American Federation of Labor (AFL) is an organisation of trades and labour unions, formed in 1881 in Pittsburgh, Pennsylvania.

170:16 **an almost Pentecostal suddenness;** Cf. Acts ii. 1–4.

170:19 **Oh, hot stuff! Hot dog!** ... *Perro caliente!* US slang: 'Great stuff! Wow!' ... Literally, 'Hot Dog!' (Spanish).

170:27 **cross ourselves** ... **Absit omen.** Roman Catholic ritual, making the sign of the Christian cross to secure divine protection. Similarly, 'Absit omen' (Latin) translates as 'May there be no [ill] omen.'

170:32 **Jonah in the whale's belly,** Cf. Jonah i.17 – ii.10. Jonah likens the whale's interior to 'the belly of hell' (ii.2, *KJB*).

170:37 **Rudolph Valentino** Rudolpho Raffaelo d'Antonguolla Guglielmo (1895– 1926), Italian actor who was called the first Hollywood 'Latin Lover', a cult hero in silent films like *The Four Horsemen of the Apocalypse* – in which he played an Argentinian womaniser (1921) – *The Sheik* (1921) and *Son of the Sheik* (1926). Although sometimes accused of bringing effeminacy to the screen hero, he was the idol of women viewers.

171:4 **Wrigley's** William Wrigley, Jr (1861–1932), developed Wrigley Spearmint and Juicy Fruit gum in 1893 in Chicago. He was known as an innovative promoter, the largest single-product advertiser of his day. Chicago's Wrigley Building was built in 1924.

171:8 **Ramon Novarro's face** ... **skin-you-love-to-touch.** Ramón Samaniegos (1899–1968) – whose stage name did not always bear the acute accent mark – was a Mexican-born actor often called the 'Second Valentino', a 'Latin Lover' who starred in silent Hollywood films like *The Arab* (1923). 'A Skin You Love to Touch' was the advertising slogan for Woodbury's Facial Soap, in one of the early US magazine 'ads' to use 'sex appeal' (1911). Quintanilla's own typescript refers to this slogan and to Novarro and Valentino.

171:10 **Pullman window!** See note on 131:6. The Pullman travellers could look out of the train windows while reclining in bed.

171:12 **enchiladas.** The enchilada developed in Mexico from an indigenous dish, a stuffed maize tortilla served with a piquant chili sauce; the Spanish added ingredients like beef and cheese to the filling.

171:14 **the dark-eyed flour-faced creatures** See also the Mexican 'flappers' in *The Plumed Serpent* with their 'face-powder and bobbed hair', 'their dark faces curiously macabre in the heavy make-up, approximating to white, but the white of a clown or a corpse' (114:32, 35–7).

171:20 **Golly!** Slang euphemism for the exclamation 'God!'

171:22 **the invisible unicorn that protects virgins** In one medieval legend, the unicorn – a mythological beast with a single horn – can tell true virgins from false ones, killing the false but sparing the genuine. The claim is probably an extreme variant of an entry in the *Physiologus* (third or fourth century AD), a bestiary in Alexandrian Greek, translated widely in the Middle Ages. In most versions, a unicorn will present itself only to a virgin, laying its head in her lap – and the two were sometimes allegorised as Christ and the Virgin Mary.

171:23 **Pancho Villa,** 'Pancho Villa' was the name assumed by Doroteo Arango (*c.* 1878–1923) to perpetuate the name of a dead bandit leader with whom he rode as a young man. Although the flamboyant Arango (Villa) had been a fugitive in his native Durango, he led an army against Porfirio Díaz (see note on 131:10) during the Mexican Revolution, became governor of the state of Chihuahua and aspired to the Mexican presidency. He was assassinated soon after DHL's first trip to Mexico. Quintanilla's own typescript refers to Villa.

171:27 **Little Bull, Arizona... Old Hat, Illinois.** Fictitious locations, probably suggested by names like Little Rock (Arkansas) and Medicine Hat (Alberta) – distant echoes of American Indian names. 'Old Hat' is also slang for something that is old-fashioned. 'Little Bull' is named in Quintanilla's own typescript.

171:29 **Cold slaw,** Cole slaw, a dish of shredded cabbage with mayonnaise or vinaigrette, gets its name from the Dutch 'koolsla' for 'cabbage salad' ('kool' derived from Latin 'caulis', 'sla' from Old French). It was a favourite of Northern European immigrants to America.

171:32 **San Juan Teotihuacán!... sprinkle him with a new tag.** The name of the village adjoining the pyramids near Mexico City (see note on 131:33)... slang for 'baptise him with a new name'.

172:1 **The snake crawled on, leaving his tail behind him.** On the Uroboros, see note on 16:5.

172:7 **Garn!** Cockney slang, apparently a contraction of 'Go on!'

172:12 **that tail will buzz... a rattler:** When defensive, a rattlesnake (a 'rattler') makes a buzzing sound by 'rattling' hard, shell-like segments of its tail. See also note on 80:26.

New Mexico

175:1 **New Mexico** The essay's first publication, in *Survey Graphic*, bore these editorial comments on its first page: '*Back of desert, the mountain; back of American and Spaniard, the Indian and the elemental life of his cosmos; "mountain life, cloud-life, thunder-life, air-life, earth-life, sun-life."—It remained for Lawrence to experience religion in New Mexico; it liberated him from the "era of materialism and mechanical developments." And this article, written by the novelist for Survey Graphic shortly before his death, carries his critique of modern civilization as it comes in contact with the Indians of our Southwest and confronts native cultures re-emerging below the Rio Grande*' (p. 153). The second periodical publication, in *John O'London's Weekly*, contained illuminated initials, based on Mexican designs by Oliver Holt: they include a Phoenix-like quetzal bird, with a serpent (forming a 'plumed serpent'), and Mesoamerican gods of sacrifice – although the essay's Indians are all from Southwestern US tribes (p. 423).

175:4 **the Bois... Central Park.** The Bois de Boulogne, a great urban park located on the west side of Paris, was formed in the second half of the nineteenth century under Napoleon III (1808–73) on former royal riding grounds. See also *St. Mawr* for Mrs Witt's reservations about the Bois de Boulogne (*St. Mawr and Other Stories*, ed. Finney, 25:35) and DHL's *Letters* (April 1929): 'How lovely the Bois was in the days of horses and carriage! how it is obscene with motor-cars' (vii. 241). New York's Central Park was created in central Manhattan (1857–78) as a fully landscaped urban park.

175:16 **Pekin**   Pekin, the French spelling for Peking (Beijing), capital of the Chinese Empire through five dynasties, the Republic of China (from 1911) and the present People's Republic of China (from 1949).

175:26 **a lecture with lantern-slides,**   The magic lantern was an early form of slide projector known as early as the seventeenth century but most popular in the nineteenth, when Sir Charles Wheatstone (1802–75) announced the construction of his stereopticon (1838) – one of a number of devices that used mirrors or prisms and the principles of bifocal vision to produce images in apparent motion. Brilliant illumination was achieved with 'limelight' (from firing oxygen and hydrogen squirted on limestone). In public performances, a 'soundtrack' was usually supplied by live lecturers or musicians.

176:3 **New Mexico [175:34] ... old Spanish ... pueblos ... penitentes, all that film-stuff.**   New Mexico, with its colourful history (see Appendix V:5), provided a frequent setting in early silent films – from documentaries of Pueblo Indian life (by Thomas A. Edison, 1898) through Buffalo Bill's Wild West movies (1898, 1902, 1910, 1917).

176:8 **know all about it.**   The phrase, which DHL probably supplied in one copy of the missing typescript (or possibly proofs), further develops the essay's opening theme about the boredom of 'knowing' everything. The words appear in Per1 and not in any other state of the text.

176:16 **holy Kandy ... southern Buddhism,**   The city in Sri Lanka (Ceylon) took its name from a Sinhalese word 'Kanda' for 'hill'. It was the last capital of the Sinhalese kings (from 1590 to 1815) and the home of a holy relic, a tooth claimed to be that of Buddha (see notes on 54:26 and 127:22). Southern Buddhism is orthodox Theravada Buddhism, as practised in Sri Lanka, Myanmar (Burma), Thailand (Siam), Cambodia and Viet Nam.

176:18 **Sicily ... Greek paganism**   When living at Fontana Vecchia, Taormina (1920–2), overlooking the Straits of Messina towards mainland Calabria, DHL wrote: 'The coast is all Greek – Naxos buried just below us, Polyphemos' rocks in the sea way down' (*Letters*, iii. 539).

176:22 **Tahiti ... California,**   Tahiti, part of the Society Islands, is the largest island in French Polynesia (in the South Pacific). DHL visited the capital city Papeete in August 1922, en route from Australia to the USA. Arriving in San Francisco in September, the Lawrences spent several days there, and DHL later spent two weeks in Santa Monica and two in Los Angeles (August–September 1923).

176:29 **morning of Australia,**   See also *Kangaroo*, ed. Steele: 'There was an unspeakable beauty about the mornings [in Australia], the great sun from the sea, such a big, untamed, proud sun, rising up into a sky of such tender delicacy, blue, so blue, and yet so frail that even blue seems too coarse a colour to describe it' (82:36–9).

176:36 **Calabria across the sea like an opal, and Etna with her snow**   Cf. 'the changing jewel of Calabria, like a fire-opal moved in the light' (*Sea and*

Sardinia, ed. Mara Kalnins, Cambridge, 1997, 7:6–7), and *Letters*, iii. 552: 'Calabria glimmering exquisite like a chalcedony'. Calabria occupies the 'boot' of southern Italy, jutting out between the Tyrrhenian and Ionian Seas; and Mount Etna is 10,741 feet high on the Calabrian plateau across the straits in Sicily. See also *Sea and Sardinia*, ed. Kalnins: 'Etna, that wicked witch, resting her thick white snow under heaven' (7:12–13).

176:37 **Tuscany, with little red tulips wild among the corn;** See also 'Flowery Tuscany': 'The red tulips open in the corn like poppies, only with a heavier red' (*Sketches* 233:25–6).

176:39 **mimosa in clouds of pure yellow ... foliage of Australia,** See also *The Boy in the Bush*, ed. Eggert, describing Australia: 'here and there a perfect wattle, or mimosa tree, with its pale-gold flowers like little balls of sun-dust' (93:29–30).

177:2 **the ditch to the canyon, at the ranch,** Gallina Canyon, about 2 miles from the Kiowa Ranch buildings (*Letters*, v. 224). DHL used the ditch to pipe irrigation water from the canyon.

177:4 **the blue mountains away in Arizona,** The Colorado Plateau, in northeastern Arizona and northwestern New Mexico, rises to 8,000 feet and has individual peaks over 13,000 feet.

177:9 **Mountains ... the Rockies!** The Sangre de Cristo Mountains, part of the Rocky Mountains, form one of the longest single ranges in the USA, extending from Colorado to Glorieta Pass, New Mexico, 10 miles s.e. of Santa Fe, and rising near Taos over 13,000 feet (Wheeler Peak).

177:10 **Leo Stein** Stein (1872–1947) was a well-known collector of post-impressionist art who, with his sister Gertrude Stein, hosted a Paris salon for writers and artists for several years. DHL had met him in Settignano in 1919 (*Letters*, iii. 463); and Stein later wrote to DHL about the beauty of New Mexico – probably at Mabel's urging when she invited the Lawrences to Taos.

177:23 **the Aztecs gave hearts of men to the sun.** The elaborate Aztec sacrifices assumed that the gods of the sun, moon and elements required human hearts in order to continue their cosmic lives (see Appendix V:3). See also 'Eagle in New Mexico': 'When you pick the red smoky heart from a rabbit or a light-blooded bird / Do you lift it to the sun, as the Aztec priests used to lift red hearts of men?' (*Poems* 374).

177:33 **some Bavarian peasants ... Buddhists or Brahmins:** A majority of Bavarians are Roman Catholics. Buddhists are followers of Buddha (see note on 54:26), seeking 'enlightenment', and Brahmins are members of the Hindu priestly caste (not to be confused with Brahman, the supreme source of divinity).

177:36 **to love at will.** The single word 'love' (not 'love it', as in Per1) is accepted from Per2 (as also in TCC, p. 5) on the grounds of sense. The idea is characteristic of DHL, as in the poem 'Cerebral Emotions', opposing 'People feeling things they intend to feel' and '*will* feel, / just because they don't feel them' (*Poems* 500).

178:1 **the Pera-hera . . . given to the Prince of Wales.** DHL was present in 1922 when the Prince of Wales (later Edward VIII and the Duke of Windsor) attended the Kandy Pera-hera. See also 'Elephant': 'But the best is the Pera-hera, at midnight, under the tropical stars, / With a pale little wisp of a Prince of Wales, diffident, up in a small pagoda on the temple side' (*Poems* 387). The celebration dates back to the fourth century and combines Buddhist and Hindu elements, especially processions honouring the Buddha's tooth relic.

178:14 **Cinghalese.** The Sinhalese, the ancient ruling class of Sri Lanka (see note on 176:16), converted to Buddhism but absorbed a lesser admixture of Hinduism.

178:29 **beyond tabu and totem,** Taboo (Polynesian) is a prohibition protecting certain animals and objects because of their sacred or forbidden quality. A totem (see Glossary) is an animal or plant to which a community feels peculiarly related (e.g. bear clan). Ethnologists, as well as Sir James George Frazer in *Taboo and the Perils of the Soul* (1910) and Sigmund Freud in *Totem and Taboo* (1918), saw these systems as early levels of social or psychological development that also survived in all civilisation.

178:31 **word.** One of several words in TS and TCC (p. 7) that suggest their possible descent not from either printed version of the essay but from an earlier unrevised typescript (see 'New Mexico' in Introduction, pp. lxxx–lxxxi): a different reading of handwriting would explain the separate texts 'word' and 'world'; and the former is accepted from Per2 (appearing also in TS and TCC). See also 'last', accepted at 179:39 from TCC (p. 9) instead of 'lost'. But misreadings in the typescripts include 'zeal' and 'starkly' (both p. 10), at 180:28–9, instead of 'year' and 'darkly'.

178:34 **on Albuquerque station . . . around Taos plaza** At Albuquerque's mission-style depot of the Atchison, Topeka and Santa Fe Railroad (built in 1902 by architect Charles Whittlesey) and on Taos Plaza, Southwestern Indians sold artifacts.

179:4 **beyond the pyramids, beyond Moses.** Some Egyptian pyramids at Giza are more than 4,500 years old; Moses the Hebrew prophet lived in the thirteenth century BC; born in Egypt, he died 'in the land of Moab' (Deuteronomy xxxiv. 5).

179:7 **Australian aboriginal** Indigenous people of Australia, who probably came from Asia at least 30,000 years ago, organised their families, groups and 'hordes' according to principles of totem and taboo (see note on 178:29).

179:10 **Taos pueblo** See notes on 'Taos' and on 64:39, 106:17 and 107:3.

179:18 **at San Geronimo,** Fiesta at Taos Pueblo, named for its patron saint, Jerome: see notes on 60:27 and 126:21.

179:24 **Dionysiac or Christian ecstasy.** Worship of the Greek god Dionysus included ecstatic and orgiastic practices. The Christian ecstasy is illustrated in the 'The Cathedral' chapter of *The Rainbow*.

179:29 **the little pueblo of San Felipe** Much as it was over 300 years ago, San Felipe Pueblo was built in 1706 on its present site, on the western bank of the Rio Grande 30 miles n. of Albuquerque. Ruins of an older village are nearby. The native language, Keres, is still spoken, and the economy is based on agriculture, mining and the making of pottery.

179:32 **Theocritus,** Greek poet born in Syracuse, Sicily (fl. *c.* 270 BC), originator of the pastoral poem that was continued by the Roman poet Vergil and later pastoralists. Sicily is the setting of his bucolic *Idylls* with their portrayal of shepherds and goatherds in mythic nature scenes.

179:35 **the Christmas dances at Taos,** See 'Taos' and notes on 60:27 and 64:35.

179:37 **dark calling to dark,** Probably echoes 'deep calleth unto deep' (Psalms xlii. 7, *KJB*). The word 'to' had been dropped in the first publication of the essay (Per1) but survived in the second (Per2), as also in TS (p. 9) and TCC (p. 9).

180:4 **away in the Apache country, in Arizona this time,** See 'Indians and an Englishman' and note on 114:23. But DHL is mistaken about the Arizona location unless he refers to another (unknown) episode and a location other than the Jicarilla Apache Reservation.

180:9 **back to before the Flood,** Cf. 'That which is aboriginal in America still belongs to the way of the world before the Flood' (*PS* 415:9–10).

180:17 **the Indian races,** See notes on 60:27, 115:19 and 121:8.

180:31 **pantheism** See note on 156:33.

181:18 **Trinidad** Trinidad Archuleta of Taos Pueblo worked with the Lawrences at their Kiowa Ranch, helping them to repair the ranch buildings, construct the irrigation system and tend to the property. He taught the Lawrences to dance in the Pueblo style and, in the 1930s after Lawrence's death, painted a mural on the outer wall of their main cabin.

Appendix I
Just Back from the Snake Dance

Note. Annotation has not been provided when there is a note for 'The Hopi Snake Dance'.

185:1 **Just Back from the Snake Dance** DHL's original title on MS was 'The Return from the Snake Dance', but he crossed out the first two words and wrote 'Just Back'. Willard Johnson apparently added 'Tired Out'.

185:15 **dry,** Because of an omission by the typist (probably Johnson), this punctuation was lost when he supplied the phrase 'dry raggy bits of disheartening ruin' by hand. Probably Johnson was working with both MS and TCC.

185:18 **what dire necessity . . . Cain-like stubbornness . . . extremities!** After Cain, the son of Adam and Eve in Genesis, was punished by God for killing his brother Abel, Cain responded: 'Behold, thou hast driven me out this day from the face of the earth, and from thy face shall I be hid; and I shall be a fugitive and a vagabond in the earth' (iv. 14, *KJB*). He then 'went out from the presence of the Lord, and dwelt in the land of Nod, on the east of Eden' (iv. 16).

185:26 **about three thousand bodies.** No source is known for the substitution of 'eight hundred' for 'three thousand' in *Laughing Horse* (Per). It is possible that Johnson inserted his own or Witter Bynner's estimate of the probable size of the crowd – a lower figure more likely, even today, for a crowd at Hotevilla. Yet the figure 'three thousand' was unchanged elsewhere in Per.

185:32 **Navajo women in full skirts and velvet bodices:** See note on 87:28.

186:4 **Queen Semiramis seated and waiting.** A legendary queen, wife of Ninus of Nineveh and mother of Ninyas, associated with the historical queen Sammuramat of Assyria and Babylon (reigned 811–808 BC) and with Ishtar ('Snake Goddess'). She often appears seated on a throne like the later enthroned Madonna. For the anaconda image, DHL may have been remembering Swinburne's 'Laus Veneris' (1866), in which Semiramis appears in the same stanza as Cleopatra, who is 'Wearing at breast a suckling snake of gold'.

186:9 **And what had they all come to see?** See note on 80:26. 'Just Back from the Snake Dance' includes repetition that furthers the echo of Christ's words to those who sought out John the Baptist: 'What went ye out into the wilderness for to see? ... But what went ye out for to see? ... But what went ye out for to see?' (Luke vii. 24, 25, 26, *KJB*). See also DHL's 186:39: 'And what had we come to see ... ?'

186:13 **one** The possessive 'his', as well as the description of a single snake, shows that the subject is singular in spite of the word 'six' in MS (p. 2); and the correction is adopted from TSC (p. 2).

186:18 **Old Roger is dead and is low in his grave!** A singing game in which children mime various actions to the words of an anonymous English song: 'Old Roger is dead and gone to his grave' or 'is low in his grave'. In the last stanza of most versions, the dead man responds to an old woman's applepicking by getting up and giving her 'a knock' that causes her to 'Go hippity-hop'. At the 'hippity-hop', the singers jerk their bodies imitatively and lean first to the right, then to the left. See also 'a silly game of Mrs. Mackenzie's Dead' in *Aaron's Rod*, ed. Kalnins, 163:38–9.

186:23 **renewed their snake as the eagle his youth** Cf. Psalms ciii. 5: 'thy youth is renewed like the eagle's' (*KJB*), referring to an ancient belief that the eagle could renew its plumage by flying near the sun and then plunging into a lake or fountain (later a symbolic image of baptism). See also Isaiah xl. 31: 'But they that wait upon the Lord shall renew their strength; they shall mount up with wings as eagles' (*KJB*).

186:34 **presto!** Literally, 'quickly!' (Italian), used in magic to herald sudden transformation. A variation, 'presto changeo' is synonymous with sleight-of-hand.

186:40 **like a circus?** See notes on 80:30, 105:27 and 105:30 about circuses and Wild West Shows.

187:3 **more harmless than doves?** Cf. Christ's command to his followers: 'be ye therefore wise as serpents, and harmless as doves' (Matthew x. 16, *KJB*).

187:13 **the Land of Enchantment.**   A nickname for New Mexico, based partly on
the title of a book about the state by Lillian Whiting (1906). Although the term
is used today on New Mexico car licence plates (since 1941) and as a registered
trademark of New Mexico's Tourist Bureau (since 1947), it has never been
adopted as the state's official slogan.

187:20 **What price irrigation, Jimmy?**   Possibly a satirical reference to the Indians' struggles for land and water rights in their arid reservations.

187:25 **dry up!** 'Be quiet!' (American slang).

187:28 **boy.**   In this case, an exclamation of emphasis and excitement, as in 'Oh boy!'
(American slang). 'Boy' is also a demeaning term for another, as is 'Jimmy'
when used as a generic term.

Appendix II
['Indians and an Englishman' and 'Certain Americans and an Englishman']: early fragment

Note. Annotation has not been provided when there is a note for the main text.

191:5 **and Indian**   Missing in other versions, this is one of the few substantive
differences between this fragment and the corresponding parts of the Yale
typescript which gave rise to the two main essays. See also 192:13 ('and
thorns'), also missing in other versions, and 195:9 ('humour' instead of the
'humanness' that appears elsewhere). Mabel Luhan said she did not know if
the piece was ever published and commented: 'It does not seem to me to be
very good' (*Lorenzo in Taos*, p. 52).

Appendix III
Pan in America: early version

Note. Annotation has not been provided when there is a note for the main text.

199:13 **Homer. Hermes and Aphrodite**   Homer is the name given to the ancient
Greek who is believed to be the author of *The Iliad* and *The Odyssey*, both
dating, perhaps, from the ninth century BC. He refers to the major Olympian
deities, including Hermes and Aphrodite. Hermes (Roman Mercury), mes-
senger of the gods, wore a winged cap and sandals and carried the caduceus.
He was the conductor of souls to Hades and also god of eloquence, commerce,
wealth and cunning. Aphrodite (Roman Venus), goddess of love and beauty,
was born of the foam near Cypress or Cytherea and was known for her many
lovers, including Ares (Roman Mars) and the mortal Adonis. Eros (Roman
Cupid) was her son.

200:8 **any** *original* **religion . . . Anglo-Saxon America**   See DHL's account of
the American 'Pilgrim' faith: 'into Puritanism and Calvinism had already
entered the dangerous *negative* religious passion of repression', which sought

to control 'the life-issue' (*Studies* 174:32–3, 34). One result was Transcendentalism, which was once part of the intended title for *Studies* (*Letters*, iii. 156, 160).

200:8 **Thoreau,** Henry David Thoreau (1817–62), American writer, was best known for descriptions of natural phenomena and Transcendentalist philosophy in *Walden, or Life in the Woods* (1834). Unlike Whitman, Emerson and Thoreau were regulars in the Transcendental Club of Concord, Massachusetts.

200:12 **Oversoul,** Emerson's original term, not Whitman's.

200:14 **Emersonian** *Oversoul*...**Whitman's** *All Things*...**Wordsworth's** *Nature*, Emerson's essay 'The Over-Soul' expressed his Transcendentalist doctrine of a universal spirit in everything. Whitman stated, 'All truths wait in all things' ('Song of Myself', line 648); and his prose, like 'Democratic Vistas' (1871), strongly advocated democracy for all. William Wordsworth frequently described deific or anthropomorphic features of nature. Cf. notes on 'Pan in America': 156:33 (Wordsworth), 157:4 (Emerson) and 157:2 (Whitman).

200:15 **Zeus or Ra.** Zeus was the principal father god of the Greek pantheon (see note on 82:18). Ra was the greatest of the Egyptian deities, the supreme sun god, usually depicted with the orb of the sun on his head.

200:26 **monotheism,** The belief that there is one God.

200:31 **to kiss...syphilitic prostitute,** Cf. final version of 'Whitman' in *Studies*: 'But when, in Flaubert, the man takes the leper to his naked body: when Bubi de Montparnasse takes the girl because he knows she's got syphilis: when Whitman embraces an evil prostitute: that is not sympathy' (*Studies* 160:1–4). DHL is responding not only to Whitman's references to the 'venerealee' and the 'diseas'd' ('Song of Myself', 'Song of the Open Road' and 'A Song for Occupations', *Leaves of Grass*, pp. 39, 123, 180) but also to 'La Légende de Saint Julien l'Hospitalier' (1877) by Gustave Flaubert (1821–80), in which the saint warms a leper with his body – 'mouth to mouth' – and *Bubu of Montparnasse* (1901) by Charles-Louis Philippe (1874–1909), in which the protagonist knowingly makes love to a person with syphilis. See also *Studies* 156:20–1, 159:23–37.

200:39 **Matter and Spirit dilemma.** DHL customarily traces this 'dilemma' to Platonic and later forms of idealism and to the Cartesian tradition with its emphasis on reason. See also 32:30, 82:17 and 157:2.

201:33 **no God or gods.** See also notes on 66:16 ('Indians and Entertainment') and 83:5 ('The Hopi Snake Dance').

201:36 **Greeks...intellectualisation...image-makers and idol-worshippers ...in stone,** Cf. note on 59:31. The reference to 'image-makers' and 'idol-worshippers' could recall Paul's sermon to the Greeks on Mars Hill: 'we ought not to think that the Godhead is like unto gold, or silver, or stone, graven by art and man's device' (Acts xvii. 20, 23, *KJB*).

202:13 **First Word, or Logos** 'Word' (Greek). In ancient Greek philosophy, the Logos is the controlling principle of the universe; in Christianity, 'the Word' is also associated with Christ (John i. 1). Cf. 'First Cause' in note on 14:2.

203:18 **as a bear . . . hollow trunk!"** The figures of speech referring to the bear are among clues that the hunter is conceived of as an ancient Indian hunter. Cf. 'New Mexico' on this indigenous American feeling for the bear, exceeding that for a horse (181:22–4).

204:25 **the puma,** The wild cat (see Glossary) that inspired DHL's poem 'Mountain Lion' (*Poems* 401–2). Along with the other animals and birds in this paragraph, it is indigenous to the foothills of the Rocky Mountains. Cf. 'Eagle in New Mexico', 'The Red Wolf' and 'The American Eagle' (*Poems* 372–4, 403–5, 413–14).

205:26 **space between the stars.** Mabel Luhan attributes these words to herself, claiming that, on the way to the Hopi Snake Dance in August 1924, she told DHL she would not like to be a star but 'the space between the stars' (*Lorenzo in Taos*, p. 257). But she had read this essay (MS1, p. 7) in May.

205:30 **the power of the world.** See also *Fantasia of the Unconscious*, ed. Steele: 'Men, being themselves made new after the act of coition, wish to make the world new' (136:1–2).

Appendix IV
['See Mexico After, by Luis Q.']: early fragments

Note. Annotation has not been provided when there is a note for the main text.

I By Luis Q.

209:2 **By Luis Q.** DHL wrote this designation underneath Quintanilla's title 'MEXICO, WHY NOT?' but no other title is visible (MS1, p. 1). He meant that Quintanilla should have the credit for any rewrite DHL might produce, but his own vigorous erasures have almost entirely destroyed this first effort. Appendix passages in Fragment I appear in MS1 as follows: (A) p. 1; (B) p. 2; (C) p. 2; (D) p. 3; (E) p. 4; (F) p. 4; (G) p. 5. Other barely discernible references include: 'Tramps Missions . . . and Jewish Missions', p. 3; the 'A. F. L.', p. 4; 'sneer at gringos', p. 4; 'Prophet Jonah', p. 5; and 'Promised Land', p. 5. This version also contained the young man's account of dashing upstairs in his office building 'to my window on the fourth floor—no elevators—' and of yelling 'across the flat roofs of this city of flat contradiction' to Popo (p. 4). Quintanilla's first paragraph develops his title, explaining 'MEXICO, WHY NOT?' as a railroad slogan for tourists.

209:3 **Popo** Nickname for the volcano Popocatapetl. See note on 167:33.

209:10 **ichthyopophagi** Ancient Greek geographers, from Herodotus (fifth century BC) through Ptolemy (second century AD), referred to 'ichthyophagi' as fish-eaters located in various parts of the Middle East, Egypt and western

Africa. DHL's term seems to be constructed on the principle of 'Anthro-pophagi' (man-eaters) in Shakespeare's *Othello* I. iii. 144.

209:13 **lapsus-linguaes, or lapsi linguarum.**   Slips of the tongue, failures of languages (Latin).

209:15 **slips between cups and lips.**   ['many a slip...the cup...the lip']. 'While a thing is yet in hand and at the point of realisation' (*OED*). The 'cuppe' and 'mouth' metaphor was recorded in English in 1539 in 'Proverbs of Erasmus' by John Taverner (1490–1545), and the proverb had variants, including one in *The Anatomy of Melancholy* (1621) by Robert Burton (1577–1640), Pt ii, Sect. 2, Memb. 3. It may arise from the legend of Antaeus of Argonaut fame, who went to his death before he could drink the wine of his own vineyard.

II See Mexico After by Luis Q.

210:12 **by an old...Sinai...SEE AMERICA FIRST.**   The passage was greatly revised in MS (p. 1) from DHL's original sentence in this version: 'I was terribly impressed by a sign that kept saying SEE AMERICA FIRST.' Sinai was the wilderness where Moses and the Israelites were fed with heavenly manna (Exodus xvi. 35), and Mt Sinai was the peak where Moses spoke with God (e.g. Exodus xxiv. 12–18) and received the Ten Commandments (Exodus xxxi).

210:16 **On revient toujours a son premier amour.** '   One always returns to one's first love' (French).

GLOSSARY OF SELECTED SPANISH AND INDIAN TERMS

(Longer passages are in the Explanatory notes.)

adios: Goodbye
adobe: The characteristic building material in Mexico and the Spanish Southwest, composed of mud and straw dried in the open air into bricks
agua: Water
alabados: Spanish hymns passed down for centuries through oral tradition in New Mexico and Mexico. The style of performance resembles that of Gregorian chant
alcalde: Head-man of a village (from Arabic)
amigo, amiga: Friend
Apache (Yuma and Zuni): Fighting men, enemy people
apaxtle (Nahuatl): Earthenware dish or tub
asuntos: Business, affairs
ay-de-mi: Oh my!

barrancas: Ravines, deep valleys
becerro: Bull calf
blanco: White
bonito: Pretty
borracharse: To get drunk
bueno, buenos: Good

caldo: Broth, soup
calle: Street
calor: Heat
candelabrum (or candelabro): A large multi-armed cactus with a long central spine, resembling a massive branched candlestick, common in Oaxaca
caramba: Damn
cargador: A labourer who carries a cargo – a porter, stevedore or dockhand
Castellano: The Spanish language of Castile and central Spain, not that of Spanish America but of its foreign-born upper class
centavo: A centavo was one hundredth part of a peso, rather equivalent to an English 'penny' or American 'cent', but worth half of a cent in the 1920s

chaps (from chaparreras): Warm leg covers, usually made of leather, worn by cowboys and ranch workers over trousers to protect their legs from rough brush and harsh weather

chirimoyas: Small custard apples

comido (from comer): To eat

cómo, como: How (accented when interrogatory)

cortar: To cut

coyote (Nahuatl): A 'prairie wolf', a carnivorous mammal (genus *Canis*) smaller than a wolf, native to western North America, including Mexico

cucaracha: Cockroach

día: Day

donde, dónde: Where (accented when interrogatory)

en parte: In part

en todo: Wholly, entirely

es (from ser): It/she/he is

Español or Espagnol: Spanish

están (from estar): They are

fiesta: Feast, festival, celebration

frutas: Fruit

gazeosa or gaseosa: Carbonated water

gavilán or gabilan: Hawk

gracias: Thank you

Gringo (from Griego): Greek, thus 'foreign', a slang term for a foreign or 'white' person

guava, guayaba or guayava (Arawak or Taino): A tropical fruit (genus *Psidium*) native to the West Indies and Mexico

hablo, no hablo (from hablar): I speak, I don't speak

hacienda: A large hereditary estate, targeted by Mexico's revolutionaries and dispersed by the agrarian laws of Benito Juárez and several of his successors

hay, no hay (from haber): [There] is, are; [there] is not, are not

horno: A free-standing dome-shaped oven, usually constructed outdoors of adobe, common in Southwestern pueblos and related architecture

huaraches: Customary footwear of Mexican peasants, sandals made of woven leather strips

idioma: A regional dialect within Spanish or Spanish Indian languages like Zapotec

jaguar (Tupi): A large leopard-like mammal with dark spots, native to Central and South America

jícara: A small cup
justicia: Justice

kisi (Hopi): Cottonwood bower used as a key location in dances like the Hopi Snake Dance and Antelope Dance
kiva (Hopi): A chamber for secret ceremonials, usually underground and traditionally round
koshare (Keres): Painted participants at Pueblo dances and festivals who play a clown-like role as well as impersonating ancestral and other spirits; called 'Chiffonettes' at Taos Pueblo

leche: Milk
lejos: Far, distant
limas: Limes
llevan (from llevar): Taken

maize (Arawak or Taino): Indian corn (genus *Zea*), an annual cereal grass, the great staple of agriculture in native American cultures
mañana: Tomorrow
masa: A cornmeal dough that is formed into tortillas
Mejicano, Mexicano: A citizen of Mexico
mescal (from mexcalli, Nahuatl): Liquor made from the agave plant
mesquite (Nahuatl): A leguminous Southwestern and Mexican shrub of the pea family (genus *Prosopis*), possessing dull grey leaves and spiny branches
mi: My
minas: Mines
moccasins (Algonquin): Traditional soft leather footwear crafted by native Americans
mozo: A male servant, often a youth employed in general labour around a household and yard
mucho: Much, very much
muy: Very, quite

naranjas: Oranges
Navajo, Navahu (Tewa): [People of the] cultivated fields
Niña: The genteel form of address for a female employer and also a common term for the Virgin Mary. Literally, 'Child'
noche: Night
Norte: A cold, strong northeasterly wind, intermittent around the Gulf of Mexico and extending inland

ocote: Wood from a pitch pine, often used in Mexico for torches and simple furniture
oiga: Attention

olvidar: To forget
otro: Another

paisano: Countryman, fellow citizen
palo blanco: 'White stick' or 'white wood', applied to several flowering desert trees (especially of genus *Acacia*)
panteón: Term for a cemetery
para: For (preposition), in order to
patio: A yard or garden, open to the sky but usually encircled, on three or more sides, by a home or other building, in the Spanish style
patrón, patrona: A master or a mistress of a household of servants or manager of a business; benefactor
perro: Dog
peseta: Spanish currency worth 100 centimos, in use before the Euro; also a diminutive term for the Mexican peso
peso: Mexican unit of currency, comprised of 100 centavos, worth 50 cents (US) in the 1920s
piñon: A long-lived pine tree (genus *Pinus*), often called the 'nut pine' for its edible nuts, common in the American Southwest and Mexico
pitahaya: A soft fruit from a giant cactus found predominantly in the arid regions of northern Mexico but also in southern Mexico
plaza: Square, the park-like centre of a town, a marketplace
pueblo: Village
puedo, no puedo (from poder): I am able, I can; I am not able, I can't
puma: An American mountain lion or cougar (*Felis concolor*)
psia (Zapotec): Hawk

qué, que: Which, what, that (accented when interrogatory)
qué quieres: What do you want?
qué tal: What's up? How's it going?
quién, quiénes; quien, quienes: Who (accented when interrogatory)
quiero, no quiero (from querer): I want, I do not want

real, reales: A Spanish real amounted to one-eighth of the eight-real silver coin ('pieces of eight') that colonial trade brought to the High Seas and the Americas. After the Spanish Conquest, the eight-real pieces were commonly made of Mexican silver. The eighth-part continues as a unit of measure
rebozo: A length of fabric, often decorated with embroidery, worn as a shawl

sabe (from saber): He/she/it knows
sarape, serape: A blanket-like wrap carried on the shoulder or worn in a poncho style, draped around the upper body
savannah (prob. Taino): An open, grassy plain, especially in tropical America

Señor, Señora, Señorita: Gentleman, Sir, Mr; matron, Madam, Mrs; unmarried woman, Miss
soy (from ser): I am

Taos (Tiwa): Probably refers to 'red willow trees' although the origin of the word is uncertain
tarde: Afternoon, early evening
la taza: Cup
tepache: A fermented drink derived from pineapple combined with sugar and water
tepee or teepee (Sioux): A semi-portable dwelling with a conical framework of poles and a covering of hides or other substance
tocando (from tocar): Touching, knocking, playing
tortilla: Flat, round cakes of bread dough patted very thin and cooked on a griddle; a food staple throughout Mexico
tos: Cough
totem (Algonquin): Natural object, like an animal or plant, that is revered as an emblem, guardian or sacred ancestor of a tribe or family

usted: You (formal)
Ute, from Yuttahih (Apache): Highland people

vara: A unit of measurement
Viejo: Old One
viene: Come
voy (from ir): I go (am going to)

yucca (prob. Taino): A tree-like American plant of the agave family, possessing white, bell-shaped flowers at the tips of fleshy branches; used by native Americans for food (roots and flowers), baskets (fibres), and cleansers and medicines (sap)

zaguan: A long covered entry-way, hall or vestibule
zócalo: A square or plaza, related in etymology to the architectural term for the base of a wall or column
zopilote: A large black scavenger bird like a buzzard or vulture

TEXTUAL APPARATUS

TEXTUAL APPARATUS

The following symbols are used to distinguish states of the text:

MS = Autograph manuscript
TS = Ribbon typescript
TCC = Carbon copy typescript
TCCR = Revisions by DHL in *TCC*
TCCC = Revisions in *TCC* by another hand or an indeterminate hand
Per = Periodical publication
E1 = First English volume edition
A1 = First American volume edition

When the reading of the base-text is retained, it appears within the square bracket, with no symbol unless the base-text and a later state with the same reading need to be indicated. Variant readings are recorded to the right of the bracket, in chronological sequence, noting only the first instance of each. Without other indications, the reader should assume that each variant occurs in all subsequent states of the text.

If the base-text does not provide the accepted reading, the symbol of the adopted source appears inside the bracket. In this case, the base-text is cited first on the right-hand side of the bracket, followed by first instances of other variants. If no others are given, all states subsequent to the source of the emendation have that same reading.

The following editorial symbols are used:

Ed. = Editor
~ = Repeated word in recording a punctuation variant
Om. = Omitted
/ = Line or page break
= Internal division
P = New paragraph
< > = Deletion in manuscript or typescript
{ } = Revision in manuscript or typescript
[ ] = Illegible or missing characters

Corasmin and the Parrots

The order of the texts is *MS, TCC, TCCR, TCCC, Per, E1, A1*.

11:1 **Corasmin and the Parrots** *Ed.*] Mornings in Mexico/ by D. H. Lawrence/ Friday Morning *MS* Mornings in Mexico/ by/ D. H. | Lawrence/ Corasmin and the Parrots *TCCR* CORASMIN AND THE PARROTS/ By D. H. Lawrence *Per Corasmin and the*

Parrots E1 I/ CORASMIN AND
THE PARROTS *A1*

11:2 way south] away South *TCC*
11:4 patio *MS, A1*] *patio E1*
11:6 is] are *Per*
11:6 rocking chairs] rocking-chairs *Per*
11:8 Mornings *TCCR*] Morning *MS,*
    Per
11:13 thin person] thin *TCC*
11:25 is] are *Per*
11:25 sun-burned] sunburned *TCC*
    sun-/ burned *E1*
11:25 urine,] *Om. TCC* ~ *TCCR, E1*
    wine *Per see notes*
11:28 piffing] puffing *TCC*
11:29 entrance way] entrance-way *Per*
11:34 birds] ~, *Per*
11:34 eyes] ~, *E1*
12:1 This] The *Per*
12:2 whistles] whistle *TCC*
12:2 Rosalino, in . . . so like] *Om.*
    TCC
12:3 it is *TCCR*] *Om. MS see notes*
12:4 him, *TCCR*] ~ *MS Om. TCC*
12:5 is *TCCR*] are *MS*
12:6 hidden,] ~ *Per*
12:12 patio *MS, A1*] *patio E1*
12:15 whistling] whistle *TCC*
12:20 cold, slow *TCCR*] slow *MS see note*
    on 12:4
12:23 Oh Perro] ~, ~ *TCC*
12:23 Perr-rrro] Perr-rro *TCC*
12:23 Oh Perrr-rro] ~, Perr-rro *Per*
12:32 little,] ~ *E1*
12:33 in to] into *Per*
12:34 near] near by *Per*
12:35 Wouf!!] ~! *Per*
12:36 zaguan] *zaguan E1* zaguán *A1*
13:1 day,] ~ *TCC*
13:7 Oh] ~, *E1*
13:8 strange,] ~ *TCC*
13:15 'r',] "~," *Per see notes*
13:20 'r'. *TCCR*] ~. *MS* "~." *Per*
13:25 Invictus *Per*] Invictis *MS*
13:25 still unconquered] still-uncon-
    quered *TCC*
13:26 and slower] *Om. Per*

13:28 "In] ~ *Per*
13:29 aloud!] ~ *TCC* ~,*TCCC*
13:31 unbowed."] ~. *Per*
13:38 stomach] stomachs *Per*
13:39 far,] ~ *Per*
14:7 begin *MS, A1*] begins *E1*
14:12 no-where, no-how] nowhere, no
    how *E1*
14:18 mid-day] midday *E1*
14:20 crocodiles] ~, *TCCC*
14:21 mosses] ~; *TCCC*
14:23 parrot... peacock]   parrots...
    peacocks   *TCC*   parrots'...
    peacocks' *TCCC*
14:24 flamingo] flamingoes *TCC*
14:24 snuggling] smuggling *Per*
14:27 *What?*] What? *TCC*
14:28 *wingless,*] ~ *TCC*
14:29 Curly] ~, *Per*
14:29 Corasmins] Corasmin *TCC*
14:30 the new] the undergrowth/ the
    new *TCC* the undergrowth, the
    new *Per*
14:38 great,] ~ *Per*
14:38 half-baked] half-naked *Per*
15:1 Sun] sun *TCC*
15:3 all, *MS, E1*] ~— *Per*
15:7 Corasmins] Corasmin *TCC*
15:9 mis-shapen] mis-/ shapen *TCC*
    misshapen *Per*
15:9 bird's-nest]   birds-nest   *TCC*
    birds's nest *Per*
15:13 Yap-yap!] *Yap-yap! TCCC* "Yap-
    yap!" *E1 Yap-yap! A1*
15:16 *Yap-yap*] Yap-yap *TCC*
15:16 Oh] ~, *Per*
15:16 of] of the *TCC*
15:16 Perro!] Per/ *Perro! TCC* Perro!/
    Perro! TCCR Perro! *Perro! Per*
15:17 *Oh*] Oh, *Per*
15:19 in,] ~ *Per*
15:25 Tiger] tiger *TCC*
15:25 Jaguar] jaguar *Per*
15:26 no-where] no-/ where *E1*
    nowhere *A1*
15:26 mercifully-forgotten] mercifully
    forgotten *TCC*

15:28 third Sun . . . The fourth] *Om.*
TCC *see note on* 15:30
15:28 rain,] ~ *TCC*
15:30 bust] burst *TCC* *see notes*
15:31 man] men *Per*
15:35 *words TCC*R] words *MS*
15:35 Terrible] ~, *TCC*
15:35 elephant *TCC*] elefant *MS*
15:38 *Come MS, A1*] "~ *E1*
15:38 *Perro! Perro!*] ~! ~! *Per, A1* ~!
~!" *E1*
16:5 *Here's MS, A1*] "~ *E1*
16:7 *Corasmin-pups. MS, A1*] ~." *E1*
16:8 *Hello!*] "~! *TCC* "~! *Per*
16:9 *Why*] ~, *Per*
16:10 *off. MS, A1*] ~." *E1*
16:11 Perr-rr-rro-o-o] Perr-rr-rro-oo
TCC
16:11 Oh] ~, *E1*
16:14 *Oh*] "~ *E1*

16:14 *it!*] ~! *Per, A1* ~!" *E1*
16:21 time] Time *Per*
16:23 navel-string] navel string *TCC*
16:31 him,] ~ *E1*
16:32 depth] depths *TCC*
16:34 tape measure] tape-measure *TCC*
16:37 Oh] ~, *E1*
17:4 will] *Om. TCC*
17:8 dimensions] dimension *TCCC*
17:10 And Corasmin . . . other dimension.] *Om. A1*
17:14 Oh] ~, *E1*
17:15 mozo *MS, A1*] *mozo E1*
17:16 He] We *Per*
17:18 of] of the *TCC*
17:24 clear] ~, *Per*
17:26 this world, *TCC*R] this world *MS*
the world *TCC*
17:26 our Sun, *TCC*R] *Om. MS see note*
on 12:4

Walk to Huayapa

The order of the texts is *MS, TCC, TCCR, TCCC, Per1, Per2, E1, A1.*

21:1 **Walk to Huayapa** *Ed.*] Morn-
ings in Mexico./ by D. H.
Lawrence/ Sunday Morning.
MS Mornings in Mexico/ by/
D. H. Lawrence/ Walk to
Huayapa. *TCCR* Sunday Stroll
*TCCC A SUNDAY STROLL IN
SLEEPY MEXICO/* Along the
Road to Huayapa—The Vagaries
of Voting—Searching for an
Orange/ in the Land of Plenty—
The Old Woman and the Bot-
tle/ By D. H. LAWRENCE
Per1 MORNINGS IN MEX-
ICO/ WALK TO HUAYAPA./
By D. H. Lawrence *Per2 Walk
to Huayapa E1* II/ WALK TO
HUAYAPA *A1*
21:4 mind: on] mind: On *E1*
21:4 fiestas] *fiestas* E1
21:5 patio *MS, Per2*] patió *TCCC patio*
E1

21:7 trying] try *E1* *see notes*
21:11 But *MS, Per2*] ~, *Per1, E1*
21:11 least *MS, E1*] ~, *Per2*
21:11 machine." *MS, Per1*] ~". *TCC*
21:12 saddle: *MS, Per2*] ~; *Per1,*
E1
21:12 donkey: *MS, Per2*] ~; *Per1,*
E1
21:13 called] ~, *E1*
21:13 children] ~, *E1*
21:13 Shank's] Shanks's *Per2* Shanks'
E1
21:13 pony;"] ~:" *TCC* ~"; *Per1* ~,"
Per2 ~"- *E1*
21:17 *Como MS, A1*] Come *E1*
21:17 *Señor!*] ~! *Per1* ~? *E1*
21:18 parrots'] parrots *TCC* parrot's
TCCC
21:19 Como no] *Como no* Per2 Come no
E1
21:19 Señor!"] *Señor!" Per2 Señor?" E1*
21:23 *Como MS, A1*] Come *E1*

21:23 Señor!] ~! *Per1* ~? *E1*
21:25 Como *MS, A1*] Come *E1*
21:25 Señor!] ~! *Per1* ~? *E1*
21:27 Como *MS, A1*] Come *E1*
21:27 Señor!] ~! *Per1* ~? *E1*
21:28 perfect,] ~; *E1*
21:28 clean] clear *TCC*
21:29 Capital] capital *TCC*
21:30 on] in *TCC*
21:31 So, *MS, Per2*] ~ *Per1, E1*
21:32 enclosure,] enclosures, *TCC* enclosures *Per2* enclosure *E1*
21:32 is *MS, Per2*] are *Per1*
21:32 barracks *TCCR*] a barracks *MS* a barrack *TCC*
21:33 once,] ~ *Per2*
22:1 mine] my *TCC*
22:1 unto *MS, A1*] until *E1*
22:3 pinkish-ochre *TCCR, E1*] pinkish yellow *MS* pinkish ochre *Per1*
22:5 stiffly-pleated] stiffly pleated *TCC*
22:5 their pleats ... lizard-claws of] *Om. TCC see note on 22:6*
22:6 foot-hills, *MS, E1*] foothills, *Per1* foot-hills *Per2*
22:7 savannah-coloured *MS, Per2*] savanah-coloured *TCC* savanah-colored *Per1* savannah-colored *A1*
22:7 savannah *MS, Per 2*] savanah *TCC*
22:7 valley, the] ~. The *TCCR*
22:8 *ocote, MS, Per2*] ~; *Per1*
22:8 and *MS, Per2*] ~, *Per1, E1*
22:8 rebozo] *rebozo E1*
22:9 fume,] ~ *Per1*
22:9 corn-flower blue] cornflower blue *Per1* cornflower-blue *Per2*
22:10 characteristic, *MS, E1*] ~ *Per1*
22:10 darkest, bluest] darkest blue *TCC* darkest-blue *E1*
22:11 royal-blue *MS, Per2*] royal blue *TCC*
22:12 soft, *MS, E1*] ~/ *TCC* ~ *Per1*
22:12 claws] ~, *E1*
22:14 the claws, *MS, E1*] ~ ~ *Per2*
22:14 trees, *MS, E1*] ~ *Per2*
22:15 foot-hills *MS, Per2*] foothills *Per1 see notes*

22:16 hacienda *MS, A1*] *hacienda E1*
22:16 green green] green *TCCC* green, green *Per2*
22:17 sugar-cane *MS, Per2*] sugar cane *Per1*
22:18 canyon, *MS, E1*] ~ *Per2*
22:20 Rosalino] Rosalina *A1*
22:21 Quién sabe] Quien sabe *Per1* Quien sabe *Per2* Quién sabe *A1*
22:21 Señor!] Señor? *TCCR* Senor? *Per1* Señor? *Per2*
22:22 savannah *MS, Per2*] savanah *TCC*
22:24 things.— *MS, E1*] ~. *Per1*
22:25 Indians,] ~/ *TCC* ~ *Per*
22:30 No Señor.] ~ ~, *TCC* ~, ~, *Per2*
22:32 Como no] *Como no TCCC, A1 Come no E1*
22:32 Señor!] *Señor! TCCC* Señor? *A1*
22:33 dumb bell *MS, Per2*] dumb-bell *TCCC, E1*
22:35 if a] if the *TCC*
22:36 white,] ~ *E1*
22:38 alone,] ~ *E1*
22:38 and] ~, *E1*
22:38 were] ~, *E1*
23:7 tinyness] tininess *Per1*
23:8 towers, *MS, Per2*] ~ *Per1*
23:9 wilderness *TCCR*] aloof *MS*
23:11 savannah *MS, Per2*] savanah *Per1*
23:15 twinkling] ~/ *TCCC* ~, *E1*
23:18 Is] "~ *TCCR*
23:19 going?] ~?" *Per1*
23:19 No] "~ *Per1*
23:19 Felipe.] ~. *Per1, E1* ~?" *Per2*
23:19 What then] "~ ~ *Per1* "~, ~, *E1*
23:19 called?] ~?" *Per1*
23:20 It] "~ *Per1*
23:20 Huayapa.] ~." *Per1*
23:20 Which then] "~, ~, *Per1, E1* "~ ~ *Per2*
23:20 Felipe?] ~?" *Per1*
23:20 That one!] ~ ~!" *TCCR* "~ ~!" *Per1*
23:20 she] and she *E1*
23:23 donkey, *MS, Per2*] ~ *Per1, E1*
23:24 foot,] ~ *E1*
23:25 bad] *Om. TCC*

23:26 pecker *MS, Per2*] dander *TCCC*
　　　 see notes
23:30 keen *MS, E1*] ~, *Per2*
23:31 that] *Om. TCCC*
23:34 Allan *MS, Per2, A1*] Allen *TCC,*
　　　 E1
23:34 raven.] ~: *E1*
23:35 Prophet... devil?]　　*Prophet...*
　　　 devil, ? TCCC Prophet... devil?
　　　 Per1 "Prophet... devil?" E1
23:36 Devil... you!]　*Devil... you:*
　　　 TCCC Devil... you, Per1
　　　 Devil... you! Per2
23:37 Nevermore] *Nevermore E1*
23:39 going] getting *E1*
23:40 too-much] too much *Per1*
24:1 This again *MS, E1*] ~, ~, *Per2*
24:5 in the earth, *TCCR*] like a moat,
　　　 MS
24:7 turf, *MS, Per2*] ~ *Per1*
24:7 palo-blanco] *palo-blanco E1*
24:8 flowers *MS, Per2*] ~, *TCCC*
24:8 cambric.— *MS, Per2*] fabric. *Per1*
24:9 sheer below] below, pheer below
　　　 TCC below, sheer below
　　　 TCCC
24:12 Mucho calor!"] *Mucho calor! Per2*
　　　 Mucho calor!" E1
24:12 extra-jaunty,] ~ *TCC*
24:12 big] *Om. TCC*
24:16 Adios!] *Adios! Per2 Adiós! A1*
24:17 Adios!] *Adios! Per2 Adiós! A1*
24:18 Adios!] *Adios! Per2 Adiós! A1*
24:18 like] *Om. TCC*
24:19 Adios! Adios! Adios!] *Adios!*
　　　 Adios! Adios! Per2 Adiós! Adiós!
　　　 Adiós! A1
24:20 swerving neutral *MS, Per2*] ~, ~
　　　 Per1 ~, ~, *E1*
24:21 passed, *MS, E1*] ~ *Per2*
24:23 wide his] his wide *TCC*
24:24 eyes] ~, *E1*
24:29 Gabilan!] *Gabilan! Per2 Gabilan,*
　　　 E1 Gabilán, A1
24:31 Psia!"—] *Psia!"— TCC Psia!"*
　　　 TCCC Psia!"— E1
24:32 wings!] ~. *E1*

24:35 with knees together *TCCR*] Om.
　　　 MS
24:35 rising] ~, *E1*
24:37 black, *MS, Per2*] ~ *Per1*
24:39 which] *Om. Per2*
24:40 upstream] up stream *TCC* up-
　　　 stream *E1*
24:40 stream, *MS, E1*] ~ *Per1*
25:3 abranch *MS, E1*] a-branch *Per2*
25:7 across-stream *MS, Per2*] across
　　　 stream *Per1*
25:8 bathing lad] bathing-lad *E1*
25:11 bird-like *MS, Per2*] birdlike *Per1*
　　　 bird-/like *A1*
25:14 *Becerro! MS, A1*] ~! *Per1* "~!" *E1*
25:15 bird-like *MS, Per2*] birdlike *Per1*
　　　 bird-like, *E1*
25:16 sun, *MS, A1*] ~ *E1*
25:18 there] this *TCC*
25:19 were] was *TCC*
25:22 Rosalino? *MS, E1*] ~! *TCC* ~;
　　　 Per2
25:23 El blanco?] *El blanco? Per2*
25:23 Si, agua] *Si, agua Per2*
25:23 Señora!] *Señora! Per2 Señora, E1*
25:23 dumb bell *MS, Per2*] dumb-bell
　　　 TCCC, E1
25:24 milk?—] ~? *TCC*
25:25 Si, es leche] *Si, es leche TCCC*
25:25 Señora!] *Señora! TCCC Señora!*
　　　 Per1
25:25 it is] it's *Per2*
25:29 Señora] ~, *E1*
25:29 water.] ~! *Per2*
25:31 Si, Señora!] *Si, Señora! Per2 Si,*
　　　 Señora. E1
25:31 Es panteón!"—] Es panteón!"
　　　 Per1 Es panteón!" Per2 Es
　　　 panteón." E1
25:31 panteón,] panteón *Per2 panteón,*
　　　 E1
25:33 cemetery!] ~, *E1*
25:35 absurdity, *MS, E1*] ~ *Per2*
25:36 laughter.— *MS, E1*] ~. *Per1*
25:38 midday *MS, Per1, E1*] mid-day
　　　 TCC, Per2
25:38 lane, *MS, Per2*] ~ *Per1*

25:39 irrigation water] irrigation-water *E1*
25:40 half tropical] half-tropical *Per1*
25:40 spouting] sprouting *E1*
25:40 out] into *TCC*
26:1 yellow flowers, *MS, E1*] ~ ~ *Per2*
26:3 *Ia... Ia Per1*] Iᵃ... Iᵃ *MS, Per2* see notes
26:4 brand-new] ~, *Per2*
26:5 Mines.—] ~. *TCC*
26:6 1st *Per1*] 1ˢᵗ *MS* 1st. *TCC, E1* First *Per2*
26:6 Magnolia *MS, Per1, E1*] Manolia *TCC, Per2*
26:6 4th *Per1, E1*] 4ᵗʰ *MS* 4th. *TCC* Fourth *Per2*
26:6 Enrique] Enriquez *E1*
26:7 Gonzalez] González *A1*
26:9 poinsettia *MS, A1*] *poinsettia E1*
26:11 stream-gutter] ~, *E1*
26:13 Vasquez] Vásquez *A1*
26:13 stream-bed *MS, E1*] stream bed *TCC*
26:14 tall, *MS, Per2*] the, *TCC* the *Per1*
26:14 wildly-tall] wildly tall *Per1*
26:20 half-bald] half-bold *TCC*
26:22 proudly-labelled] proudly labelled *TCC, Per2* proudly labeled *Per1*
26:24 church] churches *TCC*
26:27 white,] ~ *E1*
26:28 church; and where *TCCR*] church. Where *MS*
26:29 plaza... plaza] *plaza... plaza E1*
26:29 Zócalo] *Zócalo Per2, A1* zocalo *E1*
26:34 *Reforma*, the great church *MS, E1*] *Reforma, the great church Per1 Reforma* the great church *Per2*
26:35 plaza] *plaza E1*
26:36 big, *MS, E1*] ~ *Per2*
26:39 plaza, *MS, A1*] plaza *Per2* plaza, *E1*
26:39 long *MS, E1*] ~, *Per1*
26:40 crowding, *MS, Per2*] ~ *Per1*
27:1 pueblo] *pueblo E1*
27:6 *what*] what *E1*
27:8 presence, *MS, E1*] ~ *Per2*
27:8 village, *MS, E1*] ~ *Per2*

27:11 Soledad *MS, Per2*] soledad *Per1*
27:12 of the wild] of wild *TCC*
27:13 Gulliver's Travels'] Gulliver's Travel's *TCC* Gulliver's travel's *Per1* Gulliver's Travels *Per2* see notes
27:14 joy-ride *MS, E1*] joyride *Per1*
27:15 rather] *Om. TCC*
27:15 undersized:] ~; *E1*
27:17 his... his... his *MS, A1*] His... His... His *E1*
27:19 him,] him *TCC, A1* Him *E1*
27:19 living *TCCR*] *Om. MS*
27:19 half hidden] half-/ hidden *E1* half-hidden *A1*
27:26 thigh, *MS, E1*] ~ *Per1*
27:28 idiotically] ~, *Per1*
27:29 verger] Verger *TCC*
27:30 Outside *MS, Per2*] ~, *TCCC, E1*
27:33 government] Government *Per2*
27:33 state] State *TCC*
27:34 Votes! Votes! *MS, Per2*] Votes! Votes! Votes! *TCC, E1*
27:35 long] *Om. TCC*
27:35 sees, *MS, E1*] see, *Per1* sees *Per2*
27:35 letters, *MS, E1*] ~ *Per2*
27:37 Mark ◎! *Ed.*] ~. ◎! *MS* ~. ◎*TCCC* ~. ✕ *Per1* ~— ◎ *Per2* ~ ◎. *E1*
27:37 another: *MS, E1*] ~, *Per2*
27:37 Mark ☉! My] ~ ☉ My *TCCC* ~. □ My *Per1* ~— ☉? *P* My *Per2* ~ ☉. *P* My *E1*
27:39 red ring, *MS, E1*] ~ ~ *Per2*
27:40 blue ring, *MS, Per2*] ~ ~ *Per1*
28:2 another 8.] ~ = 8. *TCCR* ~, 8. *Per1* ~— 8. *Per2* ~ 8. *E1*
28:2 lucky bag *MS, E1*] lucky-bag *Per2*
28:3 out] *Om. TCC*
28:3 Zenón] Zenon *TCC*
28:3 Cocotilla *TCCR*] Quintanilla *MS*
28:6 side] *Om. TCC*
28:6 plaza] *plaza E1*
28:6 Hay frutas?] ~ ~? *Per1* "~ ~? *E1*
28:7 Oranges,] ~ *TCC*

28:7 bananas?] ~?" *E1*
28:7 *No, Señor.*] "No, Señor." *E1*
28:7 No fruits?] "~ ~?" *E1*
28:7 *No hay! TCCR*] *No hay. MS* No
    hay! Per1 No hay! Per2 "No hay!"
    E1
28:7 Can] "~ *E1*
28:8 cup?] ~?" *E1*
28:8 *No hay.*] ~ ~! *Per1* "~ ~." *E1*
28:8 Can] "~ *E1*
28:8 jícara] *jicara E1 jícara A1*
28:9 from?] ~?" *E1*
28:9 *No hay!*] ~ ~! *Per1* "~ ~." *E1*
28:10 *hay!*] ~! *Per1* ~ *E1*
28:10 *there MS, Per2*] there *Per1*
28:10 *any!*] ~, *TCCC*
28:11 dumb bells *MS, Per2*] dumb-bells
    TCC, E1
28:12 then?"— *MS, Per2*] ~?" *Per1, E1*
28:13 grass-hoppers   *MS,*   *Per2*]
    grasshoppers *Per1, E1*
28:14 stark *MS, Per2*] ~, *Per1, E1*
28:15 Next door] Next-door *E1*
28:15 *No hay!*] ~ ~! *Per1* ~ ~. *E1*
28:17 Para borracharse!]   *Para bor-*
    racharse! TCCR Para borracharse!
    Per1 Para borracharse, E1
28:18 Tepache] *Tepache E1*
28:20 mescal *MS, A1*] mescal, *Per1*
    mescal E1
28:20 on—] ~. *TCC*
28:21 Where, *where MS, Per2*] Where
    where TCC Where *Per1*
28:22 or] and *TCC*
28:22 see oranges *MS, TCCC, E1*] see
    orange *TCC, Per2*
28:22 trees, *MS, Per2*] ~; *TCCC*
28:24 there!"—] ~!" *Per1*
28:29 plaza] *plaza E1*
28:30 orange trees] orange-trees *Per2*
28:31 Hay frutas?] *Hay frutas? Per2*
28:32 No hay!] No hay *TCC* No hay.
    Per1 No hay! Per2 No hay. E1
28:34 No hay!] *No hay! Per2 No hay. E1*
28:35 slope] steps *TCC*
28:37 two] *Om. Per2*
28:37 bullocks: *MS, Per2*] ~, *Per1*

28:38 bare-bosomed,]   bare-bosomed
    TCC bare-bosom *Per2* bare-
    bosom, *E1*
28:39 Hay frutas?] *Hay frutas? Per2*
28:40 No hay!] *No hay! Per2 No hay. E1*
29:4 No hay!] *No hay! Per2 No hay. E1*
29:7 the Street] the street *Per2* The
    Street *E1*
29:7 Juárez *Ed.*] Juarez *MS*
29:8 For ◉.] For ▢. *Per1* for
    ◉. *Per2* for ◉. *E1*
29:9 sheds] shade *TCC*
29:9 *masa MS, E1*] masa *Per2*
29:10 tortillas] *tortillas E1*
29:10 kettle-drum *MS, Per2*] kettle
    drum *Per1* kettledrum *E1*
29:12 *Cucaracha Ed.*] *Cucaracha MS*
29:13 *almost*] almost *TCC*
29:14 Hay frutas?] *Hay frutas? Per2*
29:15 No hay!] *No hay! Per2 No hay. E1*
29:16 "Then what is there?"] *Om. TCC*
    "Then what is happening here?"
    TCCR see notes
29:19 fiesta] *fiesta E1*
29:20 god] God *Per2*
29:22 us, *MS, E1*] ~ *Per2*
29:23 appalled,] ~ *TCC*
29:25 back:] ~, *TCC*
29:29 *idioma MS, E1*] idioma *TCC*
29:31 Yes] ~, *Per1*
29:33 *idioma*] idioma *A1*
29:34 dialect *TCCR*] dialectic *MS*
    dieletic *TCC see notes*
29:34 Anyhow] ~, *Per1*
29:39 ant-run *MS, Per2*] ante-run *Per1*
30:1 us *MS, Per2*] me *TCC*
30:2 some] them *TCC*
30:6 "fiesta." *MS, Per1*] "fiesta". *TCC*
    fiesta. *E1*
30:7 gateway] ~, *E1*
30:11 Valentino *MS, E1*] Valentio *Per2*
30:11 Hay naranjas?] *Hay naranjas? Per2*
30:13 masa] *masa E1*
30:14 tortillas . . . tortillas]   *tortillas . . .*
    tortillas E1
30:15 fiesta] *fiesta E1*
30:16 man, *MS, Per2*] ~ *Per1*

30:18 Oh] ~, *Per1*
30:18 señor . . . señor] Señor . . . Señor *E1*
30:20 orange tree] orange-tree *Per2* orange-tree, *E1*
30:21 yellowish green] yellowish-green *TCCC*
30:24 do."— *MS, Per2*] ~,"— *TCC* do." *Per2*
30:27 those *MS, Per2*] these *TCC, E1*
30:28 oranges: *MS, E1*] ~— *Per1*
30:29 cents: *MS, E1*] ~— *Per1*
30:34 plaza,] plaza *Per2 plaza, E1*
30:34 down hill] down the hill *TCC*
30:35 a coyote] coyote *TCC*
30:35 zopilote, *MS, Per2*] ~ *Per1*
30:37 Adios!] *Adios! Per2 Adiós! A1*
30:38 Adios!] *Adios! Per2 Adiós! A1*
30:38 cannon-shot] cannon shot *E1*
30:39 down-hill *MS, Per2*] downhill *Per1, E1*
31:1 unchanneled] unchanelled *Per2*
31:3 juncture *E1*] junction *MS see notes*
31:3 the roads *E1*] roads *MS*
31:4 Again: *Adios!*] ~: Adios! *TCC* ~: *Adois! Per2* ~: *Adios! E1* ~: *Adiós! A1*
31:4 low, *MS, Per2*] ~ *Per1*
31:5 of *Adios!*] of *Adios! Per1* of *Adiós! A1*
31:6 up *MS, Per2*] ~, *Per1*
31:6 *must*] must *E1*
31:6 village, *MS, A1*] ~ *E1*
31:11 Hay frutas?] *Hay frutas? Per2*
31:12 Hay!] *Hay! Per2 Hay, E1*
31:12 half voice] half-voice *TCC*
31:13 shade? *MS, Per1, E1*] ~! *TCC, Per2*
31:13 No, *MS, Per2*] ~. *Per1* ~; *E1*
31:15 above.—] ~. *Per1*
31:15 guava tree *MS, E1*] guava-tree *Per2*
31:17 guava tree *MS, E1*] guava-tree *Per2*
31:21 La taza!] *La taza! Per2*
31:22 lifeless] ~, *E1*
31:24 noise,] ~— *E1*
31:24 chock! chock *MS, Per2*] ~/~ *TCC* ~, ~ *Per1, E1*

31:27 water,] ~ *TCC*
31:28 upstream,] up stream, *TCC* up stream *Per1* up-stream, *Per2* upstream *E1* up-/ stream *A1*
31:28 bodies] *Om. TCC*
31:29 below] *Om. TCC*
31:31 divides, *MS, E1*] ~; *Per2*
31:33 guava tree *MS, E1*] guava-tree *Per2*
31:34 arm] arms *TCC*
31:35 undergarment *MS, Per1*] under-/ garment *TCC* under-garment *Per2*
31:36 sarape *MS, A1*] *sarape E1*
31:36 rebozo *MS, A1*] *rebozo E1*
31:37 black *MS, E1*] ~, *Per2*
31:38 chirimoyas *MS, A1*] *chirimoyas E1*
31:38 Chirimoyas *MS, A1*] *Chirimoyas E1*
31:40 Spanish.] ~: *TCC*
32:2 This, *MS, E1*] ~ *Per2*
32:3 it."—] ~." *TCC*
32:4 lemonade, *MS, E1*] ~ *Per2*
32:5 good, we] ~. We *E1*
32:6 chirimoyas] *chirimoyas E1*
32:6 peso] *peso E1*
32:8 Señor!] ~, *E1*
32:8 No] ~, *Per1*
32:9 chirimoyas] *chirimoyas E1*
32:11 Now] ~, *Per2*
32:12 to you, *MS, Per2*] ~ ~ *Per1*
32:12 eat *TCCR*] live *MS*
32:17 said,] ~ *E1*
32:17 chirimoyas] *chirimoyas E1*
32:21 Huayapa!] ~, *E1*
32:23 wine-bottle *MS, Per2*] wine bottle *Per1*
32:24 her,] ~ *TCC*
32:25 guava tree *MS, E1*] Guava tree *TCC* guava-tree *Per2*
32:26 golden brown] golden-brown *Per1*
32:28 thought *TCC*] though *MS*
32:28 beautiful] ~, *Per2*
32:28 suave] ~, *Per2*
32:29 have,] ~; *E1*
32:33 zopilotes] *zopilotes E1*
32:34 día *A1*] dia *MS*

The Mozo

The order of the texts is *MS, TCC, TCCR, TCCC, Per, E1, A1.*

35:1 **The Mozo** *Ed.*] Mornings in
Mexico/ by D. H. Lawrence/
Monday Morning. *MS* Mornings
in Mexico/ by/ D. H. Lawrence/
The Mozo *TCC* MORNINGS IN
MEXICO:/ THE MOZO/ *By*
D. H. Lawrence *Per The Mozo E1*
III/ THE MOZO *A1*

35:2 here *TCC*] there *MS see note on*
35:7

35:3 place, *MS, E1*] ~ *Per*

35:4 patio] *patio E1*

35:7 other... not Zapotec. *TCC*]
Spanish blood. *MS see notes*

35:12 never] never never *TCC* never,
never *Per*

35:12 mothers *TCC*] mother's *MS*

35:13 have known *TCC*] know *MS see
note on* 35:7

35:14 unloveable] unlovable *E1*

35:14 myths,] ~ *Per*

35:21 then] ~, *E1*

35:22 infant god] infant-god *E1*

35:23 joyfully] joyful and *Per*

35:30 greedily,] ~ *TCC*

35:32 This then] ~, ~, *Per*

35:32 goddess *MS, E1*] Goddess
TCC

36:1 *Tarumm-tarahh!*] *Tarumm-tarah!*
TCC Tarumm-tarah! E1

36:3 him then] ~, ~, *E1*

36:3 people. *P* See] ~. See *E1*

36:4 reposing?] reposing! *TCCR, E1*
~/ *TCC* ~. *Per*

36:5 qué bonito] *qué bonito E1*

36:5 Oh] ~, *Per*

36:6 day, *MS, E1*] ~ *Per*

36:14 a lizard] the lizard *TCC*

36:20 them,] ~ *TCC*

36:20 or a] or *TCC*

36:21 phenomenon. Something]   ~;
something *TCC*

36:23 Now *MS, E1*] ~, *Per*

36:26 him; *MS, E1*] ~: *TCC*

36:33 Mexican] ~, *E1*

36:34 en la mañana... tarde... noche:]
en la mañana... tarda... noche:
TCC en la mañana... tarda...
noche— *Per en la mañana...*
tarde... noche: E1

36:35 mid-day] midday *E1*

36:37 horrible *MS, E1*] ~, *Per*

37:2 Indian] Indians *TCC*

37:2 near,] ~ *TCC*

37:2 very near *MS, E1*] ~ ~, *TCC*

37:6 Oh] ~, *E1*

37:9 truly horrible,] ~ ~ *A1*

37:10 *Mañana MS, E1*] Mañana *TCC*

37:12 fiestas... fiestas... [37:15] fiestas]
fiestas... fiestas... fiestas E1

37:16 time? *TCCR*] ~. *MS*

37:17 centavos] *centavos E1*

37:17 pesos] peses *Per pesos E1*

37:18 mean] ~, *E1*

37:18 all? *TCCR*] ~. *MS*

37:19 here *TCCR*] *Om. MS*

37:20 twelve-and-a-half centavos.]
twelve and a half *centavos. E1*

37:21 half a centavo also] also half a centavo *TCC* also half a *centavo E1*

37:24 trick] way *TCC*

37:24 centavo] *centavo E1*

37:25 mescal *MS, A1*] *mescal E1*

37:27 peoples] people *TCC*

37:35 care:] ~; *E1*

38:3 monkey-show,] ~; *TCC* ~: *Per*

38:4 certain] *Om. TCC*

38:8 save! *TCCR*] *save. MS* ~ *TCC* ~!
E1

38:10 food. Give] ~; give *E1*

38:11 eat.— *TCCR*] ~. *MS*

38:11 tortillas] *tortillas E1*

38:13 women] woman *Per*

38:13 Si Señor!] *Si* señor! *TCC Si, Señor.*
E1

38:14 *Nothing TCCR*] Nothing *MS*

38:14 *What is to be done? TCCR*] What is to be done? *MS What is to be done? E1*
38:15 *you—.*] *you* [ ]: *TCCC* you how. *Per*
38:16 is] was *TCC*
38:17 mud *E1*] *masa MS see notes*
38:17 twice? *TCCR*] ~. *MS*
38:18 Well] ~, *E1*
38:18 paradise] Paradise *TCC*
38:20 paradise] Paradise *TCCC*
38:20 Poor baby... in paradise.] *Om. TCC see notes*
38:21 better!] ~? *E1*
38:22 coming *MS, E1*] to come *Per*
38:24 noon, *MS, E1*] ~ *TCC*
38:24 Why morning, noon,] Why morning and noon *TCC*
38:25 any-time, any-when] any-/ time, anywhen *E1* anytime, any-/ when *A1*
38:27 at MS, *E1*] *Om. Per*
38:27 the other... hand. *TCCR*] God wants it so. *MS see notes*
38:29 Oh] ~, *E1*
38:30 tomorrow.] tomorrows. *TCC* to-morrows. *Per* to-morrows! *E1*
38:32 think.] ~? *E1*
38:33 white monkey-tricks] white-monkey tricks *E1*
38:35 good *MS, E1*] ~, *Per*
38:36 half amusing] half-amusing *E1*
39:7 time, time.] ~ ~/ *TCC* ~, ~! *TCCR* ~! ~! *E1*
39:9 changeless] as changeless *TCC*
39:14 four pesos] four *pesos E1*
39:15 tortillas] *tortillas E1*
39:15 Four pesos] Four *pesos E1*
39:20 Et praeterea nihil *Ed.*] Et praetera nihil *MS Et præterea nihil Per*
39:27 of the *MS, E1*] of *TCC*
39:27 patio] *patio E1*
39:27 panier basket] pannier-basket *E1*
39:28 shoulders] ~, *E1*
39:29 thus] ~, *E1*
39:34 patio] *patio E1*
39:37 watering can] watering-can *E1*

39:38 zaguan... [39:40] zaguan] Zaguan... Zaguan *TCC zaguan... zaguan E1* Zaguán... Zaguán *A1*
40:3 anticipating.—] ~. *Per*
40:3 zaguan *MS, E1*] Zaguan *Per* Zaguán *A1*
40:7 love-poem] ~, *E1*
40:10 aloud, *TCCR*] ~ *MS*
40:11 confused feelings *TCCR*] bashfulness *MS*
40:12 small, small *TCCR*] certain *MS*
40:13 Actually,] ~ *A1*
40:14 Exactly like a parrot. *TCCR*] *Om. MS*
40:17 more,] mor/ *TCC* more/ *TCCR* more *Per*
40:17 will perhaps *MS, E1*] ~, ~, *Per*
40:17 six intelligible sentences *TCCR*] *Om. MS*
40:20 an *Ed.*] a *MS*
40:20 uncertain *TCCR*] certain *MS* very uncertain *Per*
40:21 days' *E1*] days *MS*
40:22 alcalde] a alcalde *TCC* an alcalde *Per* an *alcalde E1*
40:22 head-man] headman *E1*
40:23 government] Government *Per*
40:23 alcalde] *alcalde E1*
40:24 him,] ~ *E1*
40:25 paisano] *paisano E1*
40:26 zaguan] Zaguan *TCC* zaguan *E1* Zaguán *A1*
40:26 patio,] *patio E1*
40:31 patio] *patio E1*
40:32 apaxtle] *apaxtle Per*
40:34 at night *TCCR*] *Om. MS*
40:36 huaraches] *huaraches Per*
40:38 paisano] *paisano E1*
41:1 half past] half-past *E1*
41:1 nine, *TCCR*] ~. *MS* ~ *E1*
41:1 in our very quiet house. *TCCR*] *Om. MS*
41:6 estan tocando!"—] estan *tocando!" Per estan tocando!"—* *E1* están *tocando!"—A1 see notes*
41:8 door-catch.—] ~. *Per*

41:13 mozo] *mozo E1*
41:14 two proper . . . the carter] the
carter *TCC* a cargador—a porter
TCCR a *cargador—a porter Per see
note on* 38:20
41:16 Help *TCCR*] ~! *MS*
41:16 them! *TCCR*] *Om. MS* ~, *E1*
41:17 muttering:] ~, *E1*
41:17 No quiero!] *No quiero! E1*
41:22 new] his *TCC*
41:22 monkey tricks] monkey-tricks *E1*
41:23 our] our own *TCC*
41:24 meat stews] meat-stews *TCC*
41:25 "Hé comido el caldo. *MS, Per, A1*]
"Hé comida el caldo/ *TCC "Hé
comido el caldo. E1*
41:26 Grazias! *MS, A1] Grazias! E1 see
notes*
41:26 "I] ("~ *E1*
41:26 you!"—] ~.")— *E1*
41:32 in] *Om. TCC*
41:38 cheese,] ~; *E1*
41:39 gazeosa] gazoosa *TCC, A1 gazoosa
E1*
42:1 *therefore* he . . . same footing,] *Om.
TCC see note on* 38:20
42:3 *therefore,*] ~/ *TCC* ~ *Per*
42:4 sleeve,] ~; *E1*
42:6 we!] ~/ *TCC* ~? *TCCR*
42:7 patio] *patio E1*
42:10 Monday,] ~ *E1*
42:10 Why?—] ~ *E1*
42:12 mozo] *mozo E1*
42:14 this,] ~ *TCC*
42:16 gloom,] ~ *E1*
42:16 little,] ~/ *TCC* ~ *Per*
42:18 of] and *TCC*
42:18 hate. *MS, E1*] ~ *Per*
42:20 mozo] *mozo E1*
42:21 potent hate,] ~ ~/ *TCC* ~ ~
Per
42:22 stomach,] ~ *E1*
42:25 made,] ~; *E1*
42:25 mozo] *mozo E1*
42:27 fiesta] *fiesta E1*
42:30 pitahayas *MS, A1] pitahayas E1*
42:39 of] on *A1*

42:40 villages.] ~, *TCC* ~; *E1*
43:7 village,] ~ *E1*
43:8 widowed] widow *TCC*
43:9 orange trees *TCC*] oranges trees
MS orange-trees *Per*
43:10 cooler. *P* Seeing] ~. Seeing *TCC*
43:11 photograph, *TCCR*] ~ *MS*
43:11 who had *TCCR*] having *MS*
43:18 fiesta] *fiesta E1*
43:18 could] would *TCC*
43:19 fiesta] *fiesta E1*
43:20 jícara] *jícara E1 jícara A1*
43:22 Señorita *MS, E1*] señorita *TCC*
43:25 Friday.] ~; *E1*
43:25 He] he *E1*
43:26 us,] ~ *E1*
43:28 Mexican] ~, *E1*
43:29 mozo] *mozo E1*
43:29 Back] But *TCC* Now *TCCR see
notes*
43:29 then] ~, *E1*
43:31 And *MS, E1*] Again *Per*
43:35 soldiers,] ~ *E1*
43:35 alcalde] *alcalde E1*
43:36 hill-village *MS, E1*] hill village
TCC
43:38 those, *MS, E1*] ~ *TCC*
44:1 soldiers *TCC*] soldiers' *MS*
44:8 mozo] *mozo E1*
44:9 He too *MS*] ~, ~, *Per*
44:10 village, *MS, E1*] ~ *Per*
44:14 mozo] *mozo E1*
44:17 or] and *TCC*
44:18 mozo] *mozo E1*
44:18 basket:] ~; *E1*
44:19 thousands. *TCCR*] servants. *MS*
44:23 mozo] *mozo E1*
44:23 basket, *MS, E1*] ~ *Per*
44:24 Adios a mi patron] *Adiós a mi
patrón A1 see notes*
44:25 Me *TCCR*] Mi *MS* Me *A1*
44:25 llevan."] *llevan." A1*
44:25 Oh] ~, *Per*
44:25 *me llevan! TCCR, Per*] *mi
llevan! MS* "*Me llevan!*"— *E1*
44:25 they] They *E1*
44:27 mozo] *mozo E1*

44:29 swollen *MS, A1*] swoollen *E1*
44:32 to] and *TCC*
44:34 Oh] ~, *Per*
44:37 back, *MS, E1*] ~. *Per*
44:37 begging   tortillas...swollen...
[44:39] people] *Om. Per* begging
tortillas... swoollen... people
E1 begging *tortillas*...
swollen... people *A1*
45:2 tiny] ~, *E1*

45:2 for the moment *TCCR*] *Om. MS*
45:4 strong. *MS, E1*] ~, *Per*
45:4 And *MS, E1*] and *Per*
45:4 intelligent, *MS, E1*] ~. *Per*
45:5 far more...Rosalino. *MS, E1*]
Om. Per
45:9 stand *TCCR*] they stand *MS*
45:9 *patron*] patrón *E1*
45:12 Indian-Mexican] Indian-Mexico
E1

Market Day

The order of the texts is *MS, Per1, Per2, E1, A1*.

49:1 **Market Day** *Ed.*] Mornings in
Mexico/ by D. H. Lawrence./
Saturday Morning *MS THE
GENTLE ART OF MARKET-
ING IN MEXICO/* The Curi-
ous Pageant That Fills the Market Road—Indians From the
Hills and/ Plains—Buying and
Bargaining—The Return Jour-
ney/ By D. H. LAWRENCE *Per1*
MORNINGS IN MEXICO/ *By*
D. H. LAWRENCE/ SATUR-
DAY *Per2 Market Day E1* IV/
MARKET DAY *A1*
49:3 gone. *P* Dawn] ~. Dawn *E1*
49:5 yellow *Per1*] *Om. MS*
49:6 patio] *patio E1*
49:6 and *Per1*] *Om. MS*
49:8 splendid] very splendid *Per1 see
notes*
49:8 sure,] ~ *Per1*
49:9 These tufts *Per1*] They *MS*
49:13 yucca *MS, E1*] Yucca *Per1, A1*
49:13 It too is] It is, too, *Per, E1* It, too,
is *Per2*
49:16 long *Per1*] big *MS*
49:16 bunch *Per1*] cluster *MS*
49:17 coffee berries] coffee-berries *E1*
49:20 patio] *patio E1*
49:21 sky *MS, Per2*] ~, *Per1, E1*
49:23 tree tips] tree-tips *Per1*
49:25 motion *MS, E1*] ~, *Per2*

49:29 gabilanes] *gabilanes Per1*
49:30 palo blanco *MS, A1*] *palo blanco
Per2* palo-blanco *E1*
49:33 none, *Per1*] no straight lines,
MS
50:5 visible] invisible *Per1 see notes*
50:5 ellipse. *P* If *MS, Per2*] ~. If *Per1*,
E1
50:6 bend, *MS, Per2*] ~ *Per1, E1*
50:8 wounds] rounds *A1*
50:12 sombering *MS, A1*] sombring *E1*
50:15 foot-slope *MS, Per2*] footslope
Per1, E1
50:16 dots *Per1*] specks *MS*
50:19 Saturday,] ~ *Per1*
50:20 ploughland] plough-land *E1*
50:21 palo blanco *MS, A1*] *palo blanco
Per2* palo-blanco *E1*
50:25 held] *Om. Per1*
50:25 blue] *Om. Per1*
50:26 girls *Per1*] a girl *MS*
50:27 along,] ~ *Per1*
50:27 come, *MS, Per2*] ~ *Per1, E1*
51:3 faggots of *Per1*] ocote *MS*
51:4 panier] pannier *Per2*
51:6 donkey,] ~ *Per1*
51:9 strange, ebbing current] strang
current *Per1* strange current *Per2*
51:11 nets *MS, Per2*] net *Per1, E1*
51:15 palo blanco MS, *A1*] *palo blanco
Per2 palo-blanco* E1
51:16 mesquite *MS, A1*] *mesquite E1*

51:18 overpowering *Perı*] overpassing *MS*

51:18 people:] ~, *Perı*

51:22 mist] midst *Eı*

51:23 cotton] *Om. Perı*

51:23 rebozos *MS, Aı*] *rebozos Eı*

51:24 white, *MS, Per2*] ~ *Perı, Eı*

51:25 invisible, *MS, Per2*] ~ *Perı, Eı*

51:28 Serranos *MS, Aı*] Serraos *Per2* serranos *Eı*

51:39 or banana... wind *Perı*] rain among leaves at night *MS*

51:40 market *MS, Per2*] ~, *Perı, Eı*

52:2 murmur] murmurs *Perı*

52:2 sounds *Perı*] sound *MS*

52:6 religion. *Perı*] ~ *MS*

52:7 These alone *Perı*] *Om. MS*

52:9 for *Perı*] to bring *MS*

52:9 women] ~, *Eı*

52:9 to cross *Perı*] across *MS*

52:13 covered *Perı*] *Om. MS*

52:16 forget me nots] forget-me-nots *Perı*

52:19 cherry-pie heliotrope *MS, Per2*] cherry-pie-heliotrope *Perı*

52:24 contest *MS, Per2*] contact *Perı, Eı* contract *Aı*

52:26 señorita] Señorita *Eı*

52:26 centavos! *MS, Per2*] ~. *Perı, Eı*

52:28 colours. Carefully] ~, carefully *Perı*

52:29 Señorita.] señorita! *Perı* Señorita! *Eı*

52:32 "It is much." *Perı*] "Thirty centavos? It is much. Twenty." *MS* 'It is much.' *Per2*

52:36 She *MS, Eı*] she *Perı*

52:37 Two *reales Perı*] Twenty-four *MS*

53:2 excuse. *MS, Eı*] ~, to these Indians. *Per2*

53:4 sweetened] sweet *Perı*

53:4 cheeses] cheese *Perı*

53:5 native woven] native-woven *Perı*

53:6 rebozos *MS, Aı*] *rebozos Eı*

53:6 handkerchieves] handkerchiefs *Perı*

53:6 far side] far-side *Perı*

53:8 serape] sarape *Perı sarape Eı*

53:9 a] the *Perı*

53:11 tigers, *MS, Eı*] ~ *Per2*

53:12 that *MS, Eı*] —~ *Per2*

53:12 serape] sarape *Perı sarape Eı*

53:15 Look *MS, Aı*] ~, *Per2*

53:21 reiterates: *MS, Per2*] ~, *Perı, Eı*

53:22 usually seem *Perı*] seem usually *MS*

53:24 *reales*] reales *Perı*

53:27 Instead, *MS, Per2*] ~ *Perı, Eı*

53:30 señor] Señor *Eı*

53:30 smell!" *MS, Eı*] ~' *Per2*

53:33 señor] Señor *Eı*

53:33 Señor *MS, Eı*] señor *Perı*

54:2 laughter,] ~ *Perı*

54:4 sandals,] ~ *Perı*

54:10 Díaz *Aı*] Diaz *MS*

54:10 Cortés *MS, Aı*] Cortes *Perı*

54:10 market-place *Perı*] market *MS*

54:24 gleaming,] ~ *Perı*

54:27 are *MS, Eı*] have *Per2*

55:9 strangers' *Aı*] stranger's *MS*

55:12 The Cathedral] The cathedral *Perı*

55:19 copper centavos *MS, Eı*] coppers, centavos *Per2*

55:20 these too *MS, Eı*] ~, ~, *Per2*

Indians and Entertainment

The order of the texts is *MS, TCC1-2, Perı, Per2, Eı, Aı.*

59:1 **Indians and Entertainment** *Ed.*] Indians and Entertainment/ by D. H. Lawrence. *MS* Indians and Entertainment./ By/ D.

H. Lawrence. *TCC1-2* INDIANS AND ENTERTAINMENT/ *D. H. Lawrence Analyzes the Difference Between the White Man's*

Drama and the Red Man's/ By D. H. LAWRENCE *Per1* INDIANS AND ENTERTAINMENT/ By D. H. Lawrence *Per2 Indians and Entertainment E1 V/* INDIANS AND ENTERTAINMENT *A1*

59:2 *The Potters, MS, Per2*] "The Potters," *Per1*

59:3 Reinhardt *MS, Per2*] Reinhart *Per1*

59:3 *King Lear MS, Per2*] "King Lear" *Per1 King Lear, E1*

59:3 *Electra. MS, Per2*] "Electra." *Per1*

59:14 all, *MS, Per2*] ~ *TCC1-2*

59:16 spirit-like *MS, E1*] spiritlike *Per1* spirit-/ like *Per2*

59:20 selves *Per1*] things *MS*

59:21 tragic, *MS, Per2*] ~ *Per1*

59:23 door, *MS, Per2*] ~ *Per1*

59:30 ideal consciousness] Ideal Consciousness *Per1*

60:6 summer,] Summer, *Per1* summer *Per2*

60:6 winter, *MS, Per2*] Winter *Per1*

60:7 law, *E1*] ~. *MS*

60:7 and from this to a belief in *E1*] And from universal law to *MS see notes*

60:20 ether, *MS, Per2*] ~ *Per1*

60:22 That *MS, Per1*] This *TCC1-2*

60:25 Eagle dance *MS, Per2*] Eagle dances *TCC1-2* eagle dance *Per1*

60:25 Corn dance *MS, Per2*] Corn dances *TCC1-2* corn dance *Per1*

60:29 Indians. Even... [60:31] the Indian. *P* So... all *MS, Per2*] Indians—all *Per1*

60:35 bunk. *P* You've got... [60:38] ours. *P* It is almost *MS, Per2*] bunk. It is almost *Per1*

60:39 for *MS*] for the *Per1*

60:40 common *MS, Per2*] ~, *TCC1-2*

60:40 healthy *MS, Per2*] ~, *TCC1-2*

61:2 sentimentalism *MS, Per2*] ~. *Per1*

61:2 like... eggs. *MS, Per2*] Om. *Per1*

61:7 eyes] your eyes *A1*

61:12 gods, *MS, Per2, A1*] ~ *TCC1-2, E1*

61:13 This... [61:16] admit it. *MS, Per2*] Om. *Per1*

61:19 Indian's] Indians *TCC1-2* Indian *Per2 see notes*

61:21 connection. *P* The sooner... realise and... [61:25] accomplishment. *P* The consciousness *MS, Per2*] connection. The consciousness *Per1* connection. The sooner... realize, and... accomplishment. *P* The consciousness *E1*

61:28 conscious *MS, Per2*] consciousness *Per1*

61:30 own] Om. *Per2*

61:33 Hindoos *MS, Per2*] Hindus, *Per1*

61:37 Ghost *MS, Per2*] ghost *TCC1-2*

61:38 *belong MS, Per2*] belong *Per1*

62:1 once. Can't be done. *P* So *MS, Per2*] once. So *Per1*

62:12 sounds, *MS, Per2*] ~ *Per1*

62:13 marvellous *MS, Per2*] marvelous *Per1*

62:14 seal woman] seal-woman *Per1*

62:15 beasts,] ~ *Per1*

62:20 human, *MS, Per2*] ~ *Per1*

62:20 *outside MS, Per2*] outside *Per1*

62:21 circumstances *Per1*] circumstance *MS*

62:24 chest, *MS, Per2*] ~ *Per1*

62:25 bear hunt:] bear hunt, *Per1* bear-hunt: *TCC1-2, Per2*

62:26 rain: *MS, Per2*] ~, *Per1*

62:26 grow: *MS, Per2*] ~, *Per1*

62:28 bear hunt *MS, Per1*] bear-hunt *TCC1-2, Per2*

62:28 men, *MS, Per2*] ~; *TCC1-2*

62:29 all bear *MS, Per2*] all bears *Per1*

62:33 subtle,] ~ *E1*

62:35 soulless, *MS, Per2*] ~ *Per1*

62:35 strange *MS, Per2*] ~, *Per1*

62:37 blood-stream *MS, Per2*] blood stream *Per1*

62:37 Hence, to our ears, *Per1*] Hence *MS*

62:37 absence *Per1*] utter absence *MS*

62:40 non-individual, *MS, Per2*] ~ *Per1*

62:40 Strange, *MS, Per2*] ~ *Per1*

63:1 unseizable *MS, Per2*] ~, *Per1*

63:2 throes: *MS, Per2*] ~; *Per1*

63:2 parted,] ~ *Per1*

63:3 blood-stream *MS, Per2*] blood stream *Per1*

63:5 ear, *MS, Per2*] ~ *Per1, TCC1-2*

63:6 tom-tom. *MS, Per2*] tomtom. *Per1*

63:7 amid the] amid *Per1*

63:9 forward, *MS, Per2*] ~ *Per1*

63:20 energy,] ~ *Per1*

63:20 or] and *Per1*

63:27 heart-beat. *MS, Per2*] heartbeat. *Per1*

63:33 pine-trees *MS, Per2*] pine trees *Per1*

63:35 aah-h-h-ing] a-ah-h-h-ing *Per1* aah—h—h—ing *Per2*

63:36 knows!] knows? *Per1*

63:39 circulation] circulating *Per1 see notes*

64:1 we seek, *MS, Per2*] ~ ~ *Per1*

64:1 passively, *MS, Per2*] ~ *Per1*

64:1 sleep, *MS, Per2*] ~ *Per1*

64:1 perhaps seek,] ~ ~ *Per1*

64:1 actively, *MS, Per2*] ~ *Per1*

64:2 pulling *Per1*] falling *MS*

64:2 blood, *MS, Per2*] ~ *Per1*

64:3 rhythm, *MS, Per2*] ~ *Per1*

64:7 debris *Per2*] dèbris *MS* débris *TCC1-2*

64:7 the day-Consciousness] the day-consciousness *TCC1-2* day-consciousness *Per1*

64:10 dances, *MS, Per2*] ~ *Per1*

64:11 shield *MS, Per2*] shields *Per1*

64:11 arm, *MS, Per2*] arms *Per1*

64:13 heart-pulsation *MS, Per2*] heart pulsation *Per1*

64:14 bird-tread *MS, Per2*] bird tread *Per1*

64:14 soft, heavy *MS, Per2*] soft-heavy *Per1*

64:14 towards *MS, Per2*] toward *Per1*

64:19 feet. *P* It] ~. It *Per2*

64:22 man. The creature...[64:28] hearts. *P* The other *MS, Per2*] man. *P* The other *Per1*

64:24 the single blood-stream] *Om. Per1* single existence *Per2*

64:27 our] *Om. Per1* our own *Per2*

64:29 see *MS, Per2*] ~, *Per1*

64:33 mystery. *P* Or *MS, Per2*] ~. Or *Per1*

64:34 deer dance, *MS, Per2*] Deer Dance, *Per1*

64:34 corn dance *MS, Per2*] Corn Dance *Per1*

64:35 deer dance *MS, Per2*] Deer Dance *Per1*

64:35 New Year *MS, Per2*] new year *Per1*

64:36 pueblo, *MS, A1*] ~: *E1*

64:36 long] *Om. Per1*

64:38 cotton-wood trees, *MS, Per2*] cottonwood trees *Per1*

64:40 deer-skin *MS, Per2*] deerskin *Per1* deer-/ skin *A1*

65:6 head: *MS, Per2*] ~; *Per1*

65:7 out: *MS, Per2*] ~; *Per1*

65:7 bear, *MS, Per2*] ~ *Per1*

65:8 come *MS, Per2*] came *Per1*

65:8 lines *MS, E1*] line lines *Per2*

65:8 animals, *MS, Per2, A1*] ~ *Per1* ~: *E1*

65:9 back, *MS, Per2*] ~ *TCC1-2*

65:9 boys, *MS, Per2*] ~ *Per1*

65:9 foxes, *MS, Per2*] ~ *Per1*

65:10 winter *MS, Per2*] Winter *Per1*

65:14 *being MS, Per2*] being *Per1*

65:15 dramatic *MS, Per2*] ~, *Per1*

65:15 naïve] naive *Per2*

65:17 wild *MS, Per2*] ~, *TCC1-2*

65:18 fox-skins *MS, Per2*] fox skins *Per1*

65:19 round *MS, Per2*] ~, *Per1*

65:21 wonder, *MS, Per2*] ~ *TCC1-2*

65:22 Amused *MS, Per2*] ~, *TCC1-2, E1*

65:30 ground, *MS, Per2*] ~ *Per1*

65:32 winter *MS, Per2*] Winter *Per1*

65:38 three-pulse] three-pulsed *Per1 see note on* 63:39

65:38 wide *MS, Per2*] ~, *Per1*

65:40 woman] women *Per1*

66:3 Now drama] Drama *Per1*

66:3 ceremonial *MS, Per2*] cremonial *Per1*

66:6 specific God] specific god *TCC1-2* particular god *Per1*

66:7 this God] this god *TCC1-2, Per2* such god *Per1*

66:8 *performed MS, Per2*] performed *Per1*

66:11 no god *MS, Per2*] no God *Per1*

66:16 God's Creation] God's creation *Per1*

66:17 Spirit *MS, Per2*] spirit *Per1*

66:17 Matter *MS, Per2*] matter *Per1*

66:18 of creation, *MS, Per2*] ~ ~; *TCC1-2*

66:19 bear,] bear; *TCC1-2* bears; *Per1* bears, *Per2*

66:20 deer, *MS, Per2*] ~ *Per1*

66:20 pine-boughs *MS, Per2*] pine boughs *TCC1-2*

66:22 winter, *MS, Per2*] Winter *Per1*

66:26 Godly] godly *Per1*

66:29 rattle-snake *MS, Per2*] rattlesnake *Per1* rattlesnake, *E1* rattle-snake, *A1*

66:30 a fawn *MS, Per2*] the fawn *Per1*

66:30 creation.] ~– *Per1* ~, *Per2*

66:31 There is no Creator: ... of creation, in] *Om. Per1 see note on* 66:32

66:32 mountain-lion, *MS, Per2*] mountain lion *Per1*

66:33 war-paint *MS, Per2*] war paint *Per1*

66:33 war-cry *MS, Per2*] war cry *Per1*

66:34 the old] old *Per1*

66:37 And to ... [67:5] creation, which ... [67:6] Nature. *Per2*] And to ... creation. *MS Om. Per1 see note at* 67:6

66:40 Mother] ~, *TCC1-2, Per2 Om. Per1*

67:2 mass] *Om. Per1* Mass *Per2*

67:8 no God *MS, Per2*] no god *Per1*

67:8 is, *MS, Per2*] ~ *Per1*

67:11 Ideal God *MS, Per2*] ideal god *Per1*

67:15 God Himself *MS, Per2*] god himself *Per1*

67:15 Goddess Herself *MS, Per2*] goddess herself *Per1*

67:16 God or Goddess *MS, Per2*] god or goddess *TCC1-2*

67:18 evolution, *MS, Per2*] ~ *Per1*

67:23 And *MS, Per1*] ~, *TCC1-2*

67:23 finally, *MS, Per2*] ~ *Per1*

67:24 The Indian ... [68:32] overtake him. *MS, Per2*] *Om. Per1 see also entries below*

67:27 man] a man *Per2*

67:30 warrior,] ~ *Per2*

67:33 abominations *Per2*] abomination *MS see notes*

67:33 cowards *MS, Per2*] ~, *E1*

68:10 Naked,] ~ *Per2*

68:20 on, on] ~, ~, *Per2*

68:24 strangely, *MS, Per2*] ~ *E1*

68:33 But what ... [68:36] from ours.] *Om. Per1 see notes*

The Dance of the Sprouting Corn

The order of the texts is *Per1, Per2, E1, A1*.

71:1 **The Dance of the Sprouting Corn** *Ed.*] THE DANCE OF THE SPROUTING CORN/ By D. H. LAWRENCE *Per1* THE

DANCE OF THE SPROUTING CORN/ *By* D. H. Lawrence *Per2 The Dance of the Sprouting Corn E1* VI/ THE DANCE

OF THE SPROUTING CORN
A1

71:27 door-way] doorway *Per2*

71:30 thud-thud-thud] thud—thud—
thud *Per2*

72:3 Thud-thud-thud-thud-thud]
Thud—thud—thud—thud—
thud *Per2*

73:1 silky,] ~ *Per2*

73:8 rhythmically *Per1*, *A1*] ryhthmi-
cally *E1*

73:9 out-out-out-out] out—out—
out—out *Per2*

73:25 under-shirt] undershirt *Per2*
under-/ shirt *A1*

73:27 handwoven] hand-woven *Per2*, *A1*
hand-/ woven *E1*

73:30 pine-sprays!] ~. *Per2*

73:34 downward-plunge] downward
plunge *Per2*

74:6 end] ~, *Per2*

74:6 feet] ~, *Per2*

74:7 boots,] ~ *Per2*

74:7 ankle *Per1*, *A1*] angle *Per2*

74:11 dropping] drooping *E1*

74:18 ceaseless] ceaselessly *Per2*

74:31 shirts] shirt *Per2*

75:1 pang-pang-pang] pang—pang—
pang *Per2*

75:9 emerald green] emerald-green
Per2

75:13 men dancers] men-dancers *Per2*

75:17 black-and-white *Per1*, *A1*] black
and white *E1*

75:26 corn husks] corn-husks *E1*

75:27 corn cob] corn-cob *E1*

75:28 dogs] ~. *Per2*

76:5 then] ~. *Per2*

76:9 moment,] ~ *Per2*

76:12 Kiva] kiva *E1*

76:15 one half,] one-half *Per2*

76:19 on] on the roofs of *Per2*

76:19 the low, round towers of the
kivas] the two low round
towers, the Kivas *Per2* the two
low round towers, the kivas *E1*

76:20 and take . . . dress,] *Om. Per2*

76:24 germination—not] ~, ~ *Per2*

76:34 influences,] ~ *Per2*

The Hopi Snake Dance

The order of the texts is *MS*, *Per1*, *Per2*, *E1*, *A1*, *TCC*.

79:1 **The Hopi Snake Dance** *Ed.*]
The Hopi Snake Dance/ by D.
H. Lawrence *MS* THE HOPI
SNAKE DANCE/ By D. H.
LAWRENCE *Per1* THE HOPI
SNAKE DANCE/ By D. H.
Lawrence *Per2* The Hopi Snake
Dance *E1* VII/ THE HOPI
SNAKE DANCE *A1*

79:2 Navajo country *Per1*] Navajo
Country *MS see note on* 79:3

79:3 Fe] Fé *Per2*

79:3 pueblo] Pueblo *Per2*

79:5 tract] track *E1*

79:5 tall,] ~ *E1*

79:9 half ruin] half-ruin *Per2*

79:11 is] it *Per2*

79:12 sun. P Walpi *MS*, *Per2*] ~. Walpi
Per1

79:15 rock cleft] rock-cleft *Per1*

79:21 the 17th August,] August 17th,
Per2

79:22 low] ~, *Per2*

79:22 grey sage scrub] gray sage-scrub
Per1 grey, sage-scrub *Per2*

79:24 cortège *Per1*] cortége *MS*

79:24 motorcars] motor cars *Per1* motor-
cars *Per2*

79:25 wending *MS*, *Per2*] wended *Per1*

79:27 dark-green *MS*, *E1*] dark green
Per1

79:29 mesa *Per1*] mesas *MS*

79:30 snake-dance] snake dance *Per2*

79:30 I am told *Per1*] they say *MS*

79:31 1924,] ~ *Per1*
80:3 black-beetle *MS, Per2*] black beetle *Per1*
80:3 school house] school-house *Per1* schoolhouse *Per2*
80:9 shoulders] shoulder *Per1*
80:11 motor cars] motorcars *Per1* motorcars *Per2*
80:12 bushes. *P* Hotevilla *MS, Per2*] ~. Hotevilla *Per1*
80:15 ruin] ruins *Per1*
80:15 two-storey *MS, Per2*] two-story *Per1*
80:16 window-holes. *P* It *MS, Per2*] ~. It *Per1*
80:17 parched] ~, *Per2*
80:18 thickly-built] thickly built *Per2*
80:19 peach-trees] peach trees *Per2*
80:21 the *Per1*] this *MS*
80:21 snake-dance] snake dance *Per2*
80:24 negroes:] ~; *Per1*
80:24 all] of all *Per1*
80:26 Mostly,] ~ *Per2*
80:27 *I . . . one!*]   "I . . . one!"   *Per1* *I . . . one! Per2, A1* "I . . . one!" *E1*
80:28 hair. *P* There *MS, Per2*] ~. There *Per1*
80:31 minute:] ~— *Per2*
80:33 Pavlova *MS, Per2*] Pavlowa *Per1*
80:34 ballet. *P* Or] Ballet. Or *Per1* Ballet. *P* Or *Per2*
80:36 snake-dance] snake dance *Per2*
80:36 are *MS, Per2*] *Om. Per1*
80:37 window holes] window-holes *Per2*
81:2 Church] church *Per1*
81:4 Church] church *Per2*
81:6 pet. *P* From *MS, Per2*] ~. From *Per1*
81:7 cultured *Per1*] cultural *MS see notes*
81:7 snake dance *MS, Per2*] Snake-dance *Per1*
81:11 cultured *Per1*] cultural *MS*
81:12 snake-dance] Snake-Dance *Per1* snake dance *Per2*
81:12 This] The *A1*
81:13 crowd. *P* As *MS, Per2*] ~. As *Per1*

81:14 cultured *Per1*] cultural *MS*
81:15 mouths. *P* And *MS, Per2*] ~. And *Per1*
81:16 tolerant,] ~ *Per1*
81:17 or,] ~ *Per2*
81:20 Indian's *MS, Per2, A1*] Indians' *Per1, E1*
81:20 Indians *Per1*] Indian's *MS*
81:21 snakes:] ~, *Per1*
81:23 anybody." *P* This *MS, Per2*] ~. This *Per1*
81:26 birds. *P* The *MS, Per2*] birds./ # *The Cosmic Dragon/ P* The *Per1*
81:27 the Spirit *Per1*] The Spirit *MS*
81:30 religion,] ~ *Per2*
81:32 to God *MS, Per2*] to god *Per1*
81:34 living *Per1*] dynamic *MS*
81:36 Sun *MS, Per2*] living Sun *Per1*
81:37 invisible] invincible *Per1 see notes*
81:38 inter-related] interrelated *E1* inter-/ related *A1*
81:38 emerges . . . seed] emerge . . . seeds *Per1*
82:4 vast] *Om. Per1*
82:5 gods. *P* Everything] Gods. Everything *Per1* Gods. *P* Everything *Per2*
82:9 like the] like *Per1*
82:10 incomprehensible. *MS, Per2*] ~? *Per1*
82:11 beasts? *P* It *MS, Per2*] ~? It *Per1*
82:12 says,] ~ *Per2*
82:16 American Indian] American-Indian *E1*
82:17 Not-God] not-God *Per1*
82:17 though *Per1*] but *MS*
82:19 monster *Per1*] beast *MS*
82:19 huge reptile-bird *Per1*] bird *MS*
82:21 dragon-mouthed *Per1*] *Om. MS*
82:22 feathered *Per1*] *Om. MS*
82:23 reservoirs] ~, *E1*
82:26 livingly] warily *Per1* fairly *Per2*
82:31 The serpent-striped, feathery Rain. *Per1*] *Om. MS*
82:33 make] made *Per1*
82:34 like *MS, E1*] ~, *Per2*
82:35 him, *Per1*] ~. *MS*

82:35 pitted . . . Cosmic Dragon.
Per2] *Om. MS* pitted . . . cosmic
Dragon. *Per1*

82:37 His] his *Per1*

82:37 foreordained *MS*, *Per2*] foreordained *Per1*

82:38 us] *Om. Per1*

82:38 terrific, terrible, crude Source
Per1] mysterious, terrible source
MS

82:40 Dragons *Per1*] Potencies *MS*

82:40 The Potencies or Powers *Per2*]
Om. MS ~ ~, ~ ~ *Per1*

83:1 earth] Earth *Per2*

83:1 birds] ~, *Per2*

83:3 gods.] Gods. *Per1*

83:3 They are Dragons . . . vast and
most powerful, *Per2*] *Om. MS* ~
~ ~ . . . ~ ~ ~ ~. *Per1* ~ ~
~ . . . ~, ~ ~ ~, *E1*

83:4 yet . . . in being *Per2, E1*] Yet they
are vast and more powerful *MS*
Yet . . . in being *Per1*

83:5 gods . . . are men *Per1*] god . . . is
man *MS*

83:6 evolved . . . with aeons *Per2*] *Om.
MS* evolved . . . through æons
Per1 evolved . . . with æons *E1*

83:9 hammers of *MS*, *A1*] hammers or
Per2

83:10 furnace . . . men, *Per1*] forge,
where the small gods *MS*

83:11 themselves *Per1*] ~. *MS*

83:11 into being. *Per1*] *Om. MS*

83:15 gods are] gods *Per1*

83:15 flowers,] ~; *Per1*

83:17 dragon-clutch *Per1*] powers *MS*

83:18 succour *Per1*] starve *MS*

83:18 flick him . . . destroy him . . .
existence, out . . . of chaos. *Per2*]
wither him or call him into
being. *MS* flick him . . . kill
him . . . existence out . . . of chaos.
Per1

83:20 Man is delicate . . . beyond flowers, *Per1*] He is delicate and godly,
MS

83:22 and hold . . . again conquer *Per1*]
conquer, conquer *MS*

83:24 Hence,] ~ *Per1*

83:26 by] by the *Per1*

83:28 This is . . . [83:32] gentle-hearted.
Per1] *Om. MS*

83:34 those] these *Per1*

83:35 rock] rocks *Per1*

83:35 snakes] ~, *Per2*

83:36 There] These *Per1*

83:39 The destiny . . . Spirit. *Per1*] *Om.
MS*

84:2 motor cars] motorcars *Per1* motor-
cars *Per2*

84:4 tourists,] ~ *Per1*

84:5 snake-dance] snake dance *E1*

84:7 man, *Per1*] ~. *MS*

84:7 pitted . . . dragon-cosmos. *Per1*]
Om. MS

84:10 years of] years' *Per1*

84:11 Sun] sun *Per1*

84:13 of the *Per1*] of our the *MS*

84:14 Our *Per1*] The *MS*

84:14 And we . . . stings us in . . .
plenty. *Per2*] *Om. MS* And
we . . . stings us with misery
in . . . plenty. *Per1*

84:15 *Quos vult perdere Deus, dementat
prius. P* On Ed.] *Om. MS* Quos
vult perdere, Dementat prius, dementat./ # *Ày-a! Ày-a! Ày-a!/ P* On
*Per1 Quos vult perdere Deus, demen-
tat prius./ # THE HOPI SNAKE
DANCE/ By D. H. Lawrence/
Continued from p. 692/ P* On *Per2*
see note at 84:16

84:19 cottonwood] cotton-wood *Per2*

84:20 green, *MS, Per2*] ~ *Per1*

84:20 wooden] *Om. Per2*

84:21 trap-door *MS, E1*] trap door *Per2,
A1*

84:22 twelve officiating *Per1*] officiating
twelve *MS*

84:31 the pattering . . . from *Per1*]
that comes from the breast
of the rain-mystery-monster in
MS

84:32 rain-god] rain-gods *Per1*
84:33 lurking, intense *Per1*] dynamic *MS*
84:35 source *Per1*] sun *MS*
84:38 rattle-snakes] rattlesnakes *Per1*
84:39 It is said *Per1*] They say *MS*
85:1 Hopi, *MS, Per2*] ~ *Per1*
85:3 sundown *Per2*] sundown on the Sunday *MS see notes*
85:4 Dance] dance *A1*
85:4 stand *Per1*] are still, *MS*
85:4 wait *Per1*] waites *MS*
85:7 "brotherhood" *MS, Per2*] brotherhood *Per1*
85:7 animals!] ~ *Per1*
85:7 best,] ~ *Per1*
85:8 difference.—] ~. *Per2*
85:14 long. The] ~. *P* The *Per1*
85:24 man *MS, Per2*] priest *Per1*
85:27 trap-door *MS, E1*] trap door *Per1, A1*
85:27 stamps] ~, *E1*
85:30 green,] ~; *Per1*
85:32 naked, *MS, Per2*] ~ *Per1*
85:33 smeared paint *Per1*] black *MS*
85:35 middle aged] middle-aged *Per2*
85:36 school-boys *MS, Per2*] schoolboys *Per1, E1*
85:37 men, *Per1*] men is *MS, A1*
85:37 is *Per1, E1*] and is *MS, Per2, A1*
85:37 round. *P* The *MS, Per2*] ~. The *Per1*
86:2 snake priests] snake-priests *Per2*
86:3 number. *P* They *MS, Per2*] ~. They *Per1*
86:7 third.—*MS, Per2*] ~. *Per1, E1*
86:11 to *MS, Per2*] to the *Per1*
86:11 antelope priests] antelope-priests *Per2*
86:13 Ay-a! Ay-a! Ay-a! *MS, Per2*] Ày-a! Ày-a! Ày-a! *Per1*
86:14 flat] ~, *Per2*
86:14 hand, at each shake, *MS, Per2*] hand *Per1*
86:18 time, D ~ *Per1*
86:18 heavy,] ~ *Per1*
86:23 unchanneled] unchannelled *Per2*

86:23 life-passion *MS, Per2*] life passion *Per1*
86:25 men, *Per1*] ~. *MS*
86:25 from . . . dark sun. *Per1*] *Om. MS*
86:32 core. *P* This *MS, Per2*] ~. This *Per1*
86:33 for] *Om. Per1*
86:33 antelope priests] antelope-priests *Per2*
86:35 low, *MS, Per2*] ~ *Per1*
86:38 times,] ~ *Per1*
86:38 in-sunk] insunk *Per1*
86:39 that too *MS, Per2*] -, -, *Per1*
87:2 him,—] ~— *Per1*
87:4 Indian's] Indians *Per2* Indians' *E1*
87:6 priest] priests *Per2*
87:16 away. A brief . . . performance. *P* The *Per2*] away. *P* The *MS* away. A brief . . . performance. The *Per1*
87:19 And *MS, Per2*] ~, *Per1*
87:19 therefore,] ~ *Per2*
87:20 crowd. *P* By *MS, Per2*] crowd./ # *Snakes from the Kiva/ P* By *Per1*
87:21 on] of *Per1*
87:27 full]] ~, *Per2*
87:30 hours and hours] hours *Per2*
87:31 policemen] policeman *Per2*
87:34 antelope priests] antelope-priests *E1*
87:35 antelope priests] antelope-priests *E1*
87:36 feet were] feet *Per1*
87:36 like suede *MS, Per2, A1*] like suède *Per1, E1*
87:37 pure suède *MS, Per1, E1*] pure suede *Per2, A1*
87:38 pale-grey *MS, E1*] pale grey *Per1*
87:38 the] *Om. Per1*
88:2 kiva] *Om. Per1*
88:5 Lords of . . . power of change. *Per1*] *Om. MS*
88:10 Twelve men . . . quarters: east, north, south, west, above and below *Per2*] *Om. MS* Twelve men . . . quarters—east, west, north, south, above and below

Peri Twelve men ... quarters: east, north, south, west, above, and below *Ei*

88:12 Their bodies ... snake marks] *Om. Peri see note on* 88:13

88:15 hot,] ~ *Peri*

88:20 towards *MS, Per2*] toward *Peri*

88:20 boys. *P* Then *MS, Per2*] ~. Then *Peri*

88:21 chant,] ~ *Per2*

88:22 one-two, one-two, one-two] óne-two, óne-two *Peri* one-two, one-two *Per2*

88:27 But the *MS, Per2*] The *Peri*

88:27 great] *Om. Peri*

88:28 wait for *Peri*] wait for/for *MS*

88:31 two] *Om. Peri*

88:32 antelope priest] antelope-priest *Ei*

88:34 else,] ~ *Per2*

88:34 snake-priest] priest *Peri see notes*

88:35 rattle-snake] rattlesnake *Peri, Ai* rattle-/snake *Ei*

88:36 naïve] naive *Ei*

88:36 rattle-snake] rattlesnake *Peri*

88:38 paced] passed *Peri*

88:39 snake *Peri*] serpent *MS*

88:40 leaping *MS, Per2*] heaping *Peri*

89:1 oldest,] ~ *Per2*

89:2 feather-prayer-sticks *MS, Per2*] feather prayer-sticks *Peri*

89:3 men,] ~ *Per2*

89:7 then another:] ~ ~, *Peri*

89:8 a] all *Peri*

89:8 probably, *MS, Per2*] *Om. Peri*

89:10 round,] ~ *Per2*

89:11 stooped,] ~ *Peri*

89:15 rattle-snake's] rattlesnake's *Peri*

89:19 half mesmerised] half-mesmerised *Per2*

89:22 snake] ~, *Peri*

89:23 pale] ~, *Per2*

89:27 bird like] bird-like *Peri*

89:28 antelope priests] antelope-priests *Ei*

89:30 their mouths *MS, Per2*] his mouth *Peri*

89:31 rattle-snake] rattlesnake *Peri*

89:32 ship, *MS, Per2*] ~ *Peri, Ei*

89:33 priests *Peri*] men *MS*

89:33 the snake-sticks] snake-sticks. *Peri*

89:34 snake-catchers *MS, Ei*] snake catchers *Per2*

89:35 in the air] *Om. Peri*

89:36 interim,] ~ *Per2*

89:37 very] *Om. Per*

89:40 boy's *Peri*] boys *MS*

90:4 as quietly *Peri*] quietly *MS*

90:5 behind him,] *Om. Peri*

90:7 naïve] naive *Per2*

90:13 actor-like *Peri*] dramatic *MS*

90:13 But *Peri*] And *MS*

90:14 spell, *Peri*] ~. *MS*

90:14 something ... world. *Peri*] *Om. MS*

90:17 towards *MS, Per2*] toward *Peri*

90:18 minute,] ~ *Peri*

90:20 snake] Snake *Peri*

90:22 mouth] mouths *Peri*

90:24 rattle-snakes] rattlesnakes *Peri*

90:26 whip-snakes *Peri*] whip-/snakes *MS* whipsnakes *Per2*

90:30 antelope men] antelope-men *Ei*

90:32 men *Peri*] priests *MS*

90:32 arms *Peri*] arm *MS*

90:34 bellies. *P* Yet *MS, Per2*] ~. Yet *Peri*

90:37 beauty] ~, *Per2*

90:39 in the days *Peri*] the days *MS*

91:2 out-running] outrunning *Peri*

91:10 near] *Om. Peri*

91:14 again, *Peri*] ~ *MS*

91:14 and with ... snakes, the ... priests *Per2*] into the arms of the two young priests, in a moment the two young men had armfuls of snakes again, and with these they *MS* and with ... snakes the ... priests *Peri*

91:16 towards *MS, Per2*] toward *Peri*

91:21 Arizona, submerged in light. *P* Away *Per2*] Arizona. *P* Away. *MS* Arizona, submerged in light. Away. *Peri*

91:22 on] *Om. Per1*
91:23 were] went *Per1*
91:24 diminishing, diminishing] diminishing *Per2*
91:24 towards *MS, Per2*] toward *Per1*
91:26 tiny] ∼, *Per2*
91:26 gods. *P* They *MS, Per2*] gods./ # *Specks of Gods/ P* They *Per1*
91:29 Free,] ∼ *Per2*
91:30 messages] message *Per1*
91:30 dragon-gods . . . and   withhold. *Per1*] rain-god. MS
91:31 breath *Per1*] will *MS*
91:34 feather-prayer-sticks *MS, Per2*] feather prayer-sticks *Per1*
91:37 will-power *MS, E1*] will power *Per2*
91:39 scattered, *MS, Per2*] ∼ *Per1*
91:40 dread] ∼, *Per2*
92:3 infallible] *Om. Per1*
92:4 is a] is *Per1*
92:5 call Sun] call sun *Per1*
92:8 unwillingness,] ∼ *Per1*
92:12 he is *Per1*] *Om. MS*
92:12 sustained and threatened, menaced and sustained *Per1*] sustained and threatened, sustained and threatened *MS*
92:13 Source, *Per1*] ∼. *MS*
92:13 the innermost sun-dragon. *Per2*] *Om. MS* the . . . Sun-dragon *Per1*
92:17 comprehension *Per1*] ∼. *MS*
92:17 also. *P* For the . . . snatch manhood . . . [92:20] Cosmos *Per2*] *Om. MS* also. For the . . . snatch further manhood . . . cosmos *Per1*
92:21 little Man] little man *Per2*
92:21 will] ∼, *Per2*
92:22 Conquered by . . . fears, the snakes *Per1*] The snakes, conquered by man who has overcome his fear, *MS*
92:24 his *Per1*] *Om. MS*
92:24 power *Per1*] command *MS*
92:29 rattle-snake's] rattlesnake's *Per1*
92:30 issue *Per1*] secret *MS*
92:30 Because,] ∼ *Per2*

92:34 virtue *Per1*] quality *MS*
92:35 primitive *Per1*] *Om. MS*
92:35 morality *Per1*] godliness *MS*
93:1 (so-called)] ∼, *Per2*
93:4 men] *Om. Per2*
93:7 running up *Per1*] emerging *MS*
93:10 washing] ∼, *Per2*
93:11 pool:] ∼; *Per2*
93:14 the] *Om. Per2*
93:17 rattle snake] rattlesnake *Per1*
93:18 until,] ∼ *Per2*
93:18 strike] strikes *E1*
93:19 Not enough . . . kill. *Per1*] *Om. MS*
93:21 emerges *MS, A1*] merges *Per2*
93:22 artery. *P* Therefore *Per2*] ∼. *P* Also *MS* ∼. Therefore *Per1*
93:23 in] of *Per2*
93:27 them. *P* We *MS, Per2*] ∼. We *Per1*
93:29 rattle-snake] rattlesnake *Per1*
93:30 powers. *P* To *MS, Per2*] ∼. To *Per1*
93:32 cruelty . . . things, *Per1*] *Om. MS*
93:33 and *MS, Per2*] and in *Per1*
93:34 towards *MS, Per2*] toward *Per1*
93:34 man] Man *Per1*
93:34 the godhead *MS, Per2*] the Godhead *Per1*
93:35 forever] for ever *Per2*
93:35 this *Per1*] this our *MS*
93:36 orientals] Orientals *E1*
93:36 God-head] Godhead *Per1*
94:1 To us, God . . . back. *P* To *Per2*] *Om. MS* To us and the orientals, God . . . back only the rudiments of our Godhead. To *Per1*
94:3 the Hopi . . . being, the . . . [94:5] godhead. *Per2*] *Om. MS* the Hopi . . . being. *Per1* the Hopi . . . being, the . . . Godhead. *E1*
94:6 negation] negations *Per2*
94:7 quickest *Per1*] easiest *MS*
94:7 conquerors *Per1*] ∼. *MS*
94:7 for the moment. *Per1*] *Om. MS*
94:11 unceasing. *P* This *MS, Per2*] ∼. This *Per1*
94:13 Maya] ∼, *Per2*

94:14 religion. *P* Until *MS*, *Per2*] ∼.
Until *Per1*
94:16 success *Per1*] overlordship *MS*
94:25 over, *MS*, *Per2*] ∼ *Per1*
94:26 western] Western *Per2*
94:31 on their hips *Per1*] *Om. MS*

94:32 spring *Per1*] pool *MS*
94:32 intent] *Om. Per1*
94:33 vision, *MS*, *Per2*] ∼ *Per1*
94:36 So,] ∼ *Per2*
94:38 motor cars] motor-cars *Per1*
94:39 rattle-snakes] rattlesnakes *Per1*

A Little Moonshine with Lemon

The order of texts is *TCC1*, *TCC2*, *Per*, *E1*, *A1*.

97:1 **A Little Moonshine with Lemon** *Ed.*] *Om. TCC1* A Little Moonshine With Lemon/ Lemon/ *By D. H. Lawrence Per A Little Moonshine with Lemon E1* VIII/ A LITTLE MOON-SHINE WITH LEMON *A1*
97:2 narrow world/ Like *TCC1*, *Per*] narrow/ world like *TCC2 narrow world/ Like A1*
97:3 Colossus—] Colosses— *TCC2* Colossus . . *Per* Colossus . . . *E1 Colossus . . . A1*
97:4 bright] a bright *TCC2*
97:4 shadow] ∼, *Per*
97:7 emerges] advances *Per*
97:7 feast-day] feast day *Per*
97:8 day *TCC1*, *Per*] Day *TCC2*, *E1*
97:9 Vermouth] vermouth *Per*
97:12 shall consider] consider *Per*
97:12 there] ∼, *Per*
97:13 south-east] southeast, *Per* south-east, *E1*
97:13 Fe] Fé *E1*
97:19 *nuovo*—! *Ed.*] *muovo*—! *TCC1 nuovo*—! *Per*
97:22 they] They *Per*
97:23 Catherine *Per*] Cathereine *TCC1*
97:32 tree-trunk *Per*] ∼, *TCC1*
98:1 fence.] ∼! *Per*
98:1 beyond, *Per*] ∼/ *TCC1* ∼ *TCC2*
98:3 Ranchos *TCC2*] Ranches *TCC1*
98:4 sky line] sky-line *Per*, *A1* skyline *E1*

98:5 nearly-full *TCC*, *A1*] nearly full *E1*
98:6 wolf-like] wolf-life *Per*
98:6 he] it *Per*
98:6 blazes,] ∼; *Per*
98:7 hoar *Per*] hear *TCC1*
98:9 Ranchos *Per*] Ranches *TCC1*
98:9 Taos. And] ∼. *P* And *Per*
98:11 mountains] ∼, *Per*
98:14 Goodnight] good night *E1*
98:14 spell.—] ∼. *Per*
98:14 *giù*, *E1*] *qui*, *TCC1 giu Per*
98:17 whistling] ∼, *Per*
98:18 youth.] ∼! *Per*
98:19 childlike] child-like *E1*
98:19 naive.] ∼! *Per*
98:27 night. Cows *Per*] night/ Cows *TCC1* night cows *TCC2*
98:28 It] The moon *Per*
98:28 round] around *Per*
98:31 stealthy, *Per*] stealth/ *TCC1* stealth *TCC2*
98:35 one's *TCC2*] one/ *TCC1*
98:35 one *TCC2*], ones *TCC1*
98:36 most, *Per*] ∼/ *TCC1* ∼ *TCC2*
98:36 Mountains] ∼, *Per*
98:38 me *TCC2*] me one *TCC1*
99:2 pine tree] pine trees *Per* pine-trees *E1* *see notes*
99:6 up.—] ∼. *Per*
99:8 still,] ∼ *Per*
99:15 pine tree] pine-tree *E1*
99:17 Si verra la primavera] *Si vedra la primavera Per Si vedrà la primavera E1*

99:18 Fiorann' le mandorline— *Ed.*]
Fiovann' le mandorine— *TCC₁*
Fiovanno le mandorine— *TCC₂*
Fiorann' le mandorline— Per Fio-
rann' i mandorlini— E₁ see notes
99:19 Ah] ~, *TCC₂*
99:20 wanted un poco . . . cannella e
limone – – –] wanted un poco

di chiar . . . cancella e limone—
TCC₂ wanted *P "Un poco di chiar'*
di luna, con canella e limone . . . . ."
Per wanted: *P "Un poco di*
chiar' . . . canella e limone . . . ." E₁
wanted *P "Un poco di chiar' . . .*
canella e limone . . . ." A₁

Certain Americans and an Englishman

The order of the texts is *TS₁* (to 106:2), *Per*, *TS₂*, *E₁*.

105:1 **Certain Americans and an**
Englishman *Ed.*] *Om. TS₁* Certain Americans and an English-
man/ *By D. H. LAWRENCE*
Per "Certain Americans and
an Englishman"/ by D. H.
Lawrence *TS₂* Certain Americans and an Englishman *E₁*
105:2 I *Per*] But I *TS₁ see notes*
105:2 in New Mexico *Per*] *Om. TS₁*
105:3 Bursum *Per*] Bursom *TS₁*
105:3 Bill] bill *Per*
105:5 affects *Per*] effects *TS₁*
105:4 it,] ~ *Per*
105:5 needn't. But] needn't. *P* But *Per*
105:5 Bursum Bursum Bursum!! *Ed.*]
Bursom Bursom Bursom!! *TS₁*
Bursum, Bursum, Bursum! *Per*
105:5 Bill! . . . Bill! . . . Bill] Bill, . . .
Bill, . . . Bill *Per*
105:6 Twitchell!!] ~! *Per*
105:7 Fall! you] ~, ~ *Per*
105:8 Fall!!!] ~! *Per*
105:8 Oh] ~, *Per*
105:8 now] Now *Per*
105:9 Whoa!] *Om. E₁*
105:9 Whoa Bursum *Ed.*] Whoa Bursom *TS₁* Whoa, Bursum *Per*
105:9 Whoa Bill!] ~, ~ *Per*
105:9 Lindsay] Vachell Lindsay *Per*
Vachel Lindsay *E₁*
105:10 bellowing] ~, *Per*
105:11 heed. And] heed. *P* And *Per*

105:11 solemnly sit down] sit down
solemnly *Per*
105:12 Printed] printed *Per*
105:12 Bursum Bill *Ed.*] Bursom Bill
TS₁ Bursum bill *Per*
105:14 Insomuch-as   *TS₁*,   *Per*]
insomuch-as *TS₂*
105:15 C's] C.'s *Per*
105:17 H's] H.'s *Per*
105:18 M's] M.'s *Per*
105:17 *for*] for *Per*
105:18 up,] ~. *Per*
105:18 and Bear . . . Bursum. *Ed.*] and
Bear . . . Bursum. *TS₁ Om. Per*
105:18 Then] ~, *Per*
105:18 Lamb-like] lamb-like *Per*
105:19 butting] ~, *Per*
105:23 doing] ~, *Per*
105:24 circus-tent] circus tent *Per*
105:31 *at*] at *Per*
105:32 no,] ~; *Per*
105:32 me] ~, *Per*
105:33 bewildered] ~, *Per*
106:1 head-or-tail] head or tail *Per*
106:4 defenceless *E₁*] defenseless *Per*
106:5 defenceless *E₁*] defenseless *Per*
107:12 no-man's *Per*] no man's *TS₂*
108:17 &c., *Per*] etc. *TS₂*
108:30 Guadalupe *TS₂*] Guadaloupe *Per*
see notes
108:37 Secretary *Per*] secretary *E₁*
108:38 Pueblo *Per*] pueblo *E₁*
109:1 Pueblo *Per*] pueblo *E₁*

109:23 Pueblos *Per*] pueblos *TS2*   109:37 Pueblos *Per*] pueblos *TS2*
109:33 Pueblos *Per*] pueblos *TS2*   110:1 Pueblos *Per*] pueblos *TS2*

Indians and an Englishman

The order of the texts is *TS, TSR, TSC, Per1, Per2, TCC, A1*.

113:1 **Indians and an Englishman**
   Ed.] PUEBLOS AND AN
   ENGLISHMAN/ by/ *D.*
   H. LAWRENCE TS INDI-
   ANS AND AN ENGLISH-
   MAN/ by/ D. H. LAWRENCE
   TSR INDIANS AND AN
   ENGLISHMAN/ BY D. H.
   LAWRENCE *Per1* INDIANS
   AND/ AN ENGLISHMAN/
   By D. H. Lawrence *Per2* INDI-
   ANS AND AN ENGLISH-
   MAN. *TCC* INDIANS AND
   AN ENGLISHMAN *A1*
113:2 on to] onto *A1*
113:5 South West] Southwest *TSC*
113:7 woollyness] woolliness *TSC*
113:7 motor-cars *TS, Per2*] motor cars
   TSC
113:11 motor-cars *TS, Per2*] motor cars
   TSC
113:12 high-brows] highbrows *TSC*
113:13 ecstatic,] ~; *TCC*
113:14 life,] ~; *TCC*
113:17 on to] onto *A1*
113:22 That *TS, TCC*] The *Per2*
113:25 bad on purpose] bad-on-purpose,
   TSC bad-on-purpose; *TCC* bad
   on purpose; *A1*
113:26 Pioneers,] ~! *A1*
113:26 Oh] Oh, *TSC, TCC* O, *Per2* O
   A1
113:26 high-brow] highbrow *TSC*
113:27 everything *TS, TCC*] ~, *Per2*
113:28 depths,] ~; *TCC*
113:28 not yet Gringo,] yet not Gringo,
   TSC not Gringo, *Per1* not gringo;
   TCC
113:30 tacitly: *TS, TCC*] ~, *Per1*
113:30 on,] ~; *TCC*

114:6 woollyness] woolliness *TSC*
114:7 depths,] ~— *Per1*
114:14 high-brows] highbrows *TSC*
114:19 intellect:] ~; *Per1*
114:19 republican] Republican *TSC*
114:19 democrat:] Democrat: *TSC*
   Democrat, *Per1* Democrat; *TCC*
114:20 lost] *Om. Per1*
114:20 circus-ring] circus ring *A1*
114:23 state *TS, A1*] State *Per2*
114:23 motor-car *TS, Per2*] motor car
   TSC
114:24 canyons] cañons *A1*
114:26 pine-tree] pine tree *TSC*
114:31 Da donde viene, Usted?"…..]
   Da donde viene, Usted?"… TSC,
   Per2, TCC Da donde viene,
   Ustèd?"… Per1 De donde viene
   Usted?"… A1 see notes
114:34 blanketted] blanketed *TSC*
114:39 blanketted] blanketed *TSC*
115:11 Fenimore *TS, TCC*] Fennimore
   Per2
115:12 west] West *TSC*
115:14 hats,] ~/ *TCC* ~ *A1*
115:22 pàt-pat, pàt-pat *TSR*] pat-pat,
   pat-pat *TS see notes*
115:24 mouths,] ~: *TCC*
115:24 Hie! Hie! Hie!] **Hie! Hie! Hie!**
   Per1 Hie! Hie! Hie! Per2
115:24 Hỳ-a! Hỳ-a! Hỳ-a! *TSR, TCC*]
   Hy-a! Hy-a! Hy-a! *TS, A1* **Hy-a!**
   Hy-a! Hy-a! *Per1 Hy-a! Hỳ-a!*
   Hỳ-a! Per2 see note on 115:22
115:24 Hie! Hie! Hie!] **Hie! Hie! Hie!**
   Per1 Hie! Hie! Hie! Per2
115:25 Ay-away-away!!] **Ay-away-**
   away!! *Per1 Ay-away-away!!*
   Per2 Ay-away-away! *TCC* Ay-
   away-away-a! *A1*

115:27 ecstasy *TSR*] ecstacy *TS*
115:31 aspen-twig] aspen twig *TSC*
115:34 pàt-pat, pàt-pat, pàt-pat *TSR*] pat-pat, pat-pat, pat-pat *TS* pàt-pat, pàt-pat *TCC*
115:36 pàt-pat, pàt-pat, pàt-pat *TSR*] pat-pat, pat-pat-pat-pat *TS*
115:40 pàt-pat, pàt-pat, *TSR*] pat-pat, pat-pat, *TS* pàt-pat, pàt-pat *TCC*
116:1 inwards] ~, *Per1*
116:3 song, shout *TS*, *TCC*] song-shout *Per2*
116:4 pine-trees *TS*, *TCC*] pine trees *Per1*, *A1*
116:6 pàt-pat, pàt-pat *TSR*] pat-pat, pat-pat *TS*
116:7 laughing] ~, *TCC*
116:8 shriek *TSR*] squeal *TS*
116:11 war whoop] war-whoop *Per1*
116:11 They produce... feel good. *TSR*] *Om. TS*
116:13 unbearable] unbearably *TCC*
116:21 The war-whoop! *TSR*] *Om. TS*
116:25 pine-trees *TS*, *TCC*] pine trees *TSC*, *A1*
116:25 far-off] far off *TSC*
116:28 meet.] ~? *Per1*
117:2 went *TSR*] *Om. TS*
117:6 country *TSR*] company *TS*
117:10 of the... crouching figures *TSR*] So I felt I may have been all wrong, and other folks may feel much many crouching figures. *TS*
117:15 grape juice] grape-juice *Per2*
117:16 Cowboys *TS*, *A1*] Cow-boys *Per1*
117:17 cow-girl] cowgirl *A1*
117:18 night *TSR*] dark *TS*
117:19 sportiveness *TSR*] sportiness *TS*
117:21 harmless-harmful *TSR*] harmless harmful *TS*
117:22 ridicule *TSR*] not jolly at all *TS*
117:30 together] ~, *TCC*
117:31 song yells] song-yells *TSC*
117:31 pat-pat] patpat *TSC* pàt-pat *Per1*
117:33 drink tent] drink-tent *TCC*
117:36 cowboys *TS*, *A1*] cow-boys *Per1*

117:37 cow-girl] cowgirl *A1*
117:38 gibing *TSR*] mocking *TS*
118:2 It seemed... the kiva. *TSR*] *Om. TS*
118:7 anyone's *TS*, *Per2*, *TCC*] any one's *TSC*
118:7 Within... firelight. *TSR*] *Om. TS*
118:7 And *TSR*] But *TS*
118:10 circle, *TSR*] ~. *TS*
118:10 of which... the key. *TSR*] *Om. TS*
118:13 half veiled] half-veiled *TSC*
118:15 far off] far-off *TSC*
118:18 bread cake] bread-cake *TCC*
118:19 Those nearer... restless. *TSR*] The rest of the circle came and went. *TS*
118:25 half-self-conscious] half self-conscious *TSC*
118:31 Buenos!] *Buenos! TSC*, *TCC Buenos! Per1*
118:32 Buenos!] *Buenos! TSC*, *TCC Buenos! Per1*
118:33 Que quiere?] *Que quiere? TSC Qué quiere? Per1*
118:34 No hablo espagnol] *No hablo espagnol TSC No hablo español Per1*
118:35 Oh] ~, *Per1*
118:35 eh?— *TS*, *TCC*] ~? *A1*
118:37 Church] church *A1*
119:1 church *TS*, *TCC*] Church *Per2*
119:5 There was none. *TCR*] *Om. TS*
119:6 sotto voce] *sotto voce TSC*
119:6 door. P The] ~. The *Per1*
119:7 complete,] ~; *TCC*
119:8 men were *TCR*] *Om. TS*
119:16 attention,] ~; *TCC*
119:16 it *TCR*] *Om. TS*
119:20 voice,] ~/ *TCC* ~ *A1*
119:20 plangent] ~, *TCC*
119:25 waist *TSR*] face *TS*
119:25 moccasins *Per1*] mocassins *TS*
119:27 mask-like *TS*, *Per1*] masklike *TSC*
119:29 living *Per1*] lining *TS*

119:33 chewing gum] chewing-gum *TCC*
119:35 sometimes] some times *TSC*
119:37 As for me *TSR*] And I myself *TS*
120:1 pine-tree darkness] darkness *TSC*
120:8 our tissue *TSR*] tissue *TS*
120:10 blood-shed] bloodshed *TSC* blood-/ shed *A1*

120:12 ah] ~, *Per1*
120:12 them, or] ~ ~ *Per1*
120:20 Ah] ~, *Per1*
120:24 like to *TSR*] fain *TS*
120:25 fire light] firelight *Per1* firelight, *TCC*
120:28 Just near . . . [121:8] of a] *Om. Per1*
121:6 I imagined the *TSR*] *Om. TS*

Taos

The order of the texts is *Per1*, *Per2*, *TCC1*, *TCC2*, *A1*.

125:1 **Taos** *Ed.*] TAOS/ BY D. H. LAWRENCE *Per1* AT TAOS/ An Englishman Looks at Mexico/ *By* D. H. LAWRENCE *Per2* TAOS/ by D. H. Lawrence *TCC1* TAOS./ By/ D. H. Lawrence. *TCC2* TAOS *A1*
125:3 Francisco *Per1*, *TCC1*] ~, *TCC2*
125:9 afterlife. *P* Taos *Per1*, *TCC1*] afterlife. # *P* Taos *Per2* after-life. *P* Taos *TCC2*
125:10 pueblo *Per1*, *TCC1*] pueblo* *Per2* *see notes*
125:17 Lyons, *Per1*, *TCC1*] Lyo/ *TCC2* Lyon *A1* *see notes*
125:29 good. *P* But *Per1*, *TCC1*] ~. # *P* But *Per2*
126:8 tom-tom] tomtom *A1*
126:12 slow *Per1*, *TCC1*, *A1*] ~, *Per2*
126:20 day *Per1*, *TCC1*] ~, *TCC2*
126:20 morning *Per1*, *TCC1*] ~, *TCC2*
126:21 may-pole *Per1*, *TCC1*] may-/ pole *Per2* maypole *A1*

126:26 game. *P* An *Per1*, *TCC1*] ~. # *P* An *Per2*
126:30 kodak] Kodak *A1*
126:32 kodak] Kodak *A1*
126:33 dollar,] ~ *TCC2*
126:33 see.] ~? *TCC2*
126:34 camera,] ~; *TCC2*
126:35 this] the *TCC2*
126:35 kodak] Kodak *A1*
126:36 sullenly, *Per1*, *TCC1*] ~ *Per2*
127:6 known] ~, *TCC2*
127:7 church-door *Per1*, *TCC1*] church door *Per2*, *A1*
127:15 excuses. *P* "Of *Per1*, *TCC1*] ~. # *P* "Of *Per2*
127:21 listened] ~, *TCC2*
127:33 tom-tom] tomtom *A1*
128:6 encouragers. *P* As *Per1*, *TCC1*] ~. # *P* As *Per2*
128:8 dispersed,] ~; *TCC2*
128:11 ordeal,] ~/ *TCC2* ~ *A1*
128:14 *laisser faire Per1*, *TCC1*] *laissez-faire Per2*, *A1*

Au Revoir, U. S. A.

The order of the texts is *Per*, *A1*.

131:1 **Au Revoir, U. S. A.** *Ed.*] Au Revoir, U. S. A./ by D. H. Lawrence. *Per* AU REVOIR, U. S. A. *A1*
131:2 "Say] ~ *A1*

131:3 *goodbye*] *good-bye A1*
131:5 sigh. . . ."] ~ *A1*
131:18 Any how] anyhow *A1*
131:28 Rio] Rió *Per*
131:28 Grande,] ~ *A1*

131:33 Teotihuacán *Ed.*] Teotihuacan *Per*
132:1 continent— *A1*] ~ - - - *Per*
132:2 rattle-snake] rattlesnake *A1*
132:4 rattlesnake] rattle/ snake *A1*
132:10 ricketty] rickety *A1*
132:13 Northern] northern *A1*
132:17 heart's-blood *A1*] hearts-blood *Per*
132:24 rattle-snakes] rattlesnakes *A1*
132:25 Teotihuacán *Ed.*] Teotihuacan *Per*

132:26 told— *A1*] ~ - - - *Per*
132:27 Quetzalcoatl— *A1*] ~ - - - *Per*
132:32 you:— *Ed.*] ~:- *Per* ~: *A1*
132:32 dark green] ~, ~ *A1*
133:3 pre-occupation] preoccupation *A1*
133:4 hotblooded] hot-blooded *A1*
133:11 ricketty] rickety *A1*
133:21 aboriginal] *Om. A1*

Dear Old Horse, A London Letter

The order of the texts is *Per, E1*.

137:1 **Dear Old Horse, A London Letter** *Ed.*] Dear Old Horse/ A London Letter from D. H. Lawrence *Per Om. E1 see notes*
137:2 Yesterday *Per, E1*] 110, Heath St., Hampstead, N.W. 3./ 9 Jan., 1924./ To Willard Johnson./ Dear Spoodle,—/ Yesterday *E1 see notes*
137:2 today] to-day *E1*
137:8 prick] pick *E1*
137:9 Letter] letter *E1*
137:11 belly;] ~: *E1*
137:13 O Horsie] oh Horse *E1*
137:13 Centaur] ~, *E1*
137:16 hobby Horse] Hobby Horse *E1*
137:18 Adam,] ~ *E1*
137:20 O] oh *E1*
137:21 centaur] Centaur *E1*
137:24 piecemeal] piece-meal *E1*
137:29 Fe] Fé *E1*
137:34 more. *E1*] ~, *Per*
138:1 Pale] pale *E1*
138:3 Turquoise] turquoise *E1*
138:5 the horse] the Horse *E1*
138:6 sniggers. *P* I'm *E1*] ~. I'm *Per see notes*
138:8 centaur] Centaur *E1*
138:8 who] *Om. E1*
138:11 Fe] Fé *E1*

138:15 Pan is dead. Great Pan is dead.] *Pan is dead. Great Pan is dead. E1*
405:16 centaur] Centaur *E1*
138:18 Horse] horse *E1*
138:18 forever:] for ever, *E1*
138:21 mummy-sarcophagus] mummy sarcophagus *E1*
138:25 myself:] ~, *E1*
138:25 Fe] Fé *E1*
138:30 seriously,] seriously, Spoodle, *E1 see note on 137:1*
138:30 Man] man *E1*
138:30 centaur] Centaur *E1*
138:32 Lament] lament *E1*
138:32 laugh] Laugh *E1*
138:33 lamenting. *P* In] ~. In *E1*
138:36 gentry.] ~? *E1*
138:36 Horse Sense.] ~ ~! *E1*
138:37 four-footed Sense] four-footed sense *E1*
138:38 Horse sense,] Horse-sense, *E1*
138:38 horse] Horse *E1*
139:2 that] ~, *E1*
139:9 southwest] south-west *E1*
139:11 mesas] *mesas E1*
139:16 pueblos] *pueblos E1*
139:17 centaur] Centaur *E1*
139:17 centaurs] Centaurs *E1*
139:19 got] GOT *E1*
139:20 got] *got E1*

139:22 to him] ~~, *E1*
139:22 No answer] No good! No Answer
   E1
139:22 dead] forked *E1*

139:29 got] *got E1*
139:30 Gods] gods *E1*
139:32 summoning] summonsing *E1*
139:33 Hup-a-la] Hup-a-là *E1*

Paris Letter

The order of the texts is *Per, A1*.

143:1 **Paris Letter** *Ed.*] Paris Letter/
   By D. H. Lawrence Per PARIS
   LETTER *A1*
143:12 their *A1*] ther *Per*
143:21 Elysées *A1*] Elysses *Per*
144:6 fesses] *fesses A1*
144:7 *forced*] forced *A1*
144:9 petit bourgeoise] petit-
   bourgeoise *A1*
144:15 the spunk] spunk *A1*

144:30 last.—] ~. *A1*
144:32 food] a food *A1*
145:3 built] ~, *A1*
145:18 a weariness] weariness *A1*
145:20 absolutely *A1*] abslutely *Per*
145:23 doesn't] doen't, *A1*
145:30 dynastic lie] dynastic life *A1*
146:10 permanencies] ~, *A1*
146:11 forever] for ever *A1*

Letter from Germany

The order of the texts is *MS, Per, TCC1-2, A1*.

149:1 **Letter from Germany** *Ed.*]
   Letter from Germany. *MS* D.
   H. LAWRENCE'S LETTER/
   FROM GERMANY *Per* LET-
   TER FROM GERMANY./ By/
   D. H. Lawrence *TCC1-2* A
   LETTER FROM GERMANY
   A1
149:2 tomorrow *MS, TCC1-2*] tomorrow *Per*
149:3 Germany] ~, *Per*
149:4 It's] It is *Per*
149:9 Strasburg *MS, TCC1-2*] Strasbourg *Per*
149:10 shop signs] shop-signs *Per*
149:13 cathedral-front] cathedral front
   Per
149:14 prisms] prisons *Per*
149:15 Queer, *MS, TCC1-2*] ~ *Per*
149:16 fanciful *MS, TCC1-2*] faithful
   Per
149:16 height, *MS, TCC1-2*] ~ *Per*
149:16 gothic] Gothic *A1*

149:17 card castles] card-castle *Per*
149:17 goths and alemans] Goths and
   Alemans *A1*
149:18 height] heights *Per*
149:22 steams *MS, A1*] streams *TCC1-2*
149:30 ponderous] ~, *TCC1-2*
150:3 and] ~, *Per*
150:12 two and a half] two-and-a-half
   TCC1-2
150:13 re-union] reunion *Per*
150:16 eastwards;] ~, *Per*
150:20 *Men Beasts and Gods,*] *Men Beasts
   and Gods TCC1-2 Beasts, Men
   and Gods A1*
150:22 Baden Baden] Baden-Baden *Per*
150:23 Turgenevs] Turgenievs *A1*
150:23 Dostoevskys] Dostoievskys *A1*
150:25 watering place] watering-place
   Per
150:27 Rentenmark *MS, A1*] Reuten-
   mark *TCC1-2*
150:27 Gold Mark] gold Mark *Per* gold
   mark *A1*

150:31 shop keepers] shopkeepers *Per*
    shop-keepers *TCC1-2*
150:32 tram-cars *MS, TCC1-2*] tram-
    cars *Per*
150:35 Pfennigs] pfennigs *A1*
150:35 pfennigs *MS, A1*] Pfennigs *Per*
150:36 Milliards] milliards *A1*
150:37 Marks] marks *A1*
151:2 that too *MS, TCC1-2*] ~, ~, *Per*
151:27 pre-historic *MS, TCC1-2*]
    prehistoric *Per*
151:30 youths *MS, TCC1-2*] youth *Per*
151:33 half mystical] half-mystic *Per*
151:34 loose] ~, *Per*

152:1 So,] ~ *Per*
152:9 broken, *MS, TCC1-2*] ~
    Per
152:13 barbarian] barbarians *Per*
152:14 White skinned] White-skinned
    Per
152:16 dark-eyes *MS, TCC1-2*] dark-
    eyed *Per*
152:19 Cathedrals] cathedrals *Per*
152:24 fate,] ~; *Per*
152:30 Quos vult perdere Deus, demen-
    tat prius. *MS, TCC1-2*] *Quos vult*
    perdere Deus, dementat prius. Per,
    A1

Pan in America

The order of the texts is *MS2, Per, TCC, A1*.

155:1 **Pan in America** *Ed.*] Pan in
    America./ by D. H. Lawrence.
    MS2 PAN IN AMERICA/
    By D. H. LAWRENCE *Per*
    PAN IN AMERICA./ By/ D.
    H. Lawrence. *TCC* PAN IN
    AMERICA *A1*
155:22 Pan power] Pan-power *Per*
155:30 laurels,] ~ *TCC*
155:30 him,] ~ *TCC*
155:32 forever, forever] for ever, for ever
    A1
156:4 oak groves] oak-groves *TCC*
156:8 Gradually,] ~ *TCC*
156:10 And] ~, *TCC*
156:16 last,] ~ *TCC*
156:20 excesses,] ~— *Per*
156:20 great god] Great God *Per*
156:22 everything,] ~ *TCC*
156:30 re-born] reborn *Per*
156:32 "ism";] "ism," *Per, A1* 'ism',
    TCC
156:32 Pantheists] pantheists *A1*
156:35 school child] school-child *TCC*
156:36 examination day] examination-
    day *TCC*
157:3 Pan,] ~ *TCC*
157:4 *Myself.*] ~: *TCC*

157:5 am Pan] ~ ~, *TCC*
157:7 answers:] *P* "All] ~: "All *Per*
157:8 A." *P* Aristotle] ~. Aristotle *Per*
157:15 But] ~, *TCC*
157:15 guinea pigs] guinea-pigs *TCC*
157:20 *us,*] *us TCC see notes*
157:21 to.] ~? *TCC*
157:24 all] ~, *A1*
157:27 Whereas] whereas *Per*
157:27 nothing,] ~; *A1*
157:29 Pan!] ~. *TCC*
157:30 too-much] too much *Per*
157:37 pine tree *MS2, A1*] pine-tree *Per*
157:39 storm] ~, *Per*
158:12 tapping:] ~; *TCC*
158:12 blue jays] bluejays *A1*
158:12 in] on *TCC*
158:21 life, the] ~ ~ *TCC*
158:29 pine-tree] pine tree *A1*
158:31 piney] piny *A1*
158:32 aeons *MS2, TCC*] æons *Per, A1*
159:6 one's self:] one's self; *TCC* one-
    self; *A1*
159:11 pine-tree] pine tree *A1*
159:11 a man] man *Per*
159:17 tree:] ~; *TCC*
159:27 pine-tree] pine tree *A1*
159:30 life,] ~ *TCC*

159:31 tree's *TCC*] trees' *MS*
159:32 Mo?] Mo.? *Per*
159:34 to or] ~, ~ *TCC*
159:35 life.] ~? *TCC*
160:1 stands *Per*] stand *MS2*
160:7 Oh...Oh...Oh] oh...oh...
oh *Per*
160:9 Tree, *MS2, TCC*] tree, *Per, A1*
160:13 inscrutable;] inscrutably: *TCC*
160:14 Oh] oh *Per*
160:25 here"? *Per*] ~,"? *MS2*
160:28 him.] ~? *TCC*
160:30 God] god *Per*
160:40 stays.—] ~. *TCC*
160:40 go—"] go——" *A1*
161:4 "Oh] "~, *A1*
161:5 Oh] ~, *A1*
161:6 me] ~, *TCC*
161:15 another.] ~? *TCC*
161:20 Oh] ~, *A1*
161:25 to,] ~; *Per*
161:28 connection] connexion *A1*
161:30 hunter,] ~ *TCC*
161:33 primarily,] ~ *TCC*
161:35 spell-bound] spellbound *TCC*
162:2 lambs-wool] lamb's-wool *Per*

162:5 Pan,] ~ *TCC*
162:6 defenceless *MS2, TCC*] defenseless *Per*
162:8 a rock] rock *Per*
162:12 water-fall] water-/fall *Per*
waterfall *TCC*
162:12 master,] ~ *TCC*
162:24 connection] connexion *A1*
162:28 extent,] ~ *TCC*
162:29 mechanisms] mechanism *Per*
163:17 shadows,] ~ *TCC*
163:19 "Lo *Per*] ~ *MS2*
163:21 power.—] ~. *A1*
163:22 something,] ~; *TCC*
163:34 Oh] "~, *Per*
163:35 Oh] ~, *TCC*
163:37 dark] ~, *TCC*
163:38 night.—] ~. *A1*
163:40 Oh] ~, *TCC*
164:1 Oh] ~, *Per*
164:3 me—] ~." *Per*
164:6 here] ~, *Per*
164:10 teepees] tepees *Per*
164:13 universe? *P* The] ~? The *Per*
164:18 Because] ~, *TCC*
164:19 universe;—] ~:— *TCC* ~: *A1*

See Mexico After, by Luis Q.

The order of the texts is *MS3, TCC1, TCC1R, TCC1C, TS, TCC2-4, A1.*

167:1 **See Mexico After, by Luis
Q.** *Ed.*] See Mexico After/ by
Louis Q. *MS3* See Mexico After/
by/ Luis Q. *TCC1* See Mexico After/ by/ *TS* SEE MEX-
ICO AFTER/ by Luis Q. *TCC2-
4* SEE MEXICO AFTER, BY
LUIS Q. *A1*
167:2 My home's...Mexico./ ...*cine
show*] My home's...Mexico,/
...*cine show TCC2-4 My
home's...Mexico,/ ...cine show
A1*
167:5 fact] ~, *TCC2-4*
167:8 I, *TCC1R*] I am *MS3*
167:9 am *TCC1R*] Om. *MS3*

167:12 sash!] ~? *TCC1C*
167:13 *Ay-de-mi!*] *Ay de mi! A1*
167:15 one?— *MS3, TCC2-4*] ~?
TCC1, A1
167:16 sparrow] ~, *A1*
167:16 etc.— *MS3, TCC2-4*] ~. *TS,
A1*
167:22 American?—by] ~? ~*TCC1*
167:26 F.,] ~/ *TCC2-4* ~ *A1*
167:27 Say, *MS3, TCC2-4*] ~ *TS*
167:32 à la Mexicaine] á la Mexicano
TCC1 a la Mexicano *TS à la Mexicaine TCC2-4*
168:7 Quien sabe?] Quién sabe? *TS
Quien sabe? A1*
168:11 bated *A1*] baited *MS3*

168:15 American?— *MS3, TCC2-4*] ~?
  TCC1
168:15 Quien sabe? *MS3, TCC2-4*]
  Quién sabe? *TS Quien sabe?*
  A1
168:20 window;] ~ *TCC2-4*
168:21 *Viejo!*—] ~! *TCC1* ~! *A1*
168:21 Oiga! *MS, TS*] *Oiga!* *TCC1 Oiga*
  TCC2-4
168:24 Quien sabe!] Quien sabe? *TCC2-
  4 Quien sabe? A1*
168:25 Oh] ~, *A1*
168:25 Quien sabe!] Quien sabe? *TCC2-
  4 Quien sabe? A1*
168:28 so!] ~? *TCC2-4*
168:29 then] *Om. TCC2-4*
168:33 via] *via TCC2-4*
168:36 FIRST.—] ~. *TCC2-4*
168:38 en todo... en parte *MS3*] en
  todo... en parte TCC1C, A1
  entodo... enparte TCC2-4
168:38 Quién sabe!] *Quien sabe! TCC1*
  Quien sabe? *TCC2-4 quien sabe?*
  A1
169:6 others.—] ~— *TCC2-4*
169:8 Bootleggers] Bootlegger's *TCC1*
  Bootleggers' *TCC2-4*
169:9 Tramps] Tramps' *TCC2-4*
169:10 Missions——] ~. *TCC2-4*
  ~... *A1*
169:11 Mohammet] Mohammed *A1*
169:12 à la] á la *TCC1 à la TCC2-4*
169:12 Mohammet] Mohammed *A1*
169:14 Cordilleras] cordilleras *A1*

169:16 elevators] elevator *TCC1*
169:16 sound of footsteps *TCC1R*] chink
  of silver *MS3, TCC2-4*
169:17 me *MS3, TCC2-4*] *Om. TCC1*
169:17 if] if [sic] *A1 see notes*
169:17 Mohammet *MS3, TCC2-4*]
  Mahomet *TCC1* Mohammed
  A1
169:19 still *TCC1R*] *Om. MS3, TCC2-4*
169:20 stripeyer] stripyer *A1*
169:23 Quien sabe! *MS3, TCC2-4*]
  Quién sabe! *TS Quien sabe! A1*
169:31 hundred-per-cent-plus]
  hundred-per-cent *TCC2-4*
169:36 There] ~, *A1*
169:38 after.— *MS3, TCC2-4*] ~.
  TCC1, A1
170:1 Commissioners] commissioners
  TCC2-4
170:5 Brummm!] *Brummmm! A1*
170:12 P. J. P.'s.—] ~. *A1*
170:18 Oh] ~, *A1*
170:20 Labour] labour *A1*
170:30 adios!] *adios! A1*
170:31 Tears,] ~; *TCC2-4*
170:40 course.] ~ *TCC2-4*
171:3 five-cents] five-cent *A1*
171:4 Wrigley's *A1*] Rigley's *MS3*
171:6 thirty-five] thirty-four *TCC2-4*
171:14 Bill,] ~; *TCC2-4*
171:30 Bull—!] ~——! *A1*
171:31 Teotihuacán *Ed.*] Teotihuacan
  MS3
171:32 tag.] ~? *TCC2-4*

New Mexico

The order of the texts is *Per1, Per2, TCC, TS, A1*.

175:1 **New Mexico** *Ed.*] New Mexico/
  By D. H. LAWRENCE *Per1*
  THE SPELL OF NEW MEX-
  ICO./ By D. H. Lawrence./
  With decorations based on Mexican
  originals by/ OLIVER HOLT.
  Per2 NEW MEXICO./ By/
  D. H. LAWRENCE. *TCC*

NEW MEXICO./ by/ D. H.
Lawrence. *TS* NEW MEXICO
A1
175:3 tourist trots] tourists trot
  Per2
175:3 around] round *Per2*
175:8 everywhere,] ~ *TCC*
175:14 And,] ~ *TCC*

175:15 motor-cars] ~, *A1*
175:15 hotels *Per1, TCC*] ~, *Per2*
175:16 Pekin *Per1, TCC*] Peking *Per2, A1*
175:17 etc. Poor *Per1, TCC*] ~. *P* Poor *Per2*
175:19 mucous-paper *Per1, TCC*] mucous paper *Per2*
175:20 world,] ~ *TCC*
175:20 bon-bon,] bonbon, *Per2* bon-bon *TCC*
175:21 it, *Per1, TCC*] ~; *Per2*
175:27 school-room *Per1, TCC*] school-room *Per2*
175:28 It's] "It's *TCC*
175:28 expect: *Per1, TS*] ~, *Per2* ~." *TCC, A1*
175:28 we] We *TCC*
175:29 all. *P* We *Per1, TCC*] ~. *P #* We *Per2*
175:33 Mexico. New] ~. *P* New *TCC*
176:1 Eastern States] eastern states *TCC*
176:2 desert-mesas] desert measas *TCC* desert mesas *A1*
176:2 cow-boys *Per1, TCC*] cowboys *Per2, A1*
176:3 penitentes *Per1, TCC*] *penitentes Per2*
176:3 Southwest; *Ed.*] South-/ west; *Per1* South-West. *Per2* South-West, *TCC*
176:3 put *Per1, TCC*] Put *Per2*
176:5 spaces.] ~! *Per2*
176:8 know all about it.] know it at all. *Per2 see notes*
176:14 development. Months *Per1, TCC*] ~. *P* Months *Per2*
176:17 even,] ~ *TCC*
176:22 me;] ~: *TCC*
176:24 Oh] O *A1*
176:24 away! *P* But *Per2*] away! *P #* But *Per1*
176:26 Fe] Fé *Per2*
176:30 parrots] parrot *TCC*
176:30 flying. But *Per1, TCC*] ~. *P* But *Per2*

176:33 new. *P* There *Per1, TCC*] ~. *P #* There *Per2*
176:37 corn;] ~: *TCC*
176:40 sky! But *Per1, TCC*] sky. *P* But *Per2*
177:2 canyon] Canyon *TCC* Cañon *A1*
177:3 of *Per1, TCC*] or *Per2*
177:3 Rockies, *Per1, TCC*] ~ *Per2*
177:6 houses:] ~; *Per2* ~, *TCC*
177:7 Cristo Mountains] Cristo, mountains *TCC*
177:9 Rockies! What *Per1, TCC*] ~! *P* What *Per2*
177:10 "It] ~ *TCC*
177:11 aesthetically-satisfying *Per1, TCC*] æsthetically satisfying *Per2* æsthetically-satisfying *A1*
177:11 know."—] ~." *Per2* ~— *TCC* ~.— *TS* ~. *A1*
177:12 splendid,] ~ *TCC*
177:12 vast,] ~ *TCC*
177:13 aesthetic *Per1, TCC*] æsthetic *Per2, A1*
177:13 appreciation. Never *Per1, TCC*] ~. *P* Never *Per2*
177:17 overweening *Per1, TCC*] overweening *Per2*
177:18 beautiful! Those *Per1, TCC*] ~! *P* Those *Per2*
177:21 unbearably,] ~ *TCC*
177:22 there. It *Per1, TCC*] ~. *P* It *Per2*
177:27 sun,] ~ *TCC*
177:28 religious. *P* And *Per2*] religious. *P #* And *Per1*
177:30 me] *me TCC*
177:33 Brahmins: *Per1, TCC*] ~; *Per2*
177:36 will,] ~ *TCC*
177:36 love *Per2*] love it *Per1 see notes*
177:36 will. *P* I *Per1, TCC*] ~. *P #* I *Per2*
178:1 Pera-hera] ~, *TCC*
178:3 religion, *Per1, TCC*] ~. *Per2*
178:4 uncontrollable,] ~ *TCC*
178:4 sensual experience] ~ ~, *Per2*
178:5 love: *Per1, TCC*] ~; *Per2*
178:13 Hindus *Per1, TCC*] Hindu *Per2*
178:14 Cinghalese *Per1, TCC*] Cingalese *Per2, A1*

178:21 article] ∼, *TCC*
178:22 wrapping.] ∼, *TCC*
178:22 *want Per1, TCC*] want *Per2*
178:23 And] But *TCC*
178:25 is,] ∼— *TCC*
178:26 religious self] religious-self *TCC*
178:27 Greeks] ∼, *TCC*
178:28 Europeans *Per2*] European *Per1*
178:29 tabu *Per1, TCC*] taboo *Per2, A1*
178:31 word. *Per2, TCC*] world. *Per1 see notes*
178:35 Personally,] ∼ *TCC*
178:38 really,] ∼ *TCC*
179:7 tabu *Per1, TCC*] taboo *Per2, A1*
179:10 morning,] ∼ *TCC*
179:11 figures] figure *TCC*
179:14 of: *Per1, TCC*] ∼; *Per2*
179:16 uprooted. *P* But *Per2, TCC*] uprooted. *P* # But *Per1*
179:19 seed-rattles *Per1, TS*] seed rattles *TCC, A1*
179:21 as *Per1, TCC*] and *Per2*
179:21 Indians. Never *Per1, TCC*] ∼. *P* Never *Per2*
179:24 Dionysiac *Per1, A1*] Dionysic *Per2, TCC*
179:28 depths. *P* Never *Per1, TCC*] ∼. Never *Per2*
179:29 Felipe] Filipi *TCC*
179:33 moving,] ∼ *TCC*
179:35 Taos, *Per1, TCC*] ∼: *Per2*
179:37 to *Per2, TCC*] Om. *Per1 see notes*
179:39 last *Per2, TCC*] lost *Per1 see note on 178:31*
180:2 procession. *P* Never *Per2*] procession. *P* # Never *Per1*

180:3 Apache] Apaché *A1*
180:4 teepees] tepees *A1*
180:5 Apaches *Per1, TCC*] apaches *Per2*
180:7 Apache *Per1, TCC*] apache *Per2*
180:13 contact. And one *Per1, TCC*] ∼. *P* One *Per2*
180:20 feathers, *Per1, TCC*] ∼ *Per2*
180:22 deliberately. And *Per1, TCC*] ∼. *P* And *Per2*
180:24 exerting] exerting it *TCC*
180:24 utmost:] ∼— *TCC*
180:28 year] zeal *TCC see note on 178:31*
180:29 darkly] starkly *TCC*
180:30 is god *Per1, TCC*] is God *Per2*
180:32 god is *Per1, TS*] God is *Per2, TCC, A1*
180:35 vast. So *Per1, TCC*] ∼. *P* So *Per2*
180:39 greater] great *TCC*
180:40 effort. For *Per1, TCC*] ∼. *P* For *Per2*
181:3 joy. This *Per1, TCC*] ∼. *P* This *Per2*
181:5 real] root *TCC*
181:5 religion.] ∼, *TCC*
181:5 And] and *TCC*
181:10 cosmic religion *Per1, TCC*] ∼ ∼, *Per2*
181:13 god-religion. *P* And *Per1, TCC*] ∼. And *Per2*
181:14 Mexico: *Per1, TCC*] ∼; *Per2*
181:18 oblivion. When *Per1, TCC*] ∼. *P* When *Per2*
181:28 sky-scraper *Per1, TCC*] skyscraper *Per2*

Appendix I
Just Back from the Snake Dance

The order of the texts is *MS, TS, TSC, Per, E1.*

185:1 **Just Back from the Snake Dance** *Ed.*] Just Back from the Snake Dance *MS* To Willard Johnson./ Just Back from the Snake Dance. *TS* Just Back from the Snake-Dance/ —Tired Out/By D. H. Lawrence *Per* To Willard

Johnson./ *Just back from the Snake Dance. Eı*
185:2 went *MS, Per*] came *TS, Eı*
185:3 hideous—a *MS, Eı*] ~, ~ *Per*
185:3 pale-grey *MS, Eı*] pale grey *Per*
185:4 mesas] *mesas Eı*
185:4 ancient,] ~ *TS*
185:5 bumpy] lumpy *Eı*
185:5 trail,] ~ *TS*
185:6 bobbled] bobbed *TS*
185:7 mesas] *mesas Eı*
185:8 last mesa . . . last mesa] last *mesa . . .* last *mesa Eı*
185:9 villages *MS, Eı*] Villages *Per*
185:10 edges of *TS*] edges of of *MS*
185:10 arid, *MS, Eı*] ~ *Per*
185:11 mesas:] mesas; *Per mesas: Eı*
185:11 them: *MS, Eı*] ~; *Per*
185:11 Walpi: *MS, Eı*] ~, *Per*
185:11 Chimopova: *MS, Eı*] Chimopavi, *Per*
185:11 then Oraibi, *MS, Per*] ~ ~ *TS, Eı*
185:12 last mesa: and . . . same mesa] last mesa and . . . same mesa *Per* last *mesa:* and . . . same *mesa Eı*
185:12 beyond Oraibi, *MS, Eı*] ~ ~ *Per*
185:15 pueblos] *pueblos Eı*
185:15 dry,] ~ *TSC, Eı see notes*
185:18 extremities!] ~. *TS*
185:18 Anyhow *MS, Per*] ~, *Eı*
185:18 got there *MS, Per*] ~ ~, *Eı*
185:19 pueblos] *pueblos Eı*
185:19 ruin. *TS, Eı*] ~ *MS* ~, *Per*
185:19 And *MS, Eı*] and *Per*
185:20 fair-sized *MS, Eı*] fair sized *Per*
185:21 back yard:] back yard; *Per* back-yard: *Eı*
185:21 square, *MS, Per*] ~ *TS, Eı*
185:25 cortège.] cortage. *TS* cortege,— *Per cortège. Eı*
185:25 Till *MS, Eı*] till *Per*
185:26 three thousand *MS, Eı*] eight hundred *Per see notes*
185:27 little *MS, Per*] Om. *TS, Eı*
185:28 thick *MS, Eı*] much *Per*
185:29 walls: *MS, Eı*] ~; *Per*

185:31 breeches: *MS, Eı*] ~; *Per*
185:32 bodices: *MS, Eı*] ~; *Per*
185:33 shawls: *MS, Eı*] ~; *Per*
185:33 black blouse *MS, Eı*] blouse *Per*
185:34 a black sailor hat: *MS, Eı*] black sailor hat; *Per*
185:34 half breeds:] half-breeds: *TS, Eı* half breeds *Per*
186:1 window holes; *MS, Per*] window holes: *TS* window-holes: *Eı*
186:1 posed *MS, Per*] forced *Eı*
186:3 sill, *MS, Eı*] ~ *Per*
186:4 Semiramis *MS, Eı*] ~, *Per*
186:5 match: *MS, Eı*] ~; *Per*
186:7 eyes.—] ~. *TS*
186:11 back-yard? *MS, Eı*] back yard. *Per*
186:11 Eight *MS, Per*] Light *TS, Eı*
186:11 antelope priests—] ~ *TS*
186:12 (so-called)—] ~ *TS*
186:13 one *TSC, Eı*] six *MS, Per see notes*
186:16 snake-adorned *MS, Eı*] snake adorned *Per*
186:16 feathers, *MS, Per*] ~ *TS, Eı*
186:17 game— *MS, Eı*] ~. *Per*
186:17 Roger *MS, Eı*] Rogers *Per*
186:19 massed *MS, Eı*] mussed *Per*
186:20 around. And *MS, Per*] ~: and *TS, Eı*
186:21 picked *MS, Eı*] pitched *Per*
186:24 drooping *MS, Per*] dropping *TS, Eı*
186:26 its *MS, Eı*] Om. *Per*
186:26 garter— *MS, Eı*] ~, *Per*
186:28 hang *MS, Eı*] hand *Per*
186:31 gathered, *MS, Eı*] ~ *Per*
186:32 let *MS, Per*] left *Eı*
186:32 wriggle *MS, Eı*] wiggle *Per*
186:33 pueblo] pueblos *Per* pueblo *Eı*
186:34 hey— *MS, Per*] ~ *TS, Eı*
186:35 with them *MS, Eı*] ~ ~, *Per*
186:35 mesa, *MS, TS*] ~ *Per mesa, Eı*
186:36 rocks, *MS, Eı*] ~ *Per*
186:40 cold-creamed *MS, Eı*] cold creamed *Per*
187:1 (so-called).] (so-called), *Per* (so called). *Eı*

187:1 Like *MS*, *E1*] like *Per*
187:1 wet,] ~ *TS*
187:2 naïve] *Om. TS*, *E1* naive *Per*
187:2 heads, *MS*, *E1*] ~ *Per*
187:5 distance. *P* Just *MS*, *E1*] ~. Just
   Per
187:6 South west *MS*] south west *TSC*
   southwest *Per* south-west *E1*
187:6 white *MS*, *E1*] White *Per*
187:12 the Land *MS*, *TSC*, *E1*] the land
   TS The Land *Per*
187:13 circus-ring: *MS*, *E1*] ~! *Per*
187:13 lots *MS*, *E1*] Lots *Per*
187:14 jabbering, *MS*, *E1*] ~ *Per*
187:14 Come on, *MS*, *E1*] ~ ~ *TS*

187:15 fun! *P* The *MS*, *Per*] ~! The *TS*,
   E1
187:16 South-west] South-West *Per*
   south-west *E1*
187:16 natural *MS*, *Per*] national *TS*, *E1*
187:16 circus-ground *MS*, *E1*] circus
   ground *Per*
187:16 on, boys; *MS*, *E1*] ~ ~; *TS* ~,,
   ~! *Per*
187:17 we've *MS*, *E1*] We've *Per*
187:19 Why] why *TS*
187:22 corn meal *MS*, *Per*] corn-meal
   TSC, *E1*
187:24 anyhow.—] ~. *TS*

['Indians and an Englishman' and 'Certain Americans and an Englishman']: early fragment

The order of the texts is *LT*, *TS*, *TSR*, *TSC*, *Per1*, *Per2*. Corresponding passages can be found elsewhere in this volume (see numbers after entries).

191:2 English;] ~, *TS* 113:2
191:4 'Here'] "~" *TS* 113:4
191:5 and Indian] *Om. TS see notes*
   113:5
191:8 woollyness] woolliness *TSC* 113:7
191:8 motor-cars] motor cars *TSC* 113:7
191:12 motor-cars] motor cars *TSC* 113:11
191:13 high-brows] highbrows *TSC*
   113:12
191:26 bad on purpose] bad-on-purpose
   TS 113:25
191:27 Oh] ~, *TSC* 113:26
191:27 high-brow] highbrow *TSC*
   113:26
191:29 not yet Gringo] yet not Gringo
   TSC not gringo *Per1* 113:28
191:31 says,] ~ *TS* 113:30
191:31 on] ~, *TS* 113:30
191:31 You] you *TS* 113:31
191:32 mine'—and] ~," and *TS* 113:31
192:4 buggoon] buffoon *TS* 114:4
192:6 woollyness] woolliness *TSC*
   114:6
192:7 depths, in] ~—in *Per1* 114:7
192:9 Empire] ~, *TS* 114:9

192:9 is] *Om. TS* 114:9
192:11 circus-ring] circus ring *TS*
   114:11
192:13 and thorns] *Om. TS* 114:12
192:14 high-brows] highbrows *TSC*
   114:14
192:19 pro-Indian:] ~; *TS* 114:14
192:19 intellect:] ~; *Per1* 114:19
192:19 republican] Republican *TSC*
   114:19
192:19 democrat:] Democrat: *TSC*
   Democrat, *Per1* 114:19
192:22 "But] *Om. Per2* 105:2
192:22 arrive] arrive in New Mexico
   Per2 105:2
192:23 Bill] bill *Per2* 105:3
192:24 it,] ~ *Per2* 105:4
192:24 needn't. But] ~. *P* But *Per2* 105:5
192:25 Bursum Bursum Bursum!!] Bursom Bursom Bursom!! *TS* Bursum, Bursum, Bursum! *Per2*
   105:5
192:25 Bill!... Bill!... Bill] Bill, ...
   Bill, ... Bill *Per2* 105:5
192:26 Twitchell!!] ~! *Per2* 105:6

192:26 Oh] O *TS* 105:6
192:27 Fall! you] ~, ~ *Per2* 105:7
192:27 Fall!!!] ~! *Per2* 105:8
192:28 Oh] ~, *Per2* 105:8
192:28 now] Now *Per2* 105:8
192:29 Whoa] ~, *Per2* 105:9
192:29 Bursum *LT, Per2*] Bursom *TS* 105:9
192:29 Whoa Bill] ~, ~ *Per2* 105:9
192:29 Whoa-a-a! *P* "Like] ~!—like *TS* 105:9
192:30 Lindsay] Vachell Lindsay *Per2* 105:9
192:30 bellowing] ~, *Per2* 105:10
192:31 have] have *TS* 105:10
192:31 heed. And] ~ *P* And *Per2* 105:11
192:31 solemnly sit down] sit down solemnly *Per2* 105:11
192:32 Printed] printed *Per2* 105:12
192:32 Bursum *LT, Per*] Bursom *TS* 105:12
192:32 Bill] bill *Per2* 105:12
192:35 C's] C.'s *Per2* 105:15
192:36 H's] H.'s *Per2* 105:16
192:36 M's] M.'s *Per2* 105:16
192:37 up,] ~. *Per2* 105:18
192:37 and Bear ye...Bursum] and Bear Ye One Another's Bursum *TS Om. Per2* 105:18
192:38 lamb-like *LT, Per2*] Lamb-like *TS* 105:18
192:39 butting] ~, *Per2* 105:19
193:3 doing, *LT, Per2*] ~ *TS* 105:23
193:4 circus-tent] circus tent *Per2* 105:24
193:10 Show] show *TS* 105:30
193:11 to you,] ~ ~; *TS* 105:31
193:12 No no,] ~, ~, *TS* ~, ~; *Per2* 105:32
193:12 me] ~, *Per2* 105:32
193:13 bewildered, *LT, Per2*] ~ *TS* 105:33
193:14 head-or-tail] head or tail *Per2* 106:1
193:17 motor-car] motor car *TSC* 114:23
193:20 a pine-tree] the pine-tree *TS* the pine tree *TSC* 114:26

193:22 silver and turquoise] silver-and-turquoise *TS* 114:28
193:25 "'Da donde viene, Usted?'...] "Da donde viene, Usted?"..... *TS* "Da donde viene, Usted?"... *TSC* 114:31
193:28 blanketed *LT, TSC*] blanketted *TS* 114:34
192:31 basin *LT, Per1*] ~, *TS* 114:36
193:32 blanketed *LT, TSC*] blanketted *TS* 114:39
194:1 wild,] ~ *TS* 115:7
194:3 hollow,] hollows *TS* 115:9
194:6 west] West *TSC* 115:12
194:10 Spanish; and] ~. And *TS* 115:16
194:16 drum] ~, *TS* 115:22
194:16 pat-pat, pat-pat] pàt-pat, pàt-pat *TSR* 115:22
194:18 Hy-a! Hy-a! Hy-a! *LT*] Hỳ-a! Hỳ-a! Hỳ-a! *TSR* Hỳ-a! Hỳ-a! *Per1* 115:24
194:19 Ay-away-away—!!] Ay-away-away!! *TS* Ay-away-away!! *Per1* 115:25
194:21 ecstasy *LT, TSR*] ecstacy *TS* 115:27
194:25 aspen-twig] aspen twig *TSC* 115:31
194:28 pát-pat, pát-pat, pát-pat] pat-pat, pat-pat, pat-pat *TS* pàt-pat, pàt-pat, pàt-pat *TSR* 115:34
194:30 pát-pat, pát-pat, pát-pat] pat-pat, pat-pat-pat-pat *TS* pàt-pat, pàt-pat, pàt-pat *TSR* 115:36
194:34 pát-pat, pát-pat] pat-pat, pat-pat *TS* pàt-pat, pàt-pat *TSR* 115:40
194:35 inwards] ~, *TS* 115:39
194:37 Hie!—Hie—away—awaya!] Hie! Hie-away-awaya! *TS* 116:2
194:38 pine-trees] pine trees *TSC* 116:4
194:40 pát-pat, pát-pat] pat-pat, pat-pat *TS* pàt-pat, pàt-pat *TSR* 116:6
195:2 near,] ~ *TS* 116:7
195:2 laughing,] ~ *TS* 116:7
195:3 squeal] shriek *TSR* 116:8
195:3 Ugh!] Ugh! *TS* 116:9

195:5 war whoop. *P* "Listening] war
whoop.—They produce the gobble from the deeps of the stomach, and say it makes them feel
good. *P* Listening *TSR* war-
whoop.—They . . . good. *P* Listening *Per1* 116:11

195:6 unbearable,] ∼ *TS* 116:13

195:9 humour] humanness *TS* 116:16

195:12 unconfined,] ∼ *TS* 116:18

195:13 gobble-agobble-agobble] gobble-
agobble *TS* 116:19

195:13 gobble-agobble, agobble] gobble-
agobble-agobble *TS* 116:20

195:14 man-fun. *P* "So] man-
fun. The war-whoop! *P* So
TSR 116:21

195:16 much. . . . "] ∼ *TS* 116:22

Line-end hyphenation

Of the compound words which are hyphenated at the end of a line in this edition,
only the following hyphenated forms should be retained in quotation:

13:16	little-curly-dog
22:5	royal-blue
26:21	chicken-bitten
39:13	monkey-speech
49:17	rose-coloured
51:3	net-sacks
52:14	many-coloured
64:18	drum-beats
83:31	gentle-hearted
86:12	low-toned
89:21	snake-stick
91:16	north-western
105:12	one-two-three-four-five-six-seven
105:32	lamb-like
108:11	high-brow
114:14	cross-roads
114:18	pro-Indian
116:2	*Hie-away-away*
116:36	sulphur-human
117:15	non-intoxicants
120:31	bird-tread
126:13	far-off
126:36	half-dollars
131:29	beer-bottle
156:33	sweet-and-pure
157:16	Something-or-other
159:8	earth-power
170:39	Italianino-Argentino-swoon-between-o
171:20	nice-looking
175:25	lantern-slides
179:17	fox-skin
192:32	one-two-three-four-five-six-seven
194:28	thud-thud
209:28	five-cents

A note on pounds, shillings and pence

Before decimalisation in 1971, the pound sterling (£) was the equivalent of 20 shillings (20/- or 20s). The shilling was the equivalent of 12 pence (12d). A price could therefore have three elements: pounds, shillings and pence (£, s, d). (The apparently anomalous 'd' is an abbreviation of the Latin *denarius*, but the other two terms were also originally Latin: the pound was *libra*; the shilling, *solidus*.) Such a price might be written as £1 2s 6d or £1/2/6; this was spoken as 'one pound, two shillings and sixpence', or 'one pound two-and-six' or 'twenty-two and six'.

Prices below a pound were written (for example) as 19s 6d, or 19/6, and spoken as 'nineteen shillings and sixpence' or 'nineteen and six'. Prices up to £5 were sometimes spoken in terms of shillings: so 'ninety-nine and six' was £4/19/6.

The penny was divided into two half-pence (pronounced 'ha'pence') and further divided into four farthings, but the farthing had minimal value and was mainly a tradesman's device for indicating a price fractionally below a shilling or pound. So 19/11¾ ('nineteen and eleven-pence three farthings') produced a farthing's change from a pound, this change sometimes given as a tiny item of trade, such as a packet of pins.

The guinea was £1 1s 0d (one pound, one shilling) and was a professional man's unit for fees. A doctor would charge in guineas (so £5 5s 0d = 5 gns.). Half a guinea was 10s 6d or 10/6 (ten and six).

The coins used were originally of silver (later cupro-nickel) and copper, though gold coins for £1 (a sovereign) and 10s (half-sovereign) were still in use in Lawrence's time. The largest 'silver' coin in common use was the half-crown (two shillings and sixpence, or 2/6). A two-shilling piece was called a florin. Shillings, sixpences and threepences were the smaller sizes. The copper coins were pennies, half-pence (ha'pennies) and farthings.

Common everyday terms for money were 'quid' for a pound, 'half a crown', 'two bob' for a florin, 'bob' for a shilling (or shilling piece), 'tanner' for a sixpence (or sixpenny piece), 'threepenny-bit', and 'coppers' for pennies, half-pence or farthings.